INSIDERS' G

D0826999

INSIDERS' GUIDE® TO

SAVANNAH & HILTON HEAD

EIGHTH EDITION

GEORGIA R. BYRD

INSIDERS' GUIDE

GUILFORD, CONNECTICUT

AN IMPRINT OF GLOBE PEQUOT PRESS

All the information in this guidebook is subject to change. We recommend that you call ahead to obtain current information before traveling.

To buy books in quantity for corporate use or incentives, call **(800) 962–0973** or e-mail **premiums@GlobePequot.com**.

INSIDERS' GUIDE ®

Copyright © 2011 Morris Book Publishing, LLC

ALL RIGHTS RESERVED. No part of this book may be reproduced or transmitted in any form by any means, electronic or mechanical, including photocopying and recording, or by any information storage and retrieval system, except as may be expressly permitted in writing from the publisher. Requests for permission should be addressed to Globe Pequot Press, Attn: Rights and Permissions Department, P.O. Box 480, Guilford, CT 06437.

Insiders' Guide is a registered trademark of Morris Book Publishing, LLC.

Editor: Kevin Sirois
Project Editor: Heather Santiago
Layout Artist: Kevin Mak
Text Design: Sheryl Kober
Maps: XNR Productions, Inc. © Morris Book Publishing, LLC

ISSN 1539-7378
ISBN 978-0-7627-5701-5

Printed in the United States of America
10 9 8 7 6 5 4 3 2 1

CONTENTS

ABOUT THE AUTHOR

Georgia R. Byrd, a native of the South, has been writing since her grandparents took her to visit Washington, D.C., at the age of eight. It was there that she journaled every stop of a Grey Line Tour in a Reporters' Notebook, which she still has to this day. As high school newspaper editor, she graduated and hit the journalism trail at the *Huntsville News,* Huntsville, Alabama, starting as a copygirl, promoted to a cub reporter, and later working as a sports stringer. While attending the University of Alabama in Tuscaloosa, she covered football during the days of Coach Paul "Bear" Bryant and interviewed the coach daily after practice, transmitting her articles to the *News* each afternoon by dictation. In the mid-70s, she relocated to the state of Virginia and worked as an editorial assistant for the Suffolk bureau of the *Virginian-Pilot* and *Ledger Star.* She also freelanced for the newspaper after the birth of her first child, producing the food section cover and editorial on a weekly basis.

Back in Savannah during the 1980s, with two children, she continued writing for Memorial Medical Health University's *For Life* magazine, and became editor of *The Islands Gazette* for three years. She then produced advertising supplements for the *Savannah Morning News.* She later became the first editor of the Closeup newspaper supplements, and then founding editor of *Savannah Magazine.*

Today, she celebrates her 26th year as a resident and journalist in Savannah, Georgia. Her work with *Savannah Magazine* received more than 50 regional and national awards for editing, graphic design, and art direction. Her articles have appeared in *Atlanta Magazine, Forbes, Southern Living,* and the *Atlanta Journal Constitution.* Her dream of working for *Forbes* magazine came true 10 years ago, and she has since produced advertising supplements, consulted for Forbes TV's travel shows, and worked with yachting companies all over the world promoting yachts in *Forbes.* Her graphic design and marketing skills have included publication work for the Georgia Ports Authority and other Savannah clients. She is also an author and contributor to several tabletop books, including *Megayachts of the World,* published by Edisea, Ltd., and *Romantic Days & Nights in Savannah* (Globe Pequot Press). She is the coauthor of *The History of Aviation in Savannah* (Savannah Airport Commission), and *Seasons of Savannah,* published by the Savannah College of Art & Design. She has appeared on the Travel Channel, CNN, *Good Morning America,* and the *Today Show* as a travel and yachting consultant.

Georgia is married to advertising photographer Joseph Byrd, and is the mother of Whit, 26, a police officer; and Ammie, 29, a school principal.

ACKNOWLEDGMENTS

It has been my pleasure to earn a decent living by writing about Savannah during my 26-year-old son's entire life span. To thank each and every one who has been instrumental in helping me transfer my thoughts into print would take yet another book. Here's to scratching the surface.

I begin by thanking Linda Wittish, editor of *Savannah Magazine,* for giving me my first writing assignment as a Savannahian. As a contributor to Memorial Medical Center's now defunct magazine *For Life,* I boldly applied for the position very pregnant and in desperate need of a writing job to help pay the rent. She hired me in spite of that and on the spot and hence, my first Savannah bylines began to appear in print.

I thank the group of private investors (you know who you are) who charged me with the task of filling up a weekly newspaper for "the islands" that surround Savannah—Talahi, Whitemarsh, Oatland, Wilmington, Tybee, and Skidaway. Through my work at the *Islands Gazette,* I discovered the charms of island living.

Thanks go to my father, who passed away five years ago. He was the one who pushed me out the door and into a newsroom at the ripe age of 17. No, dad. I still haven't won "one of them Pulitzers," but because you told me I had to get a summer job and that it couldn't be in a restaurant, I've managed to make stories out of simple things and earn a decent paycheck on occasion.

Former *Savannah Morning News* editor Wallace Davis offered me yet another opportunity to expand my knowledge of the city as editor of the *Islands Closeup* and later gave me the privilege of becoming *Savannah Magazine*'s founding editor. Through those experiences, I became pleasantly thrown into the forefront of events, activities, characters, and landmarks. I developed enough insight into the city that I was able to capture my thoughts and share them with visitors in three editions of *Romantic Days & Nights in Savannah,* by this publisher, the Globe Pequot Press.

The Savannah College of Art & Design gave me yet another chance to enhance my familiarity with Savannah through the book, *Seasons of Savannah.* Co-writing *The History of Aviation in Savannah* with my friends Rich Wittish and the late Delph Thorn opened another door into Savannah's untold stories of aviation. And speaking of Rich Wittish, I thank him and my friend Betty Darby for laying the tracks for seven editions of this book. Their meticulous research and careful wording has made this update much more manageable.

My friend, Eugene Downs, an artsy, fun-loving colleague and friend, always gives me new perspectives on the social aspects, fineries, and joys one can experience in a town such as Savannah.

Delph Thorn, a former copy editor for the *Savannah Morning News*, is applauded posthumously for keeping me grammatically in line, year after year, project after project. He is greatly messed, I mean, missed! (Oops! Where is he when I need him?)

I thank Frank Anderson, retired publisher of the *Savannah Morning News*, for his faith in me as a journalist and for teaching me the ultimate organizational skills as editor and overseer of the first few years of *Savannah Magazine*. Through that position, he appointed me to the Savannah Area Chamber of Commerce and Convention and Visitors' Bureau, where I sat on the board for seven years, and chaired (the CVB) for one. It was there that I truly cultivated my knowledge of the city through interaction in city politics and tourism and learned much from some of the area's most talented and highly respected business leaders.

For this edition, I am especially indebted to Erika Backus of the Savannah Area Chamber of Commerce who has endured my endless calls, emails, and opinion inquiries. Another thanks to Hilton Head Island's marketing director, Jessica Gardo, for checking behind me and assisting with questions I tossed her way about Hilton Head.

My dear friend Susan Lynah has been greatly instrumental in keeping me on track with this book's deadlines and fact-finding and assisting me throughout this update. I couldn't have accomplished this task without her encouragement and grand humor!

I thank my mother and stepfather, Ann and Raymond Duke, for their patience as I attempted to complete this project in record time. Also, thanks to my mother—a true present-day Scarlett O'Hara. She and her never-ending calls with yet "another thing to add to the book" have given you, the reader, much more to enjoy during your stay. Thanks to my sister, Jane, for forgiving me for not mentioning her in previous books! Now you can say I did!

I thank my children, Whit and Ammie (both grown), for living (and surviving) life with a journalist mother-on-deadline who burned many Pop Tarts, family dinners, and yes, even pots, during their years growing up at home.

And although the nest is empty and our home is relatively quiet, my husband, Joseph, is to be commended for enduring the long periods of silence as I write in my head and on my iPhone while we try to sneak in some quiet time. And yes, even he has endured the burned food (and pots) from a wife still hunched over the keyboard trying to help pay the rent. His encouragement, love, and endearing tolerance allowed me to survive many challenging years of sitting in this well-worn office chair tapping away as the years go by.

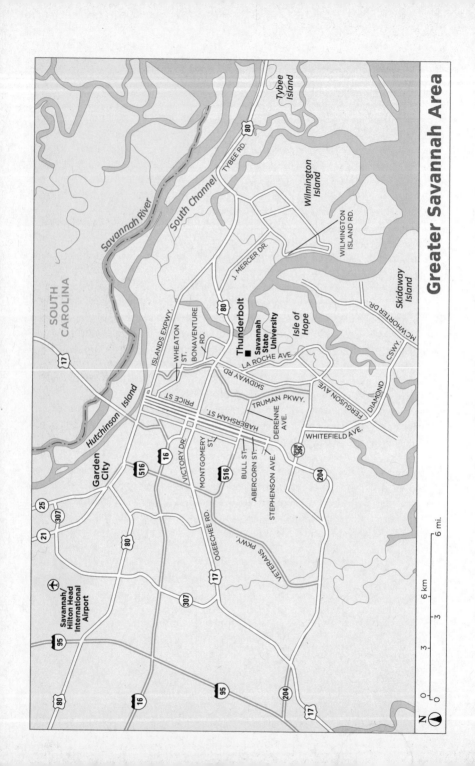

Greater Savannah Area

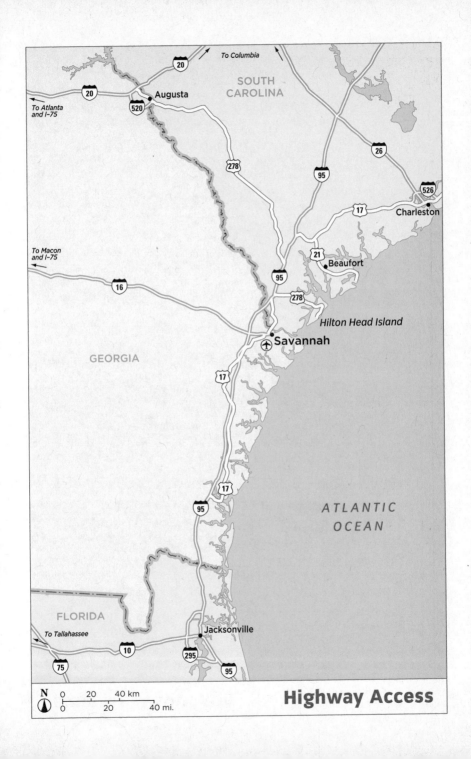

To Columbia

SOUTH
CAROLINA

20

20

To Atlanta
and I-75

520

Augusta

278

95

26

526

17

Charleston

21

Beaufort

To Macon
and I-75

16

95

278

Hilton Head Island

GEORGIA

17

Savannah

17

17

ATLANTIC
OCEAN

95

FLORIDA

To Tallahassee

75

10

295

Jacksonville

95

N

0   20   40 km
0   20   40 mi.

Highway Access

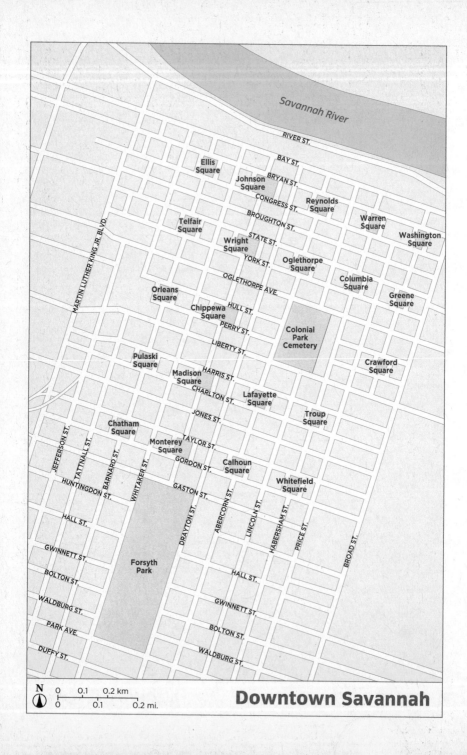

Downtown Savannah

N

0   0.1   0.2 km
0   0.1   0.2 mi.

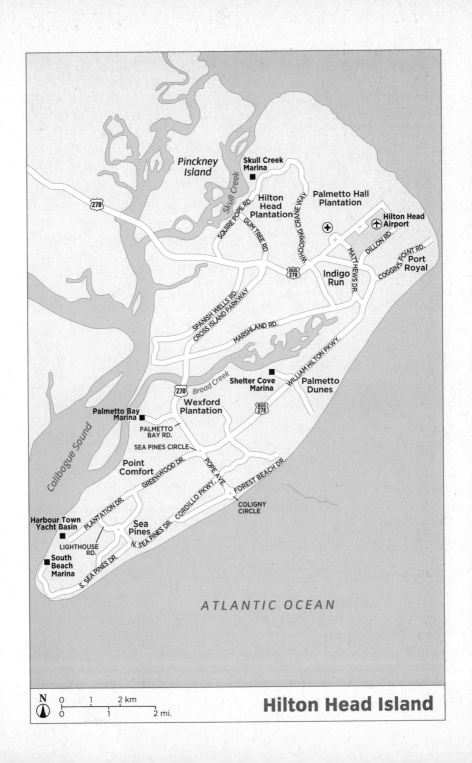

Pinckney
Island

Skull Creek
Marina

Skull Creek

278

SQUIRE POPE RD.

GUM TREE RD.

Hilton
Head
Plantation

WHOOPING CRANE WAY

Palmetto Hall
Plantation

✛

✈ Hilton Head
Airport

MATTHEWS DR.

DILLON RD.

COGGINS POINT RD.

Port
Royal

BUS
278

Indigo
Run

SPANISH WELLS RD.

CROSS ISLAND PARKWAY

MARSHLAND RD.

Broad Creek

Shelter Cove
Marina

WILLIAM HILTON PKWY.

Palmetto
Dunes

278

Wexford
Plantation

BUS
278

Palmetto Bay
Marina

PALMETTO
BAY RD.

SEA PINES CIRCLE

Point
Comfort

GREENWOOD DR.

POPE AVE.

FOREST BEACH DR.

CORDILLO PKWY.

COLIGNY
CIRCLE

Calibogue Sound

PLANTATION DR.

Harbour Town
Yacht Basin

LIGHTHOUSE
RD.

Sea
Pines

N. SEA PINES DR.

South
Beach
Marina

S. SEA PINES DR.

ATLANTIC OCEAN

N

0   1   2 km
0   1   2 mi.

Hilton Head Island

PREFACE

Twenty-five years ago my parents called and asked if I could help them find a vacation condo to rent at Tybee, a small island located about 20 minutes from Savannah. Since I was editing a weekly newspaper called *The Islands Gazette,* they looked to my expertise to find a simple, yet affordable place that offered a view of the ocean with "beachy" furnishings, modern amenities (including dishes, linens, washer and dryer, etc.), and a pool. "Something with some character and not too expensive," my dad said. "And something close to Savannah," said mom, who loved to shop and dine out.

With the windows of my Chrysler minivan rolled down, I headed east on the picturesque two-laned US 80 locals call "the Tybee road." Surrounded on both sides by marshland, I glimpsed a colorful collage of containers stacked on a massive ship making its way up the river toward Savannah. With salty breezes gusting through the van's open windows and tossing my hair in all directions, I anxiously crossed the bridge over Lazaretto Creek to Tybee Island, where I discovered the perfect getaway for mom and dad. At the north end of the beach—where rock jetties and red and green channel markers define the entrance to the Savannah River—a quaint condo development called Lighthouse Point offered an idyllic solution to their vacation demands.

This little piece of golden real estate was built on wooden stilts high above the sandy shores of the pristine north beach. Almost all of the condos faced the ocean, and most offered a view of the island's gleaming historic lighthouse. I selected a lower-level condo one flight up. I was delighted to find a spacious porch that was cradled by palm trees and situated above a carpet of dark green grass. Their grandchildren could play on the grassy lawn as the family relaxed on cushy porch furnishings. A wooden walkover leading to the beach ran alongside the grassy knoll. Sheltered on the front by sea oaks, a snow fence, and some natural flora, was a sprawling beach and the Atlantic Ocean in all its glory! As the condo's front faced the beach, the rear offered its own array of enchantments. There was a clubhouse with a screened-in room, perfect for family oyster roasts. A small, enticing pool was next to the clubhouse and proved to be the perfect diversion for my children, who would spend many afternoons laughing and splashing with their grandparents.

In short, mom and dad's proposed vacation to Savannah changed the course of their lives. My parents, who came for a weeklong visit, never left. They purchased the rental condo before moving later—at least three times—into bigger and better beach homes. Every day turned into a vacation, and their list of daily to-dos read something like this: morning walk on the beach, bike ride to the post office, neighborhood gab session in the yard, bike to the North Beach Grill to dinner. And yes, there was plenty of porch sitting in between.

In a sense, I've turned into my parents. After a quarter of a century, this city has become my perpetual vacation.

I play tourist every day even when I'm not trying. The sheer beauty of living in a historic setting replete with tropical overtones, combined with the unique mix of characters all set in a backdrop dripping with color, renders "Kodak moments" even when the day seems average. For the past 26 years, I've savored this city like it was an adventurous destination waiting to be discovered. And every day I discover new things!

Just recently, I met a friend for lunch downtown on River Street. The meeting became a cultural outing with little forethought. My short walk across Savannah's famed ballastone street from the riverside parking lot was accompanied by the bluesy saxophone serenade of a street minstrel. The "cultural outing" continued at a window-side table when a massive ship (seemingly a mere arms length away) blasted its arrival just as a basket of hot biscuits and cornbread was served. By the time dessert arrived, I had read the history of the restaurant that was printed on the place mat, watched a megayacht dock, and enjoyed the perfect picture of children dancing around the fountain.

In the many years I've lived to write about Savannah, changes have been subtle but always positive and mostly well received. This year is no different. Since the seventh edition of this book was published, Savannah has taken on a new chicness with boutique hotels blossoming all over the Historic District. Rivaling the contemporary interiors of Miami's South Beach, Savannah's historic character is now enhanced by several new upscale, contemporary eateries and hotels. There's a new "wow factor" emerging, and along with the blend of eclectic decor and fusion cuisine housed in century-old buildings, a new breed of visitor is discovering this city whose claim to fame is history. These visitors are attracting an intriguing new community of artsy residents and big spenders from all parts of the world.

While some things about Savannah have changed, there are some things that never do. Egrets with wide-span wings render astonishing sunset antics over waterways and marshes. Creek-side eateries and rustic dives entice sunburned vacationers and locals with fresh seafood spiced with secrets from old Savannah cooks. There are downtown cafes that spill onto sidewalks and plenty of outdoor benches for sitting within the Historic District's picturesque squares. There are lazy afternoons made for eating sumptuous ice-cream cones in old-time shops, and tearooms where dainty Southern sandwiches are served on antique china. Wide, expansive porches on architecturally stunning inns await guests and quiet times where rocking and reading is the course of the day. There are wooden swings planted on the beach (a mere 15 minutes from downtown) where lovers embrace ocean views, touching the sand with their toes and forgetting that they are not in some exotic locale, but rather in south Georgia on Tybee Island.

The secrets of Savannah's delights aren't so secret any more. Celebrities have relocated here and nearby. Television commentator Brent Musburger lives on Skidaway Island. Stars like Sandra Bullock and Diana Scarwid make Savannah's Tybee and Wilmington Islands their home. Ben Affleck and family own property south of the city. Gracing her squares through the years while filming are a host of stars and starlets: John Travolta, Robert Redford, Tom Hanks, Rosie O'Donnell, Demi Moore, and Miley Cyrus, whose film *The Last Song* has rendered even more notoriety to the island. More on that subject later!

Ruby Gettinger's weight-loss documentary called *Ruby* has become one of the Style Network's highest rated shows, and now in its third year, it has elevated Savannah's reputation to a refreshing high. Food Network's Paula Deen and her family offer a never-ending buffet of must-sees for the herds of starstruck fans. They flock to this city just to sample her food or catch a glimpse of the diva, her sons, and even her brother, who has found his own claim-to-fame in grilled oysters. Tourists from all over the world tag still along with followers of John Berendt's best-selling book, *Midnight in the Garden of Good and Evil*, and even after all these years, they still find the subject intriguing. There are the rich and famous who venture here quietly and discreetly to have their jets (and yachts) serviced at nearby Gulfstream and Thunderbolt Marine. And then there are just regular old born-and-bred Savannahians who just like it here and vow they'll never leave. Once you come for a visit, you might find yourself one of them.

HOW TO USE THIS BOOK

Imagine you are stepping off a train in a foreign country. Confused, frustrated, and unsure of where to go or what to do, you glance ahead and discover a smiling face and arms outstretched. Standing there to greet you is your personal guide who not only speaks the language, but has walked the streets of your destination since she took her first steps. Not only does she know every crack and crevice of the city, but, with her hand, she will lead you to some of the area's most intimate, soulful, and incredible sights—some known to many and others only to a chosen few. I'm your guide and you can trust that with my knowledge of the city, you won't get lost.

My desire is that this book will be that personal guide who will lead you through Savannah and Hilton Head Island's most popular attractions, restaurants, and accommodations, as well as those special places that only an "insider" could reveal. Before you leave home, purchase a camera bag, backpack, or purse large enough to accommodate this book, as well as your cameras, bug spray, and personal necessities. When you arrive, don your most comfortable walking shoes (flat, open-toed in summer, and flat and lined for the winter). Use this *Insiders' Guide* as a constant reference as you explore our city and parts of the South Carolina Lowcountry called Hilton Head Island.

Arranged by subjects, it is recommended that you read this guidebook in full prior to leaving home. Highlight some of your interests and familiarize yourself with the area's history that is a vital part of her present. Watch a Paula Deen cooking show on the Food Network if you haven't already done so. Count the times she says "y'all," and then practice saying it so you'll fit right in with the locals. Rent the film *Midnight in the Garden of Good and Evil,* or better yet, read the best-selling book by John Berendt. You'll be enchanted before you ever step foot here and your knowledge of the characters and places made famous by authors and screenwriters will be better appreciated. Delve into the history of the city and switch on *Ruby,* watching at least the impressive intro that showcases the city in just a few seconds.

The local area is divided into four geographical sections (Historic District, the Islands, Southside/Midtown, and West Chatham) with an explanation of the territory outlined in the **Area Overview** chapter. The maps are an excellent way to get a good overview of the geographical areas and hence guide you through the city by foot, carriage, trolley, or car. Within the chapters, **restaurants, accommodations, attractions,** and other points of interest are arranged alphabetically for quick reference. Another good way to find specific topics of interest is by looking in the extensive index in the back of the book. You'll note that the area code for almost every phone number listed is 912 (843 for places in South Carolina). Also look for Insiders' Tips—marked with an that let you in on local secrets.

This edition also reflects highways and roads that are identified by abbreviations. They include: highways, which are denoted by **I-** for interstate, **US** for approapriate two-laned (and highways that are not interstates) roads, **SR** (or an abbreviation of the state) for State Routes or State Highways. And if all else fails, ask a Savannahian for directions if you're lost. This is a city overflowing with hospitality, and you'll find that no one is too busy to help you find your way.

Moving to Savannah or already live here? Be sure to check out the blue-tabbed pages at the back of the book, where you will find the **Living Here** appendix that offers sections on relocation and real estate, retirement, education and child care, health care, and media.

In addition to giving you a full rundown on the many topics you might expect to find in a guidebook, I've included a couple of chapters regarding subjects unique to Savannah. One chapter entitled "Savannah Celebrity" will take you to the living sets of *Forrest Gump, The Gingerbread Man, Midnight in the Garden of Good and Evil,* and the more recent *The Last Song,* starring Miley Cyrus and filmed mostly on Tybee Island. Another special chapter paints the town green as Savannah's celebration of St. Patrick's Day comes to life with luck-filled advice on how and where to celebrate with the locals and a few thousand tourists.

Thanks to this guide book, visitors who fly through Savannah going to Hilton Head Island will understand that they are not in Hilton Head when they deplane in Savannah. The hour or so (depending on traffic to the island) drive to Hilton Head Island from the Savannah airport will become much less a trek of boredom as this edition also captures and highlights this popular tourist destination and offers some fun stops along the way. In turn, we have also devoted an entire chapter to Savannah's sister beach (and the neighboring islands) Tybee Island, which is part of Chatham County but very separate and distinct from Savannah.

AREA OVERVIEW

If you approach Savannah from the west after traveling the monotonous, pine-lined stretch of I-16 from Macon and follow through to the interstate's end in Savannah, you'll arrive in the midst of a lavishly beautiful part of the downtown Historic District, where architectural wonders unfold in the form of thick moss-drenched live oaks, townhomes, inns, and private residences.

If you arrive by car across the graceful cable-span bridge (called the Talmadge Memorial) that crosses the winding Savannah River and connects South Carolina to Georgia, the city unfurls like a Southern belle awaiting her suitor. Cresting the crown of the bridge, 196 feet above the water and looking down and ahead toward your destination, you'll see the city of Savannah. Be careful not to get distracted as you drive, but if you're the passenger, look over to your left. More than likely, you'll see a large yacht or two anchored at the Westin. There could be one or two colorful ferries transporting visitors to and from the Savannah riverfront over to Hutchinson Island, the home of a pristine Troon-managed 18-hole golf course. Across the river, still looking left as you descend the bridge, you'll see the gold-domed City Hall. It will glisten if the day is sunny, and the view of the Cathedral of St. John the Baptists' twin spires in the foreground will signal that you are indeed mere minutes from your destination.

Straight ahead is a network of roadways, with some of the thoroughfares leading to the city's south side and to west Chatham County, where many Savannahians live and many more do their shopping in more modern buildings. Finally, there are hints of the tropics, and palm trees and massive oaks that remind you that you are indeed in the old South.

SAVANNAH STATISTICS

Savannah is the seat of government of Chatham County, and the sixth most populous county in the largest state (in terms of area) east of the Mississippi River. Some 256,992 (*US Census Bureau 2009) people live in Chatham County, with 134,669 (*Savannah MSA 2009) residing within Savannah's city limits. About a quarter of the county's 438 square miles are unincorporated, and there are also seven other municipalities within Chatham's borders: Bloomingdale, Garden City, Port Wentworth, Pooler, Thunderbolt, Vernonburg, and the city of Tybee Island.

Due to the diverse interests and backgrounds that exist here, Savannah's major employers vary from industrial to educational and entrepreneurial. As a port community that dates back to 1733, Savannah's a city that assumes many roles, serving as a harbor, a center of higher education, a tourist destination, a site for industrial plants, a home to the military, and a breeding ground for artists and historic preservationists. Due to its history and aesthetic magnetism, the city is a virtual melting pot. For instance, take a seat on one of many benches in the squares of the Historic District and you'll most likely observe the mix: international art students hiking to and from class with projects in tow, society matrons chatting with neighbors, a herd of Girl Scouts on foot, corporate executives enjoying bagged lunches, and people like yourself watching people like yourself.

In keeping true to her military and industrial history, Savannah is home to Hunter Army Airfield and nearby (about 50 miles south) Fort Stewart military bases. Combined, the two bases employ more than 42,000 people and generate an annual direct federal expenditure of $1.4 billion dollars. The Georgia Ports Authority's (GPA) Garden City facilities comprise 1,200 acres, North America's largest single-terminal container facility. The Savannah facility alone employs 860 people for shipping terminal operations. Gulfstream Aerospace Corporation, home of the world's fastest corporate jets, is head-quartered here.

Chatham County's population is about 60 percent white, 34 percent African American, 2 percent Asian, and 3 percent Hispanic. Inside Savannah's city limits, the African-American population is the majority. The growth rate from 1990 through 2000 was 7 percent, and projections indicate the county will continue to grow until the year 2015 at an annual rate of 0.7 percent to 1.5 percent, depending on the study. Savannah's population is also getting older, with the percentage of people age 25 and younger declining and the percentage of folks age 65 and older increasing. The experts say this situation is the result of several factors,

including a lower birth rate, the aging of the baby boomers, increased longevity due to medical advancements and healthier life-styles, and the county's growing popularity as a retirement community.

Five industries account for relatively equal shares of the employment in the metropolitan Savannah area, further attesting to the area's healthy, diverse industry mix: retail trade (11.4 percent), professional and business services (11.6 percent), education and health services (13.9 percent), leisure and hospitality (12.9 percent), and state and local government (12.5 percent). Manufacturers continue to account for nearly nine percent of the area's jobs.

According to the Georgia Department of Labor's January 2009 figures, a total of 164,010 people were employed in the Savannah metropolitan area, with the region's unemployment rate at 7.4 percent. The US Census Bureau reported that the median household income in Chatham County in 2008 was $45,132.

The Savannah area is blessed with a climate classified as semitropical. Average seasonal temperatures are, in degrees Fahrenheit, 51 in winter, 66 in spring, 81 in summer, and 68 in autumn.

Although spring and fall are the most desirable times to visit Savannah, this is a city for all seasons with proper planning. For the health conscious, consider the sultry summers the perfect time to detox as humidity levels are high. This is when it's best to venture out on foot in the mornings before the sun's intensity is at its hottest. Middays are for napping and the afternoons are splendid for exploring.

Winters are brisk, and rarely is there a morning that provokes a heavy coat. If the day calls for one, more than likely you'll be

⊙ Close-up

A Gnasty Welcome to Savannah

I was standing at the first hole of a popular minigolf and arcade facility on Savannah's south side in the summer of 1977. As I dropped the golf ball for my first putt, I felt a stinging sensation on my arms, legs, scalp, and feet. Tiny bugs were flying around my face and body and I started doing a dance, of sorts.

"What's biting me?" I asked. A bystander instructed me to go inside and get a spray of Avon's Skin-So-Soft as I gyrated through the door, swatting and slapping.

I was experiencing one of Savannah's most dreaded pests, the sand gnat. This force of nature renders no easy battle. And just when the weather is perfect, the humidity is down, and the breeze lures you outside, they start their attack.

Sometimes referred to as "no-see-ums," these evil bugs feed on a human by slashing skin with its teeth and drinking the pool of blood that forms. Sounds disgusting, but you can't see this carnage taking place because your average sand gnat is about a millimeter long—so tiny it can fly through a standard window screen without grazing its wing tips. What you might see, particularly if you are prone to allergies, are small welts appearing where gnats have feasted. Try not to scratch; if you leave the bumps alone, they will disappear in about an hour.

Incidentally, the gnats biting you are females. They need the protein in blood for laying eggs. Sand gnats breed in the mud of salt marshes and are most prevalent in the spring and fall, but a few days of temperatures in the 60s can bring them out at other times. Although some folks recommend dousing yourself with Avon's Skin-So-Soft as a defense against sand gnats, entomologists say you can best fight these bugs by applying insect repellent containing the chemical compound DEET and by wearing long clothing and hats. If all of this scares you, prepare to treat these pests like the locals do. Just ignore them. Or if it's spring, buy a ticket to a baseball game!

Savannahians' love-hate relationship with sand gnats extends to the boys of summer, the city's minor-league baseball team. The management and fans of the Savannah ball club chose the Sand Gnat nickname when the team became an affiliate of the Los Angeles Dodgers organization in 1996. (As of 2007, they're affiliated with the New York Mets.) Home games are played in historic Grayson Stadium, a 4,700-seat facility built in 1927 and then later renovated. Be sure to buy a T-shirt or Sand Gnat hat to wear at home as a great conversation starter! This team's mascot—you guessed it—a pudgy, bug-eyed sand gnat, is said to be the only one of its kind in the country.

shedding it by lunchtime so stay close to your hotel or be prepared to tote your jacket as the day warms up.

More accurately, according to the Savannah Area Chamber of Commerce, the city on average experiences 67 days each year when the mercury climbs higher than 90 degrees.

Winters are fairly mild, with the temperature dipping below freezing an average of (ironically) 32 days a year. We seldom see snow, and the descent of even a few flakes is cause for excitement. The average annual rainfall is 49 inches, and Mother Nature delivers some intense downpours now and then, particularly during summer afternoon, so if this is your choice for a visit, heed this warning and bring a stylish pair of rain boots Because Savannah is in a low-lying area and much of the city's sewer system is antiquated, streets are prone to flooding when tides are high—be careful if you're driving around and get caught in a sudden storm.

Also, check the weather as you venture here between June 1 and November 30, the designated hurricane season. Being on the southeast coast, Savannah occasionally finds itself threatened by hurricanes. In recent years, the city has been spared the destruction caused by major storms. Savannah had close calls from Hurricane Hugo in 1989, Bertha in 1996, and Floyd in 1999, but the last hurricane to hit here was David in 1979, when winds as strong as 90 mph caused widespread power outages that lasted for several days.

That gives you the big picture. (For an at-a-glance version and a few extra facts, see the Vital Statistics page in this chapter.) Now let's look more closely at the four areas into which we've divided the county.

> **i** According to the Savannah Economic Development Authority, a residence in Savannah that costs $215,000 would go for $232,671 in Atlanta; $273,904 in Charleston; $462,397 in Seattle; $642,384 in Chicago; and more than $1 million in Boston and San Francisco ($1,083,836 and $1,107,397 respectively).

HERE'S LOOKING AT YOU, SAVANNAH

Historic District

In Savannah, the words *Historic District* are capitalized. That's because this area is officially designated as three distinct historic districts: the **National Historic Landmark District,** the **Victorian District,** and the **Thomas Square Streetcar Historic District.** Each designation carries clout in the realm of US cities. So when mentioning the Historic District, we're actually referring to the area of downtown where there are 22 picturesque squares with restaurants, inns, personal residences, and accommodations.

Savannah's downtown area is bordered by the Savannah River on the north, East Broad Street on the east, Park Avenue on the south, and Martin Luther King Jr. Boulevard on the west. Downtown is the oldest and most colorful part of the city—James Oglethorpe landed here when he arrived and founded Georgia more than 270 years ago. The 2.5 square-mile Historic District encompasses the 24 city squares Oglethorpe designed in his original plans. (Although his original plans called for 24 squares, there are presently 22 remaining.)

Today those squares still provide an intimate ambience unmatched by any other area of the city. Spend at least a day exploring the squares we like to call "a performance in progress." Like an ongoing film with extraordinary cinematography, they are a constant source of motion with characters changing by the minute. In summer, musicians perform on Johnson Square's monument steps for tourists and employees lunching downtown. On any given day in any given square, couples nestle on benches shaded by live oak trees with enormous branches that are laced with Spanish moss. Horse-drawn carriages click past carrying entire families on holiday and brides and grooms to and from historic churches on the weekends, enhancing the squares' theatrics. The walled gardens of homes surrounding the squares harbor history and a captivating kaleidoscope of intriguing tales and colorful characters.

Apart from the squares, downtown is also the place for fun, Southern eating at its best, and shopping on foot. The city's main thoroughfare, **Broughton Street,** was once the main shopping district and has captured the interest of locals and tourists with unique and local whimsical boutiques along with its share of chains like Gap and Banana Republic.

Downtown also plays host to festivals, with many of Savannah's major annual events being held along the river, in City Market, and at Forsyth Park, a lush, green playground on Bull Street (see our Annual Events and Festivals chapter), where a new amphitheater and cafe attract cultural and even more outdoor activities.

Downtown's **Johnson Square** is called the city's financial district, however, when you actually visit this square, you forget all about money. Situated in the center of several banks is a striking monument to Nathaniel Greene, the Revolutionary War hero. There are fountains at each end that glisten in the afternoon sunlight. The massive branches of the live oaks cover the square like a beautiful web, the Spanish moss dripping like lace on a wedding gown train, and they create a surreal ambience that is characteristic of many other areas of downtown.

Throughout downtown, striking museums such as the **Telfair Academy of Arts and Sciences** bring a little bit of a European flair to this Southern city. Enhancing the downtown area are a great number of buildings, homes, and inns that have been delicately restored to splendor by one of the community's major players, the **Savannah College of Art and Design (SCAD).**

Literal interpretations of Savannah's cartography might be a bit confusing because names don't always match up to positions. By map, the Historic District is in the northern part of town. That's because Savannah's birthplace was on a bluff on the south bank of the river, causing the heart of the city to be north of everything else. When you're in downtown Savannah, you can't go much farther north and still be in Georgia. Savannah has not grown in that direction, across the north channel of the Savannah River (which is known as the Back River), because what's over there is mostly marshland, and it's also South Carolina.

So when you're downtown on River Street gazing across the south channel of the Savannah River, you're looking at **Hutchinson Island,** a small part of Georgia that's undergone development to its advantage. Formerly a literal eyesore, the marshland has emerged in the form of a $98 million resort owned by Westin. The resort-complex towers above the flat island like a giant sand castle with a lush tropical appeal. Aesthetically, the project has been a great success and makes a splendid accompaniment to the $83.5 million Savannah International Trade and Convention Center (opened there in mid-2000).

The Westin resort complex is a 403-room, 16-story hotel that's emblematic of the growth in tourism being experienced by the city. Fueled by the popularity of Paula Deen, Berendt's *Midnight,* and by the aggressive marketing efforts of the Savannah, Convention and Visitors Bureau, and individual components of the city's hospitality industry, that growth—from 3.73 million visitors in 1995 to 6.5 million in 2009—has caused an upsurge in hotel building and expansion, a blossoming of new restaurants and specialty shops, and a proliferation of tour companies.

Because Savannah hasn't been able to expand much to the north, most early development was southward, and much recent growth has been to the east and west.

Islands

Driving eastward on US 80 toward Tybee Island, you'll pass Chatham County's inshore islands. This is where huge residential growth has occurred partly due to the island ambience, proximity to the beach, and distance to downtown. One can live on any one of "the islands" and get to work downtown in about 10 to 15 minutes, depending on the time of day and location of the workplace. Although these islands are not on the Atlantic Ocean, they're separated from the mainland and neighboring islands by salt marsh, rivers, and tidal creeks. The islands in our Islands Area are those immediately east of Savannah—Oatland, Talahi, Whitemarsh, and Wilmington—and those southeast of the city Dutch, Skidaway, and Isle of Hope. Because of its unique qualities and status as a destination for tourists, we have devoted a separate chapter to **Tybee Island,** which is also east of Savannah.

The residential development of the eastside islands took off in the late 1980s, and **Whitemarsh Island** (pronounced "WHIT-marsh") was the fastest-growing part of the county in 1996, with Wilmington Island not far behind. Growth slowed on Whitemarsh in 1997, with most of the island being built out, but residential development continued on Wilmington, the fastest-growing part of Chatham during 1998. Most of the building on these islands has been residential, although a large shopping center and three schools have been constructed on Whitemarsh in recent years.

Despite the buildup, the eastside islands, particularly **Wilmington Island,** retain a natural beauty and laid-back quality. Days are lazy and many islanders get around by bike. Spring evenings are filled with laughter and cheering from the crowds at little league baseball and church league softball games that are ongoing on Wilmington Island. It's safe enough to take an evening stroll on any of this island's streets, look up at a sky brilliant with stars, and listen to the back and forth hoots from owls. For the most part, the eastside islands remain quiet havens where folks sit on their docks and watch the marsh turn from gold to green as the seasons change; where oaks festooned with Spanish moss bend over roadways to create cool, verdant tunnels; where you can hop in your car, drive around the corner, and fetch fresh seafood from rustic markets. You can grocery shop in your flip-flops and stand in line at the banks with all your neighbors.

i Savannahians were all aglee in February 2010, when snow fell in the city and outlying areas. Snow hadn't been seen in the area since December 1989—more than a decade-long gap. That prompted many to sing one of the all-time favorite songs about wintry weather that was written by a onetime resident, James L. Pierpont. He penned the words to "Jingle Bells" and worked as an organist at the Unitarian church in Savannah.

Also representative of the eastside islands is tiny **Thunderbolt,** a quaint fishing village and its own municipality of 2,278 people living alongside the Wilmington River. This village is also home of

Thunderbolt Marine, Inc., a 25-acre site along the Wilmington River where marine skills are utilized to refit megayachts owned by the world's billionaires and registered in exotic parts of the world. Farther to the south, you'll find the gated residential enclave of **Dutch Island; Skidaway Island,** site of the Landings, a private community of upscale homes, also gated; and **Isle of Hope,** distinguished by its quaint cottages, charming Southern homes, and picturesque docks where families enjoy swimming, boating, and fishing. **The Landings** covers much of Skidaway Island with 4,800 beautifully landscaped dwellings, 2 deep-water marinas, 6 private 18-hole golf courses, a fitness center, 4 clubhouses, 34 tennis courts, and more than 40 miles of biking and nature trails. Isle of Hope is entirely residential except for the marina on Bluff Drive (see our Relocation/Real Estate chapter). **Bluff Drive** is a lovely lane running alongside the Skidaway River, and it's our choice as the Savannah area's most picturesque street. The Isle is also the location of **Wormsloe Historic Site,** the place where one of Georgia's first settlers constructed a colonial estate (see our Attractions chapter).

Southside/Midtown

Southside/Midtown is the vast area south of Historic Downtown. Note that the locals refer to the northern portion of this area as Midtown. **Midtown** starts in the vicinity of the southern end of Forsyth Park and runs south to DeRenne Avenue, although some folks might say it extends all the way to Oglethorpe Mall. Most of Savannah's **Victorian District** and all of the **Thomas Square Streetcar Historic District** are in Midtown. The districts, which are on the National Register of Historic Places, are filled with Victorian-style frame houses.

That distinction also applies to **Ardsley Park** and **Chatham Crescent,** two other areas in Midtown. Among the streets of Ardsley Park is one of Savannah's prettiest—oak- and azalea-lined **Washington Avenue.** At the eastern end of the avenue is **Daffin Park,** site of a small lake and public tennis courts and athletic fields used by recreation league teams playing baseball, softball, football, and soccer. Daffin is also home to professional athletes—the members of the city's minor-league baseball team, the **Savannah Sand Gnats** (see our Spectator Sports chapter). The Gnats play their home games at Grayson Stadium, which stands among the tall pines in the eastern portion of the park.

You'll find several shopping centers in Midtown, the main library (which has been renovated extensively), and much of Savannah's health care community. Clustered just north of DeRenne Avenue, between Reynolds Street and the Truman Parkway, are numerous doctors' offices, pharmacies, medical laboratories, and two of the city's hospitals, **Memorial Health University Medical Center** and **St. Joseph's/Candler Hospital** (see our Health Care chapter). There are a few suite-type hotels and a Fresh Market in this area of the city.

Once south of DeRenne, you are in the part of town most locals call the **Southside.** It's an area of subdivisions, churches, recreational facilities, and commercial development. Savannah's main roadway, **Abercorn Street,** evolves from a historical setting to the area's primary retail strip where shopping centers, malls, car dealerships, and fast-food restaurants fall suite. We think of Abercorn south of DeRenne as the Land of a Thousand Curb Cuts. That's an exaggeration, but not much of one. The six-lane thoroughfare is nicked by the myriad entrances and exits to

Savannah Vital Statistics

Nickname: Hostess City of the South

Mayor: Otis Johnson

Governor: Sonny Perdue

Outlying counties: Effingham, Bryan, Liberty

Population: Savannah, 343,092 Chatham County, 256,992; Georgia, 9.7 million

Area (sq. mi.): 65.1

Average temperatures: July, 82 degrees; January, 49 degrees

Average annual precipitation: Rainfall, 49 inches; snowfall, less than one-half inch

Major universities: Armstrong Atlantic State University, Savannah State University, Savannah College of Art and Design

Important dates:

> Feb. 12, 1733: Founded as capital of Georgia, the 13th colony
>
> 1734: Becomes first city in North America planned on a system of squares; also becomes site of first agricultural experimental garden in North America
>
> 1736: Becomes site of first Sunday school in America
>
> Oct. 9, 1779: Colonial army suffers crushing defeat in attempt to retake city from British during Siege of Savannah
>
> 1788: Becomes site of first African-American Baptist congregation in United States
>
> 1793: Eli Whitney perfects cotton gin on a plantation just west of Savannah
>
> May 22, 1819: Serves as embarkation point for first steamship to cross Atlantic (SS Savannah)
>
> April 19, 1862: Fort Pulaski, east of city, falls to first rifled cannon used in warfare
>
> Dec. 21, 1864: Confederate Savannah surrenders to Union forces led by General William T. Sherman at the conclusion of his March to the Sea
>
> 1886: Opens first art museum (Telfair) in Southeast
>
> 1908, 1910, 1911: Hosts Grand Prix and Vanderbilt Cup auto racing
>
> 1911: Establishes first motorized fire department in United States
>
> November 1955: Historic Savannah Foundation preservation group holds first general membership meeting
>
> July 22–Aug. 2, 1996: Hosts yachting events of Summer Olympic Games

Major area employers: Gulfstream Aerospace Corp. (5,000), Memorial Health University Medical Center (5,351), International Paper Co. (970), St. Joseph's/Candler Health System (3,300)

Famous historical sons and daughters:

Johnny Mercer, lyricist

Conrad Aiken, poet

Juliette Gordon Low, founder of the Girl Scouts

Clarence Thomas, Supreme Court justice

Major airport: Savannah/Hilton Head International Airport

Major interstates: I-95 (north-south), I-16 (east-west)

Public transportation: Chatham Area Transit (CAT)

Military base: Hunter Army Airfield

Driving laws: Seat belts mandatory for occupants of the front seat of a vehicle and all occupants younger than 18; safety restraining systems required for children younger than 6 years old, but seat belts will suffice for those who are 4 feet 9 inches and taller. Maximum speed limit under normal conditions 55 mph, 70 mph on rural interstates, and 65 mph on urban interstates. Speed limit decreases to 30 mph in business and residential districts. Headlights required between the half hour after sunset and the half hour before sunrise and when raining.

Alcohol laws: Drinking by persons younger than age 21 prohibited. Motorists 21 years and older considered under the influence of intoxicants when 0.08 gram or more by alcohol is present in the blood; for those younger than 21, the limit is 0.02 gram. Sunday sales of alcoholic beverages prohibited except in establishments that derive at least 50 percent of their food and beverage sales from the sale of prepared meals or foods. Sales of alcoholic beverages are prohibited between 2:55 a.m. on Sun and 7 a.m. on Mon and between 3 and 7 a.m. other days.

Drinking on city streets prohibited except in the area bounded generally by the city limits on the north, West Boundary Street on the west, Jones Street on the south, and East Broad Street on the east. In this area, drinking from cans, bottles, or glasses is prohibited, and paper or plastic cups containing alcoholic beverages must not exceed 16 fluid ounces.

Daily newspaper: *Savannah Morning News*

Sales tax: 7 percent (4 percent state, 3 percent local option) on the purchase of all goods and some services

Room tax: 6 percent

Information for tourists: Savannah Area Chamber of Commerce/Savannah Convention & Visitors Bureau, 101 East Bay St., Savannah, GA 31401; (912) 644-6400; www.savannah visit.com and from business establishments, used-car lots, strip shopping centers, and mega stores selling building materials, pet supplies, party goods, books, liquor, and office equipment. Interrupting this cascade of commercialism on Abercorn are the **St. Joseph's Hospital** campus and the doctors' offices that have sprung up around it (see our Health Care chapter) and the campus of **Armstrong Atlantic State University.** The area we've designated as Southside/Midtown is also home to several other institutions of higher education, including Savannah State University, Savannah Technical College, and South University (see our Education chapter).

Outdoor activities abound in the Southside. Just east and southeast of Oglethorpe Mall is **Bacon Park,** a city- and county-owned recreational complex consisting of softball diamonds, soccer fields, tennis courts, a public golf course, a stadium where high-school football teams play, an aquatic center, and a lake surrounded by a walking/jogging track. Nearby is the site of the Chatham County track and field complex inside **T. A. Wright Stadium** at Savannah State University. Among the features of this world-class facility are an eight-lane track, a dual pole vault runway, a javelin runway, a steeplechase water jump, and shot put, discus, and hammer-throw circles.

The Southside past Oglethorpe Mall is where suburbia evolved in the 1960s and 1970s, mainly in the sprawling subdivision of **Windsor Forest.** Residential growth has continued in recent years farther out Abercorn Street at **Georgetown,** one of the fastest-growing areas in Chatham County during the 1990s (see our Relocation/Real Estate chapter). This area extends almost to I-95 and includes a nice and affordable 18-hole Henderson Golf Club, where magnificent

live oaks and lush magnolia trees provide a challenging and natural place to enjoy an afternoon.

To the west of the residential and commercial development of the Southside is **Hunter Army Airfield,** a 5,400-acre military post and site of the Army's longest runway. Hunter and Fort Stewart are the homes of a Ranger battalion, units of the Third Infantry Division (Mechanized), and a Coast Guard air station. Combined, the two bases are home to more than 24,000 military personnel. The bulk of the division is based an hour away at **Fort Stewart,** the largest Army installation east of the Mississippi River. With its 11,375-foot runway, Hunter serves as a location from which troops and equipment of the Third can be deployed throughout the world.

i | As a perfect day in Savannah begins, so does an occasional unpleasant scent. Periodically wafting over the Savannah River and into downtown, this odor emanates from the industries lining the river's banks. The dominant component of the smell is sulfur dioxide, a pungent gas released during the manufacture of paper. Industry officials say they have spent big bucks attempting to eliminate the smell, and they assure us they have lessened it. The smell persists on occasion, however, especially during periods of extended wet weather. So just as locals have learned to ignore the sand gnats, they also ignore the scent, which is to some, the smell of money.

One of Chatham's municipalities is in Southside/Midtown: **Vernonburg,** a settlement of a hundred or so souls who reside on a handful of streets leading to the banks of the Vernon River. South of Vernonburg are the rustic residential communities of **Beaulieu** and **Coffee Bluff.**

West Chatham

West Chatham is to Savannah what the ports authority is to Miami. Near and along I-95, this area is home to industry, i.e., companies that produce paper products, massive structures where sleek corporate jets are built and serviced, and a European company that builds bright yellow backhoe loaders. The local daily newspaper, the *Savannah Morning News,* sits on a West Chatham site and boasts grand columns in this part of town where there are few impressive buildings. Home of the county's largest manufacturer, **Gulfstream Aerospace Corporation,** which employs 5,000 people and produces corporate jet aircraft, West Chatham, is also the site of the headquarters of the **Georgia Ports Authority,** which operates two deep water terminals on the Savannah River. Most of the cargo handled on Savannah's docks is shipped in containers, and the city is one of the busiest container ports in the United States. If you don't believe it, settle on a bench along the riverfront and watch the ships go in and out bearing containers.

Many of the people who work at the port and the industries west of Savannah live in West Chatham's four municipalities.

Of these, **Garden City** is the largest in terms of population—10,334 people call it home. **Port Wentworth,** the town closest to the river, has a population of 4,560, and **Bloomingdale** has 7,413 residents. Garden City and Bloomingdale grew considerably in 1998 when a majority of voters there opted for annexations that added about 7 square miles to Garden City and more than 1,000 acres to Bloomingdale. **Pooler,** a town of 14,875, is one of the fastest-developing parts of the region. West Chatham, long the setting for local industry, is rapidly taking on another persona—as the place where a dozen large, master-planned communities are taking shape. These communities, each covering at least 500 acres, will combine residential and commercial development with green space. The construction of up to 40,000 new homes in these areas is complete, and it's estimated that more than 100,000 people will live in these communities—with names such as Godley Station, Rice Hope Plantation, and New Hampstead—when these projects are completed over the next 20 years.

West Chatham is also the location of **Savannah/Hilton Head International Airport,** where a $68.5 million terminal was opened in 1994 (see our Getting Here, Getting Around chapter). Close by the airport are **Crossroads Business Park,** a state-of-the-art industrial park, and **Crosswinds,** a golf course that's lighted for nighttime play.

GETTING HERE, GETTING AROUND

alled one of America's most beautiful cities, Savannah sits near the mouth of the
Savannah River, which forms the boundary between Georgia and South Carolina.
Drive across the picturesque Talmadge Bridge over the Savannah River and by the time
you're back over dry land, you're in another state. Head south down I-95 for about two
and a half hours, and you've gone from Georgia's northernmost coastal point to the
Florida border—a pretty short stretch between states, considering Georgia is the largest state east of the Mississippi.

However guests arrive, Savannah is conveniently situated by road, rail, or air. Two
interstate highways pass right through: I-95, a continually busy superhighway that
stretches from Florida to Maine, and I-16, an interstate that connects Savannah to
Macon (and I-75) with some 165 miles of the wide-open interstate (translation: dull and
often lightly traveled) you're likely to find in the East. And while we call it an interstate
highway, it never leaves Georgia. Air travelers are going to find Savannah outfitted for
them in a grand style, probably several cuts above what an experienced traveler would
expect for a city this size. If you've ever navigated your way through big-city airports
like those in Chicago or Atlanta, Savannah/Hilton Head International Airport will be a
nice change. Like that of its namesake city, the pace is a little slower and friendlier at
our airport, and there are no football-field-length corridors to run through in order
to make your connections. With an atrium decor reflecting the beauty of Savannah's
squares, there are rocking chairs and park benches strategically placed to help you
pass the time. Other transportation options include Amtrak and Greyhound, which
make stops every day in Savannah.

OVERVIEW

Once you get here, there are several options
to get you around, although the best way
is still the oldest way—on foot, or as you
might hear it called, "riding shank's mare." If
you aren't interested in hoofing it, though,
you'll find a well-developed system of taxis,
a public bus system, a full array of rental car
agencies, even pedicabs, which are kind of

a cross between a tricycle and a rickshaw,
driven by strong-legged guides.

For the adventurous tourist, Segway of
Savannah offers an eco-friendly way to glide
through Savannah's Historic District. Offering
both private and self-tours, costs range from
$40 to $65

Overall, you should find Savannah to be "user friendly," no matter how you decide to get around. You won't find elaborate freeway systems with HOV lanes or throngs of harried commuters rushing to catch their five o'clock train. Sorry, Savannah's stage is set to a slower song, and her neighborly disposition makes her a city to be enjoyed at a leisurely pace.

Achieving the Southern way of seizing the day is easy: Take a deep breath and pretend there are no clocks or schedules. To a visitor, it may seem like Savannahians tackle the daily rigors of getting from one place to another in the same way. They are slow to anger and even slower to drive.

On the outskirts of town, suburban sprawl has given us a fairly recent phenomenon—some commuter-hour congestion, especially on I-16 bound for the bedrooms of Effingham County, or on Abercorn Street's southern extremes approaching the George-town neighborhood and the entrance to I-95 en route to Richmond Hill's neighborhoods in adjacent Bryan County.

So what happens if your navigation system fails or you're lost? Ask a local. More likely than not, he or she will be happy to get you headed in the right direction. Those of us who live or work in the Historic Downtown are particularly experienced at giving directions.

Directions come with caution. Although Savannah's aesthetics may lure you out at midnight, remember this: Take all precautions when walking the streets at night. Keep your wallet or purse secure, and if you're approached, never take the aggressive stand. Give the perpetrator whatever they wish to take and submit. Savannah's street crime—like that of any city—can be violent occasionally.

We have broken this chapter into two sections. Getting Here is just what you would expect: a look at the various modes of transportation to get you to Savannah. Getting Around helps you navigate once you've arrived. It includes a look at parking, public transportation, local roadways, and more.

GETTING HERE
By Air
SAVANNAH/HILTON HEAD INTERNATIONAL AIRPORT
400 Airways Ave.
(912) 964-0514
www.savannahairport.com
The Savannah/Hilton Head International Airport is about 10 miles north of Savannah. The exit number off I-95 is 104. **Delta** (800-221-1212; www.delta.com), and **USAirways** (800-428-4322; www.usairways.com) are the largest carriers and also have been with the airport the longest. Other airlines include **Continental** (800-525-0280; www.continental.com), **United Express** (800-864-8331; www.united.com), and **American Eagle** (800-433-7300; www.aa.com). Nonstop flights are available via various carriers to Atlanta, Charlotte, Newark, Cincinnati, Houston, Miami, New York (La Guardia), Washington, D.C. (Dulles), Dallas, Detroit, Chicago (O'Hare), and Philadelphia. On weekends, Pittsburgh is an additional nonstop destination from here.

The lineup at the airport is prone to change, so stay abreast of flights and airlines via the airport's website. The Airport Commission is on a constant mission to keep the flight selection competitive and cost-effective. It's also easy to confirm flight arrivals and departures because the website stays current.

Not to mislead, the proper name—Savannah/Hilton Head International Airport—is correct, even though there are currently no international flights. (The name was amended to include Hilton Head since about half of the passenger traffic is bound there.) Although the airline getting you here may change, one constant will be where you will arrive. When passengers arrive or depart, they walk through Savannah Square, a relaxing seating area patterned after Savannah's famous downtown squares.

Private Plane Service

SIGNATURE FLIGHT SUPPORT
Savannah/Hilton Head International Airport
1001 Davidson Dr., Suite 150
(912) 964-1557
www.signatureflight.com
Signature Flight Support, part of the international BBA Aviation, is open daily from 6 a.m. to 10 p.m., with additional hours available on request. It offers tie-down service for single- and twin-engine planes, along with parking for jets. Fees depend on the aircraft. Repair service is available on call.

SAVANNAH AVIATION
34 Hangar Rd.
(912) 964-1022, (800) 544-8032
www.savannahaviation.com
Savannah Aviation offers maintenance for piston aircraft as well as pilot supplies. They'll teach you to fly, rent you a plane, or arrange a charter.

Rental Cars

Passengers have a choice of several rental-car agencies on the premises, although they tend to change and you should call ahead if it is particularly important to you to deal with a specific car rental agency. A taxi starter is on duty from 8 a.m. until the last flight arrives to assist with taxi needs. Serving Savannah/Hilton Head International are **Alamo** (800-327-9633; www.alamo.com), **Avis** (800-831-2847; www.avis.com), **Budget** (800-527-0700; www.budget.com), **Dollar Rent A Car** (866-745-5063; www.dollar.com), **Enterprise** (800-736-8222; www.enterprise.com), **Hertz** (800-654-3131; www.hertz.com), **National** (800-227-7368; www.nationalcar.com), and **Thrifty** (800-367-2277; www.thrifty.com).

Taxi and Shuttle Service

The airport distributes a rate brochure (available either outside near all the cabs or inside near the baggage claim) that gives passengers an idea of what it will cost to take a taxi to local bed-and-breakfasts, hotels, motels, and inns. Maximum rates, set by the Savannah City Council, are $25 to the Historic District, $34 to Hutchinson Island, $53 to Tybee Island, $85 to Hilton Head Island, $60 to Bluffton, South Carolina, $60 to The Landings on Skidaway Island; and between $33 and $41 to Savannah's Southside. Cabbies are allowed to charge an additional $5 per passenger in Georgia and $10 per passenger after the first two bound for South Carolina.

Taxi service at the airport can be arranged by calling the taxi stand at (912) 964-8016, or by simply showing up at the cab stand curbside, which is clearly marked and impossible to miss. We've never seen the cab stand unattended. **Low Country Adventures** (800-681-8212) provides airport shuttle service to and from Hilton Head (see our Hilton Head chapter).

Shuttles are a comfortable and efficient alternative to taxis. **K Shuttle** offers scheduled shuttle service from Savannah/Hilton Head International Airport to Hilton Head.

They can be reached by calling (877) 243-2050. The rates are $44 one way and $79 round trip. All passengers arriving into the Savannah airport desiring K Shuttle services must have a prearranged reservation.

There is no scheduled provider of limousine service to and from the airport. However, there are several private limousine services in the city, and these are listed later in this chapter. If you are interested in a ride from the airport, always inquire when calling as to whether the company has a permit to serve the airport.

By Train

AMTRAK
2611 Seaboard Coastline Dr.
(912) 234-2611, (800) 872-7245
The Silver Meteor and Silver Star take turns coming into Savannah as part of their treks along the eastern seaboard. Savannah is in the New York–Miami Amtrak corridor, and travelers have a choice of several departure times each day. Note that there is no train service currently to Atlanta, an omission advocacy groups periodically tackle.

The Amtrak station is about 4 miles from the Historic Downtown. Heading west on I-16, take the Chatham Parkway exit. At the stop sign turn left, then take your first right. The station is open every day from 4:30 a.m. to noon and from 4:30 p.m. to midnight. Taxicabs are at the station when each train pulls in. Rental cars are not available at the station.

By Bus

GREYHOUND BUS LINES
610 West Oglethorpe Ave.
(912) 232-2135
Savannah is on Greyhound Bus Lines' busiest eastern corridor—the stretch between New York City and Miami. Buses depart the city 23 times a day, 7 days a week, with the most frequent departures, as would be expected, headed north toward New York and south to Miami. There are also westbound options. If you are coming to Savannah on Greyhound, you will disembark at the terminal on the far western reaches of Oglethorpe Avenue, one of the Historic Downtown's main thoroughfares. Head out the front door of the station and walk to your left along Oglethorpe—within a few blocks you will be in the heart of the Historic Downtown. If you arrive at night, use extreme caution when walking, as you would in any city. The bus station's locale used to be on the fringes of the restored Historic District, but revitalization has moved into the area, and you'll find more foot traffic and less gritty surroundings. Taxi service is available at the bus terminal.

By Car

Savannah is reachable by car via two major interstates: **I-95** from the north and south and **I-16** running east and west. I-95 is the main artery along the eastern seaboard, stretching from Maine to the tip of Florida. This interstate is extremely congested in the Savannah area during spring, when snowbirds and spring-breakers are heading south for some winter relief, so drive with caution and expect some delays near the exits. I-16 cuts an east-west path across middle Georgia before merging with I-75, which takes you into Atlanta. The following information is a helpful rundown on how to get to the main geographical sections of the city from either of these interstates.

To Historic Downtown
The best option to get to the Historic Downtown is to use I-16 heading east. There are a

couple of clearly marked exits for downtown, but we suggest the one for Liberty Street. Want to swing by the Savannah Visitor Information Center for directions and advice first? As you enter downtown from the interstate, take your first left onto Liberty Street, then your next right onto Martin Luther King Jr. Boulevard (MLK); or take the Louisville Road exit, which is near the end of the interstate and has signs guiding you to the visitor center. You are now essentially a block from the traffic light where the interstate dumped you. The visitors center on the western side of MLK, calling for a tricky left-hand turn into the parking lot. I-95 doesn't go directly into the city, so if you are traveling the north-south route, you'll need to take I-16 (the exit is clearly marked, although it features a wicked curve and tricky dual merge) for the final 10 miles or so.

To the Islands

There are a couple of options to get you to Tybee or the eastern islands of Oatland, Talahi, Whitemarsh, and Wilmington. Take I-16 into the Historic Downtown area and get on any northbound street until you reach Bay Street. Continue east on Bay Street, which, in less than a mile, merges with President Street, then becomes President Street Extension. Follow the President Street Extension until it becomes Islands Expressway. In about 3 miles, it will merge with US 80, which is the main route to Tybee and the eastern islands.

A second option to get you to Tybee, along with the eastern and southeastern islands (Dutch and Isle of Hope), involves leaving I-16 at the 37th Street exit. Take 37th Street to Abercorn Street, take a right, then proceed to Victory Drive, where you will turn left (east). To reach Skidaway Island, take

a right off Victory onto Waters Avenue. To reach the southeastern islands, look for Skidaway Road off Victory Drive and take a right to get to Dutch Island and Isle of Hope. If you continue east on Victory, it will become US 80, which will take you to the eastern islands and Tybee.

To Southside/Midtown

If you are staying near the Southside, you might want to consider exiting I-95 at SR 204 in the southern reaches of the county, about 20 miles south of the Historic Downtown. SR 204 is also Abercorn Street, the main north-south thoroughfare running throughout the entire city. After exiting, head north. After about 3 miles you will enter the Southside—the city's main commercial district, with strip shopping centers, hotels, car dealerships, and Savannah's malls.

Another option to get to the Southside or Midtown area from downtown Bay Street: Head east down Bay Street to President Street Extension. Take the ramp to Truman Parkway (south). You may exit right onto DeRenne Avenue, a main east-west thoroughfare, or depending on your destination, continue south on "the Truman" to Eisenhower or Montgomery Cross Roads. Each exit (DeRenne, Eisenhower, or Montgomery Crossroads) will eventually cross Abercorn. If you turn left on Abercorn, you'll head south and eventually hit I-95. If you turn right, you'll be driving in the direction of downtown (to the left or right).

To West Chatham

The West Chatham communities of Pooler, Bloomingdale, and Garden City are all accessible from I-16 via various marked exits. From I-95 you can also take the Pooler Parkway, which will connect you to US 80 and take you through Bloomingdale, Pooler, and Garden City.

GETTING AROUND

Once you have made it to Savannah, there are several ways you can navigate within the city—from public transportation to a comfortable pair of shoes. Following are some ideas for getting around and a few things to watch out for while traversing the town.

Sampling Savannah

Historic Downtown

Slip on your most comfortable pair of walking shoes and discover Savannah by foot. Named by *Walking* magazine as "one of the top ten walking places in America," the title is not only accurate but inviting! To add to the kudos, *USA Weekend Magazine* called Savannah "one of the ten most beautiful places in America." Savannah's squares are her most adored icons, and there are now 22 of them to explore! Recognized as America's first planned city, General Oglethorpe's design included a series of grids with wide streets connected by shady public squares. These squares served as the town's meeting places. Ellis Square was given a new and contemporary design that reflects the city's progressiveness. There are 13 main north-south streets in the Historic Downtown, stretching from the northernmost point of the city—the Savannah River—south to Forsyth Park. These streets include (listed east to west) East Broad, Houston, Price, Habersham, Lincoln, Abercorn, Drayton, Bull, Whitaker, Barnard, Jefferson, Montgomery, and Martin Luther King Jr. Likewise, there are 23 main east-west streets, starting (for our purposes) at East Broad and ending at Martin Luther King Jr. (which was formerly known as West Broad). These main east-west roadways include River, Bay, Bryan, Congress, Broughton, State, York, Oglethorpe, Hull, Perry, Liberty, Harris, Charlton, Jones, Taylor, Gordon, Gaston, Huntingdon, Hall, Gwinnett, Bolton, Waldburg, and Park.

If our streets resemble a series of necklaces, then some of them are lucky enough to have pearls in the form of squares. In fact, six of the north-south streets—Montgomery, Barnard, Bull, Abercorn, Habersham, and Houston—have these jewels, making them the most beautiful streets in the Historic Downtown. Bull Street, however, is the most commanding strand. Located in the center of the Historic Downtown and easy to spot because it begins at golden-domed City Hall, Bull Street offers some of the most notable squares in the city, including the one where Forrest Gump waited for his bus and where the main plot unfolds in *Midnight in the Garden of Good and Evil.*

It is crucial that you understand how to navigate around the squares while traveling in the Historic Downtown. It's actually quite simple to get around once you understand the basic layout. Imagine heading north or south on one of the six streets with squares. Every couple of blocks you are going to run into one. They're beautiful but they slow you down—not necessarily a bad thing—but local commuters opt for the plainer, straighter, one-way Whitaker Street to get out of town, and the equally straight, plain, and one-way Drayton Street to get in.

No, the squares aren't your standard traffic circles. There is only one lane, and traffic moves in a counterclockwise direction around a beautiful park filled with trees, benches, and in some instances, a monument or fountain. The traffic moves very slowly, so you have ample time to figure out

Getting Some Direction in Historic Downtown

Lost in Historic Downtown? Can't remember where you parked your car or how to get back to your hotel? Look for somebody doling out parking tickets. Under the "Ask Me" program, parking enforcement attendants—the ones buzzing around in those little blue-and-white carts writing parking tickets—are trained to assist tourists in need. They can give directions, help point out the nearest bathroom, even use their radios to track down misplaced cars.

Or venture over to **Ellis Square** at Bryan and Barnard Streets. This square was originally designed in 1733 and named in honor of Henry Ellis, the second royal governor. It was here that the "Old City Market" was located, and in its day, it was a buzz for merchants selling their wares. Shooting fountains now adorn the square, and modern benches are plentiful, but most helpful is a computer/touchscreen guide to the city housed in a glass kiosk. It's perfect for getting your bearings!

where you would like to exit. When entering a square, always yield to any car making its way around the square—it has the right-of-way. Once the coast is clear, enter the square driving to your right. Because we have many visitors (and not a few locals) who don't understand that part about who

has the right-of-way on the square, be cautious.

If you don't want to hit any squares, you can take a straight southbound route through the Historic Downtown on either Price Street or Whitaker Street. Both run one way. Drayton Street, a one-way northern thoroughfare, will get you all the way to the Savannah River without being interrupted by squares. These aren't, however, the prettiest routes. Note that you also will run into squares when traveling east to west in the Historic Downtown. The majority of the east-west routes pass by to the north or south of the squares, but a few intersect them. Again, when approaching a square from the east or west, you must yield to any traffic that is already making its way around the square. Once traffic has cleared, you enter the square by traveling to your right or going straight ahead. Liberty and Oglethorpe are the main east-west streets without squares, and they feature broad, tree-lined center medians. Other square-less east-west routes include Jones, Gaston, Broughton (the downtown business district's "main street"), and Bay. All of this sounds complicated. It isn't, as you will see. Yield when entering a square, travel to the right—as is quite obvious—and you'll do fine.

Islands

The eastern islands, including Whitemarsh, Talahi, Oatland, and Wilmington, are directly off US 80, which is also the only route to Tybee Island. It is a fairly wide, four-lane highway taking you through scenic marshlands before narrowing into a two-lane road as you near Tybee. Skidaway Road leads to Dutch Island and the Isle of Hope (but not, oddly enough, without some turns to Skidaway Island). Waters Avenue is the direct route to Skidaway Island. This well-marked, two-lane road is very busy and congested most times of the day. (Please see our Tybee Island chapter for more information on getting around there.) Pay particular attention to speed limits in school zones and tuck your cell phone away while driving on this road (and all others, for that matter).

Southside/Midtown

Abercorn Street is the main artery running through Savannah's Southside. It begins at the Savannah River in the Historic Downtown, and in its early stretches it is a charming, square-filled route through the Historic Downtown. It continues south some 20 miles to I-95, picking up additional lanes and additional traffic. All the motels, hotels, shopping centers, car dealerships, and other businesses in the Southside are either right on Abercorn or on a street just off this main drag. The six-lane street is heavily traveled and usually very busy. Try to avoid Abercorn during morning and afternoon rush hours—typically 7:30 to 9 a.m. and 4 to 6 p.m. If you are a road-warrior veteran of a gridlocked metropolis, however, you might find our version of rush hour amusing.

DeRenne Avenue, which becomes I-516 at its western end, is the main Southside east-west route. You will find two of the city's hospitals off DeRenne (one just off, and the other a few blocks north on Waters Avenue), along with gas stations, shopping centers, banks, and several medical offices. This road also is heavily traveled and should be avoided during morning and afternoon rush hours. Since this road serves hospital personnel, rush hour tends to start around 3 p.m. weekdays.

Victory Drive (US 80) is Midtown's main drag. It travels through residential neighborhoods and by shopping centers and Grayson Stadium, home of Savannah's minor-league baseball team, the Sand Gnats (see our Spectator Sports chapter). When traveling east, Victory Drive is the main route to Tybee and the eastern islands.

Eisenhower Drive is another major east-west road that accesses Hunter Army Airfield to the west and Skidaway Road to the east. It parallels DeRenne and Victory.

West Chatham

Bay Street, which runs right in front of City Hall in the Historic Downtown, continues to West Chatham, eventually taking you to Garden City and Port Wentworth. George Washington Highway, which turns into Augusta Road, is also another main thoroughfare for this part of town. Another route, US 80, runs through the area as well, taking motorists to Bloomingdale, Pooler, and Garden City.

Parking

When Oglethorpe designed the original city plan for Savannah, he didn't leave space for parking cars. He would probably be amused if he could see his city today, some 270 years later. You can find parking, generally, but it is not free, and it is often not as convenient as you would like in the Historic Downtown. We focus our parking information section on that part of town for a couple of reasons: It's the place most tourists want to roam, and it's the main area in the city where you have to pay to park. Venture outside the Historic Downtown to Southside/Midtown, Islands, or West Chatham, and you shouldn't have any trouble finding ample free parking. (An exception is Tybee Island, which is covered in a separate chapter.)

Despite the high volume of vehicles jostling for places in the Historic Downtown every day, a metered spot or one in a garage or parking lot usually is available. It's the daily downtown worker who finds parking an expensive nightmare, with meters vigilantly patrolled and waiting lists for monthly spaces in the city lots and prime private lots. As a visitor, you might not find a place right next to the square or shop you want to visit, but chances are good you will find one within comfortable walking distance. Utilize one of the modern parking garages to keep you from running back and forth to check the meters. Be advised that it gets more crowded as you get closer to River Street—a main tourist hub overlooking the Savannah River. And remember that no matter how good the parking situation may be the rest of the year, it is going to be tough, if not altogether impossible, to get a spot near downtown on St. Patrick's Day. (See our St. Patrick's Day chapter for more information on the perils of parking during the city's big fest.)

i If you are going to depend on parking meters, keep plenty of change handy. Meters in prime locations or those offering the longest time span often take only quarters. None of them take pennies. By the way, the meter maids in Savannah haven't taken up working on weekends—at least not yet. Conversely, the ones at Tybee Island, our beach, are most vigilant on weekends.

Parking for the majority of the Historic Downtown area (and a little farther south) is metered, costing 30 cents to $1 an hour and more, depending on location. As mentioned in other chapters, the downtown area is patrolled by vigilant parking enforcers who are out in force from 8 a.m. to 5 p.m., Mon through Fri. (Translation: It's free on weekends, provided you don't park anywhere like in front of a fire hydrant.) Leave your meter expired for even a minute or two, and chances are pretty good you are going to get a ticket. The majority of the tickets range between $8 and $15, and you have five days to pay up. After that, an additional $12 is tacked on. Wait 30 days to pay and your ticket suddenly costs you an additional $17. Parking meters are serious business in the city of Savannah, so take careful note of the time and carry change. Most merchants are friendly, but some are grouchy about making meter change. Also, messages posted on some meters claim they are checked on Saturday—which is not true.

The city's Parking Services department has gone high-tech downtown, with the installation of two new varieties of meter beyond the traditional put-in-a-coin-and-turn-the-handle versions. One requires parkers to walk to the middle of the block and buy a paper receipt from a machine, then return to the car and put it on the dashboard. Another version requires drivers to note the number of a parking space, walk to a mid-block computer, and feed in coins. If all of this sounds likely to breed confusion, you're right—it does. On the good side, the newer meters also accept currency and credit cards.

Metered parking is scarcer than ever since security concerns prompted the lifting of curbside parking near federal buildings, so read on to learn about your parking-garage options.

You won't find meters along Broughton Street, the main shopping district in the Historic Downtown. This street has undergone a slow transformation and even today, reflects modern, attractive boutiques, as well as some locally owned shops that may need a little TLC. To promote this area, the city allows free two-hour parking along Broughton Street (with a few spaces that allow only 30 minutes of parking). While there are no meters, you can be ticketed for exceeding the time limit—it is monitored.

City Parking Garages

The city operates four modern parking garages, although they are of limited use during weekday business hours because most of the spaces are taken up by contract parkers. The **Bryan Street Parking Garage** at Bryan and Abercorn Streets is the nicest of the set, and it operates 24/7. The **Whitaker Street Garage** at Whitaker and Bay Lane operates every day. The **State Street Parking Garage** at State and Abercorn Streets closes at 1 a.m. during the week—which will safely see you through dinner and most social events downtown except a steady club crawl. Hours are extended on weekends. The same hours apply at the **Liberty Street Garage** at Liberty and Montgomery Streets. Garage rates are $1 per hour with the exception of the Whitaker Street Garage, which is $2 per hour. Evening, weekend, and special event rates vary.

City Parking

The city operates a few public parking lots as well. Three are on River Street and cost $1 per hour. For easy access to the lots, from Bay Street take the Abercorn, Lincoln, or Barnard Street ramps to River Street. From the Lincoln ramp, turn left to reach the lots. From the Abercorn or Barnard ramps, turn either way on River Street to reach a city lot. Note that these are small lots; your best bet if visiting River Street is to park at the Bay Street level and walk down or ride the public

elevator between City H Regency Savannah.

There are a handful garages and lots in town. to local businesses and ha lists to get in.

Visitor Parking Day Passes

Here's a real bargain. To take the hassle out of feeding meters, the city offers a Visitor Parking Day Pass. The pass, which costs $12, is valid for 48 hours and allows visitors to park at any meter in the Historic Downtown, at time-controlled lots and parking spaces, in the five city parking garages, or at the city parking lots. The pass, which must be displayed on the driver's-side dash, is not valid in all the areas you would expect—private parking lots, hotel parking garages, sweeping zones, freight zones, bagged meters (meters that are covered to tell you that parking is not allowed temporarily), etc.

You can purchase a day pass or find out more information on parking at the Savannah Visitor Information Center, 301 Martin Luther King Jr. Blvd., or at the offices of City of Savannah Parking Services, 100 East Bryan St. (912-651-6470). The pass comes with a map showing parking locations. You can pick up a brochure outlining all the parking regulations at these locations, too.

Public Transportation

CHATHAM AREA TRANSIT
900 East Gwinnett St.
(912) 233-5767 (TDD)
www.catchacat.org
If you hear someone say they are going to "catch a CAT," they are referring to a ride on Chatham County's public bus system. Chatham Area Transit (CAT) has a fleet of buses, including nine green buses that arrived this

...r and travel on 22 routes throughout the county.

CAT offers three free services, two of which are of particular interest to tourists. There's a free CAT shuttle making its way around the Historic District to some 30 stops, including hotels and prime shopping locations and historic squares. The shuttle bus looks like a well-groomed pseudo-trolley and is wheelchair accessible. Shuttle hours are from roughly 7 a.m. to 7 p.m. every day but Sunday, when they start just after 9:30 a.m. and run to about 5 p.m. CAT also operates a passenger ferry to Hutchinson Island, which is also free (more on that later). The third free service is a shuttle originating from the city's Liberty Street parking garage, designed to make that new facility on the edge of the business district more appealing to daily downtown workers—but anyone's welcome to ride it.

As far as the regular bus service goes, you can get just about anywhere you want by catching a CAT, including the city's two malls, the Historic Downtown area, and the Islands (except Tybee). CAT buses do not, however, go to much of West Chatham. All are wheelchair accessible. There are bicycle racks with a capacity of two bikes on the front of the buses. Fare is $1.50 but you can purchase an all-day pass for $3 and literally ride any bus all day. The day pass can be purchased on the bus from the fare box. Children shorter than 40 inches tall—the height of the fare box—get to ride free (limit two free children's fares per adult), and the fare for riders age 65 and older and persons with disabilities is half price. If you plan on doing a lot of traveling around Savannah on CAT, there is a weekly CAT Card—good for unlimited rides—available for $16. You can buy tickets at the Gwinnett Street office

(although you'll never find it or get there without a car), a satellite office at 124 Bull Street, and in the Bull Street (main), Oglethorpe Mall, Carnegie, and Port City branches of the Live Oak Public Library.

Passes can also be purchased in west Chatham County at Walgreen's on SR 21 in Garden City. Regular CAT buses run each day from 6 a.m. to midnight. Bus stops are marked with bright orange signs throughout the city. Some stops have a rain shelter, some have benches, and some are just standing points. There is no service on Thanksgiving, Christmas, or New Year's Day. Its website, www.catchacat.org, is unusually well designed and informative for a government site.

CAT also operates a Links Paratransit van system for Americans with Disabilities Act (ADA)–eligible riders. ADA-eligible visitors are welcome to use the Teleride service. In order to use the door-to-door service, visitors must present an ID card from their hometown transit system that proves their eligibility. The one-way fare for Teleride costs $1.80, and they have discontinued the use of tokens. Senior citizens and disabled persons may now purchase fare passes that provide 20 rides for $15. For more information, call (912) 354-6900.

If you are in the Historic Downtown and want to purchase tokens, passes, or talk to someone about a route, stop in at CAT Central, 124 Bull St., in the county's historic courthouse.

Taxis & Limousines

The best thing to do if you want taxi service in Savannah is to call the cab company directly. In theory, perhaps, you could hail a passing cab, but we've never seen it done—when we want a cab, we telephone and ask for one or go to the cab lineups outside major hotels and the airport. There are several companies in town, typically charging a maximum of $3.50 for the first mile and $1.80 per mile thereafter.

Limousine service also is available from a variety of local companies. Limos typically cost around $65 to $85 per hour, and some of the companies require a two-hour minimum. Advanced reservations are required to ensure prompt service.

Taxi services include **Adam Cab Inc.** (912-927-7466), **Savannah Cab Company** (912-236-2424), **Yellow Cab** (912-236-1133), Checker Cab (912-236-1666), and Ataxicab (912-234-0311).

For limousines, try **A & E Luxury Limousine Service** (912-354-2982), **Low Country Adventures** (912-681-8212 and 800-845-5582), and **First City Limousine** (912-484-0455).

Bicycles

Although some would disagree and rebel by biking all over the city, at present, Savannah is not considered a bike-friendly city. In fact, because of its age, layout, and other considerations, there are only a few bike paths in town. Two of the main passages through town—Broughton Street and Bay Street—are among the most heavily traveled by car and trucks (mainly on Bay), rendering a risky ride for bikers. However, relief may be in sight. In 1997 voters passed a measure that would allow several million dollars to be used to construct a series of bike paths throughout the county. That construction is still well in the future, so don't rely on this for your upcoming trip. Until then, if you must bike, wear a helmet, follow traffic laws, and be aware that most motorists here don't

have regular experience in sharing the roadway with bikes.

For the most part, bikes are not serious commuting or traveling modes in Savannah, although the growing student population at Savannah College of Art and Design is upping the bike census. This is not to say you can't get around on a bike in Historic Downtown or a few other places—more and more people do. It is just not the preferred (or the safest) mode of transportation. If you do decide to rent a bike, observe the law. In the summer of 1999, the city banned bike riding through the downtown squares in the name of pedestrian safety, although the ban does not apply to kids on bikes.

Walking

Henry David Thoreau said, "It is a great art to saunter." Although his words were written in 1841, they remain a forging conviction among Savannahians who live in the landmark Historic District. In the afternoons when the sun is at its peak, they'll emerge from their stately homes—dogs in tow—dressed in their most casual attire and practice the art of walking. Trotting through the squares, they head south to an illustrious setting: Forsyth Park, a magical place that is cast in emerging shadows and flanked by joggers, nannies with children, and an occasional biker who has strayed from the street. Inspired by the grand park fountain that has been pictured in literally thousands of wedding albums, they follow the aura of the artists before their time, seeking a closer look at the fountain sprays that are now illuminated by the setting sun. In short, a walk through this city is a joyous occasion that remains ongoing all year long and is always serenaded by birds and solo street musicians.

Savannah Bike Paths

The designated bike paths in the city include the following (although bikes are legal on any surface street):

- West to East Corridor: 52nd Street to Ward Street to LaRoche Avenue to the entrance of Savannah State University
- North to South Corridor: Habersham Street to Stephenson Avenue to Hodgson Memorial Drive to Edgewater Drive to Hillyer Drive to Dyches Drive to Lorwood Drive to Tibet Avenue to Largo Drive to Windsor Road to Science Drive
- McQueens Island Trail: 6 miles for hiking and biking between Bull River and Fort Pulaski along US 80
- McCorkle Trail: Wilmington Island at Charlie C. Brooks Park, 7001 Johnny Mercer Boulevard

A walking tour of the city begins with your favorite shoes. Shy away from those that might bring blisters. Leave your heels in the suitcase. Tie a sweater around your shoulder and focus on the often-uneven sidewalks, scored from years of wear and the settling earth. To help find your way around on foot, we have included a walking tour in the Attractions chapter—and that's a good place to start. Here are some additional tips along with some rules to help make your steps a little more sure.

Tread Lightly on Savannah's Squares

You don't have to be in peak athletic shape to see this city's magnificent downtown by foot. Fortunately, Historic Downtown is only about 2.5 square miles, so it is fairly easy to see the entire area on foot provided you follow our guidelines.

Savannah's squares are a charming blend of splendor and whimsy, order and extravagance, and they entice visitors seeking solitude, romance, and playful adventure. Designed to create compact, cozy interludes for socializing, the squares are framed in quaint boutiques, coffee shops, and rustic eateries, and set amid a background of Southern hospitality. They provide excellent markers for walking tours. These serene settings beg for relaxed audiences. There's a story in each and every one. Benches are plentiful, and their beauty unfolds as the days change color and the breezes usher in the aura of nighttime charm.

Crossing Bay Street

Although the Historic Downtown is generally very pedestrian friendly, one area that isn't is Bay Street. This is the main street running east to west in front of City Hall. Many tourists encounter Bay Street, as it must be crossed to reach River Street, the tourist haven running along the Savannah River. As mentioned in our Bicycles section, Bay Street is a very busy, narrow four-lane road that serves as the main throughway for 18-wheeler traffic trying to make it to other areas in the city. Many visitors think they can beat the traffic on Bay Street, get halfway across, and find themselves stuck in the middle, dangerously close to traffic and unable to safely pass to the other side. After experimenting with several options, the city went with increasing the number of traditional traffic lights to get pedestrians across. Most have a button-activated pedestrian signal: Push it, wait (and wait), then move quite briskly across. A few have audio features designed to serve the blind. So, in short, resist the urge to simply cross this street; go out of your way to cross at the designated pedestrian signals.

Getting to River Street

Savannah is built on a bluff overlooking the river, even though it probably looks flat to you. River Street runs along the Savannah River, which means it's lower than the rest of the city and can present a challenge to pedestrians. One of our favorite city projects—and a favorite improvement to this area—was the 1998 installation of an elevator behind City Hall on Bay Street. The wheelchair-accessible elevator whisks riders down to River Street, avoiding the stairs and the cobblestone streets on its way. The elevator is between City Hall (can't miss that giant gold dome) and the Hyatt Regency Savannah. Part of the elevator project included the installation of a public restroom facility on the River Street level. We've stopped in periodically and have been impressed with its upkeep. There's also a small information station with a friendly question-answerer, a brochure rack, and—most importantly in Savannah's climate—a water fountain. The more adventurous pedestrian might want to skip the elevator and hoof it down the uneven cobblestones to River Street. One option to get to River Street involves treacherous stairs. There are several routes available, although—apart from the elevator—we prefer the wide, easily negotiated set that runs along the east (right-hand when you face the river) side of City Hall. All these stairs are literally hundreds of years old, and many aren't

particularly easy to navigate, such as the narrow slate steps curving along a stone wall with an aged metal railing. The steps tend to be beside the ramps that carry traffic to River Street. Be extremely careful, and if you prefer, walk down the ramps that cars use to get to the river.

Although you can avoid the tricky stairs this way, you won't avoid the cobblestone ramps, another potential pedestrian pitfall. The cobblestones, although visually charming, are not as steep as the stairs, but beware when walking on them with any type of heeled shoe. Historians will point out that these are ballast stones used to balance the weight on ships coming in and out of the port, not proper cobblestones. These roads and ramps are uneven and difficult to walk on, even for people with the surest feet and flattest shoes. If you are not above sneaking, you can duck into the elevator at the Savannah Hyatt Regency for a ride down to River Street—but you can't take a ride up without a room key.

Crossing the River

The development of the Savannah International Trade and Convention Center and the Westin Savannah Harbor Resort on Hutchinson Island—an island between Georgia and South Carolina—added some transportation challenges. You can get to Hutchinson Island easily by road, via the Talmadge Bridge. But rather than drive for several miles, the resort and convention development is literally a stone's throw, or a healthy tee shot, from River Street. The obvious solution for auxiliary transportation between the two sites was a passenger ferry, and two ferries designed expressly for the route were delivered in 2004. They're known as the Savannah Belles Ferry System, operated by the

Chatham Area Transit Authority, or CAT. The vessels are named for two historic women— Juliette Gordon Low, the Savannah-born founder of the Girl Scouts, and Susie King Taylor a former slave who started one of the first schools for blacks in Savannah. The ferries are designed to look nostalgic and operate at about 20-minute intervals. After quibbling about fares for a couple years, the ferry trip is now free. Unless you are attending an event at the Savannah International Trade and Convention Center or staying at the Westin Savannah Harbor Golf Resort and Spa (or patronizing one of its amenities), you won't really need to use the ferry. We recommend it anyway, especially if you have children in your party. It's fun to see River Street from the vantage point of an arriving sailor, and the sail across the river and back can be completed in about 15 or 20 minutes.

Ferries operate seven days a week, weather and river conditions permitting, from 7:30 a.m. to 10:30 p.m. Ferry landings are at River Street behind City Hall, at the Savannah Marriott Riverfront, and on Hutchinson Island at the convention center.

Quick Driving Tips

Here are a few suggested routes that may save you some time and frustration when getting from a few popular point As to point Bs. Note that all these jaunts are in the 15-to-20-minute range.

Historic Downtown to Oglethorpe Mall

Option One: Take Whitaker Street south about 2 miles to Victory Drive. Turn left onto Victory Drive, then right at the second light onto Abercorn Street. The mall is about 4 miles down Abercorn Street. Turn left into Oglethorpe on Mall Boulevard.

Option Two: Take Bay Street east. In less than 1 mile it runs into President Street Extension. From President Street Extension, take Truman Parkway. After a couple of miles, exit to the right on Eisenhower Drive, then turn left onto Abercorn and look for Mall Boulevard after a couple of blocks.

Historic Downtown to Savannah Mall

Take I-16 4 miles west to the Lynes Memorial Parkway exit and go south. After 2.5 miles on the Lynes Parkway, exit at the Southwest Bypass (also known as the Veterans Parkway) and continue 7.5 miles until it ends at SR 204. Turn left onto SR 204, which becomes Abercorn Street, and the mall will be some 3 miles ahead on your left. Or just take one of the options to Oglethorpe Mall and opt to stay on Abercorn instead of turning onto Mall Boulevard; Savannah Mall is only a couple miles farther, on the right.

Historic Downtown to Savannah/Hilton Head International Airport

Take I-16 west to I-95 north. The airport is 14 miles away at exit 104 off I-95.

Historic Downtown to Amtrak Station

Go west on Liberty Street, which turns into Louisville Road after less than a mile. Take a left onto Telfair Road, then a right onto Seaboard Coastline Drive.

HISTORY

Perhaps no other city owes as much to one man as Savannah owes to James Edward Oglethorpe, the English soldier and politician who founded Georgia. Oglethorpe was the mastermind and driving force behind the development of the colony of Georgia, whose first city was Savannah. He selected the site of the city and christened it, giving it the same name as the river that flows beside it. Oglethorpe supervised the first phase of the building of Savannah, and he nurtured the city during its infancy as a town. He defended it in its early years, militarily and financially.

More than that, Oglethorpe bestowed on Savannah a gift that has flourished throughout the decades and centuries since his passing. He designed and laid out the town and, in so doing, created the atmosphere that makes Savannah unique among cities. He left a legacy that has been admired and enjoyed by countless residents and visitors—a treasure that will be the pride of the city for as long as it stands.

OGLETHORPE & HIS IDEA

Oglethorpe was born into a family that had a long history of service to England. After serving in the British army and fighting the Turks as the aide-de-camp of an Austrian prince, Oglethorpe was elected to the lower house of Parliament in 1722 at the age of 25. He developed an interest in the misfortunes of the poor, in particular the plight of debtors who had been thrown into prison by creditors hoping the debtors' friends would secure their release by paying the debts. He worked for prison reform and attempted to find solutions to England's unemployment problems.

Together with John Perceval, another member of Parliament, Oglethorpe hatched the idea of giving people who were out of work a fresh start by transporting them to a new colony in America that would be located between Spanish Florida and the English colony of South Carolina. Oglethorpe

and Perceval petitioned King George II for a charter, which the king signed on April 21, 1732. The deal was not one-sided: The crown was motivated by the prospect of having colonists raise produce and procure raw materials to ship to England, while the colony served as a market for English goods. The idea of having the new colony act as a buffer between the Spanish in Florida and thriving South Carolina was not lost on the royals either. To top it all off, the colony was to be named Georgia in honor of the king.

The colony would be managed by Oglethorpe, Perceval, and 19 other trustees, who would receive no pay and no land for their involvement. There were also rules for the colony: Slavery, lawyers, and "brandies and distilled liquors" (in particular rum) were prohibited, as were Catholics. In time, all would be allowed. Those who took advantage of the free passage to Georgia offered by the trustees agreed to remain in the colony for three years, and each received a town lot for a house and 50 acres to farm. A colonist would not own the acreage and could occupy it only as long as he farmed it properly. Grants of 500 acres were available to people who paid their way to the colony.

The trustees adopted as their motto the Latin phrase *Non sibi sed allis* (Not for themselves but others). It appears on Georgia's original seal, which also bears a rendering of a silkworm crawling across a mulberry leaf; it was hoped that the colony would produce silk in abundance.

BEFORE THE ENGLISH CAME

Although Oglethorpe brought a European-style civilization to this land known as Georgia, he and his little band of settlers were very much the new kids on the block. According to Max E. White, author of *Georgia's Indian Heritage*, human beings had existed in Georgia many centuries before. White states that "the earliest evidence of man's presence in Georgia and the Southeast is in the form of fluted projectile points identical to or very similar to those found west of the Mississippi and dated to about 12,000 years ago." In addition to discovering such rudimentary tools as projectile points, modern man has found other evidence of the native peoples of Georgia—shell middens and ceremonial mounds. The middens are piles of refuse "composed primarily of mussel shells discarded by prehistoric diners." "Many times," says White, "people were buried in these shell heaps and utilitarian objects, such as bone awls, projectile points, etc., were often placed with them." The remnants of shell middens can be seen in the Savannah area at Skidaway Island State Park.

Although Oglethorpe and his Englishmen were the first Europeans to make a go of settling in southeast Georgia, others had visited before them. Spanish explorer Hernando de Soto passed through in 1539–40 during his trek across what became the southeastern United States. After de Soto's countrymen established a settlement at St. Augustine, Florida, in 1565, they built Catholic missions and churches on Georgia's sea islands, the last of which was closed in 1702. French explorer Jean Ribault—who started short-lived settlements at what are now Jacksonville, Florida, and Beaufort, South Carolina—sailed along the Georgia coast in 1562.

"Almost all of Georgia was forest-covered when the Europeans first appeared on the scene," says White. The Native Americans living there were, for the most part, members of the Creek and Cherokee nations, "practicing an economy based on agriculture, hunting, fishing, and gathering." Most were Indians belonging to the Creek Confederacy, and one of them—Tomo-chi-chi—would have a significant impact on the survival of Oglethorpe's new colony.

A WHOLE NEW WORLD

Oglethorpe and his fellow trustees recruited 114 colonists comprising 35 families for the first voyage to Georgia and the task of starting a settlement there. Oglethorpe was the only trustee to make the trip. They left Gravesend, England, on November 17, 1732, aboard a 200-ton vessel named the *Anne* and arrived in what is now Charleston, South Carolina, on January 13, 1733. The settlers then made their way south down the South Carolina coast and, after transferring to smaller boats, landed in the new colony on February 1. That was the date of Georgia's founding according to the Julian calendar. When that calendar was abandoned in favor of the Gregorian calendar 19 years later, the date became February 12—the day now celebrated as Georgia Day (see GHS's Georgia Days in the Annual Events and Festivals chapter). Oglethorpe had gone ahead of the colonists several days before their landing and had chosen a site for the town of Savannah on a 40-foot-high bluff overlooking the Savannah River—Yamacraw Bluff. In a letter to the trustees explaining his choice of the site for a city, he stated that he "thought it healthy" and wrote, "The last and fullest consideration of the Healthfulness of the place was that an Indian nation, who knew the Nature of the Country, chose it for their Habitation."

The Indians were the 100-odd members of the Yamacraw tribe of the Lower Creek nation, led by an 80-year-old chief named Tomo-chi-chi (meaning to "fly up"). The Yamacraws would prove friendly and helpful to the colonists—providing them with food, interceding with other tribes on their behalf, and aiding them in their struggle against the Spanish. The Yamacraws had come to the coast some eight years before the English, led there by Tomo-chi-chi from what is now west Georgia. Other new neighbors were the Musgroves—Mary, an Indian woman, and her husband John, who was white. The Musgroves ran a nearby trading post called Musgrove Cowpen, and they would serve as interpreters for the Europeans and the Native Americans.

The colonists spent their first night in their new home camped out in an area that is now the site of a small park at Bay and Whitaker Streets. In the following days and weeks, Oglethorpe and Col. William Bull of South Carolina laid out the new city,

and the settlers set about clearing the pine woods on the bluff with the help of black slaves from the neighboring colony. They also began cultivating a 10-acre plot that would be known as Trustees' Garden. On this parcel, at the current Bay and East Broad Streets, were planted fruit trees and the mulberry trees that were envisioned as the basis of Georgia's silk industry.

i One branch of the most heavily traveled road in Colonial America—the Great Indian Warrior/Trading Path—reached to what would become Savannah, all the way from the Great Lakes. A historical marker on Liberty Street near its intersection with Martin Luther King Jr. Boulevard states that the path "passed through here."

Things went well at the outset. By fall 1734, according to a letter from a South Carolina merchant who had visited the town, there were 80 houses and 40 more being built. During Georgia's first decade, the trustees sent more than 2,000 settlers. Other new arrivals brought diversity to the colony. Among them was a boatload of Jews from Portugal who established a Jewish congregation, Mickve Israel. It was the third founded in America and continues today as the South's oldest. Another was a group of Germans, the Salzburgers, who settled 21 miles upriver from Savannah in what is now Effingham County. Their community of New Ebenezer prospered, and the house of worship they built in 1769 is the oldest standing church in Georgia.

Also during the colony's infancy, Savannah became the site of the oldest orphanage in America with a continuous existence: Bethesda Home for Boys. The orphanage's

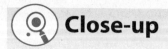

Close-up

What Are These Squares All About?

No one knows for sure what inspired Oglethorpe to design Savannah as he did. Whatever Oglethorpe's inspiration, it lives on happily in the form of Savannah's priceless jewels—her squares. Enjoy this brief summary of each:

- **Calhoun Square,** Abercorn and Wayne Streets—This square was named in honor of John C. Calhoun, a South Carolinian considered to be the Old South's greatest spokesman in the U.S. Senate. Designed in 1851, this is the only square where all of the original historic buildings remain.

- **Chatham Square,** Bernard and Wayne Streets—Designed in 1847, this square was named in honor of William Pitt, English prime minister and the Earl of Chatham during the period when Georgia was a royal colony.

- **Chippewa Square,** Bernard and Wayne Streets—This square was named for the Battle of Chippewa, an American victory in Canada during the War of 1812. Designed in 1815, the square's center offers a striking bronze statue of the colony's founder, Gen. James Edward Oglethorpe.

- **Columbia Square,** Habersham and President Streets—Named for the female personification of the United States. Designed in 1799, this square boasts a fountain from the Wormsloe Plantation, a historic Savannah settlement.

- **Crawford Square,** Houston and McDonough Streets—Named for William Crawford, a Georgia governor and U.S. secretary of the treasury, this square was designed in 1841.

- **Ellis Square,** Bryan and Barnard Streets—Named for Sir Henry Ellis, Georgia's second royal governor, this square lies at the site of Old City Market, a high-traffic zone in days gone by for merchants and townspeople. Restored after bulldozing an unsightly parking garage, this square sits at the hub of present-day City Market and is directly in the center of a revitalized area of downtown.

- **Franklin Square,** Montgomery and St. Julian Streets—This square is named for statesman and inventor Benjamin Franklin, who at one time was an agent for Georgia in London. Once home to the city's water tower, this square is flanked by First African Baptist Church and the west end of City Market.

- **Greene Square,** Houston and President Streets—Named for General Nathanael Greene of Rhode Island, a Revolutionary War hero and short-lived owner of a plantation west of Savannah, this square was designed in 1799. Second African Baptist Church is located here.

- **Johnson Square,** Bull and St. Julian Streets—This square is named for Robert Johnson, the royal governor of South Carolina who aided Oglethorpe in establishing the colony of Georgia.

- **Lafayette Square,** Abercorn and Macon Streets—Named for the Marquis de Lafayette, the Frenchman who was an important ally of the United States during the Revolutionary War, this 1873-designed square offers a fountain dedicated by the Colonial Dames of America.

- **Madison Square,** Bull and Macon Streets—James Madison, fourth president of the United States, was honored with this square named for him. Designed in 1837, a monument stands of Sgt. William Jasper, who fell during the Siege of Savannah in 1779. The granite marker denotes the southern line of the British defense during the 1779 battle.

- **Monterey Square,** Bull and Wayne Streets—Designed in 1847 and named for the Mexican city captured by U.S. forces during the war with Mexico, the square's monument honors Casmir Pulaski, a Polish nobleman who was mortally wounded while fighting for the Americans during the Siege of Savannah.

- **Oglethorpe Square,** Abercorn and President Streets—Named for James Edward Oglethorpe, founder of Georgia; this is a popular square for outdoor weddings.

- **Orleans Square,** Bernard and McDonough Streets—This square was named for the Battle of New Orleans, an American victory in the War of 1812. Designed in 1815, the fountain in the square was dedicated in 1989 by Savannah's German Society to recognize the contributions of Savannah's early German immigrants.

- **Pulaski Square,** Bernard and Macon Streets—Confederate hero Francis S. Bartow's home stands on this square named for Polish Count Casmir Pulaski.

- **Reynolds Square,** Abercorn and St. Julian Streets—This square, perfect for picnics, is one of the most colorful, thanks to beauty of the Olde Pink House and nearby Lucas Theatre. It was designed in 1733 and named for Georgia's first royal governor, John Reynolds. In 1969 the monument was changed as a tribute to John Wesley, the founder of Methodism and the Anglican minister to the colony in 1736.

- **Telfair Square,** Barnard and President Streets—The Telfair family, whose members made important contributions to Georgia in the areas of politics, business, the arts, and philanthropy, is honored in this beautiful square—another popular place for picnics.

- **Troup Square,** Habersham and McDonough Streets—Named for Georgia governor George Michael Troup, who was also a U.S. senator, Troupe Square is home to the Unitarian Universalist Church and the McDonough Row Houses. The Armillary Sphere, an astronomical device designed to show the relationship among the celestial circles, stands in the center.

- **Warren Square,** Habersham and St. Julian Streets—Boasting a 1791 design, this square was named for General Joseph Warren, a hero of the Revolutionary War.

- **Washington Square,** Houston and St. Julian Streets—Named for George Washington, first president of the United States.

- **Whitefield Square,** Habersham and Wayne Streets—Named for George Whitefield, one of the founders of the Bethesda orphanage, a traditional gazebo sits in the center amid surrounding Victorian architecture.

- **Wright Square,** Bull and President Streets—Named for Sir James Wright, Georgia's third royal governor, Wright Square boasts a rich history as a large boulder marks the grave of Tomo-chi-chi, the Yamacraw Indian chief who welcomed Gen. Oglethorpe and the first colonists.

founders, George Whitefield and James Habersham, came to Georgia in 1738 at the request of two Anglican ministers, the Wesley brothers, Charles and John, the latter of whom preached in Savannah during the mid-1730s and went on to found the Methodist church. Bethesda was situated southeast of the town on the banks of the Moon River, with the foundation of the first building being laid in March 1740. It is still in operation in a related capacity, and visitors are welcome to tour the site, a museum, and a chapel (see our Attractions chapter).

Oglethorpe remained involved with the colony during its first 10 years, and in July 1742, he led a contingent of soldiers and Indian allies in a battle that forever wrested control of the region from the Spanish in Florida. In the Battle of Bloody Marsh, his band of defenders surprised and defeated a numerically superior Spanish invasion force about 70 miles south of Savannah at St. Simons Island. The Spanish never attempted another invasion, and a peace treaty between Spain and England was signed in 1748.

Oglethorpe left Georgia on July 22, 1743, never to return. Even before his departure, Savannah began to decline as the population dwindled due to the hardships of bringing civilization to a wilderness: insects, alligators, extremes in the weather, difficulties in growing crops. The colony remained a trusteeship until 1752, when the trustees, burdened by financial problems and turnover in their ranks, relinquished their charter to the crown a year before it was to expire. As Preston Russell and Barbara Hines wrote in their lyrical *Savannah: A History of Her People Since 1733*, "Non Sibi Sed Allis had fallen on its nose. The dream was long since dead, but Savannah was here to stay."

i Among Savannah's tributes to founder James Edward Oglethorpe is a large bronze status of the Englishman in Chippewa Square. The monument is the work of Daniel Chester French, sculptor of the Minuteman statue in Concord, Massachusetts. You'll notice that Oglethorpe faces toward Florida, still guarding his beloved Savannah against an invasion from the south.

A ROYAL COMEBACK

Under control of the crown, Georgia's government changed from the benevolent dictatorship of the trustees to a more traditional setup headed by a governor and having an assembly of elected representatives. Under this arrangement, Georgia was upgraded from colony to province, with Savannah serving as the seat of government.

The first Royal Assembly met in Savannah in January 1755, and one of its first acts was to adopt a law allowing slavery. The first of Georgia's three royal governors, John Reynolds, began a two-and-a-half-year tenure in October 1754; he was succeeded by Henry Ellis, who gave way to James Wright in 1760. Wright, who ruled as governor until January 1776, was a godsend for Savannah's struggling economy. "In mere months, Wright led the youngest colony through stages of development that had required years in other colonies," states Edward Chan Sieg in his book *Eden on the Marsh: An Illustrated History of Savannah*. "Wright's administration was geared to accommodate the 'men of substance' who began to pour into Georgia from other colonies and from the plantations of the Indies. Aided by liberal credit policies and cheap labor, they transformed the coastal plains into the great plantations of legend. Wharf facilities and warehouses appeared on the bluff as shipping demands increased almost daily."

Old Fort Irish?

During your stay in our town, you might hear someone referred to as being "Old Fort Irish." This means the person is of Irish descent and grew up in the area of northeast Savannah where Fort Wayne once stood. According to local historian James Mack Adams, the fort, which was also called the Fort of Savannah and Fort Provost, was built about 1760 and was abandoned in the mid-1800s. A gas works was built on the site, and Irish immigrants flocked to the area because of low rents. The fort site at Bay and East Broad Streets is now called Trustees' Garden and is the location of shops, apartments, offices, and the Pirates' House restaurant.

The major export was rice, the growing of which had been made possible by the repeal of the ban on slavery. The idea of making Savannah a silk-production center had flopped, apparently due to a combination of mismanagement and the silkworms' problems with the climate. By 1766, Wright was estimating that the province of Georgia was inhabited by as many as 10,000 whites and 7,800 black slaves—up from a total of 3,000 people nine years earlier—and that exports of rice had tripled over a six-year span.

THE GREAT REBELLION

In the mid-1760s, many residents of England's American colonies reacted with outrage to what they deemed unfair taxation of imported items by the mother country. As the following decade unfolded, their dissatisfaction grew to the point that they sought independence from England.

The fervor for freedom took hold somewhat slowly in Savannah, but by mid-1774, it began to show itself in the actions of a group of dissidents called the Liberty Boys. Despite Governor Wright's efforts to stop them, they met several times to protest England's closing of the Boston Harbor as punishment for the Boston Tea Party. In January 1775, Noble Wimberly Jones, a Liberty Boy who had been speaker of the Royal Assembly, convened a meeting of Georgia's First Provincial Congress. Wright dissolved the body, but on July 4 a meeting of a second provincial congress was held, with the 102 delegates electing representatives to the colonies' Second Continental Congress.

In the interim, in May members of the Liberty Boys celebrated the opening shot of the American Revolution by breaking into the city's munitions room, stealing 600 pounds of powder, and shipping it to Boston to be used in the fight against the British. The powder really hit the fan on January 18, 1776, when three British warships showed up off the coast of Savannah. The newly established provincial government placed Wright under house arrest, putting an end to British rule in Savannah for the time being. The governor later slipped away and escaped on an English vessel.

On August 10, Savannahians aching for freedom celebrated the signing of the Declaration of Independence, a document endorsed by three Georgians, George Walton of Savannah and Lyman Hall and Button Gwinnett of nearby St. John's Parish. The new state of Georgia elected Archibald Bulloch as governor and completed a constitution in February 1777. Bulloch died during his first year in office and was replaced by Gwinnett.

i Downtown's *Colonial Cemetery* is the final resting place of many early settlers, including Button Gwinnett, one of the original signers of the Declaration of Independence

Savannah, being in an exposed position on the far southeastern reaches of the new United States, paid for its location on December 29, 1778, when 3,000 British troops commanded by Col. Archibald Campbell routed the city's 700 defenders. The enemy had landed below Savannah two days before and slipped behind American Gen. Robert Howe and his forces. The British sacked the city, and James Wright returned to take control of Savannah. He and a small redcoat garrison found themselves under siege in September 1779 by a force of Frenchmen, Irishmen, and volunteers from Haiti. They were joined by a contingent of American troops from South Carolina, and on October 9, the overall commander of the allied forces, French Count Charles Henri d'Estaing, ordered an attack on a defensive position southwest of the city in an area near the existing Savannah Visitor Information Center. The assault on this position, the Spring Hill redoubt, was, in the words of authors Russell and Hines, "a disaster, the bloodiest single hour in the entire Revolution."

"Through three valiant advances and the staggering retreat," they wrote, "French and Americans were slaughtered by land and naval artillery from Spring Hill redoubt

and from . . . ships in the river." The defenders lost 55 men; the attackers suffered more than 1,000 casualties, including the deaths of 2 men later immortalized in monuments in Savannah's squares—Casmir Pulaski, a Polish count who had brought a group of lancers to the fray, and Sgt. William Jasper, who fell while attempting to save the flag of his South Carolina regiment. Savannah remained in possession of the British until after the climactic Battle of Yorktown. Wright and his compatriots evacuated the city several months after that American victory in Virginia, and American forces took control of the city on July 11, 1782.

THE ANTEBELLUM ERA

The Revolutionary War left Savannah a shambles, but the city recovered and prospered in the years between the end of that fight for freedom and an even grimmer struggle in the 1860s. Much of Savannah's prosperity in the years after the Revolution and before the American Civil War was due to a machine invented in 1793 on a plantation west of the city. While serving as a tutor at Mulberry Grove—a plantation owned by the widow of Revolutionary War Gen. Nathanael Greene—a Connecticut schoolteacher named Eli Whitney perfected the cotton gin, a device for removing the seeds from cotton bolls. The machine helped revolutionize the cotton-producing industry and, in so doing, reinforced the value of slavery in the agrarian South—a circumstance that would bring disaster to the region and Savannah.

But in the early 1800s, cotton brought wealth to the city's port. On the subject of the city's transformation, Russell and Hines wrote, "In 1790 cotton exports were one thousand bales; by 1820 they were ninety thousand bales a year. In 1794 Savannah's population was 2,000 with export revenues under $500,000. By 1819 she was America's sixteenth largest city with exports exceeding $14,000,000." As Savannah prospered, its residents built elegant homes and other imposing structures. Probably the most famed of the designers of these buildings was architect William Jay, who came to the city from England in 1818, stayed for seven years, and is responsible for existing masterpieces such as the Owens-Thomas House, the Scarbrough House, and the Telfair Museum of Art (see our Attractions chapter).

Savannahians experienced some giddy high points during the years between the wars. Among the highest was the transatlantic voyage of the SS *Savannah*, a vessel that was bankrolled by local merchants and propelled by steam and sail. The ship left Savannah on May 22, 1819, and arrived in Liverpool, England, a record-breaking 29 days and 11 hours later. On the return trip, the Savannah shattered that record by four days. A much more lasting achievement involving transportation occurred in 1847 when the Central of Georgia Railroad was completed, with Savannah as its eastern terminus. At that time, "Savannah reached its antebellum zenith," stated author Edward Chan Sieg.

"Now profits really soared and Savannah enjoyed a period of unprecedented growth. In addition to cotton, other sources of income were tobacco, rice, corn, lumber, and naval stores. The population tripled, the city limits were extended, gas lighting made its appearance. Hospitals, churches, and orphanages grew in number for blacks and whites as excess wealth permitted the emergence of the charity traditions which were Savannah's birthright."

Other highly memorable moments occurred when two heroes of the revolution visited the city. In May 1791, while he was serving as the first president of the United States, George Washington came to town for four days and attended numerous get-togethers. One of these was a ball at which, according to William Harden's *A History of Savannah and South Georgia*, the Father of Our Country was "introduced to ninety-six elegantly dressed ladies." In appreciation of his stay, Washington presented the militiamen of the Chatham Artillery with two brass cannon used at Yorktown; they now occupy a spot on Bay Street just east of City Hall. The other visitor was Washington's French ally, the Marquis de Lafayette. He stopped over in March 1825 and was honored with a parade and many toasts.

Unfortunately, there were also some low points, including fires that destroyed large parts of the city in 1796 and 1820, deadly outbreaks of yellow fever in 1820 and 1854 (the epidemic of the former year killed 666), and a storm in 1804 that caused the drowning of more than 100 slaves, submerged Hutchinson Island, and greatly damaged many of the area's plantations. But as bad as those occurrences were, they were almost insignificant when compared to a disaster that was yet to come.

THE WORST KIND OF WAR

Disputes between Northern and Southern states over slavery and states' rights boiled over in the mid-1800s with cataclysmic results: the secession of Georgia and her Southern neighbors from the Union, the South's forming of a Confederacy, and the fighting of a war of the worst kind—a civil war. Although the war started in Charleston on April 16, 1861, when Confederate forces

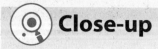

Close-up

Savannah's Priceless Jewels

The squares of Savannah lend the town a beauty and charm that's unique among American cities. But it's likely that James Edward Oglethorpe had defense as much as aesthetics in mind when he included the little parks in his plan for the city.

According to *Historic Savannah,* a survey of the city's buildings published by the Historic Savannah Foundation in 1979, "military considerations certainly played a major role" in the plan. The smallness of the squares and lots surrounding them "made the town more compact and easier to defend." The squares were also places where colonists living in nearby outposts could bring their families and livestock if attacked by Spaniards or Indians.

As conceived by Oglethorpe, the squares were at the center of the town's wards. Each ward had four "tythings," with each tything containing 10 lots for houses. In a ward, the tythings were on the northern and southern sides of the square, with the eastern and western sides of the square set aside as trust lots for public buildings. Oglethorpe laid out six wards and their squares. Four of these squares—now named Johnson, Wright, Ellis, and Telfair—were laid out in 1733, with Johnson being the first. Later, Oglethorpe laid out Reynolds and Oglethorpe Squares.

Eventually, a total of 24 squares were created. Two of them, Elbert and Liberty, have been "lost" to progress—bisected by Montgomery Street, they now exist as half squares, with one half still park like and the other half covered by public buildings. A third square, Ellis, was covered by a parking garage for 50 years but has been restored to a pristine, modern square depicting Savannah's forward progress. The square is replete with a shiny, contemporary visitor center and public restrooms. A new statue of Johnny Mercer seemingly leaning on a bench or wall, adds to the square's interest.

fired on and captured Fort Sumter, it was Savannah that, in the words of writers Russell and Hines, committed "the first belligerent act of the rebellious South."

Three months before Sumter, members of three militia outfits traveled by steamer from Savannah to Cockspur Island and seized Fort Pulaski, a large masonry edifice guarding the mouth of the Savannah River. Wrote Col. Charles H. Olmstead, who commanded the Confederates, "In due time Fort Pulaski was reached; its garrison, one elderly United States sergeant, made no defense, and the three companies of the First Volunteer Regiment marched in with drums

beating and colors flying, and so for them a soldier's life began." Olmstead and others thought Fort Pulaski was impregnable. But 15 months after its bloodless seizure, shells from rifled cannon emplaced on Tybee Island by Federal troops left the thick walls of the fort looking like Swiss cheese (see our Tybee Island chapter). After 30 hours of bombardment, Olmstead realized that holding the fort was impossible and surrendered it and its 385 defenders.

Following Pulaski's fall, the new occupants of the fort and their comrades in the Union navy began a blockade of Savannah. The city's exports of cotton and other goods were thus bottled up, and the residents spent most of the war enduring the hardships of the siege by sea and mourning the loss of relatives and loved ones who fell on faraway fields of fire. Among those who died were brothers Joseph C. and William N. Habersham, killed in fighting near Atlanta on the same day in July 1864.

i The *Green-Meldrim House* on Madison Square is the site of the meeting in January 1865 that inspired the famed "40 acres and a mule" declaration, giving black freedmen land in Georgia, South Carolina, and Florida.

Later that year came Union Gen. William T. Sherman's devastating March to the Sea across Georgia. The prize at the end of the trek was Savannah. Sherman took it on December 21, but not before a battle at Fort McAllister south of Savannah near Richmond Hill (see our Day Trips chapter) and a skirmish at what would become the town of Pooler. The Union commander also allowed a force of 10,000 badly outnumbered Confederate defenders to slip out of the city and into South Carolina. In an oft-quoted telegram to President Abraham Lincoln that the commander in chief received on Christmas Eve, Sherman wrote, "I beg to present you as a Christmas Gift, the City of Savannah with 150 heavy guns and plenty of ammunition; and also about 25,000 bales of Cotton."

Savannah was out of the war, and its citizens settled in to cope with the city's occupation by Union troops. For the most part, it was a benign affair. "The occupation was a model of order, even occasional pleasantry, with both sides generally behaving like ladies and gentlemen," wrote Russell and Hines. Regardless of this, however, some

of the women of the town refused to walk beneath the American flag.

BOUNCING BACK AGAIN

Unlike some Southern cities, Savannah survived the Civil War without being decimated by shell fire or burned to the ground, although a fire that broke out a month after the city's surrender destroyed 100 buildings. But the war took its toll, leaving the city bankrupt and its people in need of food. However, within a year of the end of hostilities, said Sieg in *Eden on the Marsh*, "Savannah was rolling again," a beneficiary of the rapid rebuilding of the South's railroads and a resurgence in cotton production. In Savannah, "exports for 1867 exceeded fifty million dollars," wrote Sieg. "The predictors of doom following the loss of slave labor were proved wrong as a rising market pushed cotton production to levels never realized" under slavery.

After the war, Savannah and the rest of the South entered into an 11-year period of Reconstruction during which radical Northern politicians hoped to build a power base with the support of former slaves. Ultimately they failed, and slavery was replaced by a caste system and the creation of a so-called separate but equal society that was more separate than it was equal. In Savannah, "blacks entered a long period of assimilation," said Sieg. "As a result, they developed their own culture, built their own institutions, formed their own business associations, created their own art, music, and literature—and in the process, developed a black elite that led the march into the twentieth century." Among the institutions founded was the Georgia State Industrial College for Colored Youth, which is now Savannah State University (see our Education and Child Care chapter).

Economically, the last quarter of the 19th century saw the rice plantations around Savannah go out of business, turpentine and rosin from Georgia's pine forests rival cotton as the city's chief export, and the port enhanced by the dredging of the Savannah River shipping channel to a depth of 26 feet from 14 feet at the end of the war. There was also a spate of disasters during the last 25 years of the 1800s: Yellow fever killed more than 1,000 people in 1876, and the city was damaged by five significant fires, a tornado, two hurricanes, and an earthquake.

RACING INTO THE 20TH CENTURY

Savannah focused international attention on itself early in the 20th century by hosting Grand Prix and Vanderbilt Cup automobile racing in 1908, 1910, and 1911. During the first decade of the new century, the city expanded in other ways: A new City Hall was built, and much of the present-day skyline took shape. In the years that followed, Savannah began stretching southward from downtown with the creation of the city's first residential subdivision, Ardsley Park, after World War I (see our Relocation/Real Estate chapter). In the black community, residents formed the Negro Civic Improvement League to clean up overcrowded neighborhoods and started their own businesses, including the Wage Earners Savings Bank, which by 1915 covered a downtown block. (The bank building is now the site of the Ralph Mark Gilbert Civil Rights Museum, which you can learn about in our Attractions chapter.)

Not all was rosy, however. By the early 1920s cotton production in the South had fizzled out as laborers moved to the industrialized North and the boll weevil decimated Georgia's cotton fields. Late in the decade came the Great Depression, and with it financial stagnation. During the 1930s, Savannah received an economic boost when the Union Bag and Paper Company set up shop just west of the city, bringing with it nearly 600 jobs and a payroll of $1 million. Union Bag, later known as Union Camp, was purchased by International Paper Company in the late 1990s and is still one of the city's largest employers. The company helped end Savannah's hard times, as did another, more far-reaching event—World War II.

ON THE HOME FRONT

Savannah contributed mightily to America's war effort. At the Southeastern Shipyard, some 15,000 workers built Liberty Ships. The city's little airport, Hunter Field, was appropriated by the military and turned into a huge air base. In 1943 it became a staging area for bomber aircraft and crews headed for duty in Europe; some 9,000 planes and 70,000 men were processed out of Hunter during the war.

With their airport gone, city officials began building another one in western Chatham County. It, too, was taken over by the government and became a training base for the crews of heavy bombers. Called Chatham Field, the base eventually became the site of Savannah/Hilton Head International Airport. Hunter continues to be used by the military and is now known as Hunter Army Airfield.

"The war turned Savannah from a sleepy, traditional, backward-looking town on a muddy river into a full-fledged, twentieth-century American city," wrote Edward Chan Sieg. "Savannahians gave what they had to the war effort, burying another generation of their youth and generously entertaining the youth of other cities." Savannah boomed, what with the influx of workers who came from the countryside to build ships and the city's popularity with military personnel from nearby bases, including the Marine Corps basic training complex at Parris Island, South Carolina.

The boom ended when the war did. The shipyard closed and most of the troops went home. "What remained was a partially deserted, once-fashionable Historic District," said Sieg. "Savannah had moved south to low-roofed suburbs, abandoning hundreds of high-ceilinged town houses to the dereliction of uncaring tenants, little or no maintenance, and, worst of all, unprofitable values. No wonder that the postwar business leaders reached the conclusion that if Savannah were to survive and flourish, the old city must make way for progress. But the preservationist attitude found its way into the lives of a handful of influential residents who became dedicated to the principle that demolition was not the only answer to decay."

PRESERVING THE PAST & MAKING PROGRESS

Savannahians reacted with shame in 1946 when Great Britain's Lady Astor called the city "a beautiful lady with a dirty face," a line that has continued to ring true occasionally to this day. They were moved to action when the town's City Market on Ellis Square was demolished in 1954 and replaced with a parking garage. The following year, a group of seven women led by Anna C. Hunter chartered the Historic Savannah Foundation for the purpose of saving noteworthy structures from destruction. By the time of the foundation's first general membership meeting in

November 1955, the organization had 700 members.

Its first project was saving the Isaiah Davenport House (see our Attractions chapter), and it was successfully followed by many others. Of the group's efforts, Russell and Hines wrote, "The foundation determined to reawaken interest in Savannah's heritage, to convince the public of the economic benefits of restoration, and to promote tourism . . . During the next decade the foundation would deluge the city with a massive public relations campaign, arrange for a professional inventory of historic buildings, establish a revolving fund, and help establish a tourism and convention bureau within the Chamber of Commerce."

i **Savannah is the home of Girl Scouting of the USA. Founded here by a woman named Juliette Gordon Low, her childhood home is called "the Birthplace" and is visited by thousands of Girl Scouts each year. The home is also Savannah's first National Historic Landmark.**

The group formulated a preservation plan that became a national model and the basis of the city's Historic Zoning Ordinance. By 1970 the foundation had saved more than 150 structures that were resold to individuals for restoration; the organization continues its efforts today from offices at 321 East York Street.

In recent years, the Savannah College of Art and Design (SCAD) (see our Education and Child Care chapter) has stepped forward as a leader in historic preservation, and their work has been nationally and internationally acclaimed. Among the many buildings the college has restored to house classrooms and offices are former public school buildings, the old Chatham County Jail, and portions of what was once the Central of Georgia Railroad complex. In the 1970s the city government beautified River Street by creating Rousakis Plaza along the waterfront and started a revitalization of the Broughton Street shopping district that is a work in progress.

Since then, Savannahians have witnessed other progressive developments, including the construction of a new airport terminal, the replacement of the aging Talmadge Memorial Bridge across the Savannah River, improvements and growth at the city's port facilities, the revitalization of the Martin Luther King Jr. Boulevard corridor, and the construction of the Savannah International Trade and Convention Center on Hutchinson Island. In 1996 and 2004, Savannah found itself back on the international stage it had trod during the time of the great auto races: in 2004 as the news media and communications center for the G-8 summit meeting held on Sea Island, Georgia, and in 1996 as host of the yachting events of Atlanta's Summer Olympic Games. Fittingly, the opening and closing ceremonies of the games in Savannah were held at the eastern end of River Street, close to where James Edward Oglethorpe and his little band of colonists landed 263 years before.

ACCOMMODATIONS

There is perhaps no better way to experience Savannah's illustrious history than to stay in one of the Historic District's many bed-and-breakfasts, hotels, carriage houses, and inns. Disguised as elaborate mansions with architecturally stunning facades, these establishments are overflowing with charm and amenities that are unique to each property. Inside each, you'll find both atmosphere and modern amenities, along with historical features, original artwork, gourmet cuisine, and innkeepers who will see that you are well pampered during your stay. There are more than 30 of these establishments to choose from, and the list is constantly expanding.

Just as Mother Nature sprays the city in pastels each spring, Savannah hotels are in full bloom year-round, offering visitors everything from contemporary and chic accommodations to historic and convenient. No matter which you choose, the hotels are gift-wrapped in the splendor of history while modern amenities like Wi-Fi, complimentary breakfasts, fitness facilities, and concierge services, abound. If you're seeking a hotel that blends with the city's historical heritage, there are several located within the Historic District that are furnished with antique replicas and housed behind centuries-old façades. Savannah hoteliers have done an excellent job marrying new accommodations with the flavor of this old city.

Most of the hotels and motels described here are situated in one of two locations: on or very near Bay Street in Historic Downtown or on or just off Abercorn Street near Oglethorpe Mall in the Midtown area. There are many other motels in several nearby locales: on or near the beach at Tybee Island, which is about 25 minutes from downtown Savannah; in the Southside on Abercorn between Oglethorpe Mall and Savannah Mall; and out on I-95, 10 or more miles from the heart of the city.

OVERVIEW

Price Code

The dollar signs indicate the average cost for a one-night stay for two adults, not including taxes, gratuities, or add-on amenities. Many establishments have both high-season and off-season rates, and they define "season" differently, so check current prices, usually posted on the facilities' websites. Most establishments charge from $10 to $25 extra for additional guests. Please inquire about additional fees when you call for reservations. Again, remember that reservations are essential.

$	less than $110
$$	$110 to $150
$$$	$150 to $200
$$$$	$200 to $250
$$$$$	more than $250

ACCOMMODATIONS

BED-AND-BREAKFAST INNS

The following listings are arranged in alpha-betical order, and prices are indicated by the dollar-sign code explained in the Price Code table above. You'll see a range of prices for some of these listings. Due to the wide variety of room options at some bed-and-breakfasts, it is not uncommon for one inn to offer both lower-priced accommodations and luxurious, upscale suites. Be specific when calling for details. The best deals are on weekday nights. If you are on a really tight travel budget, chances are many of the B&Bs listed here aren't the accommodations for you—amenities and atmosphere often come with a price tag. These entries are not meant to be an all-inclusive list of city inns. Instead, it's a guide to help you get started. Chances are there are a few newcomers who cropped up between the researching of this book and your reading of it.

AZALEA INN AND GARDENS $$$–$$$$$

217 East Huntingdon St.
(912) 236-2707, (800) 582-3823
www.azaleainn.com

Savannah's Azalea Inn and Gardens is a pleasant and pretty blend of comfort and convenience. You'll receive a warm Southern welcome from innkeepers Teresa and Micheal Jacobson, the veteran hosts at this bed-and-breakfast located in a lush part of the Historic District near Forsyth Park. This Victorian home, circa 1889, offers eight rooms, two suites, and a two-bedroom second floor carriage house perfect for small families. The inn offers several friendly touches, including fresh fruit and finger foods that are available all day long. The dining room is adorned with murals depicting Savannah's illustrious history, and the walls come to life in stories told each morning at breakfast, so be sure to ask. Breakfast is an experience in itself with some of the specialties well worth the trip. They include a beautiful orange cranberry croissant soufflé, creamy grits, and a delightful sectioned Clementine (orange) with ginger syrup and mint! Rooms are tastefully elegant and not "over-decorated" with too many knick-knacks. Several rooms offer working fireplaces and some offer spacious balconies and/or Jacuzzis. The innkeepers are particularly proud of their gardens that have been featured in several home tours. The shady courtyard garden is inviting, as is a refreshing swim in the pool after a day of sightseeing. Children over the age of 12 are welcome. The inn is nonsmoking throughout.

THE BALLASTONE INN $$$$$

14 East Oglethorpe Ave.
(912) 236-1484, (800) 822-4553
www.ballastone.com

The Ballastone is a magnificently restored, four-story 1838 mansion just off Bull Street, one of the historic area's main thoroughfares. Arriving guests will notice the beautiful Queen Anne staircase in the entryway and the warm, lavishly decorated parlor off to the right. Ceiling fans, rice poster and canopy beds, marble-topped tables, and fireplaces are some of the things you might find in one of the 16 individually decorated rooms. The Victoria Room has a massive king-size bed and whirlpool tub, while the Gazebo Room has two queen-size beds. Besides the wonderful surroundings, guests enjoy afternoon Victorian tea along with evening hors d'oeuvres. There is a terry-cloth robe waiting in the bathroom and nightly turn-down service with chocolates and cordials. In the mornings, you can choose to have continental breakfast in your room or a full gourmet breakfast served in either of the parlors or outside in the courtyard. Children 16 years of age and older are welcome at the Ballastone. The inn has been recommended by Select Registry, *Brides, Glamour, Gourmet*, and *Condé Nast Traveler*. This is one of Savannah's inns that more closely resembles a small European hotel. Jennifer Salandi is the innkeeper-owner.

i Reservations for the week of St. Patrick's Day should be made a year in advance. Bed-and-breakfast inns are perfect for your stay here during this colorful holiday!

BROUGHTON STREET BED & BREAKFAST $$$–$$$$$

511 East Broughton St.
(912) 232-6633
www.broughtonst.com

Staying at the Broughton Street Bed & Breakfast is an opportunity to have your own private home in the heart of Savannah's Historic Downtown.

This property offers three rooms and a carriage house at the quiet end of Broughton Street, downtown Savannah's main thoroughfare. The master bedroom in the front of the home includes a four-poster bed, a spacious bay window overlooking the street, and a small whirlpool bath and shower combination. The middle bedroom has a comfortable sleigh bed surrounded by the old library. The rear bedroom has a queen-size bed with a view of the small rear courtyard. The carriage-house rests on the rear of the property. It offers one bedroom and a sleeper sofa, and is decorated in a cozy, slightly more masculine style. Guests are allowed to utilize all of the house. There is a main parlor and dining room for relaxing. All the rooms are attractively decorated with antiques. The inn is not wheelchair accessible. Children are welcome. Housed in a circa-1883 town house, the inn was remodeled beginning in 1993. The home was operated as a bed-and-breakfast until 2004, and then was offered as a luxury vacation rental for families, wedding parties, and corporate retreats. It's the perfect place to stay for families or parade participants during St. Patrick's Day.

i Because of regulations passed by local government, all new bed-and-breakfast inns opening in Savannah must provide off-street parking for their guests. That may be a headache for developers (not to mention a leg up to established inns that are "grandfathered"), but guests will ultimately benefit.

CATHERINE WARD HOUSE $$–$$$$
118 East Walburg St.
(912) 234-8564
www.catherinewardhouseinn.com

From the street, the Catherine Ward House is inviting. Like a freshly painted watercolor dotted with pinks and whites of Savannah's spring azaleas, the inn is a standout among houses on its block. There's a friendly porch with hanging baskets to welcome guests. Once you step inside, you'll discover that this inn meets and exceeds all the qualities one would expect from a fine Southern lodge. With nine rooms that range from modern and chic to traditional, each offers private baths, some with double showers. Located less than a block from Savannah's resplendent Forsyth Park, the inn is equipped for business travelers and perfect those seeking a more restful stay. Nell's Room—a sunny space named for the former owner's housekeeper—offers a door leading to a private courtyard and a small fishpond. The Cosmopolitan Room is chic with a black marble hearth, warm earth tones, a wet bar, and antique Asian nightstands. Just a note: The inn does not hold a liquor license, however, guests are encouraged to bring their own liquor or wine, and the innkeeper is happy to furnish glasses and ice.

COLUMBIA SQUARE INN $$$
125 Habersham St.
(912) 236-0444
www.columbiasquareinn.com

There are two things you notice when entering the Columbia Square Inn: the wonderful wide heart-pine floorboards and the white walls. Although some innkeepers prefer lavish draperies and antiques to match, proprietor Barbara Wall's tastes are understated and elegant. There is no clutter here. The floors are nearly uncovered as are the windows, which reveal views of the fountain in the center of Columbia Square and a magnificent magnolia tree reaching to the top of the home.

All rooms in the home, which the Walls restored several years ago (they occupy the ground floor), are spacious and decorated in the same manner. A leather settee or chair is neatly arranged in front of the fireplace along with a sofa to form a comfortable sitting area in each room. There are four-poster beds and armoires, and one of the rooms has an extra bedroom and a small veranda. Mrs. Wall (Barbara) is an innkeeper who likes to give her guests their space, so everything they might need, from an ironing board to a cold drink, can be found in the rooms. There are also small refrigerators, coffeemakers, and microwaves in each. Continental breakfast is served in the rooms, but guests are welcome to spend their time in the other parts of the inn, including the parlor and dining room. Barbara says that guests are delighted and surprised by the serene ambience that exudes from their stays at her inn. There is no exterior signage. This inn is closed during the week of St. Patrick's Day. Children and pets are not allowed.

EAST BAY INN $$$
225 East Bay St.
(912) 238-1225, (800) 500-1225
www.eastbayinn.com
The striking design of downtown's East Bay Inn will catch your eye even if you're not looking for a place to stay. The exterior's tall windows and brickwork reflect the Greek Revival style, popular in Savannah around the time of the Civil War. The inn's entrance is friendly, and you're greeted with a warm welcome as soon as you step into the lobby.

As typical with most commercial buildings of the period, the facade of the first floor is cast iron, as are the interior columns. Boasting the charm of a smaller inn with a cheery ambience in all of the common areas, this inn offers incredible style and service for a more moderate price. From the ornate benches that are outside the lobby, to the rich furnishings inside, this inn, built in 1852, once served as offices for cotton merchants and housed cotton warehouses. In 1984, after several years of lying dormant, refurbishment began transforming the structure into the present-day East Bay Inn. Featuring 28 rooms—each with 18th-century-style furnishings, hardwood floors, four-poster queen-size rice beds or plantation queen beds, high ceilings, and large, beautiful windows—this inn has become one of the city's most popular. Exposed brick walls, heart-pine floors, and plenty of comfortable places to rest, read, and dine, are factors in this establishment's success. Each guest room is tastefully decorated and meticulously kept. You will feel comfortable and safe whether your visit is for business or a nice romantic getaway. This is the perfect place to book a small wedding. You can have the ceremony in a private room in the restaurant below the inn, enjoy a reception there, and book rooms for the entire wedding party.

ELIZA THOMPSON HOUSE $$-$$$
5 West Jones St.
(912) 236-3620, (800) 348-9378
www.elizathompsonhouse.com
One of Savannah's most magnificent streets is home to the Eliza Thompson House, an inn that exudes spa-like amenities in each of its 25 rooms. Set amid a canopy of live oaks and stately residences, the original home was built in 1847 and restored to

Rent a Part of History

One of the latest trends for families visiting Savannah for college graduations, weddings, and family reunions is luxurious historic homes that have been renovated for the purpose of renting out the entire home.

The **Mary O'Connor House,** at 507 Broughton St., is a fine example of one of those properties. Rates are $425 per night with discounts for a five-night stay (or longer); holidays and weekends may have a minimum-stay requirement. Rates may also vary for special-event weekends. The house is updated to the very tee, with granite in the kitchen, shiny stainless appliances, and brick walls to round out the modern conveniences. Flat-screen TVs are in all rooms, and beds are decorated with high-thread-count linens and tastefully furnished with antiques.

The home is named for Mary Flannery O'Connor who was an American author born in 1925 who wrote two novels and 31 short stories. The house has a beautiful enclosed garden, three bedrooms, and a living and dining room. For more information on this beautiful rental home, call (912) 232-6633, or visit www.savannahvillas.com.

house. Offering its guests premium soaps, bathrobes, and impeccable service, the inn is run with the efficiency and style of a small European hotel. Views from all rooms are a showcase of Savannah's natural flora: some tropical palms and flourishing live oaks adorned with hanging moss. Guests can enjoy home-cooked breakfasts outside or, on those rare occasions when the weather does not permit, in a glass-walled alcove overlooking the beautiful fountain. Wine and cheese are served in the parlor in the late afternoons, and dessert and coffee are provided in the evenings. Several guests and employees have reported seeing and hearing ghostly sightings throughout the years. Some of these include spotting Confederate soldiers in an upstairs window or a young girl wearing a white dress in the hallway. Wheelchair-accessible suites are available.

FOLEY HOUSE INN $$–$$$
14 West Hull St.
(912) 232-6622, (800) 647-3708
www.foleyinn.com

It is often the guest comments that define the success or demise of a property, and in this case, guests have praised the staff of this Savannah inn that stretches into two regal homes. The Foley House Inn's strengths—apart from a colorful, rich feel—come in the form of an outstanding staff (according to the comments) as well as luxurious amenities. The bedding is plush. The linens are fine. Several rooms offer private balconies and oversized Jacuzzis; all rooms have fireplaces. All offer plush bathrobes and lavish toiletries. When you first walk inside this 1896 brick home, you are struck by the rich burgundy and blue colors blanketing the walls and floors. The sumptuous design and detail extend throughout the parlor and all of the

historical accuracy in 1977. Extending to two buildings, a dozen rooms are located in the main house, and 13 additional rooms carry over into the courtyard and carriage

19 individually styled rooms. Look out your window, and you will see beautiful Chippewa Square. Historic First Baptist Church is across the street, and a statue of Gen. James Edward Oglethorpe, the founder of Georgia, standing in the center of the square.

Tea and hors d'oeuvres are served each afternoon in the parlor, and guests can choose to have their continental breakfast there, in the small courtyard, or in their rooms. Particularly inviting are the garden rooms on the first level. They are bright, spacious, and convenient to a lush patio area. Evening cordials are also featured, as is concierge service for making all your dining and exploring reservations. The inn offers several packages that are inclusive of tour tickets , carriage rides, and restaurants. Visit the website for a full listing. Note that the inn is not wheelchair accessible.

FORSYTH PARK INN   **$$$**
102 West Hall St.
(912) 233-6804
www.forsythparkinn.com
The stately Forsyth Park Inn is made for savoring the views of a beautiful historic park and spending afternoons sitting and sipping ice tea on the porch. Built in 1893, the inn is surrounded by the exotic flora of Savannah, from gracious live oaks that frame the exterior to flourishing palms and lush azaleas (that bloom to their fullest in spring). Innkeepers will pamper you all day long, starting with their full buffet-style breakfasts in the mornings. From fresh-fruit French toast and Florentine eggs benedict served on the verandah or in the parlor, to afternoon tea and evening wine, this is an inn that has a long following of happy guests!

Ask for room number eight, which comes with a full balcony overlooking the gardens. If you're looking for ultimate privacy, ask for the Cottage, where children of any age (and pets) are welcome. The Cottage overlooks the beautiful gardens and offers a living room with trundle bed, efficiency kitchen, and queen-size bed with private bathroom.

THE GASTONIAN   **$$$$–$$$$$**
220 East Gaston St.
(912) 232-2869, (800) 322-6603
www.gastonian.com
If there was space designated as paradise and set in Savannah, the Gastonian would be that place. This is an inn that fulfills the expectations of the most demanding traveler. Everything about the Gastonian invites relaxation and enjoyment, from the magnificent verandas that consume one side of the house to the impeccably landscaped courtyard and cheery, lavishly furnished rooms. From its lush gardens to its spacious porches, this inn has become one of the most highly acclaimed in the city. Fresh pralines are placed on your pillow nightly. Fireplaces are lit (when the weather's right). Soft music plays at the day's end. Newspapers are delivered each morning. There is a friendly concierge who orchestrates your visit, from dinner to horse-drawn carriage tours. The inn is actually two historic, wonderfully preserved mansions next to each other along Gaston Street. This striking mansion is set in a residential neighborhood is just a short walk from one of Savannah's most beautiful parks—Forsyth.

Georgian and Regency period antiques fill the main parlors, while all of the 18 rooms are styled individually. Each has a working fireplace, high ceilings, wooden floors, and Persian rugs, and is named for a noted Savannahian. In the Mary Hilyer Room, you will find a beautiful antique quilt with green and red flowers covering one wall. There is a whirlpool bath with a basket of Caswell Massey soaps and lotions nearby and a wonderful stained-glass window. French doors take you out to the veranda, where a wicker lounge chair awaits. Newlyweds often come to the Gastonian to have their pictures taken in the beautiful courtyard. There is also a sundeck with a hot tub—a perfect spot for enjoying continental breakfast.

i Did you enjoy your romantic bed-and-breakfast stay? Hang on to those business cards! Weekends at these plush homes-away-from-home are a popular and different gift for newlyweds and others who are celebrating. Of course, the price may make such a gift more feasible as a group offering from the office or a gang of friends.

GREEN PALM INN $$–$$$$
548 East President St.
(912) 447-8901, (888) 606-9510
www.greenpalminn.com
This small bed-and-breakfast plays up its name: The handful of rooms are named for different species of palm tree, and the inn overlooks Greene Square. That puts this inn on the easternmost edge of the Historic District. It is one of the smallest and most affordable of the B&Bs. The house was built in 1887, and its renovation transformed transformed it into a B&B in 1998. Look for atmospheric touches here like ultramodern bathrooms with air-jet tubs and showers (two of the smaller rooms have showers with multiple jets), a generous number of fireplaces (even in bathrooms), and British Colonial–style furniture. Guests can expect a hot breakfast as well as a delightful array of afternoon refreshments.

THE HAMILTON-
TURNER INN $$–$$$$
330 Abercorn St.
(912) 233-1833, (888) 448-8849
www.hamilton-turnerinn.com
This glamorous Victorian inn boasts notable architecture, a prime location, and plenty of romance. The mansion—with an exterior as ornate as the Victorians could get it—was built in 1873, and among its claims to fame is the fact it was Savannah's first house with electric lighting. Its location on Lafayette Square puts it square in the middle of the Historic District, with the Cathedral of St. John the Baptist as a neighbor and one of the city's most picturesque squares as its "front yard." The inn's grand-entrance steps empty onto a beautifully appointed parlor floor. The public rooms include a double parlor furnished with antiques and the front dining room, where breakfast is served. Breakfast is a full gourmet, health-oriented southern affair prepared by the inn's executive chef. Afternoon tea, evening wine with hors d'oeuvres, and late evening port are also served.

Most bedrooms boast the high ceilings and sweeping windows of the building's construction period. Exceptions, however, are on the ground floor, a level that Savannah terms the garden level. All garden-level rooms have individual private entrances from gardens. The handful of rooms here feature brick walls and a cozier feel, and some include private entrances. This is an inn that offers excellent accommodations for disabled guests with a chairlift. An open-air elevator goes from the ground level to one of the parlor-level suites.

Reservations are a must, but while you are making them, be sure to check with the innkeepers regarding their cancellation policy. Some inns charge if you cancel, on the grounds that they turned away other reservations.

JOAN'S ON JONES $$$
17 West Jones St.
(912) 234-3863, (888) 989-9806
www.joansonjones.com

Joan's on Jones is one of the most established of the smaller bed-and-breakfast inns in Savannah. Innkeepers Joan and Gary Levy have been welcoming guests to their Jones Street home since 1990. The inn features two suites, both with private entrances and ample room. You'll feel as if you have your own apartment in the heart of the city. These particular apartments are in a restored 1883 Victorian town house on one of the city's most scenic streets. The Jones Street Suite is painted a rich terra-cotta that Joan discovered in a local historic home and reproduced in her own. It is formally decorated and has pretty stained-glass windows and two fireplaces. Over one fireplace is a collection of old letters and other correspondence found behind the mantel during the restoration process. Reading lamps are over the bed for convenience, and there is a small kitchenette. The Garden Suite—just off a back courtyard that is perfect for relaxing with its lounge garden chairs—has a huge brick cooking hearth, queen-size iron bed, and exposed brick walls. There is also a full kitchen. This suite is less formal but more intimate and romantic.

Children are welcome, and well-behaved dogs are allowed in the back suite for a nonrefundable fee. Continental breakfast is served each morning.

THE KEHOE HOUSE $$$–$$$$$
123 Habersham St.
(912) 232-1020, (800) 820-1020
www.kehoehouse.com

The Kehoe House stands catty-cornered to one of Savannah's preserved architectural treasures and house museums, the Davenport House, and has a commanding view of Columbia Square. The Kehoe House was constructed for an Irish immigrant who made a fortune in the iron foundry business. As his fortune and his family grew, he built this imposing brick Victorian. After its residential days, the building served other uses, including a stint as a funeral parlor. Former football star Joe Namath was one of a group of investors who held the property for a while.

The Kehoe has 13 rooms and is known for its European-style service. Guests are treated to a gourmet breakfast, afternoon tea, and evening wine with hors d'oeuvres. The fourth floor includes a party/banquet room, which is often the scene of bridesmaids' luncheons and business meetings.

This inn is unusual in that it is outfitted with an elevator—an amenity you are sure to appreciate after you spend the day following our advice that the best way to see Savannah is on foot. Also, this inn touts its rumors of hauntings.

THE PRESIDENTS' QUARTERS INN $$$$–$$$$$
225 East President St.
(800) 233-1776
www.presidentsquarters.com

Innkeeper Jane Sales has been in the business of pleasing Savannah guests for so many years, her delightful personality and vast innkeeping experience has carried over to one of the most satisfying accommodations in the city, the Presidents' Quarters Inn. This inn is one of the city's classiest, with not only a historical relevance, but also a high "chic" factor, exemplified by bathrooms with the latest and most modern fixtures (along with updated tile). Elevators make it easy for guests to get to their upstairs rooms. Twin townhomes of this Federal-style mansion are filled with surprises, and each room is named for a president. Overlooking Oglethorpe Square, the inn seems fresh and devoid of the mustiness some historic buildings in Savannah carry with age. There are 16 rooms, and most feature baths with granite countertops, high ceilings, fine linens, and a spaciousness often overlooked by other inns. My favorite is the George Washington Suite, a two-level loft with a new wet bar, a large living space, and an upscale, tailored decor. On St. Patrick's Day, the chef's delights spill out into the courtyard, making this one of the city's most desirable and festive places to stay during the holiday. Note: If that is your wish, book early.

i Most bed-and-breakfasts provide DVD players in at least some of their suites. If aching feet or stormy weather is keeping you inside, why not check out a film made in Savannah? Check our Savannah Celebrity chapter for an inventory. Then settle back and see if you can spot your surroundings on the silver screen!

SAVANNAH BED AND BREAKFAST INN $$-$$$$
117 West Gordon St.
(912) 238-0518, (888) 238-0518
www.savannahbnb.com
This charming and well-established bed-and-breakfast was an early comer to the

scene. The circa-1853 Federal row house on Gordon Row adjoins innkeeper Bob McAlister's home in one of the most attractive areas of the Historic Downtown. McAlister is a well-known host on the local scene, and his hospitality shows in this inn's operation.

Rooms are furnished with antiques to look admire and reproductions for relaxation. (The innkeeper maintains antique chairs shouldn't be subjected to daily use, and guests shouldn't be subjected to antique chairs.) You'll love architectural details throughout. Renovation has enhanced the structure with a spacious deck that overlooks a beautiful courtyard. The garden suites are prime rooms, complete with full kitchens and living and dining areas. You really won't need that kitchen, though. A talented chef whose repertoire includes light and fluffy biscuits could be the decision maker. His famous Charlotte's Pecan Cornbread accompanies made-to-order omelets, and Col. Bob's Grits are said to please "even a Northerner." (The grits are heavy on the cream and butter, and you won't get your fill of them!) If you can get a room over St. Patrick's Day—regular returnees fill most of them—you're in for a real treat, as the breakfast party here is a favorite stopping-off point for locals (including many parade participants) heading to the festivities. Children are welcome in some of the guest rooms.

ZEIGLER HOUSE INN $$$-$$$$
121 West Jones St.
(866) 233-5307
www.zeiglerhouseinn.com
You can almost hear the "oh, how lovely" coming from guests who stay at the Zeigler House Inn! This small, cheery inn is situated in a glorious part of Savannah on Jones Street and is the perfect place to stay for a

quiet, relaxing visit to Savannah. Although there are only six rooms, they are spacious and extraordinarily furnished. A special feature, among others, is the convenience of in-room kitchens, which offer the perfect place to store (and reheat) leftovers from some of Savannah's fine restaurants.

The Inn is ideally located within a short walk to all of the major downtown attractions including shops, restaurants, Savannah College of Art and Design, museums, art galleries, Forsyth Park, City Market, and Savannah River Street.

Whirlpool tubs and private patios are unique features in several rooms. All accommodations have private baths, cable TV, CD /DVD player, refrigerator, microwave oven, toaster, and coffeemaker. Wi-Fi is available in all rooms and parking is free. Tea and hors d'oeuvres and wine are served in the afternoons Mon through Sat. Continental breakfast with homemade baked goods and fresh fruit is provided in your room.

HOTELS & MOTELS

The motels at the beach are discussed in the Tybee Island chapter of this book. The accommodations between the malls and out on I-95 represent several major chains and should offer no surprises, but if your destination is Savannah and not the House of the Mouse or some other touristy spot in Florida, we recommend that you stay closer to our city and soak up some of the atmosphere of our historic old town.

You can be in the midst of that atmosphere by taking a room at a hotel or motel in the downtown area. In most cases, you'll pay accordingly for the location, but you can find some values if you're not too picky

about the view from your room and the extras you receive. A rule of thumb: You'll pay more the closer you stay to the Historic District.

Another cost-saving option is to stay at lodgings in the Midtown area. You'll be out of the mainstream of tourism but not by much—the motels and inns in Midtown are only 5 miles from Bay Street, which is about 12 to 15 minutes of traveling time if you avoid rush-hour traffic. Although most of these establishments are geared toward people on business trips, the innkeepers are more than happy to have tourists stay with them. Another reason to take a room in Midtown is that parking is free. That's not necessarily the case if you stay in Historic Downtown, and we've indicated in our listings if and what you'll have to pay to park at a hotel or motel there.

All of the hotels and motels described in this chapter accept major credit cards and have wheelchair-accessible rooms. Almost all have nonsmoking rooms, and many do not allow pets; if a hotel or motel does not have nonsmoking rooms or does accept pets, that information is included in our listing for the establishment.

The season generally runs from mid-March through October. Some establishments decrease their rates during the hot summer months, and others jack them up on weekends, so you should call in advance to ascertain how much you'll have to spend. If you're planning to stay here on St. Patrick's Day weekend, expect to pay considerably more than you would at any other time of year and make reservations months in advance. Some places set minimum stays of two or three days that weekend. (See the St. Patrick's Day chapter for more information.)

Historic Downtown

THE BEST WESTERN PROMENADE $$
412 West Bay St.
(912) 233-1011
www.promenadesavannah.com

This is an older motel located in perhaps one of the best sections of the Historic District. The Best Western Promenade fronts Bay Street, which is at times very noisy. However, with the noise comes lower rates in comparison with many of the newer and pricier hotels nearby. It's the perfect place to bring small groups (i.e., Girl Scouts on tour, school field trips, etc.) as the rooms open to an outside walkway (hence, the name, Promenade) where there is no one to disturb. The rear building is on the western end of River Street, placing the three-story establishment about a block from the shops and restaurants along the river and in City Market (see our Shopping chapter). The establishment is a convenient stop for tour buses and trolleys that pick up at the front door.

The Promenade offers guests complimentary continental breakfasts from 6:30 until 9:30 a.m., and there's a fenced-in pool for swimming and sunning on the River Street side of the property. 87 of the rooms have two full-size beds, and the rest have king-size beds. Parking is $10 per day.

COURTYARD BY MARRIOTT $$$
Savannah Historic District
415 West Liberty St.
(912) 790-8287, (800) 932-2198
www.courtyard.com

The five-story Courtyard opened in late July 2001, adding 147 guest rooms and 9 suites to Savannah's inventory of overnight accommodations. The suites and 86 of the guest rooms offer king-size beds, with 9 of the rooms featuring spa-type bathrooms complete with whirlpool tubs. The other rooms have two queen-size beds.

The Courtyard, with a decor that's traditionally Southern in style, covers an entire block bounded by Martin Luther King Jr. Boulevard and Liberty, Montgomery, and Harris Streets. The main entrance is on Liberty, making the front door a short walk from the Savannah Visitor Information Center. The hotel's spacious courtyard—a lushly landscaped spot that creates an oasis in the heart of the downtown area—faces Harris Street and is also the site of a heated outdoor pool. Guests can relax here or at the hotel's spa, an exercise facility that includes a large whirlpool.

The Courtyard Cafe, which is in the northwest corner of the ground floor, is a roomy restaurant with plenty of windows to give diners a view of what's happening on Liberty Street and MLK. The cafe serves breakfast seven days a week, and the Camellia Room is the setting for cocktails from 5 to 10 p.m. Valet parking is available for a daily fee; no self-parking.

DOUBLETREE HOTEL
HISTORIC SAVANNAH $$–$$$
411 West Bay St.
(912) 790-7000, (800) 222-TREE
www.doubletree.hilton.com

The Doubletree Historic Savannah exudes the tradition of the finer homes of Savannah. With public areas that are bright and open, there are 150 rooms, all richly appointed with European-style furnishings. There are Irish and Celtic influences reflected throughout the common areas, and nautical hints in the rooms' decor. The hotel is an easy walk to City Market and River Street. There is an attractive restaurant and separate bar on site, a business center, free Wi-Fi, and more than 3,000 square feet of meeting space.

HAMPTON INN SAVANNAH $$$
Historic District
201 East Bay St.
(912) 231-9700, (800) HAMPTON
www.hamptoninn.com

Fully renovated in 2009, this eight-story hotel blends well with the city's Historic District buildings. The stucco, brick, and ironwork of the exterior have the look of old Savannah. The lobby has authentic gray bricks that were discovered on the site during construction. Other historical design elements include the hotel's heart-pine floors (retrieved from an old mill in central Georgia), antique and traditional furniture, Persian rugs, and a dark wood bar from England, purchased from a local antiques store. All of the hotels' 144 guest rooms have modern touches such as Cloud Nine (all white bedding), flat-screen televisions, high-speed wireless Internet service, and all rooms are equipped with a refrigerator and microwave. The Hampton is at Bay and Abercorn Streets, a block south of River Street, a location that is perfectly situated between River Street and City Market. Check out the glorious view of the Savannah River, the Eugene Talmadge Memorial Bridge, and Historic Downtown from the rooftop pool, but wear shades on a sunny day—it's bright up there! The hotel offers a complimentary, deluxe hot breakfast each day from 6 until 10 a.m. There is a courteous valet staff to park your car for $15 per day.

HILTON GARDEN INN SAVANNAH
HISTORIC DISTRICT $$-$$$
321 West Bay St.
(912) 721-5000, (877) 245-8854
http://hiltongardeninn1.hilton.com

Just a few short steps from the trendiest restaurants, nightlife, shopping, and sights of Historic Downtown Savannah is the Hilton Garden Inn Savannah Historic District. Located on Bay Street, this hotel offers a luxurious lobby. As found in most Hiltons, all rooms are equipped with the Sweet Dreams by Hilton beds, free wireless Internet, wireless phones with data ports, Herman Miller ergonomic desk chairs, MP3-compatible clock radios, and ample desk space. You'll also find a microwave and refrigerator in every guest room. Upgraded rooms feature 32-inch LCD TVs and adjustable Garden Sleep System beds. The hotel offers a breakfast buffet at the Great American Grill. There's also an on-site concierge desk, and the Pavilion Lounge serves beverages 24 hours. Other amenities include room service (for lunch and dinner), a complimentary 24-hour business center, an outdoor heated pool and Jacuzzi, a fitness center, and three updated meeting rooms for groups of 5 to 80.

HILTON SAVANNAH
DESOTO $$$-$$$$
15 East Liberty St.
(912) 232-9000, (800) HILTONS
www.desotohilton.com

One of the city's most popular and elegant hotels, the Hilton Savannah DeSoto is situated directly in the center of the Historic District. Guests will literally be at the front steps of beautiful green squares, boutiques, local restaurants and pubs, grand mansions, theaters, historic sites, and more. The Hilton Savannah DeSoto has always maintained a tradition of luxury and Southern hospitality that starts in a grand lobby replete with trademark crystal chandeliers. There are 246 guest rooms decorated in a fusion of Southern and contemporary styles, with scenic views of Savannah's

ACCOMMODATIONS

historic skyline. The hotel is the perfect place for groups, boasting 20,000 square feet of meeting space.

You'll enjoy a variety of Southern favorites at the DeSoto Grille inside the hotel, offering a lunch buffet and a diverse a la carte menu. If you're looking for something lighter, stop by for a quick Starbucks' coffee or freshly baked pastry at Beulah's, another eatery that offers wireless Internet and flat-screen TVs. In the evening, the Lion's Den Pub is both romantic and comfortable, featuring a variety of spirits served in a modern pub atmosphere. The hotel is within walking distance of River Street and City Market.

HYATT REGENCY
SAVANNAH $$$–$$$$
2 West Bay St.
(912) 238-1234, (800) 233-1234
www.savannah.hyatt.com

With an excellent management staff at the helm, you'll appreciate Hyatt Regency's hospitality whether you're dining, working out, or just hanging out in the beautiful atrium. Ironically, Gen. James Oglethorpe pitched his tent in a small park near the 351-room hotel, but that's not the main attraction of the Hyatt Regency—the hotel's drawing card is its location overlooking River Street and the Savannah River, constructed on the historic cobblestones that made the riverfront what it is today. This location places guests in the midst of Savannah's waterfront shops and festivals and affords terrific views of the river and the ships passing by. You'll pay extra for a room on the river, but it's well worth it for catching a bird's-eye view of the oceangoing vessels. On the fourth of the hotel's seven floors, you're at eye level with the decks of freighters and other ships as they make their way in or out of port.

There are also great views of River Street and the river from the Hyatt's Vu Lounge, a pleasant outdoor patio located off the lobby. The hotel's Harborside Ballroom, an 11,000-square-foot gathering place on River Street, offers floor-to-ceiling views. This is a popular setting for many wedding receptions and group meetings where guests can look out to the riverfront during their event. The Hyatt has a total of 33,000 square feet of meeting space, including two ballrooms, a junior ballroom, and breakout meeting space. The Hyatt also accommodates fitness buffs with a state-of-the-art exercise room and a heated indoor pool. Valet parking is $18 per day; there is no self-parking.

INN AT ELLIS SQUARE $$$
201 West Bay St.
(912) 236-4440, (800) 542-7666
www.innatellissquare.com

This 252-room brick facility, situated conveniently between River Street and City Market, features 57 suites decorated in a traditional style and featuring reproduction Southern accents. The inn sits on the corner of Barnard and Bay Streets and occupies the circa-1851 Guckenheimer Building. The hotel's elegantly roomy, ground-floor public areas offer comfortable chairs, large fireplaces, Dominque's Lounge, and flexible meeting space accommodating 20 to 200 people. Other features are an on-site concierge, an outdoor pool, and complimentary hot, deluxe continental

i Savannah's first hotel was a place called the Mansion House on Bay Street. According to an article from a *Savannah News-Press* magazine of 1969 stating the city's "earliest inns were the Mansion House, City Hotel, and the Screven (House), all of them operating about the middle of the last century."

56

breakfasts available daily. Garage parking is available on-site.

THE MANSION ON
FORSYTH PARK $$$$–$$$$$
700 Drayton St.
(912) 238-5158, (888) 711-5114
www.mansiononforsythpark.com

Native son Richard Kessler added the Mansion on Forsyth Park to the Kessler Collection of luxury hotels in 2005. Kessler, who was born in Savannah and grew up in nearby Effingham County, created the Mansion on Forsyth Park by purchasing the 18,000-square-foot Kayton-Granger-Huger House on the park, then buying adjacent property and building a four-story structure that houses the 126 rooms of his boutique hotel. The original brick-and-terra-cotta mansion, constructed in 1888, is now the site of the hotel's fashionable 700 Drayton Restaurant, which serves nouvelle American cuisine "with a Savannah flair." The restaurant is also home to Casimir's Lounge, the Carriage Wine Cellar, and the 700 Kitchen Cooking School. The hotel was bought by Marriott, although the sale was not highly publicized; however, it still retains its "boutique-style" and the Kessler touch.

Among amenities available to guests are the Marble Garden Courtyard, waterfall, and outdoor relaxation pool; the Poseidon Spa, which offers massage therapy, rejuvenating body treatments, facials, specialty nail treatments, a cardio-fitness facility, and men's and women's locker rooms with steam showers; and the Grand Bohemian Gallery that specializes in sales of rare art and jewelry. There's a cooking school called 700 Kitchen that offers daily hands-on classes accommodating up to 16 participants. The school is open to both individuals and groups.

THE MARSHALL HOUSE $$–$$$
123 East Broughton St.
(912) 644-7896, (800) 589-6304
www.marshallhouse.com

The Marshall House has the distinction of being one of Savannah's newest *and* oldest hotels. The 68-room luxury boutique hotel opened its doors August 1, 1999, after an extensive renovation. The hotel occupies the building that housed the original Marshall House, which was built in 1851 and closed in 1957; during its run it was also a hospital for Union soldiers.

The new Marshall House combines its historic past and sophisticated features. Rooms offer pine floors, minibars, CD players, robes, and bathrooms with pedestal sinks. Also available are a 275-square-foot boardroom; a fully-equipped business center; a 1,200-square-foot meeting room for corporate and social functions; and 45 Bistro, a fine-dining restaurant. This is yet another of Savannah's most appealing places to host weddings and receptions. The quaintness of the hotel itself, combined with the historical elements, make it quite photogenic and convenient for traveling wedding parties. Valet parking is $12 a day, with limited self-parking in a garage behind the hotel costing $8 a day.

THE MULBERRY INN $$$
601 East Bay St.
(912) 238-1200, (877) 468-1200
www.savannahhotel.com

Before there were the Mansion and the Marshall House, the Mulberry Inn was the place for weddings and receptions. Traditional furnishings, oil paintings, polished hardwood floors, and chandeliers grace the lobby, and antique furniture adds character throughout the hallways and sitting areas. Reproductions of antiques and burgundy and forest-green furnishings carry on the elegance into the 145 rooms, 25 of which are suites. The two- and three-story establishment—and a member of Historic Hotels of America—surrounds a stunning, tree-shaded brick courtyard adorned with wrought-iron tables and chairs. Then there's the name of the inn, which refers to the mulberry trees planted by Georgia's colonists in an attempt to raise silkworms. The trees grew on a site that is now Trustee's Garden, across East Broad Street from the hotel.

The Mulberry's elegant Cafe Courtyard serves breakfast, lunch, and dinner, and the inn presents a complimentary tea each afternoon from 4 until 6 p.m. Other amenities include concierge and bellman services, a secured outdoor pool, a hot tub, an exercise center, and Sargeant Jasper's Tavern, a full-service lounge. The hotel has three meeting rooms, with the largest accommodating 125 people theater-style. The inn also offers full banquet and catering services. Parking at a garage across a side street is $12 per day.

PLANTERS INN $$$
29 Abercorn St.
(912) 232-5678, (800) 554-1187
www.plantersinnsavannah.com
Built in 1912 as the John Wesley Hotel, the Planters Inn has been thoroughly remodeled but retains the elegance and charm of the early days of the 20th century. The hotel's high ceilings, four-poster beds, lavish draperies, and antique furniture give you the feeling you've stepped back in time, but the friendly staff and the services they provide will make you aware you're very much in the present. Among the extras are nightly turndown service, complimentary continental breakfasts served in the hospitality room from 6:30 to 10:30 a.m., and complimentary

wine provided in the lobby from 5:30 to 7:30 p.m. every day but Sun. Parking is available at a neighboring garage for $11.95 per night, and free valet service is offered.

RIVER STREET INN $$$
124 East Bay St.
(912) 234-6400, (800) 253-4229
www.riverstreetinn.com
Guests of this popular inn can experience a historic atmosphere in the midst of the activity of River Street. The rooms of this hotel occupy the top three floors of a renovated five-story cotton warehouse on the Savannah River. The main entrance to the inn and its "park side" rooms look out on to Bay Street. Thirty-two of the inn's 86 rooms face the river, and several of these have small French balconies you can step out onto for a grand view of the street and the waterway. (For an instant thrill, try popping out onto the balcony when you see a freighter approaching!)

The lower floors of the structure housing the River Street Inn were built in 1817 to store cotton for export, and the top three floors were added in 1853; the structure opened as an inn in 1985. Guests receive complimentary newspapers in the morning, use of an in-house exercise room, and homemade chocolates before retiring in the evening. There's a nightly wine, champagne, and hors d'oeuvres reception in the afternoon. The inn can accommodate small meetings and conferences, with seating for 12 in its boardroom, 45 in its meeting room, and 64 for dinners. There is also room for a 125-guest reception. Parking is $8 per day.

SAVANNAH MARRIOTT RIVERFRONT $$$–$$$$
100 General McIntosh Blvd.
(912) 233-7722, (800) 285-0398
www.marriott.com/savrf

The atrium at the heart of the Riverfront hotel has 7,000 square feet of carpeted space that can easily accommodate themed events and trade shows attended by as many as 500 people. As many as 108 rooms on the seven upper floors of the hotel open onto balconies with views of the atrium, the north side of which looks out on the Savannah River through expansive floor-to-ceiling panes of glass. The hotel's 15,000-square-foot ballroom is the second largest in the city, It is the largest hotel ballroom in the city and there is an additional 21,000 square feet of meeting space in the form of conference rooms and boardrooms.

The real lure of the Marriott, though, is its location on the Savannah River and the river walk at the eastern end of River Street. A total of 60 of the hotel's 379 rooms have balconies facing north to the water, and for $20 to $35 extra, you can be, as the Marriott folks say, "perched on the river" with a knockout view of passing ships. Special accommodations include rooms on the concierge floor and deluxe suites with walk-around wet bars, glass-topped dining tables, and large bathrooms featuring double vanities. Guests staying on the private, keyed concierge floor (the eighth) enjoy complimentary continental breakfasts, hors d'oeuvres in late afternoon, and a dessert buffet at night, Sun night through Fri morning.

THE WESTIN SAVANNAH HARBOR
GOLF RESORT & SPA $$$–$$$$
1 Resort Dr.
Hutchinson Island
(912) 201-2000
www.westinsavannah.com
If you fly into Savannah, this hotel will probably be the first landmark that catches your eye. The city's largest luxury hotel, the Westin, rises majestically above the Hutchinson Island waterfront across the Savannah River from the Historic Downtown. The 16-story, 403-room hotel and its riverside neighbor, the Savannah International Trade and Convention Center, are the focal points of the island's Savannah Harbor development—the centerpieces of what is seen as the creation of a "second city" just north of (across the river from) Savannah's downtown area.

Savannah decor (i.e. antique reproduction furnisings, Southern prints and accents) is carried through the guest rooms, each of which features the Westin's Heavenly Bed, an extremely comfortable seven-layer bed consisting of a pillow-top mattress set covered with luxury thread-count triple sheeting, a down blanket, and a duvet-covered comforter, with king-size goose-down-and-feather pillows. The suites on the hotel's top two floors have balconies that provide marvelous views of the City of Savannah or the PGA Tour golf course.

If you're staying for golf, the joys of playing the par 72 course—managed by Troon Golf—are almost as numerous as your spa treatment. The course plays more than 7,000 yards from its championship tees, and its clubhouse complex is the site of The Champions Grill, Legends Bar, a pro shop, an exercise facility, four Har-Tru tennis courts, locker-rooms with sauna and steam room. Additionally, The Westin's riverside oasis features a beautiful, oversized and heated swimming pool, food and beverage service, and a brand new extra large hot tub, as well as a zero-entry interactive dancing water children's feature. Cabanas are also available for rent, and include iced water and fresh whole fruit to help keep you cool under the hot Savannah sun.

The magnificent spa, the largest Westin has in North America, features 14 massage rooms, 2 steam rooms, 2 swiss shower rooms, mud baths, bodywraps, and more!

SOUTHSIDE/MIDTOWN

COUNTRY INN & SUITES
BY CARLSON $$–$$$
320 Montgomery St.
(912) 921-5335
www.countryinns.com
/savannahga_historic

You'd think you were staying in a historic inn judging by the decor of this 101-room Country Inn & Suites. Located just steps from the legendary Crystal Beer Parlor in Historic Downtown, there are an additional 12 spacious suites (850 square feet), perfect for families with children. Also convenient to the Savannah Civic Center, the hotel is only two years old and still exudes a fresh, new feeling.

Its sister hotel is located on Savannah's south side at 7576 White Bluff Rd. (912-692-0404 or 800-456-4000), and features the same amenities. Guest rooms offer two queen-size or one king-size bed, and there are three types of suites: the Jacuzzi Suite, with a two-person Jacuzzi tub, a king-size bed; the Guest Room with two queen beds or one king; and lastly, the One- or Two-Bedroom Suite, which has your choice of one room with a king or two queen-size beds, or two rooms, one with a king-size bed, and the other with two queens. All suites have a living room/sitting area, full-size sleeper sofa, microwave and minifridge. A particularly attractive feature of the Country Inn is its spacious indoor pool area, where you'll find a kidney-shaped pool, a whirlpool, and plenty of space for relaxing. The inn also offers a fitness room, a meeting room that accommodates 18 people, and a dining area where

Savannah's Boutique Hotel

Contrary to Savannah's image as the old girl with wallpapered rooms and four-poster beds, there are two really cool new "boutique hotels" in town! Both will wow you with over-the-top artwork, fabulous fabrics and textures, impeccable service, and ambient lighting that is sensual and savvy.

Going down the alphabet, **Avia** (www.aviahotels.com) is on Savannah's new hot list of contemporary places to stay. Located on the skirt tail of downtown's newest square, Ellis, this one features Italian-cotton matelasse coverlets, lush beds, in-room refreshment bars with Dean & Deluca snacks, and bathrooms that are literally spa-like retreats. Reflecting a few of the traditional building features like 9-foot ceilings, crown molding, plantation shutters, and city views, there are 151 guest rooms, and suites on the sixth (top) floor.

Just across the street on Bay, the **Bohemian** (www.bohemian hotelsavannah.com) is wowing guests who pull into a gated entryway with potted skyrocket junipers and attentive doormen. This 75-room hotel overlooks the Savannah River and also features fine luxury bedding, lots of wood, brass, and leather design elements, as well as a rooftop bar (Rocks on the River) that has become Savannah's hottest spot for drinks and a tapas-style menu.

complimentary continental breakfasts are available from 7 to 9:30 a.m.

HOMEWOOD SUITES
BY HILTON $$$$$
5820 White Bluff Rd.
(912) 353-8500, (800) CALL-HOME
www.homewoodsuitessavannah.com

The Homewood Suites by Hilton features 106 suites that are configured as either one-bedroom Homewood suites; Master suites, which have fireplaces; or as two-bedroom, two-bath suites. Each suite features a fully equipped kitchen with a two-burner stove, microwave, and full-size refrigerator; a sleeper sofa; and high-speed wireless Internet access.

Leave a grocery list at the front desk, and your shopping will be done for you and charged to your room. In addition to the three-story building and two two-story buildings housing the suites, there is a spacious lodge that can accommodate 50 people for each morning's complimentary Suite Start Breakfast, as well as the Welcome Home Reception, held from 5 until 7 p.m. Mon through Thurs, which offers guests beer, wine, ice tea, lemonade and a light meal with salad bar. A heated pool and whirlpool are situated just outside the lodge, and there is a court nearby where you can play basketball, tennis, or volleyball. If you need to burn off more energy, try the fitness center located in the lodge. The hotel also has two meeting rooms, one for up to 50 people and the other for 10, and an on-site laundry facility. Guests wishing to have a cookout will find two gas grills for their use under the huge oak tree that graces the property. Pets are allowed for a small fee; check with the hotel for particulars. The hotel is located near two modern grocery stores, Publix and the Fresh Market. It is also convenient to both hospitals.

OGLETHORPE INN AND SUITES $–$$
7110 Hodgson Memorial Dr.
(912) 354-8560, (800) 344-4378
www.oglethorpeinn.com

Although the Oglethorpe Inn and Suites (formerly the Masters Inn Suites) is near Oglethorpe Mall and nestled amid the shopping centers and office parks of the Southside, this three-story hotel looks and feels as if it belongs in downtown Savannah. This hotel is the perfect respite for families who need to stay in or near one of the city's two hospitals. It's built around an atrium decorated with palm trees, exotic plants, a gurgling fountain, and intricate black ironwork.

The Old South theme surfaces in the sitting rooms of the hotel's 51 suites. Each sitting room also contains a sofa, coffee table, easy chairs, and a small refrigerator, a microwave oven, and a coffeemaker. Six luxury suites have larger sitting rooms, king-size beds, and whirlpool bathtubs. All rooms are entered from the interior of the hotel. Guests can exercise in the outdoor pool at the rear of the hotel or in the fully equipped fitness room. Many of the guests are businesspeople, and there is a conference room capable of seating 45.

QUALITY INN
SAVANNAH MIDTOWN $
7100 Abercorn St.
(912) 352-7100, (800) 4-CHOICE
www.choicehotels.com

As its name implies, this 171-room Holiday Inn stands in mid-down Savannah, between Historic downtown and the south side. Both two-story wings of the motel flank a courtyard that includes a spacious pool area set among palms and magnolias. Some rooms have king-size beds, others have two doubles, and all were completely renovated as part of a process that was finished in March 2000. Doubles, a 110-seat lounge, is geared for the after-work and after-date crowd. The Quality Inn Savannah Midtown has a fitness room and offers same-day dry-cleaning service. The motel's several meeting rooms can accommodate up to 200 people.

RESIDENCE INN BY MARRIOTT $$
5710 White Bluff Rd.
(912) 356-3266, (800) 331-3131
www.marriott.com
This Residence Inn has 66 one- and two-bedroom and studio suites under one roof. All suites have kitchens, and each of the two-bedroom accommodations has two full bathrooms, three televisions, and a wood-burning fireplace. Kitchens are equipped with refrigerators, microwaves, and coffeemakers, and the staff will do your grocery shopping for you. Just leave your shopping list at the front desk, and the groceries will be charged to your bill and deposited in your room by 6 p.m. Copies of *USA Today* and the *Savannah Morning News* are free, as is a hot breakfast buffet served in the Gatehouse sitting area. The Gatehouse is also the scene of social hours held from 5 to 7 p.m. Mon through Thurs—complimentary snacks, beer, wine, and other beverages are served. For those seeking recreation, you can enjoy an indoor pool and whirlpool, an exercise room, and an outdoor court for tennis, basketball, or volleyball. Pets are welcome, but there is a $75 nonrefundable cleaning fee.

SAVANNAH GARDEN HOTEL $
6800 Abercorn St.
(912) 356-1234
www.savannahgardenhotel.com
At the Savannah Garden Hotel, the management serves a complimentary breakfast each

morning that gives guests the opportunity to enjoy the glassed-in dining room looking out on the pool and patio. The two-story inn, part of a small chain of motels scattered throughout the United States, has 138 interior rooms that include 10 suites and 3 Jacuzzi suites. Each suite has a bedroom with king-size bed and a sitting area/kitchen. Other rooms have either king-size beds or two queen-size beds. This property is a smoke- and pet-free facility. A 50-person meeting room is available for small groups. Direct reservations can be made through the hotel. This hotel is convenient to both hospitals.

SAVANNAH MIDTOWN COURTYARD BY MARRIOTT $$
6703 Abercorn St.
(912) 354-7878, (800) 321-2211
www.marriott.com/savch
Savannah's Courtyard by Marriott stands between two of the city's busiest thoroughfares, Abercorn Street and White Bluff Road, but the three-story hotel's beautifully landscaped grounds will give you a feeling of being away from the madding crowd. The centerpiece of the hotel is the courtyard with its quaint gazebo and swimming pool. Just off the pool is an enclosed whirlpool surrounded by lots of space for lounging, and there's a fitness room near the lobby that sports state-of-the-art exercise equipment. The Courtyard's large dining area is open for breakfast daily with a full meal priced at $9.95. There are 144 interior rooms including 12 suites. Rooms on the upper floors open onto balconies. There are two meeting rooms, each of which can accommodate 24 people seated at tables.

RESTAURANTS

Beyond the glitz of food television's Southern-cliché cooking shows, the realm of eating takes on a sophisticated flare in many of Savannah's restaurants. In other words, there's more to Savannah's cuisine than fried chicken, mashed potatoes, gravy, and lots of "y'alls." While this is a city that thrives on home cooking, there are even more culinary secrets to be found here! Word of the mild climate, romantic aura, and lower cost of living in Savannah has spread like butter on hot biscuits and, as a result, attracted gourmet chefs and creative entrepreneurs to the mix of tradition. The results: trendy cafes in historic facades, high-end restaurants, and enchanting eateries.

So how about the fare? What's new and what's Savannah's claim-to-fame with regards to dining? Apart from the Southern staples like creamy grits, cornbread, and pecan pie, many of Savannah's acclaimed provisions come from the sea. There's fresh shrimp steamed and spiced to perfection. There are crab cakes that take the cake. There's flounder served on an oversized plate, crispy and adorned with apricot glaze. And if your mouth isn't watering by now, there are hush puppies, made at least a hundred different ways.

So pull out your napkin, or better yet, bring an oversized bib. Buy your travel pants a size larger and with an elastic waist. You're about to be dazzled.

OVERVIEW

If your travels take you to nearby Tybee Island or Hilton Head, South Carolina, note that restaurants in those two locales are discussed in the individual chapters that cover those two island destinations.

Price Code

The price code is based on the cost of an average meal for two, excluding drinks, dessert, or tip.

$. . . . . less than $30
$$ . . . . $30 to $50
$$$ . . . . more than $50

RESTAURANTS

Taste of India, Southside/
  Midtown, Indian, $$, 84
Toucan Cafe, Southside/
  Midtown, Eclectic, $$, 84
Tubby's Tank House,
  Southside/Midtown,
  Seafood, $$, 85

**Uncle Bubba's Oyster
  House,** Islands, Seafood,
  $$, 81
Vic's on the River, Historic
  Downtown, Southern,
  $$–$$$, 78

Vinnie Van GoGo, Historic
  Downtown, Pizza, $$, 73
Walls' Barbecue, Historic
  Downtown, Barbecue, $, 68

HISTORIC DOWNTOWN

American

THE CAFE AT CITY MARKET   **$$**
224 West St. Julian St.
(912) 236-7133
www.savannahcitymarket.com
A classy local favorite for lunch or dinner is Cafe at City Market. This is a European-styled bistro that has maintained its popularity through the years with outstanding service, an old Savannah atmosphere, and a fabulous chef/owner at the helm. In the heat of summer, indoor dining is the choice. With original bricked walls, you'll feel cool and removed from the summertime humidity. Sinatra and Nat King Cole are often played in the evenings, making diners pause as they reminisce while they enjoy their favorite pasta, pizza, salads, or entrees. If the weather permits, dine outdoors, and you'll be sitting under an awning on an open-air deck "watching the world go by," as owner and chef Matt Maher puts it. At either location, you choose from a menu that's somewhat international in content and contains an item or two you've probably never encountered before, such as grilled cheese with artichoke hearts, mushrooms, and prosciutto ham, or black bean pizza. Also featured on the lunch menu is the perennial-favorite Southern pecan chicken salad.

  The dinner menu offers specialties such as stuffed chicken with asparagus, prosciutto ham, and provolone cheese, and Cuban tuna with black beans. There's room for 65 diners inside and 45 on the deck; you can smoke outside on the deck. Maher, who opened the cafe in 1991, recommends making reservations for dinner on weekends during the spring and summer. The restaurant is open Mon through Thurs 11 a.m. to 9 p.m.; Fri through Sat 11 a.m. to 10 p.m.; Sun noon to 9 p.m.

CHA-BELLA   **$$$**
102 East Broad St.
(912) 790-7888
www.cha-bella.com
The trend toward natural and organic cuisine meshes with a balmy, natural setting at Cha-Bella, a local favorite and off the beaten path for tourists. Anchored by a lovely patio grill, the menu is amazing and filled with fresh and artfully presented appetizers and entrees such as Georgia white shrimp Carolina gold risotto, which is pan-tossed shrimp with asparagus and a light lemon Chardonnay and tarragon sauce. The hand-rolled pasta is fresh every evening and filled with natural, organic fillings. There's a grouper dish that features a hearty mound of gently seared fish with a farm pea, sweet corn, and lump crab succotash. If weather permits, dine under the stars on the patio. There is an attractive bar inside. Hours are Sun through

Thurs from 5:30 to 9 p.m.; Fri and Sat 5:30 to 10 p.m.

CLARY'S CAFE $
404 Abercorn St.
(912) 233-0402

From the sidewalk, you'll see locals from this downtown neighborhood strolling to take their regular seats in this iconic Savannah eatery. Visitors know it as the original Clary's, the place where characters from *Midnight in the Garden of Good and Evil* congregated, but this cafe at Jones and Abercorn Streets was, as former owner Michael Faber once put it, "famous before the Book." Clary's opened in 1903 and, as a pharmacy and soda fountain, has been a hangout of Savannahians throughout its existence. Faber bought it in February 1994, during the week that *Midnight* hit the bookstores, and he renovated the building and converted the pharmacy into dining space.

As stated earlier, however, there's more to Clary's than its association with the best-selling book. Both the Midtown location (4430 Habersham St., 912-351-0302) and this one in Historic Downtown have extensive menus for breakfast, lunch, and dinner. However, the motivation for locals to flock here is Clary's famous breakfasts. Among well-loved specialties are the malted waffles and pancakes made with a special flour brought in from Michigan. For lunch, there are a variety of salads, burgers, sandwiches, and those aforementioned soups; and in the evening, featured items are the fillet of tilapia served on a seasoned oak plank, the old-fashioned pot roast, and the Triple Peaks salad, which has scoops of tuna, chicken, and shrimp salads on fresh greens with pasta salad. Hours are Mon through Fri 7 a.m. to 4 p.m.; Sat 8 a.m. to 5 p.m.; and Sun 8 a.m. to 4 p.m.

THE COTTON EXCHANGE $$
201 East River St.
(912) 232-7088

The true Savannah experience should include a visit to the oldest restaurant on River Street, the Cotton Exchange. Quartered in a 1799 cotton warehouse, this is one of several eateries where you can dine and view the massive ships carrying cargo up and down the Savannah River. The Exchange opened in 1971 and for a time offered mainly sandwiches, but the restaurant later expanded into the dinner market, which has evolved into one of its greatest draws. Among the standouts on the dinner menu are the pasta dishes and many types of seafood entrees such as the baked, stuffed flounder, and the traditional Low Country Boil (steamed shrimp, sausage, corn, potatoes) and a small side of their homemade coleslaw. Lunch recommendations include outstanding sandwiches such as the Reuben and a char-grilled hamburger they call the Congress. With your sandwich, you get a choice of a side dish, and we recommend the zesty German potato salad. Hours are Mon through Thurs and Sunday 11 a.m. to 11 p.m.; Fri and Sat 11 a.m. to midnight.

THE FIREFLY CAFE $$
321 Habersham St.
(912) 234-1971
www.fireflycafega.com

This is a precious cafe that sits on the corner of beautiful Troup Square (named for Governor George Troup). The building, circa 1869, was constructed for John J. McDonough, who later became the mayor of Savannah from 1891 to 1895. Lunches are delightful, and outdoor seating is recommended for a true Savannah experience. The oriental chicken salad is a work of art with grilled chicken breast set atop shredded lettuce that has been mixed with sesame dressing, carrots, sweet peppers, mandarin oranges, scallions, and surrounded by fried won tons. The "Firefly" Style corn chowder is one of the cafe's specialties, thick corn chowder with crab or chicken, topped with cheddar cheese, croutons, and scallions. For dinner, try the Spicy Sausage Fettuccine with a thick tomato-cream sauce. There's a child's menu, which is a good thing since children will love the outdoor seating that often brings great views of passing horse-drawn carriages. A note: Late lunches are advised as delivery trucks unloading food to this tiny restaurant are sometimes noisy and distracting. The restaurant serves brunch on Sat and Sun. Hours are Tues through Thurs, 7:30 a.m. to 8:30 p.m.; Fri, 7:30 a.m. to 9:30 p.m.; Sat, 9 a.m. to 9:30 p.m.; and Sun, 9 a.m. to 3 p.m.

**THE PIRATES' HOUSE
  RESTAURANT** $$
20 East Broad St.
(912) 233-5757
www.thepirateshouse.com
Locals have been coming here, and steering tourists here, for decades. It once flirted with a stuffier atmosphere, but its market reminded it that it did just fine in the old incarnation. The restaurant is comprised of small dining rooms that wind throughout the building. (Legend has it some are haunted!) These quarters are Savannah's link to Robert Louis Stevenson's classic *Treasure Island*. When you have children in your party, it's hard to find a classier restaurant that accommodates younger patrons. The Pirates' House does this quite well, without damaging arrangements for adults out for a dress-up dinner. The menu is varied and includes lots of seafood. Locals head for

the lunch buffet and always remember the fried chicken. The dessert menu is vast and intimidating: We suggest you consider dining here and skipping dessert, then making a return trip for dessert only before you leave Savannah. Nice casual will do for lunch, but brush up a little bit for dinner. There's full bar service. The restaurant also has a gift shop. If you're a new resident, this is a popular place to host children's birthday parties. The smaller rooms make ideal party places, and if you ask, your kids can meet a "real" pirate! Hours are 11 a.m. to 4 p.m. weekdays and weekends for lunch; dinner is served nightly from 4 p.m. to 9:30 p.m., but is open until 10 p.m. on Sat.

SOHO SOUTH CAFE $$
12 West Liberty St.
(912) 233-1633
www.sohosouthcafe.com
Food and art come together in this trendy restaurant where Savannahians sneak for lively lunches in the middle of the workday. (They're all thinking, "Don't tell the tourists.") Once occupied by an auto garage, there's no boredom here while waiting for the food to arrive. There's artwork on display throughout the entire gallery and tables interspersed between the goods. It's like dining in a glorified flea market. Soho South (which you will also hear called Soho Savannah, even though that isn't the official name) serves a sophisticated but affordable lunch. Your table might be from a patio suite or a circa-1950s dinette set. The quiche is the best in Savannah and sells out early at lunch. Salads, soups, Portobello mushroom burgers—we've never been disappointed here. Save room for the decadent desserts, which include a classic crème brûlée, homemade banana pudding, Georgia pecan pie, and a

rustic apple galette that's hard to resist. The dinner menu is more complex and expensive (salmon Wellington, pepper-crusted filet mignon), but it retains a grilled salmon BLT and a char-grilled cheddar burger. Brunch is served on Sun. Hours are 11 a.m. to 4 p.m. daily.

Asian

SAIGON RESTAURANT $$
4 West Broughton St.
(912) 232-5288

This family-run Thai/Vietnamese restaurant has transformed a storefront on the city's former main retail street into a sleek-looking restaurant for lunch and dinner. Pick the subtler Vietnamese dishes, or follow the crowd to the trendier (and spicier) Thai menu. Our Thai favorites include bai ka pao, which is stir-fried meat (choose beef, chicken, or pork) with basil, garlic, onions, and mushrooms, and the green curry, which offers a choice of meat in curry, coconut milk, and vegetables. Servings are large enough to serve two people amply. This is an excellent place for vegetarians to eat. For dessert, try the green tea ice cream. Lunch is served daily from 11 a.m. to 3 p.m.; dinner is from 5 p.m. to 10 p.m.

Barbecue

WALLS' BARBECUE $
515 East York Lane
(912) 232-9754
www.myspace.com/wallsbbq

Ninety-five percent of the barbecue pork, fried chicken, deviled crabs, and other food sold at Walls' is taken out by customers. Walls' is essentially a building with a kitchen and counter on York Lane, which runs from Price to Houston Streets between York Street and Oglethorpe Avenue. If you want to eat in,

there are three tables where you can sit. Walls' also offers fried fish, spare ribs, and vegetable plates, and all the dinners come with three sides from among red rice, potato salad, fries, cole slaw, and vegetables.

Margaret T. Weston, who runs Walls' along with her daughter Teresa, says the business was started in the mid-1960s by her parents, Richard and Janie Walls, in a building in back of their cottage on York Street. "My daddy had a wood yard and he got tired of chopping wood, but he wanted security for my mother and me—he wanted us to be able to take care of ourselves." So the late Richard Walls started his barbecue business, choosing it, says Mrs. Weston with a smile, "because it was something he could get out of." Soon after the business opened, Walls began driving a taxicab, leaving Mrs. Walls and her daughter to do the cooking, and cook they have, much to the delight of Savannahians who love barbecue. Walls' is open for lunch and early dinner Wed 11 a.m. until 6 p.m., and Thurs through Sat 11 a.m. until 9 p.m.

i Perhaps the influx of thousands of college students has something to do with it, but area restaurants are now more likely to offer vegetarian, and even vegan, options on their menus. But if the menu doesn't actually use the word vegetarian, you might want to ask—Southern cooks traditionally use "side meat" such as salt pork or ham hocks as seasoning in vegetables.

Burgers & Dogs

B&D BURGERS $
Downtown Location
13 East Broughton St.
(912) 231-0986
www.bdburgers.net

There are times when the pocketbook and appetite dictate that mealtimes stray off the beaten path to the perfect burger. As an avid traveler myself, I speak with experience in recommending an out-of-the-box burger establishment that is both inexpensive and fun! In Savannah, your search brings you to a truly unique local burger joint downtown, B&D Burgers. There are burgers named for fountains and squares. There are burgers named for Savannah landmarks and there are burgers named for famous Savannahians. There's even a burger topped with a fried egg (not exactly my choice for dinner), but depending on your own taste, this could be a prospective winner! Burgers at B&D are cooked to your liking, and accompaniments include baked beans that are rich in flavor. Order their sweet potato fries as an appetizer or Spud Mountain, fries covered with cheddar and Jack cheese, bacon pieces, chives, and, for an additional 99 cents, chili. Reaching for your Tums yet? There are vegetarian options at B&D. The Vegetarian Pizza is topped with peppers, onions, mushrooms, and cheese. There are a variety of salads, too. If you're running on empty pockets, try the B&D Challenge: Devour a three-pound triple-decker and a basket of fries in under 40 minutes, and your meal is free! A second location is at 11108 Abercorn St. (912-927-8700). Hours are daily from 11 a.m. to 9 p.m.; Thurs, Fri, and Sat until 10 p.m.; closed at 4 p.m. on Sun.

Cafes

**GOOSE FEATHERS EXPRESS CAFE
AND BAKERY**   **$**
39 Barnard St.
(912) 233-4683
www.goosefeatherscafe.com
Owner Beth Meeks has been operating this popular European-like cafe with so much success that she's now offering it as a franchise. A former hangout for writers and editors (including myself) from the *Savannah Morning News* (once located a stone's throw away), this eatery offers so many delicious items that some of us have been known to dine there twice in one day. Our favorites for breakfast? The bread pudding (although not for the calorie-conscious), is outstanding! The Belgian waffles are beautiful and tasty! There is fresh fruit with yogurt, as well as several variations of oatmeal combinations (like apples and cinnamon). For lunch, try the stuffed croissants, especially the spinach and feta or any of their trademark sandwiches such as the Hermitage, with cream cheese, cucumbers, sprouts, and tomatoes on multigrain bread. Winter begs for their tasty soups served in homemade bread bowls and accompanying sandwiches exploding with fresh vegetables. Be forewarned that you must stand in line (sometimes long, but always moving fast) to order. You'll take a tray with your drinks and a number and wait for your meal to be brought to the table. The Express opens at 7 a.m. weekdays and 8 a.m. weekends, closing at 2:30 p.m. every day.

Fine Dining

GARIBALDI CAFE   **$$–$$$**
315 West Congress St.
(912) 232-7118
www.garibaldisavannah.com
The list of Savannahians' favorites extends to Garibaldi a festive place that has played host to wedding celebrations, birthday galas, reunions, and friendly get-togethers for many years. In short, Garbaldi is usually the first place that comes to mind for locals seeking a special night out. Like a delightful European bistro, Garibaldi is located in what was once a Germania Fire House (circa 1871).

It was reported that volunteers celebrated their firehouse with "toasts and jokes for several hours." This is precisely what Garibaldi is about today. Don't expect a quiet romantic dinner but rather a loud place where conversation and laughter defies traditional downtown restaurants. The dinner and wine list is filled with impressive selections. For an appetizer, try the Corn Crab Cakes with mango relish and mango mint sauce. Don't leave Savannah without savoring the diamond-scored Crispy Scored Flounder, an entire fish that is fried to a crisp and adorned with an apricot shallot sauce. (Other restaurants may claim to offer a similar dish, but no one prepares it better than Garibaldi.) Reservations are available, and dress is business attire on up. Dinner only. The restaurant opens at 5 p.m. daily.

French

BROUGHTON & BULL $$$
2 East Broughton St.
(912) 231-8888
www.broughtonandbull.com
Located on busy Broughton Street, this is the alternative to down home Southern comfort food. A trendy, high-end bistro and wine bar, Broughton and Bull is fast becoming the talk of Savannah's elite. The decor is contemporary and the atmosphere, relaxing and low-key, while the food is creatively comprised of Southern basics that are artfully presented. For an appetizer, savor the fried green tomatoes and crab salad, oh, so delicious! The resraurant offers lunch and dinner. Lunch entrees range from a variety of fresh seafood sandwiches and salads. For dinner, try the seared scallops, jumbo crab cake, and crab-stuffed Carolina trout. Desserts are dazzling!There is an extensive wine list and reservations for dinner are

highly recommended. Hours are (lunch) Tues through Sat, 11:30 a.m. to 4 p.m.; dinner, Mon through Thurs, 5 to 10 p.m.; Fri and Sat, 5:30 to 11:30 p.m.; Sun 5 to 9:30 p.m. A complimentary glass from a select group of house wines is served during early dining hours, 4 to 6 p.m. weekdays and several entrees are discounted. An added treat: Gayle Thurmond, a popular Savannah pianist and singer, performs from 6:30 to 9:30 p.m. Fri, and Sat evenings from 7 to 10 p.m.

CAFE 37 $$
205 East 37th St.
(912) 236-8533
www.cafe37.com
Cafe 37 is an adorable 10-table French cafe that is perfect for a girls' lunch out with a little antique shopping on the side. Housed within an antique shop, there's a small outdoor seating area and a menu that exudes freshness. The breads are freshly baked, making each sandwich a soulful experience. There's a "small plates" dinner menu that changes weekly; an example would be rib eye and potatoes with a brandy-cream sauce for $14. There's a nice selection of wines. Take care to lock your car and be wary of your surroundings as this neighborhood has been prone to crime. Hours are 11 a.m. to 3 p.m. Tues through Sat; 10 a.m. to 3 p.m. Sun.

Fusion

SKYLER'S $$
225 East Bay St.
(912) 232-3955
www.skylersrestaurant.com
The co-owners of Skyler's—Nguyen Nguyet and Charles Coolidge—like to say their restaurant is "where East meets West." Nguyen, who's better known to patrons and friends as Ms. Moon, is a former resident of Vietnam,

and Charles is a native of Atlanta; they worked together as chefs at the Hyatt Hotel here and developed a cooking style Coolidge deems a "fusion of Asian-Continental cuisine with coastal dishes." They took that style with them when they left the hotel and opened the original Skyler's on State Street in 1990. The restaurant quickly outgrew that location, and Ms. Moon and Coolidge moved it in 1993 to the cellar of the East Bay Inn, where there was more room and the ambience of a onetime cotton warehouse—brick floors and walls and a ceiling dominated by thick wooden beams. Skyler's specializes in crab cakes, roast pork, teriyaki chicken, and Caesar salad, and seats its customers in Windsor chairs that make eating here an extremely comfortable experience. The main dining room accommodates 70 people, and there's a banquet room with seating for 60. Access to the restaurant is through the lobby of the East Bay Inn. Skyler's is open for lunch on weekdays (11 a.m. to 3 p.m.) and serves dinner Wed, Thurs (6 to 9 p.m.), Fri and Sat (6 to 10 p.m.).

ELÊ FINE FUSION $$$$
7815 US 80 East
(912) 898-2221
www.elerestaurant.com
Elê opened in 2009 and since then, has established itself as one of the finer dining options in Savannah and surrounding islands. Well worth the drive from any part of town, this very contemporary and upscale eatery offers an enticing sushi bar and live music throughout the week. However striking the interior is, the draw for this restaurant is its food that is fresh and gourmet-like in its presentation as well as taste. Appetizers include a lightly battered and fried oyster plate, served with sweet chili sauce

and cucumber salad ($11.95). The crispy logster spring rolls ($11.95). If you're indecisive, try Elê's tasting for two for $14.95 and $22.95 for four. You'll get a wonderful platter with chicken and steak kabobs, pot stickers, chicken spring rolls, and fried shrimp. Entrees are the real treat at Ele. The Red Curry Chicken ($15.95) comes with red and green bel peppers, green beans, snow peas, bamboo, lime leaves, and basil, a sumptuous blending of spices! Ele's steaks are cut, prime and premium grade and prepared and served with a red wine and portabella reduction sauce and steamed vegetables ($29.95 or $34.95, depending on the cut). Kobe steaks are pricey ($69.95 and $89.95) but well worth the price. These cuts are massaged with sake and so tender you can cut with a fork. Desserts change weekly and you are urged to save room! Hours are Mon through Thurs, 5 to 10 p.m.; Fri and Sat, 5 to 10:30 p.m.; Sun, 5 to 9:30 p.m.

Greek

OLYMPIA CAFE $$
5 East River St.
(912) 233-3131
www.olympiacafe.us
This authentic Greek restaurant is a welcome respite from the glare and bustle of River Street. Although it resembles a fast food–type eatery from the outside, on the inside brick walls and flooring, lots of plants, and soft lighting add to the atmosphere, but that's all incidental to the food. Favorites here include red snapper Aegean served with tomato sauce, spices, and feta cheese. Lamb chops marinated in olive oil and herbs before char-grilling are another favorite. Spanakopita is one of those dishes by which a Greek restaurant is measured, and you'll find this version of the flavored spinach

pastry measures up well. On the lighter and less-expensive side of the menu, you can choose gyro sandwiches and chicken kebobs. Don't be confused when you arrive—Olympia Cafe also operates a quick-and-casual take-out place on one side and a 35-flavor ice-cream parlor on the other. Hours are 11 a.m. to 9:30 p.m. daily.

Moroccan

CASBAH MOROCCAN RESTAURANT $$
118 East Broughton St.
(912) 234-6168
www.casbahrestaurant.com

If you're looking for a little local excitement that is out of the Savannah norm and convenient to the Historic District, bank on the many rave reviews and check out this unique-to-Savannah restaurant. Dinner at the Casbah turns into an evening-long event in which the food—which is very good—is only a small part. Proprietor Sami Samur has re-created a bit of the atmosphere of Morocco in what started out as an abandoned storefront on the city's main shopping street.

The decor is now lush, dark, and romantic, with hassocks and other plush upholstered seating, floor-to-ceiling drapes, and a balcony from which a belly dancer descends. Guests are escorted to their seats, where a waiter opens and closes the meal by washing their hands from a decorative pitcher filled with rosewater. The dancer comes on for short intervals throughout the evening, and the performances we've witnessed were interesting, entertaining, and quite decorous. The menu is heavily weighted with dishes like lamb cooked in honey and almonds, but even the less-adventurous palate will find an option here. Many dishes are variations on kebobs, in lamb, beef, or chicken (we opted for the dish featuring all three). For the appetizer course, we had a salad sampler, which features six different salads or relishes. Reservations are strongly recommended. Allow plenty of time for dinner—at least a couple of hours. Dress ranges from dress-casual to business attire, but women may feel more comfortable in pants, given the seating arrangements. There is a small gift shop selling Moroccan items like tangines (cooking vessels). Open for dinner 5:30 to 10:30 p.m. daily.

Pizza

SPANKY'S PIZZA GALLEY & SALOON $
317 East River St.
(912) 236-3009
www.spankys.tv

Ansley Williams, Alben Yarbrough, and Dusty Yarbrough opened the first Spanky's on River Street in 1976, intending to bring pizza to the area. They also served burgers and chicken sandwiches at the restaurant, which is housed in what had been a cotton warehouse. According to Williams, the chicken breasts used for the sandwiches were too large for the buns on which they were served, so the restaurateurs sliced off the excess chicken and, not wanting to be wasteful, battered and fried the strips of meat and sold them as "chicken fingers." Their concoction was a hit with locals and has become a mainstay of eateries throughout southeast Georgia. The success of the River Street location led to the opening of Spanky's restaurants in other parts of the state and locally on the Southside near Oglethorpe Mall (308 Mall Way, 912-355-3383), in Pooler (200 Governor Treutlen Rd., 912-748-8188), and Spanky's Beachside on Tybee Island (1605

Strand, 912-786-5520). There's yet another version located on Wilmington Island with the name Molly MaGuire's. Don't be fooled. This, too, is a Spanky's spinoff serving the same signature fingers and spuds. Veteran customers will vouch that Spanky's Spuds, which are circular-sliced potatoes that are battered and fried, are high on the Savannah "don't miss this list". A warning: if you're not a fan of loud and boisterous restaurants with a sports bar atmosphere, you'll probably want to stay away from Spanky's. Spanky's restaurants are open daily for lunch and dinner. Hours are 11 a.m. until midnight.

VINNIE VAN GOGO $$
317 West Bryan St.
(912) 233-6394
www.vinnievangogo.com
Vinnie's serves pizza with real character—thin crust with fresh ingredients, including such options as spinach, artichoke, and broccoli, for dinner only. Experiment with pesto instead of regular sauce. A regular 14-inch pie is $10 to start, plus $1.50 for each ingredient. Dine in the cramped interior or at outside tables overlooking City Market (semi-enclosed when it's cold). Pizza is available by the slice, and one of those with the excellent spinach salad is an ample meal. A personal favorite among the pizzas is feta, sun-dried tomato, and black olive. Beer is available. Get the wine list: Cork and screw-top are your options. Your most casual duds are probably too dressy for Vinnie's, but the food's tops. Cash only. I repeat, cash only. No debit cards. No credit cards. Delivery via bicycle available downtown. Hours are Mon through Thurs from 4 to 11:30 p.m.; Fri and Sat from noon to midnight; Sun, noon to 11:30 p.m.

Pub Fare

B. MATTHEW'S $$
325 East Bay St.
(912) 233-1319
www.bmatthewseatery.com
Claiming the rites as "the oldest tavern" in Savannah, this former home that was once a raucous bar called the Lamp Post is thriving with old-city atmosphere and charm, a publike lunch and dinner menu, and a healthy array of imported beers on tap and in bottles. Starting with breakfast, their pancakes, omelets, and egg dishes are light and tasty! Sun brunch features an artichoke-and-goat-cheese omelet and apple, pecan, and bourbon chutney pancakes (served 9 a.m. to 3 p.m.) Lunch favorites include a Black-eyed Pea Cake Sandwich, a spicy combination served on fresh bread, and an apple-pecan chicken-salad sandwich, and entrees like pecan-crusted chicken. Owner Brian Huskey bought the restaurant in 2006 and has constantly upgraded the facilities, making it one of downtown Savannah's brightest spots! Resist the urge to sit outside as the noise from trucks passing on Bay Street will spoil the pleasures of dining outdoors. Hours are 8 a.m. to 9 p.m. Mon through Thurs; Fri and Sat 8 a.m. to 10 p.m.; happy hour is from 4 to 7 p.m.; Sunday brunch is from 9 a.m. to 3 p.m.

CRYSTAL BEER PARLOR $$
301 West Jones St.
(912) 349-1000
www.crystalbeerparlor.com
Savannahian John Nichols revived the tradition of the Crystal Beer Parlor last year, much to the delight of a close following of generations of fans. As best as he possibly could, Nichols tackled the challenge of returning it to the original look of an early-1900s burger joint with a vengeance, livening up the old

place, while keeping the hometown feel alive. The original restaurant was one of the first American eating establishments to serve alcohol after the repeal of Prohibition. Today the walls are covered with photos of early Savannah. There's a Monroe Room, named for Monroe Whitlock, who was a server there for 45 years. Of course there's a bar here that serves a variety of draft and bottled beers. The rich and creamy crab stew is a specialty. The restaurant serves lunch and dinner Sun through Thurs 1 a.m. to 10 p.m., and Fri and Sat 11 a.m. to 11 p.m.

SIX PENCE PUB $$
245 Bull St.
(912) 233-3156
www.sixpencepub.com
With the charm of a true British pub, the Six Pence offers specials each day. Patrons have a particular liking for the shepherd's pie; the sausage (bangers, in England) and mashed potatoes; the French-onion and potato soups; a meat pie made with mushrooms, peas, onions, and carrots; and beer-marinated beef. So if you're looking for Savannah-fare, you may want to dine somewhere else.

With a generous selection of beer on tap, the pub is filled with conversation-starting memorabilia, with most of it adorning the walls and bar. From the Toby mugs to the coronation collectibles dating from 1898 to the pub signs, some of which are more than 200 years old, there's also a must-see ship's bell that's a replica of the one on the *Titanic*—a souvenir gift from that ill-fated vessel's maiden voyage. The pub also has its own ghost, a fellow who reportedly hangs out in the basement and has a penchant for turning faucets and light fixtures on and off. Nicknamed "Larry" by former Six Pence owner Wendy Snowden, this apparition has

the appearance of a young man from the late 1800s. Hours are Mon thourgh Thurs 11:30 a.m. to midnight; Fri and Sat, 11:30 a.m. to 2 a.m.; Sun 11:30 a.m. through 10 p.m.

Southern

ALLIGATOR SOUL $$$
114 Barnard St.
(912) 232-7879, (912) 232-8038
www.alligatorsoul.com
Alligator Soul is a sterling example of Savannah's snare enticing culinary talent. This is a restaurant that has been spared national notoriety, but should deservingly be on the "talked about" list. Establishing roots in Savannah from Seattle, Washington, the late executive chef Hilary Craig, and his wife, Maureen, transformed this former 1885 (below-the-ground) grain warehouse into a cozy, romantic place to enjoy gourmet cuisine. Today Maureen and a new co-owner /chef, Christpher DiNello, shine in carrying on the love of Southern cuisine that Hilary started. Attracted by an eclectic menu, locals and tourists have kept this eatery thriving through a recession, enjoying the fabulous creations served at this Barnard Street eatery, located just north of Telfair Square. Try the fried green tomatoes—tasteful and beautiful with a crisp Parmesan-and-cornmeal crusted covering, served sizzling over a delicious chipotle mayonnaise and garnished with a sweet relish. For dinner, I recommend the shrimp and grits—shrimp sautéed in lemon butter and Creole spices and served over stone-ground grits with Tasso ham and cheese. Save room for dessert! The Alligator Soul Banana Beignets are served hot, and are perfect with coffee if you desire. Made with fresh bananas lightly coated with tempura batter, quickly fried, and served with banana ice cream, roasted cinnamon wonton crisps,

and candied pecans, this dish is one of many reasons to dine here. Open nightly, Mon through Sun, 5:30 p.m. to "10-ish".

i If you decide to get a take-out meal along River Street (or anywhere else near the water), resist the urge to share it with that single begging seagull that will invariably show up. Otherwise, hordes of its friends will arrive, and you will have no peace. Also, beware if you sit on a River Street bench (beneath the canopy of the riverfront stores). Seagulls have been known to leave their mark when you least expect it.

HUEY'S $$
115 East River St.
(912) 234-7385
This is a chain with a local flair! Huey's brings the Big Easy to Savannah with its New Orleans–style cuisine. With floor-to-ceiling windows right on the sidewalk, Huey's also offers a great view of the Savannah River, a circumstance that makes a breakfast of café au lait and beignets something special. For those unfamiliar with "N'awlins," beignets (pronounced "ben-yeas") are delectable French doughnuts.

Huey's also has some specialties for breakfast eaters with heartier appetites, including eggs Benedict and eggs Sardou, the latter consisting of a bed of creamed spinach with artichoke hearts on a toasted English muffin with two poached eggs topped with hollandaise sauce. For lunch and dinner, there are such dishes as red beans and rice served with andouille sausage, and muffuletta, a sandwich made with freshly baked bread, Genoa salami, capocollo

ham, provolone cheese, and an olive dressing. The food is zesty but moderately spiced; if you want more zip, there's Tabasco sauce on your table. Hours are Mon through Thurs, 7 a.m. to 10 p.m.; Fri, 7 a.m. to 11 p.m.; Sat 8 a.m. to 11 p.m.; Sun, 8 a.m. to 10 p.m.

THE LADY AND SONS $$
102 West Congress St.
(912) 233-2600
www.theladyandsons.com
Paula Deen, host of the Food Network's *Paula Deen's Home Cooking*, is Savannah's most recent celebrity. Be sure to sample the food that made Paula famous here at her restaurant and remember, there are no guarantees that the diva will be there to meet you in person. (You can read more about Deen's kitchen-based empire in our Savannah Celebrity chapter later in this book.)

There's an appealing menu at this Southern comfort-food eatery, but unless you're going to be in town long enough to return repeatedly, skip it and go directly to the buffet. This is the slow-cooked, perfectly seasoned stuff that Southerners consider real home cooking, which may define why there aren't many locals eating there. (They're eating it at home, too!) Fried chicken, squash casserole, seasoned greens, fried green tomatoes, hoecakes (ask if you don't know), cheese biscuits—you get the picture. Hours are Mon through Sat, 11 a.m. to 3 p.m.; Sun (lunch buffet only) 11 a.m. to 5 p.m. Holiday hours are as follows: St. Patrick's Day, noon until when they decide to close; Christmas Eve, 11 a.m. to 3 p.m.; closed Dec. 26, Dec. 31, Jan. 1; reopening Jan. 2 and 3 with normal hours.

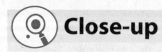

Close-up

Regional Cuisine Offers a Taste of Savannah

When you're in Savannah, you might run across some cuisine you're not likely to find in other parts of the country. Two examples, the **Lowcountry shrimp boil** and the **oyster roast,** combine food with other elements you might have noticed being mentioned throughout this book: Savannahians' love of getting together and their fondness for being outdoors.

You can order Lowcountry boil in a restaurant, and the same goes for oysters, but perhaps the best way to experience them is by attending an outdoor party at which they are the featured components. Lowcountry boil—also known as Frogmore stew because it supposedly originated in Frogmore, South Carolina, which is about 90 minutes northeast of Savannah—consists of smoked sausage, corn on the cob, and shrimp all boiled together in a large pot. Some cooks add other ingredients, with new potatoes seeming to be the most popular.

Oysters served at an oyster roast are roasted on a big piece of tin or steel that's supported by cinder blocks. A red-hot fire is built under the sheet of metal, and the oysters are placed on it and covered with wet cloth—burlap sacks do nicely. The oysters will steam open in about 20 minutes, and they're ready to eat. Special oyster knives are used to help dig the oysters out of their shells, and it's a good idea to wear gloves to prevent being cut by the oyster's tough exterior.

The Southerner's way is to enjoy a Lowcountry boil or oyster roast by standing around a long table on a crisp day in autumn, chatting with friends, and diving into a pile of oysters or a big heap of sausage, shrimp, and corn that's been dumped on a table covered with newspaper. It doesn't hurt, by the way, if grilled hot dogs are nearby for those who aren't fans of the oyster.

i You can take care of some of your souvenir shopping while you dine out. Many restaurants sell sauces featured in their prize dishes, or cookbooks drawing from their menu.

MRS. WILKES' DINING ROOM $$
107 West Jones St.
(912) 232-5997
www.mrswilkes.com

This restaurant is worth the wait because dining at Mrs. Wilkes' is about more than eating lunch; it's about experiencing the true, Southern Sunday lunch around the dinner table with family and friends. (At least they'll be your friends once lunch is over.) It's so special that President Barack Obama "popped in" with his entourage and dined with a table of surprised guests! Traditional Southern home-cooking restaurants in Savannah started at Mrs. Wilkes', and daughter Marcia Thompson does a fine job of seeing that her parents' famous traditions are ongoing. If you must visit one of the two restaurants during your stay in Savannah, try this one first. Although the notoriety is not as recent (as Paula Deen's), this place has been highly praised by national and international media through the years. You'll partake of the same Southern fare, only family-style and minus the Hollywood (although Mrs. Wilkes as been featured all over the networks.)

Among other foods associated with this area are **Savannah red rice,** a dessert called **trifle,** and a cookie known as the **benne wafer.** The benne wafer has a taste all its own because it's made with benne seeds, which is what folks in the Lowcountry call sesame seeds. Trifle, a gift of the English colonists to Savannah, consists of pound cake that's been sprinkled with sherry, layered with custard, and topped with whipped cream.

Savannah red rice goes great with fried chicken and seafood. The following is a recipe for this distinctly local dish provided by Martha Giddens Nesbit, who edited and wrote much of the food section of Savannah's daily newspaper for more than a decade and is the author of the *Savannah Collection* and *Savannah Entertains* cookbooks.

In her recipe, which serves four people, Martha uses four slices of bacon that have been fried crisp, crumbled, and reserved, one chopped onion, one chopped celery stalk, a cup of raw rice, one 16-ounce can of tomatoes, three-quarters of a cup of water, a teaspoon of salt, and a quarter-teaspoon of cayenne pepper.

Fry the chopped onion and celery in bacon fat, then remove some of the fat, if desired, and add the rice, tomatoes, water, salt, and pepper. Combine the ingredients and transfer them to a one and one-half-quart baking dish. Bake at 350 degrees for 20 minutes or until the rice is soft but not dry. Stir in the reserved bacon and serve hot or at room temperature.

Something else you're likely to encounter during mealtimes in Savannah is sweetened ice tea, which we call just plain ol' **"sweet tea."** Savannahians drink it year-round, and here's a good way to make a gallon-size pitcher full: Place three family-size tea bags in the basket of your automatic coffeemaker and brew up a full coffeepot of tea. Put about a cup of sugar in the pitcher and pour the hot tea on top. Stir it up and add a full coffeepot of water and stir again. When it cools, you've got sweet tea.

At our most recent visit to Mrs. Wilkes', the tables were loaded with fried chicken, barbecue chicken, beef stew, sausage, baked ham, collard greens, snap beans, black-eyed peas, squash, rice and gravy, okra and tomatoes, mashed potatoes, candied yams, pickled beets, apple salad, and macaroni salad. Mrs. Wilkes' doesn't take credit cards, and smoking is prohibited. Dinner is not served daily, but parties and catering can be arranged in advance. Hours are weekdays 11 a.m. until 2 p.m. Be sure to arrive early to avoid waiting.

**THE OLDE PINK HOUSE RESTAURANT
& PLANTERS TAVERN $$$
23 Abercorn St.
(912) 232-4286**

Savannahians who have traditionally enjoyed the Olde Pink House for its ambient downstairs bar and elegant, historical feel, are elated by the restaurant's expansion, an open outdoorsy bar with tables that spread out onto the sidewalk and under a canopy of trees. In fact, it's fast becoming one of the trendiest and most in-demand places to dine in town. As the dining rooms inside have sometimes felt restrictive and crowded, the outdoor Pink House is exceptional. If it's winter, start downstairs in the Planters Tavern, a more casual and comfortable dining place and home to the restaurant's wine cellar. A fireplace is usually lit on each end of the room and there is live piano music nightly.

The Olde Pink House serves regional cuisine in several elegant dining rooms occupying the upper two floors of the building. Examples of this type of cooking are the roast duck with wild berry sauce and Hoppin' John, she-crab soup laced with sherry, Caesar salad with corn bread oysters, crispy scored flounder with apricot shallot sauce, and grilled pork tenderloin with collards and yams. Reservations are definitely recommended. If you're interested in dining in the restaurant's most romantic spot, ask for a table by a window in the second-floor Office Room—it has a view of picturesque Reynolds Square. Ask your waiter or waitress to share some of the varied ghost stories that are unique to this establishment. Hours are Sun through Mon, 5 to 10:30 p.m.; Fri and Sat, 11 a.m. to 11 p.m.

VIC'S ON THE RIVER $$–$$$
26 East Bay St.
(912) 721-1000
www.vicsontheriver.com

What a refreshing place to dine on the riverfront! Vic's on the River is not typical of other Savannah restaurants that are housed in historic buildings and oftentimes dark, musty, and cramped. Because this was once the top floor of a cotton warehouse, the rooms offer a spacious and airy feel with plenty of room to dine without bumping into the table beside you. The food is as refined as the atmosphere. Appetizers include a crab cake with corn, black-eyed pea salsa, traditional remoulade, and chervil; crispy calamari with pickled peppers and a citrus chile glaze with feta cheese;

and fried green tomatoes ($8 to $10). A favorite lunchtime entree is local shrimp and smoked cheddar stone-ground grits with smoked bacon and rosemary barbeque ($13). The dinner menu standouts include many of the same entrees only doubled in price. There are also brown sugar–cured pork chops, a braised lamb shank, and a grilled rib eye ($23 to $28) for land lovers. There's a bar within the restaurant, and the view of the Savannah River is outstanding. Hours are 11 a.m. to 4 p.m. for lunch; dinner is served 4 p.m. to 10 p.m. Sun through Thurs, and 4 to 11 p.m. Fri and Sat. There is valet parking.

i Dr. Irving Victor, or "Dr. Vic" to his friends, launched Vic's on the River a few years ago to the delight of his patients and fans! Dr. Vic is a native Savannahian and obviously has a taste for fine eating establishments. His medical career in Savannah spans more than 40 years. As the former chief of staff at both hospitals, Memorial and St. Joseph's/Candler, he is the founder of Emergency Medical Services in Chatham County.

Surf 'n' Turf

BELFORD'S SAVANNAH SEAFOOD
& STEAKS $$$
315 West St. Julian Street
(912) 233-2626
www.belfordssavannah.com

Everything on the menu at Belford's is exceptional. Testifying to this statement are entrees such as shrimp, greens, and grits; a double-cut pork chop; and the stuffed filet—grilled filet mignon stuffed with shrimp and finished with béarnaise sauce. The crab cakes are among the city's best and, in fact, a consecutive award winner by professional writers. The light and airy atmosphere promotes casual dress. At first glance, Belford's architectural strengths are a standout, with the tall, arched, unadorned windows lining the City Market and Congress Streets. The restaurant is housed in a former produce warehouse once frequented by local grocers The name is derived from the Belford's Wholesale Food Company, which was an integral part of City Market in the early 1900s, and a portrait of the Belford family is among the framed artwork decorating the eatery. Brick walls, highly polished wooden floors, captain's chairs, and tables covered with linen add to the classical feel of the place. Belford's serves lunch and dinner daily, and breakfast Mon through Sat, with brunch on Sun. Hours are as follows: breakfast, 8 to 11 a.m.; lunch, 11:30 a.m. to 3 p.m.; dinner, 5:30 to 10 p.m.; Sun brunch, 11:30 a.m. to 3 p.m.

THE RIVERHOUSE RESTAURANT $$$
125 West River St.
(912) 234-1900, (800) 317-1912
www.riverhouseseafood.com
The Riverhouse and its bakery occupy four bays of an old cotton warehouse near the west end of River Street, and the bricks and thick wooden beams of the building lend charm to the upscale but casual atmosphere. Operated by the Harris family, which established it in 1982, the Riverhouse specializes in fresh seafood. Featured dishes include the grouper Florentine, which is served atop angel-hair pasta, and Atlantic salmon crowned with whipped potatoes and baked. Among the appetizers are the seafood strudel—a light pastry filled with spinach, feta, shrimp, and crabmeat—and shrimp served on grits with a tasso gravy. The restaurant serves lunch and dinner, and "dessert only" customers are welcome any

time in the bakery. Always save room for dessert here. The restaurant's forte is its Southern Pecan Pie, Praline Cheesecake, and Fudge Walnut Pie (with ice cream if you like). Lunch (11:30 a.m.) and dinner (starting at 5 p.m.) are served. Hours are Mon through Thurs 11 a.m. to 10 p.m.; Fri and Sat, 11 a.m. to 11 p.m.; Sun 11:30 a.m. to 10 p.m.

THE SHRIMP FACTORY $$$
313 East River St.
(912) 236-4229
www.theshrimpfactory.com
This restaurant near the eastern end of River Street offers what owner Cheryl Harris Power likes to call "fine casual dining," meaning the atmosphere is relaxed but replete with special touches such as the salad being tossed tableside. The Shrimp Factory prides itself on its seafood, steaks, and chicken dishes, and as might be expected, you can find shrimp served "in so many ways" here—fried, with crab au gratin, with deviled crab, with sausage Creole, and with scallops. Pecan pie is a specialty of the house, as is the pine bark stew, which is best described as a "Southern bouillabaisse." The restaurant occupies the bottom floor of a warehouse built in the 1820s for storing cotton, rosin, and other products, and the building's heart-pine ceiling beams and rafters and brick walls give the Shrimp Factory a rustic feel. Hours are Mon through Thurs and Sun, 11 a.m. to 10 p.m.; Fri and Sat, 11 a.m. to 11 p.m.

ISLANDS
Pizza

BASIL'S PIZZA AND DELI $
216 Johnny Mercer Blvd.
(912) 897-6400
www.basilspizzaonline.com

This restaurant on Wilmington Island prides itself on being family operated (the name is derived from the Greek name of a son/grandson of the owners) and specializes in pizza and Mediterranean dishes. Among the combination pizzas are the Greek, eggplant Parmesan, and gyro varieties, and the menu also includes Hellenic-inspired fare such as dolmades and spanakopita. Basil's also offers delicious pasta, salads, and a broad array of sandwiches, and the pasta salad—made with bacon and broccoli—is as good as it gets. Basil's occupies a storefront in the Wilmington Island Shopping Center at the heart of the island. Basil's offers an excellent selection of domestic and imported beers. The restaurant has seating for 80 and a special kid's room with a television and videos playing. There's outside seating on a screened-in porch. Hours are Mon through Thurs, 11 a.m. to 9:30 p.m.; Fri and Sat 11 a.m. to 10:30 p.m., and Sun, noon to 9 p.m.

Seafood

DESPOSITO'S SEAFOOD $
Macceo Dr., Thunderbolt
(912) 897-9963
If you're looking for a dive that has awesome steamed seafood, this is the place. On evenings when the weather's nice, Desposito's owner David Boone opens the windows of the enclosed porch of this little cinderblock and wood eatery at Thunderbolt. You can sit out there at tables covered with newspaper and eat boiled shrimp, crab legs, and steamed oysters as the breeze from the nearby Wilmington River wafts through the place.

Desposito's also serves deviled crab; homemade chili, pecan pie, and potato salad; and the Lowcountry basket, which is filled with shrimp, corn on the cob, sausage, and the aforementioned potato salad. In addition to the porch, there's a dining room and a bar that serves beer and wine. Desposito's is open for dinner daily except Mon and for lunch and dinner on Fri, Sat, and Sun. MasterCard and Visa only are accepted. It's on the eastern side of the Wilmington River and north of US 80. Open Tues through Thurs, 5 to 10 p.m.; Fri to Sun, noon to 10 p.m.

DRIFTAWAY CAFE $$
7400 Skidaway Rd.
(912) 303-0999
www.driftawaycafe.com
The Driftaway Cafe is a casual place resembling someone's back porch that's been decorated with beachy knickknacks. The interior is cute without being cloying, with murals of local water scenes on the walls and a massive sculpture of a raging shark bursting through one wall. The best tables overlook the marsh at the rear, where you can see a real creek and a fake waterfall, a cat (or could it be a raccoon?) with some kitschy statuary scattered around. From the porch, you can also view (on a good night) some really large snapping turtles in the creek and the butterflies feasting on the landscaping.

Enough about the scenery. The menu covers salads, sandwiches, and full entrees, but you should start with the Herb River Crab Dip, a creamy blend of cheeses brimming with (real) crabmeat and spices. The dip is served with toasted bread and it's a good thing they don't bring you much of it or you would forgo the entree and lick the dip bowl clean. There are chicken and steak dishes on the menu, but stick with seafood. There are shrimp quesadillas ($11), butterfly shrimp (fried and tossed in firecracker sauce, $11) and an Atlantic salmon grilled and served with jerk-grilled asparagus ($13). The fish tacos ($12) are phenomenal: grouper strips flash-fried in batter and served on flour tortillas with lettuce and some perfectly seasoned sauce. For a more formal meal, go for the crispy scored flounder, which is flash-fried and served with lots of spicy apricot sauce. Sides range from dressy (grilled asparagus) to down-home (homemade potato chips). There's a full bar and a large wine selection. Lunch and dinner daily, 11 a.m. to 10 p.m. Mon through Thurs, and open to 11 p.m. on Fri and Sat. Sun brunch (heavy on egg dishes) starts at 10 a.m., and they close at 9 p.m. that day. Note that this place is in the Sandfly Community on the way to Skidaway Island.

THE FLYING FISH   **$$**
7906 US 80 East
(912) 897-2009
Williams Seafood, a cherished restaurant on Talahi Island's shores and just off US 80 East, burned to the ground in 2004. The restaurant was adored by islanders and tourists who often stood in long lines for fried fish, generous portions of hush puppies, and a favorite—fried shrimp. On Sundays when church would let out, there was a literal race to reach this establishment before the crowds arrived in droves. Once the ashes were cleared after the fire consumed the place, there was a huge void where the restaurant once stood. And just as mourning of its demise escalated, Wanda and Tommy Williams, descendents of the original owners (their grandparents), opened the Flying Fish just down the road from the original restaurant. Hooray! The Williams' hush puppies, fried fish, and fried shrimp have been revived in a tropical-like atmosphere where flip-flops and T-shirts define the dress code. Don't expect anything fancy about this place

as all food is served on throwaway dishes. Be sure to try cheese grits with grouper fingers, fish tacos, and any of their fresh seafood with the Williams' trademark—perfectly sweetened tea. There's a full bar and a decent beer selection and several outdoor tables if you're coming from the beach. Hours are 11:30 a.m. to 10 p.m. daily.

UNCLE BUBBA'S OYSTER HOUSE   **$$**
104 Bryan Woods Rd.
(912) 897-6101
www.unclebubbasoysterhouse.com
Paula Deen, the star cook from the Food Network and The Lady and Sons Restaurant, is the figure behind this restaurant, which she opened with her brother, Bubba Hiers. Uncle Bubba's opened in 2004 in a renovated restaurant building on the marsh just off US 80, about halfway between town and the beach and visible from the highway. It features good marsh views and an extensive patio deck where food is served, weather permitting (and it usually is). The decor aims for a sort of retro-diner feel. It has also served as a filming site for Paula's party-themed series on the Food Network.

As you can probably tell from the name, they're big on seafood here. A signature dish is char-grilled oysters, which involve open flame, butter, and Parmesan cheese ($8 for a half dozen, $13 for a dozen). Char-grilled oysters, you say? This dish is worth the trip to Bubba's. Well, I can vouch for these as I've eaten my weight in this dish! With just the right spices (Bubba's secret) and a lemony flavor to top it off, if you're an oyster lover, this is a dish you must try if you're in Savannah. Paula's Fried Chicken Plate ($13) is filled with the signature home-style cooking Deen serves up at her downtown restaurant, so if you've missed the opportunity to try her downtown restaurant, order this. Eating at Uncle Bubba's satisfies your Deen craving with a lot less hassle. Another plus, the parking at Uncle Bubba's is free and plentiful. Hours are seasonal. Summer hours are (starting President's Day) Sun through Wed, 11 a.m. to 9 p.m.; Thurs through Sat, 11 a.m. to 10 p.m.; closed from 3 to 5 p.m. daily (although the bar is open during those hours). Starting Labor Day, Sun through Wed, noon to 8 p.m., Thurs through Sat, noon to 9 p.m.

SOUTHSIDE/MIDTOWN

American

CAREY HILLIARD'S RESTAURANT $
3316 Skidaway Rd.
(912) 354-7240
www.careyhilliards.com
That there are six Carey Hilliard's in Savannah should tell you something about the popularity of these restaurants, which provide casual dining in an atmosphere geared toward families. Founder Carey Hilliard opened his first establishment in 1960 on Skidaway Road in what had been an A&W Root Beer stand. The drive-in, curb-service feature was retained, and all six restaurants offer it today. Order from your car, and you receive many of the amenities you would by dining inside, including china plates and silverware. Barbecue has always been, and still is, a big seller at Carey Hilliard's, which serves lunch and dinner, but seafood dishes account for about half the orders these days. Among customers' favorites are the fried shrimp, oysters, and deviled crabs. Seating at the restaurants averages 250. Beer and wine are available. Check their website for information on their other restaurant locations. Hours are 11 a.m. to midnight daily.

Asian

HIRANO'S RESTAURANT $–$$
4426 Habersham St.
(912) 353-8337
Japanese cuisine became a major hit in Savannah with the opening of this small storefront restaurant on Habersham Street. Folks stand in line for a chance to order simple, fresh food from a limited menu. Large servings and reasonable prices are hallmarks here. The teriyaki chicken, served with rice and salad, runs less than $5, so if you pick your items carefully, this can be a budget meal as well as a real treat. Combination plates carry higher prices.

The food is prepared at open griddles behind the counter—this is not one of the showy knife-twirling restaurants. If you are eager to get started at the Habersham site, opt for a seat at the counter overlooking the cooking. Those seats come open more quickly than the small stock of tables. The Habersham location has a separate sushi bar, but call ahead if you are interested—it tends to keep shorter hours. Both the Hirano's serve a delicious California roll of avocado and cooked crab rolled in rice for those who are wary of traditional sushi. A second location is at 13015 Abercorn St. (912-961-0770). Hours are 11 a.m. to 2 p.m. daily for lunch; 5 to 9 p.m. nightly, except Sun when the restaurant closes at 8 p.m.

Barbecue

BARNES RESTAURANT $$
5320 Waters Ave.
(912) 354-8745
The folks at the two Barnes restaurants pride themselves on the fact that everything— from the barbecue sauce to the potato salad to the sweet ice tea—is homemade.

The sauce on Barnes's chopped pork and sliced beef barbecue is made according to a recipe developed by restaurant founder Nesbert Barnes and perfected over the years by his son, Hugh; it's spread on meat that's slow-cooked at low temperatures over oak and hickory wood. There's a step-by-step guide for making the tea and an employee specifically designated to perform the task; if the tea maker is not present on a given day, the manager gets the job.

Today families, businesspeople, and retirees flock to Barnes for the barbecue and the tea for lunch and dinner. Chicken fingers, ribs, shrimp salad, and onion rings are other big sellers. Barnes serves lunch and dinner, and you're likely to encounter a line of customers waiting at the Waters Avenue restaurant if you get there around noon. Hours are Mon through Sun, 10 a.m. to 2 p.m.; dinner, 2 to 10 p.m.; 10:30 a.m. to 10 p.m Sun.

JOHNNY HARRIS RESTAURANT $$
1651 East Victory Dr.
(912) 354-7810
www.johnnyharris.com
Stepping into the main dining room at Johnny Harris is like fox-trotting back into the late 1930s and the 1940s, when this establishment was an elegant supper club on the outskirts of Savannah. The bandstand that occupied the middle of the floor is gone, but the room retains the charm of that bygone era. Remaining from those good old days are the dark wood paneling of the Old English decor and a 30-foot-high ceiling adorned for a starry, night-sky effect. You can also still slip into one of the booths lining the perimeter of the oval-shaped room and place an order by pushing a service button that illuminates a green light overhead.

The restaurant has been a favorite of Savannahians for decades, and many patrons bring their grandchildren and great-grandchildren so they can experience the atmosphere, service, and food—in particular the barbecue, fried chicken, prime rib, and crabmeat au gratin (meat of the crab's claw folded in a cream and cheese sauce). Johnny Harris is the oldest restaurant in Savannah and one of the oldest in Georgia, but you'll notice it's not in the Historic Downtown. It's in Midtown, on Victory Drive just east of Bee Road. That intersection is where the original restaurant was built in 1924 by a Southerner from out of town named Johnny Harris; the original wooden building was torn down, and the brick structure that houses the existing restaurant was built in 1936. Johnny Harris died in 1942, and the restaurant has been run by the Donaldson family of Savannah ever since. You might also consider purchasing some of the restaurant's barbecue sauce to take home with you. It's bottled hot and sold at Johnny Harris and other outlets in Georgia, South Carolina, and Florida, and it is shipped worldwide via mail order. Hours are Mon through Thurs 11:30 a.m. to 9:30 p.m.; Fri through Sat, 11:30 a.m. to 10:30 p.m.

Cuban

RANCHO ALEGRE $
44 Posey St.
(912) 691-0110
www.ranchoalegrecuban.com
Rancho Alegre is our nominee for Savannah's biggest culinary surprise. After all, who would expect to find a restaurant tucked away just off Abercorn Street near the eastern end of the Hunter Army Airfield runway, amid auto-repair shops and wholesale houses—one that serves Cuban cuisine, no less. But there it is, occupying what was

once a residence before the commercialization spawned by nearby Oglethorpe Mall caught up with it. This restaurant serves a variety of exotic-sounding dishes featuring chicken, beef, pork, and seafood, such as pollo a la Juliana (pepper chicken strips), ropa vieja (shredded beef slowly cooked in Creole sauce), masas de cerdo fritas (fried pork chunks), and camarones al ajilio (garlic shrimp). Most entries are accompanied by rice, beans, and fried sweet plantains. We're betting this is also one of few places in town where you can get Cuban coffee, flan, and fried yucca. The Rancho Alegre serves lunch and dinner Mon through Sat.

Eclectic

TOUCAN CAFE   **$$**
531 Stephenson Ave.
(912) 352-2233
www.toucancafe.com
Nestled in the woods off Stephenson Avenue, the Toucan Cafe combines eclectic food, an interior that pulsates with the high-impact colors of the tropics, and an exterior that has a classic Mediterranean look. The cuisine reflects the influences of several exotic cultures—Jamaican jerk chicken and Jamaican jerk tilapia, both of which are served with black beans and mango salsa; chicken farfalle and shrimp farfalle, both served in a basil cream with bow-tie pasta; and Hellenic stuffed chicken, made with spinach and feta cheese, served over rice, and topped with marinated baby peas. Those are just a few of the dishes offered by owners Steve and Nancy Magulias who, in late 1998, moved the cafe to newly built quarters on Stephenson from a small storefront in nearby Eisenhower Plaza where the

Toucan had been located since 1994. The Toucan Cafe serves dinner and lunch Mon through Sat; reservations aren't required but will be accepted for parties of five or more. Hours are Mon through Sat, 11:30 a.m. to 2:30 p.m. and dinner, 5 to 9 p.m.; closed Sunday.

Indian

TASTE OF INDIA   **$$**
401 Mall Blvd.
(912) 356-1020
Savannah has a substantial Indian community, including college professors, physicians, hoteliers, and operators of retail shops. As a result, the city has a small handful of Indian restaurants. Our favorite is Taste of India. The restaurant's quarters formerly housed a barbecue restaurant, so there's something just a little incongruous about lush Indian decor against a knotty pine background. But instead of appearing overdone, the overall effect is one of exotic luxuriance.

The menu is varied, with vegetarian dishes heavily represented. You can also choose from chicken, lamb, goat, and seafood entrees. On the appetizer side, we recommend pau bhaji, a paste of mashed vegetables in garlic sauce that you eat on bread, or chicken samosa, a spiced meat pastry. For entrees, dishes we've personally experienced and can recommend include lamb sagwala, which resembles a lamb stew in a creamy spinach base. Less-adventurous souls can safely opt for the chicken curry. Taste of India is open for lunch on weekdays, when it serves from a buffet, and for dinner seven days a week. It has a full bar. Hours are Mon through Fri, 11 a.m. to 3 p.m.; dinner daily and weekends, 5 to 10 p.m.

Seafood

FIDDLERS CRAB HOUSE & OYSTER BARN $$
7201 Hodgson Memorial Blvd.
(912) 351-2274
www.liveoakrestaurants.com
This big restaurant opened in 2007 as part of the local chain that includes several seafood restaurants on River Street and elsewhere. This is a standout among Southside's local restaurants. The rustic-looking building includes an off-the-roof water cascade that cools an outdoor patio, and a "moat" that should entertain the kiddies. Inside, the decor is rustic nautical, with walls made of old deck wood and tables with seashells buried in polyurethane. Check out the walls—they're a tribute to Savannah's family fishing and processing businesses, most of which are gone with the tide these days.

Look here for simple seafood dishes—not particularly fancy, creative, or gourmet dishes, but plain, affordable, and basically good. Prices and the interesting surroundings make this a good family location (although there is a full bar and a band on weekend nights). The grilled grouper Caesar salad (market price) is excellent, as are the grouper fingers. The house salad is tasty, and there are some steak and seafood options for those averse to seafood. Hours are Sun and Mon, 11 to 9 p.m.; Tue through Thurs, 11 a.m. to 10 p.m.; Fri and Sat, 11 a.m. to 11 p.m.

TUBBY'S TANK HOUSE $$
2909 River Dr.
(912) 354-9040
www.tubbystankhouse.com
Tubby's specializes in fresh seafood, much of it caught by part-owner Stan "Tubby" Strickland, a sport fisherman with a knack for hauling in mahimahi, grouper, tuna, and wahoo.

In fact, says fellow owner Ansley Williams, Tubby's is a seafood restaurant because of Strickland's ability as an angler. Williams says that in 1994 when he, Strickland, and managing partner Ray Clark decided to start a new restaurant, they settled on opening a seafood place because Strickland "was catching so much fish we needed a place to distribute it." The result was Tubby's, a rustic-looking restaurant perched on the bluff at Thunderbolt.

In addition to the aforementioned sports fish, Tubby's serves shrimp, scallops, oysters, and Tubby's Tank Out, a seafood platter that, according to Williams, "is more than one human can eat." Burgers, chicken, and a variety of salads are available for those not inclined toward eating fish. Tubby's serves lunch and dinner seven days a week, hosts oyster roasts on Thurs nights during the winter and Thurs sunset parties in the summer, and offers dancing in the back room on Thurs, Fri, and Sat nights. A second Tubby's is at 115 East River St. (912-233-0770). Hours are Mon through Thurs 11 a.m. to 10 p.m.; Fri and Sat, 11 a.m. to 11 p.m.; Sun 10 a.m. to 9 p.m.

Southern

ELIZABETH ON 37TH STREET $$$
105 East 37th St.
(912) 236-5547
www.elizabethon37th.net
This 1900s Southern mansion that is both elegant and refined was made famous by the original owners, Elizabeth and Michael Terry. Now the operation is run under the same high standards by brothers Greg and Gary Butch, who were long-time employees of Elizabeth on 37th. With an incomparable menu starting with appetizers like a black-eyed pea patty with greens and tomato

relish, mozzarella and tomatoes served warm with pecan pesto, and seasonal soups that are standouts, there's still prestige that comes with saying you're "dining at Elizabeth's." The atmosphere could be summarized as sophisticated and maybe a wee bit snobby. My favorite entree is the Spicy Savannah Red Rice with Georgia Shrimp and Half Moon River clams, sausage, grouper, and okra—a fancy way to say, Lowcountry boil . . . with okra ($28.95). Another highlight is the Coastal Grouper Celeste, crisp sesame-almond crusted grouper with peanut sauce and roasted potato ($32.95). This is a place that truly transforms the area's finest seafood into not-to-be-duplicated dishes. Before you leave, opt for the Chocolate Pecan Torte, a dark chocolate cream in a crushed pecan crust, topped with chocolate whipped cream. There is an elegant private dining room. Dress is business casual and reservations are always suggested. Hours are 6 to 9:30 p.m. nightly. Reservations are required.

SWEET POTATOES $
6825 Waters Ave.
(912) 352-3434
www.toucancafe.com/sweetP.html

This casual restaurant, which offers lunch and dinner, is the downscale relative of the pricier and fancier Toucan Cafe (also described in this chapter)—but the food is still outstanding. The decor is simple and consists of bright paint and simple artwork. Basic meat and vegetables, cooked Southern-style, are the mainstays here. There's a rotating list of daily specials, but you can count on some standard dishes as well. I recommend the vegetable plates, for which you select up to four dishes, simply because it is so hard to find restaurants that offer good selections of vegetables and cook them

properly. Consider the dilled lima beans or the collards. True to its name, the restaurant offers some variant of a sweet potato dish every day—baked sweet potatoes, sweet potato soufflé, mashed sweet potatoes, even sweet potato salad. If you're a fan of fresh-water fish, try their fried catfish, cooked crispy (and not greasy). Beware, however, of the occasional offering of something called Wisconsin-style sweet potatoes—they are proof of the fact that while you can combine sweet potatoes and cheddar cheese, you really shouldn't. Hours are Mon through Sat, 11 a.m. to 9 p.m.

WEST CHATHAM
Seafood

LOVE'S SEAFOOD RESTAURANT $$
6817 Basin Rd.
(912) 925-3616

Love's is in southwest Chatham County, 14 miles from the Historic Downtown, but city dwellers are more than happy to make the ride to this restaurant on the banks of the serene Ogeechee River. A major reason for the pilgrimages is Love's fried catfish, 90 percent of it caught in the river and all of it battered with a fine cracker meal that makes it so light it seems to float off the plate.

Love's also serves steak and chicken fingers in an atmosphere that's rustic but upscale; however, the main draws here are the catfish and seafood, in particular the fried shrimp, shrimp and flounder stuffed with crabmeat, and the seafood fettuccine. Beer, wine, and mixed drinks are available. It's open Tues through Sat for dinner and Sun for lunch and dinner; it's closed on Mon when the owners have, as they put it, "gone fishing."

NIGHTLIFE

avannah's bar and entertainment scene falls into three general categories: River Street, a restored area along the Savannah River that was refurbished with just this sort of thing in mind; City Market, a restored quadrant of the Historic Downtown that's heavy on clubs and bars as well as shops; and a variety of watering holes and entertainment sites scattered along routes to the south of the city (the Southside, in local parlance).

If you don't have something very specific in mind (say, jazz or a sports bar), our advice is to follow your ear, literally. Visitors will fare better on River Street and in City Market, where there are lots of nightspots clustered together. You can follow the music you hear spilling out the doors and wander conveniently from site to site. Which brings us to the question of alcohol and the law. Savannah's folklore stresses the city's hard-drinking reputation, with tales that the town was never dry, even during Prohibition (which lingered long in Georgia, where some counties are still dry). You'll probably get tired of locals telling you the favorite question posed to a newcomer is, "What do you drink?"

Also note that city ordinances prohibit open bottles or cans on the street, but (as of this writing) if you want to wander out of a River Street watering hole or a City Market club, most places are glad to provide you with a plastic or foam cup. This practice, pretty unusual based on our experience with other cities, is under hostile scrutiny from Savannah City Council, however, so check with your bartender before you wander out with a cup of beer in case things have changed. (Remember, this go-cup leniency is in the city of Savannah, not the other municipalities.)

OVERVIEW

We've spent a lot of space covering alcohol, but we don't mean to give you the impression that all nightlife has to do with booze. We've included coffeehouses, which are growing in popularity, as well as movies and other activities. Also, Savannah is home to an active Alcoholics Anonymous family: If you want to catch a meeting and talk firsthand about alcohol-free nightlife in Savannah, call (912) 354-0993 for the extensive schedule.

The bars listed here are a sampling, but we think we've included at least something for everyone.

BARS

BERNIE'S
115 East River St.
(912) 236-1837
www.berniesriverstreet.com

NIGHTLIFE

This is a longtime riverfront hangout with a pub-like atmosphere that is truly Savannah. Situated within a pre–Civil War cotton warehouse, there's live music, a hefty beer selection, and easy access to the ballastone sidewalks outside where you'll dash out to view passing ships. Order a Bloody Mary and enjoy the astonishment when the bartender serves it to you in a Mason jar with a sprig of pickled okra! Now, that's Southern! Hours are Mon through Thurs 11 a.m. until midnight, Fri to Sat 11 a.m. to 3 a.m.

CHURCHILL'S PUB & RESTAURANT
13 West Bay St.
(912) 232-8501
www.thebritishpub.com

An after-hours kitchen fire drove this little bit of England out of its original home several years ago, but it's back in new (well, not new, but different) and expanded quarters. The massive carved mahogany bar will make you feel manor born! Downstairs there are pool tables and dartboards. All in all, it's a nice, friendly place to have a drink, and the management is proud to point out that it's British owned.

Churchill's is also a restaurant that serves dinner, including such British fare as bangers and mash or roast beef with Yorkshire pudding. The menu also includes more conventional items such as fish dishes and sandwiches. They claim to have 20 beers on tap (we didn't count, but there's obviously no shortage). Churchill's opens at 5 p.m. Sun through Fri and at noon on Sat. There's a fabulous rooftop bar so be sure to check it out if the weather is cooperating.

COACH'S CORNER
3016 East Victory Dr.
(912) 352-2933
www.coachs.net

The sports bar has become an American institution, and Coach's Corner is a fine example of a place where you'll find a pleasant mix of locals, students, sports fans, and a waitstaff that's been there for years (well, most of them). Don't expect the latest in audio /video capabilities as this is a small, locally owned sports bar, however, the pluses are many. Dark and cool, there are booths lined up on both sides, several pool tables, and an outdoor seating area and stage where bands and special events are held during the year. The true flair of Coach's is that no matter what obscure sporting event you're searching the airwaves for, the staff will more than likely find it for you. The chicken fingers (and chicken finger salad) are tender and lightly breaded, but the real draw here is the wings! They are possibly Savannah's most popular. Dress is always casual. Come by the Victory Drive site—it's in Thunderbolt, on the way to and from the beach—during Oct of a good season for the Atlanta Braves, and you can catch a giant motorized tomahawk chopping away, backed up by an occasional live chopper. Oh, and be sure to wear your colors! Happy hours (with discounted drink specials) are 11 a.m. to 7 p.m. Mon through Fri. Closing time varies.

KEVIN BARRY'S IRISH PUB
117 West River St.
(912) 233-9626
www.kevinbarrys.com

Savannah prides itself on its Irish heritage, not just during the elaborate St. Patrick's Day observance, but year-round. Just check out this pub. The stone-walled setting is dark and atmospheric, brightened considerably by a constantly changing program of authentic Irish performers every night (although we suggest calling ahead if this is essential to your evening; we've seen the schedule shift around a bit over the years). Count on acceptable food (including such Irish fare as potato soup and corned beef and cabbage), standard drinks, and an impressive collection of bottled and draft beers and ales. There's even a small gift shop for Irish goods. Brush up on your Irish history (and learn who the real Kevin Barry was) by reading the captions to the framed photos of figures who were either historic freedom fighters or long-dead terrorists, depending on your outlook. Hours are Mon through Sat, 11 p.m. to 3 a.m.; Sun, 12:30 p.m. to 2:30 a.m.

i Dressed up for an evening on River Street? You won't want to risk cobblestones in dressy shoes, so if you park above the street—as you probably will have to—take the municipal elevator down to the river level. It is tucked between City Hall and the Hyatt Regency Savannah Hotel.

MIDNIGHT SUN WESTIN SAVANNAH HARBOR RESORT
Hutchinson Island
1 Resort Dr.
(912) 201-2000
www.westinsavannah.com
The Midnight Sun is the bar inside Savannah's Westin Savannah Harbor Resort, and it was designed with both local color and the view in mind. From within this clublike atmosphere, you can look out on both the hotel pool and the Savannah River, with River Street and Savannah's skyline beyond it. The name comes from a song by Savannah's favorite son, lyricist Johnny Mercer. So do the names of many of the drinks, and if the song title comes with a color, you'll find

the drink color coordinated. (See what we mean by local color?) They even dub the martinis here "Mercertinis." The bar is open to the general public, not just hotel guests, and it adds another dimension to a River Street outing to take the ferry (hey, it's free!) across to enjoy the ambience and view Savannah from an angle few but sailors have enjoyed until recently. Hours are noon to midnight, Mon through Thurs; Fri and Sat, noon to 1 a.m.; Sun, 12:30 p.m. to midnight.

MOON RIVER BREW PUB
21 West Bay St.
(912) 447-0943
www.moonriverbrewing.com
This brewpub is Savannah's only on-premises microbrewery. It's also a decent place to eat. On the one hand, they serve both lunch and dinner, and it's a lot more serious than typical bar munchies—City Hotel Cheese Quesadillas, for example. On the other hand, if made-on-the-premises beer is its reason for being, it's a nightspot. Whichever side of the debate you agree with, know that you can get up to nine different (varying seasonally) fresh microbrews here in Imperial pints and half pints. The building is pretty cool itself. The home of the former City Hotel, the first post office in Savannah, where the first post office was also housed. The building also served as a branch of the Bank of the United States. During the War of 1812, Winfield Scott, the Marquis de Lafayette, the first three commodores of the U.S. Navy, and naturalist John James Audubon stayed there. There is said to be a ghost, so be sure to ask your waitress or waiter for details! Hours are 11 a.m. to 11 p.m. (except they don't close until 1 a.m. on weekend nights) and 10 p.m. on Sun. The daily happy hour is 4 to 7 p.m.

PINKIE MASTER'S LOUNGE
318 Drayton St.
(912) 238-0447

Looking for a true dive in the city? This modest neighborhood watering hole is legendary in Savannah as a political bar. Journalists once plied local sources with alcohol here; Jimmy Carter (yes, that Jimmy Carter) once gave a speech standing on the bar. What you'll find today is a small bar where regulars talk back to the television set. There's an eclectic jukebox, darts, and a few game machines, along with the beer and the booze. We have friends who swear by this place, and you can't say it doesn't have plenty of atmosphere: Christmas decorations that never come down, a stuffed crow (at least we hope it's stuffed—maybe it's just dead), a rogue's gallery of politician's photos, and a soft-focus nude painting about which any of the regulars is willing to tell you lies. Drinks are cheap, the air is thick, and there's a sign above the bar reading TIPPING IS NOT A CITY IN CHINA. Looking back over this, we sound like we're running the place down, so we better 'fess up that we occasionally go here even when we aren't researching this book's various editions, and it's always interesting. There's a lot to be said for a place that refuses to gloss up for tourists. Hours are Mon through Sat, 4 p.m. to 3 a.m., also open Sun after noon.

SAVANNAH SMILES
314 Williamson St.
(912) 527-6453

Savannah Smiles brings something different to the Savannah night scene. It features "Rock 'n' Roll dueling pianos" in an audience participation format that is a mix of rock 'n' roll standards and light comedy (with food and drink in addition, of course). The show starts at 9 p.m., and the bar opens around 7 p.m. For ages 21 and up. Okay, so it's a bit hokey, but you're on vacation and you're never going to see these people again anyway, so have fun. If you don't leave here without singing along to at least one song, then you need to take a happy pill. This is a place that will make you happy, even if you're not. Finding it can be a bit of a challenge—Savannah Smiles is sandwiched between West Bay Street and River Street, sort of behind the Quality Inn, and chances are you won't be able to find a local who ever heard of Williamson Street. Closed Mon and Tues. Hours are 7 p.m. to 3 a.m. Wed through Sat.

i A walk on the beach can be a romantic conclusion to an evening out. Stroll out onto the Tybee Pier and Pavilion, lean against the rail, and watch the moon rise out of the Atlantic Ocean.

VU LOUNGE
2 West Bay St.
(912) 238-1234

Before or after a nice dinner at one of the classier River Street restaurants, you may not be in the mood to nightcap it at one of the street's sing-along suds pubs. This is a nice alternative—a dressier place for a drink. The decor is upscale and subtle, the drinks are fine, and there's usually an inoffensive and unobtrusive musical lounge act. The whole thing would fall into the "very nice but forgettable" category if not for the view (hence the name). This bar is inside the Hyatt Regency Savannah (see our Accommodations chapter) and has glass walls overlooking the Savannah River (literally—this portion of the hotel overhangs River Street). If you are lucky (or determined enough to stay put for a while), you'll get to see one of the giant container ships headed to or from the port upriver. Granted, you can see them from the street, too, but from the Vu's vantage point, you're more on eye level with the oceangoing giants. Hours are Mon through Thurs, 2 p.m. to midnight; Fri and Sat, 2 p.m. to 2 a.m.; Sun, noon to midnight.

WET WILLIE'S
101 East River St.
(912) 233-5650
This high-volume River Street bar caters to the younger sector. The drinks are frozen concoctions with names like the infamous spring break potion, Sex on the Beach. Beware! Grain alcohol gives a single drink here the punch of at least two conventional alcoholic beverages. There's a light food menu, a small dance floor, and lots of loud recorded music. During the summer, students pour out onto the street in front of Wet Willies. It's definitely the "in" place, according to those patrons. Hours are Mon through Thurs, 11 to 1 a.m.; Fri and Sat, 11 to 2 a.m.; Sun, 12:30 p.m. to 1 a.m.

BILLIARDS

B&B BILLIARDS
411 West Congress St.
(912) 233-7116
On the fringe of City Market, this is a popular spot to shoot some pool and hang out with friends. Look for a mix of students, middle-aged locals, and the occasional tourist Hours are 2 p.m. to 2 a.m. Fri and Sat; closing at midnight, Mon through Thurs.

CAPONE'S
1100 Eisenhower Dr.
(912) 354-4848

This suburban pool parlor is also a bar and restaurant, and its location next to a shopping center multiplex makes it a good place to kill time before or after a movie. If you want to do any serious playing on weekends, arrive before 9 p.m.—that's when the wait for tables (there are 17 of them) starts to add up. Open afternoons and evenings; hours vary.

COFFEEHOUSES

GALLERY ESPRESSO
234 Bull St.
(912) 233-5348
www.galleryespresso.com
This is one of the city's first (and a personal favorite) on the coffeehouse scene. Coffee, both plain and in its multiple new forms, is augmented by a menu of baked goods and sandwiches, even wine. There's an occasional poetry reading or casual performance. The walls are home to displays by local artists, and the exhibits have grown in quality and importance over the years. Cozy and a good people-watching spot. The outdoor tables are particularly popular when the weather allows. Bring your laptop. It's usually open until 1 a.m. on the weekends. Hours are weekdays, 7:30 a.m. to 10 p.m.; weekends, 8 a.m. to 11 p.m.

THE SENTIENT BEAN
13 East Park Ave.
(912) 232-4447
www.sentientbean.com
A friend once said the Sentient Bean is a little piece of New York transplanted to Savannah. We don't know about that, but we do know that if political advocacy has a center in Savannah, this must be it. Of course it serves coffee (fair trade and organic, to boot) and light food, but that's the least of it. It hosts live music, film screenings, poetry slams,

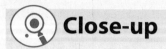

Close-up

Club One and Lady Chablis: Anything but a Drag

In a city as inherently conservative as Savannah, you wouldn't expect tourism and the gay nightlife scene to intersect. You would be wrong.

Club One Jefferson has been the most prominent social setting, under various names, for Savannah's gay community since the 1980s. Its dance and performance scene had attracted occasional bolder and curious straights, but for the most part, Club One was a world unto itself.

Lady Chablis changed all that.

The flamboyant drag queen (is there any other kind?) caught the eye of author John Berendt when he was writing the book that would become the phenomenal best seller *Midnight in the Garden of Good and Evil*. The self-titled "Grand Empress of Savannah" is featured prominently therein. That alone was enough to make the performer famous, but then she went on to play herself in the movie version.

As the cult following for "the Book" grew, its readers flocked to Savannah. They wanted to gawk at the Book's houses, tour the Book's cemetery, and buy the Book trinkets. Most particularly, they wanted to get a look at the Lady Chablis.

And that presented the folks at Club One with a dilemma: How could they tap into that market without scaring the tourists back to Peoria, while at the same time keeping the flood of book fanciers from displacing their regular clientele? Fortunately, they've come up with a smooth compromise. When Chablis is in town, they put on an earlier, somewhat tamer version of her show, reserving the stronger material for the later shows. It works well: Tourists get a sample of the strong stuff without a full dose, and the regular customers do not find their entertainment diluted, since the club's gay scene doesn't get moving until later anyway. Actually, the crowd has changed since

speeches, classes, and what have you. The schedule stays pretty full, and attendance can be pretty good, too. You might want to drop by just to read the flyers on the walls to keep up with events geared toward the young, the liberal, and/or the involved. There is both indoor and outdoor seating. The Sentient Bean is next door to Brighter Day, Savannah's oldest organic food store, and at the north end of Forsyth Park. Hours are 7 a.m. to 10 p.m. every day.

MOVIE THEATERS

Savannah has typical movie offerings for a city its size, nothing more and nothing less. The blockbusters and major releases open here the same weekends they open everywhere else, but you may have to wait longer (or even until video) to catch, say, the Sundance winners or other nonmainstream fare. Our favorite is the Victory Stadium 9, the newest multiplex and currently the one doing the best job of cleanliness, upkeep, and enforcing civility.

Savannah has 48 movie screens scattered among five multiplexes and a small two-screen independent. If that sounds like a lot of screens, don't get excited: Duplication eats up a lot of them. The daily newspaper has show times, but we've saved ourselves this phenomenon began, and you're likely to find a mix of gays and straights at the bar and on the dance floor.

Chablis no longer lives in Savannah, but she was booked for at least a dozen shows at Club One in 2009. The act is a big enough draw to rate its own page and multiple mentions on the club's website (www.clubone-online.com). The show bar is upstairs, and it's perfectly adequate and at times a bit uncomfortable. It's an old building and the stage is set in a very small room. There are small tables on the front and along the sides and several rows of seats. Don't fret if you don't get a front seat—the place is small enough for you to see from all angles. You'll have to fetch your own drinks from the bar on the upstairs level. Check the speaker location before you sit down: The room is small, but the speakers are big.

A drag show consists of female impersonators in drop-dead glamorous gowns and jewelry, dancing and lip-synching to recorded music. The Lady Chablis emcees when she is there and performs several numbers. At the conclusion of the early show, Chablis comes back out to sign autographs, so bring your copy of the Book or Chablis' own book, *Hiding My Candy*.

Club One Jefferson has shows every weekend. Other performers vary, but drag shows are staples, along with the occasional beauty pageant or striptease act. Shows start Thurs at 11:30 p.m., Fri and Sat at 10:30 p.m. and 12:30 a.m., and the Bay Cafe (lower level) offers shows on Sun at 9:30 and 11:30 p.m. Elsewhere in Club One Jefferson, you'll find multiple dance floors, full restaurant service, and a full bar. Dance music downstairs is Top 40, while the main level has techno and house music.

Pretty much anything goes by way of dress, but it's predominately casual. The club takes major credit cards and has an ATM on-site. Club One's at 1 Jefferson St., just off Bay Street at the edge of City Market. It's rare because it is open seven days a week. Hours are 5 p.m. to 3 a.m., closing an hour earlier on Sun.

disappointment more than once by calling the recorded message to double-check. You'll find those numbers in the listings that follow. "Do," the entertainment section in the *Savannah Morning News*, contains listings to help locate the theaters, all of which are outside the Historic Downtown. Ticket prices don't vary by more than a quarter or so—expect to pay in the range of $8.50 to $10 per person for a prime-time adult ticket. Child, senior, and matinee tickets are available at discounts. Theaters offer same-day advance-purchase options, and the newer ones even let you buy a day ahead and with credit cards. Most screens include stadium seating, meaning auditorium seating that is pitched so that you can see over the person in front of you. They've also upscaled their amenities.

The **Lucas Theatre,** a restored movie palace in the Historic District that primarily hosts touring shows and concerts, periodically runs movies, usually on a theme: holiday movies, for example, or movies made in Savannah. Savannah College of Art and Design, better known locally as SCAD, operates **Trustees Theatre** on Broughton Street and occasionally shows movies that have become campus standards or are film show entries. SCAD also hosts an annual film festival in that theater, showcasing some genuinely avant-garde stuff.

CARMIKE CINEMA 10
(10 screens)
511 Stephenson Ave.
(912) 353-9904

EISENHOWER CINEMAS
(6 screens)
1100 Eisenhower Dr.
(912) 352-3533

REGAL CINEMAS SAVANNAH 10
(10 screens)
1132 Shawnee Ave.
(912) 927-7700

VICTORY STADIUM 9
(9 screens)
1901 East Victory Dr.
(912) 355-5000

WESTSIDE CINEMAS
(2 screens)
403 Hwy. 80
Garden City
(912) 966-9101

WYNNSONG 11
(11 screens)
1150 Shawnee St.
(912) 920-1227

ICE CREAM PARLORS

LEOPOLD'S ICE CREAM
212 East Broughton St.
(912) 234-4442
www.leopoldsicecream.com

Okay, what's an ice-cream parlor doing in a chapter on nightlife? After all, we could have put it in the Restaurants chapter, since Leopold's also serves soup and sandwiches. But the thing is, it is open at night near theaters and various places of activity, and it's nice to have somewhere to go after dark where the focus isn't on the bar. Leopold's is an institution in Savannah, dating back to 1919, but the operation hasn't been continuous. Stratton Leopold reopened it with new digs within the old fixtures, and it's a real trip back in time. They make their own ice cream, along with fountain delights like banana splits and hot fudge sundaes. There are tables outside as well as in the nostalgic interior. Check out the decor: Leopold is a major Hollywood producer when he isn't making ice cream (really!), and he's decorated the place with memorabilia from movies he's been involved with. Hours vary to as late as 10 or 11 p.m., and it's an easy walk from both the Lucas and Trustees theaters.

SHOPPING

The late Malcolm Forbes once said of shopping, "It is more fun to get than to receive," and that saying holds true if you're rambling around in Savannah. So with that being said, clinch your environmentally friendly tote and hit the streets of Savannah!

Shopping in Savannah can be a joy or a disappointment depending on where you're from. If you've traveled here from New York, L.A., Atlanta, or Charlotte, stay within the realms of historic downtown where you'll find many one-of-a-kind shops and boutiques. The malls here may not be worth your while. If you're from a small town, start downtown and then, head to one of Savannah's two malls (on the south side of town).

Savannah is the regional shopping center for a large chunk of southeast Georgia; many people (outside of Brunswick, that is) consider it the only real metropolitan area until you get to Jacksonville, Florida (two-and-a-half hours down I-95) or in-state to Macon (three hours west on I-16).

With all this retail territory to cover, it stands to reason we had to be selective about what is included in this chapter. We'd like to share with you the rhyme and reason of what was left in and what was left out. First of all, we chose not to provide a comprehensive list of grocery stores, shoe shops, and chain stores that are in every town (i.e., Wal-Mart). Your hotel concierge or bed-and-breakfast host can point you in the right direction if you need one.

Instead, we've tried to concentrate on the needs of recreational shoppers while still steering the retail-impaired to the places where travelers are most likely to get the things they need. We've included shops that stock items of local or regional interest. Then, we've added places that I consider unusual or interesting. Next, we've included some of the places that we like to browse and buy for ourselves. One note: As you're searching Savannah's shops for the perfect item to take home, don't forget about the dog sitter!

ABOUT LOCATIONS

Before launching into our own category-by-category rundown of stores, here's a quick review of the major shopping locations with a few pointers along the way.

River Street

River Street is literally along the Savannah River. It is reached by street ramps that lead down from the bluff-level Bay Street. In between these two levels is Factors' Walk.

River Street is a major part of Savannah's tourist scene, and you'll find it is a prominent player for restaurants, nightlife, and annual events. But don't forget shopping! This restored waterfront strip features a steady progression of shops all along its length, beginning at the west end across from a small out-of-commission power plant (whose smokestacks make handy landmarks) and extending eastward many blocks until you reach the Waving Girl statue that is a local riverfront landmark. **Factors' Walk,** which parallels River Street halfway up the bluff, also features shops, although more widely scattered.

Parking is scarce. There are a few small private lots, where you pay as you enter. There's limited street-side parking on the various streets leading to River Street. Lots of motorists park illegally along River Street itself, but it's a bad idea—the city has cracked down on the long-winked-at practice.

Opt to park in the parking garages that are within walking distance of Bay Street and City Market. The City of Savannah operates five parking garages. A favorite is the new **Whitaker Street Garage** across the street from the Hyatt Regency Savannah. This underground garage was built in 2008 and is located on Whitaker Street between Bay and Bryant streets. The garage has four levels underground and space for 1,065 vehicles. In my experience, it's never been filled. The daily rate is $2 per hour and well worth it for a clean and shady place to start the day. If you're heading down to River Street, cross Bay Street (at the light at Whitaker and Bay) and trot over to the Visitors' Elevator that runs alongside the Hyatt. Once you ride down to street level and leave the elevator, you'll find yourself dropped off on the tricky ballastones of River Street. Wear appropriate footwear and opt for the elevator on your way back up. The stairs (located in each block) are steep and irregular, and once you get to the rocks, you'll find them as hard to walk on as they are to drive over. The going is much smoother once you get to the River Street level where there are pedestrian-friendly sidewalks. There are public restrooms to your left as you reach River Street.

Don't expect much in the way of bargains on River Street but do expect some really cool shops. There are a variety of stores here to keep you busy for several hours. From tropical clothing to candy, charming eateries, and lots of merchants selling Savannah-themed memorabilia, you'll find it all.

City Market

This restored area in the commercial section of the Historic Downtown runs from Barnard Street to Montgomery Street, north of Broughton Street. The complex is made up of nightclubs, restaurants, art galleries, and shops. The stores here tend to be more thematic—cat-motif merchandise, New Age, outdoor furniture and gifts, and so on—than their cousins a few blocks away on River Street.

Broughton Street & Historic Downtown Areas

Broughton Street was where Savannah shopped before malls seized control of the retail world. It suffered the same fate as Main Streets all across America but has begun a comeback as a home to restaurants, college activities, and trendy shopping, including a slew of antiques dealers. In fact, some of the very best recreational shopping in the city can be done on Broughton Street. New upscale offerings stand side by side with the small low-end shops that kept the street going in its hard-luck days, things like wig shops and cut-price clothing shops. You'll also find two of Savannah's retail grand dames still in place. When other stores abandoned the main drag for suburban malls, **Globe Shoe Company** (17 East Broughton St.) and **Levy Jewelers** (101 East Broughton St.) dug in. These stores are where Old Savannah bought her shoes for debutante parties and her bridal silver, and while both stores now have other locations as well, they never closed their doors on Broughton.

You'll find plenty of intriguing stores scattered throughout the Historic Downtown. One quaint congregation of interesting shops is at the intersection of Bull and Liberty Streets near the Hilton Savannah DeSoto Hotel. The intersection of Jones and Whitaker Streets forms the nucleus for another appealing set of shops that mostly specializes in arts and home decor. They call themselves, collectively, the **Downtown Design District,** and capitalize on their proximity to both Mrs. Wilkes' eatery (see our Restaurants chapter) and Monterey Square (see our Savannah Celebrity chapter). You'll also find individual shops, especially antiques shops, sprinkled throughout the Historic Downtown.

Looking back over all these areas, let's put it in perspective: River Street is strong in local color and has lots of shops together, where you can walk out one door and into the next. There's a variety of merchandise aimed at all age levels, and the compact location makes it easy to keep groups— be they children or merely hard-to-herd adults—together. Broughton Street's offerings aren't as likely to appeal much to children and are more widely spaced, but the merchandise is actually several cuts better, and oddly enough, the prices are more reasonable. City Market falls between these two descriptions, but it's heavy on the souvenir shops, and you can stop by the other Historic District shops as you make your way around the city on tours, and so on.

MALLS & SHOPPING CENTERS

Savannah has two malls, both south of downtown in a heavily trafficked (by Savannah standards) area of suburban and chain-store development. There are various ways to get to them, but the most direct route from downtown and the one hardest to get lost on is straight out Abercorn Street from town. About 6 miles from the Historic Downtown, you'll spot Oglethorpe Mall on your left (you really can't miss it). Another couple of miles south, and you'll spot Savannah Mall on the right.

As for that ubiquitous American retail staple, the strip shopping center, Savannah has its share scattered mainly in the Southside/Midtown area. Because you know what to expect in most of these—a grocery store, major discount retailer, chain or local drug store, etc.—we have left most of them out as a rule. However, there are a few exceptions, with interesting stores or interesting stories, which we have included here.

OGLETHORPE MALL
7804 Abercorn St.
(912) 354-7038
www.oglethorpemall.com
Oglethorpe Mall is the city's original mall, and this one is thriving, with Sears, JCPenney, Belk, and Macy's as its anchors. There are more than specialty stores here, mostly on a single story, although some of the anchors have a second level. There's ample parking,

but the multilevel parking deck comes in handy around the holidays and when it rains. You'll find a predictable array of stores inside (Gap, Victoria's Secret, CD stores, etc.), along with a few restaurants and a food court. Barnes & Noble and its daily 9 a.m. to 11 p.m. hours—complete with coffee shop—have made this an unlikely but popular late-night adult hangout.

If you are traveling with kids who are young (or look young), you need to be aware of mall policies requiring adult supervision of anyone age 16 or younger during most weekend business hours. From 4 to 9 p.m. on Fri, 1 to 9 p.m. on Sat, and noon to 6 p.m. on Sun, those younger than age 17 must be accompanied by a parent or guardian at least 21 years old. Anyone age 21 or younger will be asked for ID, with mall management considering driver's licenses, official state ID cards, college student ID cards, passports or visas, and mall employee IDs as acceptable identification.

SAVANNAH MALL
14045 Abercorn St.
(912) 927-7467
www.savannahmall.com
Savannah still calls Savannah Mall, which opened in 1990, "the new mall," although by most cities' standards it isn't new anymore. Actually, this mall almost became known as "the mall that's in trouble," as its stock of anchor stores dwindled from four to one. But some savvy lease coups, drawing on stores not usually thought of as mall staples, have given the new mall a new lease on life. First of all, the Bass Pro Shop took over what had been a two-story department store site. Now, it's a megastore for hunters, anglers, campers, and other outdoors types. There's both an outdoor and an indoor waterfall and

massive aquariums featuring large examples of fish native to local waters (the long-nosed gar is one ugly fish, you'll discover). The space is so big they sell boats indoors.

Our count shows that Savannah Mall's specialty stores include a Hallmark shop, Bath & Body Works, Victoria's Secret, Gap/ Gap Kids, Gymboree, and mall-brand stores with several restaurants. Behind the mall are neighboring rival multiplexes totaling more than 20 movie screens, so the mall is a convenient place to kill some time while waiting for Hollywood's latest. Mall hours are Mon through Sat, 10 a.m. to 9 p.m., Sun, noon to 6 p.m.

HABERSHAM SHOPPING CENTER
Habersham Street at 60th to 63rd Streets
This small strip shopping center runs along both sides of Habersham Street, from just after its intersection with 60th Street to 63rd Street. It appears modest at first glance—a small grocery store, a pharmacy, a dry cleaner, and other businesses clearly set up to serve the surrounding established neighborhoods—but look closer and you'll find some interesting specialty shops. They include Punch and Judy, a children's store, and Merry Times, a card and gift shop. Other entries include Rum Runner's Bakery, and some nifty restaurants such as a Clary's, a sister to the downtown Clary's (see Restaurants) and Bella's, a small Italian bistro.

ABERCORN COMMONS
8108 Abercorn Extension
www.abercorncommons.com
At first glance, this V-shaped strip shopping center won't strike you as anything special. It looks new and houses several nationally known names like Michael's, Home Goods, Books-a-Million, and Panera Bread (along

with some still unleased space). What makes it interesting isn't immediately apparent: This is Savannah's first LEED-certified (Leadership in Energy and Environmental Design) retail development.

Developers took an aging and down-at-the-heels shopping center that wasn't living up to the potential of its location and, instead of just bulldozing it, tackled it as a "green" project. Demolition was held to a minimum, and conscious efforts were made to recycle or repurpose demolition debris to keep it out of landfills. New buildings were designed to be energy efficient, pavement was made permeable, and xeriscaping, or the use of landscaping plants that can survive in the climate without artificial irrigation, was called into play. The stores that are moving into this work-still-in-progress include a mix of local and national names, some of which we mention in more detail later (like Wild Birds Unlimited). But really, when was the last time you went to a shopping center where the parking lot design was actually interesting and significant?

ABERCORN WALK
Abercorn Street and Janet Drive
This narrow, deep strip shopping center is on Abercorn, just slightly south of the major intersection of Abercorn and DeRenne, which marks the southward sprawl of retail in Savannah. The stores here are going to sound familiar to veteran shoppers: the Fresh Market, Ann Taylor LOFT, Chico's, Jos. A. Bank, and Talbots. The significance is the upscale nature of the collected stores. It also rates mention because the Fresh Market is Savannah's first specialty grocery store (unless you count downtown's organic food shop, the venerable Brighter Day). You could hardly move in Fresh Market for the first month

it was open, thanks to all the people who turned out for the novelty of unfamiliar produce, imported chocolates, and a deli case stocked with fancy takeout. We bought salmon there, and found it was wrapped and tied with the care and finesse rivaling anything we've managed to do with Christmas presents.

SHOPPING SAVANNAH

Anything south of, say, DeRenne Avenue is dubbed the Southside by Savannahians. This is where you'll find the strip malls, discount houses, shopping centers, mega stores, etc. The **Savannah Festival Factory Outlet Center** (11 Gateway Blvd.; 912-925-3089; www.savannahfestival.com), a typical example of this new kind of strip mall, is at the far southern edge of the city, where Abercorn is better known as SR 204 and passes under I-95. This outlet center includes a Springmaid /Wamsutta factory store, Bugle Boy, and Bass Shoes, among many others.

East and west of Savannah, you'll find mainly grocery stores and other retail outlets in support of the suburban residential development there, with a few interesting shops thrown in and a large spate of beach-oriented shops at the end of the road on Tybee Island. (Check our Tybee Island chapter for more on shopping there.)

Now that we've roughly covered the general shopping areas, let's get more specific. We've divided our featured stores into categories. Join us on a quick shopping trip.

Antiques

In this section, we cover a sampling of both high-end and low-end antiques dealers. Serious collectors with serious budgets should seek out the upscale places; collectors and browsers will have better luck in the more mainstream, less expensive stores.

ABERCORN ANTIQUE VILLAGE
201 East 37th St.
(912) 233-0064
www.abercornantiques.com

This rambling yellow Victorian home houses collections from more than 50 dealers. Look for French country furniture, statuary, oil paintings, crystal, jewelry, and so on. This is a good browsing location with a wide price range—stuff for the serious collector and less-pricey offerings as well. Lately, this veteran store has taken on a more design-oriented feel. Hours are 10 a.m. to 7 p.m., Mon through Sat, and 11 a.m. to 4 p.m. Sun.

THE ATTIC
224 West Bay St.
(912) 236-4879

Looking for antique fishing lures? Good examples can fetch $65 and up, and you'll find them among some of the other sports antiques here, along with fencing masks and old skis. It's an eclectic stock of mainly American antiques and collectibles—furniture, jewelry, glassware. It's not what you would call high end, but it's fun. The location itself is of interest to fans of *Midnight in the Garden of Good and Evil,* since it was the location of the financially ill-fated Emma's, a piano bar that is featured in that best seller. Hours are 10 a.m. to 5 p.m. Mon through Sat.

COBB'S GALLERIES INC.
122 East 37th St.
(912) 234-1582

This popular antiques shop keeps outgrowing its quarters. It is now located in a Victorian mansion at the corner of 37th and Abercorn Streets, the allegedly haunted Krouskoff House. That's appropriate, because owner Al Cobb wrote a book, "Danny's Bed," about a haunted bed that wreaked havoc in his household; you can buy a copy in the shop. Most of the stock is more conventional: an extensive collection of art pottery, about a thousand cookbooks, sports memorabilia, collectible liquor decanters, what have you. What's surprising about this shop is the sheer volume. Hours are Mon through Sat, 10 a.m. to 4 p.m.

HABERSHAM ANTIQUES & COLLECTIBLES MARKET
2502 Habersham St.
(912) 238-5908

What was once a Savannah grocery store now holds a collection of some 70 antiques dealers who fill their booth space where Savannah's Ardsley Park matrons once bought canned goods and prime cuts of meat. The expansive building now holds old books, glassware, some antiques, and even vintage clothing. It's a great place to spend a rainy afternoon. Once a year, the enterprise expands, spreading to the neighboring parking lot with a spring festival that brings other vendors in booths. Hours are 10 a.m. to 6 p.m. weekdays and 10 a.m. to 5 p.m. on Sat.

LEE SMITH ANTIQUES AND DESIGN
916 East 72nd St.
(912) 352-4151
www.leesmithantiques.com

One of Savannah's most highly reputable antiques dealer, Lee Smith opened his 20-year-old warehouse and collection to the public, and if you're shopping or just browsing, it's worth a stop to view his collections of English and continental pieces from the 18th and 19th centuries and fine art, porcelain, rugs, high-quality reproductions and custom, made-to-order pieces. The 4,500-square-foot warehouse is located at 916 E. 72nd Street in midtown. Smith is not just a dealer. His relationships with auction houses, antique "pickers," estate attorneys, and individual collectors, have resulted in pieces that are one of a kind. He's also been retained to assist in liquidating some of the largest and most prominent estates in this area, including that of the late Jim Williams, one of the foremost dealers in the country, and the estate of well-known artist Myrtle Jones, also the author of a pictorial autobiography *A Savannah Experience*. Additionally, Smith has relationships with small, high-quality domestic workshops in Great Britain and offers reasonable shipping services. There's an in-house interior design service and a separate division that handles real estate staging. Smith also has a small shop at the entrance to the Ford Plantation in Richmond Hill. The address is 50 Ford Way, Richmond Hill, GA 31324. Contact the Savannah location at (912) 352-4151 for hours at the Richmond Hill location.

SAVANNAH GALLERIES
30 East Bryan St.
(912) 232-1234
www.savannahgalleries.com
Native Savannahians own this gallery—in operation since the 1960s—where you'll discover more than 10,000 square feet of high-end antique English, French, and American furniture, silver, porcelain, and Oriental rugs. Pieces range from elegant marquetry to rustic painted pine accents. The staff is friendly and will assist you in finding and building antique collections. They'll also clean, repair, and appraise your antique and modern Oriental rugs. Hours vary.

Bookstores

THE BOOK LADY
6 East Liberty St.
(912) 233-3628
Used and rare books are what you will find at the Book Lady, a quaint bookstore ideal for browsing. Besides art, architecture, religion, fiction, and the usual fare, you will also find sections called Pretty Books and Nice Old Books among the lot. There are also several local titles on Savannah and the area. For that hard-to-find book, the store offers a search service. Hours are Mon through Sat, 10 a.m. to 5:30 p.m.

E. SHAVER BOOKSELLER
326 Bull St.
(912) 234-7257
Book lovers will delight in this independent bookstore, which occupies the ground floor of a Historic District home. The shop has become a fixture for both downtown residents and tourists. An impressive array of hardcover and paperback books is available, and the knowledgeable staff offers solid advice.

Local titles are well represented. The shop also offers an efficient book search service for older titles. A whole room is devoted to children's titles. Limited gift offerings include museum-style note cards, tote bags, and appointment calendars. This is what bookstores were before there were megachains. Hours are Mon through Sat, 9:30 a.m. to 5:30 p.m.

EX LIBRIS
228 Martin Luther King Jr. Blvd.
(912) 525-5770
www.exlibrisbkstr.com
Ex Libris is first a beautiful place to shop! Part of it is a coffeehouse, another part is a

book and gift shop, owned and operated by the Savannah College of Art and Design. The shop is on the western edge of the Historic Downtown and may be a little out of your way, but it's worth the trip. After browsing through art books, posters, framed art, and many other eclectic and fun items you most likely won't find anywhere else in Savannah, you can sit and relax on the gigantic leather sofa and simply enjoy the beautifully restored building. A magnificent stairway takes up the center of the building and is the focal point of the room, along with "pillars" made out of hundreds of old books gracefully (and carefully) stacked. The store is especially beautiful during the Christmas season, when the college opens its holiday shop and offers decorations and other festive items. Hours are Mon through Fri, 8 a.m. to 6 p.m.; Sat, 10 a.m. to 4 p.m.; closed on Sun. Store stays open from 8 a.m. to 8 p.m. following Labor Day.

i Sales taxes in Georgia vary by county, ranging from a minimum of 4 percent (the state's share) to as much as 7 percent, depending on local voter willingness to up the ante. In Chatham County (which includes Savannah and Tybee Island), it's 7 percent as of 2010. Because the state exempts its share of the sales tax on groceries, expect to pay only the local sales tax on these.

Candy

When we travel and need a gift for a hostess, or even a quick sugary snack, we often opt for pralines. No one can claim these super-rich candies (made of sugar, butter, cream, and pecans) are good for you, but at $14 and up per pound, your purse will probably stop

you before you do yourself too much harm. You can find them made and sold in two shops on River Street. Although the shops would scream to hear it, we can't taste any difference. Pralines are available at shops in Savannah's malls, but the ones on River Street taste better.

RIVER STREET SWEETS
13 East River St.
(912) 234-4608
www.riverstreetsweets.com
Savannah's oldest candy store, established in 1973, is located on the historic Savannah riverfront. Pralines are made right here, in full view, and there's usually someone near the door to offer you a sample. Display cases showcase other store specialties: confections of chocolate and nuts, spiced pecans, divinity, etc. There's a wide array of gift baskets and special packaging and an efficient shipping service. Hours are 9 a.m. to 11 p.m. every day.

SAVANNAH'S CANDY KITCHEN
225 East River St. and 318 West St. Julian Street
(912) 233-8411
www.savannahcandy.com
Kids of all ages will run rampant in this large candy store, which fills several rooms. In addition to pralines and other store-made specialties, you'll also find gourmet jelly beans and a staggering selection of other mass-produced candy—the kinds you remember from childhood and assumed no one sold anymore. Choose from a wide selection of decorative tins to fill with goodies. Prepare to spend more than a few minutes here to take your time in selecting a bag of goodies to take back to the hotel. (This store also offers gift shipping if you'd prefer

that your purchase awaits you at home.) Hours are 9 a.m. to 11 p.m. every day.

Clothing

GAUCHO
251 Bull St.
www.gauchosav.com
(912) 232-7414
When browsing through Gaucho, you might be reminded of those who believe you can never be too rich or too thin. Don't be discouraged, there's something there for every taste (and size), and you probably won't see these beautiful wares in a department store.Gaucho has a wide selection of hats and accessories, along with hand-painted blouses and, in the back, shoes. A second location is at 18 East Broughton St. in a beautifully restored site. Hours are Mon through Sat, 10 a.m. to 6 p.m.; Sun, 1 to 5 p.m.

i Shopping for Georgia lottery tickets? Your best bets are small convenience stores and gas stations. Most lottery vendors have prominently displayed signs. Time your lottery shopping spree so that you avoid 6 to just before 7 p.m.—that's when the daily drawing for the Cash 3 game is held, and there's a line of hopeful last-minute gamblers at many lottery outlets.

JEZEBEL
25 East River St.
(912) 236-4333
This upscale ladies' clothing boutique features casual and formal clothing for the Southern woman. Comfortable linen pants, dresses, and shirts perfect for weathering 90-degree temperatures are Jezebel hallmarks. Brands include Flax and Cut Loose, among others. Long flowing dresses, pants,

and shirts with pretty prints are included in the mix, along with extravagant costume jewelry, shoes, hats, and more. Another location is at the Twelve Oaks Shopping Center, 5500 Abercorn St. (912-354-8889). Hours are Mon through Sat, 10 a.m. to 6 p.m.; Sun, 11 a.m. to 5 p.m. for both locations.

Gifts & Fun Shops

BASKETS, BEARS & T'S . . . OH, MY!
305 East River St.
(912) 232-4546
The title of this cozy shop pretty well describes the stock. The collection of stuffed animals includes both collectors' treasures and high-quality children's toys. Look for brands such as Ty, Russ, Boyd's Bears, Enesco, and other, smaller lines. Upstairs you'll find 2,500 square feet devoted to baskets of every imaginable shape, size, and material. T-shirts include both Savannah-themed versions and witty (but not vulgar) novelty shirts. Other stock includes dolls (such as the Susan Wakeen line), books of local interest, and plenty of furniture perfect for toys. Other gift and novelty items are scattered in among it all—things that owner/manager Carol Devine describes as "silly stuff . . . things that strike me at the moment." Hours are 9 a.m. to 10 p.m. every day.

BYRD COOKIE COMPANY AND GOURMET MARKETPLACE
6700 Waters Ave.
(912) 355-1716
www.byrdcookiecompany.com
You can buy these well-known local cookies all over town, but the advantage of choosing them from this shop is that you can sample the wide range of flavors here: Key Lime Coolers, Benne Bits, raspberry, butter cookies, and so on. They're sold in decorative tins ($9.45

each) that are excellent choices for those obligation gifts. One is sufficient for a solid token gift, or you can assemble a collection if you need something more impressive. A locally popular favorite is the benne wafer, a subtly sweet concoction made of unhulled sesame seeds. There are oodles of gifts here, including a selection from the Gullah Gourmet line of easy-to-cook Southern treats (unique to this area). If you show up during a production run, you can even watch the manufacturing process through a glass window. In addition to Byrd Cookies and the Seckinger-Lee line of cookies and snacks that Byrd also produces, this shop features an array of clever gifts (most with a culinary theme), a selection of other gourmet food items, and fresh flowers. Note that it is closed Sat but open on Sun, noon to 5 p.m., and Mon through Fri, 9 to 5 p.m. Shipping is available.

CHARLOTTE'S CORNER
1 West Liberty St.
(912) 233-8061
This eclectic gift shop offers a little bit of everything, spread out over four rooms. There are lots of shirts—T-shirts, tank tops, sleep shirts, sweatshirts. Fancy children's clothing featuring appliqués and smocking—the things that grandparents buy—are well represented in the stock. A line of fun clothes for adults is included, and there are plenty of toys. Woven afghans are offered in various motifs, including local ones. In addition to a line of *Midnight in the Garden of Good and Evil* merchandise, there are local souvenirs including other Savannah books, ornaments, and prints by local artists.

Because Savannah hosts the largest St. Patrick's Day celebration outside of New York City, this shop carries more upscale St. Patrick's Day merchandise year-round and has

become the "must go-to store" for anyone looking for something sophisticated with an Irish motif. Owner Charlotte Parrott also sells a variety of products that depict Savannah and its landmarks, as well as interesting jewelry, dolls, wedding gifts, and home decor items. Hours are seasonal. Summers open every day from 10 a.m. to 6 p.m.; after Labor Day through May, 9:30 a.m. to 5:30 p.m. every day.

GO FISH
106 West Broughton St.
(912) 231-0609
www.savannah.gofishretail.com
This is a cheery shop filled with inspiring handicrafts that are reasonably priced. It grew out of a missionary family's interest in helping the artisans they encountered in Third World countries and has expanded to a small chain (primarily in Georgia, Florida, and South Carolina) of stores selling Christian T-shirts and imported clothing, jewelry, and handicrafts. The friendly owners, Debbie and Lloyd Ryysylainen, welcome shoppers and carry the torch for the store's mission and focus. As illustrated in the literature scattered throughout the store, the Christian-themed T-shirts, handmade home accessories—Indonesian woodcarvings, etc . . . are all priced very low. There's also a colorful like of line of elongated and brightly painted animal sculptures beginning at $25 and going up in height and price. There are, of course, a lot of fish items (paintings, carvings, etc.). The stock also includes beaded jewelry and clothing made from batik fabrics. Go Fish is a great place to bring traveling groups of adults and/or school children. There are lots of affordable gift selections. Hours are seasonal: 11 a.m. to 4 p.m. from Labor Day through Christmas, and summers, Mon through Thurs 10 a.m. to 6 p.m., and Fri and Sat, 10 a.m. to 7 p.m .

HALF MOON OUTFITTERS
15 East Broughton St.
(912) 201-9393
www.halfmoonoutfitters.com
This unique outdoor clothing and equipment company has transformed a rather pedestrian storefront on the city's former main shopping drag to a modern and appealing space. It fills two levels, and the renovation job is worth a trip inside even if you aren't interested in camping, kayaking, or backpacking. All the gear is here, from clothing to kayaks themselves, along with food supplies and a large collection of books. The shop was acquired by Half Moon Outfitters, a small chain of outdoor stores based in South Carolina. The staff is made up of friendly, knowledgeable young people who practice the lifestyle they sell, which makes them good sources of information if you are in need of advice on where best to camp, canoe, or what have you in this vicinity. Hours are Mon through Sat, 10 a.m. to 7 p.m.

i Combine shopping with the national pastime. The Savannah Sand Gnats organization, the local minor-league baseball team currently associated with the New York Mets, sells a variety of caps, shirts, and so forth with the team's attractive (but pesky) logo.

MACK'S 5 AND 10 CENT STORE
Medical Arts Shopping Center
4800 Waters Ave.
(912) 354-3025
There's an old-time dime store in every town, and this one is right in the center of Savannah. This classic dime store opened in 1946 and moved to its current location in 1962, where not much has changed since.

Although this is a fun store for browsing, it has a practical side too because, crammed into a tiny space, it somehow manages to have everything. When we needed pinwheels for a photo assignment, we knew, without question, we could find them here. People come here for stuff they still want but can't find elsewhere—things like hair nets, soft peppermint sticks, or flyswatters with wire mesh flaps. There are all sorts of housewares, along with plastic flowers, inexpensive toys, greeting cards, embroidered hankies, and cardboard cutouts for elementary-school bulletin boards.

Contemporary merchandise isn't ignored. You can find toys here for children in Memorial Health University Medical Center across the street. By the way, Mack's can still legitimately call itself a five-and-dime: Look hard enough, and you can still find items for these prices. We spotted tiny plastic animals for a dime and plastic rings and individual candies for a nickel. It's a fun place to shop if you're visiting someone in any of the nearby hospitals. Call for hours.

THE PARIS MARKET & BROCANTE
36 West Broughton St.
(912) 232-1500
www.theparismarket.com
If ever there was a beautiful store in downtown Savannah—carefully and lovingly restored to its full potential—this would be that store. The merchandise here is appealing, but the Paris Market is worth a visit just to see the primo restoration of the building that houses it. We remember when this store started as a small, crowded room-size shop in what is now called the Downtown Design District. Today, it occupies two spacious floors in a retail "palace" on a prominent corner of downtown's main street. The

ground floor has nostalgic wood flooring and is crowded with a dazzling collection of chandeliers. Downstairs, the floors are brick, and mirrors and other elegant furnishings are showcased. It is a great setting for merchandise, and the selection includes some surprisingly affordable things. We especially liked the filigree-scrolled initial ornaments outlined in pearls at $10 each (but alas, they were out of the B and the D). The stock is a mixture of new and vintage. There's also linen, dishes, soaps, decorating books, and more, much of it with a French or Parisian theme. In short, this is a nifty place to pick up a gift, or for the house-proud to groom their nests. Hours are 10 a.m. to 6 p.m., Mon through Sat, and Sun, noon to 5 p.m.

SAILS & RAILS
125 East Broad St.
(912) 232-7201
www.savannahsailsandrails.com
It's hard to miss Sails & Rails in its new location on East Broad Street. It's the shop with the brightly displayed kites, flags, and wind socks blowing outside. This unique shop includes dozens of kites, along with flags from around the world and decorative ones for your front porch. Wind socks—ranging from those with pictures of snowmen on them to others shaped like whales—are also for sale, along with things for toy-train enthusiasts. The new shop stands literally on the line between poverty and gentrification—with a nice bed-and-breakfast as a near neighbor, and a public housing project and low-income health clinic on the other side of the street. It's worth your while to drive or walk to this store, which was once more conveniently located on River Street. Although the current location isn't as desirable, the character and friendliness of

the staff, combined with flags beyond your imagination, make it just as popular to locals and tourists. Hours are Mon through Sat 10 a.m. to 5 p.m., closed on Sun.

SAVANNAH ART WORKS
1213 US 80, #4, Tybee Island
(912) 786-9080
www.savannahartworks.com
We struggled with whether to put Savannah Art Works in with the art galleries in our Arts and Culture chapter, or to put it here with gift shops. You could build a case either way, but since the affordable, artistic gifts and creations outnumbered the pricier wall pieces, we're calling it a gift shop. You may disagree, but either way you won't be disappointed with this entertaining and colorful shop. You'll find graphic cartoon dog prints and attractive and useful pottery, along with tiny 4-inch-square mini-paintings. Jane Wood, who owns the shop with Beth Martin, coils aluminum into an attractive and affordable (starting at $15) collection of vases, candelabra, and sconces. There's also plenty of stuff for deeper pockets. On our last visit, the back wall featured a display of dramatic black-and-white sketches ($125 and up), a trio of long and narrow paintings portraying either flying or falling vegetables (starting at $750), and fabric art done as pillows, purses, and wall hangings (up to $275). It's a friendly, well-positioned shop (you'll pass it if you do any serious walking in Savannah) and appears to be very supportive of local artists and craftspeople. Call for hours.

TRUE GRITS
107 East River St.
(912) 234-8006
Specializing in all sorts of nautical and Civil War items, there are lots of Savannah

souvenirs packed into this rustic store. There are more than 250 different varieties hot sauce, each label claiming to be deadlier than the other. You'll also see plenty of shirts, toys, mugs, and plates with Savannah scenes. Also, you'll find items with nautical themes: lighthouse figurines and lighthouse needlework kits; large, realistic wooden ship models; tables made from hatch covers or using four-bladed brass props as bases; and antique telescopes. Civil War merchandise includes replica swords and hats, many history books, and three different versions of Civil War–themed chess sets. Hours are 8:30 am. to 11 a.m. every day.

WILD BIRDS UNLIMITED
8108 Abercorn St., Suite 210
(912) 961-3455
http://savannah.wbu.com

Located in Savannah's midtown, this is a store for bird watchers and enthusiasts. Stock up on birdseed, feeders, houses, binoculars, toys, gifts, and CDs here. This shop is geared to those who want to watch birds in the wild (including their own backyards), so it doesn't handle pet bird supplies. Some of the feeders and birdhouses double as lawn sculptures, including ornate, copper-roofed models. You'll also find a small stock of educational toys, and such unique items as hummingbird feeders and houses especially designed for butterflies and bats. Hours are Mon through Sat, 10 a.m. to 6 p.m., and Sun noon to 5 p.m.

i If you've got military privileges, you'll find a PX and commissary at Hunter Army Airfield in Savannah.

Home & Food

ECLECTIBLES!
10 West Broughton St.
(912) 443-9292

Look here for whimsical decor and light-hearted art: Stock ranges from comical garden sculpture on stakes in the $32–$36 range to large serving trays with hand-painted olive motifs at $72, and some large cloisonné bells. Days and hours of operation are a bit erratic here. It's best to call for hours or drop by and be surprised when the store is open!

i Roadside produce stands as well as regular grocery stores are good places to pick up Vidalia onions. These famous mild, sweet onions are grown only in and around nearby Vidalia and have acquired a dedicated national following of gourmets.

ONE FISH, TWO FISH
401 Whitaker St.
(912) 447-4600
www.onefishstore.com

This little shop expanded to a bigger one and then got bigger still, offering an array of trendy and unique gifts and other unusual merchandise. We spotted gourmet goodies and gifts for pampered pets, and a few little jars of jellies and condiments for their human counterparts. The stock also includes trendy purses, ceramic flowers, and tons of other superfluous-but-so-desirable types of products. Look here for lavish linens and personal pampering items. One storefront down, but still within the same building, you'll find Circa Lighting, where you can buy lamps and lighting fixtures from a variety of periods and styles. It all adds up to a quaint and cozy little corner in which to browse. The restoration work, which stopped well short of the polished at a rustic and shabby-chic European look, merits a visit even if you are not in a buying frame of mind. Hours are Mon through Sat, 9:30 a.m. to 5:30 p.m.

PEANUT SHOP OF SAVANNAH
407 East River St.
(912) 232-8612

This is the perfect place to stock up on salty delights for your afternoon munchies attacks. Peanut brittle, roasted peanuts, and plain ol' peanuts, along with hard candy and Key lime jelly, are just some of the many things you will find inside the Peanut Shop. If you aren't sure what kind of peanuts you want, don't worry, there are usually several samples out so you can try before you buy. Hours are Sun through Sat, 10 a.m. to 9 p.m.

24E
24 East Broughton St.
(912) 233-2274
www.24estyle.com

Broughton Street and the directions it has taken with revitalization never cease to amaze us. In the street's shabbier days—post-mall and pre-refurbishment—inexpensive furniture stores and very expensive rent-to-own furniture places were one of the standard fixtures of the place, along with vacant storefronts. Now, those are mostly gone, and scattered along Broughton are a handful of upscale, high-fashion furniture stores where style (and price) rival anything you might find in a major metropolitan area.

The finest of the new lot is 24e, which has put its address to modified use as its name. In over two floors of what was once two separate storefronts, you'll find displayed everything from knickknacks (ceramic penguins that shop co-owner Ruel Joyner Jr. calls a season signature item) to truly unique furnishings. On the upstairs level, we found Italian leather sofas, overstuffed chintz armchairs, platform beds, and undulating chaise lounges. The accessory/gift-type stuff is on the lower level, including extremely expensive perfume lamps

and reasonably priced glassware. Hours are seasonal so call prior to visiting; typically Mon through Thurs 10 a.m. to 5 p.m.; Fri and Sat 10 a.m. to 6 p.m., Sun noon to 4 p.m. The website features much of the store's inventory.

Thrift & Flea Markets

This kind of shopping isn't for everyone, just the most dedicated bargain hunters. If you don't mind rolling up your sleeves, these places can be real treasure troves. Of course, you'll occasionally come away empty-handed, but if you are into the thrill of the chase, you won't mind a bit.

WILMINGTON ISLAND GOODWILL
310 Johnny Mercer Blvd.
(912) 897-3901
www.goodwill.org

If you're prone to travel to flea markets and garage sales on Saturday mornings, then you'll love shopping at this Wilmington Island Goodwill store. Spacious and organized, there's plenty to see and buy here at this bargain haven: from clothing to shoes, exercise equipment, dishes, videos, and furniture. The store is open Mon through Fri, 9 a.m. to 7 p.m.; Sun, noon to 6 p.m.

KELLER'S FLEA MARKET
5901 Ogeechee Rd.
(912) 927-4848
www.ilovefleas.com

Ever wonder where people buy velvet wall-hangings depicting the Last Supper, wild stallions, and dogs playing poker? We've found them here ($10 each). In fact, if you go often enough and search diligently, we're convinced you can find just about anything in one of the 400-plus booths. Some are just tables under shed roofs; others are enclosed mini-stores. Don't expect anything fancy—this is the base of the food chain in retail shopping. Still, we've made some real finds here and had fun people watching.

Among the booths you'll find the equivalent of yard sales, estate sales, and salvage sales. Some have new merchandise, including designer label stuff that doesn't appear very convincing and pure junk that isn't masquerading as anything else. Handcrafters, small-scale importers, and collectors set up here. Go early on Saturday, and you'll see the antiques dealers scouting for stuff they'll clean up (and mark up) for their own shops.

One section features exotic birds, reptiles, puppies, and chickens, but real animal lovers should give that section a wide berth. The market is open every Sat and Sun 9 a.m. to 6 p.m. Vendors set up at 8 a.m. and if you care to sell your own goods, spaces are only $5. Ogeechee Road is also US 17, and the market is in the county's far southwestern section. About 2 miles past Savannah Mall, you'll spot the exit for US 17. Take the exit, turn left at the end of the ramp, and you'll soon see the market on your left. Dress is casual.

Tobacco

SAVANNAH BULLDOG CIGAR COMPANY
244 Bull St.
(912) 232-2650
This smoking specialty shop stocks tobacco in all its forms, and chances are you don't realize how many forms that is. There are between 180 and 200 different types of cigars in stock at any given time, along with 30 blends of pipe tobacco (including their own custom blend, the Savannah Bulldog). Cigarettes include imported Dunhills, Export A (Canadian), and the American-made, additive-free Nat Sherman cigarettes in various sizes and shapes. The inventory even includes Indonesian clove cigarettes and Darsham Bidis,

which is Indian tobacco wrapped in eucalyptus and flavored with strawberry or vanilla.

The most distinguishing feature at Savannah Bulldog Cigar Company, however, is the lounge, a small, comfortable room at the rear of the store with leather sofas and big-screen TV. Here customers from Savannah's business district (and tourists, of course) can relax with their smokes. Individual locker-size humidors with full temperature and humidity control are available for rental to house customers' personal tobacco collections. And, true to the name, you'll find one or more English bulldogs on the premises when you call. Hours are Mon through Sat, 10 a.m. to 7 p.m.

VERDERY'S LAMPS AND YE OLE TOBACCO SHOP
130 East Bay St.
(912) 236-1178
This is a very cool family-owned store that has been in operation for several years. Lamps and tobacco might sound like a strange combination, but the way the shopkeepers see it, it gives them something for both male and female shoppers. On the lighting side, they offer custom lamps and shades, along with repairs and restorative work. For tobacco enthusiasts, there's a walk-in humidor with more than 100 brands and 200 sizes of cigars, ranging in price from 65 cents to $29.95 each. The pipe tobacco selection includes Verdery's own custom blends. In addition to the usual line of American cigarette brands, they have imported Dunhills, Gauloises, and others, along with clove cigarettes and additive-free versions. The store also stocks pipes and leather goods for smokers. A second location is at 280 Eisenhower Dr. (912-691-0807). Hours for both locations are Mon through Sat, 9 a.m. to 6 p.m.

ATTRACTIONS

We've decided to devote an entire chapter to one of the favorite Savannah pastimes, walking. This one could be addicting so be forewarned. Make sure your camera battery is fully charged and your feet are adorned in your most comfortable walking shoes. Then, set your sights high. Savannah's splendor is best viewed in the early morning or late afternoon.

First, a little direction. Since most of the city's best-known attractions are situated in the Historic Downtown, this walking tour will take you to her most beautiful sights.

Here's the format: There are detailed listings of many of the popular historic sites downtown, and in between, explicit directions will appear in italics on how to get from one location to the next. The tour takes in a little more than 2.5 miles; how long it takes depends on how fast you walk and whether you decide to take a detour or two and further explore some sites. Along the way, you'll be treated to sitting spots on attractive benches that will allow you to take leisurely breaks. (If you stumble on a place that catches your fancy and is not listed in this chapter, chances are you can find out more about it in our Restaurants or Shopping chapters.) For another great dining option, pack a picnic before setting out. Each square you encounter—and we will cover nine—is perfect for relaxing near the magnolia trees while enjoying a good sandwich

There's a basic map at the front of this book. If you need a further visual aid, several good maps of the Historic Downtown are available in shops around town and typically cost less than $5. The Savannah Visitor Information Center, located in the 300 block of Martin Luther King Jr. Boulevard near its intersection with Liberty Street, or the Savannah Area Chamber of Commerce offices at Drayton and Bay Streets (912-644-6400) also provide a free visitors' guide that has a great map.

Following our Insiders' Historic Downtown tour, there's information on other guided touring options in the city, plus a variety of other interesting attractions to explore both in Savannah's downtown and the outlying areas: the Islands, Southside, and West Chatham.

INSIDERS' HISTORIC DOWNTOWN WALKING TOUR

Whether you're approaching the Historic Downtown via the Talmadge Bridge or you're already there and wandering around on foot, you can't miss the gold dome on top of City Hall. The tour begins at this landmark on Bay Street and the northern tip of Bull Street. So look up (or down, depending on your vantage point), and when you spot

ATTRACTIONS

the gold dome, head in that direction. Once you arrive, don't be shy—wander inside for a quick look around. You'll be glad you did, and the office workers don't mind a bit. Also note that there are several ideal guided walking tours listed on the Convention and Visitors Bureau website: http://savannahvisit.com/getaways/tours/listing/0/419. Fees will vary with each walking tour. The one we share here is for an individual, self-guided tour.

Victory Drive and Washington Avenue

If you're venturing south of the Historic Downtown to do some sightseeing, be sure to take a drive down portions of two streets in Midtown—**Victory Drive** between Abercorn Street and Waters Avenue, and **Washington Avenue** between Bull Street and Waters.

You'll see stately homes set amid huge, graceful oak trees on both streets and, if you hit it just right during the springtime, medians and yards bursting with the color of azaleas in bloom. Palm trees were first planted along Victory Drive in 1906 when it was called Estill Avenue, and this thoroughfare—which starts at Ogeechee Road, runs to the Wilmington River, and continues to Tybee Island as US 80—was once reputed to be the longest avenue of palms in the nation. When Estill Avenue was widened and extended in 1922, it was renamed Victory Drive in honor of the Americans who fought and died in World War I.

CITY HALL
Bay and Bull Streets
(912) 651-6410, (912) 236-7284
Local architect Hyman Wallace Witcover designed and built City Hall in 1905 for an estimated $205,167. This price was to include statues of chariots and horses on top of the structure, but budget constraints prevented them from being built. The exterior is composed of several materials, including rough-hewn granite blocks, colored limestone, and polished granite. The dome, rising 70 feet, was originally copper. However, in 1987 a local philanthropist donated $240,000 to the city, allowing the dome to be gilded with thin layers of 23-karat gold leaf. The gold was applied to the dome, cupola, and clock hands. The dome was renovated in 2007–08, so if it seems extra shiny, you'll know why. Usually, most of the faces of the clock have the right time—but if your group is splitting up to tour, don't depend on it for your rendezvous time!

Inside the foyer you will find a lovely and intricate mosaic on the floor. Look up in the foyer, and you will see more detailed tiles. Go farther into the rotunda and look up for a pretty, circular view all the way up to the fourth floor and the stained glass in the dome. The original building directory is also in the rotunda on a giant tablet. Today, Savannah city offices are located throughout the community, but the second floor of City Hall is much like it was when the building was originally built. It still houses the mayor's office, clerk of council offices, and the council chambers. The stern and imposing council chambers have even stood in for courtrooms in a couple of Hollywood productions.

After leaving City Hall, head south on Bull Street. Look to your left while crossing

111

Bay Street. The huge building on the corner opposite City Hall is the United States Custom House.

UNITED STATES CUSTOM HOUSE
1 East Bay St.

The magnificent columns in front of the Custom House each weigh 15 tons. Across the street are cannons presented to the Chatham Artillery in 1791 by George Washington.

In 1972 the structure was designated a historic custom house by the U.S. commissioner of customs. As you walk by, notice the wonderful ironwork fencing that not only decorates the building but also guards it. It is just one of many fine examples of wrought iron you will notice throughout your walking tour. Although it is a landmark, it's also the working home of the Customs office, busy tracking the business of Savannah's port.

Continue south on Bull Street in the direction of Johnson Square.

JOHNSON SQUARE
Bull Street, between Bryan and Congress Streets

This is Savannah's first square. It is named for Robert Johnson, the governor of South Carolina who helped the Georgia colony get established. During the early days of the colony, this was the center of activity for the city. In the center is a monument to Revolutionary War hero Gen. Nathanael Greene, who died in 1786; his grave is here as well. Today the square is the center of banking in Savannah. Stand in the middle and you will be surrounded by several banks. If you need to pick up some cash, this is a good spot to find an ATM. This is also a popular square for downtown workers to lunch in, and in spring and early summer there is often lunchtime musical entertainment.

On the eastern side of the square, look for pairs of gigantic green doors and majestic columns. They belong to Christ Church.

CHRIST CHURCH
28 Bull St.
(912) 232-4131

Christ Church is known as Georgia's Mother Church. It was founded in 1733, on the exact spot where the first Christian religious service in Georgia was held. The current church replaced two churches that were destroyed. In 1735 John Wesley, the founder of Methodism, served as pastor here and founded what is believed to be the world's first Protestant Sunday school.

Also interesting: Christ Church has one of the rarest church bells in the entire country. It is known as a Revere Bell and was created by Paul Revere and Sons, the company owned by the noted "British are coming" patriot. It is one of about 130 Revere bells, the majority of which are found in New England states; only a handful made it to the South. The bell in the tower is actually the third Revere Bell the church has owned. The first, purchased in 1816 for $716, cracked during shipment. The second cracked the second Sunday it rang. The third bell, as they say, was the charm. The church didn't have any significant problems with the third bell until 1995, when repairs needed to be made to the apparatus holding the bell. After a two-year repair job, the bell was rung again in early November 1997.

Continue heading south on Bull Street, crossing Congress Street and proceeding to Broughton Street. This is Savannah's original business district, and after decades of decline, it is becoming a shining example of urban redevelopment. Look east and west to see many trendy shops and a restaurant selection that ranges from Thai to Moroccan to Italian (not to mention a good ol' hot dog place as well). Take a detour if you are hungry. If not, continue south on Bull Street to Wright Square, the second square on our trip.

WRIGHT SQUARE
Bull Street, between State and York Streets

Wright Square is named for Sir James Wright, the last royal governor of Georgia. The monument in the center is for William Washington Gordon, one of the founders of the Central of Georgia Railroad. (The railroad's offices used to be about a block away; you will pass the site on this walking tour.) The large boulder, taken from Stone Mountain near Atlanta, marks the grave of Tomo-chi-chi, the Yamacraw Indian chief who was instrumental in helping the founders get established in their new colony.

Taking up the entire western side of the square is the federal courthouse. Made of Georgia marble, its architecture is a conglomeration of many styles: Spanish, French, Italian Renaissance, and Romanesque among them. On the eastern side of the square, you'll see the old Chatham County Courthouse, a light-colored brick building designed in 1889 by noted Boston architect William G. Preston. It now houses county offices. On the same side as the courthouse is Lutheran Church of the Ascension.

LUTHERAN CHURCH OF THE ASCENSION
21 East State St.
(912) 232-4151

Massive red doors lead into Lutheran Church of the Ascension, formed in 1741 by German settlers. The current church was built between 1875 and 1879 and was designed by George B. Clarke, using Norman and Gothic styles. One of the church's most striking features is the Ascension Window, depicting the Ascension of the Lord.

JULIETTE GORDON LOW BIRTHPLACE
142 Bull St. (corner of Bull Street and East Oglethorpe Avenue)
(912) 233-4501
www.girlscouts.org/birthplace

The Juliette Gordon Low Birthplace gives visitors an authentic glimpse of what life was like in the 1800s for one of Savannah's most prominent families—one that just happened to include Juliette Gordon Low, founder of the Girl Scouts.

But the Low Center isn't just about the Girl Scouts. This beautifully restored home, Savannah's first National Historic Landmark, is full of the Gordons' original belongings—from Georgian Revival chairs in the dining room to a painting of Niagara Falls by moonlight, a souvenir the Gordons bought some years after their honeymoon. When entering the main hallway, you will immediately notice the beautiful winding staircase with a rose-colored bull's-eye glass window in the background; it was installed in 1886 to give more light in the stairway. In the library is a brass chandelier original to the home. The south parlor, decorated in striking yellow, red, and green, has a pier mirror, installed in 1884.

Construction on the home began in 1818 in the newly fashionable English Regency style. William Washington Gordon and his wife, Sarah, were the first of four generations of the Gordon family to live in the home. William Gordon served as mayor of Savannah and is credited as a founder of the Central of Georgia Railroad. The house was eventually inherited by William Washington Gordon II and his wife, Eleanor Kinzie

Gordon, the parents of Juliette Gordon. Juliette spent her childhood here.

After passing through another generation of Gordons, the house was threatened with demolition in 1953. A concerned group of local Girl Scouts, including youngsters and adults, appealed to the national organization to save the birthplace of their founder, and the building was purchased by the Girl Scouts. It was restored and opened to the public three years later. Today, thousands of Girl Scouts from around the world make the pilgrimage to Savannah to visit the home of the group's cherished founder. The house is open from 10 a.m. to 4 p.m. Mon through Sat (closed Wed from Nov to Feb) and from 11 a.m. to 4 p.m. on Sun. Cost is $8 for adults and $7 for students ages 6 to 18. Recent renovations, which include a small elevator, have made the mansion relatively accessible to the handicapped, unusual among historic attractions.

Continuing south on Bull Street, you will pass the offices for the local school district on the left, housed in a rambling brick building that once housed a school and still sports nice frescoes above its entrances, and Independent Presbyterian Church on the right.

INDEPENDENT PRESBYTERIAN CHURCH
25 West Oglethorpe Ave.
(912) 236-3346
www.ip.csav.org
This church was founded in 1755 and is considered one of the most important Federal-style churches in the country. The original was designed by John Holden Greene of Rhode Island. It burned in 1889. The current building has an elevated mahogany pulpit, and the four Corinthian columns of the sanctuary were made from a single tree trunk that was carefully selected through

exhaustive searches in the South. It's worth a peek inside just to view the pulpit. Woodrow Wilson married Ellen Axson, granddaughter of the church's pastor, here.

Continue south to Chippewa Square.

i For movie buffs, this is the square where Forrest Gump sat waiting for the bus. The bench was placed on the far northern tip of the square. Next time you see the film, notice that traffic in the square is moving in the wrong direction!

CHIPPEWA SQUARE
Bull Street, between Perry and Hull Streets
General James Oglethorpe is immortalized in bronze in the center of this square. First Baptist Church, organized in 1800, is on the northwestern corner of the square. Across the park on the northeastern corner is the Savannah Theater, home of a professional theatrical group that presents musical programs five days a week.

The beautiful building on the southwest corner is known as the Philbrick-Eastman House and is a fine example of Greek Revival architecture. It served as home for many prominent families; today, it houses a law firm. While walking south through the square, look to your left along West Perry Street, and you will notice a row of magnificently restored private homes, among the many you will see on your trip today. You are getting into the more residential portion of the Historic District.

Continue south on Bull Street. After crossing Perry Street, notice a dolphin downspout on the home to your right. These interesting adornments to lovely houses are a common sight throughout Savannah. There are several boutiques, a coffee shop, and a few lunch spots in this area. Duck in to Gaucho to look for women's high fashion. (Check the Shopping and Restaurants chapters for more information.) Farther down Liberty Street is the Hilton Savannah DeSoto, built on the site of the DeSoto Hotel, which was razed in 1966. Next is Madison Square.

MADISON SQUARE
Bull Street, between Harris and Charlton Streets

Madison Square is named for James Madison, the fourth U.S. president. When entering Madison Square you will notice the Sorrel-Weed House on the northwest corner of the square. It was completed in 1841 and is an example of Greek Revival architecture. In 1997 the home was purchased and underwent an extensive $2 million renovation that restored it to its original condition. This renovation included painting the home its original bright orange color, which did not please neighbors and members of a local historic review committee. However, the homeowner won out, as you will see when walking by.

On the northeastern corner is E. Shaver Bookseller, a popular locally owned bookstore. If you need a break, this could be a good place to take it. On the southeastern edge of the square is a gigantic redbrick building that once was the Savannah Volunteer Guards Armory. This structure and the large building across the street on the southwest corner of the square—the old Scottish Rite Temple—are now owned by the Savannah College of Art and Design. The armory was the first building the art school founders purchased when they came to town in the late 1970s. At the time, there was an old restaurant inside, so complete renovation was needed. It was the first in a long list of buildings purchased and restored by the

school; you'll find them throughout the Historic Downtown. Today the armory houses classrooms and Exhibit A, an art gallery that features artwork by students and professors and, at times, work by famous artists. It is open to the public free of charge. (For more information on the Savannah College of Art and Design, see our Education and Child Care chapter.)

Look to the northwest corner of the square. The Gothic brick mansion is the Green-Meldrim House.

GREEN-MELDRIM HOUSE
1 West Macon St.
(912) 233-3845, (912) 232-1251

Built in 1853 by architect-builder John S. Norris for a wealthy cotton merchant, the Green-Meldrim House is best known as being headquarters for Gen. William T. Sherman, who gave the city of Savannah to President Lincoln as a Christmas present. The famous telegram to Lincoln, dated December 22, 1864, reads, "I beg to present to you as a Christmas Gift, the City of Savannah with 150 heavy guns and plenty of ammunition; and also about 25,000 bales of Cotton."

Today the home serves as a parish house and is owned by its neighbor, St. John's Church. When you walk by, notice the beautiful and elaborate ironwork and the oriel windows that give light from three sides. Inside are American black walnut wooden floors, elaborate moldings, marble mantels, and other original adornments. The home is open for tours from 10 a.m. to 4 p.m. on Tues, Thurs, and Fri, and 10 a.m. to 1 p.m. on Sat year-round. Admission is $7 for adults, $2 for students.

Continuing south on Bull Street, you will pass Jones Street, considered one of Savannah's most picturesque roadways. Notice the brick streets and wonderfully restored

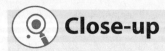

Close-up

Savannah's Mercer House Opens Its Doors to Public

During the height of the popularity of the book *Midnight in the Garden of Good and Evil*, **Mercer House** was under a sort of subdued siege. A thriving and opportunistic tourism subculture centered around the book was cashing in on the obsessive interest of fans. Nowhere could have been of more interest to those fans than Mercer House, the heart of John Berendt's loosely woven collection of Savannah stories centered around the colorful history of this magnificent mansion where among years of lavish Savannah parties, a fatal shooting occurred.

The sudden fame of Mercer House escalated when the "Midnight" book became a film. Tour buses blared their version of the story outside the sedate mansion that became the private residence of the late Jim Williams' sister, Dr. Dorothy Williams Kingery. Fans posed for pictures outside the house, or clambered up on the gate and low surrounding wall for better looks. Images of the house were reproduced on souvenirs of varying taste levels.

Kingery, the new owner of the house, fought to restore the respect of her brother's home. She trademarked the facade of the house in an effort to deter its commercial exploitation. She even put the home on the market briefly, at a multimillion-dollar price.

The closest fans got for many years, at least legally, was through a gift shop in the home's carriage house. This two-story structure to the rear of the house was once the workshop where Williams worked on antiques. So things stood for the first decade after the publication of Berendt's book. An even larger percentage of the people featured in the book have died by now. The fan fervor had died down some, although even today you can find tours and a gift shop dedicated to all things *Midnight*. Then, in 2004,

homes. It is well worth a short detour. It is also home to one of Savannah's most noted restaurants, Mrs. Wilkes', which is known for its Southern fare (see our Restaurants chapter).

Next is Monterey Square.

MONTEREY SQUARE
Bull Street, between Taylor and Gordon Streets

This is the final square on Bull Street. Its name commemorates the Battle of Monterey in the Mexican War. The square was laid out in 1847. In the center is a monument honoring Casmir Pulaski, a Polish nobleman who was killed during the American Revolution. He may or may not be buried under the monument that honors him; historians disagree. The monument was rededicated in 2001 after a restoration period of several years that saw its foundation standing empty.

During filming of the movie *Midnight in the Garden of Good and Evil*, set designers brought in their own monument. Now, when you see Monterey Square on the big screen, you'll know the monument is not the original. The square is surrounded by other significant sites used in the movie, including the home where the book's main plot unfolds, the Mercer-Wilder House, quietly, with no fanfare and an extremely low-key approach, Kingery opened the first floor of Mercer House (now increasingly known as the Mercer-Williams House) to paying guests.

The Mercer-Williams House is now the only private, occupied residence in Savannah that invites paying guests to tour it. Tours enter through the Carriage House, where a guide leads small groups through the courtyard and into the home's first floor. At the moment, you'll sample the replendence of the house, decorated with one-of-a-kind antiques and rare furnishings and accent pieces that were a part of Jim Williams's collection. British Colonial pieces are among the most distinctive. Kingery is enthusiastic about sharing the truth of the home's history and the tour guides are endorsed by her. They are knowledgeable about the home's interior features and the antiques displayed there.

At $12.50, the Mercer-Williams House is the priciest of the downtown house museums, although the price hasn't gone up in the three years it has been open. But it's also among the more interesting and beautiful. This is a tour of Williams's house, and it focuses on his impressive role in the preservation and restoration of Savannah's architectural treasures. It is not—repeat, not—a facet of the *Midnight in the Garden of Good and Evil* notoriety. You won't hear the book mentioned, and questions about the subject should be withheld as a courtesy and out of respect to the family. The front of the house has no sign or other indication that it is open to tours. The carriage house is directly behind the house, and a small, discreet sign gives tour details. The shop is worth a browse, too. It offers home decor and gift items of good quality, not extravagantly marked up. Although it isn't really a book store, the things we've bought on our few visits have all been books. And, as a sign of how much things have changed, that small stock of books on sale now includes *Midnight in the Garden of Good and Evil*.

commonly known as Mercer House, which is on the western edge of the square.

MERCER HOUSE
429 Bull St.
www.mercerhouse.com
Cited by Historic Savannah Foundation as nationally significant for its architectural style, this home was designed by John S. Norris and completed in 1871. The striking ironwork—including cast-iron window pediments, eight cast-iron balconies, and the sidewalk fence—is one of the house's signature features. The house was named for Confederate Gen. Hugh Mercer, songwriter

Johnny Mercer's great-grandfather, but General Mercer sold the house. He never lived there nor did any member of the Mercer family.

In 1970, after the house was neglected and empty for many years, Jim Williams, the antiques dealer, Savannah preservationist, and the central character in the book and film *Midnight in the Garden of Good and Evil* finished a complete restoration of the home. Today the private home is owned by Dorothy Kingery, sister of the late Williams. She opened the home to limited public tours in 2004. Tickets are $12.50, and entrance is through the carriage house. Tickets may be purchased on their website, where you will also find hours and contact information. For more details, see our Close-Up in this chapter.

Looking past Mercer House, on the south-west corner of the square, you will notice row houses along Gordon Street. One of these homes—7 West Gordon Street—has also had a brush with celebrity. If you are a fan of the PBS show This Old House, *you may be famil-iar with the renovation that took place here in 1996 at the home of Mills and Marianne Fleming. For several months, Norm Abram, Steve Thomas, and the rest of the crew from the popular series were in town helping restore the 1884 home, which made headlines when it was built for being one of the first homes in the city to have indoor plumbing. Across the square from Mercer House, on the eastern side of the square, is Temple Mickve Israel.*

TEMPLE MICKVE ISRAEL
20 East Gordon St.
(912) 233-1547
www.mickveisrael.org
Temple Mickve Israel began with a group of Spanish–Portuguese Jews who came to Savannah in 1733, just five months after the founding of the colony. It is the site of the first Jewish congregation in the South and the third in the entire United States. It is also the only Gothic synagogue in the country. The temple was designed by Henry G. Harri-son and houses the oldest Torah in America. There are also hundreds of documents, his-torical books, and letters from Presidents Washington, Jefferson, and Madison in the museum adjoining the temple. Tours of the sanctuary and museum take place Mon through Fri from 10 a.m. to 1 p.m. and 2 to 4 p.m. at a fee of $5 per person.

Continuing south on Bull Street, you will pass the George Armstrong House on the northwest corner of Bull and Gaston Streets. This massive building, constructed in 1920, was given to the city in 1935 and converted into Armstrong Junior College, predecessor of Armstrong Atlantic State University, which subsequently moved to Savannah's South-side. (For more on Armstrong Atlantic, see our Education and Child Care chapter.) Today it houses a law firm.

Across the street, on the northeast corner of Bull and Gaston Streets is the Oglethorpe Club, one of Savannah's most elite and private clubs. Straight ahead is Forsyth Park.

FORSYTH PARK
Bull Street, between Gaston Street and Park Avenue
This 30-acre park is an amazing postcard brought to life and filled with color! With azaleas, magnolia trees, walkways, and park benches, the park is one of Savannah's most beautiful spots. The park was laid out in 1851. One of its most recognizable and often photographed features is the white fountain near the center. Visit on the weekend, and you might see a bride and groom getting pictures taken beside the ornate swans and other creatures in the fountain.

The monument in the center of the park was erected by the United Daughters of the Confederacy and honors those killed during the Civil War. The park is also home to a Fra-grant Garden for the Blind and is surrounded by beautiful and elaborately restored homes, many of which are Victorian in style. Across from the northwestern corner of the park is the Georgia Historical Society.

GEORGIA HISTORICAL SOCIETY
501 Whitaker St.
(912) 651-2125
www.georgiahistory.com

Dr. William Bacon Stevens, a physician who later became the Episcopal Bishop of Pennsylvania, and attorney I. K. Tefft are generally credited with organizing the Savannah-based Georgia Historical Society. The pair was soon joined by Dr. Richard D. Arnold, a founder of the American Medical Association. In 1839 the group incorporated one of the country's oldest (and the Southeast's first) historical societies.

Nearly 170 years later, the realization of their efforts can easily be seen in thousands of historic documents, artifacts, newspapers, and other source materials documenting Georgia's past. Visitors to the society will find everything in its massive archives, from copies of letters Gen. James Edward Oglethorpe wrote to the Trustees of the Colony, to the grapeshot that killed Casmir Pulaski and was extracted from the Polish war hero's leg. There are minutes from the first Georgia Medical Society meeting, held in Savannah in 1804; photographs from the now-defunct YWCA; and family letters such as the one written by Garnett Andrews about the cotton gin Eli Whitney had invented.

The society also publishes, in cooperation with the University of Georgia, the highly acclaimed Georgia Historical Quarterly, a collection of scholarly articles. Entry to the Georgia Historical Society is free. The building is open to the public from 10 a.m. to 5 p.m. Tues through Fri and on the first and third Sat of each month, from 10 a.m. to 5 p.m. It is recommended that you call to confirm hours as they do change.

This is the midpoint of the walking tour. Time to travel north for the next portion of the tour, heading back in the direction of City Hall, where we started. Continue 1 block east onto Gaston Street, crossing Drayton Street. Check out the many beautifully restored homes. Head north by turning left onto Abercorn and stay on this street until you reach Calhoun Square.

CALHOUN SQUARE
Abercorn Street, between Taylor and Gordon Streets
The first of the Abercorn Street squares on our tour was named for John Calhoun, a South Carolina statesman. It was laid out in 1851. When entering the square, you can't help but notice Wesley Monumental Methodist Church on the southwestern corner of the square. This Gothic Revival church was named for John and Charles Wesley, early figures in the history of Methodism. The sanctuary was built between 1876 and 1890. It features a Wesley Window opposite the pulpit, which contains the busts of the men for whom the church was named.

On the southeastern edge of the square is the Massie Heritage Interpretation Center.

i You can see the whole world in Savannah, and it's sitting right near one of the city's busiest intersections—the meeting of Abercorn Street and DeRenne Avenue. The world we're talking about is what Savannahians refer to as "the Globe," a steel sphere that's 60 feet in diameter. The Savannah Gas Company erected it in the mid-1950s as an emergency holding station for natural gas and soon painted it to depict Earth's oceans and continents, with an arrow pointing to Savannah.

MASSIE HERITAGE INTERPRETATION CENTER
207 East Gordon St.
(912) 651-7022
www.massieschool.com

Honored as Georgia's oldest school in continuous operation, the Massie Heritage Interpretation Center is also the only remaining original building from Georgia's oldest chartered school system. The Greek Revival structure is listed on the National Register of Historic Places. It was completed in 1856 and is known for its gable roof, wood cupola, and cornice, among other features. Today, an enrichment program is offered to increase student understanding of Savannah's historic and architectural heritage. The center is open to the public from 9 a.m. to 4 p.m. Mon through Fri. Self-guided tours are $5; guided tours are $8.

LAFAYETTE SQUARE
Abercorn Street, between Harris and Charlton Streets

This square, which was laid out in 1837, was named for Marquis de Lafayette, who visited Savannah in 1825. There are several significant buildings on this square, but when you enter it, you can't help but notice the Cathedral of St. John the Baptist, located near the northeast corner.

CATHEDRAL OF ST. JOHN THE BAPTIST
223 East Harris St.
(912) 233-4709
www.savannahcathedral.org

A few private moments in this magnificent cathedral should be on your priority list of Savannah's must-sees. This magnificent Gothic cathedral with its twin spires is one of Savannah's most noted landmarks. It is also the oldest Roman Catholic church in

Georgia and the seat of the Diocese of Savannah. The parish organized in the late 1700s and erected its first church on Liberty Street. It wasn't until 1876 that the cathedral was built; tragically, it was destroyed by fire 20 years later.

When the cathedral was rebuilt, the original designs were used. One of the cathedral's most striking features is its stained glass. Most of it was executed by Innsbruck Glassmakers in Austrian Tyrol and installed around 1900. Other features include an Italian marble altar, the stations of the cross (which were imported from Munich), and the coat of arms of Pope John XXIII. The building just underwent a massive restoration, indoors and out, and is now fully open in its restored glory. The mass schedule is as follows: Sat, noon and 5:30 p.m.; Sun 8 a.m., 10 a.m., and 11:30 a.m.; Mon through Fri 7:30 a.m. and noon; holy days 7:30 a.m., noon, and 6 p.m.; Sun Latin Mass 1 p.m.

THE ANDREW LOW HOUSE
329 Abercorn St.
(912) 233-6854
www.andrewlowhouse.com

On the northwest corner of Lafayette Square is the Andrew Low House, built in 1848 by Low, a wealthy cotton merchant. Low's son, William McKay Low, married Juliette Gordon, founder of the Girl Scouts. In fact, the carriage house in back of the home is the first official headquarters of the Girl Scouts of the U.S.A. Juliette Low left the building to the organization following her death.

The stunning home, with its elegant front gardens and beautiful ironwork, is built of stucco brick. It is now owned by the National Society of the Colonial Dames of America in the State of Georgia, whose members also donated its furnishings. Even the three-tiered fountain in the center of the square was donated by the organization. Some of the home's most noted guests have included Robert E. Lee and William Makepeace Thackeray. The home is open for tours from 10 a.m. to 4:30 p.m. Mon through Sat (closed on Thurs), and from noon to 4:30 p.m. Sun. Cost to tour the house is $8 for adults and $4.50 for students, Girl Scouts, and Girl Scout leaders.

THE HAMILTON-TURNER INN
330 Abercorn St.
(912) 233-1833
www.hamilton-turnerinn.com
The Hamilton-Turner House is a Second Empire chateau built in the 1870s by a former mayor of Savannah. The Lafayette Square home was the first house in the city to get electricity and has many distinctive features, including a mansard roof and cast-iron balconies. In 1969 it was scheduled for demolition, but those plans were abandoned after the Historic Savannah Foundation stepped in. It has changed hands several times since then. (Read more about its current incarnation in our Bed-and-Breakfast Inns chapter.)

FLANNERY O'CONNOR HOUSE
207 East Charlton St.
(912) 233-6014
www.flanneryoconnorhome.org
Noted Southern author Flannery O'Connor was born in this high-stoop, 19th-century home on the outskirts of Lafayette Square. She lived here as a child until 1938. The parlor floor has been restored to its original appearance and houses a small museum dedicated to the author. The home is open from 1 to 4 p.m. every day except Thurs, and there is a $5 admission charge.

Continuing north on Abercorn Street, cross Liberty Street. On the east side of Abercorn Street is Colonial Park Cemetery.

COLONIAL PARK CEMETERY
Button Gwinnett, who signed the Declaration of Independence, and Edward Green Malbone, painter of miniatures, are two of the notable Georgians buried in this cemetery, the second public burial ground in Savannah. The cemetery, which takes up several blocks in the Historic Downtown, opened in 1750; it closed to burials 100 years later. Visitors are welcome to tour the cemetery and glimpse the old tombstones and inscriptions.

After exploring the cemetery, continue north on Abercorn Street, crossing Oglethorpe Avenue. As you cross Oglethorpe, you will pass the city's fire department headquarters. Next is Oglethorpe Square.

OGLETHORPE SQUARE
Abercorn Street, between State and York Streets
Oglethorpe Square was named for Georgia's founder, James Edward Oglethorpe. It was laid out in 1742. On the northeast corner of the square is one of Savannah's most famous museum houses, the Owens-Thomas House.

OWENS-THOMAS HOUSE
124 Abercorn St.
(912) 790-8880
www.telfair.org
Taking up an entire block on the eastern edge of the square is the Owens-Thomas House, considered to be one of the finest examples of English Regency architecture in the country. The home, with its columned entrance portico, brass inlaid staircase, and more, was designed by architect William Jay from 1816 to 1819 for cotton merchant Richard Richardson.

The home is made largely of tabby—an indigenous, concretelike material made of lime, oyster shells, and sand. The exterior is English stucco. The interior, which includes three rare built-in marble-top tables that belonged to the Richardsons, has many stunning features, including an entryway with a brass inlaid staircase and a drawing room with an unusual ceiling that makes the room appear to be round. The carriage house, also open for tours, is one of the earliest intact urban slave quarters in the South and opens into an English-inspired parterre garden.

In 1830, after the home had been used as a boardinghouse, George Welchman Owens, a congressman and former mayor of Savannah, purchased it for $10,000. The property remained in the Owens family until it was bequeathed to what is now the Telfair Museum of Art. The home is open 10 a.m. to 5 p.m. Mon through Sat, and from 2 to 5 p.m. on Sun. The cost to tour the house is $15 for adults; $14 for AAA members, senior citizens, and military. Students (K–College) are $5, and children under 5 are free (as are members of the Telfair). Note that this house museum is part of the Telfair's three holdings—the other two are art museums, and the best bargain is the $15 adult ticket that gets you into all three attractions.

i **Want to see all of Savannah's museums for free?** Plan your trip to Savannah around Super Museum Sunday. Every year the museums open up their doors free of charge to anyone who wants to stop by. You even get free transportation provided by the county's bus system. Not a bad deal. (See our Annual Events and Festivals chapter for more information.)

One of Savannah's other noted museum houses is just around the corner from the Owens-Thomas House on East State Street. If you would like to detour to this house, head east on State Street and cross Lincoln. One block on your left will be the Davenport House.

ISAIAH DAVENPORT HOUSE
324 East State St.
(912) 236-8097
www.davenporthousemuseum.org

As you walk around today in the Historic Downtown enjoying the beautifully restored homes and other sights, know that it was the Davenport House that was largely responsible for the preservation of the national treasure that is the Historic District. In the 1950s, when developers came up with a plan to demolish the house, sell the brick, and put in a parking lot, seven local women banded together to stop it. That group, which later became the Historic Savannah Foundation, raised $22,500 to purchase the home; such were the beginnings of restoration efforts in Savannah.

At the time of the rescue purchase, the home was a tenement, divided into small apartments and full of people. The Federal-style home was originally built in 1820 by master builder Isaiah Davenport, who used the home as a kind of showcase for his work. One of the incredible features of the house is the delicate and ornate molding and plaster work found throughout. The Davenport House is open from 10 a.m. to 4 p.m. Mon through Sat, and 1 to 4 p.m. Sun. Cost is $8 for adults, $5 for children.

After viewing the Davenport House, head west on State Street to Abercorn Street. Again, travel north on Abercorn. As you cross Broughton Street, you'll notice a large building on your right. Savannah College of Art and Design has transformed this former department store into a library. Continuing along Abercorn Street, you will come to the Lucas Theatre.

LUCAS THEATRE
32 Abercorn St.
(912) 525-5040
www.lucastheatre.com

This Savannah landmark, built in 1921, served not only as a theater but also as a general center of entertainment for the city. It had floors of imported marble, a dome ceiling surrounded by 600 incandescent lights, and 36 ornate boxes. However, it deteriorated with the rest of downtown after World War II. A group of citizens—Lucas Theatre for the Arts Inc.—banded together to reopen the theater and has been raising the millions of dollars needed to complete the project. As part of their fund-raising efforts, when the crew filming *Midnight in the Garden of Good and Evil* was in town in 1997, it participated in a fund-raiser for the theater. Among those in attendance were director Clint Eastwood and actor Kevin Spacey. The theater is now in full operation (see our Arts and Culture chapter for more information) under the management of Savannah College of Art and Design. Check the schedule and plan to enjoy the beauty of this theater if there's an event going on during your stay.

After passing the Lucas Theatre, you will enter Reynolds Square, the last square on our walking tour.

REYNOLDS SQUARE
Abercorn Street, between Bryan and Congress Streets

Reynolds Square was named for Capt. John Reynolds, who served as governor of Georgia in 1754. In the center is a statue of John Wesley, the founder of Methodism. On the northwestern corner of the square is the Olde Pink House, a popular eatery.

Continuing north on Abercorn Street, you will reach Bay Street. Look to the west and you will once again see the dome on City Hall, where the tour began. Directly across Bay Street is Factors' Walk and River Street.

FACTORS' WALK AND RIVER STREET

Bay Street Factors' Walk is named for the cotton brokers (or "factors") who bought, sold, and shipped their wares along the banks of the Savannah River. This unique row of buildings, built on the bluff overlooking the water, rises two or three stories on the street side and three or more stories over the riverfront.

The focal point is the old Cotton Exchange, a redbrick building with the name Cotton Exchange etched along the top of the facade. It was built in 1886 by William G. Preston and was one of the first buildings in the United States to be erected entirely over a public street. At one time this building was where the world price for cotton was set. While the brokers set the price of cotton, the lower floors served as cotton and naval warehouses with entrances at several levels, including on River Street.

Today both River Street and Factors' Walk are full of shops, restaurants, and galleries, all housed in the restored warehouses. It is a favorite spot for visitors. Take a stroll on the river for a fitting end to our tour.

GUIDED TOURS

Savannah abounds with guided-tour companies. Their offerings are varied—general history, ghosts and hauntings, African-American history, you name it. Modes as well as subjects vary: travel by air-conditioned minibus, open-sided pseudo trolley, horse-drawn carriage, riverboat, or plain old shank's mare (walking, in other words). The latest addition to the local tour scene is the Segway, those motorized "people movers" that look like a scale in a doctor's office, except they carry you around.

This is a very fluid industry. New tours are added constantly, schedules and itineraries change, etc. Although the following is not a comprehensive listing, it will get you started.

> **i** Florence Martus is forever immortalized by the Waving Girl statue on River Street. For many years during the late 1800s and early 1900s, she greeted the ships that passed through the port of Savannah by waving a white cloth during the day and a lantern during the night, hoping to be the first to greet her returning husband (or, by some accounts, her returning fiancé). The Altrusa Club erected this statue in her honor.

Boats

SAVANNAH RIVERBOAT COMPANY
9 East River St.
(912) 232-6404, (800) 786-6404
www.savannahriverboat.com

This hour-long cruise takes you up and down the Savannah River on a replica riverboat, either the *Savannah River Queen* or the *Georgia Queen*. It's one of many ways for a tourist to get a firsthand look at the industrial and shipping side of the city—the bread and butter for many of us who live here. You can also get a waterfront perspective on historic structures. River Street from the water lends itself to good panoramic photos, however, realize that the tours may not be narrated. Depending on river traffic, you may get to see some of the massive ships that make the port of Savannah among the busiest in the nation.

The daytime sightseeing cruise is narrated. Wear sunscreen! This company also offers a variety of other cruises, keyed around dinner and dancing, Sunday brunch, or even gospel music with a buffet dinner. You'll need to check the website for current themed cruises since they vary. Prepaid reservations are required for most tours, except the daytime sightseeing. Note: All cruise schedules are subject to change, vary seasonally, and can be affected by the weather.

Buses

Although most tours will take credit cards, some bus drivers do not have the means of processing them. If you plan on paying by plastic, mention that while making your reservations, because it may impact your selection of pickup locations. Also, prices don't include tips for the guide/driver, which most of the brochures and onboard signs shamelessly hustle for; they are strictly optional.

OLD TOWN TROLLEY TOURS OF SAVANNAH
234 Martin Luther King Jr. Blvd.
(912) 233-0083, (888) 910-8687
www.trolleytours.com

It's exciting to tour the city in an open-air vehicle, and Old Town Trolley Tours of Savannah offers colorful and comfortable trolley-style vehicles. This 90-minute tour offers re-boarding options throughout the Historic Downtown on orange and green trolley-style vehicles. A one day ticket costs $25 for adults and $10 for children. Most popular is the Paula Deen Tour where adults pay $49 and children, $25. The tour company also operates a gift shop downtown. It also offers a ghost tour on a trolley, Ghosts and Gravestones, for $25 for adults and $10 for children.

The Gospel Cruise

After several years of hearing about the Monday night **Gospel Dinner Cruises** advertised by the Savannah Riverboat Company, I ventured out to see if there was any truth to the positive reviews I had read. First, let me say this: These riverboats cruise waters along a working, industrial pathway, so if you're expecting to see postcard-like settings along the way, be forewarned. The Georgia Ports Authority's various working terminals and supporting shipping vendors will consume more space in your camera's memory than any wildlife or old buildings. You may pass working barges, and briefly, old Fort Jackson, but other than the historic cotton warehouses along River Street, there's not much beauty to behold.

The cruises board around sunset, which can be spectacular from the boat's third deck. This is where you'll want to enjoy your pre- and post-dinner time. Although the advertised boarding time is 6 p.m., board around 6:30 so you can spend a little time exploring the vessel's outside decks and maybe catch a dolphin or two in between the rustic commercial riverfront industrial sites. On Gospel Night, you'll be greeted to the sounds of about a dozen singers from varying Savannah churches who have been livening up the riverboat for the past six years. There are several lead singers, and let me tell you this, they can sing! From old hymns like "Tis So Sweet to Trust in Jesus," to favorites like, "Swing Low, Sweet Chariot" and "This Little Light of Mine," you'll be rocking right along with them as you dine on Southern favorites like fried chicken, mac and cheese, greens, and biscuits, buffet style. When it's all said and done and the group has sang its last amen, you'll wonder why you even thought about a view.

OGLETHORPE TROLLEY TOURS
215 West Boundary Rd.
(912) 233-8380
www.oglethorpetours.com

This group offers a 90-minute narrated, on-off trolley tour of Historic Savannah for $15 for adults and $10 for children. They also offer a Land and Sea Savannah Package, which includes a one-hour narrated Sightseeing Riverboat Cruise along the Savannah River. Historic Savannah Haunted Trolley Tour and a Haunted Savannah Package are also available. Tickets for these are from $15 to $29 for adults and $18 to $39 for children.

Horse-Drawn Carriages

Although children generally don't jump up and down at the prospect of a guided tour of historic sites, we've found horse-drawn carriages up the appeal significantly. Who knows? You may be lucky enough to see a chartered and decorated carriage ferrying a bride and groom from a wedding at one of the Historic Downtown churches. Tours are not given during the threat of thunderstorms, rain, or extreme heat.

ATTRACTIONS

CARRIAGE TOURS OF SAVANNAH
(912) 236-6756
www.carriagetoursofsavannah.com
Narrated tours are about an hour in length. Options include a daytime historic tour ($20 for adults, $10 for those ages 5 to 11), evening historic or ghost story tours ($20 for adults, $10 for children), and private carriage tours for couples (call for pricing). Tours depart from City Market.

HISTORIC SAVANNAH CARRIAGE TOURS
100 Aberdeen St.
(912) 443-9333
www.savannahcarriage.com
Pickup service can be arranged at hotels or at downtown locations. Fees are $20 for adults and $9 for children. Variations include private romance (Wine and Roses Tour) and Champagne Proposal tours. Departure is from the Hampton Inn at Bay and Abercorn Streets, or for private tours, by arrangement in the Historic District.

MAGNOLIA CARRIAGE COMPANY
802 Wheaton St.
(912) 232-7727
This company specializes in private tours including weddings, and romance is their specialty. All public tours are $20 per person and depart from City Market. Call for reservations.

Walking

FREEDOM TRAIL TOUR
P.O. Box 1484
Savannah, GA 31402
(912) 398-2785
This tour is available seven days a week, with two tours daily in the winter and an extended schedule during other months.

Prices are $20 for adults and $12 for children, with discounts for seniors. The tour lasts about two hours and visits historic churches, the Ralph Mark Gilbert Civil Rights Museum, slave burial grounds, and sites of particular importance to African Americans. Departures are from the Visitors Information Center, 301 Martin Luther King Jr. Blvd.

GHOST TALK, GHOST WALK
4401 Montgomery St.
(912) 233-3896, (800) 563-3896
The ghost tour is the mainstay (there are actually two different versions). They depart from Reynolds Square, beside the statue of John Wesley (one wonders what the famous preacher would have thought of it). Tours depart at dusk, varying according to the time of year, so call for information. Fees are $10 for adults and $5 for those younger than age 12. Other available tours include a Civil War version, a botanical tour, a historic architecture walk, and a literary walking tour. Rates vary; check when you make reservations.

THE SAVANNAH WALKS
37 Abercorn St.
(912) 238-9255, (888) 728-9255
www.savannahwalks.com
This walking-tour firm offers a varied menu with different meeting points. Be sure to check on these things when you make your reservations. Fees are $15 for adults and $7 for children ages 6 to 16. Options include general tours, a Midnight tour, a ghost tour, a Civil War walk, and one featuring gardens. The historic homes walk is slightly higher ($22 adults, $14 children) because it includes admission to one of the city's house museums.

SIXTH SENSE SAVANNAH
(866) 666-3323
www.sixthsensesavannah.com

Lots of companies offer Savannah tours on a ghostly theme. This walking-tour company does it with a mixture of deadpan seriousness and arch humor (like the phone number, which spells out 666-DEAD). This company does not adopt the "all in fun" approach of many other ghost tours: These folks profess to believe and even offer metaphysical readings on premises. The tour host is Shannon Scott, who has hosted some cable network TV programs on hauntings. Scott helped convince the American Institute of the Paranormal to hold its annual convention in Savannah in 2002, and the group went on to bestow its "America's Most Haunted City" title on us. Tours start at 7:30 and 9:30 p.m. Prices start at $20 for adults and $12 for children 12 and under.

TOOTSY TOURS
140 Johnny Mercer Blvd., Suite 12
(912) 898-3111
www.tootsytours.com

The company offers specialty tours for Girl Scouts and for those with specific interests, such as black heritage, Jewish history, and natural history. They'll tailor a tour to fit your business meeting's downtime schedule, too. They also do regional tour work. Prices differ with the degree of customization.

OTHER SAVANNAH ATTRACTIONS

It almost seems like Savannah Attractions are endless! One of the most distinctive draws of this city is that many of her attractions are either free or cost very little. So keep your hiking shoes on and discover what lies beyond the walking tour.

Historic Downtown

BEACH INSTITUTE
502 East Harris St.
(912) 234-8000
www.kingtisdell.org

The Beach Institute was established in 1865 by the American Missionary Association to educate newly freed slaves. Built in 1867, it was the first school in Savannah for African Americans and became a public school in 1919. The institute is an African-American cultural center and houses art, sculpture, and artifacts relating to the cultural contributions of black Americans. The star of its exhibits is the 238-piece collection of wood carvings by the late Ulysses Davis, a Savannah folk artist. Stay tuned to an updated schedule for lectures and other fascinating programs via the website. The Beach Institute is open from noon to 5 p.m. Tues through Sat. Admission is $4 for adults, $2 for children.

FIRST AFRICAN BAPTIST CHURCH
23 Montgomery St.
(912) 233-6597
www.theoldestblackchurch.org

Overlooking Franklin Square is First African Baptist Church. This church, which is still active, is descended from the oldest African-American congregation in the United States. George Leile, a slave, began making missionary visits to plantations up and down the Savannah River as early as 1774. A permanent congregation was formed at Brampton Plantation in 1788—the first black missionary Baptist church in Savannah.

Eventually, the congregation constructed the current building. It is the first brick building erected in Georgia by African Americans for African Americans; it was built by slaves who worked on it at night after being in the fields all day. The sanctuary has beautiful stained-glass windows framing the back of the altar, which displays pictures of the founding pastors. In the balcony are original pews with markings left by the slaves who built the church. The staff of this church is friendly and will invite you to visit their Sun services at 7:45, 9:15, and 10:30 a.m.

KING-TISDELL COTTAGE
514 East Huntingdon St.
(912) 234-8000
www.kingtisdell.org
Built in 1869 by W. W. Aimar, this cottage, with its original gingerbread ornamentation, is in the Beach Institute neighborhood of the Historic Downtown and serves as a museum dedicated to preserving the African-American history of Savannah and the sea islands. Inside the small home you will find art objects, documents, and furniture of the 1890s. It is open from noon to 5 p.m. Tues through Sat. Admission is $3.50.

RALPH MARK GILBERT CIVIL RIGHTS MUSEUM
460 Martin Luther King Jr. Blvd.
(912) 231-8900
www.savcivilrights.com
More than 40,000 people toured Ralph Mark Gilbert Civil Rights Museum during its inaugural year of 1996. The museum chronicles the story of Savannah's civil rights struggles during the 1940s, 1950s, and 1960s. Along with traveling exhibits and special programming, it spotlights how Martin Luther King Jr. Boulevard, formerly known as West Broad Street, was once the center of the city's thriving black business community. Besides educating the community, the museum also serves as an educational resource for southeastern coastal Georgia.

Development of the museum took place over several years. More than $1.7 million went into the museum, which included the renovation of the Wage Earners Savings Bank building, where the museum is housed. The Wage Earners Bank is believed to be the second bank for African Americans in the nation. The museum is the brainchild of the late local historian and activist W. W. Law. It is named after the Reverend Ralph Mark Gilbert, a pastor at First African Baptist Church, who pioneered Savannah's modern civil rights movement. Admission is $8 for adults, $6 for seniors, and $4 for students. (For information on the museum's annual anniversary celebration, look under May in our Annual Events and Festivals chapter.) Hours are Tue through Sat, 9 a.m. to 5 p.m. Guided tours are available upon request.

i The Pirates' House at 20 East Broad St., which is now home to a restaurant (see our Restaurants chapter) featuring a mysterious maze of rooms, is a former seaman's tavern built in 1794. Peer down into the secret tunnels and you might find a dead pirate!

THE ROUNDHOUSE RAILROAD MUSEUM
601 West Harris St.
(912) 651-6823
www.chsgeorgia.org
Your children will love seeing the locomotive collection at the Roundhouse Railroad Museum! It houses the oldest and most complete antebellum railroad manufacturing and repair facilities still in existence in the United States. Take a moment and imagine you are standing there in the 1800s. Watch as the area's largest staff of professional historic preservationists works daily on more

than a dozen historic structures. This site was the Savannah repair shop for the Central of Georgia Railroad, and thirteen of the original structures, which were built beginning in the 1830s, are still standing. Included are a massive roundhouse and operating turntable (where the engines were turned around) and the 125-foot brick smokestack. Various activities are offered daily at the site, including tours inside rail cars, a train-ride tour of the museum, and rides on a hand car; call for schedules. Take a ride on the train and check out the progress of the future Savannah Children's Museum in one of the hard-hat preservation areas. The site is a National Historic Landmark operated by the Coastal Heritage Society. It is open daily from 8:30 a.m. to 5 p.m.; weekends, 9 a.m. to 5 p.m. Admission is $10 for adults and $4 for children age 6 or younger. Children younger than age 5 are free.

SAVANNAH HISTORY MUSEUM
Savannah Visitor Information Center
303 Martin Luther King Jr. Blvd.
(912) 651-6825
www.chsgeorgia.org
Cool off and delve into Savannah's colorful past at the Savannah History Museum, located in the old passenger station of the Central of Georgia Railroad that also houses the Savannah Visitor Center. The structure, a National Historic Landmark, features a variety of exhibits, including an 1890 steam locomotive that is still sitting on the original Central of Georgia tracks. A genuine antique cotton gin is on display, along with artifacts from the Civil War and other eras. Enjoy a colorful film that provides an overview of the city's history in the small theater. The museum is open from 8:30 a.m. to 5 p.m.

The Battlefield Memorial Park

After your visit to the Round-house Railroad Museum, walk the grounds nearby where 800 troops fought and died in 1779, when soldiers from three different armies battled for control of Savannah. Within this area, approximately 2,500 British defenders faced down the Allied force of 5,500 French and American troops who fought fiercely, and when the battle was over, more than 8,000 troops fought and many died or were wounded, and Savannah remained in the hands of the British. It's quite a sight to view the granite markers that represent the soldiers who lost their lives. There's also a wooden sign greeting visitors at the Spring Hill Redoubt, a representation of the British fortification in the battle. There is no charge to walk the grounds, however, donations are always accepted. The Battlefield Memorial Park is a joint project of the City of Savannah and the nonprofit Coastal Heritage Society that has raised more than $500,000 for the memorial.

weekdays and 9 a.m. to 5 p.m. on weekends. It costs $4.25 for adults and teens, $3.75 for children ages 6 to 12. Kids younger than age 6 are free.

SHIPS OF THE SEA MUSEUM
41 Martin Luther King Jr. Blvd.
(912) 232-1511
www.shipsofthesea.com

Scarbrough House and its related garden (a true undiscovered treasure) have added a lot of tone to this museum, previously housed on River Street. The exhibits are more formal now, showcasing paintings and intricate models. The collection also includes scrimshaw, ancient navigational tools, and a china cat figurine with its own risqué story to tell. Learn about Savannah's maritime history while exploring this museum. The home, built in 1819 for the principal owner of the *Savannah*, the first steamship to cross the Atlantic Ocean, was designated a National Historic Landmark in 1974. Cost is $8 for adults, $6 for children age 7 and older (if you have a college ID you can get the discounted rate). Children younger than age 7 get in free. The museum is open from 10 a.m. to 5 p.m. Tues through Sun; closed Mon.

TELFAIR MUSEUM OF ART
121 Barnard St.
(912) 790-8827
www.telfair.org

The Telfair is the oldest art museum in the South. Its permanent collection of paintings, prints, sculpture, and decorative arts is housed in a mansion designed by English architect William Jay for Alexander Telfair, son of Georgia governor Edward Telfair. The family lived here until 1875.

Among the museum's holdings are paintings by Childe Hassam, Frederick Frieseke, and Gari Melchers, along with Robert Henri, George Bellows, and George Luks. The museum also has a decorative arts collection that includes American and European objects from 1790 to 1840, including a rare Philadelphia suite of maple furniture, a secretary-bookcase commissioned from Duncan Phyfe of New York, and a dining table ordered from Thomas Cook of Philadelphia.

The Telfair is open from 10 a.m. to 5 p.m. Mon, Wed, Fri, and Sat; 10 a.m. to 8 p.m. on Thurs; and noon to 5 p.m. on Sun. The museum is closed Tues. Cost is $12 for adults, $8 for seniors, $5 for college students, and $4 for children ages 5 to 12. Children younger than age 5 are admitted free. Chatham County residents are admitted free on Sun, but the regular rates apply to all others. Local governments or the museum periodically sponsor free admission on selected days.

Islands

OATLAND ISLAND EDUCATION CENTER
Oatland Island NO.
711 Sandtown Rd.
(912) 898-3980
www.oatlandisland.org

A visit to Oatland gives you a good idea of what Georgia's first European settlers might have seen when they landed in 1733. Walk the 1.75-mile trail through the center's 75-acre forest of oaks, pines, and magnolias, and you'll encounter enclosures providing natural settings for animals native to the state: shorebirds, alligators, panthers, birds of prey, white-tailed deer, black bears, timber wolves, and bison. The enclosures are large and wooded, and the inhabitants are often hard to spot, but getting a look at them in their environment is worth the effort. The trail leads you to the Heritage Homesite area, where two log cabins (built in 1835, moved to Oatland, and restored there) convey a feeling for life on the farm during pioneer days. Another Oatland feature is a small barnyard where youngsters can see and feed farm animals. Be sure to check out the Wolf

Wilderness Exhibit where you can view, first-hand, a pack of five wolves!

Although Oatland's main focus is on teaching students from local and out-of-county public and private schools, it is open to the public from 10 a.m. to 4 p.m. every day of the week. Guests can remain on the grounds until 4:30 p.m. Oatland hosts special events on selected Sat, such as its annual Harvest Festival, The Sheep Shearing Festival, , and the Halloween Hike (see our Annual Events and Festivals chapter). Admission to Oatland is $5 for adults and $3 for children (ages 4 to 17), and seniors age 65 and older, and active military also pay $3. Children under the age of 4 are admitted free. Sandtown Road runs south off Islands Expressway 4 miles east of Historic Downtown. The tour of the center's animal habitats is self-guided and takes about 90 minutes.

OLD FORT JACKSON
1 Fort Jackson Rd.
(912) 232-3945
www.chsgeorgia.org
Georgia's oldest standing brick fortification perches right on the banks of the Savannah River—built there so its guns could fire on any vessel coming into Savannah—and chances are good you'll get an up-close view of an oceangoing ship during your visit. This is a great place to pose for personal pictures and then walk on the parapet of the fort and investigate the structure's many nooks and crannies. Two powder magazines and most of the casemates are open to the public, and they contain displays of weaponry and tools used at the fort and artifacts from the CSS *Georgia*, a Confederate ironclad whose remains lay on the river bottom a few hundred feet away. Inspect 11 cannons. The 9-inch Dahlgren cannon is the largest

functional piece of Civil War–era heavy artillery in the United States. Cannon-firing programs are presented daily from June 15 through Aug 15; call for more information.

For a thorough rundown on the history of the fort, watch the 15-minute film that's shown in one of the powder magazines. The fort is not on an island, but we've placed it in this section because it's 3 miles from the Historic Downtown on the way to the eastside islands. To get there, take President Street Extension (also known as Islands Expressway) east to the red, white, and blue Fort Jackson sign; then turn left onto Woodcock Road and follow the brown signs to the fort. The fort is open from 9 a.m. to 5 p.m. seven days a week, but it is closed on Thanksgiving, Christmas, and New Year's Day.

Southside/Midtown

BETHESDA HOME FOR BOYS
9520 Ferguson Ave.
(912) 351-2005
www.bethesdaforboys.org
Bethesda, America's oldest children's home, reposes on 600 oak-filled acres overlooking the Moon River (yes, that Moon River, the one made famous in the song by Henry Mancini and Savannahian Johnny Mercer). You can stroll or ride around the well-kept grounds of the main campus and visit the Bethesda museum and chapel, but the home's administrators ask that you report to the office after you arrive so that they know you're there. The museum—located in what was once the dining room of Burroughs Cottage, which was built in 1883 and is the oldest standing building at Bethesda—contains documents and artifacts pertaining to the history of the home and of coastal Georgia. Whitefield Chapel was completed in 1925 and is named for George Whitefield,

⊙ Close-up

Wormsloe Historic Site

You'll be amazed and astounded when you drive up to this magnificent attraction. After driving under a large masonry arch at the entrance to Wormsloe, you'll travel down an "avenue of oaks," a wide, crushed-stone road lined with majestic live oak trees. After 1.25 miles, the road narrows to a walking trail. At this point, you'll find a parking lot and the Wormsloe museum. Discover the last architectural remnant of the Oglethorpe era in Savannah at **Wormsloe Historic Site** (Isle of Hope, 7601 Skidaway Rd., 912-353-3023; www.gastateparks.org), which is at the end of Skidaway Road on the doorstep of the Isle of Hope, about 10 miles south of the Historic Downtown.

Continue on foot down the trail about 0.25 mile, and you'll be looking at the remains of a fortified house where construction was started in 1739 during the 10-year span James Edward Oglethorpe spent founding and nurturing the colony of Georgia (see our History chapter). The builder and owner of the house—a physician, carpenter, and surveyor named Noble Jones—came to the new colony in 1733 with Oglethorpe and the first boatload of settlers. Three years later, Jones leased 500 acres from the Trustees of Georgia, land that would be part of a plantation he called Wormslow. The name was changed to Wormsloe in the mid-1800s by his great-grandson, and the plantation eventually grew to cover nearly 900 acres. Jones's descendants donated 822 of those acres to the Nature Conservancy in 1972, and the property was transferred to the state of Georgia, which manages the site via the Parks and Historic Sites Division of the Department of Natural Resources.

The house Jones completed in the mid-1740s was a five-room, one-and-one-half-story dwelling built into a fort-like rectangular wall intended to protect its inhabitants from attack by the Spanish. The house and wall were made of tabby, a concoction of oyster shells, lime, and sand mixed with water. You can see parts of the foundation of the house and large portions of the wall. Other points of interest at Wormsloe are the museum and theater, where you can learn more about the site and the early days of the colony; a stone monument marking the first Jones family burial plot; nature trails; and the Colonial Life Area, which contains re-creations of outbuildings characteristic of Wormsloe's early period. This area is also the site of living-history demonstrations and programs presented during special events (see our Annual Events and Festivals chapter).

During your drive down the avenue of oaks, you may notice an elegant, two-story frame house on the eastern side of the road. This structure was built in 1828 and is home to the ninth generation of Jones's descendants; it is closed to the public. Wormsloe is open from 9 a.m. to 5 p.m. Tues through Sat and from 2 to 5:30 p.m. on Sun. Admission is from $2.50 to $5. This site is operated as part of Georgia's state parks system.

After you visit Wormsloe, take a few minutes to drive through nearby Isle of Hope, a community of narrow streets and beautifully preserved houses. Turn right after leaving Wormsloe, and you'll be on Parkersburg Road, which meanders through Isle of Hope until it reaches Bluff Drive, one of the prettiest streets in the Savannah area. A jaunt down Bluff Drive, which runs alongside the picturesque Skidaway River, is worth the time it will take to make this short detour. (For more on Isle of Hope, see our Relocation & Real Estate chapter.)

one of the home's founders. It's a reproduction of Whitefield's church in England, and with its straight-back wooden pews, brick floor, and airy interior, the chapel is a small but beautiful place in which to spend a few moments in meditation. The chapel is open year-round; museum hours are from 9 a.m. to 5 p.m. Mon through Fri. There's no admission but donations are accepted.

SAVANNAH AREA COUNCIL OF GARDEN CLUBS, INC.
1388 Eisenhower Dr.
(912) 355-3883
See more than 900 varieties of trees, shrubs, and flowering plants when you visit this Savannah Area Council of Garden Clubs project on the Southside. The clubs maintain 10 acres of gardens featuring roses, perennials, herbs, and vegetables, and separate gardens devoted to flowering plants that bloom during the different seasons of the year. There's also a garden for plants such as ferns that grow best in spots that don't get much sunshine. Some of the plants are labeled, so neophyte gardeners will be able to tell what they're looking at. A tabby walkway meanders through the gardens, and a small pond and a nature walk add to the ambience of this spot, which is nestled in a fairly well-developed part of town. The garden center is headquartered in an 1840s-era farmhouse that was moved to the Southside from a downtown location in 1991. The center and gardens are on Eisenhower Drive at its intersection with Sallie Mood Drive. Hours are from sunup to sundown seven days a week. Admission is free, but donations are appreciated. Call ahead for info on upcoming events or to schedule a private function.

i Savannah's "Queen of Southern Cuisine," Paula Deen, and her husband, Michael Groover, were wed in 2004 at Bethesda Home's Whitefield Chapel in a highly publicized ceremony. The airing of the wedding on the Food Network brought additional fame to the tiny chapel (and to the happy couple), which was built in 1925 to serve the school's students. An ornate stained-glass window adorns the chapel's altar, adding to the reverent ambience.

West Chatham

BAMBOO FARM AND COASTAL GARDENS
2 Canebrake Rd.
(912) 921-5460
Called the Bamboo Farm through the years by Savannahians because of the groves of the tropical plant grown there, the facility has a large collection of daylilies, a xeriscape garden, a cottage garden, and bamboo, of course—140 varieties of it. The bamboo collection is the largest in the United States open for viewing by the public, and there's also a grove of giant timber bamboo—the reason the farm was purchased for the U.S. Department of Agriculture in 1918. The bamboo grove, where stalks can reach a height of more than 70 feet and a diameter of 6 inches, originated with three seedlings planted on the site in 1890; 25 years later, it attracted the attention of plant explorer David Fairchild, who bought the 46-acre farm where the bamboo grew and donated it to the government. The farm offers a self-guided walking tour that will take you to (among other botanical treasures) the bamboo collection and grove, beds of ornamental and turf grasses, an experimental grove of different species of banana tree, a collection

of crape myrtle trees that's probably the largest in coastal Georgia, and a variety of other interesting trees.

The Bamboo Farm and Coastal Gardens holds a number of special events throughout the year, most of which require reservations, and makes available a 650-seat, open-air pavilion and a 100-seat conference hall. The farm is open from 8 a.m. to 5 p.m. Mon through Fri, from 10 a.m. to 5 p.m. on Sat, and from noon until 5 p.m. on Sun. Admission is free, and donations are accepted. The facility is on US 17, about 13 miles south of the Historic Downtown.

MIGHTY EIGHTH AIR FORCE HERITAGE MUSEUM
175 Bourne Ave., Pooler
(912) 748-8888
www.mightyeighth.org

It's not unusual for veterans of World War II aerial combat to leave this museum's Mission Experience exhibit with tears in their eyes. This re-creation of an Eighth Air Force bombing mission brings back vivid memories to those who flew over Europe—recollections of heavily defended targets, stricken aircraft, and fallen comrades. The panoramic, eight-screen theater and its B-17 flight are a featured part of the 90,000-square-foot museum in Pooler near the intersection of I-95 and US 80 (exit 102 from I-95).

Besides the Mission Experience, the museum's exhibit area contains presentations featuring more than 15 units that were part of the Eighth; a mural and a scale model depicting a World War II bomber base in England; areas dealing with escape and evasion, prisoners of war, and the contributions of African-American airmen; a diorama portraying the raids on the Ploesti oil fields; a

PT-17 Stearman trainer and a Messerschmitt Komet rocket plane on static display; and several other theaters. There's also a research library stocked with books pertaining to aviation and air warfare, an art gallery, Memorial Gardens, a chapel, store, and restaurant. The museum is open from 9 a.m. until 5 p.m. daily except for New Year's Day, Easter, Thanksgiving, and Christmas. Admission to the exhibit area is $10 for adults and teens and $6 for children ages 6 to 12, with those younger than age 6 admitted free. There are discounts for members of the military, senior citizens, and groups of 20 or more. The library is open from 10 a.m. to noon and from 1 to 4 p.m. Mon through Fri.

SAVANNAH-OGEECHEE CANAL MUSEUM AND NATURE CENTER
681 Fort Argyle Rd.
(912) 748-8068
www.savannahogeecheecanal.com

The Savannah-Ogeechee Canal, which played a role in the commercial development of Savannah during the 1800s, lay virtually forgotten for a century until a group of Chatham Countians reclaimed a third of it from the tangle of foliage that had grown over it. These volunteers started their work in 1992, and now, organized as the Savannah-Ogeechee Canal Society, they oversee the continued development of the waterway as a historic and recreational area.

You can get a splendid idea of what the southern portion of the canal was like by visiting the society's museum and 184-acre nature center, which is on Fort Argyle Road (better known as SR 204), a little more than 2 miles west of exit 94 off I-95. The museum, a converted bungalow, has two exhibit rooms, one depicting the history of the canal and another displaying reptiles and amphibians that inhabit the area the waterway runs through.

Within view of the museum is Lock 5, which is on a trail you can follow for 0.4 mile along the canal south to Lock 6 and the Ogeechee River; this trail is the towpath that horses and mules trod while pulling barges more than 100 years ago. The Tow Path is one of several trails you can walk while at the nature center. The museum and nature center are open from 9 a.m. to 5 p.m. each day of the year. Admission is $2 for adults and $1 for students and senior citizens; children age 5 and younger are admitted free.

SAVANNAH CELEBRITY

Local characters and tales of eccentricity and crime, food addictions, and, toward the other extreme, home cooking have all been a healthy boost to Savannah tourism. Fans have trekked to the city to catch a glimpse at the city's celebrities and/or their hangouts, and the tourism industry has responded with specialty tours, souvenirs, classes, and books (like this one).

The tales of scandal and crime refer to John Berendt's nonfiction best seller, *Midnight in the Garden of Good and Evil*, published in 1994. Set in Savannah, it tells a series of tales about Savannah's local and oftentimes crazy characters and their peculiarities, and focuses mainly on a shooting and the subsequent series of trials.

The home cooking referenced is found on the Food Network and also downtown in Paula Deen's restaurant (and empire), constructed out of fried chicken, cheese biscuits, and several thousand pounds of butter, her favorite ingredient. In less than 20 years, Deen has gone from being a struggling, newly divorced housewife to a queen of media, resulting in an earned business empire that includes her two Food Network television programs, two restaurants, a growing library of cookbooks, her own magazine, a cooking school, and a line of products ranging from pots and pans to furniture.

In 2009, the small screen turned to a different subject, Ruby Gettinger, a Savannahian who once weighed 700 pounds and who has come public with her story of food addiction and weight loss. Now completing its fourth season, Ruby has captured the hearts of fans of the Style Network with her show *Ruby*, about her journey to weight loss and newfound personal revelations. Her weight loss of more than 350 pounds (as of 2010) has inspired many to replicate her journey in their own lives. The show's opening segment always showcases Savannah's most striking settings.

While all three of these diverse phenomena have drawn tourists to Savannah, there's been a steady trail of them since the 1990s when Berendt's novel kicked off the on-screen and print phenomena. Hotels have sprung up in places that were once derelict, and Savannahians can hardly wait to see who'll be discovered next!

COOKING UP A FORTUNE

Paula Deen has built a national reputation and business empire on her homestyle cooking skills and capricious personality. She's taken Savannah along with her for the ride. Tourists make a beeline for her two Savannah restaurants, the tour that focuses on her career, and shops that sell her cookbooks, gift items, even her magazine. And, as the Next Big Thing after the *Midnight* phenomenon, it is appropriate that *Midnight* author John Berendt had a role in her discovery and subsequent success. He was fond of Deen's cooking, and he wrote the introduction for her first professionally published cookbook back in 1998, when his own book was still the center of attention in Savannah.

The Paula Deen story is a rags-to-riches tale that reads like the script for a sappy TV movie—except that it's true. The mother of two sons, she found herself divorced and unemployed in 1989. Lacking other job skills, she fell back on the Southern cooking techniques she had learned in her grandmother's kitchen.

She started small, as the Bag Lady. Assisted by her sons, she packaged bag lunches for office workers in the downtown area. The next step in the climb was her own restaurant, run out of a nice but nondescript motel on Savannah's Southside, the section of town known for its strip shopping centers, suburbs, and adjacent military base. As she continued working her way up the ladder of the food business, she opened **The Lady and Sons Restaurant** in downtown Savannah, right in the middle of both the local business district and Savannah's tourist hub. From the very first day, her restaurants drew crowds, and that meant lines at the buffet. It was a simple restaurant with some gimmicks apart from the buffet. The waitresses were performers. As you slurped a mixture of honey and butter that drenched Deen's hot biscuits, a waitress would appear with a pitcher of tea and as she poured your refill, she would also break into song. The lunch hour downtown that started out as a lot of good eating and innocent fun was about to explode. That was the day Paula's tiny establishment that had evolved from a paper bag was named the number-one place to eat in the country by USA Today. Even if things had stopped right there, the Deen story would have been an inspiring entrepreneurial tale.

The lines grew longer every day, first with businessmen and later tourists jostling to get platefuls of fried chicken, collards, squash casserole, hoecakes, cheese biscuits, and other comfort food. She was making money and had built a sterling reputation for the quality of her food. She could have stayed a purely Savannah success story—but bigger things beckoned.

Deen had some successful appearances on a television shopping network, hawking her book and a line of seasonings. But her big break came with the advent of a regular show on the Food Network, a cable channel for foodies. Suddenly, Paula Deen went from being a good cook with a local following to a celebrity chef with a national following. And there was more to come on the heels of the program Paula's Home Cooking.

Success prompted Deen to move her restaurant a few blocks to a historic building she purchased and renovated, where she could serve bigger crowds and house more business enterprises. Her national fan following has followed her to Savannah, where it keeps her already-crowded The Lady and Sons Restaurant packed. Now there's another TV program, Paula's Party, filmed at **Uncle Bubba's Oyster House.**

Those business enterprises keep coming. Deen understands marketing across various media—she's on TV, in cookbooks, in her own magazine, at personal appearances. You'll even find her in the movies, where she had a small part in Elizabethtown, starring Orlando Bloom.

Maybe you are visiting Savannah in search of all things Paula, in which case we can steer you to the things that will feed your fascination. Maybe you don't have cable television and don't follow the celebrity chef scene—we can still steer you to some of the best country/Southern dishes in creation, well, except for my own Mama's, and that's a close tie. Read on for details on the Deen scene. Here's to a start, appropriately enough, with the food.

THE LADY AND SONS
102 West Congress St.
(912) 233-2600
www.theladyandsons.com
www.pauladeen.com
This is Deen's flagship restaurant, and the one essential, cannot-miss stop for any serious Deen fan. You'll find it described in more detail in our Restaurants chapter. We will warn you that the place is very popular and requires some planning ahead. They start taking names for lunch seating at 9:30 a.m. You must get your name on a waiting list in person at the hostess station at the restaurant on Congress Street. You cannot make phone or online reservations (except for groups). Lunch is served from 11 a.m. to 5 p.m. Mon through Sat; dinner starts promptly at 5 p.m. Sun hours are 11 a.m. to 5 p.m. only (lunch buffet only). If, however, you get your name on the list, you do get seated. And as time has passed, the staff has learned better how to cope with the steady stream of fans. After all these years, the buffet is still great and packed with steaming hot favorites: fried chicken, mashed potatoes, green beans, corn, sweet potatoes, and the list goes on and on. Parking is available in the nearby parking garages; Whitaker Street is the most convenient.

UNCLE BUBBA'S OYSTER HOUSE
104 Bryan Woods Rd.
(912) 897-6101
www.unclebubbas.com
This is the second restaurant with which Deen is affiliated, named for her brother and

launched after it became obvious the Lady's star was rising. If you can't get a table downtown, this is the next best thing to sampling her food and possibly, catching a glimpse of Paula. Her brother, Earl (called "Bubba") will more than likely greet you at the front door during lunch hours, but his schedule is almost as busy as hers. When he's there, he'll shake your hand and tell you how much he appreciates your patronage. The focus here is seafood, although a selection of Deen's country cooking is also available. Read more under Uncle Bubba's entry in our Restaurants chapter. This restaurant serves as the lunch location in the Paula Deen Tour.

THE PAULA DEEN TOUR
Old Savannah Tours
514 Berrien St.
(912) 234-8128
www.oldsavannahtours.com
This highly specialized tour will thrill Paula Deen fanatics, and it won't necessarily bore indulgent spouses and family members either. But if you haven't visited Savannah before and you aren't passionate about this celebrity cook, take another tour. For one thing, it is $49 for adults and $25 for ages 12 and under, a whopping price by local standards (but that's misleading, because it also includes a meal and souvenirs). For another thing, this tour can last from two to four hours, which (even if it does include lunch) takes a big bite out of a day.

The Deen tour cashes in on celebrity, just like similar theme tours cashed in on the popularity of *Midnight*. The difference is, anyone could launch a *Midnight* tour (and plenty did, and still do). But there is only one Deen tour, because the process virtually requires her blessing.

The tour passes through the Historic District and goes by places that were prominent in the development of Deen's career. Stops also include shops Deen recommends (usually food related), lunch at Uncle Bubba's Oyster House, and a trip to the grounds of Bethesda Home for Boys, the historic orphanage whose grounds were the scene of Deen's televised wedding. Another local family-owned food business, Byrd Cookie Company (producers of Savannah's well-known benne wafers and other treats) is included on the tour except on Sat, when it is closed in deference to the Seventh Day Adventist faith of the family behind it.

One of the prize benefits of the tour is a VIP seating pass to the Lady and Sons, Deen's flagship restaurant. The tour's pass lets participants bypass the usual wait, either for dinner that night or later in their visit.

There's no guarantee you'll meet Paula Deen on the tour (in fact, you probably won't, although it does happen), but it's not unusual to meet one of her two sons or her brother, Earl Hiers (Uncle Bubba). Call for times and be sure to reserve a seat by phone or online.

i Savannah cannot lay claim to the origins of celebrity cook Paula Deen's thick Southern drawl, so prominently showcased on her Food Network program. She is originally from Albany, Georgia. In Savannah, we pronounce Albany much the same way a New Yorker would pronounce Albany. But a native of Albany, Georgia, will tell you he or she is from "AWL-benny."

COOKING WITH PAULA DEEN MAGAZINE
Hoffman Media
1900 International Park Dr., Suite #50
Birmingham, Alabama 35243
www.pauladeenmagazine.com
If Martha Stewart has her own cooking and lifestyle magazine, why not Paula Deen? The publisher behind the glossy magazine is Hoffman Media, which also publishes two other food-oriented periodicals, *Taste of the South* and *Southern Lady*. The magazine has a central core of recipes, flanked at the beginning and end of the magazine by photo spreads and feature stories on Deen, Savannah, and other places in her life.

Meanwhile, if you want more Deen reading material, she has seven cookbooks in print already, along with what is described as a biography on her journey from troubled homemaker to successful entrepreneur, *It Ain't All About the Cookin'.* Also, there's a free newsletter you can sign up for at www.the ladyandsons.com.

Still haven't had your fill of this celebrity cook? She's marketing a line of sauces and mixes, aprons, furniture, cookware, magnets, even a line of coffee under her husband's name, Captain Michael's Coffee. You can buy at the store in her restaurants or via her website.

MIDNIGHT IN SAVANNAH

Although Savannah's *Midnight in the Garden of Good and Evil* phenomenon is not as all-consuming as it once was, it is still a viable tourism force. Spending 216 weeks on the *New York Times* best-seller list, Berendt's work yielded an insurmountable financial windfall for the city. With *Midnight*'s curiously appealing set of character sketches loosely held together by a lurid murder case, the

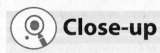

Close-up

Good Fortune for Lovers of "the Book"

"Bonaventure" means "good fortune," which may strike you as a strange name for a graveyard. But once you visit this serenely beautiful place, chances are the name will seem more appropriate. **Bonaventure Cemetery** plays a prominent role in John Berendt's *Midnight in the Garden of Good and Evil*. It is here in this lush Victorian graveyard that the book's narrator drinks martinis and gets his introductory course on Savannah society (although alcohol is prohibited in the cemetery). The massive cemetery stands under vast canopies of moss-draped shade where live oaks, thick with age, stand guard by row upon row of elegant statuary and headstones, culminating in a scenic waterfront view. The graves made famous in the book include the Aiken family plot. Here, the parents of Pulitzer Prize–winning poet **Conrad Aiken**—killed in a murder-suicide—are buried. Conrad Aiken's own grave, marked by a bench engraved with poetry, stands alongside. Not too far away, you'll spot the graves of famed Savannah lyricist **Johnny Mercer** and his wife, Ginger.

This is the culminating point for the guided tours of Book sites. If you happen to be a nonfan of the Book, and you were swept along by a fervent spouse or group, hang in there. The 160-acre graveyard is well worth seeing in its own right.

Bonaventure was once an elegant plantation, but the grand home burned down more than once. Local folklore has it that the roof caught fire during a dinner party, and the guests finished the meal outdoors by the light of the burning house. If you are looking for ghost stories, there's a tale that you can still hear the revelry and breaking glass of that party at certain times. You'll find these tales repeated in the Book. The property became a cemetery in the 1800s and was put into city hands in 1907. It is still an active cemetery with an occasional burial, but the few remaining spaces are generally taken—don't get attached to the place.

Many important figures from the history of Georgia and the nation are buried here. There's **Noble Jones,** who arrived with James Oglethorpe at the beginning of the colony; several members of Georgia's **Liberty Boys;** and a number of prominent physicians, including **Brodie Herndon,** chief surgeon of hospitals for the Confederacy and the first doctor to perform a Caesarean operation in the United States. **John Walz,** sculptor of many of the impressive funerary statues in Bonaventure and other local cemeteries, is buried here. Ironically, there is no headstone at his grave.

New York author created a phenomenon in the tourist world. His work gave rise to a plethora of themed-guided tours and silly souvenirs, and at the height of its popularity, *Midnight in the Garden of Good and Evil* created enough of a furor to drive a statue out of a graveyard and make a drag queen into a local celeb.

Midnight in the Garden of Good and Evil deals with homosexuality, murder, voodoo, weird social customs, and charismatic con men—not necessarily the most flattering portrayal imaginable. However, it was eagerly embraced by the local populace as well as the reading public.

If you want to visit Bonaventure Cemetery without a tour, here are some fairly detailed instructions. How you get there depends, of course, on where you start. Because we reasoned most visitors would be starting from the Historic Downtown, we launch our trek at the intersection of Bull and Liberty Streets, right beside the Hilton Savannah DeSoto Hotel. Set your trip odometer there; you have about 3.5 miles to go. Liberty Street is a major east-west thoroughfare downtown. Follow it east. You'll quickly leave the Historic District and pass through areas that include low-income housing and small industry. Don't be distracted by the large cemetery to your left shortly after you leave downtown—that's Hillcrest. The road forks just beyond that, so bear right. It will be fairly obvious in doing so that you are staying on the same road. The road assumes different names as you travel—from Liberty to Wheaton to Skidaway.

Immediately past a complex five-way intersection, you'll see the only real turn you'll make, a left onto 36th Street. It's identified by a street sign hanging between double traffic lights, and there's a turn arrow to help you make the turn in the increasingly heavy traffic you'll encounter. A McDonald's stands on the right just past this intersection; if you go past it, you've missed the turn. Just after you get on it, 36th Street merges into Bonaventure Road so seamlessly you probably won't even notice. Bonaventure Road is a narrow, two-lane road that winds through neat, modest housing and is lined by massive trees that are literally on the edge of the road. Pay attention!

In just under a mile, where the road curves away to the right, you'll see the cemetery gates. Don't be distracted if a Forest Lawn Cemetery billboard is still in place in the vicinity. The sign on the gate identifies Bonaventure. There's a large, framed map just inside the entrance, but it gives locations by grave site number, not name. Instead, depend on the small wooden signposts stationed along the lanes between the plots. Book fans are looking for the sign marked Aiken and the nearby Mercer. The wooden marker signs are easy to follow.

Park with care, as there is a lot of tour-bus traffic. There's a small lot behind the office building just inside the gates if you are the hiking kind; there's also a grassy parking area for a few cars that's near the water and not far from the Aiken plot. Although we haven't heard of any trouble, it's an isolated spot between tours, so it's probably a good idea to lock your car and bring a friend.

Perhaps the locals just want their 15 minutes of fame, which *Midnight in the Garden of Good and Evil* certainly gives to Savannah and its residents. It seems that normally reticent people are willing to put up with the public airing of any amount of dirty laundry as long as it brings Clint Eastwood to town to film a movie about it.

The real answer, however, probably lies deep within a cash register. The city has discovered that the coattails of a best seller with a fan following are a comfortable and profitable place to ride.

There are still a few opportunities for the Book fans to sample in person what they've experienced in print. One sure sign that the phenomenon is well past its peak, however, is this—the prices on the guided tours have not gone up. The whole phenomenon might have had longer legs if the movie version had been more successful.

For the duration, we'll follow local practice and continue to call Berendt's novel, the Book—a shorthand we have all adopted in self-defense, since an eight-word title takes a while to say in a Southern drawl, and locals have trouble pronouncing Berendt's name.

A Little Background

Midnight in the Garden of Good and Evil was published in January 1994. Berendt, a columnist and former editor at *Esquire,* had spent several years living off and on in Savannah, collecting the stories that make up the Book. The unifying thread of the Book is the four murder trials that followed the fatal shooting of a young man.

Random House quickly had a hit on its hands. The Book hit the *New York Times* bestseller list in March 1994 and pretty much stayed there for four years.

Ah, but is the Book as true as it claims? That brings to mind what the character Huck Finn had to say about the Tom Sawyer story: that it was "mostly true but with some stretchers." The time lines, for example, are a little out of sync, and the slant of the stories can still spark debate among locals. Several of the names of central figures are pseudonyms, and that told-as-true tale about the dead cat, the dinner party, and the stomach pump is a classic urban legend—consider it modern folklore.

With book sales so brisk and a larger-than-life cast of characters on the page, it was inevitable that Hollywood would go gardening. In May 1996, director Clint Eastwood began filming the screen version with Kevin Spacey in the Williams role, John Cusack as Berendt, and the Lady Chablis (the aforementioned drag queen) as the Lady Chablis. The story got a revision for the screen, and the city got an out-of-season face-lift, as the squares involved in the shooting were decked out in Christmas greenery in a month that qualifies as full summer in Savannah.

So now fans of the Book have had a refresher course, and those who haven't read it at least have an idea of what we are talking about. Let's move on to how visitors to Savannah can walk inside Berendt's pages.

Tours

If you want to cover a lot of Book territory relatively quickly, the tour buses are your best bet. We're describing them in plural here because they offer essentially the same thing: a two- to two-and-one-half-hour tour that is mainly a drive-by of important sites from the Book, capped off with a cemetery visit. Be aware that tours have a tendency to run longer than advertised, so allow for plenty of time. All tours require reservations, which can be made by phone. If this is an important event for you, call well in advance—while these tours aren't as popular as they once were, you can never tell. The various tour companies take the major credit cards, but because tour drivers usually don't handle anything other than cash transactions, ask where you'll pay if you plan to use a credit card—it might affect which of the pickup locations you specify.

Tours pick up at the **Savannah Visitor Information Center,** 301 Martin Luther King Jr. Blvd., which has reasonably ample parking. Park your car (take valuables with you, or take a risk) and look for the large parking slots near the center's front door, marked with signs identifying the tour company that uses that spot—that's where you'll board. Major downtown hotels and some bed-and-breakfasts in the Historic Downtown also serve as pickup locations. Get details when you make your reservations.

Remember that Book-related tours are just part of a wider tour menu offered by each company. Others include ghost tours, walking tours, Civil War–themed tours, carriage tours, Savannah history tours, and the like. (See our Attractions chapter for more on other types of guided tours.) The city of Savannah requires that tour guides pass a test and hold a license. On a typical tour, you'll drive by **Mercer House,** the mansion that was the site of the Book's fatal shooting; **Club One,** performance venue for the Lady Chablis (see our Nightlife chapter for details); various homes where lawyer and professional partier Joe Odom stayed, often without the owners' knowledge; the jail where Williams was held (now replaced by a structure outside town); the modern county courthouse where the first three trials were held; the ornate old federal courthouse that stands in for it in the movie version; and so on. The walking versions can't range far enough to include **Bonaventure Cemetery,** so choose another walking tour and opt for wheels if you are a Book fan—it just isn't the same without the graveyard.

Along the way, you'll get a chance to see the city's more conventional attractions as well, and chances are the tour guide will throw in a few comments about those. The highlight of all the tours is a visit to Bonaventure Cemetery, which you can read about elsewhere in this chapter. To connect with a Book tour, consult our tour listings in the Attractions chapter.

Seeing it on Your Own

The following are some tips on what you can see solo with regards to the Book. There's no shortage of maps in Savannah (hardly surprising in a city with a thriving tourism industry), and there's a good one in this very book. With a copy of the Book in hand and the map of the Historic Downtown you'll find at the front of our guide, you can find major Book sites such as Monterey Square.

Easily Accessed Sites

Now that you have a map, we'll list a few of the most easily found sites. We'll start with two general outdoor sites, where you can stand on the sidewalk and gaze, then move on to places you can actually get into.

MONTEREY SQUARE
400 block of Bull St., bounded by Taylor and Gordon Streets
This square is home to many of the central events in the Book, but it's worth a good look on its own merits. The massive central monument to Polish Count Casmir Pulaski, a hero of the American Revolution, has finally been returned to its pedestal, after a seemingly endless delay during its restoration. The absence was so long that when the movie of *Midnight* was filming on location, prop makers had to fake a version of the monument.

THE MERCER WILLIAMS HOUSE MUSEUM
429 Bull St.
(912) 236-6352, (877) 430-6352
www.mercerhouse.com

This magnificent mansion looks out on the square from Bull Street. This is where the late Jim Williams lived and is now home to his sister. It remains a private residence, so respect the owners and stay outside the gates unless you are on a prearranged tour. The Mercer House was designed by New York architect John S. Norris for Gen. Hugh W. Mercer, great-grandfather of Johnny Mercer. Construction of the house began in 1860, was interrupted by the Civil War, and was later completed, circa 1868, by the new owner, John Wilder. In 1969, Williams, one of Savannah's earliest and most dedicated private restorationists, bought the then-vacant house and began a two-year restoration. This house is one of the more than 50 houses Mr. Williams saved during his 30-year career in historic restoration in Savannah and the Lowcountry. Previously open only to benefit local historic and charitable organizations, the house has reopened to the public for the first time since its restoration was completed. Tickets for tours of the house are available online. Admission is $12.50 for adults and $8 for students. See the Close-up in our Attractions chapter for details. Mercer House had claims to fame well before Williams's misfortunes. While lyricist Johnny Mercer ("Moon River," "That Old Black Magic," etc.) never lived there, he had close family ties to it.

Jackie Kennedy Onassis once showed up to tour it, and the Book claims she concluded that tour with a request for directions to the nearest Burger King. (It's a cute story, true or not, and if you believe it and want to follow in the footsteps of the rich and famous, the nearest Burger King is in the 600 block of Martin Luther King Jr. Boulevard.) There's a Carriage House behind Mercer House that is open Mon through Fri 10 a.m.

to 4:30 p.m.; Sat 10 a.m. to 5 p.m.; and Sun 10:30 a.m. to 4 p.m.

INTERSECTION OF BULL AND GASTON STREETS

Remember, the Book maintains nothing counts unless it's North of Gaston Street (NOGS, for short). This is where Bull Street hits that great divide. The sweeping white brick building on the western side of Bull is **Armstrong House,** which crops up in the book several times, most prominently as the offices of the lawyer who handled Williams's defense. On the eastern side you'll see the **Oglethorpe Club,** which also turns up in said Book. This is the city's most exclusive private club, with rigid membership requirements that include white skin, blue blood, and money that's yellowed with age.

CLARY'S CAFE
404 Abercorn St.
(912) 233-0402
Clary's was the setting where Berendt first encountered the Luther Driggers character, who tried to make goldfish glow and enjoyed toting about a bottle of poison. At the time, Clary's was a drugstore with a lunch counter. The drugstore is long gone, but the restaurant has grown. (Read more about it in our Restaurants chapter.) Clary's has opened a second location farther south in Midtown, but there's no Book connection.

CLUB ONE JEFFERSON
1 Jefferson St.
(912) 232-0200
The Lady Chablis performs in the drag show here periodically. For more details, check out the Close-up in our Nightlife chapter.

TELFAIR MUSEUM OF ART
121 Barnard St.
(912) 232-1177
www.telfair.org

This local art museum is the new home for the *Bird Girl* statue pictured on the cover of the Book. The figure once stood guard over the Trosdal family plot in Bonaventure Cemetery, and neither the statue nor the Trosdals are in the print version of the story. Family members had the statue removed when Book tourists overran the family plot to pose for photos beside it. (By the way, photography is not allowed inside the Telfair, a common enough prohibition by museums.) The Telfair is worth a visit in its own right (see our Arts and Culture chapter). Admission costs are $15 for adults, $14 for seniors and veterans, and $5 for children (kindergarten to college), kids under the age of five get in free.

i If you are looking for artsy souvenirs at low prices, the Telfair Museum of Art has a limited selection of posters, postcards, and the like for sale at token prices. For something even cheaper (i.e., free), look for the postcard reproductions that SCAD uses to announce gallery openings. We've found them stacked for giveaway in the college galleries and downtown coffee shops and eateries.

Souvenirs

The variety of Book souvenirs is impressive. Here's a very partial list: a woven afghan featuring book scenes, bookmarks picturing one of Joe Odom's rubber checks, paintings of Mercer House, a video "tour" with interviews of some of the real-life characters, coffee mugs and jewelry featuring the *Bird Girl* figure, a limited-edition candle shaped

like the cover statue, postcards depicting the Lady Chablis, and miniature cookies in a tin patterned after the book cover. Several T-shirts are on the market.

We've listed a store that devotes a large percentage of its stock to Book items, but you can find the same stuff in any number of general gift shops along River Street and even in scattered suburban and mall stores. The only specific recommendation we make on these things concerns the cookies. If you want Byrd Cookie's Key Lime Coolers in the Byrd Girl commemorative tin ($10.95), check out our Shopping chapter. Byrd Cookie operates a gift shop as part of its bakery, and it stands to reason this would be the cheapest place to get the cookies. Besides, at Byrd's you can sample the Key Lime Cooler and the other flavors available.

"THE BOOK" GIFT SHOP
127 East Gordon St.
(912) 233-3867
www.midnightinsavannah.com

This shop occupies the garden floor (which is what we in Savannah call the ground floor of a building, topped by the parlor floor, followed by a second floor, which is really the third floor, and so on) of a building at Abercorn and Gordon Streets. Wander through several rooms to see a mix of Book souvenirs and general gifts. Stock includes shot glasses bearing the name of the Married Women's Card Club, which aptly illustrate the Southern idea of tackiness.

You'll find elements of a Book shrine along with the merchandise. The back room boasts some not-for-sale items such as a painting by Williams, a chair he once owned, a large collection of clippings about the phenomenon, and so on. Deborah Sullivan is the owner. The shop is open Mon through

Sat, 10 a.m. to 5 p.m.; and Sun, 12:30 to 4 p.m. Also, you'll find several tours that originate from the store. There's a new *Midnight* cookbook for $26.95 that is available at the store or by ordering online.

i Early in the Book, lawyer and confidence man Joe Odom describes the Georgia-Florida football game as one of only two high holidays in Savannah, the other being St. Patrick's Day. For the record, Georgia broke a seven-game losing streak in that important series in 1997 and stunned the odds makers with a 37 to 17 victory—exactly three weeks before the scheduled debut of the *Midnight* movie.

HOLLYWOOD IN SAVANNAH

Savannah has hosted at least 40 film or television projects since 1975, and it formalized the whole process by establishing a film liaison office at City Hall in 1995. The city endured a 10-year dry spell until 2010 when Robert Redford produced a Civil War period piece called, *The Conspirator*, and the Nicholas Sparks' novel, *The Last Song*, brought some big name stars to Tybee Island for four months of filming and production. That boost energized the city, and hopes are for more to come in the near future.

Some of those earlier productions have been among the most critically acclaimed movies of our day and all have starred the biggest names on the silver screen. Some have launched catchphrases into the lexicon of popular culture ("Life is like a box of chocolates . . .").

Examples of the outstanding ones include *Glory*, the historically based account of African-American soldiers in the Civil War that won three Oscars; *Forrest Gump*,

which claimed six Oscars and solidified Tom Hanks's superstar status; and *Roots*, which became the standard against which all miniseries are still measured, was filmed here in part. Going back even further, to 1962, when location shoots were rarer, the original *Cape Fear* was partially filmed here. City Hall and the downtown business district and Isle of Hope were on display. This original movie, since remade, featured Robert Mitchum at his creepiest.

If you want to experience some of Savannah's movie past in person, there's some interesting spots. Go to **Chippewa Square,** for example, where Bull Street flows around a statue of General Oglethorpe. Here is the filming site of the waiting-for-the-bus scene that was so crucial in *Forrest Gump*. Don't waste time looking for the bench—although Savannah's squares have plenty of real benches, that one was a movie prop. It was situated on the square's northern face, looking down Bull Street. Back in the movie's heyday, you could spot the occasional fan positioned there, hovering with his or her backside perched on empty air, "sitting" on the nonexistent bench for a Kodak moment.

i The first decade of this century hasn't seen any major movies made in Savannah. When movie stars are in town these days, chances are they are watching movies, not making them—the Savannah Film Festival, a project of the Savannah College of Art and Design, always draws a celebrity audience. See details in our Arts and Culture chapter.

The Legend of Bagger Vance had all the right ingredients for a mega hit: star director (Robert Redford), star actors (Will Smith, Matt

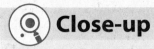 # Close-up

Savannah Filmography: 1975–2010

Note that accompanying dates are filming dates, not necessarily release dates.

2009–10: *The Last Song*

2009: *The Conspirator*

2000: *The Gift*

1999: *The Legend of Bagger Vance*

1998: *Forces of Nature; The General's Daughter*

1997: *The Gingerbread Man; Midnight in the Garden of Good and Evil; Claudine's Return*

1996: *Wild America*

1995: *Something to Talk About*

1994: *Now and Then*

1993: *Forrest Gump; Camilla*

1990: *Goldenboy; Love Crimes*

1989: *The Rose and the Jackal; Flight of the Intruder; Glory*

1988: *The Return of Swamp Thing; The Judas Project*

1987: *My Father, My Son; 1969; War Stories*

1986: *Pals*

1983: *Solomon Northup's Odyssey*

1981: *All My Children; Tales of Ordinary Madness*

1980: *The Slayer; White Death; Scared to Death; When the Circus Came to Town; Fear; East of Eden; Mother Seton*

1979: *Gold Bug; The Ordeal of Dr. Mudd; Orphan Train; Hopscotch; Carny*

1978: *The Double McGuffin*

1977: *The Lincoln Conspiracy*

1976: *Roots*

1975: *Gator*

Damon, etc.), and lovely sets and costumes from its Depression-era setting. As is so often the way with Hollywood, the film was only a moderate success.

At the moment, Savannah's biggest brush with movie fame is a producer. Savannahians know Stratton Leopold best as the native son who came back home a few years ago and relaunched his family's ice-cream parlor, not as a successful movie producer at home on such sets as *Mission Impossible 3* or the latest in the *Star Trek* franchise. That fact speaks well for both Savannah and Leopold.

LEOPOLD'S ICE CREAM
212 East Broughton St.
(912) 234-4442
www.leopoldsicecream.com

The Leopold brothers who launched this successful ice-cream parlor back in the day merit a photo display at the front of the shop. Stratton Leopold's successful and high-powered movie career is memorialized toward the back. Here you can see a movie camera, posters of the many films Leopold has been involved with, and a display case with trinkets and props from those films, including the famous "rabbit's foot" that Tom Cruise pursued so desperately in the latest and best of the *Mission Impossible* movies (it looks suspiciously like the vacuum tubes we use at the drive-thru at the bank.)

The real star here is the food—home-made and hand-dipped ice cream like that the parents of aging baby boomers courted over. Tutti-frutti is the version of local fame. The sandwiches are nothing to sneeze at, and you can get a real banana split or milk shake, too. The shop keeps late hours, so you can usually catch it open after a show at the nearby Lucas Theatre or other downtown outing.

This isn't the original location of the locally famous original, but walk through the door and you'd never know it. The latest Leopold saved the original fittings and has put them back into use.

ST. PATRICK'S DAY

You'll know it's March if you choose this month to arrive in Savannah. The flowers will be in full bloom, painting the town with blazing colors. Strolling locals will shed their winter coats in exchange for green sweaters. Irish tunes will ring from the walls of St. Vincent's Academy as the girls practice their salute to the upcoming St. Patrick's Day Grand Marshall. Sidewalks will be adorned with green and white souvenirs that spill out of shops proclaiming that the day is upon us. Closer to March 17 (St. Patrick's Day), fountains will turn to green, and the demeanor of Savannahians will turn from ho-hum to jovial. It's a time when the Irish Catholic community comes together, and those who aren't join in the festivities.

On the morn of St. Patrick's Day, even the most introverted will come out. Adorned with everything from "boingy" shamrocks to green beads, green and white buttons, and fake beards and moustaches, some celebrants even dye their dogs green. On St. Patrick's Day in Savannah, people eat green grits and drink green beer, which tends to make some of them feel a wee bit green the morning after. On St. Patrick's Day in Savannah, people give themselves over to a wonderful green giddiness that permeates the atmosphere. I'm convinced that you'll love it!

WHY ST. PATRICK'S DAY?

You might be wondering why St. Patrick's Day has evolved as the most festive day of the year in Savannah, and why a city of fewer than 150,000 people has ended up playing host to some 700,000 to close to a million revelers on that day.

These are valid questions—ones on which we can only speculate. It's not enough to say that a large segment of Savannah's population is, or has been, Irish or of Irish descent. That's true of lots of cities that don't make anywhere near the fuss over St. Patrick's Day as does Savannah.

Part of the reason for the popularity of the day might stem from the fact that it's been celebrated here for a long time, longer than in most American cities. According to the late William L. Fogarty, who wrote a

history of the local observance entitled *The Days We've Celebrated*, the first celebration here was in 1813 when the Hibernian Society, formed by Irish Protestants seeking to help their impoverished countrymen, held a private procession. The city's first public procession, which is recognized as Savannah's first St. Patrick's Day parade, was also held by the society and took place in 1824.

"Why and how this celebration could possibly have carried on these many years is perhaps one of the most fantastic mysteries of all," wrote Fogarty in 1980 as he attempted to answer questions regarding the parade's origin. "I don't know of anyone who could really give the actual reason . . . Perhaps the answer would be the 'Pride of the Irish' has sustained it."

The observance was, for many years, mainly an Irish Catholic religious celebration aimed at honoring Patrick, the priest who brought Christianity to the Emerald Isle in the fifth century. Although the celebration remains religious in nature (many Savannahians begin the day by attending morning mass at the Cathedral of St. John the Baptist on Lafayette Square), the observance has become more secular over the years and has been adopted by other segments of the population, leading to the saying that "everyone's Irish on St. Patrick's Day."

Another reason for celebrating the day in a big way might have to do with its occurring at a time of year when Savannah is blessed with some of its best weather. The normal high temperature on St. Patrick's Day is 70, and the normal low is 49. There is a saying around here to the effect that "it never rains on St. Patrick's Day in Savannah." This is usually the case, although it doesn't always hold true: We recall one year when we stood and watched the parade with ice-cold rain running down our green-shirted necks, with only mint-tainted virgin mimosas (that's champagne mixed with orange juice) to keep us from deserting our posts.

On most St. Patrick's Days, however, the often dreary days of winter are over, and folks are just itching to get outside and cut loose. What better way to do so than with a citywide party?

IT'S MORE THAN JUST A DAY

The celebrating that is part of St. Patrick's Day festivities in Savannah occurs over a span of three or four days. St. Patrick's Day is always observed on March 17, and the annual parade is held on that day except when it falls on Sunday—in that case, the parade is on Saturday, March 16. An

especially rare exception occurred in 2008, when an extremely early Easter put March 17 in Holy Week, leading to the observance being rescheduled for March 14. Some people celebrate by holding parties and get-togethers in their homes or by attending the invitation-only functions of Savannah's Irish societies. The latter range from the early-morning shenanigans of the Sinn Fein Society—which features green grits, Irish whiskey, and a master of ceremonies who continually announces "The bar is open"—to the comparatively staid, black-tie banquet held by the Hibernian Society.

The Hibernians pride themselves on their ability to attract banquet speakers of considerable note. In 1978 the Hibernian banquet speech was delivered by former Georgia governor Jimmy Carter, who at the time happened to be employed as president of the United States. Another, shorter speech Carter gave that day is the basis for one of Savannah's better St. Patrick's Day stories. In the mid-1960s, Carter developed a friendship with local character and bar owner Pinkie Masters. Pinkie—who reveled in telephoning local newspaper reporters and impersonating another character, one-time Georgia governor Lester Maddox—was fascinated with politics, and he became a fervent Carter booster. Carter didn't drink alcoholic beverages, but when he visited Savannah, he would invariably stop and see Pinkie at his lounge on Drayton Street near what was then known as the DeSoto Hilton Hotel (see our Nightlife chapter for more about this well-known bar). Masters died in the latter part of 1977, and Carter was unable to attend the funeral, which drew a huge number of political dignitaries. When Carter came to Savannah on St. Patrick's Day 1978 for the 8 p.m. Hibernian banquet, he arrived in late afternoon at the Hilton, where a large crowd waited to greet him.

According to author William Fogarty, Carter's "first act" upon his arrival "was to sneak out through the [hotel's] underground parking garage, cross Drayton Street, and enter Pinkie Master's bar unannounced. Needless to say, Pinkie's family and friends who were operating the bar were flabbergasted, as were the customers in the bar." Carter "climbed upon the bar, where they have since added a plaque, and spoke to the crowd, then returned to the hotel. He had paid his respects to Pinkie."

The public partying on St. Patrick's Day occurs at Pinkie's and other watering holes throughout the city, but the bulk of the celebrating takes place on River Street, in City Market, and along Bay Street.

Most of the merrymaking happens on the day of the parade and the weekend closest to it. When the parade is on a Monday, Tuesday, or Wednesday, the partying will be on that day, the weekend before, and the day or days before. When the parade is on a Thursday or Friday, the celebrating will be on that day, the day before, and the weekend following. On parade day and weekends, River Street and City Market are packed with celebrators.

City Market (912-232-4903; www.savannahcitymarket.com) hosts free live music and dancing in the courtyard. It's a very laid-back party that can last as long as five days, depending on when St. Patrick's Day falls. On St. Patrick's Day itself, the bands begin just as the parade passes nearby.

The **Savannah Waterfront Association** (912-234-0295; www.riverstreetsavannah.com) hosts St. Patrick's Celebration on the river with 9 blocks of food booths, nationally known entertainment, and lots of people.

Be prepared to literally rub elbows with fellow partiers as quite a crowd gathers here. Admission is free, and for legal drinkers a wristband can be purchased for $5 to drink beer outdoors. The wristband practice was begun in 1999 in an effort to curb underage drinking and, despite some initial outcry, the wristbands have become a fact of life. However, each year, there's controversy over where, when, and how far the "wristbanding" should reach, so it's best to check the City of Savannah website (www.ci.savannah.ga.us) for the latest rules and regulations.

This festival goes on for several days from 10 a.m. to midnight, spanning the closest weekend to St. Patrick's Day and reaching its peak on the day itself.

i The water of the Forsyth Park fountain is traditionally dyed green each year for St. Patrick's Day, but don't expect the Savannah River to be treated in similar fashion. The last and only attempt at turning the river green occurred in 1961 with less than desirable results. A thousand pounds of the chemical Uranine was used, and the outcome was a striped effect.

The St. Patrick's Day holidays are also a time of traditional events such as the investiture of the parade grand marshal on the first Sunday in March, the gathering of Irish descendants at the Celtic Cross on the following Sunday, and the laying of a wreath at the Sgt. William Jasper Monument on the afternoon before the parade. There are also family-oriented events emphasizing Irish heritage and culture such as the Savannah Irish Festival at the Civic Center in mid-February and the Tara Feis festival in Emmet Park on Bay Street on the Saturday before the parade. For the athletically inclined, there's the St. Patrick's Day Rugby Tournament, held in Daffin Park on the weekend closest to the big day. (For more about all these events, see our Annual Events and Festivals chapter.) The focal point of the festivities, however, is the St. Patrick's Day parade.

THE PARADE

Savannah's St. Patrick's Day parade is the third oldest and one of the largest in the United States. It dates back to 1824, and only New York City's (1762) and Philadelphia's (1780) have been in existence longer. There are more entries—usually about 250—in Savannah's parade than those in Chicago (200), Philadelphia (101), Boston (100), or New York (75). With 10,000 marchers, Savannah has fewer than New York (250,000) and Chicago (15,000) but as many as Boston and more than Philly (9,700).

Savannah's parade covers a lot of pavement: specifically, 2 miles, making it almost as long in distance as the parades in Boston and Philadelphia (2.6 miles) and longer than New York's (1.5) and Chicago's (1). As you can imagine, given the number of people who march and how far they have to walk, the local parade takes quite awhile to unfold—almost three-and-a-half hours. That being the case, it's a good idea to bring lawn chairs or stadium cushions so you can be as comfortable as possible while you watch, particularly if you arrive early and stake out a viewing spot closer to where the parade ends than where it begins. The farther you are from the starting point, the longer you'll have to wait for the first marchers to reach you, maybe as long as an hour.

Speaking of beginnings and endings, the parade starts at 10:15 a.m. at **Abercorn and Gwinnett Streets** and ends at **Bull and**

Harris Streets. The route of march is north on Abercorn to Broughton Street, east on Broughton to East Broad Street, north on East Broad to Bay Street, west on Bay to Bull, to the finish line. We think you'll find this event to be as enjoyable and festive as you can imagine, but don't go expecting to see something akin to the Tournament of Roses parade or Macy's Thanksgiving Day bash. There are floats in Savannah's parade, and they seem to be more numerous and elaborate each year, but you won't see anything that remotely resembles what you'd watch in Pasadena, California, on New Year's Day or on the streets of New York during the pre-Christmas holidays.

What you'll see in Savannah on St. Patrick's Day is more like a small-town parade dotted with a few big-name bands and participants, yet, it is possibly one of the country's most user-friendly parades. One of the reasons we Savannahians keep going back year after year is to watch relatives, neighbors, and coworkers as they march or ride by and wave and yell at each other. You'll see a lot of young girls and even grandmothers stepping out of or into the line of march as they shake hands and hug necks. And you're likely to see a woman or two dash from the sidelines to plant kisses on the cheeks of marchers, particularly those in uniform and especially members of the U.S. Army Rangers (home-based at Savannah's Hunter Army Air Field) and Benedictine Military School aggregations.

High-school marching bands, numerous glad-handing politicians riding in convertibles, some beauty queens, several military color guards, the parade grand marshal, a gaggle of past grand marshals, and a multitude of men, women, and children of Irish descent, all dressed up in their best greenery and marching in family groups or as members of Savannah's many Irish societies create the lineup. Keep your eyes peeled for one of our favorite entries, the "Irishman at Large." You'll see college cheerleaders and dance teams, officials of the Catholic church, bagpipers, and detachments of soldiers, sailors, marines, and veterans' groups. People will be waving at you from more than 20 floats representing a variety of organizations and businesses.

Among our favorite parade units are those of the Shriners of Savannah's Alee Temple. The most outlandish of the Shriner groups is the Oriental band, which consists of a group of pillars of the community clad in colorful burnooses, jackets, and pantaloons and shod in brogans that have been spray-painted gold, turned up at the tips, and decorated with tiny bells. Other crowd pleasers from the Shrine are its Dune Cat Unit, whose members zip around in souped-up go-karts, and the Keystone Kops, who hand out citations to spectators amid much frenzied whistle blowing and scurrying around.

The parade occasionally has visiting celebrities, including, in recent years, units from the New York Police Department and the Budweiser Clydesdales.

In short, the Savannah's St. Patrick's Day parade is comprised of lots of enthusiasm, a world of pride in being Irish, and the smiles of thousands of people having one heck of a good time.

i You can drink alcoholic beverages in public in the parade festival area (bordered by River Street on the north, East Broad Street on the east, Jones Street on the south, and West Boundary Street on the west), but drinks must be in paper, Styrofoam, or plastic cups of no more than 16 ounces in volume.

The parade is an all-year planning project by the St. Patrick's Day Parade Committee, and you can get a progress report on the upcoming edition of the parade at **www .savannahsaintpatricksday.com.**

PRIME PARADE-WATCHING

Some Savannahians have made careers out of saving spots in the squares for family tents. The whole process has become quite a chore, if the truth is told. That being said, the City of Savannah and the police department have been clamping down on "camping out in the squares" in recent years. Today no one is allowed to stake out their parade-watching plot until 6 a.m. the day of the parade. It's quite a sight to see the clock strike 6 and a mad rush for space, but it happens. Watch it on the news and save your energy. There are lots of spaces up and down the stretch if you'll just take your time (but get there at least by 8 a.m.).

Here are some good places for parade watching, as detailed by the *Savannah Morning News*.

- The 600 block of Abercorn Street—where "the parade's performers aren't tired yet. The bands step higher; the people waving from their floats aren't yet suffering from arm fatigue."
- East Broad Street between Broughton and Bay Streets—"a good place to see the picturesque variety of parade spectators . . . SCAD (Savannah College of Art and Design) students tend to be in full bloom around here. Green dogs abound. So do green people."
- Bay Street between East Broad and Bull Streets—"The closest convenient spot for those who've been cavorting down by the river."

We would also like to make this suggestion: To obtain a unique view of the parade, try getting a spot on the southern side of Calhoun Square (Abercorn and Gordon Streets), Lafayette Square (Abercorn and Charlton Streets), or Oglethorpe Square (Abercorn and York Streets), or on the northern side of Wright Square (Bull and State Streets) or Chippewa Square (Bull and Hull Streets). You'll be watching the parade come straight at you rather than viewing it from the side, and it's a perspective that can be quite enjoyable.

> **i** In a quest to win strings of green beads from male onlookers, some females persist in baring portions of their anatomy on St. Patrick's Day, but this is behavior that will bring about their arrest if observed by the constabulary.

PARKING ON ST. PATRICK'S DAY

If there is a downside to St. Patrick's Day, it might be locating a place to park. Metered spaces are free on this holiday, but vacant ones won't be easy to find unless you get to town real early. Another option is to park in one of the city's garages, which you can do all day for $10; here, too, an early arrival is mandatory. The garages are at Whitaker, State and Abercorn Streets, at Montgomery and York Streets, at Bryan and Abercorn Streets, and at Liberty and Montgomery Streets.

An alternative to parking downtown is to park away from the area and take a **Chatham Area Transit** bus into the city. There are regular bus routes to and from downtown (see our Getting Here, Getting Around chapter). A special shuttle runs nonstop continuously from the parking lot of Oglethorpe Mall to downtown on St. Patrick's Day for a nominal fee. The public transit organization here is the Chatham Area Transit Authority, known by the acronym CAT, and the slogan of the day is "I caught a CAT on St. Pat's." Friends who have tried this say it's not the ideal way to get downtown, but if patience is your attribute, give it a try.

Whatever you do, don't park on the parade route in a lot or space that's designated for use by a business or private individual. If there's a sign saying your car will be towed, that's probably what will happen, and you'll have to pay a minimum of $85 to get your vehicle back.

ANNUAL EVENTS & FESTIVALS

Savannahians love to party. They love their history. They also love getting outdoors and taking advantage of coastal Georgia's congenial climate. Is it any wonder, then, there's almost always something going on in Savannah? That something might be a festival attracting thousands of people or the commemoration of a historic event drawing a few hundred, but a week seldom passes in which there's nothing to do in Savannah.

We admit things slow down a tad during the summer months because of the heat, but that doesn't mean you can't get out and enjoy yourself. Grab your suntan lotion, cooler, and lounge chair, and head for a day at the beach on nearby Tybee Island, just as Savannahians have been doing for more than a century.

Savannah's biggest party is its celebration of St. Patrick's Day, a green-hued blast bringing about a half-million visitors to the city in mid-March. It's such a big deal we've devoted an entire chapter to it. But because we want to be sure you don't miss any of the fun, we've included in this chapter's brief looks at significant happenings on that great day for the Irish and the days leading up to it.

OVERVIEW

As we indicated earlier, finding a parking space in Savannah can be a hassle, and the problem intensifies when a festival is held in the downtown area. It's a good idea—particularly if you're attending an event on River Street, where parking is extremely limited—to arrive early, find a spot on a street or in a lot a few blocks from the festival, then hoof it to your destination. Savannah is a city that's ideal for walking, and your stroll to and from the festival could be one of the most enjoyable parts of your day.

We need to mention one other thing before taking you through our month-by-month rundown of events and festivals: Dates, times, and admission fees can change, so it's best to call ahead for the most current information. The telephone numbers included

with the following write-ups are the numbers of the individuals, organizations, or agencies sponsoring or coordinating the events.

JANUARY
Historic Downtown

EMANCIPATION DAY SERVICE
Historic First Bryan Baptist Church
(912) 234-6293, (912) 236-3173
www.firstbryanbaptistchurch.com
By holding a special church service on New Year's Day, Savannah's Emancipation Association commemorates the signing of the proclamation that ordered the freeing of slaves in the Confederate states. During the 11 a.m. gathering, held at a different church each year, a participant reads the Emancipation

ANNUAL EVENTS & FESTIVALS

Proclamation, a mass choir sings hymns, and speakers deliver addresses concerning the significance of that historic day in 1863. Call for additional information.

MARTIN LUTHER KING JR.OBSERVANCE DAY ACTIVITIES
Various locations
(912) 234-5502
This month-long tribute to civil rights leader Martin Luther King Jr. features a parade through downtown starting at 10 a.m. on the third Monday in January, the national day of observance for King Day. The observances wind up with the Freedom Ball at the Savannah Civic Center on the last Friday of January. For more information or for the parade route and schedule, visit www.Savannahnow.com or call the number above.

i If you're looking to uplift your spirits during what can sometimes be a depressing time of year—late January—consider attending "Hymns for Hope," a musical program usually held on the Sunday before Super Bowl Sunday. Featuring local church choirs and gospel singing groups, this presentation takes place in the afternoon or early in the evening. Admission is $10 and benefits the Interfaith Hospitality Network of Coastal Georgia, a volunteer organization that aids homeless families. You can contact the network and get the specific details on "Hymns for Hope" by calling (912) 790-9446.

HEART AND STROKE GALA
7130 Hodgson Memorial Drive, #101
(912) 790-2900
The American Heart Association's premier fund-raiser has a different theme every year

and is held in late January or in early February, which is Heart Month. Tickets are $150 or $175 per person, and they entitle guests to a cocktail party with open bar at 6:30 p.m. and dinner with wine and beer at 8 p.m. A band plays popular dance music until midnight, and live and silent auctions add to the festivities.

FEBRUARY
Historic Downtown

GHS'S GEORGIA DAYS
Various locations
(912) 651-2125
www.georgiahistory.com
This observance celebrating Georgia's founding and heritage unfolds during the first two weeks of February and usually focuses on the twelfth of the month—the day on which the first colonists landed in 1733. Georgia Week opens on the first day of February with a ceremony in a downtown square featuring a portrayal of a significant figure in the history of the state and wreath-layings at monuments throughout the city. Programs at historic sites and a lecture focusing on the aforementioned historic figure are part of the celebration, which is presented by the Georgia Historical Society (GHS) in partnership with Chatham-Savannah public schools.

On the morning of Georgia Day, February 12, schoolchildren dressed as colonists and the Native Americans who welcomed them walk in a procession from Forsyth Park up Bull Street to City Hall on Bay Street. The Georgia Day Luncheon follows, with tickets priced at $25 (in 2010 and subject to change in 2011); the other events are free. Georgia Day is contingent on receiving funding from the state. Contact the Georgia Historical Society regarding events and further information.

BLACK HERITAGE FESTIVAL
Various locations
(912) 351-6320
www.savannahblackheritage
festival.com
www.savstate.edu

Various musical groups entertain with performances of gospel, reggae, blues, and jazz, and craftspeople gather at the Savannah Civic Center on the Grand Festival Day (a Saturday) to sell items related to African culture during this event, which is held during a week in early Feb. Funded by Savannah's Department of Cultural Affairs this event is star-studded with local celebrities and usually starts at noon and ends at 4 p.m. The concert portion of the show highlights the multifaceted contributions of African Americans in the areas of music, the performing arts, and cuisine. Admission is free. Stay tuned to the website for news of the current year's event.

SUPER MUSEUM SUNDAY
Various locations
(912) 651-2125
www.georgiahistory.com

More than 40 of the area's museums, educational institutions, and historic homes open their doors and invite the public in at no charge during this event, which serves as an activity of the Georgia History Festival (once known as the Georgia Heritage Celebration and Georgia Days) and always occurs on the Sunday before Georgia Day. Hours are from noon until 4 p.m. To determine if a specific museum participates in this program, contact the museum ahead of time. (You can find museums and their telephone numbers in the Attractions chapter.)

Islands

COLONIAL FAIRE & MUSTER AT WORMSLOE
Wormsloe Historic Site
7601 Skidaway Rd.
(912) 353-3023

Historical reenactors clad in the garb of Georgia's colonists make music and demonstrate craft skills, such as making candles and musket balls, at this program held in an open area near the marsh overlooking the Skidaway River. At the visitor center, you can view artifacts excavated from Wormsloe's tabby ruins and watch an audiovisual show about the founding of the 13th colony. The program takes place from 10 a.m. until 4 p.m. on the first Sat and Sun in Feb. Admission is free.

Southside/Midtown

SAVANNAH IRISH FESTIVAL
Savannah Civic Center
Liberty and Montgomery Streets
(912) 651-6556
www.savannahirish.org

This family-oriented event uses song, dance, and recitation to emphasize the heritage of the Irish and the contributions of Irish immigrants here and throughout the United States. In addition to the main stage, where much of this activity takes place, there are stages for children's entertainment and readings and discussions involving Irish culture and history. Vendors market Irish clothing, jewelry, and artifacts, and members of local Irish organizations prepare and sell food, including shepherd's pie, Irish stew, and other ethnic dishes. The festival is on the second or third weekend in Feb from 10:30 a.m. to 8 p.m. on Sat, and from noon until 7 p.m. on Sun. Admission to the festival is $12 per day or $16 for a two-day ticket. Children age 4 and younger are admitted free.

MARCH

Historic Downtown

FIRST SATURDAY
Rousakis Plaza
River Street
(912) 234-0295
www.riverstreetsavannah.com

Browse through the wares of artisans and craftspeople from throughout the Southeast and listen to various forms of music during First Saturday on the plaza on River Street. While enjoying the breeze blowing off the Savannah River, you might find yourself staring at a large cargo ship as it glides along the waterway, so close you'd swear you could reach out and touch it. The 40 to 60 open-air arts and crafts booths on the plaza offer a variety of treasures, everything from original oil paintings and watercolors to rocking horses fashioned from wood scraps. If you can't turn up something that catches your fancy among the artists' booths, visit the shops in the renovated cotton warehouses lining River Street.

Hungry? You have your choice of restaurants dishing up a variety of cuisine. The Savannah Waterfront Association presents First Saturday festivals from 9 a.m. to 6 p.m. on—what else?—the first Saturday of each month, with the exception of January and February. Some are part of expanded, more distinctive festivals: the Savannah Seafood Festival in November, Oktoberfest in October, the Fine Arts Festival in May, and Christmas on the River in December (see subsequent listings for more details on these festivals). Admission is free.

GRAND MARSHAL INVESTITURE CEREMONY
Savannah Civic Center
15 East Liberty St.
(912) 233-4804

The St. Patrick's Day Parade Committee presents the parade grand marshal with his sash and recognizes civic dignitaries at this ceremony. The event takes place at 2:45 p.m. on the first Sunday in March, one week after the committee elects the leader of the parade. There is no charge for admission.

CELTIC CROSS CEREMONY
Emmet Park
Bay and Price Streets
(912) 233-4804

Members of the city's Irish organizations gather at the Cathedral of St. John the Baptist for mass at 11:30 a.m. on the second Sunday of the month, then march in procession to Emmet Park, where they lay a wreath at the Celtic Cross and listen to a speech about their heritage. The cross, officially named the Irish Monument, was carved from a single piece of Irish limestone in County Roscommon, Ireland. The Savannah Irish Monument Committee erected the Celtic Cross in 1983, the 250th anniversary of the founding of Savannah and Georgia, to commemorate Georgians of Irish ancestry. The ceremony starts about 1 p.m., and it's open to the public.

TARA FEIS
Emmet Park
Bay and Price Streets
(912) 651-6417
www.savannahga.gov/arts

The city of Savannah's Department of Cultural Affairs puts the emphasis on family-oriented activities at this Irish festival on the

Saturday before St. Patrick's Day. Irish music and dancing, crafts demonstrations, storytelling, and poetry recitations fill the spotlight. Youngsters can participate in hands-on activities with a Celtic touch and enjoy carnival rides. Alcoholic beverages are prohibited in an effort to enhance the family-day atmosphere. The event, in sun-dappled Emmet Park, runs from 11 a.m. until 5 p.m., and admission is as free as the Irish mist on a day in Killarney. In case you're wondering, *feis* is pronounced "fesh."

SGT. WILLIAM JASPER MEMORIAL CEREMONY
Madison Square
Bull Street, between Harris and Charlton Streets
(912) 233-4804
On the eve of the St. Patrick's Day Parade, the parade grand marshal and his aides recognize the contributions of the military by walking from Johnson Square down Bull Street to Madison Square, where they lay a wreath at the monument honoring Revolutionary War hero William Jasper. A band or two that will be participating in the parade, often bagpipers, usually accompanies them. A 21-gun salute is fired during the ceremony, which occurs about 4:30 p.m.

ST. PATRICK'S DAY PARADE
Various downtown streets
(912) 233-4804
Savannah's biggest annual event lasts upwards of four hours and involves thousands of participants. Some 250 units take to the streets for the parade, including marching bands, floats, and the city's numerous Irish organizations. The parade starts about 10:15 a.m. at Forsyth Park and winds its way around several of Savannah's squares and down its main thoroughfares. (For more information, see our St. Patrick's Day chapter.)

ST. PATRICK'S AT CITY MARKET
Jefferson and St. Julian Streets
(912) 232-4903
www.savannahcitymarket.com
City Market celebrates the big day with live music and dancing in the courtyard. This laid-back party occurs over a span of time that includes St. Patrick's Day and can last as long as five days, depending on when the holiday falls. On St. Patrick's Day, the bands crank up as soon as the parade passes nearby. It's free.

ST. PATRICK'S DAY ON THE RIVER
Rousakis Plaza
River Street
(912) 234-0295
www.savwaterfront.com
The Savannah Waterfront Association sets up food booths on the plaza and brings in nationally known entertainers to perform, but the biggest attraction of St. Patrick's Day on the River isn't eating or listening to music—it's being part of the crowd that jams River Street. This 9-block party is free for nondrinkers, and it's the place to be during St. Patrick's Day festivities if you like to rub elbows with people—literally. Those wishing to drink beer outdoors will have to purchase $5 wristbands. The merrymaking is at its peak on St. Patrick's Day and the weekend closest to the holiday; the party cranks up about 10 a.m., and food sales and scheduled entertainment end at midnight.

THE SAVANNAH TOUR OF HOMES AND GARDENS
Parish House of Christ Church
18 Abercorn St.
(912) 234-8054
www.savannahtourofhomes.org
This granddaddy of Savannah's seasonal tours brings you to a different neighborhood on each day of its four-day run. Each three-hour, self-guided walking tour takes you to approximately six private homes and/or gardens in the Historic District. Hours are from 10 a.m. until 5 p.m. on Thurs, Fri, and Sat, and from 11 a.m. to 4 p.m. on Sun, and participants are encouraged to stroll from site to site at their own pace and in any order they choose. Special events such as luncheons, seminars, cemetery tours, and teas are also presented, and they vary from year to year. The event is held in late March. Begun in 1935, the event is sponsored by the Episcopal Church Women of Christ Church, along with Historic Savannah Foundation, and proceeds benefit outreach ministries of the churchwomen and the foundation's preservation efforts. The fee for each walking tour is $40, and it's essential to order tickets for the tours and other activities ahead of time. The tours always—yes, always—sell out. You pick up your tickets at tour headquarters, the Parish House of Christ Church.

SAVANNAH MUSIC FESTIVAL
Various locations
(912) 234-3378
www.savannahmusicfestival.org
The Savannah Music Festival—formerly known as Savannah Onstage—enhances the beauty of the city with two-and-a-half weeks of jazz, classical, blues, gospel, zydeco, and other traditional American performances during late March and early April.

The cornerstone of this steadily growing festival is the American Traditions Competition, which features solo vocalists presenting music that has played a significant role in forming the cultural heritage of the United States. Each year additional major events are incorporated into the festival. Recent performers include Jazz at Lincoln Center Orchestra with Wynton Marsalis, guitarist Buddy Guy, bluegrass singer and mandolinist Ricky Skaggs, the Dave Grisman Quintet, the Tallis Scholars, the Blind Boys of Alabama, and the Derek Trucks Band, and among recent productions were a new and imaginative version of George Gershwin's *Porgy and Bess* and *An Evening With Beethoven*, featuring actress Mia Farrow and the Beaux Arts Trio. The festival also reaches students with free concerts and provides pre-concert talks, films, and lectures about the heritage of American music to children and adults.

Islands

SHEEP TO SHAWL FESTIVAL
Oatland Island Wildlife Center
711 Sandtown Rd.
(912) 395-1212
www.oatlandisland.org
While musicians fiddle and strum up a storm on the porch of a log cabin built in the 1830s, visitors watch an old-fashioned sheepshearing. This activity on a Sat in Mar takes place at the center's Heritage Homesite and is an ideal activity for families.

The main events occur about 11:30 a.m. and 2 p.m. when workers clip the sheep with hand-operated shears. Members of the Fiber Guild of the Savannahs card wool from the previous year's shearing, spin it into yarn, and, using a 150-year-old loom, weave yarn spun beforehand into a shawl. The shawl is raffled off, and the winner is announced near the end of the festival, which runs from 10 a.m. until 4 p.m. The center invites children to try their hands at carding and spinning wool. Anyone interested in viewing Oatland's wild and domesticated animals can walk the facility's 1.75-mile nature trail and visit the barnyard. Admission is $ 7 for adults and $ 5 for children, seniors, and the military.

Southside/Midtown

ST. PATRICK'S DAY RUGBY TOURNAMENT
Daffin Park
Victory Drive and Bee Road
(912) 234-5999
www.savannahrugby.com

Billed as one of the largest tournaments of its kind in the United States, this event is staged by the Savannah Shamrocks rugby club on the weekend closest to St. Patrick's Day. About 75 teams participate. There's no charge for roaming the sidelines and learning about this sport that's akin to American football and has been called "a ruffians' game played by gentlemen." The action starts about 9 a.m. on both days of the tourney, which was first held in 1979.

SPRING GARDENING FESTIVAL
Bamboo Farm and Coastal Gardens
2 Canebrake Rd.
(912) 921-5460
www.bamboo.caes.uga.edu

Swing into the planting season at the Bamboo Farm (see our Attractions chapter) by attending this program, which features garden exhibits and talks on horticulture. Also on the agenda are a container-gardening competition and a silent auction, and plant vendors will be on hand, perhaps offering that hard-to-find plant you've been looking for. The festival is held from 9 a.m. to 3 p.m. on a Sat in late Mar.

APRIL

Historic Downtown

SAVANNAH GARDEN EXPOSITION
Roundhouse Railroad Museum
601 West Harris St.
(912) 233-7787
www.savannahgardenexpo.com

During this festival in mid spring, flowering plants and greenery adorn the bays where mechanics once repaired steam locomotives. Growers, antiques dealers, and other merchants selling products to help your garden flourish set up shop in the bays. Exhibition gardens fill another portion of the Roundhouse, and window boxes created by local horticulturists brighten a long brick wall of the 19th-century railroad complex.

Lectures, seminars, gardening demonstrations, children's activities, and walking tours of Savannah add to the Expo, which is held from 10 a.m. to 5 p.m. on a Fri and Sat in early Apr. Tickets can be purchased in advance for $8 per person online or for $10 at the gate, and proceeds benefit the Historic Savannah Foundation and the Isaiah Davenport House Museum.

NOGS HIDDEN GARDENS OF SAVANNAH TOUR
Garden Club of Savannah
(912) 961-4805
www.gcofsavannahnogstour.org

For more than 20 years, the members of the Garden Club of Savannah have, via this tour, enabled folks to glimpse a part of the city they would not otherwise see. As its name implies, this self-guided walking tour is your chance to get a look at some of the elegant gardens hidden behind the walls and gates of downtown homes. Chosen because of their beauty and unusual arrangement, eight gardens are opened to the public by their owners for only the two days of the tour.

You buy your tickets online, by mail from the Garden Club (P.O. Box 13892, Savannah, GA 31416), or at the Hilton Savannah DeSoto Hotel. A splendid way to end your walk is by finishing at the Harper-Fowlkes House on Orleans Square and attending the tea served there, a treat included in the $40 ticket price. A visit to the Massey Heritage Center and its garden is included on the tour, which is presented on a Fri and Sat in late Apr, about the time Savannah is in full bloom. The gardens are open from 10 a.m. until 5 p.m., and light refreshments are served at the tea from 2 to 4 p.m. By the way, NOGS stands for North of Gaston Street, the locale of all the gardens on the tour.

SIDEWALK ARTS FESTIVAL
Forsyth Park
(912) 525-5231
www.scad.edu/experience/events /sidewalkarts/
The normally sedate slabs of the sidewalks leading through Forsyth Park pulsate with color for one previous day in late April, when the Savannah College of Art and Design stages its Sidewalk Arts Festival. SCAD students, alumni, prospective students, children, and preteens cover the concrete with chalk drawings, creating an immense art exhibit on the ground. You'll see everything from reproductions of famous masterpieces to the flights of fancy of five-year-olds as you stroll through the park. Nearly 1,000 artists participate. Other attractions include the music of various bands and art projects for young children and preteens. The festival starts at 11 a.m. and ends at 5 p.m.

CONFEDERATE MEMORIAL DAY
Forsyth Park
(912) 232-3945
www.scvsavannah.com/Events /2010ConfederateMemorialDay
An observance that began in 1866 with women decorating the graves of husbands, sons, and brothers who fell while wearing the gray and butternut of the Confederacy continues in Savannah with a gathering at the Confederate Memorial monument in Forsyth Park on the Sun closest to Apr 26, the day Gen. Joseph E. Johnston surrendered the last Confederate army at Greensboro, North Carolina. Civil War reenactors fire a 21-gun artillery salute, and there is a performance by a fife and drum corps. The solemn ceremony takes place in early afternoon.

West Chatham

STAND UP FOR AMERICA DAY
Various locations
Port Wentworth
(912) 965-1999
www.portwentworthga.com
Residents of the west Chatham County town of Port Wentworth show their red, white, and blue colors from early morning until midnight on a Saturday in April devoted to patriotism and fun. A parade featuring go-karts and bicycles decorated by youngsters starts at 10 a.m. near the city's elementary school, winds its way through town, and ends next to the fire station on Cantyre Street. That's also the site of a late-morning rally, craft sales, activities for children, and the fish weigh-in for the Savannah River Spring Classic. A nighttime street dance goes on until midnight and includes a fireworks show about 9 p.m. Festivities start at 7:45 a.m.

MAY

Historic Downtown

FINE ARTS ON THE RIVER
River Street
(912) 234-0295
www.riverstreetsavannah.com
Artists from throughout the nation display their paintings, photographs, and crafts during this festival on River Street's Rousakis Waterfront Plaza the end of April or on the first weekend in May. Wine tasting, live music, and sales of food prepared by River Street restaurants add to the festivities. Admission is free to this event, a production of the Savannah Waterfront Association.

KIRKIN' O' THE TARTAN
Independent Presbyterian Church
25 West Oglethorpe Ave.
(912) 236-3346
www.ipcsav.org
The Kirkin' O' the Tartan service begins with a procession of bagpipers and Scottish descendants bearing tartan banners representing their clans. After their entry into the church, the reading of scripture, the presentation of the banners, and a special sermon, there is more piping on the green outside the church. The service is at 11 a.m. on the second Sunday of May, and it's an occasion when many worshipers, Scottish and otherwise, rededicate themselves and their families to God.

SCOTTISH GAMES AND HIGHLAND GATHERING
Bethesda Home for Boys
9520 Ferguson Ave.
(912) 233-6017
www.savannahscottishgames.com

Although tests of strength and dexterity are the focal point of the Scottish Games, there's more to the event than brawny lads tossing long poles ("cabers") and heaving sheaves of hay into the air. Aye, there are winsome lassies performing the dances of the Highlands, and stouthearted bagpipers playing their melancholy tunes. Also, members of more than 50 Scottish clans bring a touch of plaid to the green fields of the Bethesda Home for Boys as they gather to parade, socialize, and celebrate their heritage during this festival on the first Saturday in May. The event runs from 9 a.m. to 3 p.m. The tickets are $12 for adults and $10 for teens, $5 for children younger than age 12. Tickets, maps, and directions may be found on the website.

RALPH MARK GILBERT CIVIL RIGHTS MUSEUM ANNIVERSARY CELEBRATION
Ralph Mark Gilbert Civil Rights Museum
460 Martin Luther King Jr. Blvd.
(912) 231-8900
www.savcivilrights.com
Workshops and lectures inside the museum and activities held at a local church in late May emphasize the museum's founding in 1996. Workshops, lectures, and traveling exhibits deal with aspects of African-American heritage, and so do the activities, which include a food festival and entertainment by dancers and musicians. Admission to the museum is $4 for adults, $3 for senior citizens, and $2 for students.

Islands

WAR OF JENKINS' EAR OBSERVANCE
Wormsloe Historic Site
7601 Skidaway Rd.
(912) 353-3023

Wormsloe emphasizes the military aspect of life in the Georgia of the 1740s with living-history demonstrations on the last Saturday in May. In a program running from 11 a.m. to 4 p.m., members of the Wormsloe militia depict the lives of soldiers who fought in the War of Jenkins' Ear—England's struggle with the Spanish for possession of the southeastern portion of North America between 1739 and 1742. Admission is $4 for adults, $3.50 for senior citizens, and $2.50 for children ages 6 to 18. Those age 6 and younger are admitted free.

West Chatham

SUNDAY SUPPER IN THE STRAWBERRY PATCH
Bamboo Farm and Coastal Gardens
2 Canebrake Rd.
(912) 921-5460
www.uga.extension.com/bamboo
Held the first Sunday in May at the peak of strawberry-growing season, this Bamboo Farm fund-raiser gives folks a chance to get outdoors and enjoy a good ol' Southern supper—fried chicken, rice and gravy, fresh squash, field peas, Vidalia onions, sliced tomatoes, corn bread, ice tea, and strawberry shortcake, of course. The meal is served at the lakeside pavilion at the Bamboo Farm (see our Attractions chapter), but the berries are fresh from the farm's strawberry patch. It's a dessert combination that's tough to beat.

Those attending also enjoy self-guided tours of the gardens, and there's live entertainment and a silent auction. You need to make reservations for this get-together, which starts at 4 p.m.; cost of the meal is $20 per person.

JUNE

Historic Downtown

FIRST SATURDAY
Rousakis Plaza
River Street
(912) 234-0295
www.riverstreetsavannah.com
See our March listing for more information on this monthly event.

i If you happen to be near Johnson or Wright Squares around noontime on a Friday during the summer, amble on over and you'll likely be treated to some mighty fine sound provided by members of the local chapter of the American Federation of Musicians. From ragtime to jazz, their performances make lunchtime a special outdoor treat. They're on their outdoor "stages" from 11:30 a.m. to 1:30 p.m. during most of June, July, and August.

SAVANNAH ASIAN FESTIVAL
Savannah Civic Center
Montgomery and Liberty Streets
(912) 651-6417
www.savannahga.gov/arts
A response to the contributions of Savannah's growing Asian community, this one-day event features displays and entertainment reflecting the heritage of people of Chinese, Filipino, Indian, Japanese, Sri Lankan, Nepalese, Korean, Thai, Pakistani, Taiwanese, and Vietnamese descent. A Vietnamese dragon dance ceremony, an Asian fashion show, martial arts demonstrations, and Vietnamese fan dancing are highlights. Representatives of the Asian cultures, some of them clad in native dress, display and sell arts and crafts at tables set up in the

Civic Center arena and host workshops. You can purchase samples of Asian cuisine at food booths, and among the offerings are Chinese egg rolls, Indian curry, Thai beef, Filipino rice cakes, Vietnamese shish kebob, Japanese sushi, and Korean cucumber salad. The festival runs from 11 a.m. until 5 p.m. on the first Saturday in June. It's sponsored by Savannah's Department of Cultural Affairs, which means admission is free.

JULY
Historic Downtown
FIRST SATURDAY
Rousakis Plaza
River Street
(912) 234-0295
www.riverstreetsavannah.com
See our March listing for more information on this monthly event.

FANTASTIC FOURTH CELEBRATION
River Street
(912) 234-0295
www.savwaterfront.com
The sky above the Savannah River explodes in fireworks as folks gather on the plaza to celebrate the nation's birthday on July 4. Technicians shoot off shells 3 to 6 inches in diameter, including the largest projectile fired in Georgia, from nearby Hutchinson Island Bring a radio and tune in to (FM) KIX 96.5, MIX 102.1, E 93, MAGIC 103.9, the Ticket and WBMQ as the fireworks will be choreographed to music simulcast live on these local radio stations. Come early to stake out a good spot for viewing the show, and bring lawn chairs and a picnic supper to participate in what resembles a gigantic

tailgate party. While you're waiting for the fireworks, you can listen to live music and people watch. The free event opens about 5 p.m., and the rockets start bursting in air about 9:30 p.m.

AUGUST
Historic Downtown
FIRST SATURDAY
Rousakis Plaza
River Street
(912) 234-0295
www.savwaterfront.com
See our March listing for more information on this monthly event.

OLD FORT JACKSON LABOR DAY LOWCOUNTRY BOIL AND AUCTION
Old Fort Jackson
1 Fort Jackson Rd.
(912) 232-3945
www.chsgeorgia.org
An evening of fun, history, and food at the oldest standing brick fort in Georgia on the Saturday before Labor Day. The easygoing event takes place within the brick walls of the structure, which was manned in the War of 1812 and used during the Civil War as a headquarters for the Confederacy's defense of the Savannah River (see our Attractions chapter). A silent auction is offered, and visitors can chow down on Lowcountry boil, barbecue, and all the trimmings. The young-sters enjoy themselves scampering around in what amounts to a walled playground, and there's a cannon firing to further liven things up. Proceeds from the sale of food and drinks are used for the preservation of the fort.

Islands

TOOLS AND SKILLS THAT BUILT THE COLONY

Wormsloe Historic Site
7601 Skidaway Rd.
(912) 353-3023

Wormsloe staff members in Colonial attire demonstrate carpentry, blacksmithing, cooking, weaving, flint knapping, leatherworking, woodsmen's skills, pewter casting, and other abilities essential to the development of Georgia. This living-history program is offered from 10 a.m. until 4 p.m. on the last Saturday and Sunday of August. Admission is $5 for adults, $3.50 for senior citizens, and $2.50 for children ages 6 to 18. Those age 6 and younger are admitted free.

SEPTEMBER

Historic Downtown

FIRST SATURDAY AND SALTWATER SHOOTOUT FISHING TOURNAMENT

Rousakis Plaza
River Street
(912) 234-0295
www.riverstreetsavannah.com

River Street serves as headquarters for the Saltwater Shootout Fishing Tournament during September's First Saturday event. In addition to enjoying the crafts, music, and food that are hallmarks of each First Saturday, festivalgoers can also watch anglers bring in their day's catch for weighing as the three-day tournament unfolds. Participants in the competition, an endeavor sponsored by the Greater Savannah Sports Council, compete during the first Friday, Saturday, and Sunday of September.

SAVANNAH JAZZ FESTIVAL

Forsyth Park
(912) 625-5419
www.savannahjazzfestival.org

Forsyth Park and other venues heat up with the sounds of jazz during the last full week in September when many of the finest musicians in the Savannah area and the South perform their special brand of American music. The park's the place to be for Blues Night on the Thursday of the festival, for lively presentations on Friday night and Saturday afternoon and evening, and for a special Sunday afternoon session for children. The festival is funded by the city's Department of Cultural Affairs and organized by the Coastal Jazz Association, a nonprofit, community organization that depends on volunteers to run the event. Sessions are free.

ℹ️ Wear comfortable shoes to outdoor festivals, especially those on River Street, where you'll be walking on the ballastones and uneven pavement. Be careful if you use the steps leading from Bay Street to River Street—they seem to have been designed for people with long legs and short feet.

SAVANNAH PRIDE FESTIVAL

Rousakis Plaza
River Street
(912) 234-1134
www.savpride.com

This celebration of alternative lifestyles moves around a lot. After five years at a smaller venue, it built its way up to River Street and later to Johnson Square. The festival features dozens of entertainers and guest speakers addressing topics pertinent to the gay, lesbian, bisexual, and transgender community. More than 60 vendors are on hand, including folks representing community service agencies and those involved in sales of food, arts and crafts, and other merchandise. The event, held on a Saturday in early-Sept, starts at noon and progresses into the evening.

Islands

MEDIEVAL FESTIVAL
Oatland Island Education Center
711 Sandtown Rd.
(912) 898-3980
www.oatlandisland.org
The clanging of sword fighting interrupts the normally serene environs of the Oatland Island Education Center on a Saturday in September when the Medieval Festival takes place. Costumed reenactors wield those weapons and also tell stories, roam through crowds of festivalgoers singing minstrel songs, and give demonstrations involving gypsy dancing and shooting a crossbow. Children's games and crafts and visits to a medieval village round out the activities, held from 10 a.m. until 5 p.m. Admission is $5 for those four years old and older, with kids younger than four admitted free.

Southside/Midtown

BETHESDA LABOR DAY FESTIVAL
Bethesda Home for Boys
9520 Ferguson Ave.
(912) 351-2040
www.bethesdahomeforboys.org
Held on Labor Day under the large, shady oaks at the Bethesda Home for Boys (see our Attractions chapter), this gathering for families offers live entertainment, kiddie rides, games, craft sales, and hot dogs and hamburgers, the last being made from Bethesda's

homegrown beef. Special features have included antique automobile shows and live entertainment. Admission is free, but there is a $2 fee for parking. You buy tickets for games and food, and the prices won't set you back much. The festival runs from 10 a.m. until 4 p.m.

OCTOBER

Historic Downtown

OKTOBERFEST
Rousakis Plaza
River Street
(912) 234-0295
www.riverstreetsavannah.com
If you happen to have a dachshund handy, you might want to enter it in the **Wiener Dog Race,** a comical competition that's become a featured part of the Savannah Waterfront Association's Oktoberfest event. Some 200 low-slung pooches "sprint" down the 50-foot racecourse as they seek to win prizes for their masters. The race—run in heats of four to six dogs until an overall winner prevails—benefits the local Friends of the Animals organization and costs $7 to enter. Watching is fun even if you don't have a dog running: Some pups never get out of the starting gate, and others wander around instead of heading for the finish line. The race is staged on the Saturday morning of the festival, which occurs during the first weekend of the month.

There will also be German food and music and plenty of beer. Booths manned by employees of River Street restaurants sell Wiener schnitzel, sauerbraten, bratwurst, and German chocolate cake, but there is also food for those whose tastes aren't Teutonic. Oompah-band members decked out in lederhosen and Tyrolean hats provide much of the music, and festivalgoers are invited to join them in doing the arm-flapping, head-bobbing "Chicken Dance." Also, a headline entertainer usually performs at Oktoberfest. Admission is free, but the food is not. Hours of operation are 9 a.m. to midnight on Fri and Sat, and 9 a.m. until 6 p.m. on Sun.

PICNIC IN THE PARK
Forsyth Park
(912) 651-6417
www.savannahga.gov/arts
Wine and dine under the stars and enjoy a pops classical concert by the Savannah Sinfonietta at this event on a weekend evening in early October. The more elaborate your picnic meal at tree-filled Forsyth Park, the better. Judges rate the best picnic, and festivalgoers seek to outdo one another with table settings and setups ranging from the elaborate to the unexpected. Candelabra, chandeliers, and chafing dishes make appearances, and some folks opt to embellish their picnics with formal rugs and dining room suites. Others get creative, building tropical huts for luaus or laying out an early Thanksgiving spread. If you prefer to simply sit on a blanket and nibble on a sandwich, that's okay, too. The concert and your seats on the grass are free of charge, courtesy of Savannah's Department of Cultural Affairs; you provide the food and drink.

SIEGE OF SAVANNAH MEMORIAL
Revolutionary Battlefield Park
303 Martin Luther King Jr. Blvd.
(912) 651-6895, ext. 2
www.chsgeorgia.org
The Coastal Heritage Society uses this celebration to commemorate the climactic battle of the Siege of Savannah (see the History chapter), which was fought on the site of the Savannah History Museum and the nearby historic Roundhouse Railroad Museum. The ceremony is held about 7 a.m. on the first Saturday in October, with living history demonstrations offered throughout the weekend. Admission is free.

HISTORIC SAVANNAH FOUNDATION GALA
Location varies
(912) 233-7787
www.historicsavannahfoundation.org
One of Historic Savannah Foundation's major fund-raisers starts with cocktails in private homes and moves to a site in one of the city's historic neighborhoods for a black-tie dinner party. The event is held in late October or early November, but the date and location vary. Check the website for updated date and ticket information.

SHALOM Y'ALL JEWISH FOOD FESTIVAL
Forsyth Park
(912) 233-1547
www.mickveisrael.org
Congregation Mickve Israel presents this opportunity to sample Jewish foods such as blintzes, potato latkes, matzo ball soup, knishes, kosher hot dogs, pastrami sandwiches, challah bread, and, of course, bagels with cream cheese and lox. These delectable items are sold from booths set up in Forsyth Park.

While you're strolling the park, be on the lookout for a booth manned by Arnold Belzer, the rabbi of the temple, who'll be dishing up portions of his own specialty, a type of stir-fry he calls "Ahmein Lo Mein." Live entertainment and activities for children add to the event, which runs from 11 a.m. until 4 p.m. on a Sunday in late October. Admission is free, and you purchase food and beverages by buying tickets at the park, or you may call in advance to pick up tickets before the festival. Note that the best food sells out early.

SAVANNAH FILM FESTIVAL
Trustees Theater
216 East Broughton St.
(912) 525-5050
www.scad.edu/filmfest
Hosted by the Savannah College of Art and Design, this presentation of film and video productions takes place during a week's time in late October and/or early November. The latest in feature-length films, shorts, animations, documentaries, and student work are screened at the Lucas Theatre and Trustees Theater in downtown Savannah, with workshops and gatherings at various other venues. Look for the trendy, the indie, the oldie, you name it. This week is always good for celebrity watching. Every year, the stars who attend to pick up awards become more A-list.

Islands

HALLOWEEN HIKE
Oatland Island Education Center
711 Sandtown Rd.
(912) 898-3980
www.oatlandisland.org
If you're seeking a tamer Halloween experience for your child, take advantage of this walk along the trails and through the "Friendly Forest" at Oatland Island Education Center. As they frolic through the woods, young trick-or-treaters meet adults costumed as animal characters, who greet the children with hugs and goodies. Admission is $5 per child, and the center provides

bags for collecting treats. You or another adult must accompany your child, and the little ones are encouraged to wear costumes and comfortable shoes. The center holds the hike on the Friday and Saturday before Halloween.

Southside/Midtown

SAVANNAH FOLK MUSIC FESTIVAL
Various locations
(912) 786-6953
www.savannahfolk.org
The focal point of this completely free three-day musical jamboree is a concert at the Roundhouse Railroad Museum in downtown Savannah. The concert consists of four to five acts featuring nationally recognized musicians. Folks such as singer-musicians Tom Rush, Mike Seeger, John Jackson, and Robin and Linda Williams have graced the stage. Don't let the threat of rain scare you away; the museum affords plenty of shelter, so inclement weather won't stop the singing, picking, and grinning.

The signature event of this three-day musical festival is Sun, Oct 10, 2 to 7 p.m. at historic Grayson Stadium and stars internationally acclaimed folk singers, plus the winner of the "Youth Song Writing Competition" (held the Friday before) and a silent auction. The traditional Folk fest at Ellis Square is Fri, Oct 8.

There are two events on Sat (Oct 9). The schedule is as follows: 2 p.m., the finals of the "Youth Song Writing Competition" will be held at the First Presbyterian Church, 520 E. Washington St., followed by the "Old Time Country Dance" at Notre Dame Academy gymnasium from 8 to 11 p.m. For more information, check the website.

SAVANNAH GREEK FESTIVAL
Hellenic Center
14 West Anderson St.
(912) 236-8256
www.stpaul.ga.goarch.org

When we think of the Savannah Greek Festival, we can taste the baklava melting in our mouths. Those scrumptious pastries are just a sample of the tasty concoctions offered for sale at the Hellenic Center adjacent to St. Paul's Greek Orthodox Church in midtown Savannah during the third Thursday, Friday, and Saturday in October. Among other favorites of the festival's patrons are the Greek salad, gyro sandwiches, and a spinach pie called spanakopita. While you're enjoying the food, sit back and watch the Hellenic Center's dance groups perform. You can also tour the church. Festival hours are 11 a.m. until 9 p.m. Call or visit the website for updated admission pricing.

COASTAL EMPIRE FAIR
520 West 63rd St.
(912) 354-3542
www.coastalempirefair.com

During 11 days in late October and early November when the weather turns chilly, the Coastal Empire Fair comes to town. The fairgrounds off Montgomery Street glow and throb with the lights and sounds of thrill rides, sideshows, and game booths. The 60-odd rides include about a dozen kiddie rides. This Exchange Club Fair Association extravaganza also features livestock shows, flower shows, and home demonstrations in skills such as canning and quilt making. The $20 admission fee allows you to hop on as many rides as you wish. Call or check the website for updated fares.

BAMBOO FARM ANNUAL FALL FESTIVAL
Bamboo Farm and Coastal Gardens
2 Canebrake Rd.
(912) 921-5460

Paint your face, buy some plants (perennials and fall annuals), or purchase sugar cane syrup at this celebration of autumn in late October at the Bamboo Farm. For those seeking a bite to eat, there's a snack bar and a smoked pork luncheon featuring greens, roast pork, sweet potatoes, corn bread, and ice tea, and a hot-dog lunch. The kids will enjoy hayrides, pony rides, a bounce house, and storytelling in the cottage garden. Adults might opt for the garden lecture and plant vendors. The last few years have featured workshops on the findings of an ongoing research program on growing bananas in Savannah—it can be done, with luck and skill.

NOVEMBER

Historic Downtown

SAVANNAH SEAFOOD FESTIVAL
Rousakis Plaza
River Street
(912) 234-0295
www.riverstreetsavannah.com

Fresh seafood prepared at booths on River Street's Rousakis Plaza is the main attraction of this event on the first weekend in November. Menus feature shrimp, crab, and crayfish—much of it caught in local waters. Festivalgoers munch away as they check out sales of arts and crafts, boogie to the beach and Cajun music provided by bands playing on the plaza's main stage, and enjoy the oyster-shucking contest. Hours are 9 a.m. to midnight on Fri and Sat, and 9 a.m. to 6 p.m. on Sun. Admission is free.

FESTIVAL OF LIGHTS
Savannah Station
601 Cohen St.
(912) 236-7423
A fund-raiser for the programs of the non-profit Parent and Child Development Services of Union Mission, this event on an evening in mid-November features a cocktail party and silent and live auctions. Held in the quaint brick surroundings of Savannah Station on the western fringes of the Historic District, this celebration for people of all faiths costs $100 per person to attend.

TELFAIR ART FAIR
Telfair Square
121 Barnard St.
(912) 232-1177
www.telfair.org
The Telfair Museum's annual fair attracts artists from throughout the United States. They compete for cash awards and sell their creations to the public from displays under tents set up around Telfair Square. You can find paintings, sculpture, photographs, fabric, jewelry, and other fine arts at this exhibition, which takes place early in November. Hours are 10 a.m. until 5 p.m. on Sat, and 12:30 to 4:30 p.m. on Sun. The fair is free.

Islands

CANE GRINDING AND HARVEST FESTIVAL
Oatland Island Education Center
711 Sandtown Rd.
(912) 898-3980
www.oatlandisland.org
Get a glimpse of the pioneer life of 1830s Georgia and do some early Christmas shopping by ambling through the Oatland forest and visiting the Heritage Homesite on a Saturday in November. At the end of your walk through a wood thick with oak, magnolia, pine, and vines of the Muscadine grape, you'll find yourself in a small clearing where sugar cane is being processed. Farmers grind the cane into juice at a mill powered by a horse, then boil it into syrup. You can watch the entire operation, then buy a bottle of the sweet-smelling nectar to pour on your Sunday morning pancakes.

You might also want to poke your head into the cozy interiors of the two log cabins at the site and watch weavers at work and costumed women preparing corn bread, or you might hunker down on a bench and listen to members of the Savannah Folk Music Society as they perform songs from Georgia's past. Complete your day at Oatland by walking the nature trail to the wild-animal habitats and visiting the center's barnyard. If you need to get off your feet for a while, take a hayride through the forest. The festival opens at 10 a.m. and closes at 5 p.m. Admission is $5 for persons four and older; those younger than age four are admitted free.

DECEMBER
Historic Downtown

HOLIDAY OPEN HOUSE
City Market
Jefferson and St. Julian Streets
(912) 525-2489
www.savannahcitymarket.com
On the first Friday evening of December, the courtyard at City Market glows with the soft light of more than 500 luminarias as shop owners open their doors and offer complimentary refreshments to visitors. Strolling carolers sing Yuletide classics while Father Christmas—resplendent in his green velvet robe and red velvet cape and hat—talks

with children about the spirit of the season and their plans for the holidays. This festive atmosphere takes place at City Market's Holiday Open House, which starts at 6 p.m. with the lighting of the luminaries and ends about 9 p.m.

CHRISTMAS FOR KIDS
City Market
Jefferson and St. Julian Streets
(912) 515-2489
www.savannahcitymarket.com
It's been said that Christmas is for children, and City Market takes that to heart by offering a program for young people from 11 a.m. until 2 p.m. on the first Saturday of the month. This event gives youngsters the opportunity to make ornaments to take home, have their faces painted, enjoy a petting zoo, decorate cookies, and visit with Father Christmas in the Carriage Tours of Savannah Cinderella Carriage, and a choir performance. The entertainment varies from year to year, with puppet shows, a petting zoo, and performances by cloggers in the mix. Carriage Tours collects toys for their annual Toys for Tots promotion. It's all free.

CHRISTMAS ON THE RIVER
River Street
(912) 234-0295
www.riverstreetsavannah.com
Usher in the Christmas season on the first Saturday in December by shopping for gifts created by artists and craftspeople and watching a lighted parade starring Santa Claus. The arts and crafts vendors start selling at 9 a.m. on the riverfront plaza, and the parade begins at 6 p.m. on the western end of River Street. The parade lasts from an hour to 90 minutes and also includes high-school

bands, color guards, floats, dance troupes, antique cars, and last, but most important, St. Nick riding in a carriage. After the parade, Santa poses for photos, and strolling musicians and local choirs perform throughout the day. Enjoy the parade but keep an eye out for flying candy flung from the floats to youngsters lining the route. Arts and crafts booths remain open until 6 p.m. In keeping with the spirit of the season, there is no charge for admission to this holiday festival.

i Get a unique view of activities on River Street and stay out of the crowds by renting a hotel room facing the Savannah River, but be prepared for some late-night noise from musicians and merrymakers.

SAVANNAH RIVER BRIDGE RUN
Various downtown streets
(912) 355-3527
www.savannahbridgerun.com
Participating in the Savannah River Bridge Run will give you a unique view of Savannah—on foot from the Eugene Talmadge Memorial Bridge, a 1.4-mile span that rises 196 feet above the water. New races have been added to the 5K and 10K runs—Double Pump, Kid Race, and Team Challenge. Check out the website for additional information and schedules, registration, and packet pickup dates. You can register ahead of time and save money or enter on the day before the race. Nearly 2,000 people compete in these races. The race is particularly popular as it offers runners a safe way to see the sights from the towering bridge that is normally closed to foot traffic. Savannah's terrain is flat, so the steep slope of the bridge is another novelty for local runners.

DOWNTOWN NEIGHBORHOOD ASSOCIATION HOLIDAY TOUR OF HOMES AND VICTORIAN TEA
Hilton Savannah DeSoto Hotel
15 East Liberty St.
(912) 236-8362
www.dnaholidaytour.net
Many of the homes on the tours offered during this mid-December event are decorated for Christmas in ways reflecting the lifestyles of their owners. The self-guided walking tours are on Saturday afternoon and evening and Sunday afternoon, with a different set of six to nine private homes featured on each day. The sponsoring Downtown Neighborhood Association selects homes in the Historic District that present a diversity of architectural design and decor. The Saturday evening tour runs from 11 a.m. to 4 p.m., and candles light the interiors and exteriors of many of the residences visited. The Saturday afternoon and the Sunday tours run from 12:30 p.m. to 3:30 p.m. Tickets are $30 per tour, and they can be picked up on the days of the event in the lobby of the Hilton Savannah DeSoto Hotel. Call ahead to find out more about what's available.

NEW YEAR'S EVE AT CITY MARKET
City Market
Jefferson and St. Julian Streets
(912) 525-2489
www.savannahcitymarket.com
A live band creates a party atmosphere at City Market during the hours leading up to midnight on New Year's Eve. It's an outdoor party and filled with all the color Savannah can muster. For Savannahians, this is as close as it gets to being in Times Square. The event is free, and the partying starts about 7 p.m. and lasts until 1 or 2 a.m.

Islands

COLONIAL CHRISTMAS AT WORMSLOE
Wormsloe Historic Site
7601 Skidaway Rd.
(912) 353-3023
A Christmas celebration, 18th-century-style, complete with caroling and dancing, and the burning of the Yule log, is one of the highlights of the Savannah holiday special events. This holiday program on the second Sunday in December runs from 2 to 5 p.m., and admission is $5 for adults, $3.50 for senior citizens, and $2.50 for those ages 6 to 18. Children younger than age 6 are admitted free.

Southside/Midtown

CHRISTMAS AT BETHESDA
Bethesda Home for Boys
9250 Ferguson Ave.
(912) 351-2040
www.bethesdahomeforboys.org
The boys of Bethesda (see our Attractions chapter) present a reenactment of the Magi's visit to the baby Jesus and sing Christmas carols during a program at their chapel. The boys and their guests then move to the gymnasium for an Old English Christmas celebration featuring the bringing in of a Yule log and visits from the Switch Man, who gives switches to kids who've been bad; the Cookie Lady, who gives cookies to kids who've been good; and Santa Claus, who has gifts for all the residents of the home. This observance occurs on an evening two weeks before Christmas and gets started about 6 p.m. The event is free and open to the public; donations are accepted.

KIDSTUFF

Savannah is the place to bring your kids when you want them to put down their Wii controller, walk away from the television, breathe in the salt air, and discover all the fun they've missed staying stuffed up inside. Although the romance and historical elements of this city are plenty to satisfy the more mature visitor (and this is indeed nothing close to Disney World), there are lots of fun options for play when the kids have to come along.

That's great news for many travelers. Here are some suggestions to get them out in the air, and keep them safe, occupied, and entertained while they're here. The beach is within easy striking distance, a water-oriented outdoor lifestyle that puts crab traps and fishing poles in the youngest of hands, a fanatically organized system of youth sports that covers all the major games (well, not ice hockey—this is the South, you know), a local theater scene that makes room for kids, you name it. Savannah also offers that increasingly rare opportunity of growing up in a place that has a sense of identity and uniqueness.

In this chapter, we'll focus on history, wildlife, sports, flavor, and last, but not least, the paranormal (yikes!). If you are traveling with children, we recommend spending at least part of your stay at Tybee Island, the local beach. We've got a whole chapter on options there. Any child who tags along dutifully on historic site tours and antiques shopping rounds deserves a chance to dig in the sand and splash around in the ocean, even in winter. Shark tooth scavenging is an awesome way to spend a cold but sunny afternoon!

HISTORY FOR KIDS

You'll need your video camera to capture your child's face as he stares into the sunlit spray of a fountain, tossing pennies into the flow. The mesmerizing task can be an activity that accompanies a picnic under the live oaks in Johnson Square. This is just one of many activities that will make fond vacation memories.

When the picnic ends, sign up for a tour! Enlist the help of a carriage tour driver to color up the commentary and opt to see Savannah by horse-drawn carriage. If you're

dying to do one of the Midnight tours based on the best-selling *Midnight in the Garden of Good and Evil,* make sure the guide's patter isn't going to be too explicit and think about leaving Junior at home. What does that leave in the tour category? Two really good options: **carriage tours** (as mentioned above) or **ghost tours.** If your children are old enough—say, at least second or third grade—you should check out the ghost tours, especially the walking or carriage versions. The stories are tame enough that they are unlikely to inspire screaming nightmares. Actually, these popular tours have proliferated in recent years, and gotten hokier and sillier in the process, perfect for a group of mischievous children.

i If you visit in the summer, the various branch libraries are in full swing with summer programs for kids. Call (912) 652-3600 to find the branch nearest you. Visitors are always welcome, and with a temporary card (cost $25), you can even check out books, videos, and tapes.

With younger children, you can add interest to historic sightseeing with the help of a bright, intriguing book for children, *Savannah Safari* (www.savannahsafari.com), the work of locals Polly Wylly Cooper and Emmeline King Cooper. It is a slim paperback volume, designed to serve as a coloring book if you so desire, that sends kids on a scavenger-style hunt for "animals" while touring the Historic District. The "animals" are the iron downspouts shaped like dolphins, the sculptured herons in the Forsyth Park fountains, and so on. Stretch the interest for older children by chipping in one of those disposable cameras so they can photograph their "animal" finds.

Savannah Safari is $6 and available in local bookstores, which you'll find listed in our Shopping chapter. It's time to don your backpack, hold that little hand, and gallop off to a wonderland that they'll love, even if it is in an old city.

JULIETTE GORDON LOW BIRTHPLACE
142 Bull St.
(912) 233-4501
www.girlscouts.org/birthplace

If your children are, have been, or aspire to be Girl Scouts, don't miss this wonderful house museum. In fact, it's your best bet among the museums for entertaining children. The birthplace and childhood home of Juliette "Daisy" Gordon Low is a virtual mecca for Girl Scouts from throughout the country, and you'll spot field trips full of them trooping around Savannah all the time. As a result, the staff at the center is experienced in the art of entertaining children without boring their adult escorts.

The elegant and beautifully preserved home of the wealthy Gordon family, which includes a masterpiece of a garden, works well for both age groups. The home is open for tours from 10 a.m. to 5 p.m., Tues through Fri. Closed on Wed, Nov through Feb, and on major holidays. The cost is $8 for adults and $7 for children. (Read more about it in our Attractions chapter.)

SHIPS OF THE SEA MUSEUM
41 Martin Luther King Jr. Blvd.
(912) 232-1511
www.shipsofthesea.org

The kids can learn all about Savannah's maritime history at this museum, which has been relocated to one of Savannah's historic old residences. The more upscale setting probably lowered the kid appeal here, but it should still work for kids. Cost is $8 for adults, $6 for students and seniors. Family rate is $20 (two parents and any siblings under 18). Children younger than age seven are free. The museum is open from 10 a.m. to 5 p.m. Tues through Sun; closed Mon.

WILDLIFE

THE AQUARIUM AT SKIDAWAY ISLAND
30 Ocean Science Circle
(912) 598-FISH (3474), (912) 598-2496

River Street Kidstuff

River Street, especially by day, can appeal mightily to the young tourist. All along the river are lots of shops, and while they are stocked with expensive gift items with the usual tourist-area markup, there are also plenty of wares geared toward kid tastes and kid pocketbooks. Follow them from shop to shop here and watch them buy candy and trinkets.

If luck is with you, your young entourage will get to spot one or more of the giant container ships, escorted by a team of tugboats, on its way upriver to the Georgia Ports Authority. These ships are such an imposing presence that even jaded teenagers will stop in their tracks to stare.

Scout out Georgia's marine life at the Aquarium at Skidaway Island. This small facility, operated by the University of Georgia Marine Extension Service, also includes a picnic area (which you may appreciate, because it is quite a drive out to Skidaway) and a walking trail. See 200 live animals—including fish of all shapes and sizes, turtles, and maybe even a small shark in the many wall tanks lining the exhibit hall. You owe this one to your kids if they have never seen a live flounder, our candidate for weirdest-looking fish in the world. Then go outside for a stroll along the Jay Wolfe Nature Trail, which passes by scenic marshes. The aquarium is open from 9 a.m. to 4 p.m. on weekdays and noon to 5

p.m. on Sat. It is closed on Sun and holidays. The cost is $4 for ages 13 and older, $2 for children and seniors; children ages three and younger enter free.

BULL RIVER CRUISES
8005 Old Tybee Rd.
(US 80 East)
Tybee Island
(912) 898-1800, (800) 311-4779
www.bullriver.com

This marina offers a variety of eco-cruises and charters, and bills itself as experienced in working with Girl Scout troops. Call for reservations. They're essential because these trips are keenly affected by the weather. No one can guarantee you a dolphin sighting, but it is highly likely. The real challenge is to make the trips long enough to justify the price and short enough to remain interesting if the local wildlife choose not to perform. Winter visitors are less likely to find these trips an option, although the marina will arrange custom trips, birthday parties, fishing charters, and other boating recreation excursions.

LAZARETTO CREEK MARINA & CAPT. MIKE'S DOLPHIN TOURS
US 80 East
(just across Lazaretto Creek Bridge)
Tybee Island
(912) 786-5848, (800) 242-0166
www.tybeedolphins.com

While enjoying the scenery of Fort Pulaski and the North Beach of Tybee Island, see friendly bottle-nosed dolphins playing in their natural habitat. The 90-minute tours cost $15 for adults and teens and $8 for children age 12 and younger. Diving and deep-sea/inshore fishing charters are available.

i If you dare, take your children to see the huge live alligator collection at the Crab Shack at Tybee Island. At last count, this restaurant had at least a hundred gators in captivity. These air breathers are lively and not considered to be man-eaters, despite what you may have heard. The colorful website will get your kids excited about their visit. Check it out: www.thecrabshack.com.

OATLAND ISLAND EDUCATION CENTER
711 Sandtown Rd.
(912) 898-3980
www.oatlandisland.org

You are virtually guaranteed to spot your alligator here at a natural-habitat facility operated by the local school system as an educational center. Other once-native animals—buffalo, wolves, birds of prey—and an authentic Colonial farm setting, complete with livestock, can also be seen. A self-guided outdoor hike takes you through marshes and around to the different animal and plant exhibits. Admission is $5, and free for those age three and younger. The center, which hosts many popular programs (see our Annual Events and Festivals chapter), is open from 9 a.m. to 4:30 p.m. Mon through Sat (holidays impact Sat hours). As teachers, the staff members are good with kids, so don't miss this attraction. Bring your own bug repellent, though—you'll need it. (For more on the center, see our Attractions chapter.)

SAVANNAH NATIONAL WILDLIFE REFUGE
South Carolina Hwy. 170
(912) 652-4415
www.fws.gov/savannah

Take a coastal safari through the 29,174-acre Savannah National Wildlife Refuge. It's full of freshwater marsh, tidal rivers, creeks, and bottomland hardwood swamps. While driving through the refuge, see if you can spot alligators, owls, hawks, turtles, snakes, or maybe even a bald eagle. The refuge is managed by the U.S. Fish and Wildlife Service. It is open Mon through Sat, 9 a.m. to 4:30 p.m. (except federal holidays), and visiting is free. The refuge is about 9 miles from downtown.

TYBEE ISLAND MARINE SCIENCE CENTER
14th Street parking lot
Tybee Island
(912) 786-5917 (866) 557-9172
www.tybeemarinescience.org

Stroll the beach, toss a net into the ocean, then learn about what you find during a beach discovery walk held daily at the center. A tour guide leads the way and explains about Tybee's marine life. Don't forget to check out the stuff inside the center, too— you'll find a touch tank, aquariums, and shark displays. This isn't Sea World—expect a small, personalized experience. Open from 9 a.m. to 5 p.m. daily, closing at noon on Tues. Admission is $4 for adults and $3 for children, with those under three admitted free. Check the website for the latest listing of "walks, talks, and treks" and other special programs.

OUTDOOR ADVENTURE

FORSYTH PARK
Bull Street between Gaston Street and Park Avenue

Thirty acres perfect for letting off some steam are set aside in the Historic Downtown. There are swing sets, slides, and other contraptions for youngsters needing to get rid of some energy, along with plenty of open space for just plain running, and beautiful magnolia trees and scenery for Mom and Dad to enjoy, too. May we suggest a picnic?

LAKE MAYER
**Montgomery Crossroad and
Sallie Mood Drive
(912) 652-6786**
Bring your bike and take a spin around the 1.5-mile trail at Lake Mayer, located in the 75-acre community park of the same name. While there, you can also play tennis or basketball, frolic on the playground, or feed the ducks swimming in the lake.

i You wouldn't normally think of shopping for a child in a cigar store, but hear us out: The shops sell their empty cigar boxes, starting at $2. Even adamant nonsmokers will admit there's nothing better for storing those seashells than a cigar box.

SKIDAWAY ISLAND STATE PARK
**52 Diamond Causeway
Skidaway Island
(912) 598-2300
www.gastateparks.org**
Camping sites, picnic areas, trails, an interpretive center, and three playgrounds can be found at 533-acre Skidaway Island State Park, the only state park in Chatham County. Maps of the park and trails are available at the park office. If you don't want to tackle the trails alone, free guided hikes are available with advance reservations. Park hours are 7 a.m. to 10 p.m. Office hours are 8 a.m. to 5 p.m. Cost to enter the park is $3 per car, except on Wed when it is free.

i Let the kids try their luck at fishing. The dock at the Lazaretto Creek pier is a popular "hole" and is located along a picturesque section of Tybee where there are usually fish biting on any given afternoon. Fishing gear, bait, and snacks may be purchased at Wal-Mart on US 80 at Whitemarsh Island.

THE OL' BALL GAME

SAVANNAH SAND GNATS
**Grayson Stadium
Daffin Park
1401 East Victory Dr.
(912) 351-9150
www.sandgnats.com**
If you happen to be in town during the Sand Gnats' season (early Apr through the end of Aug), round up the kids and take them to a ball game. Besides being entertained by the Gnats, the single-A affiliate for the New York Mets, kids and parents will have fun watching the dueling mascots and between-inning contests (including the classic one in which two people spin around dozens of times with their heads on the ends of bats, then try to make it to first base), munching on barbecue and boiled peanuts, and getting caught up in the atmosphere of this old-time ballpark. Games start at 7:15 p.m. on weekdays and Sat, and at 6:05 p.m. on Sun. General admission is only $7 for adults and $5 for children ages 4 to 12. Cheaper seats offer the best chance of catching foul balls. Parking is free around the stadium. (For much more on the Sand Gnats, see our Spectator Sports chapter.)

THE LIGHT AT THE END OF THE TUNNEL

TYBEE ISLAND LIGHTHOUSE
30 Meddin Dr.
(912) 786-5801
www.tybeelighthouse.org
Hike 154 feet to the top of Tybee Lighthouse for a great view of Tybee and Savannah. You'll also learn a few things about one of America's historic light stations. It opens at 9 a.m. and sells the last ticket at 4:30 p.m. (it closes at 5:30). Closed on Tues. Cost, which includes admission to the Tybee Museum, is $7 for adults, $5 for seniors, military, and children ages 6 to 17; children under 5 are free.

FOR A RAINY DAY

THE FLYING FROGS
1100 Eisenhower Dr.
(912) 356-0075
www.theflyingfrogs.com
Looking for some inside entertainmentfor children during your stay in Savannah? This establishment will keep them happy! As one of the only indoor playgrounds left in the city, kids are allowed to run wild and, in fact, are encouraged to do so. Pizza is the menu mainstay. There are also games that pay off in points that kids can amass for prizes. Admission to Flying Frogs is free. There are combinations of food and activies such as a train pass and a 12 oz. drink for $5, and there are monthly specials (check the website to view). Hours are Mon though Thurs, noon to 8 p.m.; Fri and Sat, 10 a.m. to 10 p.m., Sun 11 a.m. to 8 p.m.

ARTS & CULTURE

Savannah is an attraction for the arts and culture. With one of the country's premiere art colleges headquartered here, the city is not only a consumer of the arts but also a producer of the arts. Music, drama, and the visual arts are all well represented here, both in the form of outlets for local talent and in venues for touring artists of greater renown. Students study here to become artists (of varying sorts), and many of them stay after they graduate.

You can take your arts and culture on various levels in Savannah. You can don your designer duds and shop in ultrachic art galleries, picking up pieces by artists who never set foot on these shores; you can dress in jeans and pick up a sketch from a sidewalk artist on River Street; or you can rent a garret, buy a backpack, and enroll in art classes yourself. You can also work through the same type of strata musically as a concertgoer, a jazz follower in smoky nightclubs, or as a community band or civic orchestra performer bent on honing your talents. As for theater, you'll find several active local theater groups, thriving secular performance venues in some local churches, and, for those who prefer the role of spectator, the occasional national touring troupe.

OVERVIEW

In this chapter, we outline Savannah's major cultural organizations and venues for you. We provide plenty of telephone numbers and instructions on how to tap into specific schedules. You might also want to check out our Annual Events and Festivals chapter for further suggestions for an artsy afternoon or evening. Keeping abreast of the local cultural scene is fairly easy. The *Savannah Morning News* (see our Media chapter) offers its most comprehensive arts coverage in a Sunday Accent section. The *Morning News*'s Thursday Diversions section also contains event listings, but the coverage there tends to be more club and concert oriented.

Also, check out the Convention and Visitors Bureau's website (www.savannahvisit.com). It's an excellent resource for cross-checking event details. Again, read our Media chapter for suggestions on where to find this publication, which is free and distributed at various restaurants and businesses.

VENUES

LUCAS THEATRE FOR THE ARTS
32 Abercorn St.
(912) 525-5040
www.lucastheatre.com
The restoration of the Lucas Theatre for the Arts seemed to take forever, but it has been well worth the wait. The theater was built in 1921 and rode the popularity of the silver screen for decades. Alas, it fell into disrepair as the 1970s came on, and after some ill-fated attempts to keep it running (such as a

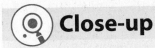 **Close-up**

Other Great Savannah Books

John Berendt's *Midnight in the Garden of Good and Evil* is not the first book to be set in Savannah, although you might get that impression from the way the city has adopted it. If you want to read more Savannah-as-a-setting books, we have some suggestions.

- *More Than Mercer House: Savannah's Jim Williams and His Southern Houses,* by Dr. Dorothy Williams Kingery (Williams's sister, an academician), reviews Williams's distinguished role in the preservation of many significant buildings in Savannah and surrounding areas and tells tales of his outstanding antiques-finding adventures. You can buy the book in the author's store or order it by mail or phone (see store listings elsewhere in this chapter).

- *Savannah Spectres and Other Strange Tales,* by Margaret DeBolt, is a collection of local ghost stories that has become sort of the standard reference work on the topic hereabouts.

- *Hooligans,* by William Diehl, was published in 1984. It never attracted as much attention as Diehl's more successful works such as *Sharkey's Machine* and *Primal Fear,* which became movies. This tale of political corruption is set in a thinly veiled Savannah: "Oceanby" for Tybee, "Isle of Sighs" for Isle of Hope, and so on. Diehl was part of a productive writers' colony on St. Simons Island, about 90 miles south of Savannah as you near the Florida border.

- *Savannah,* by Eugenia Price, is a historical romance distinguished by Price's research and a literary approach that stands far above the genre's norm. If you like what you read, you're in luck: This is the first of a four-volume saga set in Savannah. Price, who died in 1997, was another St. Simons Island author.

short stint as a dinner theater and a period when the lobby was a restaurant), the magnificent building went into mothballs.

But the Italian Renaissance–style building with its ornate interior was just too fantastic to let go, and a lengthy fund-raising campaign was started to get this grand dame back on her feet. Look for the 40-foot-wide ceiling dome, lots of gold leaf, and—a welcome sight to Savannahian eyes—the bars upstairs and down. It took 13 years to pull it off, but the end result is beautiful. The

marquee, with its chasing lights, adds an exciting touch to Savannah's nightlife, and the theater has helped spur redevelopment of nearby buildings.

The Savannah College of Art and Design (SCAD) runs the theater, and while the college does use the facility for some activities, it remains open to the public for events. This venue serves as a major host for the Savannah Film Festival and the Savannah Music Festival, and it is also the site for events sponsored by the Savannah Film Society and the

Savannah Concert Association, along with privately promoted touring productions and events brought in by SCAD but open to the general public. The theater is open Mon through Fri, 8:30 a.m. to 5:30 p.m.

SAVANNAH CIVIC CENTER
Montgomery and Liberty Streets
301 West Oglethorpe Ave.
(912) 651-6556
www.savannahciviccenter.com
The Savannah Civic Center has two main components, plus various meeting rooms and a ballroom. The arena, named for the late Dr. Martin Luther King Jr., can seat up to 9,000, depending on the event configuration. The theater, which seats about 2,500, is named in honor of Johnny Mercer, the famed Savannah-born lyricist ("Moon River," etc.). By and large, the more formal events, such as dramatic presentations or one-person shows, play in the theater, with the arena going for large-scale, pack-'em-in audiences for such events as rock or country music concerts, wrestling matches, and monster truck shows. But that isn't a hard-and-fast rule: When Mikhail Baryshnikov danced in Savannah with the touring experimental White Oak Dance Troupe, they filled the arena. The offerings at the Civic Center vary, depending on the tastes and daring of various promoters. The concert scene has become more lively with the continued growth of the Savannah College of Art and Design and its built-in audience potential. To keep up with what might be available during your visit, check the media sources mentioned at the opening of this chapter, or simply check the large billboard on the Liberty Street side of the building. The number listed here is for the box office, and tickets generally are on sale well in advance of performances.

Park Smart

The Civic Center consumes an entire block between Oglethorpe and Liberty Streets, with entrances on Montgomery Street and facing the parking lot. A word of warning about parking is in order: Popular events at the Civic Center put parking at a premium. A city-operated multilevel parking garage opened in 2005 across from the Civic Center, and it is open at night when there are performances. Because it is easier to get out of a street-side parking space, many patrons prefer to park along the surrounding streets. You don't have to feed the meters at night, but be sure not to block the crosswalks leading to the squares or make up any imaginative parking spaces—lots of parking tickets get handed out on the evenings of big performances. Also, avoid the temptation to whip into the vacant parking lots of obviously closed businesses: Many businesses choose to defend those spaces at night and will have after-hours parkers towed.

SAVANNAH COLLEGE OF ART AND DESIGN
Various addresses
www.scad.edu
You may wonder what an art college is doing under the "Venues" heading. Actually, SCAD (as it is referred to locally; see our Education and Child Care chapter for additional information) is a major player in the local arts and culture scene, not just for its own

students, but for the general public. Check out the SCAD art galleries listed later in this chapter, but first, two of the newest (including the most attractive and unique) theater entries are from SCAD. **Trustees Theater,** 206 East Broughton St. (912-239-1447), is a circa-1946 movie theater that has been refurbished and reopened as a 1,100-seat performance venue capable of handling both stage productions and movie screenings. Its basic purpose is to house performances and classes for SCAD's performing-arts majors, but it also offers performances to the public. Performers have included Tony Bennett, the Neville Brothers, and India.Arie. This is also a home venue of SCAD's annual film festival. The **Lucas Theatre for the Arts,** discussed elsewhere, is managed by SCAD.

THEATER

You have to be pretty agile to keep up with drama groups in Savannah. They come and go, and always appear to be operating on a shoestring. The amazing thing, though, is not their occasionally temporary nature—it's their resiliency. One particular group may wither away, but there's always another in the wings. Right now, we know of three independent groups, not to mention the productions put on by the City of Savannah's Leisure Services. Several churches maintain highly successful theater programs featuring secular works such as Gilbert and Sullivan offerings, and there are also collegiate theatrical groups. Armstrong Atlantic State University's Masquers produce reliably entertaining work. Check the event pages of the newspapers cited earlier for schedules and further information.

ASBURY MEMORIAL UNITED
Methodist Church
1008 East Henry St.
(912) 233-4351

This venerable church was dying out as its congregation aged and the neighborhood changed, but it got a shot in the arm when a performance-minded pastor and the congregation opened their arms to the arts community. The church social hall serves as a performance arena. Don't mistake these productions for Sunday-school projects. They're at least on a par with the other local offerings (actually, all the local theater efforts involve different arrangements of essentially the same theater performers).

Although the offerings often have a religious theme (*Godspell* and *Jesus Christ Superstar*), this group has also tackled Gilbert and Sullivan. Ticket prices vary, usually around $15. Other local churches occasionally dip into secular drama, mainly to keep their youth groups involved, but this one definitely strives for and achieves a higher level.

SAVANNAH CHILDREN'S THEATRE
2160 East Victory Dr.
(912) 238-9015
www.savannahchildrenstheatre.org

This is a thriving little theater loaded with talent! Some performances at the Savannah Children's Theatre feature only children; others have adults in some roles. Some performances are culminating events in the classes the theater teaches; roles in others are open to aspiring young actors, child and adult, free of charge. The constant is the desire to expose children to the joys of live theater, both on stage, backstage, and in the audience. It is housed in space carved out of a long-vacant department store in a small strip mall (although experience has

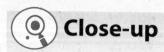

Close-up

Savannah: Style Central for Architecture Buffs

If anyone asks you about your vacation in Savannah and inquires about the architecture, whatever you tell them will be the truth. Stroll along the streets of Savannah's Historic Downtown, and you'll be looking at a blend of buildings reflecting architectural styles prevalent in America during the late 18th and 19th centuries. Among these types were Federal, which was in vogue from 1790 to 1838; English Regency, 1811 to 1830; Greek Revival, 1820 to 1875; Gothic Revival, 1830 to 1885; Italianate, 1830 to 1900; Romanesque Revival, 1850 to 1890; and Victorian, 1860 to 1915. In summary, you will view all of these architectural styles in Savannah.

Probably the city's most outstanding example of the Federal style is the **Isaiah Davenport House**, with its central hallway and arched fanlight doorway. This brick and brownstone house at 324 East State St. "reflects the balance and symmetry" of the Federal style, says Roulhac Toledano in *The National Trust Guide to Savannah*, and its double-entry stairway "must have set the standard for future graceful curving entry staircases leading to high stoops that dot the city in houses of all styles." The Davenport House, one of Savannah's many museum houses, was built in 1820; a successful effort to save it from demolition in the mid-1950s brought about the creation of the Historic Savannah Foundation preservation group. (Read more about the house in the walking-tour section of our Attractions chapter.)

The Regency style is best typified by the work of English architect **William Jay** and two of his designs, the **Owens-Thomas House** at 124 Abercorn St., and the **Scarbrough House** at 41 Martin Luther King Jr. Blvd., open to the public. The porches and columns of these buildings are prime examples of the Regency style. A commission to build the house for cotton merchant Richard Richardson is what brought Jay to Georgia, and he "went on to create a series of buildings that qualify as the state's first architectural masterpieces," says Tom Spector in his book *The Guide to the Architecture of Georgia*. These two houses "rank among the best works produced in America" during the early 1800s. The Owens-Thomas House, which Toledano deems "probably the finest example

---

taught us that theater groups in Savannah are mobile, so check the website). Past productions have included *Beauty and the Beast,* a kids' version of *Guys and Dolls,* and *The King and I.* Actually, the list of past and planned performances is long: The theater is in almost constant production mode, and plays follow on one another's heels. Ticket prices vary, and they're $10 at the moment. You can buy them at the door, but it might be just your luck that's when the young star's entire extended family attends and the theater only seats about 150. You can also buy

online. Limited concessions are available at most performances.

SAVANNAH THEATRE
220 Bull St.
(912) 233-7764
www.savannahtheatre.com
This professional troupe came to town in 2002, with a show titled *Lost in the '50s,* which was originally developed in Branson, Missouri. Since then, the bill has changed periodically, but stayed within the same framework. The group puts on an

of English Regency architecture in America," was constructed in 1819, and the Scarbrough House was completed in the same year.

Greek Revival–style buildings are reminiscent of the temples of Greece with their long front porches supported by towering columns. To see two fine models of this style, take a look at the **Aaron Champion House** at 230 Barnard St., and the **Sorrel-Weed House** at 6 West Harris St. Both houses were designed by **Charles Cluskey,** the Champion House in 1844 and the Sorrel-Weed House in 1841. Cluskey was Georgia's premier architect during the 1830s and 1840s.

Walk over to Madison Square for a look at what Toledano calls Savannah's "foremost Gothic-style house." The **Green-Meldrim House** at 1 West Macon St., which can be toured by visitors, was designed by John S. Norris and built in 1853. Exterior features are the crenelated parapet, oriel windows, and the heavily detailed iron porch. (See our Attractions chapter for more on the Green-Meldrim House.)

The **Mercer House** at 429 Bull St., is another Norris design, but it is an example of the Italianate style, which has the look of an Italian villa—low-pitched roof, wide eaves, long porch, and cast-iron balconies. The house was designed before the outbreak of the Civil War but was completed in 1871 by two assistants of Norris. (For more on the Mercer House, see our Attractions and Savannah Celebrity chapters.) Another Italianate-style residence (and another of the city's house museums) is the **Andrew Low House** at 329 Abercorn St. (see our Attractions chapter).

The Romanesque Revival style is embodied by two Savannah landmarks, the **Cotton Exchange** at 100 East Bay St. and the **Chatham County Courthouse** at 124 Bull St. Both were designed by William G. Preston. The Cotton Exchange, with its brick and terra-cotta facade and turned wooden posts, was constructed in 1886. Preston came to Savannah to build the courthouse three years later.

An interesting example of the gingerbread style of the Victorian period is the **King-Tisdell Cottage** at 514 East Huntingdon St., which now serves as a black cultural museum. It dates from 1896.

oldies-based review, changing the name and some of the program each year or so. In late November and until Christmas, it presents a holiday-themed musical. Then, it goes dark for a break of a couple of weeks and reopens with a new show. Particularly popular (and the best of its offerings) is *Broadway on Bull Street.* This show samples Broadway's greatest hits. The Savannah Theatre is billed as the country's oldest live-performance theater (stretching it a bit, since the only remnant of the original building would be the foundations of the original building, destroyed by fire long ago).

Tickets are $35 for adults, $16 for those ages 12 to 17, and $10 for those ages 5 to 11, with younger children free. You can purchase a season's pass for $60. Watch the Thursday entertainment section of the *Savannah Morning News* for discount coupons. Major credit cards are accepted, and tickets may be purchased at the number above. Performances are at 8 p.m. Wed through Sat and matinees are at 3 p.m. Sat and Sun.

i Scan the local paper for listings of performances by the Savannah Arts Academy. This public high school puts on some surprisingly professional performances, often in the spring. Its Skylite Jazz Band is particularly good.

THE PUPPET PEOPLE
3119 Furber Ave.
(912) 355-3366
www.puppetpeople.com

Puppets can be children's toys, but puppets can also be theater for grown-ups. Angela Beasley's Puppet People play to audiences of all ages. These are life-size creations that sing, dance, and vamp at everything from children's birthday parties to corporate bashes and retail openings. Beasley's been at it for 30 years, and her repertoire includes the characters around the Forsyth Park fountain, some very original Three Little Pigs, fish galore, and a Willie Nelson look-alike. These elaborate productions have been covered in the pages of *Southern Living* magazine and on cable network programming. The troupe does not perform on a regular schedule, but it is often featured at public events and festivals.

ART MUSEUMS & COLLEGE GALLERIES

SAVANNAH COLLEGE OF ART AND DESIGN
345 Bull St.
(912) 525-5527
www.scad.edu

This growing art college's campus is scattered throughout Savannah's Historic Downtown and Victorian District. Among its holdings are multiple on-campus galleries featuring rotating displays in a variety of media. Some feature the work of students, both graduate and undergraduate, or the college's faculty. Frequently, however, these galleries host works of internationally known artists such as Jasper Johns, Robert Rauschenberg, and Dale Chihuly.

The flagship galleries, most likely to feature professional work, are shopSCAD and the Red Gallery. These exhibits are free and open to the public. Times vary, particularly in keeping with the academic year, so call one of the listed numbers for hours and information on what is currently on exhibit. Also, check out the media outlets discussed earlier in this chapter for exhibit details. Following is a rundown of SCAD's galleries. Consider this list fluid. As the college grows, the roles of its various galleries are subject to change—not to mention that it keeps acquiring new real estate.

i Looking for one of the Savannah College of Art and Design's galleries? Locals, for the most part, try to be helpful when visitors ask for directions on the street, but most of us simply don't know the names SCAD gives its buildings. We don't call it Poetter Hall, it's the old Armory to us; the Jen Library is known to old locals as the old Levy Department Store and to younger locals as the Maas Brothers Department Store; Habersham Hall is the old jail. Take the online SCAD tour at www.scad .edu to learn more.

SHOPSCAD
340 Bull St.
(912) 525-5180

This gallery, housed in an old armory building in the center of the Historic Downtown was among the first of the college's now-significant real-estate holdings. This gallery concentrates on visiting national and international exhibits and is among the easiest of the SCAD galleries for a visitor to find. If you are only doing one SCAD gallery, and the details on current exhibits don't give you a reason to pick one over another, do this one. A look at the Rococo building is worth the trip by itself.

RED GALLERY
201 East Broughton Street
(912) 525-4950
This retail gallery, inside SCAD's library, features a variety of artists including SCAD alumni.

PINNACLE GALLERY
320 East Liberty Street
(912) 525-5063
This beautiful gallery space is used primarily for exhibits.

ORLEANS HALL GALLERY
201 Barnard Street
(912) 525-5063
You'll find student work for sale at this gallery, which doubles as a reception facility.

Other SCAD exhibit galleries include:

ALEXANDER HALL GALLERY
668 Indian St.

GUTSTEIN GALLERY
201 East Broughton St.

HALL STREET GALLERY
212 W. Hall St.

LA GALERIE BLEUE
3515 Montgomery St.

MAY POETTER GALLERY
342 Bull St.

PEI LING CHAN GALLERY AND GARDEN
322–324 Martin Luther King Jr. Blvd.

TELFAIR MUSEUM OF ART
http://telfair.org
The Telfair Museum of Art is actually three separate and distinct facilities operated by the same organization. The **Telfair Academy of Arts and Sciences** is a traditional art museum housed in an impressive historic mansion. The **Jepson Center for the Arts,** which merits a separate entry, focuses on modern art and has its own flashy modern building catty-cornered to the original Telfair. The Telfair also operates the **Owens-Thomas House,** a house museum covered in our Attractions chapter. We're covering both art museums here, under the heading of their parent organization.

Note that you can get better admission rates with a combination ticket for all three sites at $15 (family rate $30).

JEPSON CENTER FOR THE ARTS
207 West York St.
(912) 790-8800
http://telfair.org
The Jepson Center for the Arts adds 64,000 square feet to Telfair's assets. In addition to large galleries for traveling exhibitions, it has space for regional and community work, outdoor sculpture terraces, classrooms, a 200-seat auditorium, a cafe, and a store.

In 2006 a city that made its reputation by preserving and restoring its historic architecture also offered something significant from the modern side of the architecture spectrum. The freestanding ultramodern Jepson Center for the Arts opened on the same historic square as its parent organization, the

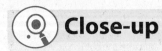 **Close-up**

Classical Music in Savannah

If classical music in Savannah were a patient on one of those prime-time hospital Dr. McDreamy soap operas on network television these days, here's what the plot line would be: A generally healthy patient who has had a few periodic health problems suddenly drops dead; initial resuscitation efforts are lackluster and unproductive; desperate measures by unheralded medical heroes revive the patient; the patient now shows signs of life but it is unclear whether they will die, survive in a diminished state, or recover. Meanwhile, the patient's friends and family (read: fans of classical music) are hanging around the waiting room, exhausted from attending one possibly premature funeral and now uncertain about whether to hold another wake or host a get-well celebration.

Okay, so we strained a metaphor there, but you get the point. The Savannah Symphony Orchestra was a proud fixture in the city for over half a century, but it closed down amid managerial disputes and financial woes in the midst of its 2002–03 season. The symphony had been in and out of financial hot water for decades but always managed to survive. There were even a handful of well-publicized musicians' strikes. With the exception of the docks, Savannah isn't known as an organized-labor stronghold, so striking violinists were a newsworthy novelty—instead of walking picket lines, they set up free ensemble concerts in downtown squares at lunchtime. And there was always this sense that the show would go on—after all, the two free outdoor concerts sponsored annually by local government were major events, the visiting artists included the cream of the touring music world, and the symphony itself was very good.

So when the symphony closed its doors in early 2003, Savannah calmly waited for a corporate white knight or private patron to ride to the rescue. Said knight/patron never showed up.

For several years, all that Savannah had of classical music was a portion of the varied schedule of the Savannah Music Festival for three weeks in the spring, a few touring performances, and an effort to keep the fall Picnic in the Park program going with a pick-up orchestra of local remnants supplemented by regional imports.

Fast forward to the present, and things are looking up. By the time you read this, they may have improved even more or failed miserably—but we've included websites so you can track the drama if this kind of music is important to you. Basically, the revival

Telfair Museum of Art. The work of international modern architect Moshe Safdie has already sparked one of the blood feuds that Savannah's arts community so loves. After a long and showy fight before the city's Historic Review Board, the Telfair got the go-ahead for the construction of the new building, which features a three-story glass wall that gives outsiders a clear view of the multilevel atrium.

Equally as different is the work on display within the new walls. The Telfair concentrates its 20th- and 21st-century collections, both owned works and traveling exhibitions, in 64,000 square feet of exhibition space. The permanent collection was bolstered on opening with the gift of more than 20 works on paper by major contemporary artists honoring the late Kirk Varnedoe, a former Museum of Modern Art curator and native efforts have gone in two different directions—one local, one tour-based. The **Savannah Sinfonietta,** a small professional orchestra with a local board that performed its first concerts in 2006–07, presented programs in two venues—donated church sanctuaries downtown in the Historic District and on Skidaway Island near the Landings, a wealthy residential community whose residents made up part of the original symphony's season audience. Audiences were skeptical at first, but the determined group was winning them over by the second season, giving reason to be optimistic about its future.

The 2007–08 Masterworks series includes six concerts, plus a Handel's *Messiah* sing-along in December, and shortly thereafter, it faded out. In 2009, the **Savannah Philharmonic Orchestra** was formed. This professional symphony orchestra was born from a strong board and enough financial support to get them off the ground. They present a full range of concerts each season, from classics to pops. The **Savannah Philharmonic Chorus** is a community-based auditioned ensemble that works regularly with the orchestra in an oratorio and opera setting, as well as performing a wide range of music from acapella Baroque to rock and pop standards. At press time, the concert schedule had not been posted, however, stay tuned and join the mailing list by signing up online at www.thesavphilharmonic.org.

The **Savannah Concert Association** (www.savannahconcertassociation.com) schedule included several concerts through April of 2010. With that season over with by the time you read this, the list of performers will give you an idea of the caliber of performance involved. The musicians included pianist Charles Wadsworth (appearing several times), pianist Hong Xu, pianist Dmitri Levkovich, violinist Chee Yun, and cellist Edward Aaron.

These concerts alternate between the Lucas Theatre and Trustees Theatre downtown, both operated by Savannah College of Art and Design (SCAD). Not only are both of these attractive venues, but they also come with an invaluable extra—professional box office service. SCAD's box office is at 216 East Broughton St. and is open during business hours during the week. Or you may call (912) 525-5050 and charge by phone. Ticket prices range from $12.50 to $35, with a special $2 rate for music teachers and students (which you must apply for in advance).

Savannahian. Included in that impressive gift were works by Jasper Johns, Roy Lichtenstein, Robert Rauschenberg, and Richard Avedon, among many others.

THE TELFAIR ACADEMY OF ARTS AND SCIENCES
121 Barnard St.
(912) 232-1177
http://telfair.org

Savannah boasts many museums, but most are either theme museums (such as the Ralph Mark Gilbert Civil Rights Museum) or house museums—interesting homes whose main attraction is the historical significance of the building itself, backed up by the re-creation of a bygone lifestyle through period furnishing. (You can find out more details about these places in our Attractions chapter.)

The Telfair, however, is a true art museum, although the house museum description certainly applies to a portion of the Telfair mansion. Housed in the Neoclassical Regency mansion designed by English architect William Jay for the prominent Telfair family (a Georgia governor was among the family members), this is the oldest art museum in the South. Think of it as having three elements: It's part house museum, part permanent collection, and part gallery for visiting exhibitions and programs.

The permanent collection includes paintings, sculpture, prints, and decorative arts. The collection includes examples of American impressionism, Ash Can Realism, and classical sculpture casts. Included are works by Childe Hassam, Gari Melchers, Robert Henri, George Bellows, and George Luks.

The museum also holds the largest existing collection of the works of Lebanese mystical poet and artist Kahlil Gibran, best known for *The Prophet*. His patroness, Mary Haskell, made her home in her later years on Gaston Street in Savannah. Because of the fragile nature of the artwork (it was done predominantly in pencil), it is only on display occasionally. On a more contemporary note, the Telfair is the new home for the *Bird Girl* sculpture featured on the cover of John Berendt's *Midnight in the Garden of Good and Evil*. Fans of the book hounded it out of its original setting in a family plot at Bonaventure.

Admission to the Telfair is $10 for adults, $8 for seniors, $5 for college students, $4 for children ages 5 to 12, and free for children under 5. Chatham County residents are admitted free on Sun, but, citing budget cuts, the museum has discontinued the practice of blanket free admission on Sun.

Hours are 10 a.m. to 5 p.m. Mon, Wed, Fri, and Sat; noon to 5 p.m. Sun; and 10 a.m. to 8 p.m. Thurs; closed Tues.

Independent Galleries

Savannah has a large stock of art galleries. We listed those with collegiate connections separately. The following list consists of independent galleries. This is only a very small sample to get you started. The Sunday arts section of the *Savannah Morning News* usually offers a current listing of shows. And you'll stumble on others by accident: Lately half the coffee shops and little restaurants in town have turned their walls into impromptu galleries. For examples of this trend, check out Soho South (in our Restaurants chapter) and the Gallery Espresso on Bull Street at Chippewa Square.

A. T. HUN
302 West St. Julian St. (City Market)
(912) 233-2060
www.athun.com
Chuck Hamilton and Grant Nelson are partners in this gallery, which also shows other artists. It's all contemporary and includes many larger pieces. The nudes that sparked the birth of the gallery aren't shocking, just a good reflection of how conservative Savannah can be. Potters, jewelers, and photographers are represented as well, and there is an affiliation with an English gallery so there is a regular exchange of international work.

Don't look here for soft watercolors or memento landscapes of Savannah. It's young, funky, and even sells T-shirts sporting a Latin phrase that translates (roughly) as "We don't do snobby." Don't be misled, however; there's good stuff here.

CHROMA GALLERY
31 Barnard St.
(912) 232-2787
www.chromaartgallery.com

This gallery, strategically located on a corner near City Market, represents many artists, but the works share some characteristics—large, bold, colorful canvases. Although there is some regional work here, locals are well represented. We're particularly fond of the electric-bright renderings of marsh scenes. The gallery also displays art glass.

GALLERY 209
209 East River St.
(912) 236-4583

This River Street gallery is the place to start your search for local artwork. Stuff here varies in quality, from some wannabe artists to the real thing. We especially like the enamel jewelry, such as a jewel-tone seahorse. In addition to paintings that run the gamut from very good to not very, you'll find fiber art and interesting and affordable ceramics. This stuff will appeal more to consumers than art museums, but what's wrong with that?

LIBRARY RESOURCES

LIVE OAK PUBLIC LIBRARY
2002 Bull St.
(912) 652-3600
www.liveoakpl.com

The opening of an $8.3 million expansion and addition to the circa-1916 main branch on Bull Street revitalized the entire library system. The building's addition is clad in marble and features park views from massive clerestory windows. The collection had drifted off into inadequacy and obsolescence until the renovation project gave it a shot in the arm—and a $3 million injection of public and private monies to stock the new shelves. While you may not think of libraries as places to visit while vacationing, there are resources here of interest to the traveler. Foremost among them is the local history and genealogy collection. Those in search of the dirt on their ancestors have been known to make the trip just to get into those records. Visitors can use the resources of the library without charge and can even check items out if they pay the $25 non-refundable temporary card fee for out-of-towners. (It's $2 if you live here.)

THE GREAT OUTDOORS

avannah's natural tropical diversions are tempting, and the loveliness of the islands with sago palms, hibiscus, and towering pines can be found throughout the city, not just in a gated park, but within the downtown, Southside, and surrounding communities. Simply said: This is the ideal place to spend time with nature. For starters, salt marshes are begging for kayaks. Embark on a trip by water, abundant with sea life and splendid birds, comical fiddler crabs, and all kinds of fish. There are the endless waterways just waiting on your discovery. Tybee Island offers a serene shoreline for surf fishing, and there's even a National Wildlife Refuge where freshwater rivers and cypress swamps intercept saltwater. The city is blessed with parks and parklike areas of every description and in every jurisdiction—national, state, regional, county, and city—and these provide settings for picnics and play and trails for hiking, biking, and jogging. Golfers and tennis players will find numerous venues that are open to the public.

Those who enjoy their recreation organized can participate in a variety of team sports offered for adults and youngsters by the county, city, YMCA, and the recreation departments of the smaller municipalities; athletes age 18 and younger can keep busy playing practically year-round, and many do. Much of this organized activity takes place at facilities at Bacon Regional Park, a 500-acre complex in Southside/Midtown. This is the site of Memorial Stadium, where many of the area's high-school football games are played; Lake Mayer Community Park; and public facilities for golf (Bacon Park Golf Course), tennis (Bacon Park Tennis Complex), youth baseball and softball (Ambuc Park, William W. Scarborough Sports Complex, and Guy Minick Youth Complex), adult softball (Allen E. Paulson Softball Complex), soccer (Chatham County Soccer Complex), swimming (Chatham County Aquatic Center), and weightlifting (Paul Anderson-Howard Cohen Weightlifting Center).

On the following pages, you'll also find information concerning the parks and activities we've mentioned. While you're reading, keep in mind that a big part of the beauty of the area's recreational offerings is that, because of Savannah's mild climate, they're available to you just about every day of the year, and most are free of charge.

PARKS & NATURE TRAILS

Historic Downtown

FORSYTH PARK
Drayton and Gaston Streets
(912) 351-3841

This downtown park on the southern boundary of the Historic District has sort of a split personality, but it's a delightful one. The northern portion consists of 11 acres filled with trees and shrubs and has an ornate fountain as its focal point. Splashing waters and shady sidewalks make this part of the park, which was laid out in 1851, a wonderful spot for strolling, relaxing on benches, and just plain goofing off.

The southern portion has a more active persona. Here you'll find a large playground, basketball and tennis courts, and wide-open spaces often used by students and locals engaged in softball, team Frisbee, and other athletic pursuits. The southern portion, a drill field for local military units before it was made part of the park in 1867, is also the site of monuments commemorating the Confederacy and honoring Georgians who served in the Spanish-American War.

Two dummy forts, structures built in 1909 and used for military exercises before World War I, straddle the line dividing the two areas. The fort on the western side of the park was renovated in 1963 as the Fragrant Garden for the Blind; the eastern fort will be converted into a restaurant.

The park was laid out on the site of a pine forest that was at the southern reaches of the city, a wood that made "sad and sea-like music, when stirred by the breeze," according to a historian of the late 1800s. Over time the pines were removed, died out, or were uprooted by storms. Of the park's numerous existing trees—44 per acre in the northern portion—a few are pines, but you'll see many more oaks, sycamores, and magnolias when you visit. Particularly impressive are the live oaks (a particular species of oak) that line the central walkway stretching from the park's northern end at Gaston Street to its southern end at Park Avenue.

The monuments are on this wide promenade, as is the much-photographed fountain, which features a female figure surrounded by water-spouting swans and tritons (men with the lower bodies of fish). The fountain, said to be the largest in the United States when it was unveiled in 1858, is modeled after one in the Place de la Concorde of Paris. A lighted sidewalk that's much favored by walkers and joggers who live or work downtown borders Forsyth. According to the city, the distance around the park is 1.5 miles. The park is also the site of major annual events, including the Sidewalk Arts Festival and the Savannah Shakespeare Festival (see our Annual Events and Festivals chapter).

i Although most city parks such as Forsyth and Daffin don't have gates that can be shut to keep people out at night, there is an ordinance stating that parks close at 9 p.m.

Islands

OLD SAVANNAH-TYBEE RAILROAD HISTORIC AND SCENIC TRAIL (MCQUEEN ISLAND RAILS TO TRAILS)
US 80 East
(912) 652-6780
www.parks.chathamcounty.org
When you walk, jog, or bicycle on this 6.5-mile trail, you're traversing the roadbed of a railroad that took passengers from eastern Savannah to Tybee Island for nearly 50 years starting in the late 1800s. Chatham County maintains the palm-lined, limestone trail on McQueen's Island and created it beginning in 1991 as part of the Rails Into Trails program, an effort to transform abandoned railroad rights-of-way into recreational areas. A trip along the entire length of the trail takes you past 18 fitness stations, past 30 wooden picnic tables, and across 10 wooden footbridges. Besides what it offers in the way

of exercise, the trail presents visitors with vistas of marshland and the south channel of the Savannah River, opportunities for fishing and crabbing, and glimpses of wildlife indigenous to the marsh. Keep your eyes peeled for creatures such as the Eastern box turtle, the diamondback terrapin, the American alligator, the red-tailed hawk, the brown pelican, and the great blue heron, and don't be surprised if you walk up on a rattlesnake or two (they enjoy sunning themselves on the trail).

The railroad was built over 17.7 miles of salt marsh, rivers, and tidal creeks by a group of investors led by Savannahian D. G. Purse, who in 1885 owned a good portion of Tybee Island and was trying to find a way to transport people there that was faster than the two-hour ride by steamboat. His solution was to build a railroad, and the idea was considered a harebrained scheme by local folks; they were convinced it was an engineering feat that couldn't be accomplished. But Purse persisted, and his Savannah and Tybee Railway began making regularly scheduled runs in July 1887.

A few years later, the line became part of the Central of Georgia Railway system and was operated from then on as the Savannah and Atlantic Railroad. The last passenger excursion was in July 1933; by then, the advent of the automobile and the construction of a road to Tybee (now US 80) had made the railway obsolete. But in its heyday, the little railroad carried thousands of Savannahians and out-of-towners to Tybee for days of sunning and swimming at the beach and nights of dancing at the Tybrisa Pavilion. The entrance to the trail places you at its midpoint and is on US 80 just east of the Bull River Bridge. The highway is well traveled, and there is not much space at the

trail entrance, so be careful when you pull off the road to park. The trail is off-limits after darkness falls and not safe, so make sure you plan to visit when you have plenty of time to complete the walk or run before dark sets in. Plans are to extend the trail all the way to Tybee Island itself, but that's in the future. For much more on Tybee's interesting past and present, see our Tybee Island chapter.)

SKIDAWAY ISLAND STATE PARK
52 Diamond Causeway
(912) 598-2300
www.gastateparks.org/Skidaway
Get back to nature on the Big Ferry or Sandpiper Trails at Skidaway State Park. Walking either will give you a good look at a maritime forest and the salt marsh, their plants, and possibly some of their animals, including fiddler crabs, egrets, deer, and alligators. The trails also take you to earthwork fortifications built as Confederate defenses during the Civil War and the remains of a moonshine still. Big Ferry can be hiked in either a 2- or 3-mile loop, with the latter taking about 90 minutes to walk. Sandpiper is a mile long, takes about 20 minutes, and can be traversed by people using wheelchairs (with a little help) and parents pushing baby strollers. A path connects the trails, enabling hikers to get in as much as a 5.5-mile walk. Contact the park for guided hikes.

The 533-acre park, created during the early 1970s and opened in 1975, is in the western portion of Skidaway Island and borders a stretch of the Intracoastal Waterway called the Skidaway Narrows. Other features of the park include a museum featuring the skeleton of a giant sloth, picnic sites, interpretive nature programs, and campsites (see the Camping section of this chapter). In addition to the picnic sites, there are five covered shelters available on a first-come, first-served basis. If you don't want to take a chance, you can reserve one at $60 a day; a group shelter accommodates 150 people and rents for $255 per day.

The park is open from 7 a.m. to 10 p.m. seven days a week. There's a $3 parking fee (more for buses) on all days except Wed, when admission is free. If you're planning to come here often or visit other state parks and historic sites in Georgia, you might consider purchasing an annual Georgia Park Pass for $30 ($15 for those age 62 and older). That will get you unlimited admission to all state parks.

Southside/Midtown

DAFFIN PARK
1301 East Victory Dr.
(912) 351-3841
When Savannah's Park and Tree Commission members conceived plans for Daffin Park in 1908, the recreational area was on the outskirts of the city. Now, Daffin is in the middle of Midtown, and it's a magnificent place for residents to stroll and enjoy the outdoors; it's shady and covered with giant live oaks, and there's a well-kept lake and plenty of benches. The park, which is maintained by the city of Savannah's Leisure Services Bureau, covers 77 acres bounded by Victory Drive, Waters Avenue, Washington Avenue, and Bee Road.

Opportunities for enjoying the outdoors in a residential setting abound at Daffin, which has a large playground; grassy fields that accommodate softball, baseball, football, soccer, rugby, and, on occasion, cricket; basketball courts; nine tennis courts; a pool; a four-acre lake where you can fish for bass, bream, and catfish; and a pavilion on the lake that can be reserved for $125 per day for a

variety of gatherings. Call (912) 351-3837 for reservations.

The eastern portion of the park is the site of Grayson Stadium, home of the city's minor-league baseball team (see our Spectator Sports chapter), and a picnic area shaded by towering pine trees. The playing fields on the southern side of the park—once the site of polo matches and a landing strip for airplanes before the city built its first airport in 1929—are also fine for flying kites, driving golf balls, and exercising Rover, when the fields are not otherwise occupied. If you're into walking or jogging, you'll find room to roam on the 8-foot-wide, 1.5-mile-long sidewalk surrounding the park. For a shorter jaunt, try the lighted sidewalk around Daffin Lake, which is a third of a mile long. A note: For safety reasons, don't walk the park at night, especially alone.

LAKE MAYER COMMUNITY PARK
Montgomery Crossroad and
Sallie Mood Drive
(912) 652-6780
www.chathamcounty.org
As the name implies, the centerpiece of this 75-acre park on the Southside is the lake, but there's more here than recreational offerings involving water. Lake Mayer is surrounded by a 1.5-mile walking and jogging track dotted with 18 fitness stations. The park grounds provide space for eight lighted tennis courts, two lighted basketball courts, an unlighted ball diamond, a conditioning course and a basketball court for people using wheelchairs, a playground, a remote-control auto racetrack, and an outdoor skating rink designed to accommodate in-line hockey games. Picnic tables are sprinkled throughout the park, and two covered areas accommodate large groups: a pavilion with space

THE GREAT OUTDOORS

for as many as 500 people and a shelter with room for 80 to 100. These can be reserved at fees of $175 and $150 respectively for five hours of usage; otherwise, they are available on a first-come, first-served basis.

Getting back to the 35-acre lake: Swimming is prohibited, but you can fish for bass, bream, catfish, and crappie if you have a freshwater license. The possibilities for boating abound; the lake is the site of the Savannah Sailing Center (see this chapter's Sailing section), which offers instruction to young people and adults, and of Red Cross classes in kayaking and canoeing. Windsurfing is permitted on the lake, which is also where remote-control boat-racing enthusiasts come to compete.

Staff members at Lake Mayer present special events throughout the year, including egg hunts and kite-making and flying contests on the weekend before Easter; fishing rodeos in April, May, and June; Senior Citizens Day in May; Family Nature Day in September; and Christmas Camp in December.

Lest we forget, numerous ducks and geese call the park home, and they are more than happy to take stale bread off (and out of) your hands. The park—created in 1972 and operated by Chatham County's Public Works and Park Services Department—is on Montgomery Crossroad near the intersection of Sallie Mood Drive. It's open from 8 a.m. to 11 p.m. in the spring and summer and 8 a.m. to 10 p.m. in fall and winter. Again, a reminder: Don't walk this park at night.

SOUTHSIDE COMMUNITY PARK
Science Drive
(912) 351-3841
Developed by the city of Savannah in cooperation with Armstrong Atlantic State

University (see our Education and Child Care chapter), this 28-acre wooded area on Scenic Drive across from the ASSU field house features a nature walk that's two-thirds of a mile long. A playground and picnic tables round out the facility. The park opens at dawn and closes at dusk.

WILLIAM E. HONEY WATERFRONT
Memorial Park
Mechanics Avenue
(912) 447-1900
The attraction of this park in the east Chatham town of Thunderbolt is the T-shaped fishing pier, a facility that gives anglers and crabbers access to the Wilmington River and its aquatic bounty. The pier extends 82 feet from high ground out over the water, and the crossbar of the "T" paralleling the riverbank is 96 feet long and 16 feet wide. If you're here to picnic and not to fish, you'll find tables and a covered pavilion where you can enjoy a meal alongside the river. The park, opened on Labor Day 1997, is named for a Thunderbolt resident who donated funds for its creation. It's at the eastern end of Mechanics Avenue, which runs off US 80. The park and pier open at sunrise and close at sunset, and there's no charge for using them.

West Chatham

L. SCOTT STELL COMMUNITY PARK
195 Scott Stell Rd.
(912) 652-6780
www.chathamcounty.org
Helicopter pilots once prepared for war on the site of this 108-acre park southwest of Savannah. Now Chatham Countians come here to play ball on the four lighted diamonds of the Jim Golden Sports Complex, shoot hoops on the four lighted basketball

courts, jog and walk on the 1-mile fitness trail, and picnic under the pines. There are also a BMX bicycle track, a tree farm, and a dog exercise area. During the early 1970s, the park site was Cu Chi Stage Field, a training area for South Vietnamese helicopter pilots stationed at nearby Hunter Army Airfield. Later in the decade, the county planted the seeds, literally, for the park by making garden plots at the site available to local residents free of charge.

You can still farm one of these 30-by-60-foot plots (there's no cost involved; you simply sign an agreement stating you will be responsible for your plot) in addition to taking advantage of the other recreational opportunities offered here since the park's completion in 1984. The fun includes fishing for bream, catfish, bass, and crappie in the pond. The park is open all year, from 8 a.m. to 10 p.m. during fall and winter and from 8 a.m. to 11 p.m. during spring and summer. Special events include garden workshops, fishing contests, Easter festivities, and a Halloween haunted house.

SAVANNAH NATIONAL WILDLIFE REFUGE
South Carolina Hwy. 170
(912) 652-4415
www.savannah.fws.gov

By traveling the Laurel Hill Wildlife Drive, you can see some of the refuge's 29,174 acres of freshwater marshes and hardwood islands, which are known locally as "hammocks." This 4-mile gravel road is open to hikers, bicyclists, and motorists, and it takes you along dikes built during the late 18th and early 19th centuries by rice planters. The U.S. Fish and Wildlife Service, which manages the refuge, maintains 3,000 acres of freshwater pools created by the dikes, areas that serve as feeding grounds for wading birds and waterfowl. Unless posted as closed, all the dikes are open to foot travel, as is the Cistern Trail, a winding path that runs off the Wildlife Drive; however, if you're planning on leaving the drive to hike or bike, call ahead to ascertain the condition of the dike system.

The Wildlife Drive is open from sunrise to sunset throughout the year, except for two days during the fall, usually in October, when it's closed to the general public to allow a deer hunt by people using wheelchairs; you should check to see if this event falls at a time when you intend to visit the refuge. The drive and the dikes are great places from which to observe wildlife, in particular birds and alligators. A marvelous time for bird-watching is late December and early January, when the refuge is visited by 13 different types of ducks in concentrations of up to 30,000 birds. The best times for viewing gators are in March, April, and October, when the big reptiles crawl onto the banks of the refuge's canals to bask in the sun.

Laurel Hill Wildlife Drive and about half of the refuge are in South Carolina but right across the Savannah River from Chatham County; the entrance to the drive is only a couple of miles from the West Chatham town of Port Wentworth on SC 170, which is SR 25 south of the river. The drive is not far from downtown Savannah. To get to it from downtown, about a 15-minute trip, take US 17 north across the river to its intersection with SC 170, then turn south on SC 170.

You can fish from the banks of the Wildlife Drive and in the Kingfisher Pond year-round and in the remainder of the refuge's freshwater pools from March 1 to November 30, but the angling at these spots isn't anything to write home about, and you'll need a South Carolina license. You'll

THE GREAT OUTDOORS

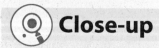 **Close-up**

See Wilderness Up Close!

Wilderness Southeast (WiSE) programs offer scheduled and private programs for getting close to Savannah nature without taking the risk of getting bit, or lost! For example, if you're into birding, you may wish to schedule a private birding tour with one of their guides. (Diana Churchill is the bird expert of Savannah, so ask for her.) A portion of every tour fee goes toward Fish Got to Swim, a science enrichment water quality course that they provide for Savannah's underserved public middle-school students. The company also offers a wide array of group (minimum of two people) coastal tours such as beaches, estuary, salt marsh, cypress swamps, and wetlands. They also investigate wildlife such as alligators, birds of all sorts, dolphins, and much less glamorous species, according to their executive director Joyce Murlless. Throughout the year they offer various water-based (paddling, motor boating, beach, and some early morning birding) programs. Here are some examples of tours they offered in 2010:

- **Alligators and Others:** On this three hour tour, participants venture to the Savannah National Wildlife Refuge Visitor's Center to discover alligators basking in the sun while great birds fish serenely nearby. A certified naturalist will share alligator stories, and you'll discover the secrets of historic rice plantations and learn the importance of maintaining the old rice paddies for wildlife. The fee is $30 per person and includes the use of binoculars and spotting scope, transportation around the wildlife refuge, and a tour of the new visitor center.

- **Blackwater River Paddle:** After basic canoeing instruction, your WiSE naturalist will lead the way downstream past stately tupelo and cypress trees. Their bright spring-green foliage and dark trunks reflect perfectly in the mirror-dark water. The tour participants will be on the lookout for turtles, herons, and noisy kingfishers diving for their next meal. There's beauty around every bend! The fee is $40 per person and includes the canoe, paddles, and basic instruction. The tour size is 4 to 16 people. Participants meet in Rincon, Georgia.

For more information, check out this organization's colorful website (www.wilderness-southeast.org) or call (912) 236-8115.

get better results fishing in the Savannah River along the refuge's boundaries, and a Georgia license will suffice if you stay in the main channels. The refuge manages hunts for deer, feral hogs, squirrels, waterfowl, and turkeys during the fall and winter. Permits to hunt there are required and can be obtained by mailing requests or applications to Savannah Coastal Refuge Hunts, Parkway Business Center, 1000 Business Center Dr., Suite 10, Savannah, GA 31405.

**SAVANNAH-OGEECHEE CANAL
 MUSEUM AND NATURE CENTER**
681 Fort Argyle Rd.
(912) 748-8068
www.savannahogeecheecanal.com
The 184-acre nature center and its several trails will give you a look at three environments: pine woods, hardwood tidal river swamp, and sand hills. Two of the trails start in the pines at the museum and follow the southern portion of the canal, which dates from 1830, faded from usage near the end of the 19th century, and has since been cleared of brush and other overgrowth. These trails—the Tow Path and the Heel Path—are each 0.4 mile long and lead you past Locks 5 and 6 of the canal to the Ogeechee River. The only bridge across the canal is at Lock 5 near the start of the paths, so don't expect to walk to the end of one and back on the other. However, a trail created as an Eagle Scout project allows you to walk from the end of the Tow Path (on the eastern side of the canal) to the 0.5-mile-long Jenkes Road Trail.

Jenkes Road, once a thoroughfare for wagon traffic, will also take you from the museum to the river. The road and the paths take you through the swamp; you can see the sand hills by walking the mile-long Holly Trail. The nature center is open from 9 a.m. to 5 p.m. daily. Admission is $2 for adults and $1 for senior citizens and children older than age five. (For more on this site and the history of the canal, see our Attractions chapter.)

TOM TRIPLETT COMMUNITY PARK
US 80 West
(912) 652-6780
www.chathamcounty.org
The first phase of this 193-acre park along US 80 just west of Dean Forest Road was

It's a Swamp Thing

Occasionally, the Savannah-Ogeechee Canal park management team will host a **"Swamp Thing Lantern Tour."** This tour is comprised of a series of reenactments from different periods of the canal's history, including the local lore about the presence of a fictional creature said to live in the area—the Swamp Thing. The program, designed to create and promote awareness of the center, is offered at different times for several hours and covers a half-mile section of trail covered in about 20 minutes. The first part of the reenactment recreates the 1831 opening ceremony of the canal. A Civil War scene follows where Sherman's army is shown stealing a local man's horse, and another illustrates Confederate defenders burning the bridge at the canal's mouth. Both scenes are dramatic!

There are others equally as enthralling, including one story with live actors about the moonshine era where participants suddenly come face-to-face with the Swamp Thing! For more information and to find out when the next tour will be scheduled, call (912) 748-8068, or visit the website, www.savannahogeecheecanalsociety.org.

opened to the public in October 1998. Visitors will find two pavilions and a 19-acre lake that's stocked with fish and circled by a paved path intended for walking, running,

---

An Eco-Friendly Day Trip

From time to time, the Friends of Ossabaw lead groups to discover the natural and human history of Ossabaw Island, the state's third largest barrier island. The island was designated a Heritage Preserve for natural, scientific and cultural study, research and education. The cost of the trip is $50 for Friends of Ossabaw, or $70 for future Friends of Ossabaw (the membership is included in the price). To register or find more information about their exciting day trips, go to www.ossabaw island.net or call (912) 210-1613.

---

and bicycling. Plans call for the eventual construction of a boathouse and docks and the creation of campsites, hiking trails, picnic areas, and a playground. When it's completed, this county-owned park will be the largest in Chatham. The park is open from 8 a.m. until dark.

RECREATION

Recreation Programs

What follows are listings for three entities that help organize a wide variety of sports activities for youth and adults in Savannah and Chatham County. Note also that most of the smaller municipalities in the county have recreation departments, some of which are extremely active. To register to play on teams sponsored by these agencies, or to find out about their programs, call their representatives in Bloomingdale at (912) 748-4522, in

Garden City at (912) 966-7788, in Pooler at (912) 748-5776, in Port Wentworth at (912) 966-7428, in Thunderbolt at (912) 447-1900, and on Tybee Island at (912) 786-9622.

CHATHAM COUNTY PUBLIC WORKS AND PARK SERVICES DEPARTMENT
7235 Sallie Mood Dr.
(912) 652-6780
www.chathamcounty.org/pwps_recreationmain.html
Operating out of offices on Sallie Mood Drive, the department's Sports Division provides league play for youngsters in a variety of sports. These include basketball (January through March for boys and girls ages 8 through 14), soccer (March through May for boys and girls ages 6 through 19), baseball (March through July for boys ages 6 through 14), fast-pitch softball (March through July for girls ages 6 through 18), and football (September through November for boys ages 5 through 12). The division also sponsors swimming and weight-lifting complexes near Lake Mayer and holds a cheerleading competition for youngsters at Memorial Stadium in December and fast-pitch softball clinics in the fall. Entry fees vary per team for participation in basketball and $150 per team for participation in soccer, baseball, softball, and football. Call for the most current information.

CITY OF SAVANNAH DEPARTMENT OF RECREATION SERVICES
7171 Skidaway Rd.
(912) 351-3852
www.ci.savannah.ga.us
The city provides team athletic competition for youngsters and adults throughout the year. Youth sports include basketball (January through March for kids ages 8 to 17),

baseball (April through July for ages 6 to 17), football and cheerleading (September through November for kids ages 6 to 12), and soccer (September through November for girls and boys ages 6 to 19). For adults, there are leagues in softball in the fall and in spring/summer, basketball from January through March, baseball from April through July, and soccer from September through November. Entry fees for youth sports are $100 per team, with no fees charged for youth basketball. Fees for adult teams can run anywhere from $390 to $490, depending on how many games are played in the sport involved and the expenses incurred by the city in providing the program.

YMCA OF COASTAL GEORGIA
6400 Habersham St.
(912) 354-5480
www.ymcaofcoastalga.org
Besides the programs you'd expect to find at the Y (such as those involving swimming and other types of physical fitness for individuals), the YMCA of Coastal Georgia, through its five branches in Chatham County, offers youngsters opportunities to participate in youth basketball, baseball, softball, and soccer. Participants are registered and teams are formed at the branches, while leagues are set up and scheduled through each branch office. For the most part, games are played at facilities owned or leased by the Y.

Programs are open to nonmembers at fees slightly higher than those charged to members, and scholarships are available. Basic fees for individuals participating in all sports vary with each location. To enroll your child in a program, contact the Y branch nearest you. The facilities are the Habersham Branch in Southside/Midtown at 6400 Habersham St. (912-354-6223), the Southside Branch at 11702 Mercy Blvd. (912-961-9622), the Tybee Island Branch at 204 5th St. (912-786-9622), and branches on the eastside islands (912-897-1192) and in West Chatham in Pooler (912-748-9622).

The West Chatham Branch is a 32,000-square-foot facility that features an outdoor pool, a day-camp facility, a Sprayground—a fully equipped playground that incorporates the use of water and two large gymnasiums. The Islands Branch on Johnny Mercer Boulevard on Whitemarsh Island is built on 50 acres and has much more room for parking than the old Islands Y, where finding a space was often a problem. This branch also houses racquetball courts and a Sprayground. Both branches also are sites of a St. Joseph's/Candler Health Systems Children's Place to Be Fit, where children of elementary-school age are offered activities while their parents work out. All the Y branches provide health-screening services free to members via the Health Connection, which is staffed by St. Joseph's/Candler personnel.

Basketball

The county offers basketball for boys and girls ages 8 through 14 at a variety of sites between January and March. The city runs basketball programs for adults age 18 and older and for youngsters ages 8 to 17 during January, February, and March. Teams play at gyms in community centers and public schools, and the youth program puts 80 to 90 squads on the floor.

The YMCA hoops program attracts about 1,600 youngsters, making it bigger than both the county's and city's. Teams of boys and girls play in leagues starting at younger than age 6 and progressing to younger than age 18, and they do their dribbling and shooting at gyms at the Y's branches, previously listed.

THE GREAT OUTDOORS

Baseball & Softball

In April, the fancy of many a youngster in the Savannah area apparently turns to . . . baseball and softball. The city's youth baseball program involves about 120 teams in 6-and-under, 8-and-under, 10-and-under, 12-and-under, 14-and-under, and 17-and-under leagues. The county hosts about 65 teams in 6-and-under, 8-and-under, 10-and-under, 12-and-under, and 14-and-under competition, and the YMCA's program accounts for 75 teams in those age groups, plus an under-6 category. Some city and county teams play into July, while the Y program ends in May. City teams play at numerous locations including the Guy Minick Youth Complex and the William W. Scarborough Sports Complex, both in Bacon Park, and on diamonds in parks and at public schools. The city also conducts an adult baseball program, with games being played from April through July at fields in Daffin Park, at Savannah State University, and at Jenkins and Windsor Forest High Schools. Fees are $480 per team.

Diamonds are also best friends to many local young women: The county's softball program for girls ages 6 to 18 will field close to 65 teams between March and July, and the Y has leagues for under-10 and under-12 teams during April and May. The county schedules its baseball and girls' softball games at the Charles C. Brooks Sports Complex on the Islands, Ambuc Park in Southside/Midtown, Runaway Point Park in east Savannah, and the Jim Golden Sports Complex in West Chatham, all of which have restrooms and offer sales of snacks and beverages. Y teams play at the Y branches.

AMBUC PARK
Sallie Mood Drive
(912) 351-6754

This 25-acre sports complex in Southside/Midtown has four lighted diamonds for baseball and girls' softball. Maintained by Chatham County, it's also the site of youth football games and soccer matches.

CHARLES C. BROOKS SPORTS COMPLEX
Johnny Mercer Boulevard
If you hear locals talk about this 20-acre county facility on Wilmington Island, they'll probably refer to it as "the landfill" because that's what it's built on. The complex has four lighted fields for baseball and softball, two multipurpose fields, a soccer field, and a football field that can be used for soccer matches. The road leading to the complex is on Johnny Mercer near that street's intersection with Quarterman Drive. The complex is filled with families during the fall and spring months as this is the site for little league sports and adult church league softball on the islands.

GUY MINICK YOUTH COMPLEX
Eisenhower and Sallie Mood Drive
(912) 351-3858
This Savannah-owned facility is the site of many of the baseball games played by teams in city leagues. Four lighted fields are also used for soccer games played by teams in the younger age groups in the city's fall program.

JIM GOLDEN SPORTS COMPLEX
195 Scott Stell Rd.
(912) 652-6780
The 25-acre Golden complex has four lighted fields for baseball and girls' softball and an unlighted T-ball field. It's part of L. Scott Stell Community Park in West Chatham.

Bicycling

We mention in several places in this book that the Historic Downtown, with its quaint streets and squares and its laid-back attitude, is an ideal place for walking. It follows that this area is also a wonderful place to see from the seat of a bicycle. But if you opt to ride a bike rather than stroll around the downtown, be aware that you'll be competing with traffic that seems to become increasingly heavier as Savannah grows in popularity as a tourist destination. To avoid the worst of the traffic, consider taking your ride on a weekend morning before the sightseeing starts in earnest. Also, be sure to observe the same traffic laws as you would when driving your car, and give serious thought to wearing a helmet. Georgia law requires kids younger than age 16 to use protective headgear; if you're older than the age limit, you can set a good example by wearing a helmet, and you might even save yourself a bump on the noggin. Keep in mind that adults are prohibited from riding bikes through Historic District squares.

i If you're staying downtown and want to pedal around the Historic District, you can rent a bicycle from the *Bicycle Link* at 408 Martin Luther King Jr. Blvd. Shop owner John Skiljon is a good source of information on where to ride, as is Mike Maynor, owner of *Quality Bikes* (1127 East Montgomery Cross Rd.) on the Southside.

Dedicated cyclists who delight in long rides will find that the city and county haven't done a great deal to accommodate them; however, there is a governmental committee on bikeways and greenways that's working to come up with facilities that will make bike riding more enjoyable. Until the committee devises some plans and officials implement them, however, bike riders will have to make do with the existing designated bike paths and bike trails at their disposal.

The city has two bike paths, each of which uses streets that are often heavily traveled by motorists:

- The West to East Corridor runs along 52nd Street to Ward Street to LaRoche Avenue to the entrance to Savannah State University.
- The North to South Corridor follows Habersham Street to Stephenson Avenue to Hodgson Memorial Drive to Edgewater Drive to Hillyer Drive to Dyches Drive to Lorwood Drive to Tibet Avenue to Largo Drive to Windsor Road to Science Drive at Armstrong State University.

The county offers a couple of trails for bicyclists:

- The McCorkle Bike Trail ambles for 4 miles over 10 acres on Wilmington Island. The eastern end of this trail is at Walthour Road near Concord Road, and the western end is on Cromwell Road just past its intersection with Wilmington Island Road.
- The McQueens Island Trail runs between Bull River and Fort Pulaski and is part of the Old Savannah-Tybee Railroad Historic and Scenic Trail (see entry in the Parks section of this chapter). This crushed-stone trail is best suited to mountain bikes.

COASTAL BICYCLE TOURING CLUB
www.cbtc.org
This group of biking enthusiasts holds organized rides just about every weekend and special rides throughout the year. The club has about 150 members who meet monthly

and receive a monthly newsletter. Annual membership fees are $25 for individuals. Members meet on the first Monday of the month at 5:45 p.m. at Tubby's Tank House restaurant in Thunderbolt.

Bird watching

Its location on the air route of migratory birds known as the Atlantic flyway makes Savannah a splendid place for watching birds. The premier spot for this activity is the Savannah National Wildlife Refuge (see entry in the Parks section of this chapter), a haven for thousands of mallards, pintails, teal, and as many as 10 other species of ducks that migrate here during the winter months. Transient songbirds and shorebirds stop by briefly during the spring and fall. The peak time for viewing ducks at the refuge occurs in late December and January. According to Pat Metz of the U.S. Fish and Wildlife Service, you might also do some worthwhile bird-watching on the beach on the north end of Tybee Island during the spring, fall, and winter and on Skidaway Island during the spring and fall. Tybee's north beach is a good place for spotting gannets and purple sandpipers during the winter, and you might find migratory shorebirds and neotropical songbirds at Skidaway Island State Park and along the 4-mile trail on the northern end of the island running from the Georgia Marine Extension Service aquarium to Priest's Landing. Wild Birds Unlimited, the locally owned franchise of the national birding supply store, has an expert staff willing to answer questions—see our Shopping chapter.

Boating

Chatham County has about 86,700 acres of tidal marshlands laced by approximately 420 miles of navigable tidal waters. In other words, the area is a paradise for boaters.

Three of the most accessible scenic waterways are the Wilmington, Bull, and Skidaway Rivers, and they'll lead you to Wassaw Sound and the beaches of Wassaw, Williamson, and Beach Hammock Islands, where you can picnic, swim, sunbathe, and look for shells. The 7 miles of beach at Wassaw, a barrier island that's part of a national wildlife refuge and accessible only by water, are most inviting, particularly the "boneyard" on the northeast end where the bleached remains of toppled trees present opportunities for taking intriguing photographs. The southernmost and northernmost ends and the ocean beachfront of Williamson Island are open to boaters, but the middle of the island is a Critical Wildlife Area closed to humans; this area is reserved for birds such as the American oystercatcher. The basically pristine beaches of these islands are about a 25-minute trip from the marinas in Thunderbolt.

When you make a landing, you shouldn't have to worry about rocks, but be aware of what the tide is doing—if it's running out, you could get stranded for several hours if you're not careful. Also, be sure you're wearing shoes when you jump out of your boat into the water so oyster shells, broken glass, or the occasional stingray won't injure you.

The county maintains boat ramps at several locations that will provide you with access to local waterways. In the Islands area, there are two double ramps at Skidaway Narrows on the Diamond Causeway, and double ramps at Lazaretto Creek on US 80 East at Tybee Island and at Frank W. Spencer Park on the Islands Expressway just east of the bridge over the Wilmington River. In West Chatham, there are two double ramps at the Houlihan

Bridge on US 25 at the Savannah River and at Kings Ferry on US 17 South at the Ogeechee River; and there is a single ramp at Salt Creek on US 17 South. All of the ramp facilities have restrooms and wooden docks. You'll find picnic areas at all the ramps (with the exception of Lazaretto Creek), and Kings Ferry has a swimming area and a playground.

Downtown Via Boat

You can reach River Street and its shops, restaurants, and other attractions by boat via the Savannah River, but make sure to stay well clear of the commercial vessels using the shipping channel. These are huge ships, and they throw huge wakes. You can tie up alongside River Street at a 300-foot floating dock alongside Rousakis Riverfront Plaza.

The rate for using this city-owned facility is $1 per foot. If you plan to stay more than three hours, you must register with the city's Revenue Department, which can be contacted by calling (912) 651-6451. If you're tying up for less than a couple hours, there's no docking fee. You'll also find a dock at the Hyatt Regency hotel that's 414 feet long and available for boats 25 feet or longer. The fee for using the hotel dock overnight is $3 per foot, and electricity, water, and cable television hookups are provided, as is use of the hotel's indoor pool and fitness center.

On July 1, 1998, the state of Georgia began enforcing minimum age limits for operators of boats and personal watercraft. Under these requirements, children younger than age 12 are not allowed to operate personal watercraft or boats longer than 16 feet.

Marinas

If you're traveling to Savannah by boat and are looking for a place to dock during your visit, or if you need somewhere to store your boat, you can choose from several marinas.

BAHIA BLEU MARINA
2812 River Dr.
(912) 354-2283
www.bahiableumarina.com
Tie up at Bahia Bleu Marina and you're within walking distance of the restaurants and stores on the bluff at Thunderbolt. This facility, on the Wilmington River near Intracoastal Waterway mile marker 583, offers more than 3,000 feet of concrete dock and 240 enclosed racks, plus an extensive ship's store, restrooms, and showers.

BULL RIVER MARINA
8005 Old Tybee Rd.
(912) 897-7300
www.bullrivermarina.com
This marina sits on the Bull River some 4 miles from the mouth of Wassaw Sound, which borders the Atlantic Ocean. The location makes the marina about halfway between Savannah and Tybee Island. The marina provides boaters with 80 deepwater slips, a ship's store, restrooms, showers, live and frozen bait, gas, and diesel fuel. It offers private charters, boat rentals, inshore and offshore fishing charters, beach and island shuttles, and dolphin, sightseeing, and nature tours. The marina is just off US 80 at the western end of the bridge over the Bull River.

HOGAN'S MARINA
36 Wilmington Island Rd.
(912) 897-FISH
www.hogansmarina.com

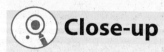 **Close-up**

Reworking the Concept of the Ideal Vacation: The Caretta Research Project

If your concept of the ideal vacation involves lazing on a sandy beach with accommodations that include air-conditioning and a hot tub, then you probably won't want to spend a week during the summer serving as a volunteer for the Savannah Science Museum's **Caretta Research Project.**

On the other hand, if you don't mind paying at least $750 for seven days and nights of no A/C, no hot water, no privacy, and lots of bugs, then working with the environmentalists who run this sea turtle monitoring program might be right up your alley.

For your hard-earned dough, your time, and your sweat, you get the satisfaction of helping save a threatened species—the loggerhead sea turtle. Depending on when you devote a week of your life to the Caretta Project, you have the opportunity to either see loggerheads crawl up the beaches at Wassaw Island and lay their eggs, or watch hatchlings scramble down the beaches to take up residence in the Atlantic Ocean.

"People say the project changes their lives," said biologist Kris Williams, who serves as director of the undertaking. After their weeks on Wassaw, "many students have changed their majors to biology to work with sea turtles," she said.

The Caretta Project—*Caretta caretta* is the scientific name of the loggerhead—has had more than 2,520 volunteers from nearly every state and about a half-dozen foreign countries participate since its onset in 1973. It's one of the oldest sea turtle monitoring programs anywhere and the only one in the United States whose volunteer sessions last an entire week and are thoroughly hands-on. Hands-on means that you'd better be ready to work if you volunteer. "We don't want people wanting to spend a vacation," said Williams.

Volunteers who participate in the sessions running from mid-May through early August spend their nights—we're talking from dusk to dawn—patrolling 7 miles of Wassaw's practically pristine beaches looking for turtles intent on digging a nest and laying eggs. Once a turtle is found, she is checked for an identification tag; tagged, if necessary; and measured. The turtle-monitoring team—which consists of six volunteers, a member of the Caretta Project staff, and an assistant—then either marks the nest and covers it with a screen to protect it from marauding raccoons or digs up the eggs and relocates them to a spot farther from the water's edge. Relocating the eggs is often necessary because erosion has caused a shelf to form along much of the beach

Situated on Turner Creek about 0.75 mile from the Wilmington River—the Intracoastal Waterway—Hogan's has more than 1,100 linear feet of dock space, a 16,000-pound boat hoist, and 272 dry-rack spaces. You'll find a store with nautical gear and fishing tackle, gasoline, restrooms and showers, live and frozen bait, a fish-cleaning facility, and ice and beverages. Hogan's also repairs engines.

ISLE OF HOPE MARINA
50 Bluff Dr.
(912) 354-8187
www.isleofhopemarina.com
On a picturesque bend of the Skidaway River sits the Isle of Hope Marina, which was established here in 1926 and installed concrete docks in 2003. The marina was the first dealer of Cris Craft boats in the nation

at Wassaw; unable to climb up the shelf, the turtles sometimes dig their nests where the tide can wash their eggs out to sea.

"The eggs probably wouldn't hatch if we didn't move them," said Williams, noting that a major aim of the project is to maximize the survival of hatchlings. Seeing the hatchlings dash for the ocean is the lure for the volunteers who take part in sessions running from late July through mid-September. "We watch the nests and try to make sure we're there to ensure the hatchlings make it to the water," said Williams, explaining how volunteers ward off predators such as coons and ghost crabs. "We usually stay up until midnight, then get up at dawn to make sure no hatchlings are stuck."

While on Wassaw, a sea island southeast of Savannah that's accessible only by boat, volunteers sleep in a rustic one-room cabin that's not air-conditioned; there's no hot water, and the shower is outside. Team members share housekeeping duties, including the preparation and cleanup of supper, the only organized meal of the day. "We eat well," said Williams, noting that suppers revolve around hearty dishes such as beef Stroganoff, pizza, spaghetti, and vegetable lasagna.

The registration fee covers a volunteer's food, lodging, and transportation by boat from Skidaway Island to Wassaw and back.

Volunteers should be 18 years old or older, but Williams said the program will accept those age 16 or even younger, provided they are highly motivated and independent types. "This is not a summer camp," said Williams. "This is a working vacation—it's not fun and games."

There's no maximum age limit, but participants in the program must be in good health and have reasonably good night vision and the ability to handle a moderate amount of walking. "Perhaps most important is your mental attitude," states the program's informational literature. "The project requires upbeat, adaptable folks who can cheerfully endure close quarters, insects, rainstorms, and the heat and humidity of a week in the subtropics without air-conditioning."

If you fit that bill and you're interested in participating, you can start the process of volunteering by calling (912) 447-8655 or writing to Caretta Research Project, P.O. Box 9841, Savannah, GA 31412. Registration information is also on the website (www .carettaresearchproject.org). Project staffers start accepting applications in January, and the sessions do fill up, so it's a good idea to get yours in early.

"It's a very rewarding experience," Williams said of the volunteer program. "We've had people coming back for their 10th and 11th years."

and was the site of the dock scenes in the original production of the movie *Cape Fear*, the first in a long line of films made in the Savannah area. There are 100 wet slips and a ship's store. Gas and diesel fuel are available, as are showers, and there's an over-the-water pavilion available for rental. It's at Intracoastal Waterway mile marker 590.

SAIL HARBOR MARINA & BOATYARD
606 Wilmington Island Rd.
(912) 897-2896
www.sailharbormarina.com
As the name implies, Sail Harbor caters mainly to owners of sailboats, but this marina on Turner Creek near the Wilmington River will also accommodate powerboats.

(For more on this facility, see this chapter's Sailing section.) There is no fuel here.

SAVANNAH BEND MARINA
Old Tybee Rd.
(912) 897-DOCK

This marina on the Wilmington River at Intracoastal Waterway mile marker 582 has transient dockage at 35 wet slips and a dry-storage building containing 262 racks for boats up to 29 feet long. The ship's store carries nautical apparel. You can relax and get a fine view of the river from one of the rocking chairs lining the porch of the store. Savannah Bend offers fuel service and has showers, laundry facilities, and restrooms. The marina is in Thunderbolt near the eastern end of the bridge over the Wilmington River.

THUNDERBOLT MARINA
3124 River Dr.
(912) 356-3875
www.thunderboltmarina.com

Yacht owners who dock at this marina, next to the boat works in Thunderbolt, get doughnuts delivered to them in the morning. The marina has more than 1,100 feet of dock space available for transient boaters. The marina offers a ship's store selling marine supplies, has gas and diesel fuel, will perform maintenance service, and provides a laundry and showers. Thunderbolt Marina is on the Wilmington River at Intracoastal Waterway mile marker 583.

Bowling

AMF SAVANNAH LANES
115 Tibet Ave.
(912) 925-0320
www.amf.com

Bowlers will find 50 lanes, a pro shop, a snack bar, and a full-service sports lounge at Savannah Lanes. This establishment in the Southside is the home of about 50 bowling leagues and two special promotions: Moonlight Bowling is from 10 to 11:30 p.m. on Sat, and Extreme Bowling, which starts at midnight on Fri and Sat and runs until 3 a.m. and from 9:30 p.m. to midnight on Sun. Prizes are awarded during Moonlight Bowling; when it's time for Extreme Bowling, the regular lighting is turned off, disco lights are turned on, and a DJ plays Top 40 dance music. Check the website for the most current offerings as they change. Daytime rates are $4.35 per game, per person. After 6 p.m. all age groups bowl for $5.60 a game. Savannah Lanes is open year-round.

AMF VICTORY LANES
2055 East Victory Dr.
(912) 354-5710
www.amf.com

A well-received promotion at this establishment—which has 40 lanes, a pro shop, a full-service snack bar, and a lounge that opens at noon—is Friday Night Extreme Bowling, which features disco lighting effects from 11 p.m. to 2 a.m. Rates are $4 per game before 5 p.m. and $4.50 a game afterward. Victory Lanes is the home of several leagues, plays host to bowlers seven days a week, and is closed only on Christmas Eve.

Camping

SKIDAWAY ISLAND STATE PARK
52 Diamond Causeway
(912) 598-2300
www.gastateparks.org

The park has 88 pull-through campsites set amid the serenity of a maritime forest on Skidaway Island. Each has water, 30 amp and a limited number of 50 amp electrical hookups, cable television, hookups, and elevated tent pads; grills and tables are provided. You can build campfires in the fire rings found at each campsite, but please don't build them on the tent pads. The park is a popular spot because of its natural beauty and also because it's only about 35 minutes from the Historic Downtown (see the state park's listing in the Parks and Nature Trails section of this chapter). Many campers use the park as a "bedroom" while they visit the city, so the sites tend to fill up on major holidays and the weekend closest to St. Patrick's Day. If you're planning to stay at the park during those times, make a reservation by calling (800) 864-7275. Fees per night for campsites are $24.

Fishing

If you like to fish, you've come to the right place. Year-round, there's somewhere in Chatham County or offshore in the Atlantic Ocean where you can wet a line and catch something. Basically, we're talking about three types of fishing: inshore and offshore, which involve fish that live in saltwater, and freshwater.

The inshore area stretches from the beachfronts into the tidal rivers and creeks and includes **Wassaw Sound.** This is where you'll find spotted trout, red drum (also known as spot-tail bass), flounder, sheepshead, tarpon, croaker, and spots in the summer and whiting in the spring and summer. If you're visiting or new to the area and want to do some inshore fishing, hire a guide to show you some good fishing holes, which local folks call "drops." There are countless drops in Chatham's inshore waters, and it pays to know where they are; if you don't, you might find yourself sitting in a boat doing nothing while anglers in a vessel less than 50 feet away are hauling them in.

It's also a good idea to consult the local tide charts before you go fishing inshore; Chatham County has a high tidal range, and when the tides are "springing" (i.e., rising to 8 to 10 feet), the fishing isn't good because the bottom is churned up and the water is muddy. Go fishing when the tides are in the 6- to 7-foot range and the water is clear. You can find tide charts on the weather pages of the *Savannah Morning News.*

i If you need information about where to find fish and how to catch 'em, drop by the Tybee Island Bait and Tackle shop and chat for a while with co-owner Ray Golden. He makes it part of his business to impart the lowdown on prime fishing spots, and he stocks a full supply of the equipment you'll need to have an enjoyable day on the water. You'll find his shop on Tybee's main drag, Butler Avenue, between 15th and Tybrisa Streets.

When you fish offshore, you'll either be bottom-fishing or trolling for sport fish. **Bottom-fishing** will net you black sea bass, grouper, and a variety of snapper. The sportfishing is seasonal, starting in spring with bluefish, followed by cobia, king mackerel, bonito, wahoo, marlin, sailfish, amberjack, tuna, and Spanish mackerel. The **sportfishing** is good into November, and some veteran anglers say the optimum time to venture out is after Labor Day. Offshore angling is best in the Gulf Stream and at a particularly fishy live bottom called the **Snapper Banks.** The Snapper Banks are about 40 miles out, and a trip there from Wilmington Island will take about two hours; the Gulf Stream, the warm ocean current that flows from the Gulf of Mexico along the U.S. coast to New England, is about an hour farther.

If you're after freshwater fish in Chatham County, head for the Ogeechee River above Kings Ferry and the Savannah River above Port Wentworth. You'll encounter large-mouth bass, shad, bluegill bream, redbreast bream, shellcracker bream, and crappie.

Georgia Fishing License

Make sure you have a Georgia fishing license, which will cover both salt- and freshwater angling; you'll be fined if you get caught without one. Licenses can be purchased just about anywhere you can buy fishing tackle, including discount department stores and online at www.georgiawildlife.org. A three-day license costs $3.50 for residents and $20 for nonresidents. Licenses that are good throughout the year are $9 for residents and $45 for nonresidents. For more information, call (800) 366-2661.

Okay, now that you have what you need, gather up your license, gear and bait and go fishing!

AMICK'S DEEP SEA FISHING
1 US 80, Tybee Island
(912) 897-6759
www.amicksdeepseafishing.com
Amick's offers mostly offshore fishing trips and can accommodate 23 passengers on its 41-foot custom-built Morgan, the *Scat*

II. Full- and half-day trips are available for private parties or individuals, and the company also has a 31-foot Morgan, the *Scamp*, for offshore fishing. Amick's is based on Tybee Island, just off US 80 at Lazaretto Creek. Open-boat trips to the Snapper Banks (approximately 10 hours) aboard the *Scat II* are $120 per person. Private weekend charters on the *Scamp* (also 10 hours) are $880 for six passengers.

COFFEE BLUFF MARINA
14915 White Bluff Rd.
(912) 925-9030
Even if you didn't take advantage of the services offered by Coffee Bluff Marina, the ride out to the end of White Bluff Road would be worth making just to get the panoramic view of the Forest River and the wide expanse of adjacent marsh. Anglers who make the trip will also find the marina's large convenience store with a supply of fishing tackle and equipment, a boat hoist, gas, oil, bait, and ice. The marina also offers boat storage in the water and in sheds, but there are no rentals. This facility is closed on Tues and Wed.

i Crabbing is a favorite pastime of many Savannahians. It's a recreational pursuit that's relatively inexpensive, and you don't need a boat to do it. All you do need is a basket net, some bait (chicken parts, such as the necks, will do fine), and a tidal creek in which to crab. If you don't want to buy the basket net, you can affix your bait to a line with a lead weight attached, but you'll probably need a dip net for getting the crabs you catch out of the water.

MISS JUDY CHARTERS
124 Palmetto Dr.
(912) 897-4921
www.missjudycharters.com

Go fishing and have fun doing it with Miss Judy Charters. Why is it fun? Owner Judy Helmey, who started skippering boats in the mid-1960s at the age of 14, says it's because her company caters to customers by making them aware of their surroundings during trips, answering their questions, showing them rod and reel operations, and swapping a fish story or two. "They get to do everything that's fun and we take care of the hard stuff," she says. The Wilmington Island–based company—started in 1947 by Judy's father, the late Sherman I. Helmey—provides inshore and offshore fishing via the *Miss Judy Too*, a customized 33-foot Sport fisher, and from a variety of other boats. Trips leave from the company's dock on Turner Creek; the entrance to the road leading to the dock is on Wilmington Island Road about a mile south of Johnny Mercer Boulevard. Weekday rates for offshore fishing parties of up to six people are $500 for a four-hour trip, $700 for a six-hour trip, and $900 for an eight-hour trip.

> **i** It is customary to cash tip the mate on your fishing charter, 15 to 20 percent. When the charter is complete, don't blame him or her if the fish didn't bite! (Don't forget to tip the fish cleaner, as well.)

Football

The county provides facilities and support for 8-and-younger, 10-and-younger, and 12-and-younger football teams that play games September through November at Ambuc Park, the Jim Golden complex, the Charles C. Brooks Sports Complex (see previous listings for these venues), and Memorial Stadium. The city's youth football program is for 6-and-younger, 8-and-younger, 10-and-younger, and 12-and-younger teams. From 40 to 50 squads participate, playing games at Daffin Park (see previous listing) starting in mid-September and finishing just before Thanksgiving.

Golf

If golf is your game, you have several public and semiprivate courses in Chatham County from which to choose—one downtown, one on the islands, four in Southside/ Midtown, and three in West Chatham. There are also write-ups on a couple of courses in nearby Bryan and Effingham Counties for those golfers who don't mind taking about a 30-minute ride to the links. The following listings will give you an idea of what's available; greens fees include cart rentals, and yardage is from men's tees.

Historic Downtown
THE CLUB AT SAVANNAH HARBOR
2 Resort Dr.
(912) 201-2240
www.theclubatsavannahharbor.com

As you might expect of a course that hosts Savannah's premier golfing event—the Liberty Mutual Legends of Golf—this layout on Hutchinson Island has an impressive pedigree. As the course matures, it becomes more and more beautiful. This semiprivate course, which opened in 1999, was designed by golfing legends Robert Cupp and Sam Snead and is operated by the highly acclaimed Troon Golf. Set on 250 acres in the middle of the Savannah River, The Club takes golfers through a marshland environment and affords them spectacular views of Savannah's riverfront. The 6,627-yard, par-72 course features wide fairways and large, flat greens, and each hole bears an intriguing name. No. 8, for instance, is "the Briar Patch," a 132-yard par 3 with lots of marsh and a long green. Snead is celebrated at No. 10, nicknamed "Slammin' Sammy." The hole has a kidney-shaped green fronted by a large bunker; it's a par 4 that covers 363 yards.

The club has a pro shop, chipping and putting green, and a driving range, and there's an attractive grill overlooking the course that serves breakfast and lunch daily and dinner on Fri. Expect to pay at least $100 for a round of golf at The Club before 3 p.m. and $45 afterward. Walking is permitted at all times.

Islands
WILMINGTON ISLAND CLUB
612 Wilmington Island Rd.
(912) 897-1615

Set amid the oaks, pines, and palms of southwestern Wilmington Island, this par-71 course rambles over 6,715 yards. Raised, undulating greens are planted in Tifton and Bermuda grass, and there's water on 10 holes, including No. 15 and No. 6, two of the course's four well-bunkered par 3s. The signature hole is 6, a 155-yard par 3 with a pond in front of the green and bunkers on the right.

Donald Ross designed the course, which opened in 1927 as part of a resort, the centerpiece of which was the eight-story General Oglethorpe Hotel on the Wilmington River. In the mid-1960s, the hotel was refurbished and renamed the Savannah Inn and Country Club, and the golf course was rebuilt and improved by Willard Byrd. The resort was later purchased by the Sheraton

corporation, which gave the property a new name. The hotel closed in 1994, but the semiprivate golf club remained open under the name of the Sheraton Savannah Resort & Country Club. In May 1998, a family-run development company based in Macon bought the hotel and golf course and changed the name of the golfing facility to the Wilmington Island Club.

The developers built a $1.5 million clubhouse—a two-story, 25,000-square-foot building featuring gym and locker rooms, a card room, a lounge-grill area, a full-service kitchen, and a banquet room capable of seating 300 people. The course was upgraded with new cart paths and a new irrigation system, and a pro shop, lighted driving range, and practice green are also part of the layout.

Only club members are allowed to walk the course. Greens fees are $56 for non-members, and the course is open only to members on Sat and Sun mornings.

Southside/Midtown
BACON PARK GOLF COURSE
Shorty Cooper Dr.
(912) 354-2625

Bacon Park's 27-hole layout presents golfers with three 9-hole courses—Cypress, Live Oak, and Magnolia—featuring narrow, tree-lined Bermuda grass fairways and elevated greens. Cypress and Live Oak carry pars of 36, while Magnolia is a 37, and the combined length of any pair of the courses is more than 6,000 yards. Donald Ross designed the original layout, which is in the midst of suburban Savannah; it's owned by the city and operated by EDR Management Inc. The clubhouse contains a pro shop and full-service snack bar, and a driving range and practice green are available. You can walk the course on weekdays and after 1 p.m. on Sat and Sun. Playing 18 holes runs from $21 weekdays to $23 on weekends.

CYPRESS COURSE

The shortest of Bacon Park's three courses at 3,001 yards, Cypress has water on seven holes, including No. 3, the signature hole. This 185-yard par 3 has a large expanse of water on the approach to the green.

LIVE OAK COURSE

The first hole is long and narrow, a 384-yard par 4 with a green that's well bunkered. The ninth hole is the longest at Bacon Park, a 522-yard par 5 with a fairway that is crossed by a canal past midpoint; there's plenty more water along the remainder of the fairway and in front of the green. The course runs 3,163 yards.

MAGNOLIA COURSE

This course starts with a long hole, a 466-yard par 5 whose green has lots of water on the right. Another interesting hole is No. 8, which is crossed near midpoint by a canal that runs down the left-hand side of the latter half of the fairway. The total length of Magnolia is 3,035 yards.

HENDERSON GOLF CLUB
1 Al Henderson Dr.
(912) 920-4653
www.hendersongolfclub.com

Henderson, opened in March 1995 and owned by Chatham County, offers a good mix of lengths among its 18 holes, ranging from just 127 yards on the 15th to 522 yards on the first hole. The course was built on farmland in southwest Chatham that contained 240 acres of wetlands, so there's plenty of water to look at. In most cases,

however, the water is an intimidation factor rather than a sheer hazard.

In laying out the 6,273-yard, par-71 course, designer Mike Young took advantage of the wetlands and an abundant number of native trees by weaving them in with fairways and greens. Some of the holes eventually will be overlooked by homes; the area is being developed as a golf community where about 350 residences in the $150,000 to $400,000 range have been and are being built.

Rapidly gaining a reputation as Henderson's signature hole is the 18th, a par 4 that's 416 yards long. Accuracy is paramount here because there's water on the entire left-hand side of the hole and to the right of the green. The 6th hole also presents a worthy challenge; it's a long (437 yards) par 4 that plays more like a par 5 because of the usual prevailing winds from the southwest. This is the hole where the ability to hit long counts most. Henderson has a pro shop, driving range, practice green, and a grill serving hot food and sandwiches. It's the home of the Savannah Golf School, which offers a variety of lesson packages and hosts golf camps for youngsters.

Walking at Henderson is permitted anytime Mon through Thurs, and after 1 p.m. on Fri, weekends, and holidays. Fees are $39 on weekdays and $48 (plus tax) on weekends and holidays. The course is off SR 204 just east of the I-95/SR 204 interchange.

West Chatham
CROSSWINDS GOLF CLUB
232 James B. Blackburn Dr.
(912) 966-1909
www.crosswindsgolfclub.com

This semiprivate club boasts the area's only par-3 course, a 1,126-yard layout that's illuminated for nighttime play. The par 3 is suitable for families, people new to golf, and the occasional player, but it's challenging enough to allow veteran golfers to sharpen up their iron play. Water comes into play on five holes, and the par 3 has undulating greens similar to the club's 18-hole course.

The larger course at Crosswinds, which derives its name from its location—less than 2 miles from Savannah/Hilton Head International Airport—covers 6,032 yards and is different from most layouts in that it has four par 5s and five par 3s and is devoid of residential development. The front nine features tree-lined fairways, while the last nine holes offer a wide-open, Scottish links feel. Water is in play on 8 of the 18 holes, and No. 3, a par-4 514-yarder, might give you fits because of a small green with lots of slope that provides the potential for putting balls in the drink.

Crosswinds, which opened for play in October 2000, has a spacious clubhouse featuring a full-service restaurant (Grille 19) that's open for lunch seven days a week and a banquet room that seats 126 people. Also on the premises are a pro shop, an illuminated driving range, and putting and chipping greens. Walking is permitted on both courses. Greens fees for the 18-hole course are $41.50 Mon through Thurs, and $51.50 Fri through Sun. Discount packages are available. Fees for the par 3, which is open seven days a week, are $30 for cart and $22.50 to walk. Hours affect rates.

The club is just off Airways Avenue near that boulevard's exit (104) from I-95.

MARY CALDER GOLF CLUB
West Lathrop Ave.
(912) 238-7100
Owned by International Paper Company and located on the grounds of the company's kraft paper-manufacturing plant just east of Garden City, this par-35, nine-hole course exists mainly for the enjoyment of employees but is open to the public. Play 18 holes, and you'll cover 5,964 yards on a course that's not difficult but does present some challenges because of its tight, elevated greens.

The course, opened in 1937 on the site of Hermitage Plantation, has a pro shop, snack bar, and two putting greens. You can walk the course anytime. Fees for 18 holes are $28 on weekdays and $30 on weekends. You reach Mary Calder from downtown Savannah by driving west on Bay Street, turning north onto West Lathrop Avenue, and entering the manufacturing complex at Blue Gate 1.

SOUTHBRIDGE GOLF CLUB
415 Southbridge Blvd.
(912) 651-5455
www.southbridgegc.com
Rees Jones designed this 6,450-yard, par-72 course, blending in the tall pines, graceful oaks, and wetlands of the West Chatham woodlands. Water comes into play on 11 holes on the course, opened in 1988 as part of the Southbridge residential community. The signature hole is No. 13, a par-3, 179-yarder involving a shot over water to an elevated green cut into three sections. The fourth hole is also challenging; it's a long par 5 typical of holes on the back nine. This hole was carved out of a thick forest. Water on the left side is involved in every shot on this 490-yarder, and bunkers guard the right side.

Southbridge is off Dean Forest Road at I-16, making it about five minutes from downtown Savannah. An antebellum-style clubhouse adorns the semiprivate course, and the building houses a pro shop and

Vickery's at Southbridge, a full-service dining room. The course rents clubs and has a driving range and putting green. Greens fees at Southbridge, which has cohosted the Georgia Open several times, are $40 on weekdays and $50 on weekends, with twilight discounts. Walking is allowed daily.

Outlying Courses
BLACK CREEK GOLF CLUB
Bill Futch Road, Black Creek
(912) 858-4653
Playing the 18-hole layout at Black Creek is a bit like competing on two different courses. The front nine has an open-links feel with its rolling hills and greens; the back nine, with its extensive wetlands, will remind you that you're not far from the coast (you're about 26 miles from downtown Savannah). Water comes into play on 11 holes on the 5,701-yard, par-72 course, which was designed by Jim Bivins of Atlanta and opened in September 1994. The signature hole, No. 15, was cut right out of a swamp and features an island-type green with a large pond in front of it and wetlands on the right and left. You want to make sure you use enough club on this par-3 140-yarder, because anything short of the green is in the water. All four of Black Creek's par 3s will test you, as will the green at No. 7, a par-4, 354-yard hole that presents a dogleg to the right.

The green is well bunkered and two tiered, with the right and left sides sloping away from you, so your shot to the pin has to hit in just the right spot. Semiprivate Black Creek—which is part of a golf community featuring homes priced from $210,000 to $350,000—features a Lowcountry-style clubhouse accommodating a spacious pro shop, a grill, and full-service bar. There's also a driving range and practice green. Walking

is allowed late in the morning and in the afternoon. You must be accompanied by a member, or unaccompanied guests must be sponsored by a member. Fees range from $57 to $110 (unaccompanied guest/weekends).

To get to Black Creek, take I-16 to exit 143 and head west on US 280 toward the Bryan County town of Pembroke. Drive about 2 miles from the interstate to Wilma Edwards Road and turn right; the entrance to the club is less than a half mile on your right.

LOST PLANTATION GOLF CLUB
1 Clubhouse Dr., Rincon
(912) 826-2092
www.lostplantationgolf.com
This semiprivate course near the Effingham County town of Rincon is a long one—7.5 miles from first tee to 18th green, so spread out that you'll never see another hole from the one you're playing. Narrow, tree-lined fairways set on rolling hills offer an abundance of hazards. There are ponds, lakes, or wetlands on 14 holes, and the Bermuda grass greens are big and protected by large bunkers. The signature hole of the 6,445-yard, par-72 course is No. 18, a 390-yard par 4 featuring a dogleg to the left and a lake that shields 70 percent of the green—on the front, left-hand side, and back.

Lost Plantation's rustic-looking clubhouse provides golfers with a well-stocked pro shop, a grill, and a card room. The course, which was built in 1988 and designed by Joe Lee, has a driving range and practice green. You can walk the course after 1 p.m.; fees are $32 on weekdays and $37 on weekends, with discounts for seniors and afternoon times.

Lost Plantation is 21 miles from downtown Savannah. You can get there from the city by taking Bay Street and SR 21 to Fort Howard Road in Rincon and turning right. The road leading to the golf course is about a mile down Fort Howard Road on the right.

Ice Skating

SAVANNAH CIVIC CENTER
Liberty and Montgomery Streets
(912) 651-6550
Believe it or not, you can enjoy this winter sport in Savannah, even at a time when it's liable to be downright warm. During December and starting on the first day of the month, the arena of the Civic Center is transformed into an ice rink where intrepid Southerners try their luck—and ankles—at skating. The rink fee of $6 (which is prone to change over the interval of a year that separates sessions) entitles you to the use of a pair of skates. Skating times vary, so call ahead for information on when the rink is available.

Running

You'll see lots of people running and jogging in Savannah, particularly during the more temperate months of autumn, winter, and spring. Good spots for running—places where you won't have to worry about colliding with motorists—are the sidewalks around **Daffin Park** and **Forsyth Park** and the jogging track at **Lake Mayer Community Park** (see listings in the beginning of this chapter). Each of these facilities covers 1.5 miles, so you can get a good workout by making a circuit or two. Some of the more experienced local runners drive out to the north end of Skidaway Island, park at the marine science center, and take to the roads there. These thoroughfares are fine for running because they are in good condition and sparsely traveled by drivers.

Savannah is the site of several major races, principally the **Savannah River Bridge Run,** a 5K and 10K race held in December (see our Annual Events and Festivals chapter), and the **Tybee Marathon** in February. If you're a competitive runner, you can probably find a race most weekends (except during the hot and humid summer months) within a two-hour radius of Savannah.

SAVANNAH STRIDERS
P.O. Box 15785, Savannah GA 31416
(912) 921-4786
www.savystrider.com
The Striders meet monthly, and many members get together for runs during the week. The club, whose membership numbers about 180, sponsors the Tybee Marathon, Half-Marathon, and 5K in February and the Women's Wellness Walk/Run 5K in September. Annual dues are $15 for individuals and $20 for families, and membership forms can be picked up at the Habersham Branch YMCA on Habersham Street. The listed telephone number is the Striders' information line, and calling it will provide you with data on club meetings and upcoming races. Members meet on the first Thursday of each month at 7 p.m. at the Exchange restaurant at 6710 Waters Ave.

Sailing

Sailing is smooth in Savannah, as you might expect from the venue for the yachting events of the 1996 Summer Olympics. The best sailing is in Wassaw Sound, which is where the Olympic competition was staged. The sound has lots of deep water and few hazards, and you can bank on getting a tradewind breeze in the afternoon. Another good place for sailing is the Wilmington River, which is the site of several local regattas. The following are great places to get started.

GEECHEE SAILING CLUB
(912) 897-5597
www.geecheesailingclub.org
The club sponsors two major sailboat races, the St. Patrick's Day Regatta on the weekend after the holiday and the Oktoberfest Regatta in early October, and organizes about seven extensive cruises for members each year.

Members meet at Tubby's TankHouse restaurant in Thunderbolt on the second Monday of each month at 6:30 p.m. About 70 people actively participate in club functions that include a heavy social agenda. Membership fees are $125 a year.

i Besides being fun and good exercise, kayaking is an excellent way to get a close look at the marshland environment. Kayaking continues to grow in popularity in coastal Georgia, and you can rent boats and paddle around the marshes by paying a visit to North Island Surf & Kayak (912-786-4000) or Sea Kayak Georgia (912-786-8732), both of which are on US 80 on Tybee Island.

SAIL HARBOR MARINA & BOATYARD
606 Wilmington Island Rd.
(912) 897-2896
www.sailharbormarina.com
Sail Harbor is on Turner Creek, right around the corner from the Wilmington River and about 7 miles from Wassaw Sound. This marina, whose office is closed Sun and Mon, has 100 wet slips, 5 of them for transients; a ship's store offering a variety of sailing

merchandise; and a laundry, showers, and restrooms.

Sail Harbor was the 1996 Olympic yachting marina, meaning it served as a shore base for officials coordinating the sailing events. The actual sailing was done from a floating marina in Wassaw Sound that was dismantled after the Olympics.

SAVANNAH SAILING CENTER
Lake Mayer
Montgomery Crossroad at
Sallie Mood Drive
(912) 231-9996
www.savannahsailingcenter.org
Youngsters and adults can learn to sail and sharpen their skills by participating in the programs offered by this community-based, nonprofit organization. The center began operations in 1993 and trained all of the volunteers who served on the water for Olympic yachting in Savannah in 1996. Courses are taught at the boathouse at Lake Mayer. The center will accept children as young as age eight if they know how to swim. The center offers instruction on Saturday during the summer and every other Saturday during the spring and fall. Individual lessons start at $40 a session, but the pricing structure includes multi-session programs that work out to be much cheaper, including one for juniors that is $100. Scholarships are available, as are discounts for multiple sessions and multiple family members.

Soccer

Youth soccer is huge here, so big that there are spring and fall seasons. The county handles the spring program from March through May and typically has 60 teams in leagues for youngsters ages 6 to 19. The city coordinates play for a total of about 100 teams in those

THE GREAT OUTDOORS

age groups during September, October, and November.

Most matches are played at the county's soccer fields on Sallie Mood Drive, but the city also stages matches at Guy Minick Sports Complex on Sallie Mood at Eisenhower Drive and in Daffin Park. There is also an autumn adult soccer program, with fees set at $420 per team.

Teams participating in city and county youth leagues are members of the Coastal Georgia Soccer Association, which can be reached by calling (912) 691-2472. The YMCA of Coastal Georgia runs its own fall soccer program, fielding about 70 teams in the under-6, under-8, under-10, under-12, and under-14 age groups. Matches are played at the Y branches in the county between September and November.

CHATHAM COUNTY SOCCER COMPLEX
7221 Sallie Mood Dr.
(912) 356-2503
Local youngsters get their kicks on eight lighted fields at this 50-acre complex on Sallie Mood Drive near Eisenhower Drive. There are three fields that are 64 by 110 yards, three that are 60 by 105 yards, and two that are 75 by 115 yards. On occasion, the larger fields are divided into smaller fields to accommodate matches being played by the youngest participants.

Adult Softball

ALLEN E. PAULSON SOFTBALL COMPLEX
7171 Skidaway Rd.
(912) 351-3852
Winter is the only time you won't find softballs flying at the city's Allen E. Paulson Complex, one of the finest facilities of its kind in the Southeast. Other times, the place

is jumping with slow-pitch activity. About 90 teams compete in Savannah's open, church, and coed leagues during the spring and summer season, which ends around Labor Day. In September the fall leagues crank up, and about 60 teams hit the five lighted, 300-foot fields; play ends around Thanksgiving. Fees for teams playing in spring leagues are $490; teams that play in the fall leagues pay fees of $390.

Swimming

CHATHAM COUNTY AQUATIC CENTER
7240 Sallie Mood Dr.
(912) 652-6793
www.aquatic.chathamcounty.org
A dome supported by air covers a 40,000-square-foot area containing an eight-lane, 50-meter pool and a six-lane, 25-yard recreational and instructional pool, both of which are accessible to the disabled. In addition to accommodating lap swimming, the large pool is used for district, regional, state, and national swim meets; there's seating for 976 spectators. The building also has men's and women's changing rooms, a pro shop, a snack vending area, and several offices.

The 50-meter pool keeps things calm with a water-motion stabilizer that minimizes swimmers' wakes, and a ventilation duct running around the inside of the center keeps the air temperature at 88 to 90 degrees and the humidity at comfortable levels. Swimmers enter the pool area through a revolving door that maintains the air pressure inside at the level needed to support the dome. The center offers a variety of programs for swimmers of all ages, those who want to develop their strokes and train for competition, and those interested in aquatic fitness. Swimming lessons are $60 for eight sessions; fees for aquatic fitness and coached swimming programs range from $40 to $85 per month. Recreational and lap swim times during the fall, winter, and spring and lap swim times during the summer run from 6 a.m. to 8 p.m. Mon through Fri, and from 11 a.m. to 6 p.m. on Sat. Daily admission passes for Chatham County residents cost $5 for adults and $3 for children ages 10 and younger and $4 for senior citizens, college students, and active-duty military personnel, with kids age 2 and younger admitted free. Rates for noncounty residents are $1 more. Confirm rates by checking the website (click on lessons) as they are subject to change.

Tennis

About 1,500 tennis players participate in the United States Tennis Association league program here, making it the second-largest program in the state next to Atlanta's. A total of 150 of the teams in the program, more than a third of those involved, play at public courts. There are courts at city and county parks throughout the area, but the biggest public tennis complexes are at Bacon and Daffin Parks.

BACON PARK TENNIS COMPLEX
6262 Skidaway Rd.
(912) 351-3850
Tucked into a wooded area on Skidaway Road, this complex has 16 lighted hard courts open from 9 a.m. to 9 p.m. Mon through Thurs and from 9 a.m. to 5 p.m. on Fri, Sat, and Sun, however, call for hours as they vary with the seasons. A pro shop sells tennis merchandise and beverages. Fees start at $5 per hour.

DAFFIN PARK TENNIS COURTS
1001 East Victory Dr.
(912) 351-3851

Daffin's six clay courts and three hard courts sit near the park's lake, so you can occasionally catch a breeze off the water. You can play for free on the lighted hard courts (available from 7:30 a.m. to 10 p.m.); there's a fee of $5 an hour for using the soft courts, which don't have lights and are open from 8:30 a.m. until 5 p.m. seven days a week. (Longer hours are available during the summer. Call for times.)

SAVANNAH AREA TENNIS ASSOCIATION
(912) 961-9862
The Savannah Area Tennis Association organizes and oversees the operation of the majority of United States Tennis Association leagues here. The board of directors of SATA meets at 6 p.m. on the third Monday of each month at the Exchange restaurant on Waters Avenue, and the meetings are open to the public. The association has about 1,500 active members. To join, contact the pros at public or private tennis facilities in the area. You'll pay a $40 USTA membership fee and a league fee of $11. Check out the group on Facebook.

Weightlifting

PAUL ANDERSON–HOWARD COHEN WEIGHTLIFTING CENTER
7232 Varnedoe Dr.
(912) 351-3500
www.co.chatham.ga.us
This facility is adjacent to Memorial Stadium in the Southside and is part of Chatham County's recreational setup. The 15,000-square-foot center is geared toward Olympic-style weightlifting and strength training for local sports teams, but it's open to the public from 9 a.m. to 8 p.m. Mon through Fri and from noon to 5 p.m. on Sat. At the center, you can lift free weights or

Team Savannah

There are bigger regional weight-lifting organizations in the nation, but Team Savannah is the largest one representing a specific locality. Team Savannah has 150 registered weightlifters and 12 coaches, including head coach Henry Meyers III. The team was founded by Michael Cohen, a former Olympian who started the organization in 1987 while serving as the strength coach for the Jenkins High School football team. Since then, Cohen's pupils have set numerous records and claimed a passel of championships. In 2004 two members of Team Savannah were part of the U.S. weight-lifting squad that participated in the Summer Olympics in Athens, Greece, and Cohen served as the women's coach. Membership is $10 monthly and open to members of USA Weightlifting, according to weightlifting center director Meyers.

train on weight machines. Coaches are on hand to answer questions, and there are separate showers and saunas for men and women. The facility opened in February 1995 and is home to Team Savannah, the largest Olympic-style weightlifting team of its kind in the United States. Monthly fees are $10 for individuals and $20 for families, with daily visits pegged at $5.

SPECTATOR SPORTS

Because there are so many opportunities to participate in recreational activities throughout the year in Savannah, most spectator sports tend to come along on a smaller scale and take a backseat to enjoying Savannah's many outdoor venues. Even so, fan interest in minor-league baseball, professional golf, and automobile racing remains strong.

Minor-league baseball has been a part of the Savannah sports scene since the turn of the century (the 20th century, that is), with the most recent in the city's long line of diamond organizations being the Savannah Sand Gnats of the Class A South Atlantic League. The Sand Gnats are affiliated with the New York Mets, and they play their games in Grayson Stadium, the city's gem of an old-time ballpark.

If you're seeking some big-league sporting action, you can find it within reasonable driving distance of Savannah. Atlanta, with its Falcons of the National Football League, Braves of Major League Baseball, Thrashers of the National Hockey League, and Hawks of the National Basketball Association, is five hours to the northwest. The NFL's Jaguars of Jacksonville, Florida, are even closer—about two and a half hours south on I-95. You can always walk up and purchase tickets at these venues. Nearer still is Hilton Head Island, the site of a major sporting event in the spring: the Verizon Heritage PGA golf tournament (although the tournament was seeking a new sponsor at press time; for more on this event, see our Hilton Head chapter).

If you're into intercollegiate sports, you'll find a lot to choose from close to home at the city schools, or you can hit the road for Georgia Southern University in Statesboro (about an hour away), the University of Georgia in Athens (four and a half hours), or Georgia Tech in Atlanta.

AUTO RACING

OGLETHORPE SPEEDWAY PARK
Jesup Road off US 80
(912) 964-RACE
www.ospracing.net

This speedway gives the green flag to stock car drivers competing in the NASCAR Weekly Racing Series every Friday night from March through September. Special racing events are held on Saturday nights.

You'll see more than 115 entries competing each week on the half-mile dirt track in Weekly Series ministock, street stock, pure stock, 440, and late-model division events. The speedway also hosts other motor sports events, concerts, and festivals on weekends throughout the year.

Oglethorpe Speedway is on Jesup Road off US 80 in West Chatham County. Tickets for Weekly Racing Series events are sold at the gate and are $12 for adults and teens and $10 for senior citizens and persons in the military. Children ages 6 to 12 are $3, and those younger than age 6 are admitted free. Parking is also free, there's a park for recreational vehicles, and primitive camping is available at no charge. The gates open at 5 p.m., and racing starts at 8 p.m.

BASEBALL

SAVANNAH SAND GNATS
Grayson Stadium
1401 East Victory Dr.
(912) 351-9150
www.sandgnats.com

The city's Class A minor-league baseball team, an affiliate of the New York Mets, plays 70 regular season games at Grayson, where the brick grandstand was built in 1941. Located at the eastern end of Daffin Park, the stadium stands amid tall pines and oaks dripping with Spanish moss, and it's a great place to sit back, relax, and enjoy the national pastime while sipping a cold beer and devouring some peanuts—the boiled variety being the most popular in this part of the world.

Savannah began fielding a professional baseball team in 1904 and is a charter member of the South Atlantic League. Since 2007 the team has been affiliated with the New York Mets. A big part of the fun of following the Sand Gnats, regardless of their affiliation, is knowing that you might very well be watching a future big-league star.

The Sand Gnats organization schedules numerous special events and promotions and giveaways of baseball caps, T-shirts, replica jerseys, bobbleheads, beer steins, backpacks, and baseball-card team sets. After-game fireworks are held several times

each summer, and it's usually the best display available locally. Games start at 7:05 p.m. on weekdays and 2:05 p.m. on Sun. General admission is $7 to $10 for adults (depending on where you sit) and $4 for ages 4 to 14, senior citizens, and military personnel; kids younger than age 3 get in free.

Reserved seats are $8, and box seats run $10, if you can get them. There are usually a couple of free games a year, with admission sponsored by a company or organization. You can reserve tickets by calling the number listed, or you can order them online. Parking is free.

BIG-LEAGUE SPORTS

For years sports fans in Savannah have been making pilgrimages to Atlanta to watch the Braves, Falcons, and Hawks in action and enjoy the big-league surroundings. However, Savannahians no longer have to drive five hours to Georgia's capital to witness sports at a top level—at least not during football season. Florida's Jacksonville Jaguars, in existence since 1996, play eight home games in a refurbished stadium that's half the traveling time of the Savannah-to-Atlanta junket. To order tickets to Braves, Thrashers, Falcons, and Hawks games, call Ticketmaster in Atlanta at (800) 326-4000. You can obtain Jaguars tickets by calling (877) 452-4784.

GOLF

LIBERTY MUTUAL LEGENDS OF GOLF
The Club at Savannah Harbor
1 Resort Dr.
(912) 236-1333
www.libertymutuallegends.pgatour.com

Held during the third week in April, the Legends of Golf brings many of the sport's all-time greats to Savannah and the par 72

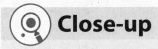

Close-up

Shoeless Joe Gets His Due in Savannah

Savannah did in 2003 what baseball has refused to do for decades—admit Shoeless Joe Jackson into a Hall of Fame.

Jackson, an all-time great outfielder who was banished from baseball following a gambling scandal involving the 1919 World Series, has been excluded from baseball's Hall of Fame in Cooperstown, New York, much to the dismay of fans who have sought his induction. His supporters point out that Jackson was never found guilty of charges of throwing the series.

But Shoeless Joe—a featured character in the films *Field of Dreams* and *Eight Men Out*—has found a place of honor in the **Greater Savannah Athletic Hall of Fame (GSAHF)**. Although not prominently displayed, his plaque and likeness adorn a wall on the second floor of the **Savannah Civic Center** (301 West Oglethorpe Ave.; 912-651-6556; www.savannahciviccenter.com), along with other members of the Hall's Class of 2003.

"There is only one athlete in any sport that interest is still being shown 80 years after he finished playing," states the inscription on his plaque. Also noted is that "his ties to Savannah began when he was sent here in 1909. . . . He loved Savannah and made it his home for years during and after his playing days."

Jackson, a native of South Carolina who died in 1951 at the age of 62, "owned and operated two businesses in downtown," his tribute states.

Shoeless Joe is among more than 200 athletes, coaches, mentors, administrators, executives, sportswriters, and organizations who have been inducted into the GSAHF since its founding by a group of 16 sports-minded residents in 1965.

The athletes participated in a wide array of sports—baseball, football, basketball, track, golf, swimming, diving, softball, automobile racing, weightlifting, and even lacrosse, kayaking, and racquetball. Those inducted range from media-mogul Ted Turner, famed as a yachtsman and as the owner of professional sports teams, to a quintet of the University of Georgia's bulldog mascots—UGA I, UGA II, UGA III, UGA IV, and UGA VII.

You can find out more about Savannah's sports history and the folks who have contributed to it the most by visiting the GSAHF, which is free and open to the public during Civic Center operating hours.

Club at Savannah Harbor course—players such as Arnold Palmer, Lee Trevino, and Chi Chi Rodriguez. Moved from north Florida to Savannah in 2003, the Legends is the second-oldest tournament on the Senior PGA tour—the event debuted in 1978—and boasted a total purse of $3 million in its first year here. Although legendary players are the main attraction of the tourney, the course is also a crowd-pleaser. Situated as it is on Hutchinson Island across the Savannah River from the city's Historic District, the Club at Savannah Harbor offers spectacular views of the town. The 18 holes, designed by Sam Snead and Robert Cupp and bearing names such as the Briar Patch and Battery Point, also have a charm of their own derived from their marshy and woodsy environment.

The event features golfers competing in three divisions—the Demaret Division for players age 70 and older, the Raphael Division for those ages 50 to 69, and the Legends, which is the main competition. Check the website for ticket and official scheduling information. Parking is free in lots at the nearby Savannah International Trade and Convention Center.

INTERCOLLEGIATE SPORTS

You can witness competition on various intercollegiate levels in football, baseball, men's and women's basketball, and women's volleyball and stay in town while doing so. Armstrong Atlantic State University, Savannah State University, and the Savannah College of Art and Design all compete in basketball; Savannah State plays football; and Armstrong, Savannah State, and SCAD field baseball and volleyball teams.

You'll have to do some driving to see the big-time college athletes compete. Georgia Southern University in Statesboro (a one-hour drive west) plays Division I-AA football and has won six national championships since 1985, the last in 2000. The GSU men's basketball team has been to the NCAA Division I playoffs twice since 1987, and the women's team has gone two times since 1993.

But the really big shows are in Athens at the University of Georgia, where the Bulldogs and Lady Bulldogs compete in the Southeastern Conference, and in Atlanta, where Georgia Tech's Rambling Wreck participates in Atlantic Coast Conference play.

DAY TRIPS

You obviously will find plenty to occupy your time in Savannah, but if you want to go roaming a bit, you'll discover lots to see and do in the rest of coastal Georgia. To get you started on your explorations of the territory to the south of Savannah, we've mapped out trips to Richmond Hill–Liberty County and to Jekyll Island.

The spotlighted sites in the Richmond Hill–Liberty County area are within an hour's drive of Savannah. It will take a little longer to reach Jekyll, which is about a 90-minute jaunt from Savannah. For those inclined to head north into the South Carolina Low-country, we've included a trip to Beaufort, a charming, history-filled town located 50 miles from downtown Savannah. Happy wandering!

RICHMOND HILL–LIBERTY COUNTY

Lovers of history and nature will enjoy a tour of Richmond Hill and Liberty County, an area of extensive marshlands, lush forests, and meandering rivers, where the past is rich in significant people and events. To adequately visit all the spots we'll be sending you to, you'll probably need more than a day. That said, you might want to split this tour into a couple of day trips or pick a few places that sound the most appealing and spend a day visiting those.

Begin your tour of the area by driving to the Bryan County municipality of **Richmond Hill,** a fast-growing town that's become a bedroom community of Savannah during the past 20-plus years. This one-time stomping ground of industrialist Henry Ford is 19 miles southwest of downtown Savannah and can be reached by heading west on I-16 to I-516. Then head south on I-516 to the Southwest Bypass (Veterans Parkway), south on the Southwest Bypass to SR 204, west on SR 204 to US 17, and south on US 17 to the highway's intersection with SR 144.

Turn left from US 17 onto SR 144 and head east through the heart of Richmond Hill; it's a mile to your first stop, the **Richmond Hill Historical Society and Museum.** The museum building, which once housed a kindergarten that was a project of Ford and his wife, is on the right on the corner of SR 144 and Timber Trail Road.

RICHMOND HILL HISTORICAL SOCIETY AND MUSEUM
SR 144, Richmond Hill
(912) 756-3697
www.richmondhillhistory.org
You'll learn the fascinating story of Richmond Hill's Henry Ford era (1925–51) when you visit this museum. The billionaire Ford purchased 85,000 acres in Bryan County in the mid-1920s, in effect buying the town of Richmond Hill, which was then known as Ways Station. Ford spent his winters there, living on a plantation that accommodated a laboratory where chemists attempted to transform agricultural products into goods

that could be used by the automobile industry.

Ford revitalized an area where moonshining was one of the major occupations; he put people to work on his plantation and at a sawmill that he refurbished, and he built medical clinics, houses, chapels, and the town's Community House. Ford also improved existing schools and built a trade school for boys and a grammar and high school for African-American youths. A museum staffer will tell you about Ford's accomplishments and their impact on the community while you look at photographs and artifacts from the period. You'll also learn about sites from the Ford era that you can visit, such as the Community House, which is now a funeral home, and one of the chapels, now a Catholic church.

Other sections of the museum depict the area's plantation era and offer displays of photos and some of the furniture used in the county's one-room schoolhouses and in a typical parlor of a Bryan County home in the early 1900s. One room is devoted to the re-creation of a country store whose shelves are filled with authentic tins and boxes that held products popular during the early 1900s, and if you're interested in the really distant past, be sure to check out the time-line mural depicting the history of the area from prehistoric times to the present. An admission fee is not charged, but donations are accepted. The museum is open from 10 a.m. to 4 p.m. Mon through Fri.

After you've looked at the displays at the Richmond Hill Museum, hop in your vehicle and head east on SR 144 to Fort McAllister State Historic Park. To reach the park, you'll drive 4 miles into the countryside on SR 144 to SR Spur 144, then turn left onto SR Spur 144; the entrance to the park is 4 miles ahead, and the drive to it will take you past upscale Lawcountry-style and ranch-style homes, some of them with backyard boat docks on the beautiful and fast-flowing Great Ogeechee River, which can be seen on your left.

i Some of the attractions on our Richmond Hill–Liberty County day trip are in somewhat remote areas that aren't near restaurants, so you might consider packing a lunch for the day. You can dine in relative comfort at picnic areas at several stops on this tour, including Fort McAllister State Historic Park, Fort Morris State Historic Site, the Midway Museum, and the Fort Stewart Museum.

FORT MCALLISTER STATE HISTORIC PARK
3894 Fort McAllister Rd., Richmond Hill
(912) 727-2339
www.gastateparks.org

This 1,725-acre park between the Ogeechee River and Red Bird Creek has two alluring identities: It's a recreational area featuring amenities for campers and picnickers, and it's also the site of an earthen fort where much of the Savannah area's most significant Civil War action took place.

Prior to 1980 these two attractions existed as Richmond Hill State Park and Fort McAllister Historic Site. That year, they were combined to form Fort McAllister State Historic Park, which today is operated by the Georgia Department of Natural Resources. There's a $3.50 to $5 parking fee to enter the park, which is open daily from 7 a.m. to 10 p.m. (campers arriving later can register at their campsites); admittance is free on Wed. There are also three homey cottages (built 14 feet above the ground) to rent at this park for $125 per night. The cottages have two double beds in each bedroom and sleep eight. There are fully equipped kitchens with microwaves and dishwashers, heat, and air-conditioning. One, in particular, also has a lovely screened-in porch that overlooks the marsh.

i Fort McAllister State Historic Park and Fort Morris State Historic Site are among the 18 bird-watching venues on the Colonial Coast Birding Trail, which stretches along Georgia's coast from Tybee Island in the north to Cumberland Island National Seashore and the Okefenokee National Wildlife Refuge in the south. You can see songbirds, wading birds, and waterfowl at Fort McAllister and Fort Morris, depending on what time of year you visit.

THE RECREATIONAL AREA

For day-trippers, the main attraction here is the tree-filled picnic ground running along a high bluff overlooking the Ogeechee River. Tall pines and hardwoods make this a shady, serene spot for walking or sitting in a glider-type swing and watching the river flow by. You'll find 50 sites with picnic tables and grills, a fishing pier that extends out over the river, and plenty of rustic-looking playground equipment for the kids in this area, which borders the main road leading to the fort. Across the road from this area is the start of a 3.5-mile nature trail complete with a primitive campsite that can be rented for $3 a night per person.

If you plan on making your visit to Richmond Hill–Liberty County last longer than a day and you like roughing it, consider staying at the park's Savage Island Campground, which has 66 campsites—54 for recreational vehicles and 12 with tent pads, and all with

water and electrical hookups, grills, and tables. Two comfort stations provide campers with toilets, heated showers, and washer/dryers, and the campground also has a playground, nature trail, and dock and boat ramp on Red Bird Creek. The RV sites rent for $20 a night, and the tent pads are $18 a night, with reduced rates for senior citizens.

The Historic Site

Fort McAllister is one of the best-preserved earthwork fortifications built by the Confederacy during the Civil War. The southernmost of the defenses ringing Savannah, the fort withstood several attacks by Union warships before being overpowered by Federal forces on December 13, 1864, at the end of Gen. William T. Sherman's March to the Sea. The site was once owned by Henry Ford, who began an extensive restoration in the late 1930s, and the fort eventually fell into the hands of the state of Georgia, which restored it to its 1863–64 appearance.

You can wander around the walls and through the interior of the fort and look inside its central bombproof, but be careful not to climb on these earthen structures, which are extremely susceptible to erosion from foot traffic. Take the self-guided tour of the fort and check out a 32-pounder smoothbore gun that fired red-hot cannonballs and the furnace where these projectiles were heated; the reconstructed service magazine, which held shells, powder, and fuses for the rebels' 32-pounder rifled gun; and the fort's northwest angle, where the attackers placed the first U.S. flag planted on the parapets.

The fort site has a museum that's part of a visitor center that opened on September 1, 2001. The museum contains Civil War shells and weapons; implements such as those used in the construction of the fort; artifacts from the Confederate blockade runner Nashville, which was sunk in the Ogeechee by the Union ironclad *Montauk;* a diorama of the assault on the fort; a display depicting life at the fort as experienced by its 230 defenders; and exhibits involving the Guale Indians, who once inhabited the area, and Henry Ford's efforts to preserve the site. The fort is open from 9 a.m. to 5 p.m. Admission rates are $4 for adults, $3.50 for seniors, and $2.50 for youths; children younger than age five are admitted free.

After visiting Fort McAllister State Historic Park, head back to Richmond Hill on SR 144 and then south to Liberty County and the Historic Liberty Trail. The first attraction on this tour of the trail is Fort Morris State Historic Site, and you can get there from Richmond Hill by turning left onto US 17 from SR 144 and driving 2 miles to I-95, heading south on I-95 for 11 miles, and leaving the interstate at exit 76. Next, turn left onto US 84/SR 38 (Fort Morris Road) and stay on it for 7 miles until you come to the entrance to the site.

FORT MORRIS STATE HISTORIC SITE
2559 Fort Morris Rd., Richmond Hill
(912) 884-5999
www.gastateparks.org

This peaceful little spot on a low bluff on the Medway River was the scene of one of the classic rejoinders in American history. During the Revolutionary War, the British besieged the American earthworks of Fort Morris and the nearby town of Sunbury, and the Redcoat commander demanded a surrender. The fort's commander, Col. John McIntosh, answered the demand in this defiant manner: "We, sir, are fighting the battles of America, and therefore disdain to remain neutral till its fate is determined. As to surrendering the fort, receive this laconic reply,

'Come and take it!'" Lacking some expected support from another British force and the exact knowledge of the strength of the troops at Fort Morris, the Redcoats did not follow McIntosh's suggestion; instead, they retreated. Fort Morris, however, eventually fell to the British and was dismantled.

A smaller earthen fort, called Defiance in honor of McIntosh's reply, was built during the War of 1812 from the remains of Fort Morris, and you can explore it by visiting this site. Strolling around the walls of the fort under the majestic oaks towering over it, you have a wonderful view of the Medway and its marshes, and you might even get a glimpse of a shrimp boat trawling in the river. The interpretive center/museum at the site tells the saga of the fort and of Sunbury, the town it was built to protect, and there's also a mile-long nature trail through marsh and scrub oak forest.

The Georgia Department of Natural Resources, which maintains the 70-acre site, offers several special events during the year, including the Independence Day Colonial Faire in July and the "Come and Take It!" reenactment in November. Admission to the site is $2.50 for adults, $2 for seniors, and $1.50 for youths ages 6 to 18; entry for children younger than age 6 is free. Fort Morris is open from 9 a.m. to 5 p.m. Tues through Sat and from 2 to 5:30 p.m. on Sun. It's closed on Mon, with the exception of federal holidays.

While you're at the interpretive center at Fort Morris State Historic Site, be sure to view the award-winning, 12-minute video, Sunbury Sleeps: The Forgotten Town of Sunbury, Ga. *This hauntingly beautiful tribute to one of Georgia's "lost towns" serves as the perfect introduction to the next stop on our day trip, the Sunbury Cemetery. The cemetery is a little more than a mile from the entrance to Fort Morris. After leaving the fort, turn right onto*

Fort Morris Road and keep to your left until you reach Sunbury Road. Turn left onto this dirt road and drive to Dutchmans Cove Road, then take a right and follow this unpaved lane a short distance to the cemetery.

SUNBURY CEMETERY
Dutchmans Cove Road, Richmond Hill

This small cemetery is all that remains of the once bustling town of Sunbury, which in 1764 had 80 dwellings, three stores, several wharves, and a trio of town squares. By 1773, Sunbury was a seaport beginning to rival Savannah as a place of commerce. That year the town saw 56 vessels clear port as compared with Savannah's 160. Sunbury also had another claim to fame: All three of Georgia's signers of the Declaration of Independence had a connection to the town—Lyman Hall lived there, Button Gwinnett resided on nearby St. Catherines Island, and George Walton was confined there when Sunbury was made a military prison after its capture by the British during the Revolutionary War.

By the end of the war, most of Sunbury had been destroyed, and the town never recovered. There were fewer than eight families living there by 1855, and all evidence of the town eventually disappeared—everything but the cemetery and the 34 grave markers that remain standing. When we visited Fort Morris, we knew when we left that there wouldn't be a great deal to see at the cemetery. But after viewing the Department of Natural Resources video about Sunbury, we felt compelled to take a look and pay our respects, so to speak. Maybe you will, too.

Now it's time to get back on the Historic Liberty Trail and head to the town of Midway. We recommend, though, that while you're on the way, you visit Seabrook Village, which you can find by turning right off Fort Morris Road onto Trade Hill Road.

SEABROOK VILLAGE
660 Trade Hill Rd., Richmond Hill
(912) 884-7008
www.seabrookvillage.org

This 104-acre site portrays the history and culture of African Americans living in coastal Georgia during 1865 to 1930. Using authentic buildings and displays of artifacts, Seabrook brings that period to life. Among stops on guided and self-guided tours of the village are Bowen's Farm, with its rice fields and a barn containing tools used in farming, gathering oysters, and making turpentine; the Ripley Corn Crib, where corn is ground into grits and meal; the Seabrook School, with its original wooden blackboard and desks made by former student John Stevens; the Gibbons-Woodward House, in which you can see a rural kitchen, a feather bed, and a replica of the original clay chimney; a mill and boiler house where stalks of sugarcane are ground by horsepower and cooked into syrup; the Delegal-Williams House, with its family photographs and local furnishings; and a train depot that was moved to the site from nearby Riceboro.

While you're visiting Seabrook, be sure to see the unusual artwork of Cyrus Bowen, with which he adorned local gravesites. Seabrook is open Tues through Sat from 10 a.m. to 4 p.m. Group tours lasting three hours and conducted by costumed guides are available, as are one-hour guided tours in the afternoon.

The next stop on our tour is Midway, which was established in 1754 by a group of Congregationalists from Dorchester, South Carolina. Their Midway Society produced governors, cabinet members, U.S. senators and congressmen, numerous ministers, and foreign missionaries. The parish they settled, St. John's, was a hotbed of patriotic fervor during the years leading up to the American Revolution, and two of its residents,

Lyman Hall and Button Gwinnett, were among Georgia's three signers of the Declaration of Independence. To get to Midway, head west on US 84 back to I-95 and stay on US 84 until you reach US 17. Turn right onto US 17. Clustered just up the road are the Midway Museum, Midway Congregational Church, and the Midway Cemetery.

THE MIDWAY MUSEUM
US 17, Richmond Hill
(912) 884-5837
www.themidwaymuseum.org
This museum gives visitors an idea of what life was like for landowners in coastal Georgia during the late 18th and early 19th centuries. The museum building is an elegant, raised cottage-style house erected in 1957 and based on a sketch made in 1828 of a home in nearby Riceboro. The rooms of the house are filled with original 18th-century furnishings; among the unique items are a walking-cane gun that fired a .45 caliber slug, and a set of musical glasses that are played by rubbing vinegar around the rims. A museum staff member will tell you about many of the items in the three first-floor rooms of the house and will play a tune on the glasses; you're free to look at the upper-floor bedrooms and displays in the ground-floor rooms on your own.

This attraction, which is operated by the Midway Museum Board of Governors, is open from 10 a.m. to 4 p.m. Tues through Sat; Sun, 2 to 4 p.m.; it's closed on Mon. Admission, which includes access to nearby Midway Congregational Church, is $6 for adults, $5 for seniors and military, and $3 for youngsters ages 6 through 17; children younger than age 6 are admitted free.

MIDWAY CONGREGATIONAL CHURCH
US 17, Richmond Hill

Built in 1792, this stately church reflects a style reminiscent of colonial New England (some of the founders of Midway were descendants of Puritans from Massachusetts who had settled in South Carolina). The existing building replaced a church that was burned by the British in 1778. The church is a short walk from the Midway Museum, and you can obtain a key from a museum staff member and take a look inside. The church has no heating system or artificial lights, but services are conducted there each April by the Midway Society. For inquiries and service times, email info@themidwaymuseum.org.

MIDWAY CEMETERY
US 17, Richmond Hill
Researchers believe Midway Cemetery was laid out in the late 1750s and that it contains about 1,200 graves. Among those buried there are James Screven, a brigadier general in the American army who was killed in November 1778 in a skirmish with the British about a mile south of his resting place, and Daniel Stewart, who attained the rank of brigadier after fighting in the Revolutionary and Indian Wars and was the great-grand-father of President Theodore Roosevelt; Fort Stewart, the U.S. Army's military reservation at nearby Hinesville, is named after him. The cemetery is open to the public, and a brochure featuring a map and self-guided tour of the site is available at the Midway Museum for 25 cents.

Midway Cemetery is also the burial site of Louis LeConte, who owned a rice plantation south of Midway where he created a botanical garden of great renown. You can reach the plantation by driving south on US 17 for 3 miles to the Barrington Ferry Road. Turn right onto Barrington Ferry and follow it for 5.5 miles to the entrance to the plantation site.

LECONTE-WOODMANSTON RICE PLANTATION AND BOTANICAL GARDENS
Barrington Ferry Road, Midway
(912) 884-6500
www.leconte-woodmanston.org

In its heyday during the early 1800s, Woodmanston Plantation covered more than 3,300 acres and was the largest inland rice plantation in Georgia. Louis LeConte came into possession of Woodmanston in 1810, and the garden he planted there gained fame throughout the United States and Europe.

The plantation was abandoned in 1869, but a restoration of a 63.8-acre site was begun in the late 1970s as a project of the Garden Club of Georgia. The project, being carried on now by the LeConte-Woodmanston Foundation, is a work in progress that so far has resulted in the creation of a 1.5-acre botanical garden featuring plants that LeConte might have grown and a 1-mile nature trail along a network of rice dams. The garden contains more than 100 different plants, including beds of older varieties of camellias and roses. Several structures that were part of the plantation—a chicken coop, a garden shed, a smokehouse, and a slave cabin—have been re-created on the site. Visitors can also stroll along a path through a three-acre bog containing flowering plants native to the area and observe rice being grown on two acres of wetlands.

The plantation is open to the public from 10 a.m. to 4 p.m. Tues through Sun, and at other times by prior arrangement, and admission is $2 per person or $5 per family. Because LeConte-Woodmanston is in a somewhat remote spot, you might want to call ahead to the listed number before you visit, and you definitely should call to make arrangements for group tours. Also, be aware that the last 1.6 miles of the drive to the plantation is on dirt roads.

The last attraction on this tour is the Fort Stewart Museum, a military museum just inside the main entrance to Fort Stewart, the huge U.S. Army post at Hinesville. From LeConte-Woodmanston, drive back to the intersection of US 17 and US 84 and head west on US 84 about 7 miles to Hinesville. Turn right onto General Stewart Way, which will take you to the entrance to Fort Stewart. The museum is on the post at the corner of Wilson Boulevard and Frank Cochran Drive.

FORT STEWART MUSEUM
2022 Frank Cochran Dr., Hinesville
(912) 767-7885
www.stewart.army.mil

Displays at the museum focus on the history of Fort Stewart and its current occupant, the Third Infantry Division (Mechanized). Fort Stewart, now the largest army installation east of the Mississippi River, was established in the summer of 1940 as Camp Stewart and served as an antiaircraft artillery training center during World War II and the Korean War. During the early 1960s, the post was the site of a variety of tests and training by military units, and in the latter half of the decade it served as a training area for Army helicopter pilots.

In the mid-1970s, the Twenty-fourth Infantry Division (Mechanized) was activated at Fort Stewart, and the unit was based there until April 1996, when the post became the home of the Third Infantry. The story of the Third's service in the two world wars and Korea is related at the museum, portions of which are also devoted to the Twenty-fourth Infantry and the military history of coastal Georgia. Uniforms, weapons, and other items used by the Third Infantry and their opponents are on display in the museum, as is a

T-72M-1 tank abandoned by Iraqi Republican Guard crewmen in an engagement with the Twenty-fourth Infantry during the earlier war in the Persian Gulf. There are also exhibits featuring Operation Iraqi Freedom and Audie Murphy, a Third Infantry hero in World War II whose exploits won him the title of "America's Most Decorated Soldier." Outside the museum, you'll find static displays of equipment used in warfare, including an M4A3 Sherman tank, a UH-1 Huey helicopter gunship, and numerous Iraqi artillery pieces and vehicles captured by U.S. forces during the Gulf War. Entry to Fort Stewart is open to civilians, and admission to the museum is free. Hours of operation are from 10 a.m. to 4 p.m. Tues through Sat. Museum-goers should enter the post via the visitor center at Gate 1 on General Screven Way.

JEKYLL ISLAND

Georgia's coastline is a fascinating and varied one. Savannah, which snugs up to South Carolina, marks its northernmost point. At the southern extremity, up against the Florida line, you'll find St. Mary's, with its access to Cumberland Island National Seashore. And in between you'll find the Golden Isles.

Four islands make up this cluster, accessible from **Brunswick,** a port and industrial city that retains a small historic district. It is the jumping-off point for the Golden Isles, reachable by causeway with one exception. **St. Simons Island** is the biggest and most developed of the Isles, with beaches, motels, restaurants, and historic sites. **Little St. Simons** is accessible only by boat and is open to a limited number of guests (by arrangement). Consisting of largely undeveloped beaches and marshlands, this island is a real treat for environmentally minded tourists. **Sea Island,** largely residential and from

a geographical point of view virtually part of St. Simons, is home to the extremely tony resort known as the Cloister.

Jekyll Island is the southernmost of the four Golden Isles and has the same appeal to the same type of traveler who is attracted to Savannah. You'll find places to eat and sleep there, but development has not destroyed the natural beauty of the island. In fact, the state of Georgia owns the place, and the business and residential ventures there are really long-term leases. However, that policy is changing—in 2007 the state opened part of the island to high-dollar development. Enjoy the beaches (which are all public, at least at the moment) and consider a trip along the extensive network of bike paths a must-do (bike rental places abound; check the lobby of larger motels). Spend the night to enhance your day trip even more. It's a beautiful island and you'll probably hate to leave! Jekyll, like the rest of the Golden Isles, is also covered with golf courses, most of which are accessible to the public at large.

The **Jekyll Island Welcome Center,** P.O. Box 13186, Jekyll Island, GA 31527 (912-635-3636, 877-453-5955), and the **Brunswick & the Golden Isles Visitors Bureau,** 4 Glynn Ave., Brunswick (912-265-0366, 800-809-1790), are two general sources that can provide additional information, including lodging details and how to get onto the golf courses. Expect to pay a $3 "parking fee" as you drive onto Jekyll. There's also a website: www.jekyllisland.com.

To get there, head south on I-95. It takes about 90 minutes. While it's not that long a trip (we know people who commute there from Savannah for work daily, in fact), it can be harrowing. This is the corridor that runs between the Northeast population centers and Florida, and it is always heavily traveled by time-conscious vacationers. Exits are clearly marked.

Jekyll and St. Simons Islands are not accessible from one another—you have to make the trip back to the mainland on the causeway and then take the other causeway to the next island. It's a pleasant drive through the marshes, watching herons and marsh rabbits, but it does take a little time.

St. Simons is a more developed beach community than Jekyll Island, but it has still retained its charm and individual character. There's a large year-round population, and they clearly cherish the winter months when the tourists aren't as prevalent. That doesn't mean visitors aren't welcome; it does mean a quieter pace of life in the winter. There's even a "downtown," a short strip of shops leading to the water and including the usual tourist stuff, an interesting toy store, a bookshop, etc. St. Simons has large, legible signs posted at key intersections, and the names of specific destinations are clearly listed. It's simple to get around on St. Simons. The King and Prince Hotel is a good lodging choice (the selection is rather limited). It's by no means as tony as the Cloister, the region's upscale resort, but they've got the amenities you'd expect in a beachside resort. The island offers multiple restaurant options, predictably leaning toward seafood. The exclusive **Cloister Sea Island** (www.seaisland.com/thecloister) resort was built just before the bottom fell out of Wall Street and launched the Great Depression. It has long been a traditional destination of the if-you-have-to-ask-you-can't-afford-it crowd. Not that there aren't bargains to be had: Honeymooners are extended the right to rent rooms on their anniversary at the rate that prevailed at the time of the wedding—so if you meet someone celebrating their 50th, they're in

high cotton. The owners tore the whole thing down a couple years ago and rebuilt it, using salvaged materials when possible. The result is a new-that-looks-old resort with stunningly landscaped grounds.

JEKYLL ISLAND HISTORIC DISTRICT MUSEUM VISITORS CENTER
Stable Road, Jekyll Island
(912) 635-4036

Georgia was originally founded as a refuge for debtors, but the richest and most powerful men in America originally developed Jekyll Island. They bought the island in 1886 and made it into a private resort where you need not apply unless your annual income included at least seven figures, all to the left of the decimal point, at a time when that was really a fortune. Names that are synonymous with American fortunes were among the Jekyll Island Club's members: Rockefeller, Gould, Morgan. And they didn't stay in rented quarters, although the club was (and now is again) a fine hotel. Instead, they built "cottages"—mansions that took advantage of beautiful views, cooling breezes, and balmy weather. This was, indeed, the playground of the rich and famous.

Types of tours vary by season. The version that does not involve entry into any of the buildings costs $10 for adults and $5 for children and runs throughout the day. A more elaborate version that allows entry into two of the cottages that have been restored with period furniture runs at 11 a.m. and 2 p.m. daily (more often in some months). Cost is $15 for individuals. The stops usually include the mansion known as Indian Mounds, where once the Rockefellers roamed. There's bad news for independent-minded travelers: Only the guided tours get inside the choice restored

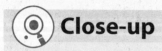 **Close-up**

Cumberland Island

If you're feeling adventuresome, prepare to unearth one of this country's best-kept secrets, **Cumberland Island.** Travel south on I-95 to FL A1A (exit 373). Turn left at the light at the end of the ramp. Then, follow FL A1A East for 14.8 miles to Centre Street. Turn left onto Centre Street and go to the waterfront. Drop off your passenger and/or luggage to meet the boat captain at Dock 3 next to the LUCY R. FERGUSON sign on the dock rail. Follow the directions on your parking pass to the parking area, then walk southwest across the train rail to the boat. (The ferry leaves the Fernandina Beach docks at 9:30 a.m., 12:15 and 5:30 p.m. daily.)

Cruising over to Cumberland Island is a treat in itself. Pack a light snack as the ferry ride takes about 45 minutes. As you make your way closer and closer to **Cumberland Island National Seashore,** you'll enjoy unparalleled views of the south Georgia shoreline. Cumberland Island is approximately 18 miles long and 3 miles wide, and is the nation's largest wilderness island. There are endless smooth, white beaches that stretch the entire length of the eastern shore, oftentimes nearly a mile wide. There are times when you'll hardly meet a soul as you stroll along the beach. Cumberland's dense forest, golden salt marshes, and pristine beaches provide sanctuary to a host of wildlife, including armadillos, bobcats, loggerhead turtles, herons, egrets, alligators, wild horses, turkeys, and hogs. There are still traces remaining of the Native Americans, Spanish missionaries, English soldiers, plantation owners, slaves, freedmen and freedwomen, and Gilded Age industrialists who called the island home over the centuries. Sand dunes are prevalent, and among them arises one of the most luxurious (and private) hotels in existence, the Greyfield Inn, a four-story, 16-room property, which is detailed below.

On the opposite end of the island stand the stately ruins of **Dungeness,** an original estate built by Thomas and Lucy Carnegie in the late 1800s. Thomas died before Dungeness was completed, leaving behind his wife and nine children. Mrs. Carnegie was a dominant figure on the island. Expanding her husband's initial acquisitions, she eventually owned 90 percent of the island. She initiated renovation of Dungeness and construction of four additional mansions built as island homes for her children. The Greyfield Inn was the home of Lucy R. Ferguson, the daughter of Thomas and Lucy Carnegie. Converted to an inn during 1962, the family still oversees the operation.

Once you arrive on the island, if you haven't booked a room in the idyllic **Greyfield** Inn (www.greyfieldinn.com), then you'll at least want to tour this magnificent treasure where John Kennedy and Carolyn Bessette spent their honeymoon in 1996 after getting married in a small historic chapel on the island. Voted one of the top 500 highest-rated hotels by *Travel and Leisure,* you'll feel right at home among the beautiful antiques, candlelit dinners, and comfortable, plush sitting areas. There's no cell phone service here, and don't even try to pick up a Wi-Fi signal. My tip is to purchase Greyfield Inn's "Georgia Golden Isles American Plan Package " that includes round-trip ferry transportation; a single/or double occupancy room (additional guests are $275 per night); all meals (breakfast, lunch, and gourmet dinner); hors d'oeuvres during the nightly cocktail hour; snacks; a naturalist-led tour; unlimited use of sports, fishing, and beach equipment; and parking. Rates are $395 to $595 per night and depend on the room you select for your stay (for one person, all inclusive). A two-night minimum is required. Call (866) 401-8581.

buildings outfitted with period furniture. Several restored buildings, however, are in use as shops or galleries and, of course, are open to the public at no charge.

BEAUFORT, SOUTH CAROLINA

Beaufort is situated between Savannah and Charleston, South Carolina, and it exudes much of the charm of those two cities, but on a smaller scale. This town of about 9,500 residents has a historic district filled with elegant homes built in the 1700s and 1800s and a quaint but bustling waterfront shopping district that's brimming with intriguing stores and unique eating places.

The Beaufort area is rich in history. The Spaniards unsuccessfully attempted to found the colony of Santa Elena here in 1559, and French Protestants, led by explorer Jean Ribaut in 1562, tried to start a settlement called Charlesfort on what is now Parris Island. It failed, and the Spanish returned to the area in 1566, building a fort, San Phillipe, and the Mission of Santa Elena at Port Royal. According to the Historic Beaufort Foundation, this settlement was, by 1580, one of the largest Spanish towns north of Mexico. It was abandoned in 1586 following attacks on Spanish Florida by the English privateer, Sir Francis Drake.

The English laid claim to the area in the 1600s and by the turn of the next century had established a foothold at Port Royal. Beaufort was founded in 1711, and in the years leading up to the American Revolution, local planters turned profits by growing rice and indigo. During the Revolutionary War, residents of the area were sharply divided over the issue of independence from Britain and allegiance to the crown. British forces occupied Beaufort in July 1779 but evacuated later in the year. Cotton planting was introduced to the area after the Revolution. Subsequent crops made rich men and women of many of Beaufort's citizens in the years leading up to the Civil War. Early in the conflict, in November 1861, South Carolina's Sea Islands were invaded by Union forces, and Beaufort and the Port Royal area fell into Federal hands. Beaufort became the main base of Union squadrons blockading the South Atlantic. During the Union occupation, the first school for black freedmen, which eventually became Penn School, was established east of Beaufort on St. Helena Island.

Beaufort is about 55 minutes from downtown Savannah by car. To get there, take Oglethorpe Avenue west and drive across the Eugene Talmadge Memorial Bridge on US 17 into South Carolina. It's 5 miles from the bridge to the intersection of US 17 and Alternate SC 170; turn right onto Alternate SC 170 and stay on it for 6 miles, where it becomes SC 170 (also SC 46). Continue 3 miles to where SC 170 leaves SC 46. Turn left onto SC 170 and enjoy the scenery—a narrow, two-lane road shrouded by the moss-covered branches of gnarled oaks. Take a good look, because this area might not be heavily forested for much longer; civilization and the developers of subdivisions and shopping centers appear to be taking over.

You'll be on SC 170 for about 20 miles, which will take you into the outskirts of Beaufort. While on SC 170, you'll pass country roads with fascinating-sounding names such as Bulltomb, Bufflehead, Heffalump, Old Bailey's, Crippled Oak, Bellinger Bluff, and Mudbar, and you'll catch glimpses of marshland and open water. You'll cross the picturesque Chechessee River, drive through relatively pristine Lemon Island, and then find yourself marveling at the majestic expanse of the aptly named Broad River, which is spanned by a bridge that's 1.4 miles long.

SC 170 will lead you to US 21 South (also known in these parts as Boundary Street); turn right onto US 21 and stay on it for a mile until you reach the traffic light at Ribaut Road. Turn right onto Ribaut Road and drive to the third stoplight, then turn left onto Bay Street, which will take you about a mile past stately homes and a bay dotted with sailboats and into Beaufort's waterfront district.

The focal points of this area are **Bay Street,** which is lined on either side with shops and restaurants, and **Henry C. Chambers Waterfront Park,** a pleasant, tree-filled swath of greenery lying south of Bay Street. The park, with its wide walkways, swinging benches, and elaborate children's playground, is a wonderful place for strolling or sitting and catching a breeze off the nearby water. Several of the restaurants that dot the south side of Bay Street open onto patios and porches that offer outdoor dining on the fringes of the park. Among these eating places are **Saltus River Grill** at 802 Bay St., which specializes in seafood; **Plum's** at 904½ Bay St., which is known for its gourmet soups, salads, sandwiches, and homemade ice cream; and **Panini's Cafe** at 926 Bay St., which features pasta, pizza, hoagies, and, of course, panini-style sandwiches.

The stores along Bay Street and on the narrow lanes running to the north off Bay provide a plethora of shopping opportunities. There are several galleries; a unique one is the **Rhett Gallery** at 901 Bay St. In addition to selling prints and paintings, this gallery offers antique maps and nautical charts and Civil War art and artifacts, including pages from *Harper's Weekly* and *Frank Leslie's Illustrated Newspaper.* Specialty shops you might

want to visit include **the Craftseller,** at 818 Bay St., which deals in local and regional arts and crafts; **the Cat's Meow Shoppe,** a gift shop on Bay Street that caters to collectors of all things feline; and **Bellavista Antiques and Interiors** at 206 Carteret St. If you're looking for books, stop in at **the Book Shop** at 808 Bay St., **McIntosh Book Shoppe** in the refurbished Old Bay Market Place at 917 Bay St., or **Firehouse Books & Expresso Bar** at 706 Craven St. Each has a good inventory that features books related to the region, and McIntosh has a large selection of rare, out-of-print editions.

Those in search of history will find it throughout town in general and in two locations in particular:

BEAUFORT MUSEUM
713 Craven St., Beaufort, SC
(843) 525-7077
Housed in an arsenal that was completed in 1798, the museum tells the story of Beaufort's history through its exhibits and displays of artifacts. Among the exhibits are those involving the Native Americans who lived in the area, the European colonization of the region, the development of the town in the era prior to the Civil War, the Union occupation during that conflict, and early-20th-century industries.

The museum has been situated in the arsenal since 1939 as the result of a WPA project to add a wing for a museum and relic room. The building was the site of National Guard musters until 1966, and it was acquired by the city of Beaufort in 1990 for the continued purpose of preserving the town's heritage and that of the surrounding Sea Islands. The museum is closed on Sun and city holidays but is open the rest of the time from 11 a.m. until 4 p.m. Admission for adults is $3, and children age six and younger are admitted free.

i While visiting Beaufort, consider taking a side trip to nearby Penn Center, a 50-acre National Historic Landmark District on St. Helena Island. Penn Center is the site of Penn School, one of the most significant African-American institutions in the United States and an active community center. The mission of the center is to preserve the history, culture, and environment of the Sea Islands. You can get there by taking US 21 east from Beaufort to St. Helena Island and turning right onto Martin Luther King Jr. Drive.

JOHN MARK VERDIER HOUSE MUSEUM
801 Bay St., Beaufort, SC
(843) 524-6334
Built in the late 1790s by one of the town's leading merchants, the two-story frame house rests on a tabby foundation and is an example of the Federal style of architecture. Interior features are the paneled reception parlor, first-floor dining room, graceful staircase, and spacious second-floor drawing room. The decor and furnishings reflect those of the period from 1790 until 1825.

The house was condemned in 1942, but public-spirited citizens spearheaded a drive to save the structure, and a restoration effort was begun in the fall of 1975. It was completed a year later. The house is open to viewing Mon through Fri with the first tour at 10:30 a.m. and the final tour at 3:30 p.m. Admission is $6 for adults and $4 for students.

The Point

You can see more of Beaufort's elegant old houses—their exteriors, at least—by visiting an area called **the Point,** which is ea. Street. This oak-filled section of town is large and doesn't take long to drive throug but it's abundantly graced with what the local historic foundation calls "Beaufort-style" homes. According to the Historic Beaufort Foundation, these homes were "designed for airiness and coolness" and "incorporated elements of Georgian and Colonial architecture as well as those of Greek Revival and semitropical Spanish." The foundation's guidebook states that the Beaufort-style home "differs from the more urban designs of Charleston and Savannah in that the Beaufort house is freestanding on a large lot, frequently with a formal garden, and is oriented to take full advantage of the prevailing southwesterly breezes. It more nearly resembles the plantation house, brought to town, as some indeed were, and adapted to the summer heat and the dampness of the Lowcountry."

A wonderful way to view these homes and the rest of Beaufort's Historic District is on foot on your own; you can pick up free maps of the area at many of the downtown shops and at the visitor center, which is at the intersection of Congress and Carteret Streets. If you're looking for something that's a little more structured, there are numerous tours available, including those provided by appointment by **the Point Tours** at 1002-B Bay St. (843-522-3576) and by **Carolina Buggy Tours** (843-525-1300), whose carriages leave from the marina area of the waterfront; and by **the Spirit of Old Beaufort,** which conducts walking tours from its gift shop at 103 West Street Extension (843-525-0459). **John Sharp** (843-575-5775) provides a spookier look at Beaufort, with a lantern-lit narrative conducted in the graveyard of St. Helena's church.

EAD,
AROLINA

Hilton Head Island, a lush playground for wealthy individuals—many who own second homes there—is also a popular destination for visitors from all over the United States. This is the South's answer to the tropics, and by all appearances, it's an island that was bred for fun! The foot-shaped barrier island is located off the Atlantic coast of South Carolina, approximately 45 miles north of Savannah, 90 miles south of Charleston, S.C., and 30 miles south of historic Beaufort, S.C. The island—12-miles long and 5-miles wide—was the first "eco-planned" destination in the United States. What does that mean? To the average onlooker who is trucking onto the island with a mini-van filled with kids, luggage, and beach gear, it means that this is a place that has been delicately preserved, where nature has collided with man in a pleasant sort of way. It's a place where you can bring your kids to escape the world of video games and opt to spend afternoons together trekking through the island on foot or bike. There are no high-rise buildings or commercial, touristy strips. Billboards are few, and even the common places that you know (like Publix, Outback, and TJ Maxx) blend discreetly into the serene natural flora. Indeed, the developers of this island are to be commended! Hilton Head can be the perfect day trip, or better yet, the perfect place for an extended vacation. If you choose to drive over for the day, you might find yourself booking a private home, villa, or condo for a longer return visit! There are simply too many things to do here, and to do them well and enjoy the ride, one must commit to a few days, at the very least. If you're coming for the week, you'll be sad when the checkout day arrives.

HISTORY

In contrast to Savannah, most of the structures on Hilton Head are less than 60 years old, the result of two momentous events in the island's history that occurred in the mid-1950s. One was the opening of a set of two bridges connecting the 42-square-mile sea island with the South Carolina mainland. The other was the start of the Sea Pines residential/resort community by a southeast Georgian named Charles Fraser.

"The opening of the bridge had a major impact on development," states Porter M. Thompson in the book *Hilton Head Island Images*. "Suddenly building materials, equipment and people were able to come and go freely—Hilton Head had lost its isolation and a new era had begun."

Sea Pines, in its basic form a residential area built around a golf course, set the tone for the other planned communities that would be created on Hilton Head and spurred the development of the island as a mecca for retirees and vacationers. Back in the early 1950s, Hilton Head was home to about 100 families, "little more than a quiet community of farmers and shrimpers," as author Richard Rutt put it in *Hilton Head Island: A Perspective*. Now the island—with its natural assets of marshes, wide creeks, hardwood forests, and 12 miles of beach—is the site of more than 10 planned communities harboring a multitude of stylish homes and upscale condominiums known locally as villas. Hilton Head boasts 25 beautifully manicured golf courses, almost 400 tennis courts, 10 marinas, 4 large hotels, a bevy of villa-style resorts and midsize hotels and motels, more than 250 restaurants, and 36 shopping areas with more than 200 shops. Permanent residents now number approximately 34,000, many of them engaged in satisfying the needs of visitors, of whom there are 2.5 million annually, according to the island's chamber of commerce.

All this growth has occurred in a manner that places an emphasis on preserving Hilton Head's natural surroundings: live oaks, magnolias, pines, palmettos, and other flora. Following ideas originally credited to Fraser, most islanders continue to adhere to the concept that buildings must blend in with the environment and that the development is as unobtrusive as possible.

Although Hilton Head's modern era begins in the 1950s, the island's recorded history goes back considerably further—to the 1500s, when Spaniards and Frenchmen visited while exploring the area bordering Port Royal Sound, the large bay on Hilton Head's north shore that's one of the world's finest natural harbors. The Spanish and French fought over the sound for almost 50 years,

with the Spaniards triumphing but never settling the area. That was left to the British, who in 1717 were responsible for the island's first English-speaking settler, John Barnwell.

Englishmen had been in the area well before that, however. In 1663 sea captain William Hilton sailed into the sound and came upon the island. He spotted a headland on the northeastern end and named it after himself. As time went on, the entire island came to be called by the name of this promontory, Hilton Head.

The settlers who came to Hilton Head in the 1700s eventually planted the land in cotton, indigo, sugarcane, rice, and other crops. They purchased slaves brought to America from Africa and used them to create large plantations. According to Richard Rutt, there were 24 plantations on the island by 1860, most of them producing cotton. Also by that time, South Carolina was on the verge of seceding from the Union and leading the South into the Civil War, a conflict in which Hilton Head would play an interesting part.

The island was invaded by Union troops on November 7, 1861, seven months after the war began, in an effort to control Port Royal Sound and establish a portion of the blockade of the Confederacy's Atlantic coast. In the Battle of Port Royal, a Union fleet of 15 warships and 31 transports and supply ships exchanged shots with 4 Confederate gunboats and 2 forts, one of them on Hilton Head. The Confederate guns were silenced, the forts were evacuated, and Union forces took possession of the island and held it until the end of the war.

The area near the fort on Hilton Head—called Fort Walker by the Southerners and renamed Fort Welles by its Federal conquerors—became a town during the Union occupation, when the population of Hilton Head

mushroomed to 40,000. "Enlisted personnel—both soldiers and sailors—constituted
the bulk of that population, or, 23–30,000
men," Rutt stated in his book. "The balance of
Hilton Head's wartime population consisted
primarily of freedmen who sought refuge on
the island, civilian dependents, and Yankee
tradesmen. The latter opened and operated
a variety of business establishments, ranging
from hotels, blacksmith shops, and theaters
to photography studios, tattoo parlors, and
bordellos."

The main street of the town, which was
located in what is now Port Royal Plantation,
was named Sutler's Row after the merchants
who lined it. The military men who paid
exorbitant prices for the sutlers' goods called
it Robber's Row, the name now borne by
one of the plantation's golf courses. Another
settlement sprang up in what is now Hilton
Head Plantation. It was called Mitchelville
and consisted mostly of tents and barracks
housing freed slaves who had fled to the
island. When the war ended, the military and
the sutlers left and, said Rutt, "the shops and
houses of Robber's Row and Mitchelville rapidly disappeared from the island, no doubt
torn down by freedmen seeking to build
homes of their own."

From the end of the Civil War until the
middle of the 20th century, Hilton Head
was a sleepy sea island largely bypassed
and forgotten by the rest of the world. All
that began to change in 1950, when Fred
Hack, C. C. Stebbins, and Lt. Gen. Joseph B.
Fraser bought 8,000 acres of pine forest and
formed the Hilton Head Company for the
purpose of selectively cutting the pines. In
1956 the company's holdings were divided,
with Fraser acquiring 4,000 acres on the
southern end of the island. A year later Fraser's son Charles, a University of Georgia and

Yale Law School graduate in his 20s, bought
his family's holdings and another 1,200 acres
and started planning and developing Sea
Pines.

Meanwhile, Hack and O. T. McIntosh,
who had purchased 12,000 acres on the
northern end of the island in the early 1950s,
began work on their own developments:
Spanish Wells Plantation and Port Royal
Plantation. (Sea Pines also used the term
plantation in its name in its early years, as
have many of the planned communities
on the island; it refers to the antebellum
plantations once located on the sites of the
communities.)

"These few men," wrote Porter Thompson in referring to Fraser, Hack, McIntosh,
and other developers, "began with the idea
that large holdings of land could be sub-
divided into lots and sold for residential
purposes. There was a twist to this. Hilton
Head is ideally suited by climate and location for resort activity, so the communities
developed would have to accommodate
both resort and residential activities. Charles
Fraser is largely credited with first developing the concept that a resort/residential
community could be successful, if a few
considerations were made. He embodied
two excellent and highly compatible interests: the understanding of development and
a love of nature and of the natural beauty of
the island."

Under Fraser's direction, Sea Pines
became, in the words of the Associated
Press, "a big-time leisure landmark, a model
for resort playgrounds and planned communities from Virginia to the Philippines."
Other developers followed his lead, creating
their own planned communities and, in the
process, transforming Hilton Head into the
world-renowned resort that it is today.

Note that the island is virtually "built out" today. Just about the only vacant land is that set aside for green spaces, so new construction generally requires demolition of something that's already there. This has led to upscale development spilling off the island and onto the mainland, in the form of gated "plantation" housing, golf courses, and shopping centers. Although this Hilton Head "sprawl" is well outside the actual Bluffton, this area is called Bluffton.

GETTING HERE

Some people arrive at Hilton Head Island by boat or fly directly onto the island, but if you're like most visitors, you'll be coming by car, either from home in your own vehicle or from the Savannah International Airport in a rental. Whatever the case, here's how to get to the island.

By Car

Getting to Hilton Head by car is fairly simple because there's only one road onto the island, **US 278,** a four-lane that runs west to east through the South Carolina Lowcountry. Finding US 278 is easy, particularly if you're arriving at Savannah International Airport and renting a car for the 40-minute drive to the island (you can find information on flights to Savannah and car rentals in our main Getting Here, Getting Around chapter). US 278 is also easy to get to if you're coming from the south or north on I-95, or if you're arriving from the west via I-16 and I-95.

US 278 intersects I-95 just north of Hardeeville, South Carolina, so once you're on the interstate, all you have to do is watch for the exit for US 278 (exit 8). Take that exit and head east; it's an 18-mile straight shot to Hilton Head. You'll be on the island in

20 minutes and at the middle of it in about a half hour. To get to I-95 from Savannah International Airport, take Airways Avenue west for a little more than a mile to the interstate. Get on I-95 and head north into South Carolina. The US 278 exit is 16.5 miles up the interstate from where you left Airways Avenue.

If you're not renting a car, you can get to Hilton Head from the airport via the **Gray Line Low Country Adventures Ltd.** shuttle service. Low Country Adventures meets all incoming flights with private-ride or shared-ride shuttles; reservations are strongly recommended. Shared-ride fares from the airport to the island are $38 per person one-way and $66 round-trip, with multiple-passenger discounts available. You can reach Low Country Adventures at (843) 681-8212 (in South Carolina) or (800) 845-5582 or www.lowcountryadventures.com.

If you're visiting Savannah and succumb to the temptation to venture over to Hilton Head for the day or spend a night on the island, you can drive there by following the I-95/US 278 route just discussed, or you can go the "back way." If you take the I-95/US 278 route, you'll be on multilane highways, and it will take about an hour and five minutes for you to get from Savannah City Hall to the Hilton Head Island Chamber of Commerce building at the middle of the island. (To get to I-95 from city hall, drive west on Bay Street through three traffic lights to Martin Luther King Jr. Boulevard, turn left onto MLK, and head south three traffic lights to the entrance ramp to I-16, then take I-16 west for 8.5 miles to I-95.)

The back way is shorter (about 55 minutes from city hall to the middle of Hilton Head), more scenic, and a little more complicated. It involves traveling on roads that are under construction. If you want to try it, take Oglethorpe Avenue west to the Eugene Talmadge Memorial Bridge and drive north across the Savannah River into South Carolina. You'll be on US 17 for 5 miles from the South Carolina side of the bridge to the intersection of US 17 and Alternate SC 170. Turn right onto Alternate SC 170 and stay on it for 6 miles, where it merges with SC 46. Continue east on SC 46 for 12 miles to US 278. Turn right onto US 278 and head east—you'll be on the island in about five minutes. Along your way on SC 46 to US 278, you'll pass through piney woods, hardwood swamps, and the laid-back, offbeat little town of Bluffton with its Squat & Gobble restaurant (worth a stop for lunch and whimsy) and 30 mph speed limit (be sure to observe it). While in Bluffton, you'll come to a four-way stop; turn left to stay on SC 46. This route is an area of active, almost exponential, development, so you will be sharing the road with cement mixers and lumber trucks. Be careful and on your first trip, it's a good idea to plan to travel in daylight.

By Boat

If you're going to Hilton Head by boat, you can get there via the **Intracoastal Waterway,** which runs along the west side of the island, however, please utilize the resources of a map or ask at the marina for specifics. There are several public marinas and harbors where you can tie up and enjoy your stay while aboard your vessel. These include **Harbour Town Yacht Basin** at Sea Pines (843-671-2704, or e-mail htyachtbasin@aol.com), **Outdoor Resorts Yacht Basin** at Intracoastal Waterway Marker 20 (843-681-3256), **Palmetto Bay Marina** at 86 Helmsman Way (843-785-4893), **Shelter Cove Marina** at Shelter Cove (843-842-7001), **Skull Creek**

Marina at Hilton Head Plantation (843-681-8436), and **Windmill Harbour** (843-681-9235). The length of the slips available at Windmill Harbour marina ranges from 25 to 70 feet, and the cost per night for docking runs from $1.75 per foot for boats under 50 feet, to $1.90 for boats over 50 feet. Call ahead for specific details for this and other marinas as prices change.

By Plane

Hilton Head has its own airport on the north end of the island. The **Hilton Head Airport** is on Beach City Road, which runs north off US 278, the island's main drag. Beach City Road is at mile marker 4 on US 278, and the entrance to the airport is about a mile from US 278. There is a fixed-base operator across the runway from the airport terminal that can accommodate private planes. The FBO is on Gateway Circle off Dillon Road less than a mile north of US 278.

HILTON HEAD AIRPORT
120 Beach City Rd.
(843) 689-5400
www.hiltonheadairport.com
Hilton Head's airport has an up-to-date, spacious terminal that is served by two commercial carriers, as of Spring 2010 (remember, air travel is a volatile business and things change a lot). The longest established there is **U.S. Airways Express** (800-428-4322). U.S. Airways Express offers 8 to 14 flights each day to and from Charlotte, North Carolina, and direct flights to and from Washington, D.C., on weekends. **Delta Connection** (843-342-5380) offers three departures daily.

Six rental-car agencies maintain desks at the airport: **Avis Rent A Car** (843-681-4216, 888-897-8448), **Budget Rent A Car** (843-689-3737, 800-527-7000), **Enterprise**

(843-689-9910), **Hertz Rent A Car** (843-681-7604, 800-654-3131), **National Car Rental** (843-681-7367, 800-CAR-RENT), and **Thrifty Car Rental** (843-689-9990, 800-847-4389). There are nine taxicab and shuttle services operating from the airport. Rates from the airport are set by the cab companies and monitored by Beaufort County: Standard rates are $12 to the Hampton Inn; $21 to Hilton Head Plantation; $21 to the Marriott/ Palmetto Dunes; $21 to Shipyard; $22 to the Holiday Inn Oceanfront; $25 to Sea Pines; $42 to Del Webb Sun City near Bluffton, South Carolina; and $80 to Savannah.

The airport has short- and long-term parking lots: Short-term rates are free for the first 15 to 30 minutes and $1 for each additional half hour, with a maximum charge of $8 for each 24-hour period; long-term rates are $1 for the first hour and $1 for each additional half hour, with a maximum charge of $6 for each 24-hour period and a weekly charge of $36.

CAROLINA AIR CENTER INC.
52 Gateway Circle
(843) 689-3200
In addition to the usual services you'd expect from a fixed-base operator, Carolina Air Center offers a shower, a nine-hole putting green, and courtesy crew cars on request. The ramp charge for single-engine aircraft is $10 per night, and 100 LL and Jet A fuel service is available 24 hours a day if you call after normal business hours, which run from 6 a.m. to 10 p.m.

GETTING AROUND

I recall driving on to Hilton Head Island for the very first time. With visions of a "beach town," dancing in my visor-shaded head, I remember asking my husband time-and-time again

when I would first see the ocean? Expecting a Daytona-like setting where high-rise hotels and condos sit right on the sand, all of which is within eyesight of the main drag, I learned that the beach itself is not within plain view. The beach is, in fact, hardly seen until you check into your oceanside hotel or villa. The main road to Hilton Head (US 278) cuts the island in parts, but it is far from scenic. Once you get to your destination, more than likely, you're within a bike ride or short walk to the strand.

The best way to get on to Hilton Head is by car, and in some cases, the car is your best way to get around once you're there. Where you're staying and where you're going will dictate whether you should drive or ride a bike. Taxi and limousine services are available, however, the surest and less costly way to assure your stay in Hilton Head is pleasurable is to rent a car.

Driving on the Island

Finding your way around Hilton Head is fairly easy, but actually finding the places you're looking for can be a challenge. At first glance that statement might not make much sense, but consider this: Most of what a visitor would be looking for can be found on or very near three main roads (US 278, Pope Avenue, and South Forest Beach Drive), but spotting a specific restaurant, shop, or motel can be difficult because of town regulations limiting signage and promoting natural beauty. Businesses are not allowed to have signs off the premises, and the signs they do have must conform to strict rules involving size and lighting. These regulations, combined with the emphasis on preserving trees and foliage and having buildings blend in, can make it easy for you to drive right past your intended destination. This is particularly true when it comes to the island's main thoroughfare, US 278, a busy four-lane divided highway also known as the William Hilton Parkway. Most everything is set back off the road on tree-lined side streets that often resemble driveways; pay close attention as you cruise along the island.

William Hilton Parkway

Once you cross the Karl S. Bowers and J. Wilton Graves Bridges to Hilton Head on US 278, you're on William Hilton Parkway, which runs east for 5 miles to the northern end of the island, then bends south and continues 6 miles to Sea Pines Circle. This 11-mile stretch passes restaurants, motels, shopping centers, other businesses, and the entrances to resort communities such as Hilton Head Plantation, Port Royal, Palmetto Dunes, and Shipyard.

To aid motorists, the town has placed mile markers along the parkway, with the lower-numbered markers closer to the bridges and the higher-numbered ones closer to the traffic circle. In some write-ups on businesses on the parkway, we've included a mention of the mile marker nearest the business being discussed.

Sea Pines Circle

When you enter this traffic circle from William Hilton Parkway, you'll encounter exits to the Cross Island Parkway one-quarter of the way around, Greenwood Drive halfway around, and Pope Avenue three-quarters of the way around. Greenwood Drive is the main road leading into the Sea Pines Resort community. The stretch of the Cross Island Parkway directly west of the circle, also known as Palmetto Bay Road, was widened into a four-lane highway in 1997.

Pope Avenue

Pope Avenue runs east a tad more than a mile from Sea Pines Circle to Coligny Circle. On Pope, you'll find a variety of restaurants, stores, shopping plazas, another entrance to Shipyard, and the entrance to the public parking lot at Forest Beach.

Coligny Circle

The Coligny traffic circle is practically on Forest Beach, and it routes motorists from Pope Avenue to South Forest Beach Drive (one-quarter of the way around the circle) and North Forest Beach Drive (three-quarters of the way around). North Forest Beach Drive is residential and leads to many of the older vacation homes and permanent residences on the island; short side streets run east to the beach, but access is private and public parking is a no-no.

South Forest Beach Drive

There are several resorts and restaurants along South Forest Beach Drive, which leads to another entrance to Sea Pines. Access to the beach via the side streets is private unless marked otherwise.

Cross Island Parkway

The Cross Island Parkway, a four-lane toll road that bypasses the southern portion of William Hilton Parkway and alleviates traffic congestion on that heavily traveled thoroughfare, opened in January 1998. The 6-mile, limited-access highway stretches from near the intersection of William Hilton Parkway and Spanish Wells Road, at mile marker 2 in the northwestern portion of the island, to Sea Pines Circle. Part of the Cross Island Parkway is a 65-foot-high bridge that crosses Broad Creek at Palmetto Bay. The toll for riding the length of the parkway (one way) in a car has been set at $1; it's $1.75 for three-axle trucks and $3.25 for five-axle trucks. Planners say the road saves motorists anywhere from 8 to 10 minutes in travel time.

Biking on the Island

Hilton Head has some 50 miles of paved public bicycle paths, and there are many more miles of paths within the island's resort communities. Among the public paths are those that run along William Hilton Parkway from Gumtree Road (just past mile marker 2) to Sea Pines Circle for 9 miles, along both sides of Pope Avenue from Sea Pines Circle to Coligny Circle for a total of 2 miles, along North Forest Beach Drive from Coligny Circle to the end of North Forest for 1.3 miles, along South Forest Beach Drive from Coligny Circle to Sea Pines' Ocean Gate for 1.4 miles, along the Cordillo Parkway from South Forest Beach Drive to Pope Avenue for 1.1 miles, and to the Folly Field Beach Park (see the Public Beach Access and Parking section in this chapter) from William Hilton Parkway for 0.8 mile. A 3.5-mile path along Gumtree and Squire Pope Roads in the northwestern part of the island was completed in 1998, as were a 1-mile stretch on Point Comfort Road and 1.1 miles of pathway on Arrow Road in the southern portion of the island. Also open for riding are a 2.2-mile path along Beach City Road and the wider paths along North and South Beach Drives.

You can make arrangements to rent a bike through the resort where you're staying or by calling one of the more than 20 bike rental outlets that can be found in the Yellow Pages of the local telephone directory. In season, expect to pay $25 to rent a bike for a week and $9.50 to $12 for a day.

Taxis & Limousines

In addition to the taxicab and limousine companies that serve the Hilton Head Airport, there are several other limo operators on the island, including **Camelot Limousine & Tours** (843-842-7777).

Taxi rates are not regulated by the city of Hilton Head and vary from company to company and point to point. To find out how much a trip will cost, tell the dispatcher where you are and where you're going and ask what the fee will be. Rates for limousines run from $65 to $75 per hour with a two-hour minimum.

Bus Service

The island is served by the buses of **Beaufort County's Lowcountry Regional Transportation Authority** (LRTA), but this public transportation service is mainly a means of getting working people from towns on the mainland on and off Hilton Head. These buses serve Hilton Head in the early morning and in the late afternoon, meaning the LRTA is not a means of conveniently getting around the island throughout the day. However, there is a limited-demand response system through which riders can schedule transportation by calling (843) 757-5782 (a round-trip to Bluffton using this system can range from $6 to $10).

Public Beach Access & Parking

All beach access points, with the exception of Burke's Beach, are ADA approved. In additional, public restroom facilities are available at each beach access point or nearby community park. As far as parking on the rest of the island goes, there is an abundance of parking in the lots of restaurants, shopping centers, motels, and other commercial establishments, much of it shaded by trees, which can be a blessing in the summer months.

Alder Lane Beach Access

This access point is on South Forest Beach Drive. Metered parking for the access is on Woodward Avenue, which is across South Forest Beach Drive from Alder Lane. The meter fee is 25 cents for 15 minutes. There are 23 spaces.

i The town of Hilton Head's Green Guide asks that visitors help safeguard the island's flora and fauna by, among other things, staying off sand dunes and refraining from picking dune plants, feeding dolphins, or tampering with turtles' nests.

Burke's Beach Access

This access is at the end of Burke's Beach Road, which runs off of William Hilton Parkway between mile markers 6 and 7. There are 13 metered spaces here, with fees set at 25 cents for 15 minutes, and there are 200 free spaces at nearby Chaplin Community Park.

Coligny Beach Park

The access at Coligny Circle offers about 30 metered spaces and a parking lot with about 350 spaces. The meters allow you to park 15 minutes for a quarter. Rates when the lot is manned by an attendant—usually on Fri, weekends, and holidays—are $4 per day.

Driessen Beach Park

Located at the end of Bradley Beach Road, which intersects William Hilton Parkway just past mile marker 6, this access has a lot with 212 spaces where parking is 25 cents per half hour. The lot is about a half mile from the parkway.

Folly Field Beach Park

This access is on Starfish Drive, which runs off Folly Field Road. Parking at the 52 spaces here is metered, and the rate is 25 cents for 15 minutes. Folly Field Road also runs into William Hilton Parkway at mile marker 6; it's a little more than a half mile from the parkway to the access.

Islanders Beach Park

This facility is on Folly Field Road about a mile from William Hilton Parkway. All the 150 spaces here are reserved for persons having annual beach passes (there are also 30 such spaces at Driessen Beach). Passes are available only to local residents or property owners; they cost $30 for a two-year pass and can be obtained at Town Hall near the entrance to Wexford Plantation, or at Facilities Management at Gateway Circle off of Dillen Road.

Pinckney Island National Wildlife Refuge

Travelers intent on hiking, bicycling, and observing wildlife will find a pleasing venue in the form of the Pinckney Island National Wildlife Refuge, located off US 278 a mile west of Hilton Head Island. The refuge offers more than 14 miles of trails and accommodates large concentrations of wading birds and an active bald eagle nest. Pinckney Island, the largest land mass in the refuge and the only one open to the public, covers 1,200 acres. Admission is free. The refuge is open every day however it is recommended that you exit prior to dark.

SOURCES OF INFORMATION

**HILTON HEAD ISLAND–BLUFFTON
CHAMBER OF COMMERCE
WELCOME CENTER**
100 William Hilton Pkwy.
(843) 785-7110
www.hiltonheadisland.org

The chamber of commerce staffs a welcome center at this site just past mile marker 1 on William Hilton Parkway. Stop here and you'll find displays and brochures involving shopping, dining, lodging, long- and short-term rentals, golf, tennis, fishing, real estate, tours, and events. There's a video display that will introduce you to the island in several different languages (you make the choice) and a large-scale map of the island, plus smaller maps of Hilton Head and the surrounding areas that you can take with you. The center is open from 9 a.m. to 5:30 p.m. daily.

The welcome center shares a building with the Coastal Discovery Museum, which offers exhibits involving the area's history, native crafts, and wildlife. Admission is $2. There's also an art gallery exhibit room. Museum hours are from 9 a.m. to 5 p.m. Mon through Sat and 10 a.m. to 2 p.m. Sun, and there's a museum shop featuring books on the Civil War and topics of local interest.

ACCOMMODATIONS

When you vacation at Hilton Head, you have the option of staying at hotels, motels, villas, or private homes that are being rented out by their owners. I prefer the villa rental or selecting hotels with kitchen suites. The costs are comparable with hotels, but on the downside you'll have to purchase your own staples as opposed to hotels where you'll receive daily maid service and on-site eateries and restaurants. Another upside of

Harbour Town Lighthouse

The Harbour Town Lighthouse, Hilton Head's most enduring symbol, stands 93 feet tall and is visited by a quarter-million people a year. The observation deck perches 66 feet above the base floor of the lighthouse on Calibogue Sound, and you reach it by climbing 110 steps. Completed in 1970, the lighthouse was the first one built on the Atlantic coast in more than 150 years. Flashing a white light every 2.5 seconds, it's a navigational aid for the sound and the Intracoastal Waterway, even though it's not operated by the U.S. government. (It's run by the company that owns Harbour Town.) The structure is open daily from 8 a.m. to dusk, and there's a $1 fee to tour it, which is highly recommended. The views will be etched in your fondest vacation memories.

condo rental is that they are more spacious than standard hotel rooms. You'll get more for your money and there are literally hundreds of condos for rent, even if you're on a budget. The hotels and motels range from modern, well-maintained establishments on the island's main thoroughfares to full-blown resorts situated in or adjacent to Hilton Head's luxurious golf communities. The villas are fully furnished condominiums set in apartment buildings and town houses, many of them with pools and locations close to beaches, golf clubs, and tennis courts.

There's plenty to choose from—Hilton Head has more than 3,000 hotel and motel rooms, 6,000 villa units, 1,000 time-share units, and an array of rental homes ranging from oceanfront mansions to laid-back cottages. Here's a rundown of hotels and motels—places that offer nightly accommodations; for information on villas, time-shares, and private homes, which usually rent for longer-term stays (anywhere from three nights to two weeks), we suggest calling one of the island's numerous central reservations services. Among these are the **Hilton Head Condo Hotline** (843-785-2939, 800-258-5852), **Hilton Head Accommodations and Golf Hotline** (843-686-6662, 800-444-4772; www.hiltonheadusa.com), and **Hilton Head Vacation Rentals** (843-689-3010, 800-476-4485).

In general, rates for accommodations are higher from the end of April through September, although some places raise their prices starting in February, and others lower them after Labor Day. Call ahead to see what's available (well ahead if you're planning on staying during the summer, especially on weekends) and ask about special deals—many of the larger establishments have a variety of vacation packages from which to choose. Be aware that some motels and hotels will give you a lower rate if you stay with them early in the week when they might be struggling to fill up their rooms.

Most of the hotels and motels surveyed don't allow pets and have nonsmoking and wheelchair-accessible rooms; exceptions are noted.

Price Code

We have included a dollar-sign code with each entry denoting a price range for the average one-night stay, in season, for two adults. These prices do not include tax, gratuities, and add-on amenities such as room service.

$	less than $100
$$	$100 to $120
$$$	$120 to $175
$$$$	$175 to $225
$$$$$	more than $225

Unless we've indicated otherwise, you'll have to pay to play golf or tennis at the resort where you're staying. Most places have packages or special deals involving these sports, and you should inquire about these if you intend to play. The following properties are listed alphabetically.

COMFORT INN SOUTH FOREST BEACH $$
2 Tanglewood Dr.
(843) 842-6662, (800) 522-3224
www.choicehotels.com
(Type in Code: SC173)

The Comfort Inn South Forest Beach is a convenient and inexpensive place to stay that is also pet friendly and located five minutes (by foot) from the beach. The five-story hotel is comfortable and clean and is a pleasant place to stay. There is a nice pool on the premises and many activities (such as a water park) within walking distance.

The 153-room hotel is situated on six acres graced by three lagoons, sits well back from South Forest Beach Drive, a block from the Coligny traffic circle. Guests can partake of deluxe continental breakfasts from 7 to 10 a.m. in the registration building, which also houses 900 square feet of meeting space. Some of the rooms have refrigerators and microwave ovens, and there's a store (Bi-Lo grocery store) nearby where you can purchase food items. Golf packages are available. The hotel charges a pet-cleaning fee of $25 for the first night, and $10 for each additional night. There is a new business center and a free shuttle to the beach during the summer months (May through Aug).

CROWNE PLAZA RESORT $$$$$
130 Shipyard Dr.
(843) 842-2400, (800) 334-1881
www.cphiltonhead.com

If you've ever stayed in a Crowne Plaza, you're familiar with all the little details that make this hotel a special place to stay. For starters, the beds and linens are a part of this chain's image. There are sleep aids like masks, special aromatic sprays, and turn-down service. The Hilton Head Island version of Crowne Plaza incorporates the hotel's standard delights with the aesthetically pleasing elements that are unique to this island paradise. For example, the grounds at this Crowne Plaza are spectacular, with small islands of colorful flowers planted throughout and around the beautiful palm, pines, and live oaks. Built in a U-shape on the ocean in Shipyard Plantation, the Crowne Plaza opens onto a breezy courtyard filled with subtropical gardens, extensive green spaces, and lagoons crossed by graceful wooden bridges. One bridge is a favorite spot for couples saying their wedding vows (The hotel has its own notary public.) The large courtyard is also the location of a pool, outdoor hot tub, toddler's pool, and Dockers, which serves light fare and drinks open-air-style and around the pool

Amble down to the beach, and you'll pass by the beach snack bar, which specializes in snow cones and hot dogs. Nearby is the hotel's 7,000-square-foot outdoor pavilion, which is popular for meetings, dinners, and those weddings we referred to.

The Crowne Plaza has 340 rooms, including 9 suites, with views of either the island, the courtyard, or the ocean. Portz, a more upscale restaurant within the resort complex, is romantic and offers ambience plus some outstanding favorites: a delicious shrimp bisque (with just the right amount of dry sherry), and a variety of hand-cut steaks with truffle butter. Brellas Café offers breakfast, lunch, or dinner indoors or on a waterside terrace. It's a less-expensive option. A traditional breakfast buffet is served there, and guests will be anxious to line up for the hotel's signature Southern Pecan Sticky Buns!

The hotel's leisure activities department operates Camp Castaway, a structured and supervised program for children ages 3 to 12. Among the many activities provided are shell hunts and turtle feedings for the youngest kids, games on the beach and in the pool for those ages 6 to 12, as well as bike tours. The program runs from May 28 thru Sept 4 (Wed through Fri 6:30 to 10 p.m.). The cost is $45 per child with the second child receiving $10 off (minimum of two children). For more information, call (843) 842-2400, ext. 7620, by 5 p.m. the day of the program. Adults seeking opportunities to exercise can find them at the Crowne Plaza's fully equipped fitness center (with Cybex training equipment) and adjacent indoor pool and at Shipyard's golf courses and tennis courts.

DAYS INN $
9 Marina Side Dr.
(843) 842-4800
www.daysinn.com

An older and more serene place to stay for families on a budget, the Days Inn offers 14 suites with a nice touch—French doors separating the bedroom from the large sitting room. The other 105 rooms at the three-story motel off US 278 just past mile marker 9 have king-size and double beds, and there is a small pool and fitness center. Guests in quest of another form of recreation might opt to play the adjacent Pirates Island miniature golf course. The motel's complimentary continental breakfast awaits guests in a dining room off the lobby from 6:30 to 10 a.m. The Days Inn is centrally located and near a slew of restaurants and shops.

HAMPTON INN $$
1 Dillon Rd.
(843) 681-7900, (800) HAMPTON
www.hamptoninn.com

If you're not particularly interested in going to the beach, the Hampton Inn might be for you. This two-story, 115-room motel just off US 278 at mile marker 5 caters to business travelers and people visiting the island for the golf of it. And if you do desire to take a dip in the ocean, the Atlantic is only a little more than a mile away at the Folly Field Beach access. There's an outdoor pool for those who want to stay close by to do their swimming, an indoor putting green, and a small but well-equipped exercise room for the fitness minded. The Hampton Inn, like all other Hampton Inns, offers deluxe, complimentary continental breakfasts from 6 to 10 a.m. and free copies of USA Today. Some of the rooms have kitchenettes with microwave ovens and small refrigerators, and some have whirlpool baths. Ask for the family suite where a special children's room is connected to a king suite. A special feature of the Hampton is the "afternoon snack" of fresh-baked cookies.

HILTON HEAD MARRIOTT
RESORT & SPA $$$$$
1 Hotel Circle
(843) 686-8400, (800) 228-9290
www.marriotthiltonhead.com

If you're searching for a nice hotel that's right on the ocean and in the midst of lots of family activities, the Hilton Head Marriott is an excellent choice, and the views of the Atlantic Ocean are spectacular. Situated within Palmetto Dunes resort, this hotel stands 10 stories high and is the largest oceanfront resort on the island between Atlantic City, New Jersey, and Palm Beach, Florida. The property is overflowing with lush foliage, offering guests a tropical feel wherever they stroll. Boasting spacious and updated rooms (there are 512), this is also a popular place for group meetings with 46,000 square feet of meeting space.

There's an Adventure Club for kids ages 6 to 12 that will give mom and dad a little time of their own. The Adventure Club provides fun (including nature walks and sand sculpting) via half-day and full-day programs available from Memorial Day to Labor Day. Rates are $35 for morning sessions; $55 for afternoon sessions, which usually include an off-site activity such as kayaking; and $85 for the entire day.

There's an abundance of dining options within the Marriott's premises. Poolside, guests will find the **Ocean Blu Restaurant,** a great place to order sandwiches, wraps, salads, and tropical drinks during the day. In the evening, Ocean Blu turns elegant-casual as the sun begins to set. From hazelnut-crusted sea bass to pan-seared fresh swordfish, this is a convenient and fun place to dine without ever leaving the property. For indoor dining, there's **the Cafe** for breakfast (fresh fruit, traditional eggs and bacon, oatmeal, yogurt, and muffins), lunch (an excellent selection of low-carb options are offered), and dinner (burgers and sandwiches), and Conroy's for dinner and Sunday brunch. **Conroy's Lounge** overlooks the ocean and offers nightly entertainment. Named for the author Pat Conroy, who is a nearby resident, try the jumbo lump crab cakes, a specialty. If you're in need of snacks, try the Grocery, an offbeat little convenience store on the hotel's lower level. Other shopping opportunities are found at the Coastal Coffee Boutique. If you crave exercise, you can work out in the Marriott's well-equipped fitness center, play a round of golf at one of five courses within walking or shuttle distance, or hit the courts at the **Palmetto Dunes Tennis Center.** Be sure to ask about bike rentals at the hotel and enjoy the miles of trails within Palmetto Dunes.

HILTON OCEANFRONT
RESORT $$$$$
23 Ocean Lane
(843) 842-8000, (800) 845-8001
www.hiltonheadhilton.com

Try the tropics with a Southern accent. The Hilton Oceanfront Resort combines the best of both worlds for a spectacular holiday on the ocean. Oversized guest rooms decorated in traditional Southern themes (shades of green, wooden accents, striped fabrics) are designed to give you a "beach house" feel with all the amenities of a luxury hotel, including full mini kitchens, private balconies, wireless Internet service, and in-room safes. Open hallways are tranquil with flowing ocean breezes, and a maze of lagoons winding their way through the flourishing greenery give this beachfront Hilton Hotel at Palmetto Dunes a semitropical aura. The extra-large rooms have equally spacious

balconies, each with at least a partial view of the beach and sea. All 296 rooms have ceiling fans in dining areas and separate vanities in bathrooms. Oceanfront suites offer the same amenities, only with 1,000 square feet of space and a separate bedroom, living and dining rooms, and extra-spacious balconies that overlook the beach. The five-story hotel is built in a horseshoe shape that opens onto the beach, and the nooks and crannies of the spacious garden within the horseshoe feature small courtyards, rambling wooden decks, and plenty of seating for quiet afternoons spent reading or napping.

Dining options are abundant here. For a fun and casual oceanfront cafe, try the **Buoy Bar.** There are fun tropical-themed drinks galore, artfully presented chilled salads, outstanding burgers, and an unspoiled view of the ocean! **The Palmetto Market** is new and boasts a trendy, luxurious atmosphere. This is where you'll dine for breakfast, lunch, and dinner. The **Lavazza Coffee Bar and Cyber Café** is filled with freshly baked items, deli sandwiches, and specialty desserts, and you can bring your laptop if you need to catch up on business or correspondence. There's also an adults-only pool for those seeking a quieter atmosphere. For more relaxation, try one of the two oceanfront whirlpool baths or the variety of services at the **Ocean Tides Spa and Fitness Center.** With kayaking so popular on the island, the Hilton offers 10 miles of lagoons! When the day is over, schedule a treatment at the Ocean Tides Spa (843-341-8056). The Coastal Cabana Massage is performed in a private cabana beside the ocean. The 50–80 minute treatment is available for singles or couples. Call for rates.

The hotel offers special rates for golf and tennis at the courses and courts at Palmetto Dunes, and special activities for children via

Seaside Adventures Club. This day and evening camp program from Memorial Day to Labor Day is for kids ages 4 through 12 and is priced at $45 per child for a full-day session, $35 per child for a half-day session, and $30 per child for an evening session. The Hilton has 15,000 square feet of meeting space and the shorehouse open-air pavilion, and there's a shuttle from the hotel to all the activities Palmetto Dunes and nearby Shelter Cove Harbour have to offer.

HOLIDAY INN OCEANFRONT $$$
1 South Forest Beach Dr.
(843) 785-5126, (800) 423-9897
www.hihiltonhead.com
A view of the Atlantic Ocean from poolside is a plus at this moderately priced oceanfront hotel. This family-friendly spot also accepts pets, and kids eat free at the on-site restaurants. The contemporary decor of the inn's 202 rooms (all of which have refrigerators and open onto interior hallways) carry out the beach motif, as do the five-story motel's eating and drinking places—**Grouper's** restaurant, which has plenty of windows and great views of the ocean; the **Island Eatery,** which stands on a concrete peninsula jutting into the pool and serves lunch fare and ice cream; and the poolside **Tiki Hut** beach bar, which offers live entertainment. There's a banquet room with an ocean view—perfect for receptions and family reunions for up to 400 guests.

The inn offers numerous recreational activities, some of them free and many intended for the younger set. A children's program that runs from Memorial Day to Labor Day provides kids with activities such as relays on the beach, sand-dollar painting, and underwater treasure hunts. The inn also has a children's pool, kids' playground, and

Dolly the Dolphin, a mascot who greets guests and interacts with youngsters. The hotel is near several restaurants, including Antonio's Italian Cuisine, an island favorite!

INN AT HARBOUR TOWN $$$$
7 Lighthouse Lane
(843) 363-8100, (800) 732-7463
www.seapines.com
As you check into your room at the Inn at Harbour Town, you'll feel special—there to greet you is a personal handwritten letter along with chocolates in a gold box. At this instant, you'll become one of many who will probably return due to the service at this hotel. Although there are 60 rooms, butlers will serve you throughout the day, doing most anything you ask. From bringing you drinks and sandwiches to seeing that business papers are mailed, shoes are shined, and pants are pressed, these "services" are only a part of the delights of this inn. There are Anichini Egyptian-cotton linens and duvet covers, complimentary shoe shine service, iPod docking stations, granite vanities, Molton Brown toiletries, plush robes, and complimentary newspapers, for starters. Some rooms offer fabulous views of the Harbor Town Golf Links, and others open on to the beautiful palms and tropical landscaping. The butlers, some of them wearing Scottish attire in keeping with Harbour Town's Highlands heritage, are a big part of the concept of patterning the Inn at Harbour Town after small, fine European hotels. Make sure you save time to enjoy the plush furnishings in the Player's Library where you can read, catch up on business, or enjoy a sporting event on the large wide-screen TV.

The inn, which opened in late November 2000, also has much to offer in the way of recreation. The hotel overlooks the first tee of the famed Harbour Town Golf Links, and the Sea Pines Racquet Club is a short stroll from the front door. Guests have access to the pool next to the Racquet Club and can take advantage of a complimentary shuttle service that will take them anywhere in Sea Pines at any time of day.

The inn serves a continental breakfast from 7 to 11 each morning at a cost of $9 per person, and there are lots of restaurants nearby, including the Harbour Town Grill and the eateries at the Harbour Town yacht basin. The Inn is a AAA Four-Diamond resort.

MAIN STREET INN $$$$
2200 Main St.
(843) 681-3001, (800) 471-3001
www.mainstreet.com
Emulating a fine European hotel, the Main Street Inn is indeed a delightful retreat in the midst of a modern-day island destination located just off US 278 between mile markers 3 and 4. Elegance abounds in this inn. There are rich (and comfortable) furnishings, antique accents, fresh floral arrangements, a grand piano, and beautiful heart-pine floors. In short, it's a captivating place to stay. The Royal Queen Suite is bright and cheery with an iron bed and gold-framed artwork perfect for a couple seeking a spot for a romantic getaway. The Deluxe Queen rooms have fireplaces and balconies large enough for a wrought-iron table that's a perfect spot for breakfast.

The additional 32 rooms are luxuriously appointed with classic furnishings: wooden armoires handmade on Hilton Head; beds adorned with Italian linens, goose-down pillows, and comforters; and baths featuring pedestal sinks and Italian marble floors and shower walls. The inn's crowning glories are the four Courtyard King rooms with

their whirlpool tubs, glassed-in showers, and pine floors fashioned from the 150-year-old beams of a Lowcountry mill. In some Kings, French doors in the bathroom open onto an intimate courtyard abounding with fig vines, fruit trees, and jasmine. Guests staying in rooms on the upper two floors can step outside onto wide verandas complete with rocking chairs. From there, you'll see the Charleston-style gardens of the courtyard and an inviting pool designed for swimming laps; the view beyond is of the lush 15th green and 16th fairway of Hilton Head Plantation's Bear Creek Golf Course and of the forested wetlands of a nature preserve.

Your stay includes buffet breakfasts with eggs, bacon, fresh fruit, and pastries served from 7:30 to 10:30 a.m. in the dining room /library, the dining room/lounge, or the courtyard. If all this isn't relaxing enough, try a massage, which is available on-site. For a first-hand look, the website offers a virtual tour of all rooms and exterior gardens.

PARK LANE HOTEL $$$
12 Park Lane
(843) 686-5700
www.hiltonheadparklanehotel.com
Formerly the Residence Inn, this freshly renovated hotel lies on a quiet wooded area in the Central Park office complex just off US 278 between mile markers 9 and 10, convenient to area businesses and in the midst of Hilton Head's shopping and business district. Completely renovated in 2009, each of the 156 "Carolina-decorated" suites has a fully equipped kitchen with granite countertops (including a full-size refrigerator), fireplaces (in some), and trendy loft suites that are perfect for lengthier stays or for hosting guests. The lofts boast an enlarged dining area, a sleeper sofa, and a bedroom with

its own bathroom. Take note: There are no dining options here so you'll need to come prepared with your own staples. Pets are accepted with a $50 nonrefundable deposit; there's a limit of two pets.

THE QUALITY INN & SUITES $$
200 Museum St.
(843) 681-3655, (800) 995-3928
www.hhqualityinn.com

Located on the rapidly developing north end of the island, the Quality Inn boasts many of the features you might expect to find at a full-service hotel, along with a modern, clean look that compliments Hilton Head's building ordinances. The hotel blends in with the discreet environment and offers travelers a less expensive way to sample Hilton Head. Among the amenities here are an outdoor pool, a putting green, 2,000 square feet of meeting space, and same-day valet, laundry, and dry-cleaning service. There's an Applebee's restaurant on the property, and the motel serves a complimentary continental breakfast daily from 6:30 to 9:30 a.m. The 127-room motel, which is on US 278 at mile marker 3, is also pet friendly.

SOUTH BEACH MARINA INN $$$
232 South Sea Pines Dr.
(843) 671-6498, (800) 367-3909
www.sbinn.com

Called South Beach due to its location at the southern tip of Hilton Head Island, the inn is small and rustic and decorated in the spirit of New England. In fact, were it not for the distinctly Southern foliage and marshlands within view, you might imagine that you are, in fact, in New England. The charming, 17-room hotel is part of a small complex of shops and restaurants patterned after a fishing village on Nantucket

Island, Massachusetts. The rooms of the inn, a nightly rental property at Sea Pines, reflect the Yankee atmosphere via the highly polished heart-pine floors, brass beds, and colorful rag rugs.

All of the one- and two-bedroom accommodations have kitchenettes, and most have separate, cozy living rooms that will make you feel as if you've found a second home. Although the inn is deep within Sea Pines, the village and marina offer just about everything a vacationer would need. You could park your car and not leave, except to play a round of golf on the nearest course, which is a five-minute drive. At your front door is the marina on **Braddock's Cove,** which offers various recreational opportunities for hire—boat rentals, charter fishing, parasailing, kayaking, and windsurfing. Also, just outside your doorstep, you will find a pool, a dozen tennis courts, and 15 miles of paved trails for hiking, bicycling, jogging, and in-line skating. You can walk to the beach in three to four minutes, and there are six restaurants within the village. All rooms are on the second floor; there are no wheelchair-accessible accommodations.

WESTIN RESORT
HILTON HEAD $$$$$
2 Grasslawn Ave.
(843) 681-4000, (800) WESTIN1
www.westinhiltonhead.com

The architecture of the sprawling Westin radiates the charm of a classic, turn-of-the-century seaside hotel and is designed to complement the historic cities of Savannah and Charleston. A feeling of Southern hospitality carries throughout the five-story oceanfront hotel at Port Royal Plantation. The lobby features polished woods, palms, elaborate chandeliers, and Asian porcelains, and a mix of comfortable seating offers an ambience characteristic of the homes of the Old South. The Gazebo Lounge looks out on the hotel's spacious courtyard, where swans swim in a pond set amid lush foliage. In the cooler months, the lounge and its comfy drawing-room furniture and wood-burning fireplace beckon to guests. When the weather's warm, the courtyard is the place to be. You'll find two pools (a round pool and a lap pool) and extensive wooden decks where you can sunbathe and have a bite to eat at calypso-themed Turtles Beach Bar & Grill or Turtles Poolside, where you'll get in the island spirit with tropical drinks and Caribbean fare (and even a massage by the pool if you like). There are pools galore, including an outdoor heated pool, a main outdoor pool, an outdoor whirlpool, and an indoor pool with a hydraulic lift for the physically impaired. Take advantage of the Westin Workout, powered by Reebok Gym.

Those seeking outdoor recreation can find it at the nearby Port Royal Golf Club, which has three championship courses (see the Golf section of this chapter), or at the Port Royal Racquet Club, which offers grass, clay, and hard-surface courts. A shuttle service is provided from the hotel to both sites. For youngsters ages 4 to 12, the Westin Kid's Club operates from Memorial Day weekend through Labor Day weekend.

There's fine dining during the evening at Westin's **Ocean Grill,** an outstanding place with fresh seafood that is served any way you like it; casual dining and cocktails in the late afternoon and evening at **Turtles,** which also offers an ocean view; and family dining throughout the day at the **Carolina Cafe,** which features a nightly seafood buffet, an 18-foot-long dessert table, and Sun brunch.

RESTAURANTS

Just as Hilton Head's resplendent image of gleaming white beaches, live oaks dripping with moss, and colorful flora convince you to spend a vacation here, come with the knowledge that this is an island that also shines for connoisseurs of fine cuisine. There are outdoor cafes set amid a backdrop of the dunes. There are restaurants rich in ambience. There are open-air seafood eateries on the rims of marinas, and yes, bakeries that will lure you with promises of sumptuous pastries. So save room for this chapter filled with tempting dining options. Note that smoking is banned in all bars and restaurants in Hilton Head.

All restaurants listed (in alphabetical order) take most major credit cards.

Price Code

You can expect restaurants to be more expensive on Hilton Head Island than in Savannah. The price code is based on the cost of an average meal for two, excluding drinks, dessert, or tip.

$..................less than $30
$$ .... $30 to $50
$$$ .... more than $50

ALEXANDER'S $$–$$$
76 Queens Folly Rd.
(843) 785-4999
www.alexandersrestaurant.com
Located on a lagoon at Palmetto Dunes, Alexander's invites a business-casual dress code in three splendid settings: a delightful, enclosed porch with magnificent lagoon views, an alluring wine bar with a fireplace, and a friendly dining room replete with a variety of tropical plants that accentuate a fine collection of vintage Harleys. This restaurant will fast become one of your vacation

highlights. Enticing entrees include Macada-
mia Nut Flounder (with ginger-butter sauce
and sweet chili glaze), Shrimp and Grits
(a Lowcountry favorite with pan-sautéed
shrimp with andouille sausage, red bell-
pepper cream sauce, and fried cheddar grits,
Southern Fried Chicken (a boneless chicken
breast with Dubliner macaroni and cheese
and lemon thyme pan gravy). This is just a
small sample of some of the over-the-top
specialties. There are more than 100 selected
wines from which to choose, and dinner
starts at 5 p.m. nightly. An early dinner (5
to 5:45 p.m.) offers outstanding specials at
reduced prices. Reservations are suggested.

THE BARONY GRILL   **$$$**
2 Grasslawn Ave.
(843) 681-4000
With its cozy hunt-club atmosphere, the Bar-
ony Grill provides an ideal setting in which
to celebrate a special occasion. High ceil-
ings, brick archways, comfortable chairs, and
elegant table settings create an ambience
that's refined yet relaxed.

A special feature is the wine-tasting
room, where diners can find assistance in
selecting the wines that will best comple-
ment their meals. The room—with its sand-
colored stucco walls, polished wood floors,
and wrought-iron wine racks—is also a spot
where patrons can simply enjoy the experi-
ence of tasting various wines.

The Barony specializes in chops and sea-
food, and among diners' favorite dishes are the
pan-seared grouper and smoked prime rib. For
starters, there are appetizers such as lobster
bisque, roasted Carolina quail, and the onion
soup, which features a three-cheese melt.
Desserts, including the crème brûlée, are hard
to miss—they're displayed on a large marble-
and-iron table situated at the entrance.

The Barony—located on the first floor of
the Westin Resort Hilton Head at Port Royal
Plantation—serves dinner Wed through Sun
and is closed during Dec, Jan, and Feb.

BIG BAMBOO CAFE   **$**
Coligny Plaza
1 North Forest Beach Dr., Suite 210
(843) 686-3443
www.bigbamboocafe.com
Owners of this establishment might be
accused of packaging all the fun you can
think of having into one cool place. For
starters, there's live music several times a
week (check the website for details). For
instance, at press time, Wednesdays are Reg-
gae Night, and Beatles' music is played every
Friday starting at 6:30 p.m. (by the Beagles!).
Then, there's the decor that may take you by
surprise. According to the legend of the Big
Bamboo, which appears on the front of the
cafe's menu, this restaurant on the ocean
side of Coligny Plaza shopping center has
been constructed as closely as possible to
the configurations of the original Big Bam-
boo, a bar and grill opened on the Pacific
island of Tarawa in 1944 by ex–fighter pilot
Jimmy Phipps. From the bamboo of the bar
to the thatched palm fronds and camou-
flage netting of the ceiling to the World War
II regalia tacked on the walls, Hilton Head's
version of the Big Bamboo reflects the feel of
the real thing—if there had been a real thing,
that is. You see, the Big Bamboo of the Pacific
is a figment of the imagination of a former
owner, albeit one that has been brought
vividly to life on Hilton Head.

What is real about this 85-seat dining
room and bar is the food. There's a TGIF-like
mix of dishes available, ranging from the
roasted turkey sandwiches to the barbecue
ribs, Greek pasta, and seafood fettuccine.

Harder to believe is an item called the War Dog—a hot dog stuffed with cheddar cheese, wrapped with bacon, dipped in beer batter and fried, then tucked in a toasted roll and smothered with chili, cheddar cheese, and onions. Hours are 11:30 a.m. to 4 p.m. for lunch. Dinner starts at 4 p.m. through 10 p.m. The restaurant is closed on Sun.

THE BRICK OVEN CAFE $
25 Park Plaza
Office Park Road
(843) 686-2233
www.brickovenhhi.com
Gourmet pizzas and pastas from this rustic establishment, combined with a cool, friendly atmosphere give this restaurant in Park Plaza on Office Park Road an identity all its own. Among the pizzas on the menu are scampi, five-cheese, and mesquite-grilled chicken varieties, but you can also create your own. Dining parties are encouraged to share two or three dishes designed for that experience, including sesame-crusted tuna, calamari, and tempura chicken fingers. The wine list is extensive and offers numerous good values. There's a tempting early bird menu (5 to 6 p.m.) for $12.95. From slow-roasted prime rib to rosemary-rubbed pork tenderloin and chicken Alfredo (or scampi), each entrée comes with a choice of soup du jour or house salad. Child-friendly, the Brick Oven Cafe feeds your under-10 child for free every Tues. Hours are from 5 p.m. to 1 a.m. daily.

CAFE AT WEXFORD $$
Village at Wexford
1000 William Hilton Pkwy., Suite B
(843) 686-5969
The food and atmosphere of a cafe in the French countryside await you at this restaurant in the Village at Wexford near mile marker 10 on William Hilton Parkway. Wood floors and lots of brickwork give the 60-seat cafe an intimate aura. The menu offers a wide selection of country French cuisine; among the most popular entrees are the veal sweetbreads, which are sautéed in cream sauce with mushrooms and strips of ham; the cherry-glazed roast duckling; and the potato-onion-crusted fillet of grouper. For an appetizer, try the pâté de foie gras. The cafe serves lunch Mon through Fri, dinner Mon through Sat, and brunch on Sat and Sun. Reservations for dinner are required.

CHARLEY'S CRAB $$–$$$
2 Hudson Rd.
(843) 342-9066
www.muer.com
There was a time when I wouldn't travel to Hilton Head Island without dining at Charley's Crab. The food is always spectacular and the presentation like a graphic illustration brought

---

The Sweet Stuff

Make this bakery a sure stop when your sweet-tooth attacks. **Signe's Heaven Bound Bakery & Cafe** at 93 Arrow Rd. is indeed one of Hilton Head Island's main attractions. The mouth-watering creations are the truly angelic pastries and other goodies, such as the banana nut bread and the Key lime pound cake, but Signe's also serves breakfasts, salads, and hot and cold sandwiches. There's seating inside or on the outdoor deck and a long list of loyal fans cheering, "Just like heaven."

to life. Open-air decks and screened porches make this restaurant overlooking Skull Creek a splendid venue for waterfront dining. The location—just off Squire Pope Road about 1.5 miles from William Hilton Parkway—and the name clue you into the fact that Charley's specializes in seafood dishes such as caramelized catfish, crab cakes, and shrimp and grits. Steak, chicken, and pasta entrees also hit the mark. The fried green tomatoes—served with rock shrimp and crawfish salsa—constitute a can't-miss starter. Charley's, which has three dining rooms and a bar in a rustic setting, serves dinner nightly, lunch Mon through Fri, and brunch on Sun.

CHARLIE'S L'ETOILE VERTE $$–$$$
8 New Orleans Rd.
(843) 785-9277
www.charliesofhiltonhead.com
If you're looking for a restaurant that has colorful character, fine cuisine created with the freshest ingredients, the charm of Europe, and a staff that locals know and love, Charlie's L'Etoile Verte fits the bill. And if you ask any islander where to eat on Hilton Head, the first word out of his or her mouth is more than likely to be "Charlie's." This busy bistro near Sea Pines Circle serves lunch Tues through Sat 11 a.m. to 2 p.m., and dinner Mon through Sat, 5 to 10 p.m.

Charlie's is billed as a "French kitchen" (*l'etoile verte* means "green star" in French), but this eclectic-looking cafe serves, as its affable owner Charlie Golson puts it, "whatever we feel like cooking"—"we" being Golson, his entree chef, and his dessert-and-appetizer chef. The three of them put their heads together and brainstorm during the day, a process that creates a menu that's different each night, written in longhand, and copied for distribution to diners.

Served cafe-style on linen covered tables with fresh flower sprays, among the most popular selections are the chicken salad, Cobb salad, rack of lamb, pompano with mango sauce, and triggerfish in Parmesan crust. The Carolina red trout (with horseradish beurre blanc) is also tasty. Charlie's specializes in more than a dozen types of fish cooked in many ways.

CQ'S RESTAURANT $$$
140 Lighthouse Rd.
(843) 671-2779
www.cqsrestaurant.com
CQ's is a story and then an experience before it is a restaurant. As the first structure built with careful environmental forethought within Harbour Town, the restaurant was originally designed by Ralph Ballantine in 1970 for his studio. A transplant of Chicago and a recognized advertising illustrator, Ballantine's work includes illustrations of the Jolly Green Giant and the "good hands" of Allstate, as well as the bull of Schlitz Malt Liquor fame. The restaurant was built from several materials from different Lowcountry buildings, i.e., roof beams from an old Savannah house and flooring from a Jasper County church. Modeled after a local rice barn, the two-story building also includes spindles from the staircase that reportedly once graced the interior of a house of ill repute in Savannah. Originally called Bal's Place, (a name for the studio), the building evolved into a restaurant at the urging of Bal's friend, "Sig" Winehandle, and te establishment is named after Sig's son, Courtney Quentin. Today each dining room reflects a name that is representative of its heritage. There's the Plantation Room, the Heritage Room, the Cotton Room, the Rice Room, and the Indigo Room.

Many of the dishes are American Southern, and among the featured entrees are the venison, lobster pasta, and crab cakes. The mouthwatering appetizers include seafood bisque and baked brie. There's also an extensive wine menu. CQ's has outdoor seating on a deck. Reservations are highly recommended at this well-known establishment, which serves dinner seven days a week. Hours are 5:30 to 10 p.m. every day April through Oct; 5 to 9:30 p.m. daily Nov through March.

THE CRAZY CRAB　　　$$–$$$
104 William Hilton Pkwy.
(843) 681-5021
www.thecrazycrab.com
Colorful and festive, Hilton Head Island's two Crazy Crab restaurants serve fresh seafood and steaks in a rustic wharf-side surrounding offering splendid views of the water. At the Crazy Crab on the William Hilton Parkway near mile marker 1, the view is of picturesque Jarvis Creek and its marsh. The other Crazy Crab is among the shops alongside the Harbour Town Yacht Basin in Sea Pines (Lighthouse Road, 843-363-2722), overlooking the scenic marina. The menus at both restaurants are the same, with the mainstays being the fried shrimp and the steamed seafood pot, which consists of half a Maine lobster, crab legs, shrimp, and oysters. They are open for lunch and dinner seven days a week.

HILTON HEAD BREWING COMPANY　$
7-C Greenwood Dr.
(843) 785-3900
Billed as South Carolina's first brewpub since Prohibition and the only one on the island, this establishment in Hilton Head Plaza just off the Sea Pines traffic circle always has

five handcrafted beers ready for drinking: South Atlantic Pale Ale, Calibogue Amber, Old Duck Dark, Raspberry Wheat, and a seasonal brew. Although the pub takes on the atmosphere of a bar late at night, the restaurant offers casual dining for families at lunch and during the evening. Watching the turtles, ducks, and geese in the pond outside the pub's enclosed porch will keep the kids entertained. The menu yields a large variety of choices, including hand-tossed pizzas, burgers, steaks, huge sandwiches, and their award-winning chicken wings. The pub has room for about 155 customers, including seats for 60 on the porch. On Wed evenings the staff removes the tables and chairs from the area around the large bar and a DJ presides over Disco Night. Hours are 11 a.m. to 10 p.m. Mon through Fri, 11 a.m. to 2 a.m. weekends,

i It was once said that one shouldn't consume an oyster unless the month of consumption had the letter *r* in it. South Georgians and South Carolinians bank on this. You won't find many of us eating oysters in May, for instance. This is, however, folklore, and the rumor mill was probably born in the days when there wasn't adequate refrigeration and much spoilage resulted. So no matter what month it is, although there are always risks in eating raw shellfish, enjoy your "or-sters," as we jokingly call them.

HUDSON'S ON THE DOCKS　　$–$$
1 Hudson Rd.
(843) 681-2772
www.hudsonsonthedocks.com
The emphasis at Hudson's—a fixture on the Hilton Head restaurant scene since 1967—is

on fresh seafood, much of it caught locally, including shrimp hauled in on the boats you might see tied at the docks just outside. The vessels and Skull Creek can be viewed from the main dining room, one of three at the 335-seat restaurant, which also has an oyster bar. Forty percent of Hudson's business involves shrimp—fried, steamed, or boiled—but the steamed oysters, scallops, and crab cakes (made with 100 percent lump backfin meat) are also big sellers. As you might expect, the dining rooms at Hudson's have a nautical look, and the tables and the oyster bar are made from shrimp-boat doors, the wooden pieces of equipment used in trawling.

The Oyster Factory Dining Room occupies the site of an oyster processing plant built in 1912 and bought by J. B. Hudson in the 1920s. The Hudson family added shrimp to the processing operation in the mid-1950s and opened the restaurant with 95 seats in the latter half of the 1960s. Brian and Gloria Carmines purchased Hudson's in 1975 and have expanded it since then.

Hudson's serves lunch and dinner daily. If you're visiting during an *r* month, try the steamed oysters in the shell or steamed crab legs. The Lowcountry Crab Dip is habit-forming with fresh tortilla chips as an appetizer. The butterflied fried local shrimp is exceptional—and ask for a napkin to dab the cocktail sauce off of your chops! The mud pie dessert is really enough for four (although they say two). The restaurant is off Squire Pope Road about 1.5 miles from Squire Pope's intersection with the William Hilton Parkway between mile markers 1 and 2.

JULEPS RESTAURANT $$
14 Greenwood Dr.
(843) 842-5857

The name is Southern and so are the surroundings at Juleps, which has the look of the fine old homes of Charleston. The food is continental, says owner/host Sam Cochran, but prepared with Southern ingredients by his chef and wife, Melissa. This combination produces entrees such as Kentucky bourbon rib eye steak, roasted stuffed quail, jumbo shrimp stuffed with lump crabmeat, sautéed trout N'awlins with shrimp and crawfish, and Dixie cornmeal flounder. Among the appetizers are coconut pecan shrimp, which comes with a spicy citrus dipping sauce; and corn, crab, and sweet potato fritters. Specialty drinks can be ordered from the bar, including—what else?—mint juleps.

This restaurant in the Gallery of Shops near the Sea Pines traffic circle serves dinner seven days a week. Reservations are recommended, and the owners request that diners wear shirts with collars.

KENNY B'S FRENCH QUARTER CAFÉ $
70-A Circle BiLo Center
(843) 785-3315
Kenny B's brings a touch of the Quarter to Hilton Head at its eatery in the BiLo shopping plaza at the intersection of Pope Avenue and Cordillo Parkway. The cuisine is Creole with some Lowcountry tweaking, and murals, ceiling fans, and lampposts create a Big Easy atmosphere. Entrees lend to the aura—there's crawfish parade; voodoo pasta, which features seafood over penne; and Taste of the Bayou, a medley of N'awlins favorites (gumbo, jambalaya, red beans and rice, and shrimp étouffée). Drop by Kenny B's daily for breakfast, lunch, or dinner.

MARLEY'S ISLAND GRILLE $
35 Office Park Rd.
(843) 686-5800
www.marleyshhi.com

The food is as colorful and tasty as the atmosphere is fun at Marley's Island Grille. With indoor or outdoor dining, the festive atmosphere is enhanced with theatrics from the tropics as chefs prepare your dinner in the restaurant's open kitchen. If you watch, you'll marvel as they toss, chop, and create masterful culinary creations from the wood-fired grill and steaming kettles. As the reggae plays, your fresh shellfish—shrimp, mussels, clams, or a combination of all three—will merge with ingredients like traditional tomato sauce, an island curry, the house ale, and Old Bay, or in a broth of garlic butter and sherry. Try one of these other intriguing-sounding seafood dishes: tortilla-crusted tilapia, sesame-seared yellowfin tuna, or voodoo-spiced swordfish. From the wood grill, there are the red chili–rubbed flank steak, Havana cabana chicken, and Australian rock lobster. Famous for its drink selections—margaritas, house-made sangria, and other tropical drinks—Marley's is open each evening; it's located in the Park Plaza shopping complex just southeast of Sea Pines Circle. Check the website or call for live entertainment schedule.

OLD FORT PUB $$$
65 Skull Creek Dr.
(843) 681-2386
www.oldfortpub.com
If you're looking for a romantic setting for a meal, your search ends at the Old Fort Pub. Set on a bluff along Skull Creek amid a tangle of live oaks, this restaurant offers evening-time diners candlelight, classical music, a rustic Lowcountry atmosphere, and spectacular sunsets over a creek and its marsh. There are great views of the water from the first-floor dining room, bar, and outdoor deck that get even better as you ascend to the second-floor Sunset Room and the rooftop widow's walk, a wooden deck reached via a cast-iron spiral staircase. Up there in the treetops, you'll find an ideal place for small cocktail parties, marriage proposals, and wedding ceremonies.

Old Fort Pub serves Lowcountry cuisine for dinner seven days a week and offers brunch on Sun; reservations are a must in the evenings and should be made three to four days in advance. The dinner menu includes dishes such as Atlantic salmon, wild shrimp and pasta, and herb-crusted rack of lamb.

While you're at Old Fort Pub, which was built in 1974 in a style inspired by the architecture of the Lowcountry, take time to stroll around the remains of Fort Mitchel, a Civil War gun battery on the site adjacent to the restaurant. Pathways wind through what were once the bunkers and moats of a fortification constructed by the Union Army after it captured the island in November 1861.

The restaurant is in Hilton Head Plantation on the northwestern part of the island (see the Planned Residential Communities section of this chapter). To get there, take William Hilton Parkway to Squire Pope Road, which is between mile markers 1 and 2. Turn north on Squire Pope and stay on it until you reach the Hilton Head Plantation gate; the guard there will give you a pass and directions to the restaurant. Old Fort Pub is a AAA Four-Diamond restaurant.

THE OLD OYSTER FACTORY $$
101 Marshland Rd.
(843) 681-6040
www.oldoysterfactory.com
With its floor-to-ceiling windows, this multilevel restaurant offers splendid views of beautiful Broad Creek and the adjacent marsh

from its 270 seats. Built of pegged timbers on the site of one of Hilton Head's oyster canneries and opened in 1989, the restaurant serves steaks and seafood, including oysters from surrounding waters prepared several different ways. At times you can view small family boats cruising by, continuing the tradition of shrimping that started generations ago. Shrimp is part of one of the restaurant's big sellers—the seafood medley, which also consists of scallops, oysters, and choice fish fillets. Another popular dish is the salmon *en croute* (in pastry), but you'll have to ask your server about it—it's not on the menu. The Old Oyster Factory is open for dinner daily and provides live entertainment on the dock from May through Sept.

ℹ️ A good source of information concerning the island's eating places is *Hilton Head Island Restaurants* magazine, which you should be able to find at rental villas, hotels and motels, shops, grocery stores, and other locations, including the chamber of commerce welcome center on William Hilton Parkway near mile marker 1. This free booklet of some 176 pages has listings for more than 100 restaurants and reprints of menus. The centerfold of this guide is a map that will help you locate these eateries.

REILLEY'S $
7-D Greenwood Dr.
(843) 842-4414
www.reilleyshiltonhead.com

The laid-back atmosphere of the Reilley's in Hilton Head Plaza on Greenwood Drive is what you'd expect from a restaurant that has a deck once called the "Barmuda Triangle." First-class rustic, this is a restaurant that could

double as a Boston bar. With dining that is indoors or outdoors, locals have labeled it "an institution." Reilley's menu, adorned with shamrocks and leprechauns, lists a wide variety of offerings including several variations of Blarney Burgers and Super Sandwiches. If you're in the mood for a dinner, flip to the Longtime Favorites section, where you'll find steaks and a couple of dishes suited to Gaelic tastes—the corned beef and cabbage and the cottage pie, which is ground chuck seasoned with mushrooms and onions and topped with peas, homemade mashed potatoes, and cheddar cheese.

Reilley's takes credit for organizing the island's first St. Patrick's Day parade, a celebration started in 1983, the year after the restaurant opened in the Gallery of Shops. In 1995 the restaurant moved to its existing location in Hilton Head Plaza just south of the Sea Pines traffic circle. Reilley's serves lunch and dinner daily and offers a champagne-and-eggs brunch on Sat and Sun. The menu and atmosphere are much the same at the Reilley's at Port Royal Plaza on Mathews Drive (843-681-4153), but there's no deck.

SAGE ROOM $$$
13 Heritage Plaza
(843) 785-5352
www.thesageroom.com

Although the Sage Room nestles in one of the least-conspicuous locations of any restaurant on the island, that hasn't kept locals from flocking there. And if you make the effort to find it, you'll see why. Contemporary with shiny stainless accents, white linen tablecloths with black accents, this restaurant is an experience in behind-the-scenes food prep. The chefs work in an open kitchen, turning out a variety of dishes featuring seafood, fowl, and steak, plus Colorado rack of lamb and roasted pork tenderloin. Appetizers include some you won't encounter often—butternut squash soup, , and the snow-pea martini (sautéed snow peas with a pineapple soy reduction). The Sage Room serves lunch Mon through Fri, and dinner Mon through Sat. As for that location, it's in the northwestern corner of Heritage Plaza, which is on the north side of Pope Avenue close to Coligny Circle.

SANTA FE CAFE $$–$$$
700 Plantation Center
(843) 785-3838
www.santafecafeofhiltonhead.com
A delightful rooftop cantina is one of the highlights of the Santa Fe Cafe. With white-washed adobe walls (inside and out), fire-places, and tiled floors, this is a place for quiet conversation and fresh, authentic southwestern cuisine. Owner and chef Jim Buckingham spent his younger days in the Southwest, and he brings his appreciation for that region to his cooking. The upscale southwestern cuisine of his Santa Fe Cafe is spicy food based on many types of chiles, resulting in dishes such as grilled pork tenderloin with smoked habañero barbecue sauce, black beans, and sweet potato fries; herb-roasted free-range chicken with jala-peño corn-bread stuffing and roasted-garlic mashed potatoes; and grouper with chipotle (smoked chile) Parmesan au gratin. After several years of operating a limited chain of Mexican restaurants, Buckingham decided to concentrate his efforts on one establish-ment and in 1993 opened this cafe off William Hilton Parkway near mile marker 8. The stylishly southwestern Santa Fe serves dinner seven nights a week (5 to 10 p.m.) and lunch Mon through Fri (noon to 2 p.m.); reservations are accepted.

STEAMERS SEAFOOD COMPANY $$
1 North Forest Beach Dr., Suite 28
Coligny Plaza
(843) 785-2070
www.steamersseafood.com
With a pleasant outdoor deck and live enter-tainment seven nights a week, Steamers has become a Hilton Head tradition since 1991. Boasting an island decor, this reasonably priced eatery has grown its beer selection to 250 beers from around the world. That coupled with fresh fish, shrimp, lobster tails, and certified Angus beef make it one of the locals' favorite places to dine. For shellfish lovers, there's a platter consisting of steamed oysters, clams, shrimp, crawfish, mussels, and snow crab. Barn and dock wood and cor-rugated tin on the walls and bars complete the pier-side look, and there's also a 70-seat raw bar for fans of steamed and raw seafood.

Steamers, which serves lunch (11:30 a.m. to 4 p.m.) and dinner daily (4 p.m. until the last diner is full and content!), offers unique appetizers such as Savannah Seafood Dip (an awesome blend of shrimp, crabmeat, and Parmesan) and Tuna Bits (medallions of fresh yellowfin tuna blackened with scallions and tomatoes).

STELLINI ITALIAN RESTAURANT $$
15 Pope Ave., Executive Park
(843) 785-7006
This "little star" of an Italian restaurant shines forth from a wooded nook off Pope Avenue. Owner Joe Pesce and his partners have cre-ated the comfortable look of the Little Italy section of New York City at Stellini. Especially inviting is the 40-seat Carolina Room, a porch with views of the surrounding forest. The res-taurant also has a main dining room for 50. The menu provides an extensive selection of northern Italian fare, including chicken

pancetta, a chicken breast sautéed in a light cream sauce with pancetta bacon and broccoli over angel-hair pasta; veal Sorrento, medallions of veal sautéed in white wine topped with eggplant and melted mozzarella cheese in marinara sauce over angel hair; and zuppa di pesce, clams, shrimp, scallops, mussels, calamari, and grouper in marinara over linguine. One item you won't find on the menu is a special that's offered often: the veal chop stuffed with prosciutto and mozzarella. Pesce suggests making reservations to dine at Stellini, which opened in 1988. The restaurant is open Mon through Sat for dinner starting at 5:30 p.m.; closed on Sun. Call during the winter months as they close briefly.

THE TAPAS RESTAURANT $$
11 Northridge Plaza
(843) 681-8590
Ever wanted to try something a companion is eating but felt self-conscious taking it from him or her? When you dine at the Tapas, such behavior is not only acceptable, it's expected. Tapas are appetizers in Spanish cuisine, and the small dishes served at this cozy, elegant bistro in Northridge Plaza off William Hilton Parkway between mile markers 4 and 5 are perfect for sharing. Don't be overwhelmed when you see the menu of more than 50 items. Each colorful presentation is prepared on small plates, almost like an appetizer so treat each dish as it is an appetizer. For instance, if you're dining with three other people and each of you orders three different selections, you may be tasting up to twelve different dishes. A word of warning if you've never dined at a tapas restaurant: Keep a mental tally of the meal as you go along so the final bill won't be shocking.

Among the dishes you might try are the veal Antonia (tenderloin of veal sautéed with garlic and mushrooms deglazed with sherry), and lobster seafood cake, served with sweet potato french fries and tangerine-balsamic drizzle. The Tapas, although housed in a shopping center, is filled with surprising ambience. The ceiling is filled with a multitude of hanging wicker baskets, which makes it feel a little like being outside. The 56-seat restaurant is open for lunch Tues through Fri, and for dinner nightly; reservations are strongly suggested.

TRUFFLES CAFE $
71 Lighthouse Rd.
(843) 671-6136
www.trufflescafe.com
Islander Price Beall has owned and operated this casually elegant restaurant (and two other similar ones) since this one opened

---

Feel Free to Pig Out

If you need a bite to eat while traveling the "back way" to or from Hilton Head Island, consider stopping at the **Pink Pig** restaurant (843-784-3635) on Alternate South Carolina Highway 170 at a crossroads identified as Levy. This shockingly pink cinder-block eatery specializes in barbecue and is open for lunch and dinner Wednesday through Saturday. You'll chuckle when you enter the front door to pink pigs hanging from all directions! You can't miss the place. Just look for the pigs on the simple one-story building on your right and come hungry.

in 1983. With seating for 150, Truffles is larger than the typical cafe but retains the atmosphere of a bistro. It is jovial, and there are linen-covered tables and island artwork on the walls. The food is American in style, with specialties like chicken potpie made with fresh vegetables (broccoli, carrot, mushroom, sweet bell pepper) in white wine sauce and pasta New Orleans—a chicken breast served over pasta tossed with a spicy cream sauce. Other favorites of regular customers are the ribs, grilled fish, pasta dishes, and Caesar and Monterey salads, both of which feature grilled chicken. Lunch and dinner are served daily. Hours are 11:30 to 2:30 Mon through Fri; 5 to 10 p.m. dinner daily; happy hour, 5 to 6:30 p.m. There is also a location at Sea Pines Center.

THE WATERFRONT CAFE   **$$-$$$**
160 Lighthouse Rd.
(843) 671-3399
www.waterfrontcafehhi.net
The Waterfront Cafe sits at the foot of the lighthouse in Harbour Town and is open all day long, starting with a superb breakfast at 8 a.m. Watch the morning sun sparkle on the Calibogue Sound where you'll view a mile-long expanse of sea from the panoramic window. Lunch starts at 11 a.m. (continuing through 2:30) and the menu is "oh, so, Southern." Try the Low Country She Crab Soup and the Calibogue Shrimp Salad with baby shrimp tossed with fresh dill in a lemon caper crème fraiche, with coleslaw, macaroni pie, or fresh fruit. For the health-conscious, the grilled vegetable salad is outstanding. Since the restaurant sits at the boaters' entrance to the Harbour Town Yacht Basin at Sea Pines, the Waterfront Cafe is a wonderful place to watch the yachts check in and out of the harbor. Maybe you'll spot a celebrity!

Favorites for dinner (4 to 10 p.m.) include the Carolina crab cakes and blackened grouper. The restaurant offers a three-course special that gives you a choice of grilled salmon, classic chicken Marsala, and seafood potpie (my recommendation). The Waterfront Cafe also has outdoor dining in an area at the base of the Harbour Town Lighthouse and overlooking the marina. Reservations are recommended for dinner. The restaurant is open from 8 a.m. to 10 p.m. seven days a week from mid-Feb to Oct. Call for hours Nov through Feb.

NIGHTLIFE

Hilton Head is a resort that caters to families who are on the go throughout the day and to golfers with early-morning tee times, so it's not exactly a hotbed of nightlife activity. Evenings are mostly spent with a good book, a family round of Monopoly, or ample porch sitting. If you're visiting there, you might find yourself actually searching for nightspots and maybe even commenting about how sleepy the island appears. There are, however, nightspots at several hotels and motels, including the **Regatta Lounge** at the Hilton, **Signals** at the Crowne Plaza (located in the breezeway near Brellas Cafe and Portz), and **Conroy's Lounge** at the Marriott. Some of Hilton Head's restaurants also have lounges where you can hang out and catch live entertainment.

There are three movie theaters on the island: Coligny Theatre in Coligny Plaza, Northridge Cinemas at 435 William Hilton Pkwy. at mile marker 5, and Park Plaza Cinemas in the Park Plaza Shopping Center off Greenwood Drive. Coligny Theatre has 1 screen, Northridge has 10, and Park Plaza has 5.

 # Close-up

Hilton Head's Gone Gator

If you get near a body of fresh or brackish water on Hilton Head, which is hard not to do given the preponderance of the island's lakes and lagoons, there's a good chance you will see a creature that looks as though it has crawled right out of *Jurassic Park*. This is the American alligator, the largest reptile on the North American continent and one of the oldest surviving vertebrates on the planet.

Alligators abound on Hilton Head, where developers have provided readymade homes for them by creating the waterways that decorate the island's communities and golf courses. "If there's a mud puddle in the Lowcountry, there's an alligator in it," says Dean Harrigal, who coordinates the alligator nuisance program in the area. There have been no formal surveys of the alligator population on Hilton Head, but there are probably 2,000 to 4,000 gators living on the island, says Walt Rhodes, the alligator project supervisor for the South Carolina Department of Natural Resources.

Alligators, which are protected by state and federal law, can grow to a length of 12 feet, but most of the gators removed from Hilton Head under the nuisance program are from 6 to 8 feet long, according to Harrigal. Even so, if left alone, alligators pose little threat to humans, say Rhodes and Harrigal. "Gators are naturally shy of people," says Rhodes. According to the two alligator experts, humans are more of a threat to gators than vice versa.

If the state receives a complaint about a gator on Hilton Head, and the animal is deemed a nuisance because of its behavior or location, the reptile will be removed. Removed, in this case, means destroyed, not relocated. Relocating a gator doesn't work because of the animal's strong homing instinct: Gators have been known to travel as much as 30 miles to return to their nesting areas, Rhodes and Harrigal say. About 50 gators are removed from Hilton Head each year because of complaints against them, but the two say that wouldn't be the case if people were more tolerant of the animals,

If you've spent your day knocking a tennis ball around, pedaling a few miles on bicycle paths, and frolicking in the surf, and you still haven't pooped out, you might consider these other nighttime entertainment options:

THE JAZZ CORNER
The Village at Wexford
(843) 842-8620
www.thejazzcorner.com
This nightspot is literally tucked away in a corner of the Village at Wexford shopping complex. When you walk through the door (if you can get inside despite the lines of people trying to get in), you'll immediately put on your happy face! Although tiny in size, this establishment defines fun and offers live jazz and Dixieland music and fine dining each evening of the week. Dinner is available, with entrees averaging $20 and including dishes such as crispy flounder, seafood-stuffed salmon, Oysters Gillespie (named for trumpeter Dizzy, no doubt), and veal piccata. If you're out for dinner, it's recommended to dine early rather than later when the joint gets jumping! In fact, although the food is delicious, this is a great

who were here first (present-day gators are direct descendants of a creature that lived in what is now Florida during the Miocene epoch, which occurred 25 million years ago). People don't like gators for a number of reasons. For one thing, the alligator's appearance is not in its favor. The gator looks like a big lizard, only uglier, and it seems to have a malevolent smile permanently plastered on its bumpy face. "It's not Bambi," says Rhodes. "It's not warm and fuzzy, it's cold and scaly." For another, most people don't know much about alligators and their relatively placid temperament. Folks confuse gators with the crocodiles found on other continents, in particular the 14-foot crocs seen devouring water buffaloes in sensationalized nature flicks. Gators, says Rhodes, "will let you alone if you let them alone, and they'll see you first."

Humans have a tendency to bring out the aggressiveness in gators by feeding them. If a person feeds a gator enough times, the beast's golf ball–size brain begins to associate the human with food. This is, if you'll pardon the phrase, a recipe for disaster that can be harmful to the human involved and fatal to the gator. It's also against the law: If you're caught feeding an alligator, you can be fined $200 or sentenced to 30 days in jail. There are cases of humans provoking gators into attacking them. Rhodes tells of a golfer who hit his ball near a gator that was sunning itself on a Hilton Head fairway, then smacked the animal with his golf club in the process of recovering the ball. The gator bit the golfer. "The gator did what you would do if someone hit you with a golf club," says Rhodes. There have been reports of people being pursued by gators, but Rhodes says he's handled in excess of 3,000 of the animals and has never been chased.

Rhodes's rules for coexisting with gators: Don't feed them; they find plenty to eat in the form of insects, crustaceans, fish, and snakes. Don't tease them. For goodness sake, don't try to pet them. Look at them all you want but do so from afar. "Give the animal the respect it deserves," says Rhodes. "It has as much right to be here as the deer, squirrels, and people."

after-dinner place to go. Although the focus is on the smooth jazz of the 1950s and 1960s, there's plenty of swing-era music. The Jazz Corner makes the most of an abundance of local talent while also presenting well-known performers such as pianist-singer Mose Allison and vocalist Tierney Sutton.

THE LODGE
Hilton Head Plaza
7 Greenwood Dr.
(843) 842-8966
www.hiltonheadlodge.com

The island's only cigar bar has an interior resembling a hunting lodge, and it's high on the popularity list of beer fans. With 36 rotating taps (and growlers to go), it's a popular place for locals and a quite festive place for visitors to the island. You can satisfy your competitive instincts at the billiards tables or try some shuffleboard, or you can relax in front of one of the two fireplaces with a drink from the full bar or a cigar from the Lodge's large stock of smokes. In addition to wine by the glass, single malts, ales, cognacs, and bourbons, the bar serves a specialty drink— the chocolate martini. This establishment in Hilton Head Plaza, off Greenwood Drive near the Sea Pines traffic circle, opens at 5 p.m. daily.

SHOPPING

The shopping is plentiful on Hilton Head, which has stores of every description located in large shopping centers, in strip malls, and along the island's out-of-the-way streets and byways. To get you started, we've provided rundowns on a few of the bigger shopping areas and pointed out some of the stores you can find there. Also, Hilton Head offers two clusters of outlets. Both are located as follows: From Savannah, take I-95 to Hwy 278, South Carolina exit 8. Proceed for 13 miles. Tanger Outlet Center 1 (under renovation) is on the right, 2 miles before the Hilton Head Bridge. Tanger Outlet Center 2 is on the right, 1 mile before the Hilton Head Bridge. Tanger 2 offers more than 50 different stores with highly discounted items (www.tangeroutlet.com); open Mon through Sat, 10 a.m. to 9 p.m., Sun 11 a.m. to 6 p.m. Knock yourself out.

Shopping Centers

COLIGNY PLAZA
124 North Forest Beach Dr.
(843) 842-6050
www.colignyplaza.com
Sometimes it takes a rainy day to encourage you to change directions during a vacation on Hilton Head Island. It's those days that call for a trip to Coligny Plaza, one of the island's most popular places to shop, dine, and peruse the more than 60 retail stores and eateries. As the island's oldest and largest shopping center, it covers nearly nine acres at the Coligny traffic circle on the south end of the island.

The Plaza mixes specialty shops with conventional businesses such as a hardware store and a Piggly Wiggly supermarket. Among the specialty stores are Black Market Minerals, a rock and mineral shop; Jamaican Me Crazy, a clothing store that's Caribbean in character; the Shell Shop; the Island Fudge Shop, where sweets are made before your eyes; the Coligny Kite and Flag Company; and the Magic Puppet & Toys Too. There are also a plethora of clothing stores, with the emphasis on beach and sportswear.

More than a dozen eating places offer everything from Italian cuisine at the Just Pasta cafe to seafood at Steamers Seafood Company (see listing in the Restaurants section of this chapter) to sandwiches at the Art Cafe, Coligny Deli, and the Earle of Sandwich.

i On summer evenings, Coligny Plaza stages puppet shows and other family-oriented entertainment in the piazza off North Forest Beach Drive. The shopping center also hosts special events during the year, including an Irish festival held in conjunction with the island's St. Patrick's Day parade; a Halloween festival, during which shop owners dress in costume and open their doors to trick-or-treaters; and appearances by the Easter Bunny and Santa Claus, with the latter arriving at the shopping center via fire truck.

HARBOUR TOWN
Harbour Town Yacht Basin
(843) 363-5655
www.harbourtown.com
The iconic lighthouse at Harbour Town is your marker to spend an afternoon browsing the shops there. With more than 20 shops and eating places gracing the north side of

beautiful Harbour Town Yacht Basin, there's plenty to entertain you all within a pleasant walk. When you're not busy wandering in and out of shops such as Camp Hilton Head I and II (souvenirs, casual clothing, and hats), Knickers' (classic and casual men's apparel and accessories), the Cinnamon Bear County Store (unique foods and gifts), the Planet Hilton Head nature store (Crocs, Jibbitz, collegiate ceramics, books, and local artwork), and Radiance (an upscale women's store); or dining at restaurants such as the Crazy Crab or CQs, you can relax outside by plopping down in one of the many rocking chairs and watching the activity in the boat-filled marina. The Harbour Town shopping complex is in the Sea Pines Resort and hosts a variety of on-site entertainment during the summer months.

THE MALL AT SHELTER COVE
24 Shelter Cove Lane
(843) 686-3090
www.mallatsheltercove.com

As Hilton Head's only enclosed mall, this one has seen its share of hard times in the past two years. Several stores have closed, however, there are still some very strong ones that are thriving, making it worth your while to stop and shop. Those stores are attractively housed in the tropical mall setting featuring potted palm trees and other plants. Anchoring the northern end of the mall is a department store you might not expect to find on a Southern sea island—an Off 5th/Saks Fifth Avenue Outlet. At the southern end of the shopping center is the other anchor, Belk (for women and juniors); scattered in between are Belk for men, children, and home goods; and several stores offering high-quality apparel including Ann Taylor, Banana Republic, Talbots, Express, Jos. A. Bank, the White House

/Black Market, Chico's, Swim 'n Sport, and Victoria's Secret. The mall is off William Hilton Parkway near mile marker 9.

PINELAND STATION
430 William Hilton Pkwy.
(843) 681-8907
www.pinelandstation.com

This upscale shopping center, which dates back to 1979, was completely renovated in 1997. It wends its way over 10 acres on the north end of the island. Covered walkways lush with foliage and potted plants connect the four retail buildings, and there's a special events staging area set among gardens, a fountain, a waterwheel, and the center's well-known duck pond.

Shoppers will find stores offering apparel, including, Low Country Baby, Tradewinds (ladies' apparel), and Tanner (another ladies' fine apparel shop); several shops dealing in home accents and gifts, including Island Baskets, a Stein Mart; a Starbucks coffee shop; Vic's Tavern; and four restaurants—Le Bistro Mediterranean, Il Carpaccio Ristorante & Pizzeria, Ichi Sushi Japanese Cuisine, and a highlight, the French Bakery and Cafe. Pineland Station, which has more than 100,000 square feet of retail space, is between mile markers 4 and 5 on the parkway.

VILLAGE AT WEXFORD
1000 William Hilton Pkwy.
(843) 842-2240
www.villageatwexford.com

If you're looking for upscale variety, you'll find it at the Village at Wexford, where the majority of the 30 stores and eateries are locally owned. This quaint-looking stucco retail-and-office complex sits on nine wooded acres off the parkway near mile marker 10, and houses Le Cookery kitchen accessories, an Audubon

Nature Store, Mum's the Word florist and gift shop, Pretty Papers stationery store, and Smith Galleries, which deals in artwork and jewelry. Several stores offer women's apparel, including Patricia's, and there's a men's clothing store, Teague's. Island Child specializes in clothing and shoes for children. The restaurants at the Village at Wexford range from those offering fast food to those devoted to casual and fine dining; at one end of the spectrum are Wendy's and Subway, with the, the British Open Pub, Antonio's, and the Hugo's at Wexford (see this chapter's Restaurants section) at the other. The center is also the site of the Jazz Corner.

Bookstores

BARNES & NOBLE
20 Hatton Place
(843) 342-6690
This branch of the nation's largest bookseller opened in July 1998 and offers islanders and visitors more than 175,000 titles, a mind-boggling selection of magazines, and a cafe where you can sit, read, and drink juice, tea, or coffee and munch on gourmet cookies. Special features of the 20,250-square-foot store are the storytime sessions for children on Wed and Sat at 10 a.m. The store's Special Order Express service will order any book from more than 1.2 million in print, and deliveries usually take place within seven days. This spacious store is just off William Hilton Parkway between mile markers 3 and 4.

PORT ROYAL BOOKSTORE
Village at Wexford
(843) 842-6996
It you enjoy browsing through bookstores with unique character and a great selection, owner John Stern refers to his small but well-stocked bookstore at the Village at Wexford shopping center as being old-fashioned—one where you can sit in a comfortable chair and read a book or have the staff special-order a hard-to-find volume. Stern constantly peruses catalogs in an effort to maintain an extensive inventory of books covering a wide range of topics, including the "War of Northern Aggression," which is what some Southerners still call the Civil War.

The store rents best sellers by the day or week, a service designed with vacationers in mind. While you're at the store, take a gander at Stern's collection of miniature lead soldiers, which is displayed near the front of the shop. Hours are 10 a.m. to 6 p.m. daily.

RECREATION
Golf

Hilton Head is heaven on earth for golfers. There are 25 courses on the island, many of them world-class and all of them overflowing with natural beauty. Seventeen are open to the public, and information on these follows.

The courses we've described have amenities such as pro shops, practice greens, and driving ranges. Many of these courses do not allow walking, but we've pointed out which ones do and to what extent. The greens fees listed include carts, and they reflect rates during the most popular playing times (generally spring and fall).

The rates included are for players not staying at the resorts associated with the courses. You can make arrangements to play these courses by calling directly, through the resort where you're staying, or via central golf reservation services such as **Last Minute Tee Times** (843-689-2262, www.lmteetimes .com), and the **Golf Island Call Center** (888-465-3475, www.golfisland.com). Public and private courses are noted.

i These reservation services are extremely busy so make sure you check details for both services online, first, and if possible. There are times when the phone lines are tied up due to demand, so reservations for two or more players can be made online. In some cases, phone reservations must be made from 7 to 10 p.m. the night before the planned outing.

COUNTRY CLUB OF HILTON HEAD (PUBLIC)
70 Skull Creek Dr.
(843) 681-2582
www.hiltonheadclub.com

Many of the greens on this par-72, 6,543-yard course at Hilton Head Plantation run near the Intracoastal Waterway, and the 12th is right on it. Designed by Rees Jones and built in 1985, the course has two holes that are almost 600 yards, including the uphill, par 4, 556-yard 18th. Greens and fairways are Bermuda grass. Greens fees are $92.

GOLDEN BEAR GOLF CLUB (PUBLIC)
72 Golden Bear Way
(843) 689-2200
www.goldenbear-indigorun.com

What a great name for a golf course! Interestingly enough, the chief architect of this Jack Nicklaus design was not the Golden Bear himself but the late Bruce Borland. Players of this 6,643-yard layout at Indigo Run will find a real challenge in the 11th hole—it runs 430 yards and features a long dogleg to the left and water on the left side of the green. This par-72 course has fairways and greens of Bermuda grass set among lagoons and stands of pine and hardwoods. Be wowed as you tackle the course amid towering pines and mature cypress. Among the amenities are a bar and grill. You'll spend $65 to play this course.

OYSTER REEF GOLF CLUB
155 High Bluff Rd.
(843) 681-1745
www.hiltonheadgolf.net

This course was rated one of the top 25 new courses in America in 1983 and was designed by Rees Jones. The sixth hole at Oyster Reef—a par 3, 160-yarder—overlooks Port Royal Sound, giving golfers a fine view of that majestic body of water on the northern side of Hilton Head. The par-72 layout, which is the work of Rees Jones, covers 6,440 yards at Hilton Head Plantation. The greens were converted to Tif Eagle Bermuda grass in 2000. There are 9 ponds and 66 bunkers for players to contend with. At the end of a round, players can relax at the club's bar and restaurant. Greens fees run $80.

PALMETTO DUNES GOLF COURSES (PUBLIC)
1 Trent Jones Lane
(843) 785-1136, (800) 827-3006
www.palmettodunes.com

Palmetto Dunes offers golfers three 18-hole courses from which to choose, each of them named for their heavy-hitting designers: Arthur Hills, George Fazio, and Robert Trent Jones. You can cover them on foot if you want to. Unrestricted walking is allowed at all times of the day. Rates on the Fazio and Jones Courses run $95, while the Hills Course is $148.

ARTHUR HILLS COURSE AT PALMETTO DUNES

This heavily wooded par 72 was reconditioned during the mid-1990s, with all the greens being rebuilt. One of the most interesting holes is the 12th, a par 4 that's bordered by water along one side. The course measures 6,122 yards. The fee to play is $80.

GEORGE FAZIO COURSE AT PALMETTO DUNES

This course is ranked among the Top 100 in the country. Located inside Palmetto Dunes, it offers a 432-yard 1st hold and 462-yard 18th hole and is the only par-70 course on Hilton Head Island. The Fazio Course covers total 6,239 yards and is characterized by rolling fairways and lots of long par 4s—there are only two par 5s and three par 3s. The 18th is a challenge, ending with a hole where two bunkers provide a significant challenge.

ROBERT TRENT JONES COURSE AT PALMETTO DUNES

Don't be surprised to view kayakers paddling quietly in the lagoons that run throughout this scenic course. If you like playing by the water, you'll enjoy this 6,570-yard course, which provides a winding lagoon system tied into 11 holes and a great view of the ocean from No. 10. Other hallmarks of this par 72 are open fairways and large greens. Doug Weaver is the pro and will be happy to offer pointers to steer your game to perfection!

PALMETTO HALL PLANTATION CLUB (PUBLIC)
108 Fort Howell Dr.
(843) 689-4100, (800) 827-3006
www.palmettodunes.com

The Palmetto Hall Plantation Club offers golfers the opportunity to enjoy a Lowcountry-style clubhouse and 36-hole courses designed by Arthur Hills and Robert Cupp. The 16,000-square-foot clubhouse is a repository of historic artifacts (both Lowcountry- and golfing-related), antiques, and paintings, and features a grillroom with the aura of a club. Greens fees for the par-72 courses are $95.

Triple Play

Rather than paying individual greens fees for each course within Palmetto Dunes, book an **Unlimited Golf Package** that includes private villa accommodations and golf! You can play on three legendary courses: the Robert Trent Jones Course, the George Fazio Course, and the Arthur Hills Course. Stay four days and three nights in select resort villas starting from $225 per person, per night, and receive three rounds of golf per person on three championship golf courses (includes green fees, cart fees, and warm-up range) with complimentary repeat rounds available on the same course, same day based on availability. For more information, call (866) 380-1778.

ARTHUR HILLS COURSE AT PALMETTO DUNES

The signature hole here is No. 18, a 434-yarder with water running up the left side of the fairway. It's a challenging par 4. Another hole featuring plenty of water is the 5th, but the water on this beauty is on the right side. The hole runs 490 yards and is a par 5. This 6,257-yard course was opened in 1991. Walking is prohibited. If you book your reservation through Last Minute Tee Times (843-689-2262), the fee is $80.

ROBERT CUPP COURSE

Unrestricted walking is allowed on this 6,042-yard course, which was unveiled two years after the Arthur Hills layout. Vistas of marshlands and forests of oak and pine are features of this par-72 course, along with its straight lines and sharp angles. The course, which opened in 1993, was renovated and reopened in the fall of 2005.

PORT ROYAL GOLF CLUB (PUBLIC)
10 Clubhouse Dr.
(843) 689-1760
www.hiltonheadgolf.net
This golf club at the Port Royal resort community has three 18-hole courses—Barony, Planter's Row, and Robber's Row—plus a bar and restaurant. Greens fees run $90 in the morning, $60 after noon, and $45 after 2 p.m.

PORT ROYAL / BARONY COURSE
The long drivers will take a backseat to the shot makers on this 6,223-yard course, which has many small greens. The Barony, which was designed by George Cobb, presents players with a test of skill at No. 12, a par-4, 411-yard hole with water on both sides of the fairway.

PORT ROYAL/PLANTER'S ROW COURSE
Willard Byrd was the designer responsible for Planter's Row, where golfers finish on a par-5, 511-yard hole featuring woods and water. If that's not enough of a challenge, consider No. 12, a narrow, 419-yard hole where you've got to cross water to get to the green. The course measures 6,284 yards, and par is 72.

PORT ROYAL/ROBBER'S ROW COURSE
Robber's Row represents a team effort by designers George Cobb and Pete Dye. The course was built in 1967 and reconfigured in 1994 by Dye, who added several water hazards. This par-72 course runs 6,311 yards.

SEA PINES RESORT (PUBLIC)
www.seapines.com
Sea Pines is the home of three of the island's most popular golf courses, including the Harbour Town Golf Links, which is the site of Hilton Head's number-one sporting event, the Verizon Heritage. Walking is allowed on all three courses.

HARBOUR TOWN GOLF LINKS (PUBLIC)
11 Lighthouse Lane
(843) 363-8385, (800) 955-8337
The signature hole at Harbour Town is the one you've seen countless times on television—the windswept 18th, a par 4 on Calibogue Sound where shots to the green often end up among the fiddler crabs in the adjacent marsh. Consistently ranked among the world's top courses, this one was designed by Pete Dye and Jack Nicklaus and has some outstanding par 3s. The yardage at this par-71 course totals 6,040. Greens fees run $250, however, realize that this is one of the country's premier and challenging courses, so expect pricey fees.

OCEAN COURSE (PUBLIC)
100 North Sea Pines Dr.
(843) 842-8484, (800) 955-8337
The 15th hole on this oldest and newest of island courses offers a terrific view of the ocean. It's the oldest course because it was designed by George Cobb in 1962 and was remodeled by Mark McCumber in 1995. Greens fees for this par- 72, 6,172-yard layout run $114.

HERON POINT COURSE (PUBLIC)
100 North Sea Pines Dr.
(843) 842-8484, (800) 955-8337
You'll encounter wide fairways and lots of lagoons, trees, and marshes when you play

this par-72 course, which was redesigned by Pete Dye and reopened after a year of work in September 2007. The previous name was Sea Marsh. Greens fees are as follows: Aug 1 through Sept 19, 6:30 a.m. to 6:30 p.m., $83; Sept 20 to Nov. 28, 6:30 a.m. to 6:30 p.m., $98; Nov. 29 through March 6, 6:30 a.m. to 6:30 p.m., $70.

i If you should somehow run out of golf courses to play on Hilton Head, be advised that there are several fine off-island layouts nearby. Among them are four on US 278, the road to the island—Eagle's Point (843-815-3100), Hilton Head National Golf Club (843-842-5900), Island West (843-689-6660), and Old South Golf Links (843-785-5353).

SHIPYARD GOLF CLUB (PUBLIC)
45 Shipyard Dr.
(843) 689-GOLF, (800) 2-FIND-18
www.hiltonheadgolf.net
Shipyard offers three interconnecting 9-hole courses appropriately named for three types of sailing vessels: Brigantine, Clipper, and Galleon. There is water involved on 25 of the 27 holes, which have Bermuda grass fairways and greens. There's a bar and restaurant on the premises. Greens fees are $90 in the morning, $60 after noon, and $45 after 2 p.m.

BRIGANTINE COURSE
The work of designer Willard Byrd, the Brigantine is a 3,054-yard, par 36 surrounded by private homes and rental condominiums that blend in with the natural environment. You'll be challenged by No. 6, a long par 4; and No. 9, which is a par 5 that runs 494 yards and has water on one side of the fairway. Resort rates during summer months are as follows: $105 in the morning, $80 after 11

a.m.; $63 after 1 a.m., and $50 after 3 p.m. The nine-hole rate is $40.

CLIPPER COURSE   PUBLIC
The 3,302-yard Clipper has a tough 9th hole with lots of bunkers. Water comes into play on all the holes except No. 6, which is a par 4, 415-yarder. George Cobb also designed this course, which carries a par 36. Resort rates during summer months are as follows: $105 in the morning, $80 after 11 a.m.; $63 after 1 a.m., and $50 after 3 p.m. The nine-hole rate is $40.

GALLEON COURSE
The Shipyard Golf Club consists of three 18-hole golf courses that have interconnecting nines. The Clipper/Galleon Course is the larges of the three. The greens are large and well bunkered. This George Cobb–designed, par-36 course is best known for No. 2, a par 5 with an elevated green fronted by water and with bunkers all around. Total yardage for the course is 3,146. Resort rates during summer months are as follows: $105 in the morning, $80 after 11 a.m.; $63 after 1 a.m., and $50 after 3 p.m. The nine-hole rate is $40.

Tennis

If you fly in on through the Savannah airport, you'll be surrounded by avid tennis players heading to "the island" for tennis vacations. This is a sport that brings thousands to Hilton Head to improve their game. The options for playing, as well as for formal instruction, are plentiful! Among those open to the public for play are the following:

PALMETTO DUNES TENNIS CENTER
6 Trent Jones Lane
(843) 785-1152, (800) 972-0257
www.palmettodunes.com

An array of instructional programs and daily round-robin tournaments are featured at the tennis center at Palmetto Dunes. The tournaments are billed as "lively afternoon social competition with the emphasis on fun." There are 23 clay and 2 Pro Bounce (a cushioned hard surface) courts, 8 of which are lighted.

Reserved rates are $25 for Palmetto Dunes' guests and $30 for players not staying at the resort. Walk-on rates (noon to 4 p.m.) are $20 from noon to 4 p.m.

PORT ROYAL RACQUET CLUB
15 Wimbledon Court
(843) 686-8803

The Port Royal Racquet Club is the only tennis facility on Hilton Head—and in all of South Carolina, for that matter—offering all three Grand Slam–type playing surfaces. There are 10 clay courts, 4 cushioned hard courts, and a new croquet court! The club offers a variety of instructional programs and will custom design clinics for individuals and teams.

Located at Port Royal Plantation, the club has a well-stocked pro shop that provides a varied selection of men's and women's tennis wear and the latest in equipment. Reserved rates for clay and hard courts are $25 per hour. You'll need reservations for the croquet court and the fee is $12 per person.

SEA PINES RACQUET CLUB
5 Lighthouse Lane
(843) 363-4495, (800) 732-7463
www.seapines.com

Programs and instruction take center court at the Sea Pines Racquet Club, which *Tennis* magazine has ranked number two in the country. The flagship program is the Smith Stearns Tennis Academy, named in part after Stan Smith, the former U.S. Open and Wimbledon champion who serves as the club's touring pro and tennis consultant.

There are various programs for every age group, and 23 clay courts are available for play. The club has five instructors led by the genial Job de Boer, who specializes in teaching groups.

The club dates from the early 1970s. The pro shop offers players the latest in tennis fashions, equipment, and footwear. Court fees are $25 per hour for a reserved court.

Sea Pines Resort gives their guests two hours complimentary each day. The website has a full listing of instructional packages, including several children's tennis programs.

VAN DER MEER SHIPYARD TENNIS RESORT
116 Shipyard Dr.
(843) 686-8804, (800) 845-6138
www.vandermeertennis.com

Twenty courts set amid the lush surroundings of Shipyard Plantation await the tennis buff at this racquet club, which the United States Tennis Association presented with its Outstanding Tennis Facility of the Year Award for 1997, and continues to live up to the honor today. There are 13 clay courts and 4 hard-surface courts outdoors and 3 DecoTurf courts indoors (a total of 5 courts have lights). The club also offers a variety of tennis getaway weeks and weekends, stroke of the day sessions, daily drills, and intensive drills available year-round. The intensive drills are geared for players with 4.0-plus ratings and are designed to take skills to the next level.

The club, owned by premier tennis teacher Dennis Van der Meer, holds exhibitions by tennis professionals on Mondays from March through October, with admission and refreshments free. The Shipyard

Racquet Club has a large pro shop displaying an extensive variety of items, and it's also the site of the United States Professional Tennis Registry's International Tennis Symposium and $25,000 Championships, which are held annually during the middle of February.

Reserved rates for the club's clay courts are $25 per hour, with walk-ons paying $18 per hour from noon to 4 p.m. Fees for hard courts are $20 per hour reserved, $15 walk-on. Covered courts must be reserved, and fees are $40 per hour.

VAN DER MEER TENNIS CENTER
19 DeAllyon Rd.
(843) 785-8388, (800) 845-6138
This tennis center operated by well-known instructor Dennis Van der Meer provides a multitude of programs for adults and junior players in all stages of development, from beginners to aspiring professionals. There are 17 hard-surface courts, of which 4 are covered and lighted, with fees for an hour of play set at $15. The center has a pro shop and is the headquarters of the Van der Meer Tennis University, which offers training programs for tennis teachers. The center is on DeAllyon Road, which runs off Cordillo Parkway on the south end of the island.

ANNUAL EVENTS & FESTIVALS

The island's most significant annual events occur during the spring. The most exclusive and highly publicized is the The Heritage of Golf, from April 18–24. If you're a fan of the sport, you won't want to miss this event, on one of the most picturesque venues in the country. Tickets and information are updated online at www.theheritagegolfsc.com so refer to the website for additional inquiries.

FOOD AND WINE FESTIVAL
Hilton Oceanfront Resort
Palmetto Dunes
(843) 686-4944, (800) 424-3387
www.hiltonheadhospitality
association.com
The Hilton Head Hospitality Association produces several events featuring food and wine, including their Food and Wine Festival which is typically held annually Feb 4–7. In 2010, the 25th anniversary of the Hilton Head Island Wine and Food Festival was a huge success. There were wine-pairing dinners, cooking demonstrations, and island chefs showcased their talents at the Grand Wine Tasting. Stay tuned for current and future plans by visiting the website.

ST. PATRICK'S DAY PARADE
Pope Avenue
www.stpatricksdayhhi.com
What started as a march by a few residents of Irish descent in 1983 has matured into the largest free spectator event held on the island. Some 20,000 onlookers gather to watch the two-hour parade, which is held on the Sunday before St. Patrick's Day or on the day itself when the holiday falls on Sunday. If you go, expect to see marching bands, in the neighborhood of 30 floats, dance groups, a bagpipe band or two, local dignitaries, and maybe even Budweiser's Clydesdale horses. The parade starts at 2 p.m. at Coligny Circle and proceeds west on Pope Avenue to Office Park Road and into Park Plaza. Tom Reilley started the celebration when he and a few friends decided to march in honor of St. Patrick. Because they didn't have a parade permit, Reilley and his pals ran into some legal troubles with local officials, but they managed to straighten things out and resumed marching in 1985. Since then the

parade has grown into the family-oriented event that it is today. Visit the website for more information.

THE HERITAGE OF GOLF
Harbour Town Golf Links
11 Lighthouse Lane
(843) 671-2448, (800) 234-1107
www.theheritagegolfsc.comHilton Head's Heritage of Golf brings the PGA's 132 invited players and 125,000 spectators to famed Harbour Town Golf Links in the Sea Pines Resort during four days in April. In one of golf's most picturesque sites, this course has attracted international media since it started in 1969. The list of Heritage champions of the past includes Jack Nicklaus, Greg Norman, Nick Price, Hale Irwin, Tom Watson, and Arnold Palmer, who won the tournament in its inaugural year of 1969 when it was known as the Heritage Classic.

Attending the Heritage involves more than watching a golf tournament. The event is usually held during the second week in April, when the weather is generally lovely and nature is putting on a springtime show. It's a terrific time to get outdoors, amble around the verdant Harbour Town course, visit the shops and restaurants at the Harbour Town Yacht Basin near the first tee and 18th green, gawk at the high-priced boats docked in the marina, and observe the hordes of spectators doing all of these things. Sometime during their day at the course, those attending are invariably drawn to the 18th hole, which overlooks Calibogue Sound and has the Harbour Town Lighthouse as part of its backdrop, to see how the players finish up and deal with the wind blowing off the water.

During the three days leading up to the tournament, which starts on Thursday and ends on Sunday, there are two pro-am events and a pro-am fishing tournament. On the Monday afternoon before Thursday's first round of play, the Heritage presents opening ceremonies focusing on golf's Scottish origins and the game's long history in South Carolina (the South Carolina Golf Club of Charleston was founded in 1786 and is reputed to be the oldest membership golf club in America). The defending champion, tournament board members clad in plaid, and bagpipers from The Citadel military college parade along the yacht basin to the 18th green, where the defending champ gets the tourney under way by smacking a ball into Calibogue Sound as a Civil War–era cannon is fired.

A grounds badge, which is good for admission to the tournament grounds for the entire week of Heritage events, costs $115 but could go higher. A clubhouse badge, which gives you access for the entire week to the grounds, the clubhouse, and the Heritage Pavilion, a hospitality tent, averages $145. Practice round badges enable you to attend all the events leading up to the four-day tournament. Also, there are patron plans available for large groups of spectators; for details on these, contact the Heritage staff at the phone numbers listed for this entry. Parking for the Heritage is in lots within Sea Pines, and spectators are shuttled by bus to Harbour Town. The parking and the bus service are complimentary.

ARTS & CULTURE

Hilton Head has for years radiated a vibrant cultural presence. Some 20 community groups—ranging from the Hilton Head Art League to the Hilton Head Orchestra—foster and promote an appreciation of the visual and performing arts. The community

HILTON HEAD, SOUTH CAROLINA

created a new artistic resource, the Arts Center of Coastal Carolina, which has become the cultural hub of the island.

ARTS CENTER OF COASTAL CAROLINA
14 Shelter Cove Lane
(843) 686-3945, (843) 842-ARTS
www.artscenter-hhi.org

A big-city facility on a resort island, this $10 million visual- and performing-arts center offers theatrical productions, performances by musicians and dancers, art shows, education programs, and community-service programs.

Each year the center's 350-seat Elizabeth Wallace Theater hosts up to six productions. Among the previous presentations were *Say Goodnight, Gracie,* a one-man Broadway show; and *Bjorn Again: The Abba Experience.* Check the website for current events. The theater complex has dressing and costume rooms and a green room. A rehearsal hall has seating for 150.

The center brings islanders a series featuring local talent and regional and national touring companies. Six to eight art shows are exhibited annually in the center's 2,300-square-foot Walter Greer Gallery, which has 12-foot-high ceilings and flexible lighting for showcasing art. Through its education program, the center cosponsors residencies by professional artists in area schools and brings children on field trips to the center for performances. The center also offers services and assistance to artists and art groups from throughout the island, providing technical support and space for a variety of organizations.

The center further serves the island by presenting free events such as the Community Christmas Tree Lighting, Family Fiesta Latina, Youth ArtsFest, and Gullah-Fest.

For tickets to individual events, visit www.artshhi.com/html/tickets.html or call (843) 842-2787.

HILTON HEAD ART LEAGUE
430 William Hilton Pkwy.
(843) 681-5060
www.hhal.org

As part of its mission to provide artists with opportunities to hone their skills and exhibit their works, the Hilton Head Art League presents "minishows" every four weeks at its gallery in the Pineland Station shopping complex. Each of these exhibits features the work of a league member, and each opens with an evening reception. The league sponsors two major art shows annually at the Walter Greer Gallery of the Arts Center of Coastal Carolina. One of the shows is juried, and the event attracts more than 700 entries from throughout the Southeast. The league also presents workshops that attract nationally known artists from throughout the United States (call 800-995-4068 for information). The Hilton Head Art League was started in 1972 by a handful of local artists. Today there are more than 950 members, 250 of whom are artists.

HILTON HEAD ORCHESTRA
32 Office Park Rd.
(843) 842-2055
www.hhorchestra.org

The 65-piece Hilton Head Orchestra presents a 10-concert Monday Master Series, a 5-concert Sunday Series, and several special events, and sponsors a youth orchestra and international piano competition. About 40 percent of the musicians are from the local area, with the others traveling from Southern cities such as Savannah; Charleston, South Carolina; and Jacksonville, Florida, to participate in performances. Concerts are held at the First Presbyterian Church at 540 William Hilton Pkwy. Mary Woodmansee Green serves as the orchestra's music director/conductor, having assumed that role in July 1998. Prior to coming to Hilton Head, she was the music director and conductor of the Kennett Symphony and Philadelphia Festival Orchestras, the Delaware Valley Chorale, and The Mary Green Singers. The orchestra was founded in the winter of 1982 by a handful of local musicians who incorporated the organization as the Hilton Head Chamber Orchestra later in the year. The name was changed to Hilton Head Community Orchestra in 1983; six years later, it became the Hilton Head Orchestra. The Hilton Head Youth Orchestra was organized in 1996. The Hilton Head Island International Piano Competition was also started in 1996. The competition is held early in March at the First Presbyterian Church. About 150 pianists apply, with 24 selected as quarter-finalists.

REAL ESTATE

They're luxuriant and they're extravagant and many are recognized by stately gated entranceways, classic fountains, and striking landscaping. These are Hilton Head's 11 planned residential communities that cover 65 percent of the island. Many of the island's golf courses (see subsequent listings) are located within or associated with the communities, as are the four largest hotels and many of Hilton Head's homes, vacation villas, tennis courts, and marinas. Security is strictly enforced, so if you're planning to take a joy ride to view the properties inside, be prepared to be stopped. You won't get too far.

Some communities are more private than others: A few admit only residents and their guests; others are accessible to vacationers staying at hotels and villas within the communities and to golfers playing on courses that allow public participation. Sea Pines, which is the site of several restaurants and two shopping areas, allows the public to visit at a charge of $5 per car.

As we've mentioned before, the buildings in these communities are, in most cases, designed to melt into the landscape; stucco and wood are used extensively as building materials, and painting is in muted colors. The grounds surrounding these structures are often left in as natural a state as possible. In most communities, architectural review boards must approve buildings. This section comprises sketches of the island's 11 planned communities, listed in alphabetical order. For each we've provided, when possible, an address, telephone number, and/or website of a source for additional information: either a sales office, an administrative office, or the office of the property owners' association.

Hilton Head Plantation

Hilton Head Plantation is the second-largest planned community on the island, covering 4,000 acres on the northern tip of Hilton Head between Port Royal Sound and Skull Creek, which is part of the Intracoastal Waterway. Within the plantation's borders are 4,400 residential lots, four 18-hole golf courses, a beach fronting on the sound, the Whooping Crane Pond and Cypress Nature Conservancies, the Seabrook Farm garden plots, and tennis courts and swimming pools.

On the Skull Creek side of the plantation are Skull Creek Marina, a deepwater facility with 180 boat slips, the Old Fort Pub restaurant, and Fort Mitchel, a historic site that was a Union gun battery during the Civil War.

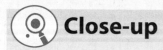 **Close-up**

Palmetto Dunes: A Sample Resort Itinerary

To truly enjoy South Carolina's pristine beaches at Hilton Head Island, it's best to reserve a private home or villa (depending on your budget) at any of the island's splendid resorts. I recently played tourist at one of Hilton Head Island's most highly acclaimed developments, **Palmetto Dunes,** a 2,000-acre resort that boasts activities for every age. From fishing in the surf to kayaking in the man-made lagoons, biking, swimming, or just sitting, the wide array of activities available in this natural setting combined with an attentive staff make this place ideal for spending family time together far away from the distractions of home. The resort offers 3 miles of beach bordering the Atlantic Ocean; 5,000 homes and villas, more than 500 of which can be rented by vacationers; three 18-hole golf courses; a world-class tennis facility; an 11-mile lagoon system (for endless kayaking); and two of the island's "big four" hotels—the 512-room **Marriott Beach and Golf Resort** and the 324-room **Hilton Oceanfront Resort** (see listings under this chapter's Accommodations section). There are accommodations for all sizes of groups and price ranges, and throughout the well-manicured resort, you'll encounter personalities that you'll not forget when the trip is over. I sampled a two-bedroom condo in the oceanfront Barrington Court building. The fourth floor condo was spacious, bright, and decorated "island-style." The master and second bedroom (each with a private bath) were separated by a large living/dining area. The full kitchen was stocked with cookware, dishes, silverware, washer/dryer, and the living area opened to a huge porch with comfortable seating that overlooked the pool, lagoon, and ocean. A flat-screen television included a DVD player and even a video setup for children. The cost ranged from $260 nightly (Jan to Apr, with a three-night minimum) to $440 nightly (June to Aug with a seven-night minimum). The condo was only secondary to the vast array of activities available at this resort. I tried them all!

I highly recommend that you plan an itinerary that is inclusive of all sports offered, whether you're familiar with them or not. For instance, if tennis is your game (or not), call the tennis facility at Palmetto Dunes (843-785-1152) and reserve a spot in tennis pro Tapi Hayrinen's Cardio Tennis class. Hayrinen is a delightful chap from Finland who will help you burn some calories while having fun, all set to music! Whether you're a novice to golf or a pro wannabe, golf pro Doug Weaver will gently lead you through the tips for a winning round. There are bikes for every age so make sure you schedule some time to cruise the island's bike trails and request your bikes when you make the

Two of the golf courses within the plantation (the Country Club of Hilton Head and Oyster Reef) can be played by the public.

Outside the plantation's main gate, which is off William Hilton Parkway near mile marker 3, is Main Street, a development of shops and professional offices. The Hilton Head Plantation Property Owners Association is within the plantation at 7 Surrey Lane, and the telephone number there is (843) 681-8800. The website is www.hiltonhead plantation.com.

reservation. That way they'll be waiting for you at the condo's bike rack. There are bikes with child seats and even bikes for little ones.

If you're a beach bum, try lunch or sunsets at the **Dunes House,** an open-air restaurant with full bar right on the beach! Colorful and casual, the restaurant features gourmet salads, homemade hamburgers, and fresh seafood entrees and appetizers. It's also the site of weddings and receptions as there is full beach access from the restaurant's deck. This favorite beachfront destination also offers public restrooms and limited on-site parking.

The best way to travel to and from the Dunes House (and all over the island) is to ride your bike or take the free **Dunes Buggy** shuttle. To reserve a ride on the free shuttle from Mar 28 through Sept 30, please call (843) 689-4222. The Dunes House is also available year-round for private celebrations, including family reunions, weddings, holiday parties, and birthday parties. To book a special event at the Dunes House, contact Nicole Guy, Events Manager, at (866) 650-4130.

Even if you've never been in a kayak, you'll enjoy trying this sport, as I did for the first time. Start with scheduling your outing at **Palmetto Dunes Outfitters** (843-785-2449). A guide will lead you through some of the 11-mile maze of lagoons for any length of time that you desire. There are two-seater kayaks available, as well as canoes. Call for pricing. Just a note about traveling the resort at night. There are no street lights, so utilize the Dunes Buggy for all your nighttime travel within the confines of Palmetto Dunes.

All three of Palmetto Dunes' golf courses—named for designers Arthur Hills, George Fazio, and Robert Trent Jones—are accessible to the public (see listings in this chapter under Golf), as are the 23 clay and 2 hard courts of the Palmetto Dunes Tennis Center. Homes in Palmetto Dunes range from $500,000 to over $5 million. Palmetto Dunes was started in the late 1960s and acquired in 1979 by the Greenwood Development Corporation, which since then has created the Shelter Cove Harbour yacht basin and retail complex and the Leamington community. Shelter Cove—a marina surrounded by shops, restaurants, and villas built in the style of a Mediterranean village—opened in 1982 and is directly across William Hilton Parkway from Palmetto Dunes. Leamington, covering 400 acres within Palmetto Dunes, is a private community with security gates that's centered on the Arthur Hills golf course. Development of this area was begun in 1986. You'll find the Palmetto Dunes sales office at the entrance to the community, which is off William Hilton Parkway near mile marker 8. The phone number is (843) 842-1111.

Indigo Run

Most of the homesites at this 1,775-acre development on the northern portion of Hilton Head Island border one of two 18-hole golf courses: the Golf Club at Indigo Run, a members-only layout designed by Jack Nicklaus and his son, Jack Nicklaus II, and opened in 1996; and the Golden Bear Golf Club, which was designed by Nicklaus's company and can be played by the public (see listing in this chapter's Golf section). All property owners at Indigo Run are entitled to join Golden Bear, and membership includes access to Sunningdale Park, which has six tennis courts, an

Olympic-size pool, a kiddie pool, and a large playground for children. Membership in the Golf Club is open to owners of homesites and homes in Indigo Run.

As of November 2009, there were 804 homes on the 1,517 acres comprising Indigo Run's private residential community. These residences represent a wide range of styles and construction materials and are valued at $450,000 and up. Fifty of Indigo Run's homesites are in the River Club section along the banks of Broad Creek, and many owners of homes there have backyard boat docks. Sixty-four homesites are located in Broad Pointe, where the residents have access to a waterfront park including a pool and boardwalk. There are no villas at Indigo Run, and the only rentals allowed are long-term arrangements of a year or more. For more information, contact the Indigo Run Community Owners Association by calling (843) 689-7300.

Long Cove Club

Established in the early 1980s, Long Cove Club on Hilton Head Island has been recognized as a friendly private community. Small by design, the natural beauty and casual elegance are a true reflection of this community's relaxed and unpretentious Lowcountry lifestyle. There's a championship tennis facility, state-of-the-art marina (with direct access to the Atlantic Ocean and the Intracoastal Waterway), a spacious dog park, community pool and complex, and a nationally acclaimed golf course designed by Pete Dye.

Long Cove Club is the first residential community on Hilton Head to establish a charitable endowment fund. The Long Cove Club Community Endowment Fund was established in 2003 by the Long Cove Club Board of Directors in collaboration with the Community Foundation of the Lowcountry and awards grants which fill needs in the areas of health, housing, hunger, and education in the local community. For more information, visit their website at www.long coveclub.org or contact the Administration Building at (843) 686-1070.

Palmetto Hall Plantation

Palmetto Hall is a strictly residential, golf-oriented community covering 775 acres in the northern portion of the island. Most of the 500 homesites border the fairways of the plantation's two 18-hole golf courses—the Arthur Hills and Robert Cupp Courses—both of which are open to the public (see listings in this chapter under Golf). Started by Greenwood Development Corporation in 1991, Palmetto Hall is now a part of the Heritage Group and offers its residents a 14,000-square-foot clubhouse and an activities center with pools, tennis courts, and a children's playground. Palmetto Hall Plantation is one of the few plantations allowing its 550 members to own private carts for transportation.

The homes here, all of them single-family residences, reflect the style of the Lowcountry with their verandas, dormers, and colorful shutters. Residences range up to $900,000. Palmetto Hall is also the site of more than 100 acres of nature preserves. For information on home sales, call (843) 342-2582 or visit www.hiltonheadgolf.net. Palmetto Hall's main gate is on Beach City Road about a half mile from the road's intersection with William Hilton Parkway at mile marker 4.

Port Royal Plantation

Living on the beach (or having easy access to it) is the main drawing card of this 1,000-acre community in the northeastern corner of the island. There are 2.5 miles of beach stretching along the plantation on the east and southeast—1.5 miles on the Atlantic Ocean and the rest on Port Royal Sound. The eastern side is the site of the actual Hilton Head, the bluff where English sea captain William Hilton looked out on the sound while exploring the region; it's the spot for which the entire island was eventually named.

Port Royal was one of the island's first planned communities, and the 920 homes within its gates reflect a wide variety of sizes and styles. They range in value from $500,000 to $5 million; most are in the $750,000 to $2 million-plus range, and those on the ocean-front average about $3.5 million.

Another big attraction at Port Royal is golf. There are three 18-hole courses: Planter's Row, Barony, and Robber's Row, which are open to the public on a rotating basis (see listings in this chapter's Golf section). Residents of the plantation can be members at all three courses. Also outside the plantation but considered part of the Port Royal resort complex are the Port Royal Racquet Club, which has grass, composition, and hard-surface tennis courts; the 412-room Westin Resort Hilton Head hotel (see listing in this chapter's Accommodations section); and the villas at Island Links, Ocean Palms, Port Royal Village, Royal Dunes, the Links and the Lyons, Crown Reef, and the Barony Beach Club. The property owners' association office is at 10 Coggins Point Rd. just before the main gate, which is off William Hilton Parkway near mile marker 5. The phone number is (843) 681-5114, or visit www.hiltonhead golf.net for more information.

The Sea Pines Resort

A Hilton Head architect once called Sea Pines the "daddy rabbit" of planned residential/ resort communities. It's an apt description of the largest and oldest of the island's major developments—the first community of its kind in the nation.

The Sea Pines Resort covers 5,200 acres on the south end of Hilton Head and was started in 1957. It's the site of the island's first golf course, the Ocean Course, one of three courses in the community, all of which can be played by the public (see the Golf section in this chapter). The most popular of these courses is the Harbour Town Golf Links, which is the site of the island's biggest annual event, the Verizon Heritage, a PGA tour event that brings many of the world's best golfers to Hilton Head for four days during April. (See this chapter's Annual Events section for more on the Heritage.) The racquet club has 23 courts and offers comprehensive programs of tennis instruction under the direction of former Wimbledon champion and U.S. Olympic men's coach Stan Smith.

The Sea Pines Resort is the site of Hilton Head's best-known landmark, the red-and-white striped lighthouse at the Harbour Town Yacht Basin. Villas, shops, and restaurants ring the basin at Harbour Town; it's one of two marinas in Sea Pines, the other being at South Beach, where you'll find a New England–style village with shops, restaurants, and all sorts of water sports. Both marinas provide access to Calibogue Sound. More shops and places to eat are available at Sea Pines Center.

Within the borders of Sea Pines are a 605-acre nature preserve, 5 miles of beach, the ruins of the Stoney-Baynard Plantation, two swimming pools, the Lawton Stables equestrian center, and a beach club that has an open-air grill, an oceanfront bar, a gift shop, live entertainment and dinner nightly in season, and picnic tables. The Sea Pines Resort offers 10,000 square feet of meeting space at the Plantation Club Conference Center, the Harbour Town Clubhouse, and the new Harbour Town Conference Center.

Sea Pines has nearly 3,500 single-family homes. A total of 530 villas and homes are available for rent by vacationers, and the new Inn at Harbour Town provides luxurious accommodations for those seeking a hotel-type setting. To learn more about the Sea Pines Resort, visit the welcome center at 32 Greenwood Dr. or the website at www.seapines.com, or call (843) 785-3333 or (888) 807-6873. The welcome center is right outside the community's main gate, which is on Greenwood Drive just south of the Sea Pines traffic circle.

Shipyard Plantation

Shipyard has a mixture of single-family residences, condominiums, time-share units, and commercial developments within its 834 acres. There are about 265 residences ranging from patio homes starting at $400,000 to larger houses on golf courses that start at $500,000. The plantation, in the southeastern part of the island, is the site of more than 1,400 villas grouped in 22 different villa regimes.

The Shipyard Golf Club consists of 27 holes on 3 courses open to the public: Brigantine, Clipper, and Galleon (see this chapter's Golf section). Residents and guests have other forms of recreation available, particularly tennis and the beach. The Van der Meer Shipyard Racquet Club boasts 20 championship courts, and the eastern side of the plantation is on the Atlantic Ocean.

Shipyard's ocean side is the site of the 340-room Crowne Plaza Resort Hotel (see this chapter's Accommodations section) and a beach club community house for residents. The plantation is also the home of the Hilton Head Health Institute, a resort for folks seeking to change their lifestyles by learning how to control their weight, reduce stress, and become more physically fit.

Ironically, Shipyard has no marina; its name is derived from the cotton plantation that once occupied the site. Administrative offices are at 10 Shipyard Dr., and the phone number is (843) 785-3310. They're just outside the main gate, which is off William Hilton Parkway near mile marker 10. There's a website at www.spoa.com.

Spanish Wells

There are some 200 single-family lots at this 350-acre community on the western portion of the island; the houses at Spanish Wells are on lots of at least 1 acre.

Spanish Wells is the most secluded of the island's communities; it's at the end of Spanish Wells Road, nearly 3 miles from William Hilton Parkway. The private golf club has a nine-hole course, two tennis courts, and a swimming pool. Many of the homes at Spanish Wells are on Calibogue Sound or Broad Creek, and those on Brahms Point, a narrow finger of land at the southwestern reaches of the community, have views of both bodies of water. The community derives its name from the wells from which Spanish explorers drew fresh water while visiting Hilton Head. Also of historical note is the fact that Spanish Wells is the site of Battery Holbrook, a Civil War gun emplacement. To learn more about Spanish Wells, call the property owners' association at (843) 842-4138.

Wexford Plantation

Wexford Plantation is one of the island's most glamorous private residential communities. The emphasis is on privacy at Wexford, where rentals are prohibited and admittance is open only to residents, their guests, and prospective home-buyers. This golf and yachting community covers 525 acres near the middle of the island. All of the 459 lots at Wexford are sold, and about 340 homes had been built as of summer 2005, most of them two-story, British Colonial–style houses valued from $750,000 to $5 million.

About a third of the homes are on the plantation's scenic 35.5-acre harbor, which winds through the center of the community and is lock controlled to keep the water calm and at a minimum of 8 feet deep. The harbor, with slips accommodating yachts up to 66 feet long, provides access to Broad Creek. Most of the other homes are on Wexford's 18-hole golf course, a layout by Willard Byrd that's reserved solely for members and their guests and was restored to its original design. Other amenities take the form of a harborside clubhouse graced with pink Georgian marble and Tiffany glass skylights; a pool with a patio that overlooks the water; six tennis courts, four of them lighted; and a croquet lawn. Sales offices are at 2 Town Center Court and can be reached by calling (843) 686-8800 or (800) 345-2392; you can also reach the executive office at (843) 686-8810 or www.wexfordplantation.com. Wexford's main entrance is off William Hilton Parkway near mile marker 10.

Windmill Harbour

Designed for boating enthusiasts, Windmill Harbour covers 172 acres in the northwestern portion of Hilton Head. Unlike the island's other planned communities, Windmill Harbour has no golf course, but it does have a 15.5-acre yacht basin with 260 boat slips. The harbor, the site of the South Carolina Yacht Club, has a lock system that keeps tides and currents to a minimum; the lack of movement of water also inhibits the growth of barnacles on the bottom of boats, allowing their owners to save on maintenance costs. The harbor lies on Calibogue Sound, which is part of the Intracoastal Waterway.

Eighty percent of the homesites at Windmill Harbour have views of the water. Among the residences at Windmill Harbour are estates on lots of an acre or more, villas, patio homes, and condominiums, all of them reflecting architectural styles seen in the historic district of Charleston and the South Carolina Lowcountry. Prices for condos start at $300,000; homes run from $500,000 to $2.5 million and up.

Residents seeking recreation other than boating can find it at the community's sports center, which provides an Olympic-size lap pool, seven clay tennis courts, and extensive workout facilities. The elegant building that serves as headquarters for the yacht club overlooks the harbor and offers a meeting place where members of the club can dine and attend cookouts, oyster roasts, and parties. Although Windmill Harbour is mainly a private community, the yacht basin is open to the boating public, and residents can rent out their dwellings for periods of 60 days or more. Shorter-term rentals are prohibited. The sales office is at 2 Harbour Passage Patio inside the main gate, which is off William Hilton Parkway just after you cross the bridges to the island. You can reach these offices by calling (843) 681-5600 or (877) 681-5600. You can also see more about Windmill Harbour at www.richardsongroupllc.com.

TYBEE ISLAND

The drive out to Tybee Island from Savannah is a bit like being on a small adventure. With marshland on both sides, the natural setting is captivating, often luring drivers to pull over to the side of the road to take a quick photo of an egret standing in the mud with its neck outstretched or a turtle hatchling trying to cross the road. (This is not recommended.) The scene is often mixed with a little bit of disbelief as you make the 8- to 10-minute-long trek to this oasis called Tybee Island. Once you've arrived, you'll know it, as you'll quickly slow your speed down to 35 mph and begin taking in the colorful wooden signs, salty docks, and cheap souvenir shops that tell you that you've left civilization.

There are some things about Tybee that haven't changed in the past couple decades. They are all good things. City Hall is still City Hall. The North Beach is still vast, and beachcombers are few. The ships still blow their horns as they make their way into the mouth of the Savannah River right off Tybee's coast. You can still get a smooth ice cream cone (and chocolate dip) from a vendor on Butler Avenue, the main drag. And there's still plenty of beach to lie on, even when it's the Fourth of July.

Those things that have changed are also few. The mayor is a young whippersnapper that nobody thought could win but who did win, and is doing a darned good job. The permanent amusement park has gone and given way to condos, but a floating carnival has filled the void of a vacant lot during the summer. In 2009, the movies came to Tybee and stars like Miley Cyrus brought the Nicholas Sparks novel, *The Last Song*, to life. Lots of Tybee citizens were involved and hence, the nickname "Tybee-wood" was born.

While other beach communities succumb to high-rises, slick resorts, and gated communities with lawns pristine enough to putt on, Tybee has stubbornly resisted. Look around the town's beachside shops during summer and you'll see kites and flags hanging out the doors of souvenir shops that hawk seashells and bargain T-shirts for less than $10. You'll see sunburned kids slurping snow cones to music wafting from the Tybee pier. And you'll see locals strolling the strand every day because that's what they do.

HISTORY

Tybee is a place where folksy eccentricity is celebrated, and many things have been practiced. Gambling was one of those things practiced in back rooms throughout Tybee until being exposed and cleared out in the early 1960s. A decade or so later, nearly every bar in town was shut down for staying open too late on Saturday night. Seems people were having too good a time to remember that selling beer on Sunday was illegal. That's the thing about Tybee islanders—they just sort of do their own thing.

Through the years, there have been nicknames for Tybee that may, or may not, have been quite fair. Somehow, "Redneck Riviera" just doesn't seem appropriate for this beautiful place, where you can wear flip-flops year-round and everybody knows your name. Bluntly put, there are places at Tybee that are a little scruffy, but if you'll get your nose out of the air, you'll learn to appreciate the quirky appeal as the art of the island. You'll find million-dollar beachfront construction next door to cinder-block shacks (and don't necessarily assume the owners of the fancy home are the richer: Tybee knew shabby before it was chic). This is a beach run by locals who are glad to see tourists, and even happier to see them leave. Tybee is a beach of rituals. One such example is the Beach Bums Parade, wherein locals on makeshift floats armed with large-scale water guns do battle with spectators spraying garden hoses, marking the beginning of the tourist season—a fun, messy launch to the crowds of summer. Later, mid-September ushers back in "Tybee time," when the residents have the place to themselves and the particular pleasures of a warm winter beach.

If you think Tybee—with its whimsical cottages and wacky storefronts is colorful, just wait until you read about her past. This island served a role in several wars and has been home to Lt. Col. George C. Marshall (creator of the Marshall Plan) and to a quarantine station for people with infectious ailments. In the early 1800s, scientists believed the marshes in and around the island held harmful vapors or miasma, which rose from the marsh vegetation and were carried by the wind into Savannah. However, it was also widely theorized that the vapors were counteracted by the healing properties of sea air. That was a notion that eventually played a role in Tybee's foray into tourism in the late 1880s.

Native Americans were the first Tybee islanders. They settled this small island (2.5 miles long and about 0.6 mile wide) and also are generally credited with giving the island its name, which means salt, though there are other competing theories. Next came the Spanish in the 1500s, followed 200 years later by Georgia's founder, Gen. James Edward Oglethorpe.

Because of its location at the mouth of the Savannah River, Tybee was important strategically. Soon after his arrival, Oglethorpe ordered the construction of a lighthouse, which was completed in 1736. During the War of 1812, the lighthouse (see Things to Do in this chapter) was used to warn Savannah of possible attack by the British, but this attack never materialized. A fortress known as a Martello Tower, designed with round walls that supposedly would deflect cannonballs, was built on Tybee Island in 1815 to help guard the Savannah River from attack. It was one of only a few such structures in North America.

On the western end of the island, a quarantine station was set up to house sick passengers coming in off ships. This is how Lazaretto Creek got its name. *Lazaretto* is an Italian word for an institution or hospital for those with contagious diseases. "They kept them in quarantine there for four months," said James Mack Adams, local Tybee historian. "If they got sick and died, they buried them right there."

In 1829 construction began on Fort Pulaski (see the Things to Do section in this chapter). The fort, now a national park, stands off US 80 as you approach Tybee. It was constructed of 25 million bricks and has walls 7.5 feet thick. Robert E. Lee was one of the engineers who planned and supervised construction. During the Civil War, Union forces attacked the fort using a new weapon called "rifled cannon." It took only 30 hours of bombardment for the fort to fall into Union hands. The attack had such devastating effects on the brick fort that after the surrender, all forts like Pulaski were considered obsolete.

ℹ️ **Tybee hasn't had a major hit from a hurricane in more than 100 years. The most damaging hurricane occurred August 27, 1881. It landed with a massive storm surge that covered the island and destroyed nearly every structure in its path.**

Following the war, Tybee turned its attention toward tourism. In its early years, Tybee was reached by boat, a voyage that could take two hours from Savannah. That changed in 1887 with the construction of a rail line through the marsh and over various creeks and rivers between the island and the mainland. That same year Tybee was officially incorporated as Ocean City. A year later it was changed to Tybee, only to be changed in 1929 to Savannah Beach. It wasn't until many decades later, in the early 1970s, that it became Tybee again. A reference today to Savannah Beach is likely to raise the locals' dander.

Day-trippers, as they were known, would come on the train, rent bathing suits from a local hotel, and spend the day at the beach. Some would arrive later in the day to dance to Big Band music supplied by outfits playing at one of the island's biggest attractions: the Tybrisa Pier. When the Tybee

Road opened in 1923, the stream of people coming to the island continued to grow. In a column that ran in the local newspaper in 1931, E. B. Izlar reflected about the "good old days" on Tybee. "The decline of mosquitoes, of picnickers, of bars and of yardage in women's bathing suits constitute the most radical changes in reviewing the past thirty years on Tybee Island," the column stated. "Today, Mr. Izlar declares that mosquitoes, except in the dense wooded places, are rare, and he bears out his statement by remarking that he has only seen three this season."

Reminiscing on the bathing suits of the early years, Mr. Izlar lamented the time when suits were sold for $2.50 to $4 a dozen (except, of course, when special suits for women were as high as $12 a dozen) in the days when women "wrapped up" to cover everything. As for bars, Mr. Izlar said that though they abounded in bygone days, there was little disorder—only friendly fights. "There was not even need for a jail in those days."

While the islanders focused on tourism, the U.S. War Department began construction of Fort Screven on the north end of the island. The fort was made up of seven gun batteries that ended up being fired only for practice, not for war. During World War I, part of the Eighth Infantry Regiment was assigned to Fort Screven. One of its commanders was Lt. Col. George C. Marshall, who after leaving Tybee became a five-star general and served as secretary of state, secretary of defense, and author of the Marshall Plan for rebuilding western Europe after World War II.

In the meantime, Savannahians were beginning to build houses at the beach for the summer months. The ocean breezes would give them relief from the city's sweltering summer heat. Many of these magnificent old beach homes can still be found on the island today, and many are still owned by descendents of family members who were the original owners. Current resident Walter Parker recalls how empty the island was in those days. "I can remember in the winter you could go for several blocks before you saw a light on," said Parker. "No one lived here year-round."

Eventually, that began to change, and Tybee's year-round population slowly grew. However, several factors—beach erosion, pollution, the closing of Fort Screven— resulted in several years of decline on the island beginning in the 1940s. Residents cultivated an outlaw attitude during this era by engaging in back-room gambling and illegal drinking, which got the attention of the news media. It also helped fuel the island's reputation in some circles as Georgia's unruly stepchild. Eventually, local and state law enforcement agencies cracked down to curb Tybee's wanton ways. The pollution, gambling, and other sins were eventually cleaned up, and Tybee once again became a popular tourist spot.

Since 1980 or so, the island's year-round population has been on the rise to its current level of around 4,000. Today, locals who have called Tybee home for generations live among a thriving community of artists and writers, most of whom migrated during the 1980s. There are also many retirees whose hometowns are places far away from Tybee. Every socioeconomic group is represented, from the poor to the very wealthy.

"I think Tybee is an easy place to live," said Parker. "I think it has more than its share of characters . . . But it has a small community feeling and most want it to stay that way."

GETTING HERE, GETTING AROUND

Tybee is about 18 miles east of Savannah. There is only one road to get you there: US 80. You can reach it from the Historic Downtown by heading east on Bay Street. In less than a mile, it will run into President Street, then President Street Extension. After about 3 miles, it merges with US 80 East. From Midtown, hop on Victory Drive and head east—you are also on US 80 East.

After entering Tybee, US 80 turns into Butler Avenue, the community's main street, which will take you past hotels, beach houses, and the small downtown area. You will know US 80 has become Butler Avenue after going around a fairly sharp curve that keeps you from driving into the ocean. You can't miss it. Follow Butler a mile or so farther into downtown, and you will be deposited in a city parking lot next to the pier.

Most places you need to visit on Tybee should be accessible from this main strip. Near the beginning of Butler Avenue, streets running east and west are numbered, starting with 1st Street at the northern end of the city and ending with 19th Street at the southern end. These are crossed by north- and south-running streets that are named and numbered, starting with Butler Avenue closest to the beach and ending with 6th Avenue.

i Geologically speaking, Tybee is very young—only about 1,000 years old. Savannah's other islands, including Wilmington and Skidaway, are more than 40,000 years old.

If you are going to spend the day at the beach on Tybee, you will have to pay for parking from 8 a.m. until 8 p.m. Parking today at Tybee has gone high tech, or at least as high tech as you can get at Tybee. There are pay-and-display meters so you can purchase time, print out a receipt, and display it on the dash of your car. The rates are $1.50 an hour and you can purchase up to three days worth of parking with a credit card on these machines. If you receive a parking citation, you may pay in person at City Hall, over the phone by calling (912) 786-4573, ext. 102, or online by clicking the Online Payments button at www.cityoftybee.org. If you're experiencing problems with a meter or pay station, or if you need to dispute a ticket, call Parking Services at (912) 786-4573, ext. 135. The streets closest to the beach are metered at $1 an hour, and all meters require quarters.

The city operates three parking lots, all accessible from Butler Avenue: at the end of Tybrisa (which used to be 16th Street), 14th Street, and at North Beach. The parking lots, and the streetside spaces near them, also are equipped with pay-and-display meters. Officially, parking is patrolled every day year-round from 8 a.m. until 8 p.m. In reality, and in typical Tybee fashion, it's a more practical system: starting up about 8-ish or 9-ish and depending on the weather or crowds. If it's raining or the crowds are light, the parking enforcers may knock off early, but be aware that you're taking a gamble if you assume they have. Like the Savannah authorities, the parking enforcers are very generous when doling out tickets and are fairly vigilant. So if you don't want an expensive ticket, don't leave your meter expired. It usually isn't too much trouble finding parking on Tybee, except for a few very busy weekends. Planning a longer stay? Parking stickers that allow you to park in all lots and at all meters without further payment are available. Property owners get them free; other frequent visitors buy them from Tybee City Hall for $100 a year. Tybee's parking services can be reached at (912) 786-4573, ext. 121, with office hours beginning at 9 a.m.

ACCOMMODATIONS

Affordable hotel rooms, sprawling beach houses, and ocean-view condos are some of the choices you'll find when searching for accommodations on Tybee Island. Tybee is known as a family beach, so a lot of what is available is geared toward those lugging not only beach chairs but high chairs as well. Regardless of where you land, more likely than not you'll be within comfortable walking distance of the beach.

Tybee's season runs typically from the middle of April through the middle of September. After that, the streets become less crowded and rates go down. Stay during the peak season, especially on weekends, and the rates are going to be higher. A few weekends, including July 4, are especially busy. Weekend hotel rates are considerably higher than weekday rates.

Tybee's accommodations scene is very atypical. There's a healthy scattering of hotels, but few in the way of major national chains and none that you would consider truly upscale. (In fact, lots of them are rather shabby, although you'd never guess it from their rates.) Nor is development moving in that direction. When a developer breaks ground on Tybee these days, chances are that developer is building condos. These run the gamut from strictly investment properties to purely private residences, but it's safe to say the tourist housing market on the island is skewing increasingly to condo rentals. At least one motel has converted to condos, in fact.

While we list some Realtors who can help land you in a beach house and condo, some owners handle property rental on their own. Most simply post a FOR RENT sign in the front yard—when you're in town, pick one of these places that you like and jot down the number for future reference. Some private owners also put listings in the *Savannah Morning News* (see our Media chapter for more information), so check there as well. Our listings begin with hotels and motels, we throw in a couple of bed-and-breakfasts, then move on to rentals. Note that Tybee's rental market for houses and condos, just like its real-estate market, is booming—so rates are volatile and could well climb between this writing and your reading.

Price Code

Our price code is designed to make it easier for you to gauge the cost of staying at one of Tybee's hotels, motels, or bed-and-breakfasts. The dollar sign indicates the average cost for a one-night stay for two adults during peak season, typically mid-April through mid-September. Weekends cost more.

$..................less than $50
$$ ....$50 to $100
$$$ ....$100 to $150
$$$$ ....more than $150

Hotels and Motels

There are only a handful of middle-class hotels and motels to choose from on the island. Most are smaller chains with names you will recognize and offer standard, sometimes modest accommodations. In all honesty, the majority of the few hotels on Tybee are plain, and far from luxurious. In other words, the term *renovation* might be defined as new bedspreads and curtains at Tybee,

so don't expect the Ritz here. The ones we list have nonsmoking and wheelchair-accessible rooms and come with free parking. Although Tybee is outside Savannah, it shares area code 912.

BEST WESTERN DUNES INN $$–$$$$
1409 Butler Ave.
(912) 786-4591, (888) 678-0763
The Best Western Dunes Inn is across the street from the beach and a block or so away from Tybee's small-town shopping district, where you can find everything from a new swimsuit to suntan lotion. This motel offers spacious rooms comfortably furnished with two double beds or one king-size bed. Some have balconies overlooking the pool, and a few kitchenettes are also available. Complimentary coffee is served every morning.

DESOTO BEACH HOTEL $$$–$$$$
212 Butler Ave.
(912) 786-4542 (877) 786-4542
www.desotobeachhotel.com
The only thing old about this place is the name, which once served one of Tybee's oldest hotels. Completely renovated in 2010, this is a delightful place to stay with freshly painted rooms, upgraded linens and furniture, and rooms that range from two bedrooms with queen-size beds, oversized balconies, and kitchenettes (Hernando DeSoto Suite) to deluxe rooms with two queen-size beds. The old is gone, but on this narrow sliver of land between condo developments, careful design has led to 37 rooms, most of which are technically ocean view and a few of which have a magnificent view. The hotel is on the ocean side of Butler, and it is one of the first motels or hotels you will encounter when driving onto the island. There's an oceanfront pool and a game room

that's partially open to the elements. Rates in season range from $130 to $210.

HOWARD JOHNSON
ADMIRAL'S INN $$$–$$$$
1501 Butler Ave.
(912) 786-0700, (800) 793-7716
A nice, two-story hotel, Admiral's Inn has 41 spacious rooms, a swimming pool, and is across the street from the ocean. The standard room comes with two queen-size beds, but if you need a little more space, deluxe king rooms with sitting areas are available. For those coming to Tybee after tying the knot, there is also a bridal suite. The hotel's meeting room holds up to 75 people.

Computer, phone/fax, and copy service are available for those unfortunate souls who have to work while at the beach. The hotel is within comfortable walking distance to "downtown Tybee."

OCEAN PLAZA BEACH
RESORT $$–$$$$
15th Street and Ocean Front
(912) 786-7664, (800) 215-6370
www.oceanplaza.com
This is Tybee's largest hotel, with 215 rooms, suites, and nearby luxury condos at the Brass Rail (offered under the umbrella of the Ocean Plaza). There are two swimming pools on property at the Ocean Plaza. It is also one of the few properties that offer direct room views of the ocean. Head out your door, walk through a parking lot, and within a few steps you are on the sand. Located on the southern end of the island, there are actually three buildings at Ocean Plaza, including two four-story structures facing the ocean. The rooms are spacious and decorated in bright pastel colors. All oceanfront rooms have balconies overlooking the Atlantic.

Many room options are available, including a single room with a king-size bed, one-room suites with queen-size beds, and two-room suites with one king-size and one double bed. Kitchenettes are also available. Regardless of the room type, all come with a choice of poolside or ocean-view location. Rollaway beds can be rented for $10, and cribs cost $5. The Ocean Plaza offers free HBO and a conference center. The Dolphin Reef Restaurant, bridging two of the motel buildings, serves breakfast, lunch, and dinner seven days a week.

RIVER'S END CAMPGROUND AND
R.V. PARK $
915 Polk St.
(912) 786-5518, (800) 786-1016
www.cityoftybee.org/campground.aspx
This little campground is full of charm and has great access to the beach. The City of Tybee Island bought the park in 2006 to preserve its use as a campground, fearful of impending condo development. Aside from the unusual ownership arrangement, this is a standard campground. There are close to 100 RV sites with water and electric and 18 primitive campgrounds. Among the amenities are a swimming pool, air-conditioned bath houses, cable, Wi-Fi, a laundry, and similar touches. Rates start at $29 a night for the primitive campsites, and go up to $45 for the most utility-rich RV sites. Rates are cheaper by the week, and even cheaper by the month. The campground stays pretty busy, so book early.

SAND CASTLE INN $$–$$$
1402 Butler Ave.
(912) 786-4576, (866) GA-BEACH
The Sand Castle Inn is within walking distance to Tybee's "downtown." It is on the

beach side of Butler Avenue—Tybee's main thoroughfare. The motel offers a pool and free continental breakfast each morning. The rooms are fresh, with bright colored bedspreads and white walls. Although just a short stroll to the beach, none of the rooms have ocean views.

Bed-and-Breakfast

THE LIGHTHOUSE INN $$$$
16 Meddin Dr.
(912) 786-0901, (866) 786-0901
www.tybeebb.com
Susie Morris and her husband, Stuart Liles, opened this charming B&B in the fall of 2000 in a circa-1910 home they have restored. It features three fully decorated guest rooms and baths, as well as a front porch for relaxing. The couple lives on the ground floor. The location is close to the north beach (a less-developed segment of Tybee's beaches) and the lighthouse (as the name no doubt cued you). The North Beach Grill is also close by, and beach access is just a few short steps away.

Rentals

TYBEE BEACH VACATION RENTALS, INC.
Solomon Properties
211 Butler Ave.
(912) 786-0100, (800) 967-4433
www.renttybee.com
Solomon Properties is a local company of Realtors with several private condos and homes for rent. Their offices are on the right after you round the bend (US 80/Butler Avenue) heading toward downtown Tybee. Like all the rental agencies listed here, inside the offices are lists of properties, pictures, rates, and other valuable information. The rental

rates seem outrageous compared with what they were a few years ago—$1,700 a week for a two-bedroom house that is near but not on the beach was a landlord's dream in, say, 1997. It's a reality today.

TYBEE COTTAGES
P.O. Box 1226
Tybee Island, GA 31328-1226
(912) 786-6746
Tybee residents Jim and Becky Heflin represent several appealing rental properties at Tybee Island. From quaint two-bedroom cottages decorated with typical brightly colored, Caribbean type furnishings to two-story classic Tybee beach houses with their white-slat woodwork and expansive porches, most properties are located right on the beach or come with a pool, and each is supplied with all the conveniences you'll need for a pleasant stay: i.e., linens, dishes, cookware, and washer/dryer. Ideal for wedding parties and groups, there are several properties that are also pet friendly (for a small deposit). All properties can be viewed on their website.

TYBEE ISLAND REALTY
1016 First St.
(912) 786-7070, (800) 379-2298
www.tybeeislandrealty.com
John and Judy O'Neill, a husband-and-wife team, own this real-estate company, which also deals with several private rentals. You can stop in at the offices, located on your right a mile or so after crossing Lazaretto Creek Bridge into town, and pick up one of their rental brochures. Again, these give all the information you need: pictures of available properties, price ranges, and lists of amenities. When we stopped by, they had many listings—everything from oceanfront

condos for $1,175 per week to beachfront homes that sleep 14 for $2,500-plus a week. Many rentals were also available nightly.

TYBEE ISLAND RENTALS, INC.
US 80 and Second Avenue, Savannah
Tybee Island
(912) 786-4034, (800) 476-0807
www.tybeeislandrentals.com

Beach homes, condos, and cottages of all shapes and sizes can be rented from Tybee Island Rentals. Check out the varied selection at their offices, located about 2 miles past the bridge onto Tybee. If you are looking for a romantic getaway for two or a place to bring the whole family for a week at the beach, you should be able to find something that suits your needs. Choices include everything from a five-bedroom, six-bath home overlooking the ocean for $2,200 a week to a one-bedroom efficiency for $375. Remember that rates are seasonal.

RESTAURANTS

Tybee's restaurant scene is evolving. Locals don't have to be that old to remember when most eateries were burger and ice-cream joints where you could come in your bathing suit, and where you were likely to find the door locked shortly after Labor Day. Those places are still there, but they have been joined by a few reasonably priced family restaurants. One thing you won't find (and another personification of Tybee's individuality) is much in the way of fast-food franchises—with the exception of an Arby's. A burger joint on Tybee would be named something like Earl's instead of McDonald's.

Price Code

The price code listed below is based on the cost of an average meal for two, excluding drinks, dessert, or tip. Of course, prices vary to either extreme on most menus and you can tip the bill over into the next category.

$.................less than $30
$$ ....$30 to $50
$$$ ....more than $50

BREAKFAST CLUB $
1500 Butler Ave.
(912) 786-5984
www.tybeeisland.com/dining/brclub/
Default.htm

If you want to get a table at the Breakfast Club without waiting in line, you may have to get up a little early, especially during the summer months. Lines start forming outside this very popular eatery about 7 a.m. on weekends. During the week, sleep in much past 8:30 a.m., and you will most likely find yourself waiting outside with a handful of other people. Regardless, it is worth the wait. As the line (which moves fast) attests, this diner on the southern end of the island near downtown is one of Tybee's best. For more than 20 years, members of the Farrow family have been serving up breakfast specialties like chorizo con huevos (flour tortillas, sausage, sharp cheese, salsa, and sour cream) and pecan waffles, which are light and crunchy and the talk of the beach. For $8.95 you can get the surf and turf omelet, complete with fresh rib eye and local shrimp with garlic butter. While omelets are a menu favorite, you will also find many other choices, from grits to burgers. Chef Jodee Sadowsky, who purchased the diner from his mother, Helen Farrow, was named one of North America's 101 best cooks in

Cooking Across America. After the season, when the locals reclaim the island, you'll find them sitting here, sharing the gossip. Warning: This place doesn't look like much but don't let that mislead you. Hours are 7 a.m. to 1 p.m. daily, year-round.

THE CRAB SHACK $$
40 Estill Hammock Rd.
(912) 786-9857
www.thecrabshack.com

Going to the Crab Shack is as much about atmosphere as it is about seafood. Located in Chimney Creek, a hamlet off US 80 just past the Lazaretto Creek Bridge (you can't miss the signs), the Crab Shack's motto is, "Where the Elite Eat in Their Bare Feet." What started as a small, rustic restaurant on the marsh has grown into a giant tourist favorite. Now they've even added a licensed live alligator habitat. While munching on giant servings of seafood delicacies such as Georgia blue crab, snow crab, golden crab, Alaskan king crab, shrimp, and oysters, you can sit out on the huge porch overlooking the marsh. Oak trees decorated with white lights give the Crab Shack a casual, relaxed, fun flair. If you want to try a local specialty, try the Lowcountry boil, which includes boiled shrimp, corn, potatoes, and sausage. As for drinks, the frozen margarita is a good choice along with the piña coladas and daiquiris. Dress is beach casual. The restaurant can handle parties of up to 150 people and boasts a separate gift shop, dubbed (what else?) the Gift Shack. Hours are noon to 10 p.m. daily, year-round.

FANNIE'S ON THE BEACH $$
1613 Strand
(912) 786-6109
www.fanniesonthebeach.com

This restaurant and outdoor bar, which commands an ocean view across a parking lot, added an upstairs outdoor deck for dining and a band on the weekend. It's open for lunch, dinner, and late night. Specialties include a shrimp burger—a concoction made of ground shrimp, sautéed onions, and celery. Quesadillas are meals, not appetizers, and include shrimp and scallop varieties. They also offer sandwiches, salads, and burgers, but the staff considers the pizzas to be the signature dish. You can get everything from the standard version to one sporting smoked salmon, capers, cream cheese, scallion, black olives, and sun-dried tomatoes. After dark, the club atmosphere comes to the fore, and the band cranks up in summer, playing for a diverse crowd. Hours are Mon through Fri, noon to 11 p.m.; noon to 2 a.m. weekends. Call for hours Oct through March.

THINGS TO DO

A vacation to Tybee Island should first be filled with lots of time for reading, shuffling about on the beach, kite flying, fishing, and of course, dining on the excellent seafood at local restaurants. The South Beach, where the most development (restaurants, shops, entertainment, etc.) and largest crowds are, and North Beach, which is more residential in nature, are your two options for hanging out on the beach. Go south for people watching, north for shelling. You're at South Beach when you park in Tybee's downtown, main-drag Strand area. North Beach parking is across from the lighthouse and behind the museum. At low tide, you can walk from one to the other, but if you miscalculate the incoming tide, it can be a long walk around.

During the season, Tybee's beaches have lifeguards. Hours and days depend on the weather and crowds. The lifeguard stands

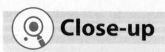 **Close-up**

Hitting the Beach with "Crawfish" Crawford

There is good news for swimmers diving into the ocean off Tybee, according to John "Crawfish" Crawford, a University of Georgia educator and expert on Tybee and its marine life. The 30 to 40 species of sharks lurking in the waters offshore probably aren't that hungry. "We have well-fed sharks here," said Crawford. "The water is full of plenty of food which they would rather eat instead of fooling with something the size of a human being."

Words to live by. Although shark attacks are so rare they are nearly unheard of on Tybee, Crawford says to reduce your risk even further by avoiding swimming during twilight hours when sharks typically feed. Also, don't use a flutter kick—to a shark it could sound like a wounded fish.

Besides sharks, beachgoers might encounter an abundance of other marine life on Tybee, according to Crawford. Some of the more common things you might come across during your day at the beach include:

- **Sandpipers**—These tiny, fleet-footed birds seen running up and down the beach are born and nest in the Arctic tundra. They fly all the way to Tybee just to engage in a little 50-yard beach dash for food.

- **Ghost Crabs**—Look near the dune line, and you might see whitish-colored crabs scurrying—then disappearing—into a hole. Besides spending their time digging their hole homes, these crabs serve as beach garbage collectors, picking up parts of dead fish and others things cluttering their front yards.

- **Jellyfish**—Several different species of jellyfish live in our waters. The cannonball variety has a brown rim around the edge, and you can't be stung by them. The sea nettle, which comes out typically in the late summer and has long wispy tentacles, is responsible for the most stings off Tybee. If you get stung, putting meat tenderizer on the sting helps ease the pain, according to Crawford.

- **Ghost Shrimp**—If you run across tiny holes just above the low-tide line, you most likely have encountered a ghost shrimp. These tiny shrimp live in a network of burrows that twist and turn in the sand and are only three-fourths of an inch in diameter. Those little brown things you see near the entrance of the hole are their droppings.

- **Sand Dollars**—These small disks are actually live animals. Many people mistakenly take them home while they are still alive, Crawford said. If you find a sand dollar on the beach and it is a greenish color on top and reddish on the bottom, it is still alive, so leave it on the beach. A white color indicates that the sand dollar has died.

- **Stingrays**—If you happen to see a stingray while swimming in the surf, don't panic—they aren't aggressive and won't bother you a bit. If you happen to be unfortunate enough to step on a stingray, however, they do consider this an attack and will sting. To avoid such a confrontation, shuffle your feet back and forth while walking in the surf. This gives them enough time to realize you are coming and head in a different direction.

- **Sea Turtle Nests**—Sea turtles regularly nest on Tybee Island. The city's public works department patrols the beaches for the nests to mark them with wire so people don't run over them. If you do come across a nest, don't disturb it.

are clustered near the public parking. Early on, they're only staffed on weekends. Don't take it for granted that there's a lifeguard on duty, and even if there is, they call it a day when the crowd starts to thin. Be careful! Ocean swimming at Tybee Island can be tricky, even for the strong swimmer. Tybee is prone to riptides.

Beach regulations prohibit glass containers or cans. Dogs aren't allowed on the beach, either, and you'll get a ticket if you bring one. The beach is patrolled by officers in shorts and T-shirts, either walking or on all-terrain vehicles.

Vendors on the beach rent canvas rafts, umbrellas, boogie boards, and the like.

FORT PULASKI NATIONAL MONUMENT
US 80 East
(912) 786-5787
Explore a 19th-century fort from top to bottom at Fort Pulaski. Located about 15 miles outside Savannah on the way to Tybee, the fort is remarkably preserved and gives a fascinating glimpse into coastal warfare. The fort was completed in 1847 and considered the ultimate defense system of its day. Audio stations provide information on the fort's pivotal role in the Civil War and how it changed defense strategy worldwide after an attack by Union forces. The 5,600-acre monument also provides picnic areas, a boat ramp, and nature trails, along with panoramic views of the Atlantic Ocean and scenic salt marshes. Bring your camera—this is one of the area's most photogenic spots. Expect to see abundant wildlife such as white-tailed deer that roam freely on the island, and alligators, turtles, and small marine life that inhabit the moat. There are numerous trails so bring a picnic if you're prone. The fort is open from 9 a.m. to 7 p.m. but closes two hours earlier

in the off season (Sept to May). The cost is $3, and the admission fee is good for up to six days of visitation. Children age 16 and younger enter free. There are group rates for commercial vehicles: one to six passengers, $25.

LAZARETTO CREEK MARINA
US 80 East, just across Lazaretto
Creek Bridge
(912) 786-5848, (800) 242-0166
www.tybeedolphins.com
You'll be thrilled to see wildlife up close on Captain Mike's dolphin tours at Lazaretto Creek Marina. There are also fishing, diving, and sunset cruises. Dolphin tours are $15 per adult and $8 per child (12 and under); offshore fishing ranges from $250 to $850, depending on the length of the trip. Boats are not wheelchair accessible. Tours are conducive to weather and wind conditions so it's best to call and confirm.

THE TYBEE ARTS ASSOCIATION
P.O. Box 2344
Tybee Island, GA 31328
(912) 786-5920
www.tybeearts.org
This nonprofit group is dedicated to developing and promoting arts throughout the area. Besides operating the Lighthouse Gallery near Tybee Lighthouse, the organization holds exhibits and gives art classes for adults and children. Adult classes can include pottery, stained-glass making, and painting, while children's classes include wearable art, make-your-own puppet, sand and beach art, and painting and drawing, among others. Weekly classes are $60; times vary. Stay tuned for current events posted on the organization's website.

Hole-In-One

There's no golf at Tybee. There are no water parks. There is no putt-putt course here. The fun lies within your imagination. However, if you're looking for a fun place to take your family that is clean and safe, try the **Island Mini Golf** on US 80 and Walthour Road (912-898-3833; www.island-minigolf.com). There are bumper go-karts, softball and baseball batting cages, a Moonwalk bounce, a clean and refreshing arcade with snacks and hot dogs, a private party room, and an 18-hole miniature golf course!

TYBEE ISLAND BRANCH LIBRARY
Live Oak Public Library
405 Butler Ave.
(912) 786-7733

Chances are there aren't too many public libraries around with an ocean view. Granted, you have to have pretty good eyes to see it, but the view is there, along with an impressive entryway sculpture by ironwork artist Ivan Bailey. (Look up!)

Local library regulations are very kind to guests. Here, as elsewhere in Chatham County, nonresidents can buy a temporary library card with full privileges for $25, valid for nine weeks. Some paperbacks and children's books can be borrowed without a card. (Library cards are free to residents.)

The collection includes books, magazines, audiobooks, and videotapes. The branch is not large, but it has access to the library system's full collection, if you can wait for delivery.

TYBEE ISLAND LIGHTHOUSE
30 Meddin Dr.
(912) 786-5801
www.tybeelighthouse.org

Throughout history there have actually been four Tybee Island lighthouses. The original was completed in 1736, but it sat too close to the shore and was washed away during a storm. Hurricanes, fires, and even an attack by Union forces during the Civil War led to partial or complete destruction of two other stations. In 1866 the fourth Tybee lighthouse—a combination of old and new—was authorized. It used the lower 65 feet of the 1773 Tybee light as the base, then 94 more feet were stacked on top. The light, a first-order Fresnel lens, was displayed for the first time on October 1, 1867, and it has been there ever since. It is one of only two of the 15 original light stations built in Georgia that is still functioning.

Learn about the history of the lighthouse in the newly renovated facilities and take a 154-foot climb to the top for a wonderful view of the area. Hours are 9 a.m. to 5:30 p.m. daily (last ticket sold at 4:30 p.m.) except Tues, when it is closed. Closed for major holidays (St. Patrick's Day, Thanksgiving, Christmas, and New Years Day). Cost is $7 for adults, $5 for seniors, military, and children ages 6 to 14; children younger than age 6 get in free. The price includes admission to the Tybee Museum.

i The Tybee Lighthouse was one of five southeastern lighthouses featured on a set of U.S. postage stamps in June 2003.

TYBEE ISLAND MARINE SCIENCE CENTER
14th Street
(912) 786-5917
www.tybeemsc.org
Learn about Tybee's marine life at the Tybee Island Marine Science Center. Located just steps from the sand in the 14th Street parking lot, the center has aquariums with species indigenous to the area, such as starfish and jellyfish. There is a small library, a touch tank, and displays featuring such things as sharks and shells—always favorites with the kids. Don't expect anything polished or Sea Worldish, but it is informative. Beach walks are one of the most popular programs offered. Folks are invited to stroll the beach to learn about the things that inhabit it. The center staff also throws a seine net into the ocean to see what they might catch. The center is open from 10 a.m. to 5 p.m. daily, closing at noon Tues. Adults $4, children $3. Fees for "walks, talks, and treks" are $10; $9 for members. Kids ages three and younger are free.

TYBEE MUSEUM
30 Meddin Dr.
(912) 786-5801
www.tybeeisland.com
Besides learning about Tybee's history, visitors to the Tybee Museum get to walk around one of the few remaining structures at the former Fort Screven. Inside Battery Garland, one of the original seven-gun batteries built at the fort, you can learn about hundreds of years of Tybee lore—from the arrival of Native Americans to Tybee's role in the Civil War to the beginning of tourism on the island. Open from 9 a.m. to 5:30 p.m. daily (although the last ticket is sold at 4:30 p.m.); closed Tues and major holidays (note

that St. Patrick's Day is a major holiday in these parts). Admission is $7 for adults; $5 for seniors, active military, and children ages 6 to 17; children ages 6 and younger get in free. The fee includes admission to the Tybee Island Lighthouse just across the street (see listing).

TYBEE PIER AND PAVILION
16th Street
This $2.5-million wooden pier was unveiled in time for the 1996 Summer Olympics, when the yachting events were held in the area. It was built in almost the exact location of the Tybrisa, Tybee's former pier and pavilion that was known for its Big Band concerts before it burned down. Wander out to the end of the pier, and you will witness anglers casting into the ocean to see what they might catch. You can rent fishing poles and bait on the pier, and you can pick up a snack, too. The pier's pavilion, a large wooden platform you cross before heading out over the ocean, is also a popular spot for concerts. Concerts are often free (and even when they aren't, you can sit on the beach and listen in). It's also a good place for a romantic evening stroll without getting your feet wet.

i Like to collect seashells? According to expert seashell hunters, Tybee's North Beach provides the best bounty.

SHOPPING

Tybee isn't exactly a shopper's paradise, but you can buy what you need. Beach essentials and tacky souvenirs are easy to come by in a variety of stores clustered around the action. Some places merit more attention, however, and we mention a few of them here.

T. S. CHU CO.
6 Tybrisa St.
(912) 786-4561

T. S. Chu emigrated from China early last century and slept in the dunes until he got things going financially. And get them going he did. His early enterprise has grown to a prosperous local retail empire. For the most part, it's convenience stores and gas stations. But the original store remains on Tybee, a sprawling, dimly lit, and unconventional place that sells tourist junk and beach supplies near the door and lightbulbs, hammers, dishpans, and other housewares and hardware farther inside.

TYBEE MARKET
1111 Butler Ave.
(912) 786-4601

The mark of a dedicated Tybee Islander is a refusal to leave the island unless he or she absolutely has to. That makes Tybee's only grocery store (aside from numerous convenience stores) a godsend for some. It's small, and the selection is limited, but it serves the purpose. If you are whipping up a complex recipe in your vacation digs, you might have better luck in the conventional supermarkets you drove past on the suburban islands on your way out to Tybee.

REAL ESTATE

Like the Historic Downtown in Savannah, Tybee has been one of the most popular places to buy real estate in the last few years. The small-town atmosphere, along with its ideal climate and proximity to Savannah, has made this island community attractive as a year-round residence for many. However, the real estate downturn of 2009 seems to have slowed things down a lot here. Prices plummeted, and foreclosures were plentiful.

Many investors walked away with bargains. The outlook, however, is improving, and as of May 2010, homes are starting to sell again.

This interest has led to much development and a few growing pains. After a large hotel went up on the beach, a movement was started to restrict the height of all development on Tybee to avoid a resort full of high-rises. Many residents want to keep the beach community what it is—a small town by the sea.

i Wonder why the new homes here (and some of the older ones) are built so high off the ground? It leaves ample room for an open parking area under the house, but the real reason is the building codes that require lifting the finished floor out of the reach of floods.

It's difficult to identify distinct neighborhoods on Tybee. There's basically a mix of old and new all over the island. In some neighborhoods, you might find older beach houses next door to modest, one-story homes. A few doors down there could be two or three new homes or a set of two or three new town houses. Near Fort Screven or North Beach, you will find a few new housing developments that can offer large two- and sometimes three-story homes with ocean views and wraparound porches on fairly large lots. A few streets away there could be a modest home needing quite a lot of work. It's worth noting that streets often don't follow a particular pattern on Tybee; many are dirt roads that zigzag, and in some cases just stop.

Tybee's older beach homes are usually found along Butler Avenue, the city's main thoroughfare, which goes to the southern end of the island. Here the streets follow a grid pattern with the numbered streets increasing the closer you get to downtown. Again, in many blocks, there is a smattering of new homes followed by several older ones. During the last few years, many older homes have been torn down to make room for condos, townhomes, and the like. Single-family homes on the island range from around $200,000 for older, modest homes to $500,000 for new construction to the-sky's-the-limit on oceanfront. All new homes must be built several feet off the ground to prevent flooding. The realty companies listed earlier are ready to assist you with inquiries concerning the Tybee Island real-estate scene. Call for more details.

LIVING HERE

In this section we feature specific information for residents or those planning to relocate here. Topics include real estate, education, health care, and much more.

RELOCATION & REAL ESTATE

Savannah is a popular relocation destination. Retirees come here, drawn by the weather, the availability of military benefits resources, the golf. Military discharges often opt to stay. Vacationers get hooked on what they see and come back year after year, finally pulling up stakes elsewhere and putting down roots here. And, in a phenomenon we probably couldn't document but which we would vouch for after 20-plus years of anecdotal observation, people who are reared here return to live here, despite the appeals of better-paved career paths, larger cities, and lower humidity. See a Savannah girl marry a beau from college in the Northeast and then strike out for California? Sure. Give her a few years—she and that husband will be back here to raise their kids.

If you are looking to relocate yourself, you want an area that has shown up on relocation radar. It's not that you are looking to follow the rest of the migrating herd—it's just that when you look at an area with a tradition of welcoming in new populations, you find a relocation industry already in place. The banks are all going to have packets welcoming you to the community; everyone from the voter registration folks to the library is going to be versed in helping newcomers; and chances are your kid won't be the only new face to turn up in class this year.

OVERVIEW

When you are starting out on a relocation quest, the first thing you want is information—lots of it. That's what this chapter is all about, and we'll refer you to the other chapters of this book that have details of particular information to newcomers (Education, Media, etc.), but for some other sources, consider these.

**SAVANNAH AREA CHAMBER OF
  COMMERCE**
101 East Bay St.
(912) 644-6400
www.savannahchamber.com
The chamber can provide you with its standard relocation packet via mail and free of charge. No one ever accused a chamber of being excessively unbiased, but this is still a good starting point. Materials and references will largely be restricted to chamber members, but with a few exceptions that doesn't lead to major omissions. Be sure to stress, when making your request by telephone, that you are looking for relocation info, not just tourist material, since the chamber's Convention and Visitors Bureau handles tourism materials, too.

SAVANNAH MORNING NEWS
1375 Chatham Pkwy.
(912) 236-9511
www.savannahnow.com

We wouldn't even think of relocating to a town (assuming we had a choice) without reading the daily newspaper for a period of time. You could take out a mail subscription by calling the above number. The website offers essentially the full local news content of each day's paper, and it's free and available with no sign-up hassles. But with just the Web version, you miss the community flavor that goes with all the "other" stuff—wedding announcements, the neighborhood-oriented Closeup sections, and above all, the ads. (After all, if you are going to live here, don't you want a feel for where you'll be shopping? Of course, we take care of part of that for you in our Shopping chapter, but it doesn't cover such things as grocery stores.) Whichever form you choose, we recommend this information source as a reality check, since you can usually assume a daily newspaper wasn't put together with any thought of luring in visitors or new residents.

THE BASICS

Consider this section a quick community review. You can read more in our chapters covering the area overview, history, education, and health care.

When you are talking Savannah, you are essentially talking three counties and multiple municipalities. **Chatham County** (population 251,120 in 2008, spread out over 451 square miles) is the biggest one in the area, and the sixth most populous in the state of Georgia. **Savannah** is the county seat, but you'll also find incorporated communities to the east and west—**Thunderbolt, Tybee Island, Vernonburg, Pooler, Bloomingdale, Garden City.**

Effingham and Bryan Counties make up the rest of what statisticians call the Savannah SMSA, or Standard Metropolitan

Statistical Area. Both were established rural counties in their own right before becoming bedroom communities for Savannah as well. Effingham's county seat is Springfield, but the SUVs that commute into and out of Savannah are likely coming from Guyton and Rincon, for the most part. Bryan County's county seat is Pembroke, but the smaller municipality of Richmond Hill—south of Savannah's Southside—is the town you'll hear of most often.

Other counties—hey, Georgia boasts 159 counties—play a role in the local scene, too. Most prominent is **Liberty County** (county seat: Hinesville), which is home of **Fort Stewart,** to which Savannah's Hunter Army Airfield is attached in all but geography.

On the South Carolina side, essentially two counties play in the regional mix—**Beaufort County,** with its county seat of Beaufort and townships of Hilton Head Island and Bluffton; and **Jasper County,** home of Ridgeland and Hardeeville.

Hilton Head Island pioneered the concept of planned communities designed for relocating early retirees. As the island has increasingly built up, you'll find similar upscale buildings spilling onto the mainland side, where the address is Bluffton. Next in line for the advent of gated communities will be Jasper County, which currently isn't heavily developed.

A geography review seems in order for those who are relocating from other parts of the country. Not for nothing is this section of South Carolina called the **Lowcountry,** and the land doesn't get any higher when you cross the Savannah River and hit Georgia. Invest in flood insurance wherever in this region you buy, and carefully evaluate the flood risks of any property you are considering buying. Remember that Savannah

LIVING HERE

305

and environs all fall within hurricane impact zones. True, the last hurricane to really strike Savannah was David in 1979, and that was sort of a glancing blow. But Hurricane Hugo (1989) and Hurricane Floyd (1999) prompted evacuations before striking elsewhere, and the potential is there every fall.

In fact, put drainage at the top of your list of questions when looking at property. It doesn't take a particularly heavy rainfall to cause localized flooding, if it comes during a high tide when all the drainage ditches (we call them canals) are filled up with tidal water. Paving and development have increased the flood risk and drainage problems in some areas. Investigate thoroughly.

INFRASTRUCTURE BASICS

Next up for review are infrastructure issues.

Electricity in this section of Georgia is provided by **Georgia Power,** a division of Southern Company. Natural gas is a deregulated industry in Georgia, as of several years ago. The result was a glut of marketers, confusing pricing, and billing fiascoes. Things have shaken out a bit now, but as a new resident you'll find yourself choosing among providers.

By the way, when investigating a new home, review your energy system seriously. The hot, humid summers make good air-conditioning a serious quality-of-life issue. And despite the fact that there may be a

i As a new homeowner in the region, one of the first services you are going to need is pest control. Mild winters, wet weather, and lots of green spaces all add up to bugs. Most locals make their peace with them outdoors, and wage chemical warfare inside their homes.

palm tree growing outside a house, winters can include some serious cold snaps—and many older homes lack good insulation.

The city of Savannah sells water, sewer, and garbage service to its citizens, and also sells water and sewer services under contract to various developments outside its city limits. In fact, you'll find these services provided by most municipalities. If you wind up in the unincorporated areas of the county—such as the popular Islands area—you may find yourself in an area served by a private water system, septic tanks, and private garbage contractors. Outside the city of Savannah, you may also encounter areas served by volunteer or combined pro and volunteer fire departments.

Chatham County and Savannah have consolidated their police forces. The smaller municipalities still maintain their own. All you really need to know is that 911 works countywide.

Comcast Savannah is basically Savannah's answer to television cable service and offers phone and Internet service as well (www.comcast.com).

Does your new home involve construction or remodeling? Unless you are from some very isolated portion of the country, you're familiar with the idea and basic process of getting building permits. If your tastes have led you to the Historic District, be aware that the renovation permitting process can be extremely exacting—yes, you may find yourself (or your architect) having to defend the style of door handles you choose.

SAVANNAH NEIGHBORHOODS

We've been amazed at what real-estate prices have done in the last few years here. The beach was once a bargain (unbelievable but true); not anymore. Owning a home in the Historic District takes serious money and has for years. And a curse of trendiness sometimes descends on a neighborhood, sending prices skyrocketing all out of reason, as has happened in Ardsley Park, where circa-1930s and '40s bungalows command a quarter of a million dollars. Still, you can find livable selections. A well-maintained 1960s ranch home with three bedrooms and two baths can be had on the Southside for less than $150,000, and new construction of smaller homes on freshly opened-up sections of the southwest portion of the county are marketed for $160,000.

Historic District

The Historic District is a miniature city within a city. Inside the 2.5-square-mile area you will find restaurants, churches, antiques shops, museums, banks, government buildings, art galleries, and even some wildlife—that is, if you count the hundreds of squirrels who call the many squares and parks home. (They'll practically eat out of your hands!)

Of course, there are also the houses. Hundreds of homes painstakingly restored to their original 19th-century splendor fill the area. Within a few steps in the Historic District, you are apt to encounter wrought-iron balconies, brick courtyards, and other architectural delights such as historic downspouts shaped like dolphins that empty water into the street.

In addition to being a neighborhood, this is also a tourist attraction. Be aware that this is, or could become, a drawback of sorts: slow-moving and loud tour buses that the city does not regulate heavily; onstreet parking problems; walking tours that currently are at daggers-drawn with some irate residents; and so on. The charms outweigh

the drawbacks, though (although we do admit to being taken aback, when we lived downtown, to people who would walk up to our windows and peek in as if the living room were an attraction).

The Historic District is also an area of great diversity. Some of Savannah's wealthiest and oldest families live a door or two away from art students who came to town from California or Ohio or Asia. In the Beach Institute area on the eastern edge of the district, many long-standing African-American families raise their children in homes that have been in the family for generations.

i Residents of the Historic Downtown can apply for inexpensive parking stickers, which allow them to park their vehicles at meters near their homes without getting tickets. Everyone, residents and guests alike, however, needs to watch out for the posted weekly sweeping zone times, when parking is prohibited so the city street sweepers can do their job.

The stock of run-down homes in need of renovation has fallen in the main district, although there are still fixer-uppers in the Victorian District and other historic areas outside the traditional "landmark" Historic District. Don't expect to find anything renovated for less than $250,000, although you may find some bargains in new condos, townhomes, or downtown lofts. The same housing market slowdown that has hit elsewhere in the country began affecting this area, too. Look for prices to correct to more realistic levels.

A good dose of "buyer beware" is called for when buying a historic home. Antique mantels are adorable; antique plumbing and wiring are not. If you are not familiar with the mixed blessing that comes with being the keeper of historic architecture, make sure you seek out expert advice about things like lead paint, fire escapes, and the like. And if you plan renovations of your own, any changes visible from the street will be under the watchful eye of the Historic Review Board.

The Victorian District

Just south of the Historic District lies the Victorian District, roughly bounded by Victory Drive, Gwinnett Street, Martin Luther King Jr. Boulevard, and East Broad Street. Here you will find the Victorian ladies of architecture—two- and three-story wooden houses with porches and gothic touches.

There's still renovation work to be done here, and gentrification is an active struggle here as well. Homeowners also confront the climate—Savannah's heat and humidity are a challenge to any paint job ever painted. The result is spotty: gorgeous homes next to boarded-up hulks, blocks that look homeless next to blocks that look pristine.

Some of these homes have as neighbors parts of the campus of Savannah College of Art and Design, which has spread beyond its Historic District roots to the Victorian District and even to surrounding industrial neighborhoods.

Starland

Once called "a cozy artists' neighborhood," this southernmost section of the Victorian District had not seen much in the way of restoration until a handful of visionaries began rebuilding the blighted area into a diverse and friendly mix of residence and business. The name comes from an old dairy plant in the area. Now, there are artists galore and it's become one of the city's most hip places to live and work.

Today you'll find the area still fairly early in the regeneration stages, with much of the work done by energetic sweat-investors rather than banks. There's a coffee shop, a dog park, art galleries (including a vet's office that sells art), and an eclectic feel of community.

If you are looking to buy here, come ready to do your own work—the stock of redone housing isn't large yet. But we suspect that to most Starland residents, that's sort of the point.

Southside/Midtown

Ardsley Park

Ardsley Park is Savannah's original suburb. Laid out in 1911, the development is south of the Historic District and the Victorian District in what Savannahians call Midtown. Although it was designed as a single residential subdivision, throughout the years it has grown to include a large area loosely bounded by Victory Drive on the north, Columbus Drive on the south, Bull Street on the west, and Waters Avenue on the east. Ardsley Park offers wide, tree-filled streets with many sizes and styles of older homes. Drive around and you will see large four- or five-bedroom mansions with elegant entrances, sunporches, and several fireplaces selling for $500,000 and higher. In other blocks, couples with young children live in very nice Craftsman-style bungalows with big yards. Because the area appeals to such a wide section of the community—from professionals to young families—it is a popular place to buy. In fact, as mentioned before, it is in the midst of the temporary curse of being trendy.

Looking in this neighborhood? Watch for flood-prone areas. Also, massive drainage improvement projects, ongoing for at least two years, have raised concerns about foundation damage near drilling sites. Also, don't invest without checking the after-work parking situation. Many of the bungalows either lack garages or carports, or else had them converted to living space—which means competition for street parking in some blocks is downright cutthroat. Columbus, Washington, and 52nd Streets have become fairly heavily traveled east-west routes.

An additional note: Across Waters Avenue and for several blocks behind the city's major Daffin Park is a neighborhood called Parkside, where you'll find much the same types of homes at, at least for the moment, slightly lower prices.

Gordonston

Gordonston is a small, charming neighborhood nestled into Savannah's eastside. It is a popular spot for many local professionals including professors and others working in education.

Bordered by Skidaway Road, Gwinnett Street, and Pennsylvania Avenue, it was developed in the 1920s by the brother of Juliette Gordon Low, the founder of the Girl Scouts, on property that was once part of the family farm. In some ways, it is like a miniature Ardsley Park. Similar to its bigger cousin, throughout the development you will find tree-lined streets filled with a variety of older homes on large properties with front yards and backyards. Home styles include bungalows, cottages, and large mansions, and they tend to be less expensive than those in Ardsley Park. First-time home buyers might be able to find a two- or three-bedroom bungalow for around $200,000,

while someone needing more space could find a large three- or four-bedroom home for $50,000 more.

Windsor Forest

When the city began suburban sprawl in earnest during the 1960s, south was the direction and Windsor Forest was the place. Windsor Forest is now a sprawl of neighborhoods between Savannah's malls that still reflect the look of the '60s, even after all these years. Here are classic American suburbs—ranch-style homes, split-levels, two-car garages, backyard barbecues, and so on. You can find virtually any price range here, even tony marshfront property, but it's a decidedly middle-class enclave. Here, you'll find your biggest, most elaborate grocery stores, your movie theaters, and on the nearby commercial arteries, the car dealerships and the fast-food franchises.

Georgetown

Although Georgetown debuted in 1974 on open land most Savannahians consider south of the Southside, you will still find homes going up there. More than 1,600 homes have been built throughout the development, located off the far southern reaches of Abercorn Street on King George Boulevard. There are nine subdivisions in total in the community offering a variety of home styles and prices. First-time home buyers should be able to find a two-bedroom home in Georgetown for around $140,000. Others wanting to move up to a larger house with many amenities like gourmet kitchens, Corian countertops, and hardwood floors will be able to find what they are looking for in Georgetown for $250,000 and up. There's also a pool and amenities center. Don't buy here without checking out the afternoon commute from Savannah, as this is an infamously congested route. Depending on where you're from, that traffic will either strike you as no big deal or a disaster.

Islands

The Islands area covers a lot of ground. Places such as Dutch Island and Skidaway Island, home of the Landings, are high end and exclusive (we mean that literally: They have gates). Islands such as Wilmington, Whitemarsh, and Talahi are more standard suburbia, and people who don't live there can't tell where one island ends and another begins. Tybee Island, the only one of the islands that actually feels like an island, covers a wide range of incomes and is sort of a world unto itself. (In fact, it has its own chapter in this book.)

Dutch Island

Dutch Island, an exclusive, gated enclave 20 minutes from downtown Savannah, is a popular choice for young professionals or those looking to move up to a larger home. The first neighborhoods on the island opened up in the early 1980s. Today it is home to about 300 families and is expected to reach its maximum capacity of 500 homes within the next few years. Spacious homes with pristine lawns and traditional architecture can be found throughout Dutch Island. Home sizes range from 2,400 square feet up to 12,000 square feet, while prices go from $600,000 to "the sky's the limit."

Providence Plantation is the island's newest neighborhood. Half-acre lots start at $45,000, and homes begin at $225,000. Gourmet kitchens, hardwood floors, screened porches, and fireplaces are just some of the many amenities available. There is also a pool, playground, and lagoons stocked with fish for anglers. There are no recreation fees charged to use these facilities.

Isle of Hope

This peninsula in southeast Chatham County was an early summer resort for tourists. Situated with the Herb River on the west and the Skidaway River on the east, the community is one of Savannah's most picturesque. Beautiful old cottages with white picket fences and massive oak trees in the front yards overlook the waterways, while newer, typically suburban, homes scatter throughout other neighborhoods. The very old and very new mix together nicely.

There is a small-town feel even though large developments and the hustle of Savannah are just 20 minutes away. Longtime residents live on Isle of Hope as well as young families and professionals. Home prices vary from modest, older two-bedroom bungalows around $200,000 to new three- and four-bedroom homes with all the amenities for $350,000 or more. The beautiful waterfront mansions on Bluff Drive are the stuff dreams are made of, and when one goes on the market, expect a multimillion-dollar price tag.

Long Point

More than 130 new homes have been built since 1992 at this popular Whitemarsh Island development. Conveniently located on Johnny Mercer Boulevard, it comfortably puts homeowners a short, 20-minute drive away from downtown or the Southside. Home prices start around $450,000 and climb to great heights for waterfront property and include many amenities like hardwood floors, cathedral ceilings, gourmet kitchens, and more. Styles differ throughout the development from sprawling single-story brick homes with circular drives to two-story stuccos with large front porches. Wide streets circulate through the community, and there is a guard gate that is typically occupied during the evening hours. According to local real-estate agents, when the most recent section of interior and lagoon lots opened at Long Point, 25 were sold within the first 60 days.

The Landings on Skidaway Island

Spend any time in Savannah and no doubt you will hear someone refer to "the Landings." This massive gated community takes up approximately 4,450 acres on Skidaway Island and is considered among Savannah's most prestigious developments. Started in 1972, the Landings is currently home to 6,500 residents from 45 states and 15 foreign countries. Since debuting more than 30 years ago, four phases have been built at the Landings, providing a diversity of architectural styles in a variety of prices ranging from the high $200s-plus to $1 million-plus. In Midpoint, one area of the development, you will find colonial, Federal, and Southern Lowcountry homes, while traditional, ranch-style wooden homes can be found elsewhere. Granite countertops, custom cabinets, hardwood floors, cathedral ceilings, terraces, and bay windows are just some of the many amenities available in homes at the Landings.

All the homes are on nicely landscaped lots that are often filled with trees, giving the feeling that you're living in the country, not a development with thousands of homes. The Landings' other main selling points include 6 golf courses, designed by such golfing luminaries as Arnold Palmer and Tom Fazio; 34 tennis courts; 2 marinas; and a yacht club. At the Oakridge Fitness Center there is a pool, plus fitness and exercise rooms. At the Franklin Creek Activity Center, there is a pro shop, clubhouse, 25-meter pool with hydro-spa, and a snack bar. Membership fees are required to use the various facilities.

Although all the original lots have been sold, there are usually about 100 listings, including resale homes and home sites, available at any one time, according to the Landings. Many interested people purchase a lot a few years before retirement in anticipation of eventually building a home. A more recent trend for a community made up so heavily of out-of-state retirees is the interest of affluent families already living in the area. All development at the Landings is closely monitored and must be approved by the Architectural Review Board. A number of restrictive covenants apply.

i There are dozens of neighborhood associations in Savannah. To find out information about a neighborhood group you are interested in, call the city of Savannah's Community Services Department at (912) 651-6520.

West Chatham

Southbridge

Southbridge is a 1,100-acre planned community 8 miles west of the Historic Downtown. Developed by Hall Development of Myrtle Beach, South Carolina, it is the first community of its size to open in West Chatham.

More than 500 families, including a mix of retired residents, young families, and professionals, have moved to Southbridge since its opening in 1987. As its literature explains, Southbridge is "a residential golf community blending Southern tradition with the amenities of a country club." Traditional Southern architecture is the development's hallmark. Drive around the neatly landscaped neighborhoods and you will see classic Georgian- and Federal-style wooden, brick, and stucco homes nestled among trees or along fairways on the golf course. Inside are many extras including modern kitchens, high ceilings, parquet floors, formal dining rooms, fireplaces, and breakfast nooks.

Two-, three-, or four-bedroom home options are available from roughly 1,600 to 2,400 square feet; prices range from $275,000 to $600,000. One of the latest additions to the development is Steeple Run, offering three-bedroom town houses of roughly 2,000 square feet. These run from $265,000 to $280,000 and include such features as vaulted ceilings, hardwood floors, and skylights. If you prefer, you can purchase a lot for $30,000 to $100,000 and have a home built to your specifications. You pick the home style, wallpaper, where you want it on the lot, and the builders do the rest. The developers added golf course condos and large duplexes they call "villas" in 1999.

Golf architect Rees Jones designed Southbridge's 18-hole course, which is rated one of Georgia's 25 best courses by *Golfweek* magazine. The semiprivate Southbridge Golf Club includes a 6,000-square-foot clubhouse with a pro shop, dining room, and lounge. Besides golf, there is the Southbridge Racquet and Swim Club, featuring 12 clay tennis courts, 2 hard courts, a swimming pool, and spa. Membership dues are required to use these facilities.

Godley Station

In the spring of 1999, construction began on the first homes in this planned unit, mixed-use development. It turned into an almost "instant community," with a growing population and adjacent "big box" retail all well established by 2001. Today it's an example of geometric growth. Remember the old adage about "retail follows rooftops"? This massive tract is near the Savannah International Airport and just off I-95. As predicted, this has been the major new direction for suburban expansion in Chatham County. The neighborhoods here are heavily pitched to families and have a strong sense of traditional community. The residential section, which lies partly in Savannah and partly in the West Chatham municipality of Pooler, has protective covenants, sidewalks, and community amenities such as a pool and clubhouse.

Westbrook

This new gated community in western Chatham County began home construction in mid-2001. It is part of a larger development known as Savannah Quarters, where price points start at $140,000. Westbrook, however, is clearly the upscale part of the new development, with starting prices closer to $500,000.

This community may be unique because it tore up one designer golf course and put in another. A Robert Cupp course went in first. Then, Medallist Developments assumed full ownership of the development. Golfer Greg Norman is behind Medallist, and it was decided to replace the existing two-year-old course with one of Norman's design.

Other Westside

New residential development is booming around the West Chatham municipalities of Pooler and Bloomingdale. These tend to be smaller subdivisions, not the massive planned developments like those outlined earlier—solid, middle-class homes for folks who are willing to drive a bit to get out of the city. Many of these include starter homes in the $150,000 range. It is here you'll find national homebuilders like Centex and D.R. Horton competing in what was previously pretty much a local-builders environment.

But don't get the idea that these municipalities began with these neighborhoods. These fiercely independent little communities have been around for years, housing the blue-collar workforce for the industries of Chatham County (which are clustered toward the west) and the remnants of the county's agricultural population. If you are looking to buy acreage, this is about your only remaining option in Chatham County, and you're probably too late.

Outside the County

Savannah has developed its own commuter culture as well, with people driving into Savannah from bedroom communities in adjacent Richmond Hill (Bryan County) to the south, and Rincon, Guyton, and Springfield to the west in neighboring Effingham County. Here, you'll find typical suburbia, with its typical advantages and disadvantages. A word of caution: Don't trust anyone's estimate of commuting time. Drive it yourself during peak morning and afternoon traffic times. We never thought we'd see it, but these routes are starting to develop rush-hour traffic problems.

Although Savannah doesn't approach the metropolitan gridlock of larger cities during commuting hours, it still takes time to cover distance. We've heard radio ads cheerfully tout these out-of-county addresses as "20 minutes from Savannah." Remember, Savannah is a big place, and perhaps whoever timed that trip was in a helicopter. Still, many families find the open spaces, near rural quiet, and a lightning-bug population that hasn't succumbed to mosquito spraying to be well worth a daily drive.

It's hard to leave this topic without at least mentioning the Ford Plantation in Bryan County. This literally was the Fords' plantation, as in Henry Ford. The land is being developed into ultraluxury homes designed as second or third homes for the jet set. There's a club, spa, marina, shooting, and other outdoor sports—you name it. Prices are predictably stratospheric.

REAL-ESTATE COMPANIES

Regardless of the area or price range you are considering, there are hundreds of local Realtors ready to help you with your real-estate needs. What follows is a rundown of some of the best in the area, but remember that this is a small sample. Companies are listed in alphabetical order.

You might also want to touch base with the **Savannah Area Board of Realtors** (www.sav.interealty.com). They won't recommend one member over another, of course, but they can provide information about a member's credentials. Their number is (912) 354-1513.

BARROLL AND BARROLL REALTY COMPANY
101 West Liberty St.
(912) 235-5665
www.barrollandbarroll.com
Since returning to Savannah from Philadelphia in 1981, Margery and Larry Barroll have formed a family real-estate business that includes their two sons. Together the husband-and-wife team has been in the real-estate business since 1975. Although the Barrolls live in Ardsley Park and, in fact, have purchased many homes there themselves,

they don't limit their business to that area—but it is one of their areas of expertise. Their listings are throughout Savannah and include Tybee.

CELIA DUNN REALTY COMPANY
9–13 West Charlton St.
(912) 234-3323
www.celiadunnsir.com
Celia Dunn has been selling real estate in the Historic Downtown for more than 20 years. In fact, her offices take up the bottom floor of a beautifully restored three-story home overlooking Madison Square. Besides specializing in the historic area, she and her agents sell in several other areas of Savannah, including Ardsley Park, Habersham Woods, Tybee, and Thunderbolt, and branched out into neighboring areas of South Carolina. The firm is associated with Sotheby's International Realty.

COLDWELL BANKER PLATINUM PARTNERS
6349 Abercorn St.
(912) 352-1222
www.coldwellbankerplatinum.com
This high-volume real estate firm is owned by Connie Farmer Ray. It handles property of all types in the Coastal Empire and neighboring South Carolina. The firm has six offices (that's the main address listed here) and more than 150 agents. It's hard to point to a neighborhood or price point specialty—these folks are everywhere in the residential market.

CORA BETT THOMAS REALTY
24 East Oglethorpe Ave.
(912) 233-6000
www.corabettthomas.com
Cora Bett Thomas Realty is a deluxe,

high-powered real estate firm. This office specializes in prestige and historic properties, and the clientele includes discreetly unconfirmed celebrities. Thomas is affiliated with the real-estate arm of Christies Great Estates, of British fame, for the marketing of unusual and high-end properties. The firm specializes in upscale properties, including new condo developments in the Historic District and on the waterfront. It has also expanded into planned developments in neighboring South Carolina.

DAVID BYCK REALTY COMPANY
13 East York St.
(912) 233-1276, ext. 76
Commercial and residential sales and property management are what this 25-plus-year-old company concentrates on. Although its commercial and residential departments often specialize in the Historic Downtown, its rental apartments and homes are located throughout the city, including the Southside. The company's commercial department is affiliated with a national network specializing in commercial and industrial leasing. They also work with a national relocation group with more than 900 agents throughout the country. According to owner David Byck, who has been selling real estate for more than 40 years, the company's agents strive to meet all the needs of someone relocating to Savannah, whether the person requires rental property or wants to buy a home.

JUDY NEASE REALTY
924 Wilmington Island Rd.
(912) 354-9966
www.judy-savannahrealestate.com
Judy Nease's specialty is her own backyard: She has called Savannah's eastern islands home for more than 30 years. This is also

where she sells the majority of her real estate. Nease has been in the business since 1978 and started her own company around the beginning of 1996. There are seven agents in the office, all of whom have been selling real estate for many years and have built up their own areas of expertise. The company also offers relocation services for people moving to the area.

KELLER WILLIAMS
329 Commercial Dr.
(912) 232-8580
www.kw.com

This busy Savannah real estate company handles property from marshfront lots to historic homes. Located in a central part of the city, the company was founded in 1983 in Savannah and has increased in popularity, Realtors, and properties through the years.

KONTER REALTY
22 Commerce Place
(912) 354-9314

Konter Realty is one of Savannah's largest real estate companies, with 30 to 50 agents selling throughout the city and surrounding counties. It is also one of the oldest. The husband-and-wife team of the late Lawrence and Harriet Konter founded the company in 1971 in a small, two-room office in the Historic Downtown.

There are six individual divisions under the corporate umbrella of Konter Realty, including real estate, construction, and property management. The company also manages more than 500 residential units, along with 600,000 square feet of commercial/office space. Konter builds between 50 and 60 homes each year and is also involved in light commercial development including apartments, offices, and retail buildings.

THE LANDINGS COMPANY
1 Landings Way
(912) 598-0500, (800) 841-7011

This real estate company is part of the Landings on Skidaway Island—Savannah's largest development and one of its most exclusive. Up to 20 agents are in the office, which, of course, specializes in selling homes, lots, and condos at the Landings. But you'll find their other listings all over town, too.

MOPPER-STAPEN REALTORS
31 West Congress St.
(912) 238-0874

Mopper-Stapen has been in downtown Savannah for over 20 years. During this time, the company has been involved with many properties requiring renovation—sometimes entire neighborhoods with dozens of vacant houses. Besides specializing in historic properties, the company also concentrates on commercial real estate and property management.

THE PRUDENTIAL SOUTHEAST
Coastal Properties
1 Diamond Causeway
(912) 355-4171
www.prusavannah.com

There are 28 agents in this office, which is the only Prudential affiliate in Savannah. Reva and Bob Laramy started the company in 1982 and offer many services, including relocation, property management, short- and long-term rentals, and commercial sales. The company sells real estate throughout the city from West Chatham to the Southside. However, one of their main areas of expertise is the Landings on Skidaway Island.

RELOCATION & REAL ESTATE

RE/MAX PROFESSIONALS
6813 Johnny Mercer Blvd.
(912) 897-1955
www.remax.com
RE/MAX Professionals has 10 agents specializing in Wilmington, Tybee, and other islands. Owner Lynda Werntz has been in real estate since 1978. The office is one of three RE/MAX offices in Savannah, each with its own area of expertise and services.

SHORE, BELL & SEYLES REALTY
401 Mall Blvd., Suite 102B
(912) 356-1653
http://shorebellseylerealty.com
Relocation is the specialty of Shore, Bell & Seyles Realty. As part of their relocation efforts, owners Carey Shore, Nick Bell, and Charles Seyles, who each have more than 30 years of real-estate experience, will send you a relocation packet, give you a tour of Savannah, and even pick you up at the airport if you need a lift. They handle individual and corporate moves involving several employees. The company's main areas of concentration are Dutch Island and Long Point, two high-end island developments with properties ranging in price from $200,000 to $750,000.

APARTMENTS

Due to the highly competitive apartment market in Savannah, many of the franchise complexes reflect updated and contemporary settings with incentives like reduced rent to bring in new residents. Most were built in the late 1990s, if not more recently, and will be found on the Islands and Southside/Midtown. They are clustered in the Islands area because of the local reputation of the schools there (and usually are priced higher there), and on the Southside, in large part, because that is where off-base housing for Hunter Army Airfield tends to concentrate, close to base. The complexes are listed in several free publications offered in racks at area grocery stores.

The Historic Downtown also has a healthy market. Many residents have converted part of their private homes into apartments, and there are also a few apartment buildings to choose from. With the influx of students wanting to live downtown, finding an apartment in this area has become more of a challenge. Until recently, you could find a one-bedroom apartment starting around $750 a month, and a two-bedroom for around $950. However, those prices have gone up and, depending on the apartment's size, quality, and amenities, monthly rents can go for $1,200 and up in some cases.

One of the best ways to find apartments in the Historic Downtown is to check in the *Savannah Morning News*. However, many owners don't bother advertising and simply post a FOR RENT sign on their apartment—a walk or drive around town is a good way to get leads.

You will also find houses for rent in several areas of Savannah, including Southside, Midtown, and the Islands. As the real estate slowdown has made it harder for relocating homeowners to sell their properties, they are putting them into use as rentals. The homes vary from area to area and can include everything from older bungalows to new homes in gated developments. Like apartment rentals, many of the owners simply post a FOR RENT sign or advertise in a local newspaper. Some list their homes with local Realtors. Prices range anywhere from $500 (not many of those to be had) to $2,000 a month.

EDUCATION & CHILD CARE

Savannah and Chatham County offer a wide spectrum of educational opportunities, from excellent public schools to satellite branches of many out-of-state schools and a top rated technical school. In addition to the forward-looking public school system, there are a variety of private high schools, a technical school, two state universities, and the largest art school in the United States. This chapter presents overviews of all these plus a broad look at what's available in the area of child care.

PUBLIC SCHOOLS

SAVANNAH-CHATHAM COUNTY PUBLIC SCHOOLS
208 Bull St.
(912) 201-5600
www.savannah.chatham.k12.ga.us
One of the most attractive incentives in relocating to the state of Georgia and hence, Savannah, is the HOPE Scholarship and Grant Program, one of the state's most successful education initiatives. Launched in 1993, the Georgia lottery program has contributed $3.61 billion to its major education initiatives resulting in free college education for thousands of Georgia students, a voluntary prekindergarten program for four-year-olds, and new capital construction outlays that result in updated and contemporary new facilities, technical institutes, colleges, and universities. The Savannah-Chatham school system serves more than 34,000 students in prekindergarten through 12th grade. They are enrolled at 48 schools and participate in several alternative programs. Students in the system attend 30 elementary schools, 11 middle schools, and 7 high schools, and thanks to the Georgia Lottery, more are on the way.

Twelve of the schools were added to the system between the mid-1990s and 2003 as part of an aggressive $221 million construction program. Among the facilities added was **Savannah High School,** built on the east side of town as a replacement for its namesake in Midtown on Washington Avenue. The old Savannah High, which was erected in 1937, was renovated and now houses the **Savannah Arts Academy,** which is dedicated to the visual and performing arts.

In another development involving a new school, a charter public middle school— **Oglethorpe Academy**—opened in August 1999 in west Savannah on the site of a one-time elementary school. The academy's charter is based on providing students with a rigorous curriculum and an environment— that is, a student body—that's smaller than those of other schools. Another feature calls for parents or guardians of students being asked to sign contracts obligating them to accept responsibility for their children's behavior and compelling them to participate in the educational process.

Among the school system's alternative programs are two **Corporate Academies,** which promote the academic and social development of at-risk students by means of nontraditional programs, and the **Adult Education Center,** which offers basic skills and secondary education for persons seeking to pass the General Educational Development Test or enhance their personal growth through education. The system also operates the **Coastal Georgia Comprehensive Academy** for students with severe emotional and/ or behavioral disorders and autism.

The system has an extensive academy program that enables students to concentrate on special talents and interests. Included in the program are the Montessori Academy at Ellis Elementary School; Advanced Learning academies at Bartow and Heard Elementary Schools; Fine and Performing Arts academies at Bloomingdale and Gadsden Elementary Schools, Shuman Middle School, and Savannah Arts Academy; the Traditional/Latin Academy at J.G. Smith Elementary School; the Renzulli Enrichment Academy at Mercer Middle School; and Honors academies at DeRenne Middle School and Jenkins High School. Two exciting innovations are the Children's Engineering Academy at Spencer Elementary School and the Marine Science Academy at Thunderbolt Academy. The average class size at schools in the system is 25 students. There is an emphasis on computer technology, and the system has more than 7,500 computers in its classrooms and access to the Internet at each school. The system has 278 partnerships with the business community through which businesspeople voluntarily assist individual schools in areas such as mentoring, accomplishing building projects, cleaning up campuses, and raising funds.

Two unique features of the local system are the **Massie Heritage Interpretation Center** and the **Oatland Island Education Center** (see our Attractions chapter). Massie, which is at 207 East Gordon St., is the oldest standing school in Georgia (see the Close-up in this chapter). The school does not hold regular classes, but programs on the history of Georgia are offered. Teachers arrange for their classes to attend programs at Massie. Oatland, at 711 Sandtown Rd., covers 75 acres, and its 1.75-mile Discovery Trail takes visitors through woodlands, past marshes, and to specially constructed habitats of endangered and protected animals of the state—wolves, bison, panthers, and birds of prey among them. There's a re-creation of a colonial settlement and a barnyard where youngsters can get a feel for life on the farm, past and present. The Oatland staff holds several special events throughout the year, including a festival featuring sheepshearing in March and a cane grinding festival in November (see our Annual Events and Festivals chapter). At press time, there were substantial cuts to the Savannah/Chatham County budget, however, those cuts have not been finalized so please accept this as an overview only.

PRIVATE SCHOOLS

Savannah's private high schools provide teenagers and their parents with alternatives to what's offered by the public school system. Most of the private schools are church-related, and all are focused on preparing their students for college. These schools are predominantly coed, but there is a school for girls and one that admits only male students. There's at least one private high school in each section of the city, with the majority being centrally located in the Midtown area.

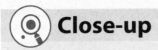

Close-up

Massie School

Supporters of Massie School, the oldest operating public school in Georgia, celebrated the facility's 150th birthday in 2006. A public school from 1856 to 1974, Massie continues to serve as a focal point of education in its role as the Massie Heritage Center, a museum for teaching Savannah's history to students and adults. Housed in three Greek Revival–style buildings on Calhoun Square, Massie offers visitors a look at a 19th-century classroom and exhibits involving the history of the school, Savannah's city plan, the preservation of the city, its architectural treasures, American Indians in coastal Georgia, and the legacy of Savannahian W. W. Law, who was a civil rights leader, historian, and preservationist.

Massie began its long life as Massie Common School House in a single building designed by architect John S. Norris, who drew the plans for many of Savannah's important structures. A western annex was added in 1872, and the eastern annex was built 14 years later. The school was listed on the National Register of Historic Places in 1977, the year it began serving as an education and resource center under the aegis of the Savannah-Chatham County Public Schools.

From its location at 207 East Gordon St., the center purports to offer local residents and visitors alike "the best orientation to Savannah's built environment." A highlight of this experience is a visit to the City Plan Room, which holds the only three-dimensional model of the city's Historic District. It's a huge layout that affords a bird's-eye view of the downtown. The room also contains maps and photographs describing the development and preservation of the city plan set forth in the 1700s by Savannah's founder, James Edward Oglethorpe. There's more to be learned about Savannah's buildings and efforts to preserve them via exhibits involving the city's classical architecture and the beginnings of the preservation movement—displays that make use of photos and artifacts.

Massie is open from 9 a.m. until 4 p.m. Mon through Fri. Self-guided tours are $5 per person; children under 12, $3; and children under 4 are free. Docent-led visits run $8. Visit the website at www.massieschool.com

BENEDICTINE MILITARY SCHOOL
6502 Seawright Dr.
(912) 644-7000
www.bcsav.net

This Catholic high school for boys dates back to 1902, when it was founded on Bull and 32nd Streets as Benedictine College. Having sons become "BC boys" is a prestigious tradition in many Savannah families, a circumstance that has led this military school for 9th through 12th graders to have an extremely faithful and active group of alumni. Sixty percent of those who attend the school are Catholic, but the remainder of the student body is as diverse as the faculty, which is composed of Benedictine priests and monks, laymen and laywomen, and military retirees. Enrollment is about 400.

Benedictine is a college-prep school, and 95 percent of graduates attend college. The school is housed in large, contemporary-style buildings on 100 acres in the Southside. It was moved there in the early 1960s; until that time, students received military training during all four years of school. Since then, however, Junior ROTC classes have been mandatory only for freshmen and sophomores and optional for juniors and seniors. More than 90 percent of upperclassmen continue to participate in JROTC, training that can give them an advantage should they elect to attend a military college or enter the armed forces out of high school.

BIBLE BAPTIST SCHOOL
4700 Skidaway Rd.
(912) 352-3067
www.bbsav.org
The administration and faculty of Bible Baptist seek to educate the whole child while emphasizing the spiritual side of students' development. Bible is taught in every class of this traditional Christian school, which has an enrollment of 380 students in prekindergarten through high school. The coed, college-prep school is a mission of Bible Baptist Church, and it's located on a 19-acre church-school complex that includes a football stadium, a lighted baseball field, and a gymnasium with two full basketball courts. Although the school is open to students of all faiths, the teaching of Christian values is stressed.

Spacious classrooms give teachers plenty of room for learning centers and computer corners, and the average class size is 16 to 20 students. Ninety percent of graduates attend college. Among school traditions are the ceremony at which juniors are presented their senior-class rings by parents or friends and attend a social gathering afterward, with parents, grandparents, and siblings invited to join in. Bible Baptist, whose founders say it was formed in reaction to the ban on prayer in public schools and what was seen as a

lack of discipline there, has a full program of varsity athletics. The school is a member of the Georgia Christian Athletic Association and Georgia Association of Christian Schools.

CALVARY DAY SCHOOL
4625 Waters Ave.
(912) 351-2299
www.calvarydayschool.com
This coed school in Savannah's Midtown is a ministry of Calvary in Savannah and is open to students of all faiths and creeds. The school and church occupy 22 acres at Waters Avenue and 63rd Street. The school started downtown with a kindergarten class in 1961 under the leadership of the Reverend John T. Tippitt Jr., and a grade was added each year. Calvary, which moved south to Midtown in 1964, now provides Christian-based education to more than 900 students in prekindergarten through 12th grade.

According to school officials, academics are blended with a strong program of athletics and other activities to help students evolve into well-rounded citizens. The student-teacher ratio is 18 to 1. The curriculum is designed to prepare students for college, and 98 percent of Calvary's graduates attend institutions of higher learning. Among the tools used in accomplishing the goal of readying students for life after high school are five computer labs, a high-school medical profession program, a middle-school technology lab, and two libraries.

The school offers a full program of athletics and has its own football stadium and track, a complex named M. C. Anderson Field. Cavalry offers before- and after-school programs for students prekindergarten through sixth grades.

i Thinking about homeschooling your child? You must first register with your local school board. You can find support for your homeschooling efforts in Savannah by meeting with members of Family Education for Christ (www.fefonline.com), which can be reached by calling (912) 355-2722. This group schedules special activities for homeschooled students. Another organization, the Kingdom Builders Co-op (www.kingdombuilderscoop.com), offers small classes for homeschoolers in a variety of subjects.

MEMORIAL DAY SCHOOL
6500 Habersham St.
(912) 352-4535
www.memorialdayschool.org
Established in 1971 by the membership of Memorial Baptist Church, this college preparatory school in the northern part of the Southside focuses on equipping each of its students for the diverse challenges and opportunities of higher education and for responsible citizenship. With a fully degreed faculty and a schoolwide pupil-teacher ratio of 12 to 1, Memorial provides more than 300 students with wireless laptop computer technology, software, and a variety of current media resources. Before- and after-school programs include remedial and enrichment activities for students through the age of 10, and there's a fully licensed day-care program for children 6 weeks to 4 years old. The school offers extracurricular activities that encourage participation in academic competitive events in debate, public speaking, drama, music, and the literary arts, and in athletic programs involving football, basketball, baseball, softball, track, golf, and cheerleading.

ST. ANDREW'S SCHOOL
601 Penn Waller Rd.
(912) 897-4941
www.saintschool.com
The secondary division of St. Andrew's is the only high school on the eastside islands. St. Andrew's includes classes for prekindergarten and up. About 500 students are enrolled at the coed, nonsectarian, college-prep school, which is on 28 tree-filled acres on Wilmington Island.

The guiding principles of the school are high standards, a personalized approach to education, multiple opportunities for discovering talents and interests, small class size, and a strong sense of community. The student-teacher ratio is nine to one, and all graduates attend college. A series of seminars, multiple counseling sessions, and school-arranged tours of various colleges assist students in making their postsecondary decisions. Limited need-based financial aid is available for qualifying families. St. Andrew's offers a broad range of extracurricular activities, including participation in athletics, with St. Andrew's competing on the varsity level in the South Carolina Independent School Association because of its proximity to similar-size schools in the Palmetto State. The school's fine-arts programs are extensive.

ST. VINCENT'S ACADEMY
207 East Liberty St.
(912) 236-5508
St. Vincent's—a Catholic, college preparatory school for girls—has been owned by the Sisters of Mercy since 1845 and is the only private high school in the Historic District. The three main buildings of the school cover a city block on the south side of Liberty Street between Abercorn and Lincoln Streets, and

St. Vincent's also includes the Walsh Hall gymnasium on Harris Street and the Peg F. Dressel Library at Liberty and Lincoln. Although the Sisters of Mercy still operate the school, the majority of the faculty consists of professional lay teachers.

St. Vincent's teaches grades 9 through 12. About two-thirds of the school's 350 students are Catholic, but St. Vincent's is open to all young women regardless of creed, race, or socioeconomic status. Classes average about 20 students, with 95 to 100 percent of graduates attending college. The school administration believes the downtown location is an asset because it enables students to experience an urban environment and brings them into direct contact with Savannah's history and culture. St. Vincent's places an emphasis on Christian values and "the acceptance of individuals as God's gift to the world," says the principal, Sister Helen Marie Buttimer. This philosophy has led to a long tradition of graduates sending their daughters and granddaughters to their alma mater, up to the fourth and fifth generations. At the same time, St. Vincent's cherishes the diversity of its student body and makes its services available to all of Savannah's young women. St. Vincent's offers an extensive program in visual arts, and the school's chorus is known throughout Savannah. St. Vincent's competes in eight varsity sports: volleyball, softball, basketball, tennis, track, soccer, riflery, and swimming.

SAVANNAH CHRISTIAN PREPARATORY SCHOOL
1599 Chatham Pkwy.
(912) 234-1653
Savannah Christian is an independent, nondenominational Christian school for students in prekindergarten through 12th grade. The school's college prep curriculum produces above-average SAT scores and a college placement rate of 100 percent, and school spokespeople say Savannah Christian also seeks "to glorify God by partnering with families, churches, and the local community in educating future generations through Christ-centered training, application, and example."

Savannah Christian maintains two campuses. The 254-acre Chatham Parkway campus hosts nearly 1,000 lower- and upper-school students and 160 day-care/preschool students. Facilities include 13 buildings with classrooms, labs, media centers, a gym, and a cafeteria; an outdoor pool; a track; five athletic fields; three playgrounds; and E.D.E.N. (Ecological Diversity for Educational Networking), a 125-acre outdoor learning center. A 14-acre campus on eastern DeRenne Avenue is home to more than 500 lower- and middle-school students, and facilities there include four buildings with classrooms, labs, media centers, a cafeteria, and two gyms. The school launches a fund-raising campaign yearly and continually upgrades its facilities and offerings with the proceeds.

SAVANNAH COUNTRY DAY SCHOOL
824 Stillwood Dr.
(912) 925-8800
www.savcds.org
Country Day strives to fulfill its motto— "Fostering excellence through knowledge, character, and service"—through a college prep program that emphasizes topflight performance in academics, the arts, and athletics. The student-teacher ratio is 10 to 1, with class sizes averaging 21 students in the lower school, 16 in the middle school, and 15 in the upper school. The coed school offers 19 Advanced Placement courses.

A broad range of athletics and extracurricular activities is offered, with the middle and upper schools fielding more than 40 sports teams. The school has 2 libraries with more than 25,000 volumes and 85 online services, 4 computer labs with 350 networked computers, 4 music and art studios, a fine-arts center, 3 gymnasiums, and a football stadium.

The Country Day campus is on 65 wooded acres tucked away in the Windsor Forest subdivision on the Southside. The school moved there in 1957 from a building on Forsyth Park that had been the home of the Pape School for Girls from 1905 until 1955, the year Country Day was chartered. Since then, it has added several buildings.

TECHNICAL SCHOOLS

SAVANNAH TECHNICAL COLLEGE
5717 White Bluff Rd.
(912) 443-5700
www.savannahtech.edu
Savannah Tech seeks to provide the local business and industrial community with highly trained workers—a service it has rendered since its founding by the Savannah Chamber of Commerce as the Opportunity School in 1929. Back then the school turned out mainly stenographers and clerks; these days, the emphasis is on providing students with the opportunity to acquire quality technical education and training that will allow them to be productive members of a global workforce.

The school offers credit, noncredit, and specialized industry services and training. Credit offerings include technical certificates of credit, diploma programs, and associate's degree programs in allied health, business, and industrial technology. The school has more than 50 different credit programs,

ranging from one-quarter programs in areas such as automotive technology and surgical technology to marketing and computer information systems. Some 4,000 students attend Savannah Tech.

The school serves four counties—Chatham, Bryan, Effingham, and Liberty. With the opening of the Army Education Center on Fort Stewart, the College has a presence on-post to serve military families with the necessary skills and education. The Liberty Campus continues to serve the educational needs of the community with programs in nursing, early childhood education, computers, and technology. The Crossroads Technology Campus in West Chatham, a key element in the development of a high-tech

The Hope Scholarship Program

There's Hope for Georgia residents entering their first year at the state's colleges and universities. The Hope Scholarship pays tuition, some fees, and up to $100 per quarter for books to students attending a state school who have earned a B average in high school. B students attending eligible private colleges in Georgia can receive Hope in the amount of $3,000 per academic year for tuition. Students can renew these scholarships in their sophomore, junior, and senior years by maintaining a 3.0 grade-point average. Hope is funded by the Georgia Lottery for Education. For more information on the Hope program, call (800) 546-HOPE.

corridor along I-95, is a catalyst for regional business development.

The college also partners with area employers to deliver programs off-site in area hospitals, specially equipped community education centers, and the public high schools. Provided are community-based studies in fields such as health care, masonry, early childhood care and education, and computer information systems. It also offers customized workforce training programs for new or expanding local industries as an economic development incentive.

COLLEGES AND UNIVERSITIES

ARMSTRONG ATLANTIC STATE UNIVERSITY
11935 Abercorn St.
(912) 927-5277, (800) 633-2349
www.armstrong.edu
Armstrong Atlantic provides more than 75 academic programs through its College of Arts and Sciences, College of Education, College of Health Professions, School of Computing, and School of Graduate Studies. The university's teacher education program has gained state and national recognition, and its economics, computer science, and chemistry programs are also particularly strong. The College of Health Professions is the regional health-professions education center for southeast Georgia. Among master's degrees are those offered in history, criminal justice, liberal and professional studies, nursing, education, public health, sports medicine, and physical therapy. Armstrong has an abundance of evening and weekend classes.

More than 7,000 students, including 810 graduate students, attend the school. They are taught by almost 500 professors. The great majority of students are commuters.

The school is situated in the Southside on 268 acres in an arboretum setting.

The school fields NCAA Division II teams in men's basketball, baseball, tennis, and golf and in women's basketball, fast-pitch softball, volleyball, soccer, golf, and tennis (the 2005 team won the national championship). Armstrong hosts more than 200 cultural events each year, including a faculty lecture series, concerts, and dramatic presentations, all of them open to the public and most of them free.

SAVANNAH COLLEGE OF ART AND DESIGN (SCAD)
342 Bull St.
(912) 525-5100, (800) 869-7223
www.scad.edu
The Savannah College of Art and Design has grown tremendously since its founding in 1979 with one building and 71 students. Today SCAD is the largest art school in the country with its enrollment of more than 7,000 students. The college has almost 60 buildings (and seemingly constantly buying more) spread throughout the Historic and Victorian Districts, many of them of historic significance and beautifully renovated by the school. The college's restoration efforts have been so striking that the National Trust for Historic Preservation awarded SCAD the National Honor Award for Historic Preservation in 1994.

The college offers bachelor's degrees in fine arts and master's degrees in arts, urban design, fine arts, and architecture. Among its 30 fields of study are historic preservation, interior design, painting, photography, furniture design, and production design. Programs involving computer art and graphic design attract scads of students, if you'll pardon the expression. The student-teacher ratio is 18 to 1.

SCAD has more than 50 student organizations and an intercollegiate athletic program fielding teams in basketball, golf, tennis, volleyball, swimming, rowing, cross-country, lacrosse, horseback riding, baseball, softball, and soccer. Although founded and headquartered in Savannah, SCAD also has campus facilities in Atlanta and France.

SAVANNAH STATE UNIVERSITY
B. J. James Drive, Thunderbolt
(912) 356-2186
www.savstate.edu

Savannah State University has three colleges—Sciences and Technology, Business Administration, and Liberal Arts and Social Sciences—offering a total of 22 undergraduate degrees and 4 master's degree programs (social work, urban studies, marine sciences, and public administration). The campus, located adjacent to the town of Thunderbolt, covers 173 acres, many of them shaded by large oak trees festooned with Spanish moss. The eastern portion of the campus is bordered by salt marsh and the Wilmington River; that and the school's proximity to the Atlantic Ocean (about 8 air miles) led to its sobriquet of "College by the Sea," which it was called for many years before its upgrade to university status by the Georgia Board of Regents in 1996. Now it's known, not surprisingly, as the "University by the Sea." The school's location also lends a uniqueness to the university's marine sciences program; the program is the only one of its kind in the state situated in a natural setting. Among features of the program is the *Sea Otter*, a 35-foot cabin cruiser that's used for exposing students to marine science research.

The school was founded in 1890 as Georgia State Industrial College for Colored Youth and retained that name until 1950, when the regents dubbed it Savannah State College. It is the oldest public, historically black college in Georgia, and Savannah State has a student body that is 90 percent African-American, but university officials say the student population and faculty become more diverse each year. There are approximately 2,900 students and 145 instructors, about 70 percent of whom hold doctorates.

Savannah State has a full-scale athletic program and competes intercollegiately in football, baseball, men's and women's track and field, men's and women's basketball, and women's tennis, volleyball, and cross-country. The school achieved Division I status in 2002.

SOUTH UNIVERSITY
709 Mall Blvd.
(912) 691-6000
www.southuniversity.edu

One of Savannah's oldest colleges, South University has grown from its humble beginnings as a two-year business college into a four-year institution offering degrees ranging from associate and bachelor's to master's and doctorates. Through its School of Business, School of Health Professions, School of Pharmacy, and a diverse offering of online programs, students can now pursue a wide variety of majors in the classroom, online, or through a combination of both.

Within the School of Business, the university offers a bachelor of business administration and bachelor of science degrees in legal studies and information technology in addition to associate of science degrees in accounting, business administration, paralegal studies, and information technology. The School of Health Professions offers a bachelor of science in physician's assistant and health-care management, master's degrees in physician's assistant, anesthesiologist assistant, and professional counseling in addition to its associate of science degrees in medical assisting and physical therapist assisting. South University was the first college or university in Savannah to award a doctorate degree through its School of Pharmacy. The School of Pharmacy was, at one time, one of only three such schools in the state of Georgia and, unlike other similar schools, it features a three-year, full-time accelerated program resulting in a doctor of pharmacy degree.

With more than 1,000 full-time students and hundreds of online students attending classes at South University, the average class size is 15 students per teacher, resulting in personalized attention from faculty who have been hired from some of the top universities in the country.

The school dates from 1899, when it was founded as a practical business college. The university was formerly located in downtown Savannah but moved to its current location on Mall Boulevard to accommodate the significant growth in students. Today, the campus covers more than 10 acres and features complete wireless computer access, student lounges, state-of-the-art classrooms and labs, and a 47-foot-high clock and bell tower that marks the center of campus.

CHILD CARE

The state of Georgia regulates the businesses of people who provide care for more than two children at a time. To comply with state law, a person who provides care for up to six children in his or her home—officially called a family day-care home—must be registered with **Bright from the Start: Georgia Department of Early Care and Learning.**

College Alternatives

Apart from the standard public and private colleges in Savannah, i.e., the Savannah College of Art and Design, Savannah State University, Armstrong Atlantic State University, Savannah Technical College, and Georgia Southern University, branches of other well-known schools and universities are springing up.

The University of Phoenix (www.phoenix.edu) has a viable campus here. Columbia College (Missouri) offers classes online and at Hunter Army Air Base (www.ccis.edu). These campuses are ideal for people who are working full-time jobs and can't take time off to attend on-campus classes.

Persons operating businesses caring for more than six children must obtain licenses. Such businesses fall within two categories: **group day-care homes,** which provide supervision and care for 7 to 18 children either in a home or another location, and **day-care centers,** which provide care and supervision for 19 or more children. To be certified or licensed, the operator of a child-care business must be at least 21 years old, have a high-school or general-equivalency diploma, and pass criminal background and fingerprinting checks. They must have completed training in first aid and in infant and child cardiopulmonary resuscitation, and they must annually undergo 10 hours of continuing education in health and safety and child development.

When you're shopping for child care, make sure the provider you're dealing with is registered with or licensed by the state. Take a good look at the facility you're visiting: Ascertain that the inspection data on the fire extinguisher is current, that the smoke alarm and telephone operate properly, and that rooms are in good repair, well lit, and spacious. Check to see if instructions involving fire drills and other emergency procedures are posted. Ask about the program offered—it should provide age-appropriate toys and activities that encourage children to use their five senses.

Chatham Academy

Chatham Academy, a private school for students in grades 1 through 12, offers a full-day program of instruction for children with specific learning disabilities and attention deficit disorders. The school, located at Royce Learning Center at 4 Oglethorpe Professional Blvd., just east of Oglethorpe Mall, serves children of at least average intelligence who have been unable to function successfully in a traditional classroom. Chatham Academy provides a low student-teacher ratio and addresses the academic, social, and emotional needs of its students in classes grouped according to age and academic functioning level. You can contact the school by calling (912) 354-4047.

CHILD CARE RESOURCE AND REFERRAL AGENCY OF COASTAL GEORGIA
7395 Hodgson Memorial Dr.
(912) 925-7575, (877) 935-7575
www.cc4children.net

A great way to start your quest for the child care that meets your needs is by calling the Child Care Resource and Referral Agency of the Coastal Coalition for Children. This agency serves a nine-county area in coastal Georgia and assists parents searching for child care by presenting them with lists of referrals of licensed and registered child-care providers. Parents are also provided with information on how to choose quality child care, and these services are provided at no cost to families.

Parenting counseling is also available from Lutheran Ministries, which administers the A+ Parents program. This program provides support for people striving to be good parents and is a collaborative effort of Lutheran Ministries and the University of Georgia Extension Service in Chatham County. Lutheran Services of Georgia is located at 6555 Abercorn St., and can be reached by calling (912) 355-9179.

IN HIS ARMS EDUCATION CENTER
7816 US 80
(912) 897-6826

Child care on Wilmington Island has expanded with the addition of In His Arms, a branch of a day-care center for ages six weeks to 12 years. The bible-based center also has another location on the campus of Bible Baptist Church and School at 4700 Skidaway Rd. The number is (912) 721-2973.

HEALTH CARE

Savannah has experienced the good fortune of being a magnet for medical care almost since its founding in 1733. According to historians Preston Russell and Barbara Hines, the city's "first civic hero" was a physician, Dr. Samuel Nunes Ribeiro, who was among a boatload of Portuguese Jews who came to the town about five months after Savannah was settled. Georgia's founder, James Oglethorpe, credited Nunez, as he became known, with saving the colonists from the fevers that had killed several of them, including the only other doctor, William Cox.

The city was the site of Georgia's first hospital, a facility incorporated in 1808, and since the mid-1950s Savannah has been served by three large hospitals, two of which merged into a single health-care system in the spring of 1997. The other hospital, Memorial Health University Medical Center, is the regional tertiary medical center, a circumstance that draws many medical specialists to the area.

The latest available statistics involving health care indicate that Chatham County is the home of 635 physicians, giving the area a ratio of 1 medical doctor for every 365 residents. Georgia's first public health agencies were established in Savannah more than 100 years ago to combat yellow fever and improve the health of poor children. Since then, public health services have been expanded to offer preventive health services to all residents of the area and to provide primary care to those who do not have private physicians.

HOSPITALS

MEMORIAL UNIVERSITY MEDICAL CENTER
4700 Waters Ave.
(912) 350-8000
www.memorialhealth.com

This 530-bed hospital in Savannah's Midtown offers tertiary care to residents of 35 counties in southeast Georgia and southern South Carolina. In this role, Memorial provides the region with several one-of-a-kind facilities and services, including the area's only pediatric intensive care unit (part of the Backus Children's Hospital), the only perinatal testing center, the only emergency helicopter service (LifeStarOne), the only ambulance specially equipped for sick newborns (Angel 3), and the only Level 1 trauma center, meaning the medical center offers extensive, immediate, round-the-clock services for emergency, life-threatening needs.

Memorial's Women's Health Institute is one of only six perinatal centers in Georgia, and the Neonatal Intensive Care Nursery is among only six in the state. The hospital's Curtis and Elizabeth Anderson Cancer Institute is southeast Georgia's referral source for cancer treatment, and its Heart and Vascular Institute is the regional coordinator of comprehensive cardiovascular services. Memorial's 50-acre campus is also the site of the Georgia Eye Institute, the Georgia Ear Institute, and the Rehabilitation Institute, which provides a comprehensive regimen of services for people recovering from illnesses and injuries.

Memorial opened in 1955 as a 300-bed general hospital. As a regional referral center, it now ranks in size among the top 5 percent of hospitals in the United States and employs more than 4,000 people, with about 1,000 of those working for CareOne, Memorial's home-care organization. Care-One brings home care to patients in 37 counties throughout southeastern Georgia and southern South Carolina, with its nurses providing services ranging from giving simple medications to highly technical care. Memorial is also a teaching hospital.

St. Joseph's/Candler Health System

This health-care system was created in April 1997 as the result of the merger of Savannah's two oldest hospitals, St. Joseph's on the Southside and Candler in Midtown. The system offers general services and a wide range of specialized care, with St. Joseph's specializing in cardiovascular, oncology, and neurological services and orthopedics, and Candler specializing in oncology, pulmonology, outpatient surgery, the treatment of digestive diseases, and women's and children's services. Candler's Telfair Hospital is the area's only hospital dedicated to women. (By the way, there are only three general hospitals in Savannah: the Telfair Hospital at Candler, like the Backus Children's Hospital at Memorial, is merely a part of the larger hospital.)

In 1998 St. Joseph's/Candler opened the Children's Place on the campus of Candler

Emergency Services

If you have an emergency or need general information about community resources, here are agencies you can contact. For emergencies requiring ambulance, police, or fire departments, call 911.

- Alcoholics Anonymous, (912) 398-2977
- Crime Stoppers, (912) 234-2020
- First Call for Help, (912) 651-7730
- Georgia Medical Society, (912) 355-6607
- Helpline Georgia (crisis line), (800) 338-6745
- Poison Hotline Center, (800) 282-5846
- Rape Crisis Center, (912) 233-7273
- Safe Shelter, (912) 234-9999
- Savannah Runaway Home, (912) 234-4048

Hospital. This pediatric acute-care program serves the special needs of sick children and their concerned parents. The Children's Place utilizes a kid-friendly decorative theme in which each unit is adorned in primary colors from floor to ceiling. The hospital also offers the "Bearly Sick" program to employees' children (and to some extent to the larger public); it provides child-care services for mildly ill children who are too sick to go to school or day care. Also in 1998, the health system introduced its Care Call Center, which enables you to obtain a physician referral and information about treating minor health problems by dialing (912) 819-3360. A major addition to the system is the Nancy and J. C. Lewis Cancer and Research Pavilion, a $24 million, freestanding facility that opened in January 2005. The pavilion, located on Reynolds Street across from Candler, provides subspecialty cancer care and specialized research.

ST. JOSEPH'S HOSPITAL
11705 Mercy Blvd.
(912) 819-4100
www.stjosephs-candler.org
This general acute-care hospital dates from 1875 when the Sisters of Mercy of the Roman Catholic Church took over operation of the Forest City Marine Hospital, a facility in downtown Savannah that specialized in the treatment of sick seamen. A year later the operation was moved to more spacious facilities at Taylor and Habersham Streets and was renamed St. Joseph's Infirmary. It was named St. Joseph's Hospital in 1901 and expanded several times before a new facility was built on the Southside in 1970.

In the years between the move south and the merger with Candler, St. Joseph's accomplished a $7 million expansion of its Emergency and Outpatient Building and opened its Sports Medicine Center, Multiple Sclerosis Clinic, and Diabetes Management Center. The hospital is situated on 28 acres and is affiliated with the Mayo Clinic Jacksonville and Nemours Children's Hospital in north Florida.

CANDLER HOSPITAL
5353 Reynolds St.
(912) 692-6000
www.stjosephs-candler.org
One of the longest continually operating hospitals in the United States and the first

in Georgia, Candler was founded in 1805 and chartered in 1808 as the Savannah Poor House and Hospital. A new facility of the same name was built on Gaston Street in 1819, used as a Confederate hospital during the Civil War, and renamed Savannah Hospital in 1872. The first school of nursing in Savannah was established there in 1902, and 28 years later the Methodist Episcopal Church purchased the hospital from the city and renamed it Warren A. Candler Hospital in honor of one of its bishops.

During the 1960s, the hospital was renamed Candler General Hospital and expanded through the purchase of the Telfair Hospital (which became its obstetrical unit) and the Central of Georgia Railway Hospital. Construction of a new hospital at DeRenne Avenue and Reynolds Street began in fall 1978, and it was opened in late 1980. Its name was changed to Candler Hospital in 1992, with the word General being dropped to reflect the hospital's growth in specialized health-care services. Candler is affiliated with the Emory University System of Health Care.

i Savannah has two services you can contact for help in finding doctors and obtaining free information about hospital services and your health. They are the Care Call Center at (912) 819-3360, and NurseOne at (912) 350-9355.

WALK-IN CLINICS

If you find yourself in need of medical care during your visit to Savannah, there are clinics where you can obtain treatment without having an appointment. These facilities are in addition to the emergency rooms at the three local hospitals.

IMMEDIATE MED
10410 Abercorn St.
(912) 927-6832

Immediate Med handles minor emergencies and comprehensive family medical care at its clinic in the Southside on Abercorn Street. The clinic is open from 9 a.m. to 9 p.m. every day except Sun, when the hours are 1 to 9 p.m. (Note that hours change from time to time; call ahead.) Major credit cards are honored, but Medicare and Medicaid are not accepted.

URGENTONE–GODLEY STATION
110 Medical Park Dr.
(912) 748-1515

Memorial University Medical Center is the hospital behind these organizations. They offer physicians to handle urgent medical problems—the non-life-threatening kind. Hours are 9 a.m. to 9 p.m. daily, although we recommend calling to make sure nothing has changed. Note that the Savannah Mall location at 14089 Abercorn St. (912-350-2121), in an outparcel location beside the mall, is on Savannah's far Southside, while the Godley Station location is in Pooler, one of the municipalities in the western part of the county.

HOSPICE CARE

Several organizations in Savannah offer specialized care for the terminally ill and assistance to members of their families, such as respite care and bereavement counseling.

Hospice Savannah Inc. (1352 Eisenhower Dr., 912-355-2289), which introduced this type of care to the area in 1980, provides living quarters for patients who cannot be cared for at home, as do **Spanish Oaks Retreat** (8510 Whitefield Ave., 912-356-0234), and **Heritage Park of Savannah** (12825 White Bluff Rd., 912-927-9416).

COMPLEMENTARY MEDICINE

Although it's nowhere near a hotbed of complementary medicine, Savannah shows signs of beginning to catch on to this style of healing. More than two decades ago, at least one physician in town was practicing nutritional medicine, but an awareness of and growth in complementary medicine took shape in the 1990s. Now there are a handful of full-fledged acupuncturists available and several medical doctors learning acupuncture techniques. You can avail yourself of the services of a slew of chiropractors, and there are also practitioners of osteopathy, herbal medicine, massage therapy, aromatherapy, and shiatsu (Japanese pressure-point massage).

If you're looking for practitioners of complementary medicine, a good place to start is the **Brighter Day** (1102 Bull Street, (912) 236-4703) natural foods and organic produce store at Bull and Park Streets. Owners Peter and Janie Brodhead don't make recommendations pertaining to practitioners, but they do maintain a "community bulletin board" that might steer you in the right direction.

MEDIA

Need to delve deeper into the lives of Savannahians, the social agendas here, or see what festivals and events are on tap for the future? Well, you're in luck. Savannah media outlets include everything from slick city magazines to newspaper tabloids with all the latest. There's a TV affiliate for each of the major networks, cable access, radio stations in formats from country to classical, a daily newspaper, and several weeklies, monthlies, and specialty publications, even two city magazines.

To go along with this, Savannah has a solid journalism tradition. In the early 1980s, a now-defunct weekly won the Pulitzer Prize in editorial writing. In the days when such things were economically possible, there were competing daily newspapers in Savannah, and desktop publishing and niche markets periodically keep some variety moving in the print world.

As for TV, when you add all the morning, midday, evening, and nightly local newscasts up, they total at least 10 hours each weekday (and it keeps growing). Savannah has joined national media trends with absentee corporate ownership. The last locally owned television station was sold in 1998, meaning that all the major daily print and television media outlets now are owned by companies headquartered elsewhere. Radio has joined the trend. With a handful of exceptions—one independent holdout, two college stations, a public radio affiliate, some AM residue—three national corporations own all local FM radio stations.

NEWSPAPERS

Dailies

In addition to the *Savannah Morning News*, you can also get daily delivery of the *Wall Street Journal* and the *New York Times* (depending on which neighborhood you live in). Ironically, however, you can't get home delivery of the *Atlanta Journal-Constitution*, the major paper from the state capital, in most neighborhoods, but you can buy it at convenience stores, newsstands, and vending boxes. (Check our Shopping chapter for info on where to get really out-of-town newspapers.)

SAVANNAH MORNING NEWS
1375 Chatham Pkwy.
(912) 236-9511
www.savannahnow.com

Savannah's daily newspaper is the *Savannah Morning News*. It's part of Morris Communications, which owns several other Georgia papers (in Athens and Augusta, where the company is headquartered) as well as Jacksonville's *Florida Times-Union* and a host of other newspapers and publications.

Don't be confused if you hear the paper called the *News-Press*. Until 1996, the same company put out the *Savannah Evening*

Press, and the combined weekend editions were known as the *News-Press*. The Press may be several years dead, but habit dies hard in Savannah, and we still use the name from time to time.

Recent years have seen an emphasis on modern design and less focus on breaking hard news. Regular readers know where to find the regular features—the automotive section on Saturday, food coverage on Wednesday, a pullout entertainment tabloid called *Diversions* on Thursday, and lots of special sections on Sunday. Cost is 75 cents for single copies daily ($1.50 Sun) and $18.20 monthly for home delivery.

i Looking for work? The serious job ads are in Sunday's *Morning News*—the weekday stuff is pretty run-of-the-mill. You might also want to track down one of the city's two African-American newspapers. Companies that are meeting corporate affirmative action commitments often make a special effort to advertise in those publications.

The editorial pages feature a mix of local and nationally syndicated columns, but the real star of these pages is editorial cartoonist Mark Streeter, who takes on local, national, and international topics with razor-sharp points, humor, and humanity.

A popular feature is "Vox Populi," consisting of a selection of anonymous phoned-in comments that are alternately rants and raves, reasoned commentary, whimsical observations, or frightening evidence of social disintegration.

Diversions, a tabloid that runs every Thursday, includes listings on everything from what movies are playing in local theaters to concerts, gallery exhibits, and more. A favorable review of a restaurant in *Diversions* will pack the place for a while.

Monday's edition usually includes a map showing locations of local reported crimes from a couple weeks previously.

The *Morning News* puts a lot of effort into its website, www.savannahnow.com, as well. Included here is a feature portion where people can post their own photos from events.

The *Closeups* are a selection of weekly neighborhood newspapers published as sections in the regular paper (the *Islands Closeup*, the *Intown Closeup*, etc.) for subscribers in those areas.

The *Morning News's* facilities in the western suburbs include a large lecture hall where the paper occasionally hosts public forums and lectures.

Ethnic Newspapers

Savannah has two weekly newspapers devoted to covering the African-American community. These papers had their roots in the days of segregation, when mainstream papers did not cover the black community. As that has changed, these papers have evolved. Although they still have news content—often of social events, church activities, achievement, or coverage of the historically black Savannah State University—they also devote a large portion of their pages to political commentary and opinion columns. Of the two papers, the *Herald* is the dominant.

SAVANNAH HERALD
1803 Barnard St.
(912) 232-4505
This weekly newspaper was founded in 1945. The *Herald*'s motto is "Publishing Positive

MEDIA

News for and about Savannah's African-American Community." Inside you will find local news stories, church news, sports, and editorials.

In "Around Town," columnist Jettie Adams fills people in on a variety of subjects, like who is having a birthday and the accomplishments of local children. The *Savannah Herald* is published on Wednesday, when 8,500 copies are distributed. Subscriptions are by mail, and the paper sells in vending boxes throughout town. Copies are also distributed at the larger African-American churches.

THE SAVANNAH TRIBUNE
916 Montgomery St.
(912) 233-6128
The *Tribune*, as it is known, is Savannah's other weekly newspaper devoted to the black community. Publisher and editor Shirley B. James includes local, state, and sometimes national items pertaining to African Americans. The *Tribune* is published on Wednesday. Subscriptions are predominantly by mail but it does have boxes as well.

Other Newspapers

COASTAL ANTIQUES AND ART
1375 Chatham Pkwy.
(912) 236-9511
This monthly tabloid, distributed free throughout town, was purchased by the *Savannah Morning News's* parent company in 1999. The ads are more useful than the editorial content if you are antiquing in Savannah.

COASTAL SENIOR
1375 Chatham Pkwy.
(912) 236-9511

This monthly publication, distributed free at racks throughout town, subtitles itself "Lifestyles of the 50+." Like its sister publication, *Coastal Antiques and Arts,* it was acquired by the *Morning News's* parent company in 1999. Content is all geared toward older readers and includes advice columns from local physicians, schedules of senior-oriented events, and the like.

i The Savannah *Pennysaver* is a "shopper"—an ad-oriented publication with little or no editorial content. It gets tossed on just about every lawn in town Wednesday night and is especially valued for its garage-sale ads and lists of miscellaneous merchandise for sale: exercise machines, collector's dolls, used appliances, whatever. We aren't making this up: We really did once spot an ad in there offering to sell a parrot or trade it for a boat motor.

CONNECT SAVANNAH
1800 East Victory Dr.
(912) 238-2040
www.connectsavannah.com
This weekly newspaper is an alternative news voice, but its major focus is the entertainment and cultural scene. Expect some longer feature stories and a more-outspoken editorial voice. Coverage here better serves younger, edgier readers. The format is tabloid, but it has a magazine-style cover to introduce its lead story. This publication conducts a very thorough, and apparently valid, readers'-favorite contest each year: If you are going to pay attention to posted brags like "Voted Best Sushi Restaurant," you're safer if you stick with this publication's version. *CONNECT Savannah* is available free at newspaper boxes, restaurants, and nightclubs. The website is particularly useful if you are

looking for a quick rundown of what's happening on the entertainment front that particular evening.

LA VOZ LATINA
5960 Ogeechee Rd.
(912) 925-7328 (Español)
(912) 925-7308 (English)
www.lavozlatinaonline.com
This monthly tabloid serves the growing Hispanic population of Savannah and surrounding region. The articles appear in both Spanish and English, although the ads are only in Spanish. (We loved the ones for Chinese restaurants.) Recent articles covered a string of robberies targeting Hispanics, gardening features, travel pieces, and coverage of local Hispanic organizations. *La Voz Latina* can be picked up free at a variety of locations—we find it at restaurants, both Mexican and otherwise.

MAGAZINES

SAVANNAH MAGAZINE
1375 Chatham Pkwy.
(912) 652-0291
Savannah Magazine is owned by Morris Communications, which also owns the city's daily paper, but it has its own staff. This slick city magazine, which targets upper-middle-class and professional residents, is published eight times a year (every two months starting with January plus two other editions focusing exclusively on local interior design). The magazine was launched in the early 1990s, which means it has been around long enough to get all those tiresome stories about the 10 most eligible bachelors out of its system. Content is all local and ranges from pithy pieces such as the best lawyers in town (can't you imagine what those who

were left out had to say?) to soft decorating features. It also covers the city's charity festivals and other annual events—sort of like the old-time society pages with better production values—and carries a regular listing of city events of all types.

i Want to read the latest without buying all these publications? Read the periodicals at any branch of the Live Oak Public Library or online via each publication's website. (You'll find more information on the library in our Arts and Culture chapter.)

SKIRT!
1375 Chatham Pkwy.
(912) 525-0741
www.skirtmag.com
A Savannah/Beaufort/Bluffton/Hilton Head edition of this magazine showed up on the local scene, one of the several different publications from the same people who bring you the *Savannah Morning News*. It's aimed at women—intelligent, well-heeled women who like to shop. At first glance, this publication appears extremely lightweight, but there is espresso beneath that froth. The articles are hyper-short, the photos are big, and the essays tend to meditative pieces on self-discovery, all put together with a more liberal flavor than is typical in Savannah. But the ads share the stage in this publication (and you know how painful it must be for a writer to acknowledge that!). Those ads cover Savannah's retail scene with surprising thoroughness, provided you are looking for trendy stuff and are not on a budget. The monthly mag, produced in a supertab format on heavy newsprint, is available free at a wide range of shops.

THE SOUTH MAGAZINE
116A Bull St.
www.thesouthmag.com

Publisher Michael Brooks launched this bimonthly magazine in 2006. It's glossier and edgier than its competition but realistically targets a different market. The audience here is just as monied as that of *Savannah Magazine,* but younger. The magazine draws heavily on Savannah College of Art and Design graduates, and the result is a dramatic showcase for photographic work. Stories range from personality profiles to meditative pieces on Confederate history and its modern-day devotees. The writing is average, but it is often upstaged by the design and photography, which are clearly in the driver's seat. Subscriptions are $19 a year, but you can pick up single copies at a wide range of local outlets for $3.95 an issue. Like its older competition, this publication comes out every two months—but its management cleverly picked to publish on the competition's off months.

TELEVISION

Weather coverage is particularly strong here—and a good thing, too, since the local National Weather Service (NWS) office fell victim to federal budget cuts several years ago, and the nearest NWS location is now in Charleston. Stations give their meteorologists good equipment and ample air time. After all, outdoor lifestyles are the norm here, and we do live in a region of "active" weather. Want to see a news team drool with excitement? Just pick a station—any station—when the area is under a hurricane watch.

Notice that in the following listings the channel numbers are broadcast channels. If you are on a cable system—and most people here are—the channel numbers are

different, but we've included the broadcast numbers so you'll know what people mean when they say "22 was at our wreck today" or "Was 11 there?" Comcast is the area cable provider (912-354-7531), having recently acquired a couple of smaller, neighborhood-specific systems. Just a note: High-definition channels via Comcast Savannah are all in the 400s.

WJCL–ABC (CHANNEL 22)
 WTGS–FOX (CHANNEL 28)
10001 Abercorn St.
(912) 925-0022

These stations are jointly managed but separately owned. Traditionally the weakest player in local news broadcasts, the stations have been devoting more effort to news in the last few years. The network affiliations are a clue to what you'll find in handling of local direction. The Fox affiliate, for example, airs its late news at 10 p.m. instead of the more traditional 11 p.m.

WSAV–NBC (CHANNEL 3)
1430 East Victory Dr.
(912) 651-0300

WSAV is the city's major runner-up in the news race and has spent quite a bit of time and money tinkering with its program. The newscast tends to be younger, and the content played more dramatically. The early morning newscast is a particularly good example of folksy without being overly cutesy.

WTOC–CBS (CHANNEL 11)
11 The News Place
(912) 234-1111

This station has been the news ratings leader so long, it calls its 6 p.m. broadcast—both arrogantly and accurately—"THE News." This station also runs a solid 90 minutes of local evening news that serves to remind that one of the virtues of news is that it is selective, not exhaustive. Still, it has the biggest news staff among the local TV stations and can generally be counted on to get local breaking news quickly.

WVAN–PBS (CHANNEL 9)
260 14th St. NW, Atlanta
(800) 222-6006
While airing the more familiar offerings, such as *Sesame Street* and *NOVA,* this PBS station also runs some very interesting local programming (on Georgia history, B&Bs, and such) in cooperation with its Georgia affiliate, Peach State Public Television.

RADIO
Adult Contemporary/Soft Rock

WAEV 97.3 FM
WYKZ 98.7 FM
WRHQ 105.3 FM

Various Oldies Formats

WGCO 98.3
WLOW 107.9

College Radio

WHCJ 90.3 FM
(Savannah State University)

Christian Contemporary

WLFS 91.9 FM
WLXP 88.1

Country

WJCL 96.5 FM
WGZR 106.9 FM

Gospel

WSOK 1230 AM
WJLG 900 AM
WHGM 1400 AM

Talk/News/Sports

WTKS 1290 AM
WBMQ 630 AM
WFXH 1130 AM

Top 40

WZAT 102.1 FM

Public Radio

WSVH 91.1 FM

Rock

WFXH 106.1 FM
WIXV 95.5 FM

Urban Contemporary/R&B

WQBT 94.1 FM
WLVH 101.1 FM
WEAS 93.1 FM
WWVV 104.9 FM
WTYB 103.9 FM

RETIREMENT

Savannah's a retiree's dream place to settle. Recreational opportunities for the active retiree abound, from the opportunity to play golf virtually year-round on a variety of courses to boating and sailing around the abundant islands that feed into the city, which are attractive, plentiful, and challenging enough to have landed the city Olympic venue status. Social opportunities are plentiful also, with a variety of organizations tailoring their offerings strictly to older members. Those who are eager to explore new educational horizons have the resources of area universities and their related programs.

Services for the changing needs of an elderly population are in place in Savannah, and they are growing in scope as the demand increases. Health care options are first class, and there are two cancer centers in the middle of the city. If you have family members who are likely to need assistance with household chores or daily supervision because of Alzheimer's disease, programs are available to help both them and you. Expanded transportation, meal, and utility programs have been established to serve the elderly who need additional help.

SENIOR HOUSING OPTIONS

Savannah, like almost any other American city, has its full complement of nursing homes. As baby boomers and their parents age, however, the trend across the country includes residential options that provide a degree of support while stopping well short of the custodial/medical role of the classic nursing home. Some may be apartment complexes catering to older residents, while others offer a full "continuum of care" program where residents live independently in a complex's houses or apartments and, as their needs increase, move on to the complex's assisted-living quarters or on-site nursing home (usually marketed under more attractive terms, such as "skilled-nursing facility"). The personal-care home, which closely approaches the nursing home, is another in this new breed of senior housing options.

The broader spectrum of options began cropping up in Savannah about 20 years ago. This has been a real growth industry in the past few years here, but only recently did the upper end of the range—a full-scale continuing-care retirement community (CCRC) complete with capital investment requirements—launch here.

These types of housing options tend to fall at the extremes of the income range, with provisions for the lowest-income seniors in public-housing high-rises on one end and luxurious private quarters with amenities and prices to match on the other, with not much middle ground.

For the purposes of this book, we selected four of the more luxurious and pricey options for further discussion: one because it is the newest and plushest of the lot, reflecting a concept familiar to people relocating here from larger population centers; another because it pioneered such options here and has proven to be a popular choice for middle-class and higher incomes; and one because it provides more affordable options while maintaining lots of amenities and resident choices.

MAGNOLIA MANOR ON THE COAST
141 Timber Trail, Richmond Hill
(912) 756-4300
www.magnoliamanor.com
This apartment complex for seniors emphasizes independence. There are 120 apartments in the three-story complex, which opened in 1990. Rents range from $1,520 for the one-bedroom, 600-square-foot units and go up to $1,920 for the 900-square-foot, two-bedroom units. Housekeeping and all utilities except telephone service are included. The dining room provides a midday meal that is designed to be the major meal of the day. Amenities include a full schedule of classes and activities, and the property includes a lakeside walking trail and other fitness options. A limited number of assisted-living units are available. It is affiliated with the Methodist church and offers a chapel and variety of spiritual activities, but it is nondenominational and sets no religious requirements for eligibility. (Richmond Hill is a bedroom community just outside Savannah's Chatham County.)

THE MARSHES OF SKIDAWAY
50 Diamond Causeway
(912) 598-5030, (800) 889-6238
www.marshesofskidaway.com
This CCRC shares a socioeconomic rung with the Landings, Chatham County's first gated,

golf course–oriented community, although there is no formal connection beyond the fact that the two developments are neighbors on Skidaway Island. For initial investments that range from $221,000 to $579,000 (depending on size/format of housing), residents buy a residential agreement in various designs of freestanding homes, duplexes, or apartments. When residents die or relocate, the bulk of the investment (given certain conditions) is returned to the resident or estate. The facility offers assisted-living options and a nursing home.

A set monthly fee buys residents a broad array of amenities, including dining privileges in one of four dining rooms, maintenance, utilities, spa and pool access, scheduled activities, and more.

i Savannah's movie theaters offer discount ticket prices to senior citizens.

SAVANNAH SQUARE RETIREMENT COMMUNITY
One Savannah Square Dr.
(912) 927-7550
www.savannahsquare.net
This facility began offering independent-living, assisted-living, and skilled-nursing housing options in 1990. Financial arrangements call for a $500 deposit and month-to-month leases for apartments and cottages at rates ranging from $2,067 to $3,560. Amenities include communal dining, transportation, security, a library, a variety of community spaces, and other services. The facility covers a total of 15 acres and, between its apartments and cottages, incorporates 200 housing units.

Golden Age & Other Senior Centers

Golden Age Centers and Community Centers are daily gathering places that provide active senior citizens with an opportunity to participate in classes and other events. Lunches are served. The centers operated by the City of Savannah are known as Golden Age Centers. Senior Citizens Inc. operates three additional centers in arrangements with the municipalities of Garden City, Port Wentworth, and Thunderbolt. Pooler has its own center. All offer very similar programs.

The following is an alphabetical listing of the **Golden Age Centers** (all of them are area code 912): **Cunningham Center,** 121 East 36th St. (651-6779); **Cuyler Center,** 812 West 36th St. (651-6780); **Frazier Center,** 805 May St. (233-4796); **Grant Center,** 1310 Richard St. (651-6785); **Savannah Gardens Center,** 2500 Elgin St. (651-6775); **Stillwell Towers Center,** 5100 Waters Ave. (351-3855); **Stubbs Towers Center,** 1301 Bee Rd. (651-6776); **Wimberly Center,** 121 West 37th St. (651-6778); and **Windsor Forest Center,** 303 Briarcliff Circle (921-2104).

The three nearby community centers operated by **Senior Citizens Inc.** include the **Garden City Center,** 100 Main St., Garden City (966-7791); the **Port Wentworth Center,** 100 Aberfeldy St., Port Wentworth (964-5411); and the **Thunderbolt Center,** 3236 Russell St., Thunderbolt (352-4846). The **Pooler Center** is at 100 West Collins St., Pooler (964-5411).

SUMMER BREEZE
351 Wilmington Island Rd.
(912) 228-4473
www.kapdev.com

This delightful assisted living home offers private cottages and spacious studio-type housing for senior citizens, with an on-site beauty salon, transportation to medical visits and shopping, a full cafeteria with first-class meals, and a setting that is on the skirts of one of Savannah's most picturesque country clubs. The staff at this facility is caring and efficient. Call for pricing.

SENIOR CITIZENS, INC.

Think of this nonprofit organization, located at 3025 Bull St. (912-236-0363; www.senior-citizens-inc.org) as a clearinghouse for senior services. Social and educational opportunities, as well as discounts provided by various merchants, are the primary benefits available to the younger segment of members. The range of services (some on a fee basis, others free or on sliding scales) runs all the way to home-delivered meals and utility assistance—whatever it takes to keep even frail and very low-income seniors independent as long as possible. The Meals on Wheels program, which delivers hot meals to housebound seniors, is excellent and affordable. Call the center for more information.

Senior Citizens derives much of its funding from federal grants, foundation donations, and personal bequests. It is also a participating member in the United Way of the Coastal Empire.

The next several listings provide information on Senior Citizens' offerings for active members of the retirement community. We follow those up with Senior Citizens' options that address social service needs.

CLUB 55
3025 Bull St.
(912) 236-0363
This separate suite within the Senior Citizens complex is designed as a social and educational center for all Senior Citizens' members. It includes meeting facilities, rooms for scheduled bridge games and other recreation, exercise facilities that include treadmills and other machines, computers for classes and Internet access, and a gathering place for health screenings, courses, and seminars on topics of interest to seniors. Dues are $12 annually. Current courses range from keyboarding to tap dancing to oil painting.

MERCHANTS' DISCOUNTS
More than 170 participating merchants and service providers offer discounts to Senior Citizens' members (and many give price reductions to any senior citizen, member or not). Maintaining a current inventory of the very fluid list of participants and the terms of their discount offers has proven to be a pretty overwhelming challenge for the Senior Citizens' staff. Participating merchants are asked to display the Senior Citizens' logo where customers are likely to see it. If a freshly updated list isn't available when you join, and if you don't see a logo displayed by a merchant, the organization encourages you to show your membership card and ask if they participate in the program. After all, even if you don't have fixed-income problems, it's nice to pay less if you have the opportunity.

RUTH F. BYCK SOCIAL CENTER
64 Jasper St.
(912) 234-6666
The Social Center's adult day-care program provides an option for families facing the hardships of caring for a loved one with Alzheimer's disease or similar chronic disorders. Residents receive social interaction, exercise, and meals while family members are freed to go to work or take a break from constant care. The center is located at the rear of the Senior Citizens' complex.

OTHER SENIOR SERVICES & ELDERHOSTEL

ELDERHOSTEL
75 Federal St.
Boston, MA 02110
(617) 426-8056
www.elderhostel.org
Elderhostel is a resource that everyone age 55 or older who travels should become familiar with. It offers noncredit educational opportunities on a wide range of topics (and we do mean wide, from phonics to history to literature). Tuition is moderate, and arrangements are made for you to stay near the class site, usually in area motels. The program is generally arranged to allot time for classes, socializing, and taking in the various sights around the host location.

Elderhostel is a particularly thriving program in Savannah, where Armstrong Atlantic State University, Savannah State University, and Temple Mickve Israel/Jewish Educational Alliance all have course offerings that take particular advantage of the Savannah area setting. Other nearby units of Georgia's university system, such as Coastal Georgia Community College in Brunswick and Georgia Southern University in Statesboro, also participate.

Costs are moderate when you consider prices include motels, meals, and, in most cases, local transportation. The offerings we scanned ranged from $705 to over $1,000, with options that can add to the price. Preregistration is absolutely essential. Local residents can get discounts because they won't need the meals and lodging. They can register through the local addresses, but we really recommend you get the catalog and handle registration through the Massachusetts office.

ARMSTRONG ATLANTIC STATE UNIVERSITY
11935 Abercorn St.
(912) 921-5439
www.armstrong.edu
Armstrong Atlantic's courses are based in two locations: at the university's Southside Savannah campus and on Tybee Island, Chatham County's beach municipality. Offerings are varied but tend to have musical themes. At Armstrong, the program has expanded into a Lifelong Learning Institute geared toward local membership. Courses are based at the Armstrong Center for Professional & Continuing Education, 11935 Abercorn St.

SAVANNAH STATE UNIVERSITY
P.O. Box 20523
Savannah, GA 31404
(912) 356-2253
Savannah State University has equally diverse offerings. The university's marshfront setting comes into play in a course on marine life of the Southeast, and other recent courses include Savannah history, phonics, and Gullah culture, which examines the language and African culture retained by a community of Lowcountry slave descendants. Among Savannah State's most popular Elderhostel offerings are its various jazz courses, taught by members of Savannah's thriving community of jazz musicians and scholars.

CONGREGATION MICKVE ISRAEL
20 East Gordon St.
(912) 233-1547
The courses sponsored by Mickve Israel tend to focus heavily on Jewish culture and history. The Mickve Israel congregation itself, as the oldest Jewish congregation in the South, is the focus of one course. Not all courses are centered on local topics, however. For example, check out "The Jewish Heritage of the American Musical."

Schedules change each quarter. Your best bet is to call. Note that some courses involve Savannah teamed with other cities.

i The Live Oak Public Library offers records and cassettes of print items to those with vision problems and can also arrange to deliver items to homebound patrons. Call (912) 652-3600 for more information.

RETIREMENT SERVICES OFFICE THIRD INFANTRY DIVISION (MECH.)
368 Hase Rd., Fort Stewart
(912) 767-3326
We've found that military retirees are well versed on the benefits they carry into retirement. They probably don't need a reminder that they retain shopping privileges at post exchanges and commissaries, and that there are active posts in Savannah for all the various military organizations. But those moving into or passing through the area might be pleased to know the extent of services available in the region, thanks to the major military presence here.

Hunter Army Air Field in Savannah is a subinstallation of Fort Stewart, which is about 40 miles southeast of the city. Some 4,300 soldiers are assigned to Hunter, and 16,000 are based at 279,000-acre Fort Stewart, the largest military installation east of the Mississippi. With that many personnel, you've got recreation facilities, and retirees have access to the Morale, Welfare, and Recreation programs at these installations. Although it is unlikely that many retirees are interested in the concerts staged for young soldiers, they may well want to know about the golf courses, skeet shooting, movie theaters, and other activities and facilities at the two military reservations. Because it is far larger, many of these will be found at Fort Stewart in Hinesville, which is an accessible commute.

On the more serious side of things, Tuttle Army Health Clinic serves Hunter for primary and ambulatory care, and the larger, full-service Wynn Army Community Hospital is at Fort Stewart. The office listed at the head of this entry is largely concerned with such major tasks as straightening out retirement check problems or arranging veteran burials at sea, but personnel there can also provide information on other retiree services.

HOSPITAL-SPONSORED CLUBS

Both of Savannah's two hospital systems offer special clubs to senior citizens, focusing not only on health care and wellness activities but also on education and social opportunities.

GENERATIONONE
7137 Hodgson Memorial Dr., Suite 12-B
(912) 350-7587
This club, sponsored by Memorial Health University Medical Center, offers health fairs and screenings, a member discount program, and visits to members hospitalized at Memorial. Classes in such areas as arts and crafts, line dancing, and bridge are scheduled, along with Senior Net computer classes and Internet access. Seminars are offered on health and retirement issues, healthy aging, and driver's safety. This group also has an active ongoing arrangement with a group-tour company. Eligibility begins at age 55. Membership is $12 per year.

SMARTSENIOR
No. 8 Medical Arts Center
(912) 352-4405
This program of St. Joseph's/Candler Health System provides health seminars, educational programs, medical screenings, and visits to members hospitalized at either St. Joseph's Hospital or Candler Hospital. That may sound a bit stodgy, but it isn't—much of this group's activity is geared toward active retirees. There's a travel club that has gone from the Bahamas to Canada and points in between, ranging from two-week excursions to overnighters to catch an Atlanta Braves game. Activities scheduled throughout the year include tours of local industry, arts and crafts classes, and line dance lessons, for example. In addition, the group provides member discounts at participating merchants. Annual dues are $12. Eligibility begins at age 55.

INDEX